To- Bill

Christmas '89

May

it

be filled

with

Good Cheer!

From - Mike

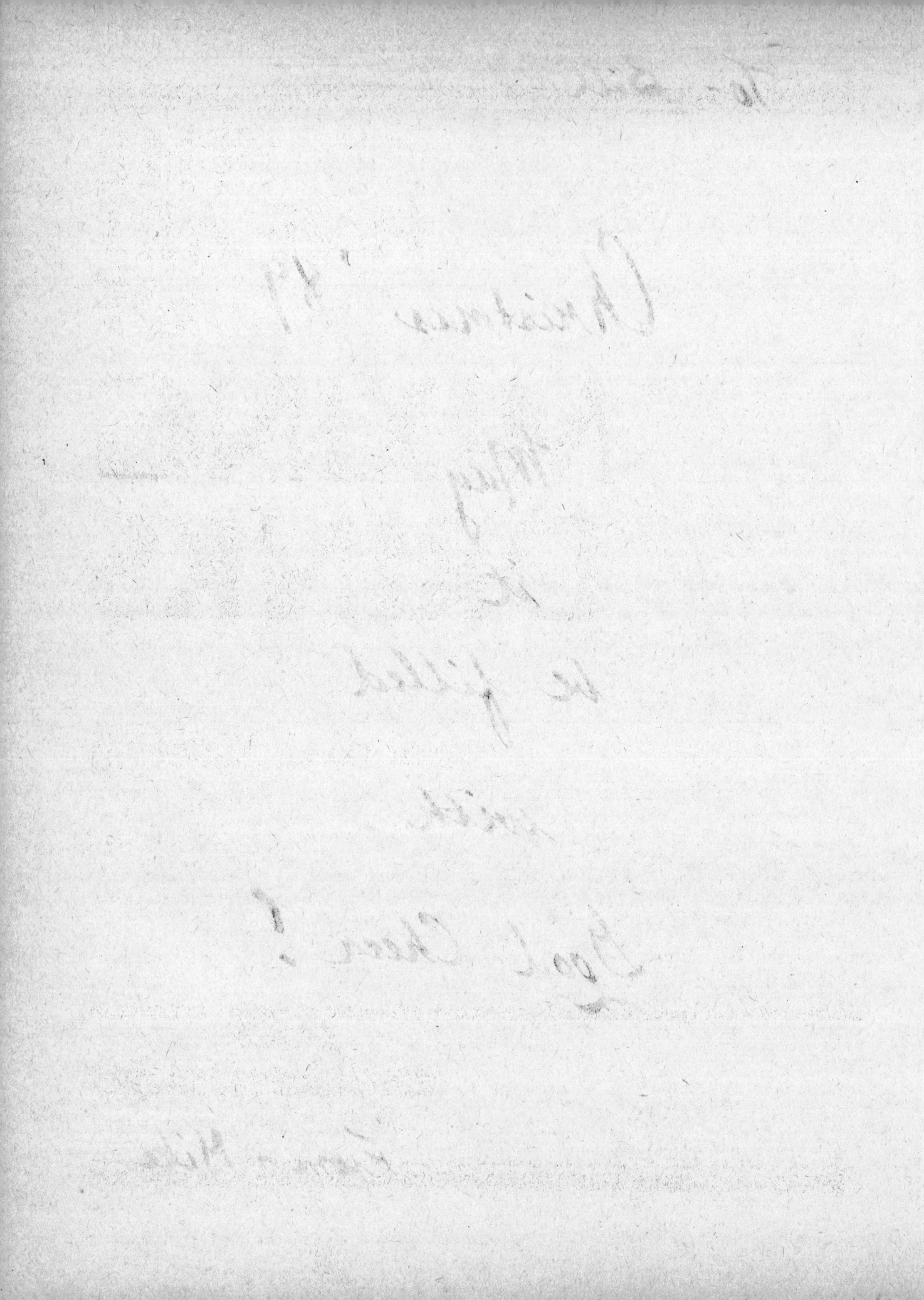

THE
FINE ART
OF
MIXING
DRINKS

Carlos C. Valerian

checkerbooks

ISBN 0-88634-044-6

© COPYRIGHT 1982 AND PUBLISHED BY

checkerbooks inc.

TORONTO   CANADA   PRINTED IN CANADA

CONTENTS

THE COCKTAIL

Stories abound about how the word "cocktail" first came to be used to describe a mixed drink. We are never going to know the true derivation of the word and must be content with its modern interpretation: Webster defines COCKTAIL as "a short, mixed alcoholic drink made in various ways and iced." In these fast-changing times this definition is no longer strictly accurate, because our repertoire of mixed drinks now includes many recipes that have no alcoholic content whatsoever. The calorie-conscious imbiber and those who are "on the wagon" have created a new demand for light, non-alcoholic cocktails.

Since the word in its present connotation has been around since 1806 it is obvious that the mixed drink has been popular for a very long time. However, the 1920s and the early '30s were the great heyday of the cocktail and hundreds of new concoctions were added during those years. This spread in popularity was due in part to prohibition in the United States. The birth of the speakeasy and the need to disguise the taste of poor quality liquor such as "bathtub gin" helped to create many exotic mixed drinks. Subsequently, the establishment of cocktail bars and the proliferation of home-built bars served to introduce "the cocktail hour" — one of the highly civilized institutions of the western world. The cocktail has also lent its name to that fabulous festivity, "the cocktail party." This convenient method of entertaining can be scaled from a small, intimate group where the host acts as bartender, up to the awesome, outsize party that requires many professional bartenders. Whatever the occasion, whatever the number of guests invited, each drink should be prepared with pride, using fresh mixes, the correct glassware and ingredients of the highest quality. The finished cocktail should be pleasing to both the eye and the palate.

While there is still wide appreciation of the Martini, the Manhattan, the Old-fashioned and other great classics, there has been over the past few years considerable change in consumer taste. The fashion for vodka drinks is relatively new and has led to the creation of Screwdrivers, Gimlets and the Bloody Mary. The liqueur Galliano, another newcomer, has helped make the Harvey Wallbanger one of the most often requested cocktails. New drinks are being invented every day, and professional bartenders vie with each other to create unusual and unique taste experiences. Forty years ago the average bartender was satisfied to know how to prepare two dozen drinks. With today's varied tastes he needs to know 100 to 150 recipes. With over 5,000 mixed drinks to choose from, the sensible host keeps a good bartender's guide close to his bar . . . after all, nothing is too good for your guest!

The various types of mixed drinks can be conveniently divided into categories. The most common are listed below with some descriptive comment.

APÉRITIF A drink of alcoholic beverage or wine taken before a meal to sharpen the appetite. Apéritifs should look attractive and they should be fairly dry.

BUCK An excellent bad-weather drink. Originally, only gin was used in making a buck, but it is just as acceptable to use applejack, or brandy, gin, rum, tequila, vodka etc. The liquor you choose is combined with ice and lemon or lime juice. A twist of lemon or lime peel is added, as well as ginger ale.

COBBLER Like the julep, the cobbler is an American invention. This drink is now a favorite everywhere — particularly on a hot day! It takes no great skill to create a cobbler, but to make it *look* delicious as well as *taste* delicious takes some imagination. To prepare, fill a glass with shaved or cracked ice, add the ingredients and stir. The glass can then be decorated with fresh fruits: berries (in season) should always be used, as well as cherries, pineapple chunks, spices and citrus fruits in wedges, twists or wheels. Always serve a cobbler with a straw.

COCKTAIL This term covers a multitude of short, cold and perfectly-blended drinks comprised of various spirits, syrups, ice and bitters. The drier varieties are considered to be apéritifs, whereas the sweeter cocktails can be enjoyed after a meal and are very often mixed with liqueurs. Cocktails should always be served in regular cocktail glasses (unless the recipe specifies otherwise) and glasses should always be chilled before using. Generally, cocktails should be well iced, mixed thoroughly in a shaker or stirred thoroughly in a mixing glass and strained into a cocktail glass. Each drink should be appropriately decorated with a fruit twist, cherry, pearl onion or olive as directed in the recipe.

COLLINS A tall, effervescent, iced drink, usually made by mixing lemon or lime juice with spirits and powdered sugar. The mixture is strained into a tall glass containing plenty of shaved ice and is then topped off with sparkling soda or water. Very refreshing!

COOLER This drink, which belongs to the Collins family, is a long, well-iced summer drink, usually made with any of the basic liquors, combined with ice, sugar and lemon or lime juice. It is served in a tall 12-oz. glass containing shaved ice and is topped off with soda water.

CRUSTA The ideal concentrated drink decorated with fruit and lemon or orange twists. A crusta may contain spirits, liqueurs, fruit juices and spices. Ingredients are well shaken with ice and strained into a 6-oz. glass with a sugar-frosted rim. The glass is prepared by running a wedge of lemon around the rim, then dipping the rim into powdered sugar.

CUP A beverage consisting of liquor, curaçao, brandy and fruit, well iced and served in a punch bowl or in a pitcher.

DAISY A drink made by combining ingredients in a mixing glass, pouring the mixture into a highball glass containing clean, shaved ice, stirring, and serving with a garnish of fruits or mint. Daisy ingredients usually include liquor, raspberry syrup, lemon juice and soda in addition to the decorative fruit.

EGGNOG Eggnogs are of American origin, but they have universal popularity. An eggnog is an almost indispensable Christmas drink, and generally a favorite for all seasons. The ingredients, which include liquor, egg, milk, sugar and nutmeg, are shaken or blended with ice and strained into a Collins glass.

FIX Fixes are medium-tall drinks in which the ingredients are "fixed" in a highball glass packed with crushed or finely cracked ice. As with the cobbler, no soda or other extender is added and shaking or straining is not necessary. The single fix of liquor, sugar, ice and lemon is an heirloom from Victorian days. These simple drink recipes, together with modern variations, can make gloriously refreshing bracers.

FIZZ Fizz drinks are long, effervescent, cooling beverages consisting of liquor, lemon, sugar and chilled soda water. The ingredients should be mixed with ice and strained into a fizz or highball glass which is then filled with cold soda. The drink is topped with a lemon slice, wedge or wheel.

FLIP A sweetened, rich, and sometimes spiced beverage that resembles an eggnog without the milk. It usually includes liquor (or ale, beer or cider), sugar and an egg. The ingredients are shaken with ice and strained into a flip glass or a Delmonico glass.

FRAPPÉ A frappé is a cool refreshing beverage consisting of liqueurs poured over finely crushed ice. Frappés may be served freshly made or, preferably, swizzled to a foam and stored in the freezer until served. When removed from the freezer the ice, which is loosely formed, will melt quickly, and the drink can be sipped from the glass or with a straw.

HIGHBALL This is a long, effervescent drink consisting of liquor poured over ice cubes in a highball glass. Chilled ginger ale or soda are added and the drink is topped off with a lemon twist.

JULEP Both Georgia and Kentucky claim to have originated juleps, but questions of origin have never been settled and Southern Colonels everywhere have created many wonderful variations. In general, a julep is a long, cold drink featuring freshly crushed garden mint, crushed ice, and either bourbon or rye whisky. The entire concoction is decorated with mint sprigs and served in a frosted Collins glass or tankard.

MULL A mull is basically hot wine, served in a mug, containing sugar and spices. Brandy, a liqueur or a fortified wine can also be added to make the drink stronger. Spices are boiled in water, then combined with wine and sugar and the mixture is heated to below the boiling point (if the temperature is too high, the alcohol will evaporate).

POUSSE CAFÉ The name of this showy little drink is derived from French words which, literally translated, mean "to push coffee." A Pousse Café is usually served after coffee and consists of several liqueurs of different colors and specific gravities. Served in a pousse café or pony glass, the liqueurs are carefully poured in proper sequence, so that each liqueur floats on the previous one. To keep the ingredients from mixing, pour them slowly over the back of a teaspoon, holding the tip of the spoon against the inside of the glass.

PUFF A good "pick-me-up" to serve before lunch. It may be made with brandy, bourbon, gin, rum, scotch or rye, but the Brandy Puff is the most popular. A puff (a combination milk-and-soda punch) is made with equal parts of liquor and milk mixed and strained into a Sour glass and topped off with chilled soda or tonic water.

PUNCH A sparkling punch bowl seems to be an irresistible center of conviviality, and is indispensable to special occasion hospitality. Punches may be served hot or cold and may contain either wine, spirits, beer, cider, rum, brandy, champagne — or no liquor at all. They can be light and refreshing, mild and heart-warming or rich and nourishing.

RICKEY Another long, cool, refreshing drink. Simple and delightful, the rickey combines the juice and rind of lime with ice cubes, soda and a choice of gin, scotch, rye, bourbon, apple brandy or rum.

SANGAREE A sangaree is made with liquor, wine or ale and just a little sugar. It should always be very well stirred and is invariably dusted with nutmeg and served in a large or small tumbler with cracked ice.

SHRUB A shrub is a ripened mixture of fruit juice, sugar and spirits. Aging is done in stone crocks or glass bottles which, if stored, should be corked tightly until served. When used, a shrub is diluted with plain or carbonated water. It should be well chilled. Shrubs are usually fortified with brandy or a Jamaican rum. Applejack can be used as well. When a shrub is made from juice derived from such fruits as raspberries, cherries or strawberries, white rum or even gin can be used.

SLING A drink usually made with either gin, whisky, brandy, applejack or rum poured over ice and sugar in a Collins or Old-fashioned glass. Lemon juice is added and the glass may be filled with water, soda or ginger ale.

SMASH A small version of a julep, served in a small tumbler or in an Old-fashioned glass. Smashes contain liquor, lump sugar, mint, ice and soda: sugar, mint and a little water are put into a glass, mint is then muddled and the sugar dissolved. Ice and liquor are added and the drink is topped off with soda and a sprig of mint.

SOUR This is a tart drink, usually served as a cocktail before a meal. A Sour is made of liquor, lemon juice and sugar shaken vigorously with ice, strained into a Sour glass, topped with soda and decorated with a maraschino cherry and an orange or lemon slice. Although the "Whisky Sour" is the most popular, a Sour may also be made of applejack, brandy, gin, rum, bourbon, tequila or vodka.

SWIZZLE A swizzle is a type of "sour" drink churned with a swizzle stick until the mixture becomes foamy and the glass is frosted. Usually served in a highball glass, a swizzle combines crushed ice, lime juice, sugar and bitters with either brandy, gin, rum or whisky.

TODDY Toddies are made with applejack, gin, rum or whisky, and may be served hot in a mug or cold in an Old-fashioned glass. They are prepared by dissolving a lump of sugar in either a glass or a mug, adding ice or hot water, the basic liquor, lemon peel and spices, such as clove, nutmeg and cinnamon.

ZOMBIE This is a strong drink, made by mixing different rums in a tall glass and adding fruit juices, sugar and crushed ice.

LIQUORS

DISTILLING

The distilling process is basically simple. Alcohol boils at a lower temperature than water. When a fermented mixture is heated to near boiling, the alcohol in the mixture will vaporize first, separating from the rest of the liquid. The vapors, trapped before dissipating into the air, are then cooled. Condensed, they form alcohol. This process was — and in some cases still is — traditionally carried out in a pot still, essentially a pot in which wash is boiled and the resultant alcohol vapors captured in receptacles.

Today, a system of continuous distillation is used to produce quantities of highly refined alcohol efficiently and economically. The modern still, known variously as the "Coffey" still (after Aeneas Coffey who patented it in 1832), the "patent" still, or the "continuous" still, is shaped like a column. The wash is fed in at the top and seeps downward, falling onto and spreading over a succession of perforated plates. Meanwhile, steam, forced in at the bottom of the column, rises and vaporizes the alcohol in the thinly-spread wash. This operation continues in a cyclical manner: hot steam vaporizes the cold wash, while the resultant spirit vapors serve to heat, and, at the same time are condensed by, incoming cold wash. Spirits processed through a pot still have a much lower proof level, and are heavier and more flavorful than those produced by a continuous still. The latter have a higher proof (more alcohol) but are proportionately less flavorful, since spirits of a higher proof content are unable to retain their taste characteristics.

PROOF

Proof refers to the measurement of alcoholic strength in liquor. There are three different methods for indicating this alcoholic strength. (1) The French system, known as the Gay-Lussac system, is by far the simplest. It indicates the volume of pure alcohol in a spirit. Thus, a bottle of liquor with a label that reads 40 per cent Gay-Lussac, means simply that the spirit in the bottle contains 40 per cent pure alcohol. (2) In the United States, absolute (pure) alcohol is taken to be 200 and proof spirit is exactly half of that. Under the U.S. system, then, the alcoholic strength of any drink can be determined simply by dividing the proof number in half: a bottle of 100-proof liquor contains 50 per cent alcohol and 50 per cent water; a bottle marked 90 U.S. proof contains 45 per cent alcohol, and so on. Note: the American system has been used in this book. (3) The British proof system is different again — and more difficult to calculate. It rates pure alcohol as 175.25 (175, in practice); proof spirit is 100 and contains approximately 57 per cent alcohol. A 70-proof spirit in Britain and other Commonwealth countries contains 40 per cent alcohol. The following table shows approximate comparisons of the three systems.

British Proof	American Proof	Gay-Lussac Metric Proof	Percentage of alcohol by volume
175	200	100	100
100	114	57	57
88	100	50	50
80	90	45	45
75	86	43	43
70	80	40	40
65	74	37	37
0	0	0	0

WHISKY

All whisky begins with one or more types of grain. The particular grain formula used will largely determine the type of whisky to be produced. One reason why Bourbon, Scotch, Irish and Canadian whiskies taste differently is, quite simply, because different grains are used in their manufacture. Bourbon, for example, is made primarily from corn, while Scotch derives most of its flavor from a blend of barley whiskies. Certain types of grain not only create taste differences, they also impart more flavor than others: smaller grains such as rye and barley will contribute much more flavor than corn. And environmental factors are important. Affected by soil and climate, corn grown in one part of a country will differ in size and composition from corn grown in another area. Other factors that determine the character of a whisky are related to production: the quality, purity and mineral content of the water used in the mashing of grains; the method of distillation; the care with which whiskies are blended; and the entire aging process. These elements, among others, contribute to the final product. Irish and Scottish distillers have traditionally used the pot still to produce a heavily-flavored "single malt" (or "pot-stilled") whisky. Today, most of the Scotch and Irish whiskies available are a blend of these heavier-bodied whiskies plus higher proof whiskies produced in a continuous still. Canadian and American whiskies are also blends of several whiskies, but all are produced at high proofs in continuous stills.

Time is another crucial factor in the making of any whisky. Depending on the country, the liquor is aged for a minimum of two or three years in wooden barrels. Many of the harsh qualities of the new whisky are absorbed by the wood; while the wood lends special characteristics of its own to the product being aged. Through this interaction and over a period of time, the whisky changes and mellows. Scotch, for example, loses some alcoholic strength and changes very little in color; Bourbon, on the other hand, gains several proof degrees during storage and takes on a deeper color as it matures.

The production of whisky throughout the world is carried on in the same basic manner, with each country retaining its own manufacturing traditions, and individual distillers within each country producing whisky according to their own formulas. Modern technology, in conjunction with centuries of experience, is producing better and better whiskies, but it is interesting to note that there remain innumerable subtleties of flavor, aroma and texture in liquor which cannot be accounted for by either science or man.

SCOTCH WHISKY

Many factors, some maintained by law, contribute to the unique characteristics of Scotch whisky. Statutes require that all Scotch whiskies have a barley malt content, that they be distilled at a certain proof and that they be aged in wood for a minimum of three years. While all Scotch whiskies are manufactured in much the same way, each has its own taste, aroma and texture, created through specific combinations of raw materials and production procedures.

Single malts are always made exclusively from barley malt (supplied by a specialist malt manufacturer) that has been kiln dried over a peat fire. Pungent smoke from the fire impregnates the malt and gives it the distinctive "smoky" flavor for which Scotch whisky is known. The malt is then crushed and mixed with warm water, resulting in a liquid called "wort." To this, yeast is added; and fermentation takes place. When this process is completed, the liquid — now referred to as "beer" or "wash" — is pumped into an enormous pot, known as a pot still, where it is heated, vaporized, condensed and re-distilled, eventually yielding whisky. The whisky is put into oak casks to age and mature before being sold.

The malted, or pot-still whisky described above is combined, in varying proportions, with "grain whisky" (a type of unmalted whisky distilled primarily from corn) to create a smoother, more consistent product: blended whisky. Today, there are only about ten "straight" malt whiskies readily available, while there are almost 2,000 blended Scotch whiskies. Differences between Scotch whiskies are mostly due to the quality and amounts of malt and grain whiskies blended together. Usually, 30% of the former is used, the balance being made up of grain whisky. Grain whisky, distilled in a continuous still at high temperatures, is lighter than the malts, and helps to temper their fullness and smokiness. Although the number and quality of grain whiskies used in a blend is important, in the final analysis, the flavor, body and texture of the blend depends more on the malt whisky contribution.

It is not uncommon in the blending procedure for distillers to use 30 or more whiskies, both malt and grain, to achieve the required taste — and it takes an expert blender to do this. The end product is always unique. Distillers in the same area, each using the same raw materials and manufacturing processes, inevitably produce distinctly different whiskies. Attempts to duplicate Scotch whiskies in other parts of the world have always failed — perhaps for lack of Scotland's water, the Highland air, the inherited skills of distillers and blenders or the old sherry barrels in which the whisky is aged. These are elements that can be found only in Scotland.

IRISH WHISKY

Most Irish whiskies available today are blends of the traditional pot-distilled whiskies and grain spirits produced in continuous stills. As with whiskies produced everywhere, special grain formulas determine the taste, aroma and texture of Irish pot-stilled whiskies.

The mash used for Irish whisky is barley (usually only half of it is malted), wheat, rye and, peculiar to Ireland, oats. The whisky is produced in very much the same manner as Scotch whisky, except for one important difference: whereas in Scotland the malt is "smoke-cured" when it is dried, Irish distillers keep their malt free of smoke when drying it. As a result, Irish whisky doesn't have the smoky flavor characteristic of Scotch.

The grain whiskies used in blending originate with corn and are produced at relatively high proofs. Although they are not a principal factor in determining the final flavor of the whisky, they do make their contribution. (Irish whisky is influenced to a greater extent by the quality of the water used in production.) On the whole, however, the basic pot-still contribution is the crucial factor. Irish whiskies are renowned for their high proof content and taste, qualities that result from the fact that in Ireland, pot-still whiskies are distilled not twice, but three times. This produces a very fine, strong, smooth liquor.

Although the Irish themselves prefer the full-bodied pot-still liquor, exports to England and North America, where palates are accustomed to lighter liquors, are mainly of the more delicate, blended varieties. Irish distillers are required by law to age their whiskies for at least three years, but most are aged for a much longer period of time. In many instances the age shown on the label of a bottle of Irish whisky indicates the age of the youngest liquor in the blend. The others may be even older.

BOURBON AND RYE WHISKY

In earlier days whisky was a frontier drink, a necessary part of a hard, rough life. Many emigrants from Scotland and Ireland took their own traditional methods of whisky-making with them when they went to America. They made whisky out of whatever grains were available and this, combined with primitive methods and lack of time, resulted in crude, fiery concoctions. As circumstances gradually changed, however, and tastes became more refined, whiskies were produced with more care and were properly aged in wooden casks. Two types of whisky dominate the whisky market in America today: Bourbon and Rye. Until the late 1800s, Rye whisky, produced mainly in Pennsylvania (and most notably by Abraham Overholt), enjoyed a greater popularity than Bourbon. But this began to change in the 1800s when higher taxes forced distillers to examine their costs: rye grain was simply more expensive than corn; and the price of Rye inevitably had to reflect this expense, resulting in declining sales.

Bourbon originated at Georgetown, in Bourbon County, Kentucky, and was made from corn, the most plentiful grain available. Today, however, Bourbon is made from a mixture of at least 51% corn (required by law), rye, wheat, oats and barley. Individual distillers have their own grain and yeast formulas as well as particular manufacturing methods. As for aging, years ago it was discovered that charring the insides of the oak barrels used to store Bourbon whisky added considerably to the taste and aroma of the liquor. Today this is standard procedure, required by law. Prolonged storage in these barrels, in humidity-controlled warehouses, also transforms the whisky to a deeper color and increases the alcoholic content.

CANADIAN WHISKY

Canadian whiskies are best described as a distinctive blend of whiskies unique in taste, aroma and lightness. Canadian legal requirements as they relate to liquor production are primarily related to tax matters and the government has set no limitations on formulas, distilling proofs or aging requirements. Free from bureaucratic interference, distillers in Canada have been able to create whiskies that are light, mellow, gentle and smooth — and extremely popular. Canadian whiskies are a blend of whiskies made from corn, wheat, barley, rye and other cereal grains. Specific grain formulas are regarded as trade secrets of individual distillers. Production methods are similar to those used in America, except for certain advantages gained through having no governmental restrictions: for example, to compensate for evaporation losses during aging, new whisky may be added to replace the amount lost. Also, Canadian whisky may be bottled in bond when two years old and may be bottled at 90 proof. Nearly all Canadian whisky is over six years old when marketed, however — and any whisky less than four years must be identified by label.

BLENDED WHISKY

Blended whisky is becoming increasingly popular and constitutes almost 50% of the whisky consumed today. Most consumers prefer it because it is a lighter, smoother and more consistent product. At the same time, the producer benefits from the trend toward lighter whiskies because it is less expensive to blend straight whiskies with cheaper neutral spirits. In addition, the producer is able to maintain greater control over the balance and quality of his whisky, and is able to duplicate a successful blending formula indefinitely.

The production of blended whiskies would have been impossible without the introduction of the continuous still, which not only allowed for the increased production of spirits, but also gave distillers an opportunity to investigate and develop new kinds of whiskies. Blended whiskies, already characteristically light in flavor and body, are being made even lighter to satisfy public demand.

The quality of a blended whisky is governed by two factors: the caliber of the whiskies and spirits used and the varieties and proportions of straight whiskies to grain neutral spirits. Whereas straight whiskies (distilled at less than 160 proof) contribute aroma, flavor and body to the product, unaged neutral spirits, distilled at proofs of 190 and above, are almost flavorless and so add lightness and smooth texture. The law requires that blended whisky contain a minimum of 20% straight whisky, but says nothing about the quality of that whisky. Nor does the law stipulate the type of straight whisky to be used. This is left up to the distiller, who, for the most part, is able to control how the whisky will taste. The law also allows the use of certain "blending materials" in blended whiskies — up to 2 1/2% by volume. This allows for considerable manipulation of taste through the addition of fruit juices or wines.

GIN

There are two basic types or styles of gin on the market. One is Dutch gin — also called Schiedam, Hollands or Geneva gin — and the other is Dry gin, labeled London Dry by gin producers in many countries. (Just as the name "London Gin" no longer has any geographical significance, the term "dry" has no real meaning — all gins are essentially dry.) Different manufacturing methods used in the production of each account for the distinct differences in character of these two kinds of gin.

All gins start out as neutral spirits distilled from grain — mainly corn. Grain formulas vary from distiller to distiller: for example, corn, rye and barley, in approximately equal parts, are used in the making of Dutch gin, while in England the formula for gin consists of 75% corn, 15% barley malt and 10% other grains. But the truth is, the grain formula used contributes to the taste of the final product *only* when the alcohol is distilled at a low proof (as in the case of Dutch gin). Otherwise, the base material, once highly refined, is indistinguishable. In making Dutch gin, juniper berries (the most important flavoring ingredient in gin) and a small amount of other aromatics are chopped and added directly to the mash of grains. Then, after fermentation has taken place the resulting liquid, or beer, is distilled and re-distilled in a pot still at a low proof. The final product is a gin which is just as dry as the so-called "dry" gins, but heavier and more pungent in taste. In fact, because the taste is so pronounced, Dutch gin is generally unsuitable for use in cocktail recipes and is best drunk chilled or straight.

To make Dry gin, the beer obtained from the grain mash is distilled in a column still. The spirit produced from this initial distillation is then re-distilled, or rectified, to eliminate all possible traces of impurities. The result is a pure spirit of a high alcoholic strength — much too strong to drink — which must be reduced with distilled water. Adding flavoring agents to the distillate is the next step in the gin-making process. To this end, the spirit is re-distilled along with a variety of herbs and spices. Distillers use their own secret blend of botanicals, a formula which may have been passed down over hundreds of years, to create the distinctive flavor of their gin. Again, the principal ingredient is always the juniper berry. These dark-blue berries give the gin a special "medicinal" quality. Coriander seed, angelica root, cassia bark, licorice, dried lemon and orange peel, cinnamon, anise, caraway and fennel are among the botanicals used to add nuances of flavor. They can be mixed into and distilled with the spirit or suspended in mesh baskets above the spirit in the still, so that when distillation begins, the spirit vapors will mingle with the flavoring oils of the botanicals. These vapors, having acquired a delicate flavor, are then condensed to yield finished gin. Another method of infusing the neutral spirits with flavor is to prepare the spirit in one still and produce a distillate from the extract of berries, roots, spices and herbs in another. This flavoring spirit and the alcoholic spirit are then combined to make gin.

A brief mention must be made of two other, less common varieties of gin: Plymouth Gin and Old Tom Gin. Old Tom — ideally used in a Tom Collins drink — is simply a sweetened version of the London Dry-type gin, and Plymouth Gin, a proprietary brand from the city of the same name, is known for its slightly strong, heavy flavor. (Sloe gin, it should be noted here, is not a gin, but a liqueur made with the sloe plum of the blackthorn bush.)

Whereas other kinds of spirits must be aged for a period of time, there is no need to age gin: it does not have to be stored away to mellow and mature. Rather, when it comes from the still, and is reduced in proof to bottling strength, it is ready to be marketed. Today gin is universally accepted, but in its earlier history it had a notorious reputation. It was imbibed (especially in London) in vast quantities, often illicitly distilled, and came to be associated with working-class alcoholism. The London "gin palaces" of the 1800s, and the Cocktail Age, following on the heels of Prohibition, did as much as anything to transform gin into a fashionable drink, as opposed to one which was merely popular.

RUM

Rum, a by-product of sugar, is produced mainly in tropical areas where the raw materials used to make it are readily available. Today most rum is made in the West Indies, particularly in Puerto Rico, Jamaica, the Virgin Islands, Martinique, Barbados and Trinidad, as well as in the adjacent area of Guyana.

To make rum, sugar cane is first crushed to yield a juice. This is boiled down to a thick syrup. When the sugar in the syrup crystallizes, the sugar is removed. What remains when it has been extracted is molasses, the substance used for rum distilling. The molasses will have retained an amount of sugar — about 5% — which must be fermented (converted into alcohol). This is done by adding water and yeast to the molasses, as well as some leftover distillate from a previous distillation. In a matter of days (the exact number depends on the type of yeast used) the fermentation process is completed: the original wash of molasses, water and yeast has been transformed into a fermented mash, containing about 7% alcohol. The next step is to refine out the alcohol, separating it from most of the other liquid. This can take place in a pot still, in which case the mash must be distilled twice, or in a continuous still. As has been noted elsewhere, these stills produce spirits of differing qualities: the continuous still yields a lighter, purer, more alcoholic spirit; whereas the pot still produces a lower proofed spirit with more character and flavor. In either case, only the middle portion of distillate — the madilla — is used for rum. The rest is collected and later redistilled to make sure no alcohol is wasted.

The rum is aged in wood for a number of years, the length of time depending on the type of rum being produced and the judgment of the distiller. Again, heavier rums, containing more residual constituents, need more time to mellow and mature than do higher-proofed rums. The neutral rums, aged for a shorter length of time, are often filtered through layers of charcoal and sand, leaving them with an even lighter taste and body. Finally, the blending of rums takes place: rums of different ages and distillations, but generally from the same type of still, are blended together to ensure a balanced and consistent product.

Rums can be divided into two categories: they are either light-bodied and dry, perfectly suited for mixing in cocktails (such rums are produced in Puerto Rico and the Virgin Islands, for example), or they are the flavorsome, full-bodied rums typical of Jamaica, Martinique and Guyana. In between are a variety of medium rums. This is not to say that each country produces only one kind of rum and not any other. Rather, certain areas are better known for a particular type. Within the two broad categories mentioned above there is a great deal of variation and individuality, for the character and quality of a rum is determined by many factors: where and how the sugar cane was grown; the quality of the water used throughout production; whether natural or cultured yeast was used (the former requiring a much longer fermentation period); and finally, how the rum was distilled, aged and blended. The special character of every rum depends upon its geographical origin:

BARBADOS RUM This fragrant rum, ideally suited to light punches and cocktails, falls midway between light rums and the heavier types.

DEMERARA RUM A dark rum produced in Guyana. Distilled in column stills instead of by the pot still method, Demerara is available at various proofs, including 151 proof.

HAITIAN RUM Made from the sap of the sugar cane instead of from the syrup. The result is a fine, flavorful, mellow rum which can be sipped, sans mixer, like brandy.

JAMAICAN RUM The typical rum of Jamaica is full bodied, richly flavored and either golden or deep mahogany in color, depending on the amount of caramel coloring used.

PUERTO RICAN RUM A light-bodied rum, usually blended, with a delicate dry taste.

VIRGIN ISLANDS RUM Another light rum. But this one is not aged for as long as Puerto Rican rum, and is not as fine.

BATAVIAN ARRACK From the island of Java, Indonesia. The unique flavor of this dry, aromatic rum comes from a combination of factors: the local water, molasses and special yeast used, and the Javanese rice cakes placed in the fermenting vats.

VODKA

Vodka is the ultimate alcoholic drink from which all impurities have been removed by distillation, rectification and repeated filtration. Its main merit is that it adds zest to whatever it is mixed with, with a minimum effect on taste and a maximum effect on morale. As a mixer it makes soft drinks hard and hard drinks harder.

Vodka — a diminutive of the Russian word for water — is believed to have originated in either Russia or Poland as far back as the 12th century. It ranks in Europe as one of the oldest and most versatile of liquors. In North America, the vodka vogue really began in the late 1940s, when a restaurant man with a large stock of ginger beer on hand created a new drink to get rid of it. He put vodka, ginger beer and a slice of lime in a mug and called the concoction a "Moscow Mule." The idea caught on. Vodka gained fame as a great mixer and before long everybody began making new drinks with it. Since that time the popularity of vodka has grown dramatically.

Like whisky, vodka is a spirit made from a fermented mash of grains. But whereas whisky is distilled at a low proof specifically to retain flavor, vodka is taken from the stills at 190 proof or higher and therefore has very little character. It is then subjected to a process which further refines it: the pure grain neutral spirits are taken from the stills, transferred to tanks and slowly filtered through columns of charcoal. This in effect renders the liquor colorless, odorless and tasteless. Finally it is reduced to 80-100 proof before bottling (vodka requires no aging.) From here, vodka finds its way into a multitude of mixed drinks, including vodka martinis, Screwdrivers and the ever-popular Bloody Mary. It can also be drunk straight. Indeed, as vodka connoisseurs know, the traditional way to take vodka is straight, ice cold, and in a single gulp from a one-ounce glass. An appetizer usually follows — a bite of smoked salmon, herring or other delicacy — before the glass is refilled.

There are many varieties of vodka available today, made in countries such as Russia, Poland, Czechoslovakia, France, England, Israel, America and Canada. Unless you are a true connoisseur of subtle variations in spirits, it should make very little difference which one you drink. All of them are, by definition, unflavored. Nevertheless, there are differences among brands, particularly among vodkas from America or Britain, for example, and those from the USSR or Poland. The latter can be described as having more character, a result of differences in water, grains and yeast, and methods and means of filtration.

BRANDY

Brandies are made from the fermented juice of grapes, as well as other fruits. But when the word brandy is used, unqualified by the additional name of a fruit, grape brandy is always understood. The finer products are blends of different brandies, each contributing distinctive characteristics of body, flavor, aroma, quality and age to the final blend. The kinds of brandy commonly known are:

COGNAC

Brandy can be made from wine produced anywhere in the world, but the most exquisite brandy is Cognac, distilled from wine made in the section of south-western France known as the Charentais, the principal city of which is Cognac. The Department of Charente is divided by law into seven brandy-producing areas. Only brandy made in these areas may be designated as Cognac. In other words, while all Cognac is brandy, not all brandy is Cognac. The large shippers of Cognac brandies — firms such as Courvoisier, Hennessey and Rémy Martin — do not own acres of vineyards. Nor do they operate distilleries. Rather, individual farmers tend their own small vineyards, harvest their own grapes and, in most cases, do their own distilling. The new, young brandies are then sold to shippers who age and blend them to their requirements.

By law, Cognac must be made from at least 90% St. Emilion, Folle Blanche and Colombard grape varieties. The result is a thin wine with a sharp, fruity taste. For conversion into Cognac, it must be double-distilled in an old-fashioned pot still. When it comes from the still, colorless and with an alcoholic strength of about 70%, the brandy is ready for aging. Here, French law becomes quite specific: the casks used for storing Cognac brandy must be made from oak trees grown near the town of Limoges or from the oak trees of the Troncais forest. This wood and the new brandy interact in special ways during storage.

Over a period of months, the brandy absorbs oxygen through the pores of the wood. Some evaporation occurs and there is a loss of alcoholic strength. But, more importantly, taste and perfume are changed and refined and the brandy, as it mellows, becomes amber in color. To create a product consistent in quality and taste, shippers then select brandies from their large stocks and blend them.

ARMAGNAC

This is the only other brandy in the world that is recognized as equal to any but the very finest old Cognacs. It is the product of the region of Armagnac, in France. Armagnac is a highly-prized brandy, considerably different in taste than Cognac. Like Cognac, it is made principally from St. Emilion, Folle Blanche and Colombard grapes. But it is distilled in a special continuous still at a relatively low proof and, as a result, is more heavily and distinctively flavored. Also, the casks in which the brandy is aged are made from local wood — black oak of Gascony — which contributes significantly to the strong, dry taste of Armagnac.

OTHER BRANDIES

Many countries produce brandy: some of the finest brandies, after the products of France, are those of South Africa; California now actually produces more brandy than France; and Australia has a flourishing trade as well. A number of other brandies are described below.

PISCO is a brandy, produced mostly in Peru, which is distilled from muscat grapes. It is usually distilled at a very high proof and aged (for a short time only) in paraffin-lined clay jars. As a result, Pisco is of a lighter color than most other brandies.

APPLE BRANDY known in France as Calvados, originated in the northwest of France in the province of Normandy. It is distilled (in pot stills) from fermented apple cider, and is aged in wood for 10 years. In the United States, however, the product is known as Applejack. It is produced in continuous stills and aged for 2-5 years in wood.

SLIVOVITZ is a brandy distilled from plums and usually originates in Hungary, Czechoslovakia, Yugoslavia and Romania. It is generally bottled at a very high proof after being aged in wood, and retains a very distinctive plum flavor.

KIRSCH or KIRSCHWASSER is a colorless brandy made from cherries grown in France, Germany and Switzerland. The brandy, which is very strong, is the distillation of cherries and pits, with no syrups added. Kirsch is primarily used in mixed drinks, in cooking and in flavoring various fruit desserts.

MISCELLANEOUS SPIRITS

ANIS

The name "anis" is a general term given to a variety of licorice and aniseed-flavored spirits known as *pastis*. Different countries have their own version of this product. In Spain it is Ojen; in Greece, Ouzo; in Italy it is called Anesone; Turkey has Raki; and France is famous for Pernod and Ricard. All of these drinks are quite strong. They are customarily diluted with water (5 parts of water to 1 part of liquor) and served in tall glasses as apéritifs or refreshers. Pastis may be described as the modern substitute for Absinthe — that legendary elixir which has been banned, because of its potency, in many countries. What makes *pastis* acceptable where Absinthe is not is simply that *pastis* is of generally lower strength.

ARRACK

Arrack — or arak, raki, arack etc. — is associated with the Far East and Middle East. In spite of the variations on its name, the basic meaning is the same: *arak* is Arabic for "juice," or "sweet." Although most forms of this spirit are essentially the same, the precise nature of arrack varies from country to country, depending on the ingredients used to make it. In Lebanon and Syria it is made from grapes; in Iraq and Egypt, from dates; in India, fermented palm-sap is used; and elsewhere the main ingredient varies from coconut juice, to palm juice, molasses, or rice.

AQUAVIT

Aquavit, which translates as "water of life," is the national beverage of the Scandinavian countries, where it is better known as "schnapps." This pungent, colorless spirit is made from grain or potatoes (in much the same way as gin) and is flavored primarily with caraway seeds plus fennel, aniseed, orange peel, lemon peel, cardamom and coriander. The specific mix of extra ingredients accounts to some extent for differences in sweetness and flavor among brands. The Danish version of Aquavit, for example, tends to be drier than the Swedish equivalent. The proper way to serve this drink is ice cold in a one-ounce glass, along with appetizers and a beer chaser. Once you have toasted your drinking companion Scandinavian-style (the word to use is *skaal*, pronounced "skol"), the liquor should be downed in one swallow: then reach for a bite of food and a swig of beer with which to wash it all down.

OKOLEHAO

"Oke", an unusual-tasting drink which is available in only some parts of North America, is made in Hawaii from sugar-cane molasses and other ingredients. Two kinds are manufactured — one white and one dark — and both are bottled at 90 proof or less. A number of cocktail recipes call for Okolehao. As well, this spirit may be taken straight, on the rocks, or in tall drinks.

TEQUILA

With a little practice, the traditional Mexican technique for drinking tequila can be mastered: the head is tilted back and sour lime or lemon juice squeezed into the mouth. A quick lick of salt from the back of the hand is followed by a shot glass full of tequila, gulped down fast. For those less adventurous souls, tequila can be mixed with a variety of ingredients to make cocktails and other drinks — the Margarita and the Bloody Maria are two of the most popular.

Tequila is made in Mexico from a plant, similar to cactus, known as Mescal. When this plant reaches maturity (after 10-12 years) the base, which resembles an oversized pineapple, is cut away. This part of the plant contains the sap used to make tequila. The "pineapples" are taken to the distillery where they are steamed, then shredded to free all the juices contained within. Fermentation of the juices takes place in large vats; and distillation is carried out in pot stills. The finished product is drawn off at about 104 proof and is bottled at 80-100 proof. Most tequila — in fact any that is white in colour — is unaged. Gold tequilas are aged for about two years in oak vats and are pleasantly mellow as a result.

LIQUEURS AND CORDIALS

Basically, a liqueur can be defined as an alcoholic beverage, the result of combining a spirit (usually brandy) with flavoring material, and adding sugar. Liqueurs should not be confused with fruit brandies. To clarify: liqueurs tasting of fruit are merely *flavored* with the essence of fruits. Fruit brandies, on the other hand, are actually *made* from a fermented mash of fruits. Another possible source of confusion — *liqueur* and *cordial* mean exactly the same thing. And in France, liqueurs may be labelled *digestifs*. The word *crème* is applied to liqueurs that are especially smooth and flavorful.

Many of the fine liqueurs we enjoy today were first developed centuries ago, by alchemists, for use as medicinal remedies, love potions, aphrodisiacs and general cure-alls. As the distillation process became better understood and more universally used, and as spices, herbs and sugar became readily available, the bitter medicines of the Middle Ages were converted into intriguing new alcoholic drinks. In the early days fruits were rarely used. Most liqueurs were based on flowers, plants and herbs. It was not until the 19th century that fruit liqueurs became popular, reflecting a gradual change in taste for lighter, richer after-dinner drinks rather than the heavier digestives of medicinal origin.

The discovery that fruits could provide a ready source of flavor opened the door to the production of a great variety of liqueurs. It was also found that the manufacture of liqueurs could be carried out virtually anywhere in the world. Despite this universality, certain countries (France and Holland in particular) have produced such excellent liqueurs that their products have become the standards of acceptance for the entire industry. Specialty liqueurs with wide general appeal have also been produced in other countries. We have, for example, Italy's Strega and Amaretto di Saronno, Germany's Kümmel, American Crème d'Yvette and Forbidden Fruit, and Denmark's Cherry Herring.

There are two basic methods by which liqueurs are made: maceration (or percolation) and distillation. When the distillation process is used, as it frequently is, to produce plant liqueurs, ingredients such as seeds, spices, herbs, peel and leaves are soaked in brandy for 1-2 days before being placed in a pot still with more brandy. The aromatic essences of these ingredients are then distilled along with the alcoholic vapors.

Maceration, which is akin to making tea, consists simply of steeping fruit in a base spirit such as brandy for a period of time, and allowing the liquid to absorb the flavor, bouquet and color of the fruit. A technique related to this, but used to make plant liqueurs, is percolation. By this method, spirits are percolated through layers of a particular flavoring agent (coffee beans, vanilla pods, for example) so that the liquid, washing over and dripping through the agent, absorbs its flavor and aroma. In either case, when the spirit, infused with the essence of the flavoring ingredients, is drawn off, the mass of fruit or vegetable matter that remains is often distilled to extract any remnants of liquor and flavor. The resulting distillate is then combined with the original infused spirit, and this mixture may even be blended delicately with other infusions or ingredients. If necessary, the product may be aged awhile; sugar syrup, water and alcohol are added as required; and, finally, the liqueur is allowed to "rest" before filtering and bottling.

While liqueurs were at one time used primarily as after-dinner drinks, in recent years they have achieved glory heights as featured ingredients in thousands of delicious cocktails. The following list of various types of the more popular liqueurs includes a brief description of each.

ABSINTHE Absinthe is an alcoholic liqueur containing oils of wormwood, anise and other aromatics. It was very popular in France in the late 19th and early 20th centuries until it was banned in virtually every country because of its potency and allegedly undesirable side effects.

ADVOKAAT This is a famous Dutch liqueur, similar in color and texture to an eggnog, but with a distinctive flavor all its own. It is a 40-proof emulsion of brandy, fresh eggs and sugar and is available in a great range of consistencies. All varieties should be shaken before use, since the ingredients have a tendency to separate.

ALMENDRADO A delightful Mexican liqueur with a bitter almond flavor.

AMARETTO di SARONNO This is a sweet, rich, tasty liqueur with a distinct almond flavor and aroma which, strangely enough, is achieved through the distillation of apricot pits. It has a fairly low alcohol content (28%) and medium sugar content. It is made in Saronno, Italy, but imitations are now being made in several other countries.

AMSTERDAM A liqueur made up of Cherry Brandy and Advokaat.

AMOURETTE A French liqueur, of a purple or violet color.

ANESONE A 90-proof licorice-flavored liqueur made in Italy and the U.S.A.

ANGELICA A Basque liqueur with a very sweet taste, flavored with angelica and other plants common to the Pyrennes foothills in France.

ANISETTE One of the oldest liqueurs known, originally used for medicinal purposes. It is a sweet, white liqueur made chiefly in the south of France and flavored with anise seeds that give it a delicate licorice taste. It has a sugar content of 40%, contains 30% alcohol and is equally popular as an apéritif, an after-dinner drink and as a favorite ingredient in cocktail recipes.

APPLE GIN A colorless liqueur made in Scotland.

APRICOT LIQUEUR An extremely popular fruit liqueur presently manufactured in France, Hungary, and the U.S.A. The flavor originates with dried apricots and the crushed kernels of their stones, treated with other ingredients through the maceration process.

AURUM A pale gold Italian liqueur with a delicate orange flavor, of medium sweetness and strong bouquet.

B AND B A popular liqueur made up of half Brandy and half Benedictine. This blend, which is dark amber in color, tastes (exactly as might be expected) like Benedictine but is drier, with a definite Cognac character.

BENEDICTINE One of the oldest and most widely known liqueurs, distilled by the Benedictine monks of Fecamp, France, since 1510. Benedictine is made of the finest brandy and a secret recipe of many plants, seeds and herbs, including cloves, nutmeg, cinnamon, peppermint, angelica root, aromatic calamun and flowers of arnica. It is highly aromatic and very sweet and many people prefer to drink it combined with brandy in equal parts — a blend know as B and B (see above). It is sold in bottles of a distinctive shape, the labels of which bear the initials D.O.M. The liqueur was dedicated by the monks to God centuries ago, with the Latin words "Deo Optimo Maximo" which means "To God, most good, most great."

BLACKBERRY LIQUEUR   Distilled from blackberries and other ingredients, it may occasionally have a small amount of red wine added. Generally bottled at 60 to 70 proof it may be served straight or mixed in cocktails.

BOLSBERRY   A pleasant, moderately sweet liqueur that derives its flavor from a mixture of fruits, among which blackcurrants (cassis) are an important ingredients.

CALISAY   A Spanish liqueur made in the Andalusia region of Spain. It is fairly sweet, with strong quinine characteristics.

CAPRICORNIA   An Australian liqueur made of tropical fruit. The name is derived from the Tropic of Capricorn, in which area the fruit is grown.

CASCARILLA   A popular South American liqueur flavored with spices and various barks.

CHANNELLE   A rare liqueur made from cinnamon and a number of other spices.

CHARTREUSE   This world-famous liqueur is usually made in green and yellow (occasionally in white) and was originally produced in La Grand Chartreuse, the old Carthusian monastery near Grenable, France. It was made there by the monks from 1607 to 1901, at which time the monks left France and settled in Taragona, Spain. Green Chartreuse, considered by many to be the world's finest cordial, is said to contain 230 separate ingredients and Yellow Chartreuse more than 120. The formulas for both are similar, although Yellow Chartreuse contains honey as well as sugar and is therefore sweeter. Today, the Chartreuse distillery and aging cellars are located in Voiron, France and the formula remains in the hands of Carthusian monks who work in the distillery.

CHERI-SUISSE   Chocolate and cherry flavors blend perfectly in this liqueur.

CHERRY LIQUEUR   A liqueur distilled from the juices of ripe cherries fermented together with crushed cherry pits to give it a distinctively bitter almond tinge. Cherry liqueurs are sweetened to varying degrees, and all are blends of cherry spirits, various brandies and flavoring essences depending on individual distillers' formulas and the legal requirements of the country of origin.

CHERRY HEERING   A popular cherry-flavored liqueur also known as Peter Heering. Made from the celebrated red cherries of southern Denmark, it has a relatively low alcoholic content and is dark red in color.

CLEOPATRA   A chocolate-and-orange-flavored liqueur.

COINTREAU   Probably the best-known and most popular orange liqueur, Cointreau originates in the Loire Valley town of Angers in France. It is a light, colorless and refreshing beverage with an extremely pleasant aroma, flavor and aftertaste. Cointreau is made of orange peels distilled in the presence of high-proof neutral alcohol with some added aromatics. It is marketed all over the world in a readily identifiable square-shaped amber bottle.

CORDIAL CAMPARI   A light yellow-colored liqueur made by the distillation of raspberries.

CORDIAL MÉDOC   A fine liqueur made of curaçao, orange, champagne, cognac and claret.

CRÈME d'ALMOND   A liqueur similar to Crème de Noyaux. It is pink in color and flavored with fruit stones and almonds.

CRÈME d'ANANAS   A fine, smooth liqueur made by steeping pineapple in brandy and flavoring with vanilla. It is bottled at 60-proof strength.

CRÈME de BANANES   Made of very ripe bananas macerated in neutral alcohol. It has an unmistakably strong banana flavor and aroma, is yellow in color and has quite a thick consistency.

CRÈME de CACAO   A very sweet liqueur with a strong chocolate flavor, made of cocoa beans, cloves, mace and vanilla beans.

CRÈME de CASSIS   A popular French liqueur made from crushed black-currants steeped in neutral high-proof alcohol for several months and finally blended with water and sugar. Crème de Cassis is quite sweet, with a strong blackcurrant taste and a low alcoholic content.

CRÈME de CIEL   A Dutch liqueur, after the style of Curacao, with a light blue coloring.

CRÈME de FRAISES   A sweet French liqueur with a flavor and color derived primarily from strawberries.

CRÈME de FRAMBOISE   A French liqueur with the flavor and coloring of raspberries, bottled at 60 proof. It is *not* the same as Framboise, which is a white, unsweetened raspberry Brandy.

CRÈME de MANDARINE   A sweet liqueur made primarily of tangerine peels. It is generally bright orange in color and is bottled at 60 proof.

CRÈME de MENTHE   A cool, refreshing and very popular liqueur made from mint leaves steeped in brandy spirits and sweetened with a sugar syrup. It is marketed in red, in green and is also available as a colorless beverage. All varieties have an identical taste, since the coloring is of neutral vegetable matter.

CRÈME de MOCHA   A light brown French liqueur made from coffee beans steeped in brandy.

CRÈME de NOISETTE   A liqueur with a taste derived primarily from hazel nuts steeped in neutral alcohol spirits.

CRÈME de NOYAUX   A French liqueur made by steeping a mixture of apricot stones, cherry stones, peach stones, myrrh and nutmeg in brandy. The resulting beverage has a distinct almond flavor and is bottled both pink and colorless.

CRÈME de PICCO   A Dutch liqueur made by macerating tea leaves in brandy. It is sweetened with a sugar syrup.

CRÈME de ROSE   An exotic French liqueur made from rose petal essences and vanilla. It is bottled at 60 proof, has a delicate taste and a delightful fragrance and color.

CRÈME de THÉ   A colorless French liqueur made by steeping tea leaves in a blend of brandy and neutral alcohol.

CRÈME de VANILLE   A sweet liqueur made by steeping vanilla beans in brandy. Brown in color, it has a strong vanilla flavor.

CRÈME de VIOLETTE   A French liqueur made from the essences of violet petals and vanilla.

CRÈME d'YVETTE   A popular violet-flavored American liqueur of relatively high alcoholic strength.

CURAÇAO   A sweet, orange-flavored liqueur made from peels of the bitter Curaçao orange of the West Indies, complemented lightly with aromatic spices steeped in brandy, and blended with neutral alcohol. Available in a variety of colors.

DRAMBUIE   A world-famous Scotch liqueur based on fine old Scotch whisky which is blended with heather honey, a secret essence of herbal oils, sugar syrup and water.

FALERNUM   A mild, colorless flavor syrup with a very modest alcoholic content. It is made of sugar syrup, almond, ginger, lime and various spices.

FIOR d'ALPE   An Italian herbal liqueur from the north of Italy, derived from wild flowers that grow on the slopes of the Alps. Bottled with a small branch in each bottle around which sugar crystals form.

FORBIDDEN FRUIT   One of only two American liqueurs (the other is Crème d'Yvette) exported to Europe. The flavoring is a mixture of grapefruit and orange steeped in fine French cognac. It has a bright red color and is bottled at 64 proof.

GALLIANO   An Italian liqueur produced in Milan and named after a hero of the Italo-Abyssinian war at the turn of the century. The flavor is gained from a distillation of various herbs and plants, aged and blended with sugar and water. It has a bright yellow coloring and a mild, clear flavor.

GINGER-FLAVORED BRANDY   A combination of fresh ginger root and brandy — perfect in a hot grog.

GLAYVA   A Scotch liqueur based on a straight grain whisky blended with a number of herbal ingredients that produce a lighter, drier beverage than Drambuie.

GLEN MIST   A liqueur similar to Drambuie but made of a blend of Scotch and Irish Whiskies. Bottled with a red seal at 70 proof and with a gold seal at 45 proof.

GOLDWASSER (DANZIGER) A colorless, sweet liqueur with a flavor obtained primarily from orange and lemon peels, coriander, cardamom, mace and other spicy herbs and plants. Each bottle contains tiny flecks of gold leaf, in keeping with the alchemists' traditional belief in the positive medicinal qualities of gold.

GRAND MARNIER Is one of the world's finest blends of champagne cognac and orange curaçao. It is golden amber in color with an orange flavor and is bottled with a relatively high alcoholic content (80 proof).

HALF AND HALF A sweet Dutch liqueur made of a blend of half orange curaçao and half bitters.

IRISH MIST An Irish liqueur based on aged Irish Whiskies, herbal extracts, Irish heather honey, sugar syrup and water. It has a light body, moderate sweetness, a pleasant aroma and a complex taste of orange, almonds and Irish whisky.

IZARRA A Basque liqueur made in Bayonne, France, just north of the Spanish border. It comes in both yellow and green colors — the former is bottled at 40 proof and the latter at 50 proof. Izarra is made from flowers and many other plants steeped in neutral alcohol spirits, distilled and finally blended with Armagnon.

KAHLUA A Mexican liqueur, very sweet and with a delightful coffee aroma and pleasant coffee flavor.

KEUCK From Turkey, a dark-brown mocha liqueur.

KÜMMEL An extremely popular liqueur with agreeable digestive properties. It has been made in Holland for centuries, although it has since been made in Lithuania and Germany as well. Its alcoholic base is always a highly distilled neutral spirit produced from grain or potatoes. It has a flavor based on caraway and cumin seeds and its sweetness varies depending on the distiller.

LIQUEUR d'OR A sweet French liqueur, similar to Goldwasser, with a flavor based on orange and lemon peel, nuts and plants. It is bottled with tiny flecks of gold in keeping with the ancient alchemists' belief in the positive, therapeutic qualities of gold.

LOCHAN ORA A liqueur based on Scotch, sweetened with honey and flavored with herbs.

MANDARINE A French liqueur with a flavor based on the dried peel of tangerines.

MARASCHINO A liqueur, originally produced in Yugoslavia, with a flavor of the Dalmatian Marasca cherry. Since 1947, however, it has been produced in Torreglia, Italy, with the flavor obtained from Marasca cherries grown in that area. In the manufacture of this liqueur, cherries, stones and stems are all used in the fermentation. The refining process of this liqueur is so demanding that approximately 12 pounds of cherries are required to flavor about a quart of the final product.

MARNIQUE An Australian liqueur, similar to Grand Marnier, with a flavor derived primarily from Mandarine oranges or tangerines.

MASTIKHA (MASTIC) A liqueur of Middle East origin with a flavor derived from the mastic shrub and aniseed.

MAZARIN A light brown liqueur, produced in France, with a flavor similar to that of Benedictine.

MELETTE A brand of anisette produced in Italy.

MIRABELLE A white French liqueur made from the Mirabelle, a type of yellow plum grown in the Alsace region of France.

MONASTIQUE An imitation of Benedictine originating in South America.

MONTE AGUILA A Jamaican liqueur with a flavor derived from rum, spiced with pimento, cloves and other spices.

OJEN A colorless anise-flavored liqueur, made in the town of Ojen in the south of Spain.

OUZO An anise-flavored apéritif liqueur made in Greece and Cyprus.

PARFAIT AMOUR An exotic liqueur of a beautiful royal purple color. Its flavor is created by blending together lemons, oranges, coriander, anise, vanilla, brandy and sugar syrup.

PASTIS; PASTIS de MARSEILLE A licorice-flavored French liqueur.

PEACH LIQUEUR   A liqueur with the color of brandy and a flavor derived from fresh and dried peaches.

PEPPERMINT SCHNAPPS   A mint liqueur, with a lighter texture and milder flavor than Crème de Menthe.

PICON   A French bitter liqueur, primarily used as an apéritif in France when mixed with soda. It is better known elsewhere as a useful cocktail ingredient.

QUETSCH   A French liqueur with the flavor of plums and a gin-like appearance.

PRUNELLE; CRÈME de PRUNELLE   A sweet, fruity liqueur made primarily from plums, green in color, and bottled at a high 80-proof alcoholic strength.

RAKI   An anise-flavored liqueur of Greek, Cypriot and Turkish manufacture bottled with an exceptionally high alcoholic content.

RICARD   Another pastis from Marseille.

ROCK AND RYE   A liqueur with a rye whisky base blended with grain neutral spirits, rock candy syrup, and flavors obtained from mascerated lemons, oranges and cherries.

ROIANO   An amber-colored Italian liqueur tasting of anise and vanilla.

ROSOLIO   This liqueur is similar to Crème de Rose.

SABRA   A popular Israeli liqueur, with a distinct chocolate flavor, made from a blend of Jaffa oranges.

SAMBUCA ROMANA   An Italian liqueur with a flavor based on elderberries and aniseed.

SLOE GIN   A lovely, mild, red liqueur made from sloeberries of the blackthorn bush.

SOUTHERN COMFORT   A velvety, 100-proof whisky-and-peach combination from America.

STREGA   An Italian herbal liqueur produced in the town of Benevento. It is light in color, of medium body and has a strong, somewhat medicinal flavor.

SWEDISH PUNCH   A Swedish liqueur with a flavor obtained from a blend of Batavian rum, spices and citrus extracts.

TIA MARIA   A light, dry Jamaican liqueur with a very pleasant coffee taste and aroma.

TIDDY'S CANADIAN LIQUEUR   A light amber, moderately sweet cordial, made of a blend of Canadian whiskies, herbals and an orange-based flavor.

TRIPLE SEC   A colorless liqueur of the curaçao family, with a flavor based on sweet and bitter oranges, complemented with spices and roots. Usually bottled with a higher alcoholic content than other curaçao-related liqueurs.

TUACA   A clear, amber Italian liqueur with a "coconut" taste. It is made from a secret formula but is known to result from a mixture of citrus fruits and milk steeped in alcohol spirits, distilled and blended with brandy.

VAN DER HUM   A liqueur, made in South Africa, that derives its flavor primarily from the South African tangerine.

VANDERMINT   A chocolate mint liqueur from Holland.

VIEILLE CURÉ   A French herbal liqueur made in Cenon, a suburb of Bordeaux. It is produced from a mixture of over 50 ingredients macerated in water and neutral alcohol, distilled and aged for up to three years and then blended with sugar syrup, honey, water and alcohol. Available in yellow and green varieties (the latter is bottled at a higher proof).

WISHNIAK   A liqueur, distilled in Poland, flavored by wild cherries and spices.

WINES OF THE WORLD

Wine can be simply defined as the fermented juice of freshly gathered, ripe grapes. It is one form of alcohol that can be made without special ingredients, equipment or chemistry, and in this sense is an entirely natural product, one that has been enjoyed and glorified for centuries. Four main classifications of wine are:

TABLE WINE (Natural, still wines)   Grapes are gathered and crushed, and the juice fermented naturally and completely before the wine is bottled. These wines are "still" in that the carbon dioxide produced during fermentation is allowed to dissipate through the wood of the casks in which the wine is stored. In time, only the still, non-volatile parts of the wine remain. Table wines are generally quite dry, with an alcoholic content of 14 per cent or less.

SPARKLING WINE   The effervescent wines such as Champagne and Asti Spumante "sparkle" because of the capture of CO_2 gas in the bottle during fermentation. These wines also have an alcoholic strength of up to 14 per cent.

FORTIFIED WINE   These are wines that have been fortified with the addition of grape brandy. The brandy not only makes the wine stronger (17-21 per cent alcohol), but it stops the fermentation process before completion so that some of the natural grape sugar remains in the wine. Fortified wine is therefore sweeter than most table wines, and is best served with dessert.

AROMATIC WINE   Wines that have been treated with herbs, roots, seeds, spices and other flavoring agents fall into this category. The best-known example is probably Vermouth. Aromatized wines make great mixers in cocktails, and are ideal served as apéritifs. Alcoholic content is anywhere from 15-20 per cent.

FRENCH WINES

BORDEAUX

France, the "Vineyard of the Earth," produces more fine wines than any other country in the world — and many of these wines come from Bordeaux, in the southwest corner of France. Within Bordeaux, there are five wine-producing districts that are of great importance: *Médoc*, northwest of Bordeaux, is the home of most of the great red wines; *Graves* produces several great reds and numerous excellent dry white wines; *Sauternes*, bounding Graves on the south, produces white dessert wines exclusively; and *St. Emilion* and *Pomerol*, east of Bordeaux, are, like the Médoc, districts producing red wines but wines generally fuller and richer in color than those of the Médoc.

Specific châteaux within these celebrated districts have become famous for the outstanding wines they produce. Château Margaux, Château Lafite-Rothschild, Château Latour, Château Haut-Brion, and Château d'Yquem are a few of the most famous. These wines, and others, are marked with the words, "Mis en bouteille au château." This phrase means that the wine was made, developed and bottled by the proprietor of the château. A wine that is château-bottled is always genuine.

BURGUNDY

The Burgundy region as a whole is comprised of four separate, wine-producing districts; the Mâconnais and Beaujolais; the Côte Chalonnaise; the vineyards surrounding the town of Chablis; and, finally, the Côte d'Or, or "Golden Slope." The Côte d'Or, which is only about 35 miles long and about a mile wide, is the most important wine-producing district in Burgundy. Among the several very fine wines produced in this district are: Le Montrachet, Muersault Corton (among the finest white wines produced in the world), Pommard, Volnay, Romanée-Conti, Richebourg, and La Tâche.

As a group, Burgundy wines are of exceptionally high quality and are therefore much imitated. Almost every country in the world has a wine which it dubs a Burgundy. People are definitely misled, however, if they associate such wines with true Burgundy. Genuine Burgundies are both robust and delicate. At their best there are only several wines which equal them. They really rank among the aristocrats of the wine world.

RHÔNE

The Rhône valley vineyards, situated just south of Burgundy, produce many delicious wines — wines that are red, white, sweet-tasting or dry, golden or rosé, still or sparkling. The red wines, for which the area is best known, are deeper in color than Burgundies and the whites have unsuspected strength. The most famous Rhône valley red wine is Châteauneuf-du-Pape, an intensely deep-colored wine with a particular sweet-bitterish taste. This wine was once the daily beverage of the Avignon Popes. Other good wines of this district are the dry Hermitage whites and Tavel wine. The latter, a rosé wine, is probably the best of its type in the world.

LOIRE

This region produces mostly rosé wines and delicate white wines. Pouilly-Fumé, Sancerre, Muscadet, Chinon and Vouvray, a light, fresh wine, are all good wines from the Loire valley vineyards.

ALSACE

The white wines from the vineyards on the French banks of the Rhine (the district of Alsace) are often called French Rhine Wines, for they do indeed resemble the Rhine wines of Germany more than they do French wines. Instead of taking on the name of the locale or vineyard where they are made, most are named after the grape from which they are produced. Thus we have Riesling, Traminer, Tokay, Sylvaner and several others.

GERMAN WINES

Germany is famous for its white wines. Most of them come from the valley of the Rhine and Moselle rivers. Four main districts produce German wines: The Rheingau, the Rheinhessen, the Palatinate (Rheinpfalz) and the Moselle. All four lie in or around the Rhine valley, where various towns and vineyards lend their names to the innumerable vintages of the region. The vineyards are the most northerly in the world. Consequently, great care and scientific culture are necessary to produce fine wines. The wines tend to be more hardy and drier than French wines, since they must develop and ripen in a very short space of time. Many of the wines originate with the Riesling vine. This vine is responsible for the characteristics of fine flavor, richness and character, and the clean, refreshing taste which most Rhine and Moselle wines share. In all, an enormous variety of German wines are available today in a great range of prices and tastes, and many of them work well as mixers in drinks.

ITALIAN WINES

Millions of gallons of wine are produced in Italy each year, mostly for home consumption. The acres planted with vines exceed those of France, since much of the total area of Italy is under vines. These vines, which grow so profusely across the land, produce many excellent wines. Some of the best known are *Barolo*, a full red wine from Piedmont in northern Italy; *Soave*, a white wine from the north; *Valpolicella*, a delicate red from Venetia, in the east; the archetypal Italian wine — *Chianti* — from Tuscany; *Orvieto*, a popular white wine; Italy's sparkling wine, *Asti Spumante*; a wine called *Lacrima Christi* ("the tears of Christ"), pressed from grapes grown on Mt. Vesuvius; and *Marsala*, a famous desert wine from Sicily. Aside from these special products there are many good Italian wines which are enjoyed simply for their clean, sound taste.

AMERICAN WINES

There are two main wine-producing areas in the United States: California and the East, particularly the Finger Lakes region of New York State. Although California wine is produced from grape varieties imported from Europe, differences in the soil and climate in which the vines are grown make California wines unique. Names such as Zinfandel, Gamay, Pinot Noir and Cabernet Sauvignon (red wines) or Pinot Blanc, Pinot Chardonnay and Riesling (white wines) signify premium wines. These wines, and others, are known as *varietals*. Quite simply, varietals are wines named after the grapes from which they are made, provided at least 51 per cent of the grape for which the wine is named was used in making the wine. Wines from the Eastern States are made from native grapes such as Delaware, Elvira and Concord, to name just a few. Also, new hybrid varieties created by crossbreeding native grapes with European vines are increasingly being used. Since the eastern vineyards are subject to short summers and long, severe winters, they yield wines that are quite different in character to those produced in California. Generally the East is known for white wines and for sparkling wines, especially champagne.

CHAMPAGNE

True champagne is made only from grapes grown in the old Province of Champagne in the northeast corner of France, just north of Burgundy and west of Alsace. It is known today as the Department of the Marne. Wines produced in other wine-producing districts of the world have been labeled champagne but, in the true sense of the word, they are not: only wine made in the French Department of the Marne is champagne. If the wine is produced in France and is labeled champagne, the cork itself will have the name Champagne imprinted on it.

Grape vines have been cultivated in Champagne for centuries; but up to the close of the 17th century only red and white still wines had been produced. Although the discovery of sparkling wines has been credited to Dom Perignon, Head Cellarer of the Abbey of Hautvillers, sparkling wines had been made before he was born. Champagne of the modern fashion, however, was originated by Dom Perignon about the year 1670. He supervised the care of the vines and the making of the wine. Some time later, it occured to him to blend together wines of various qualities in order to secure a sound standard of excellence. He also succeeded in making white wine from black grapes and by some means found a method of regulating the tendency of champagne to effervesce. By paying particular attention to the period best suited for bottling, he succeeded in producing a perfectly sparkling wine. Further, Perignon contrived to clear or fine the wine without decanting it from one bottle into another. He also received credit for being the first to use the bark of the cork tree as a stopper for the bottle instead of bits of tow dipped in oil or tallow.

Champagne is not a cheap wine because of high taxes and duties, and because it takes so long to prepare it for market. It is and always has been the wine of luxury. You should be willing to pay a good price for it, since the cheaper champagnes will probably be inferior final pressings after the first good wines have been pressed out, or else the raw, crude, produce of unfavorably situated vineyards. And since champagne is almost always a blend of several wines from various vineyards, the most important thing to know about champagne is the reputation of the blender or shipper whose name appears on the label. After all, it is his ability, proven by the quality of wines he has shipped over a period of years, that counts. The blends of each shipper are closely guarded secrets of the house, so that particular blends or cuvées of certain shippers become well known for a high grade of quality champagne.

VERMOUTH

Essentially, vermouth is a blended wine, aged and treated with herbs, roots and other botanicals to enhance its flavor. The two most popular sorts are the dry and the sweet varieties. These may be referred to, respectively, as French Vermouth and Italian Vermouth. Such titles do not necessarily denote origin, as both dry and sweet vermouths are made in France and in Italy as well as in many other parts of the world.

In making "French" vermouth, the basic white wines are relatively neutral. To these wines, other sweetened and fortified varieties (such as Brandy) are added, and the blends are placed in casks. After aging for about two years, the wine is treated with anywhere from 30-50 different herbs, roots, seeds, spices, peels and flowers in accordance with a duly tested, secret formula. It takes about four years to properly mature true vermouth and achieve a perfect blending of wines and plants. During this period the wine is refrigerated to prevent it from throwing a deposit. Then, before bottling, the vermouth is pasteurized and, finally, filtered. Altogether, the costs of bringing vermouth to this stage are enormous. Only a few houses can produce a quality product. "Italian" vermouths are sweet when compared with French vermouth. This is because the basic wine (Marsala) used in the Italian blend is sweeter and fuller than the neutral white (Herault) wines used in France. In addition, the herbs and spices used in the preparation of Italian and French vermouths are considerably different.

Vermouths of fine quality may be used as apéritifs, and there are few alcoholic beverages that are comparable as appetite stimulators, but their greatest popularity is unquestionably earned in the mixing of cocktails. Some of the more popular brands of vermouth available today are:

CINZANO A famous brand made in Turin, Italy, by Francesco Cinzano & Cia.

CHAMBÉRY Vermouth from the Savoy district of France. Several types are available, including a classic, dry vermouth; a red vermouth; and Chambéryzette, a vermouth flavored with the juice of wild strawberries.

MARTINI & ROSSI Producers of a celebrated red, Italian vermouth, as well as dry "French" vermouth and Bianco vermouth.

NOILLY PRAT Dry vermouth from Marseille, France.

PUNT E MES Produced by Carpano, in Turin, Italy, this vermouth has a distinctive bittersweet taste.

A variety of apéritif wines other than Vermouth deserve mention. These aromatic wines will be red or white in color (depending on whether their base is a red or white wine) and they will be sweet or dry depending on the botanicals and aromatics with which the wine has been infused. It can be said in general, however, that the principal flavoring agent of these apéritif wines is quinine. All share a distinctive bittersweet character. They make excellent appetizers and can also be used (instead of vermouth) as modifying agents in cocktails.

BYRRH (pronounced "beer") From France, a red apéritif wine based on wine from either Southern France or Spain.

DUBONNET A popular French apéritif wine, now also made in the United States. Both red and "blonde" Dubonnet are available.

LILLET Another well-known apéritif in red or white wine, from France.

ST. RAPHAËL France produces both a red and a white St. Raphaël.

CYNAR From the Latin word for artichoke, *cynara*. A wine apéritif with a principal ingredient of — artichoke.

POSITANO Positano is considerably drier than other apéritif wines.

PORT WINE

Genuine port wine comes from the Douro Valley near the city of Oporto in northern Portugal. In this mountainous district, the quintas, or vineyards, are built on terraces to prevent heavy rains from washing away the soil. Each quinto may be planted with as many as 15 different varieties of grapes. In the fall, all the grapes are gathered and pressed, and the 2-3 day fermentation process begins. At a specific time during this period, when a certain amount of sugar remains unfermented, brandy is added to the must. This procedure stops all further fermentation so that the remaining grape sugar acts as a sweetener in the wine itself.

The wine is then drained off into large wooden casks and stored away for two years. Should it develop into a fine, big wine capable of further improvement, it will be bottled, aged for an additional 20 years, and sold as a Vintage Port. As such it is always the wine of a single year — one in which a good vintage has been produced — and it is never blended. If the wine does not meet the exacting requirements of a Vintage Port, it is blended with other wines of different years and will be stored in wood from 8 to 20 years. During this time it may be blended again in order to maintain an established standard of quality. The longer the port remains in wood, the more the color fades: young ports (with the exception of white ports) are deep purple in color. As they mature, they become ruby and in time are left with a brownish, russet tinge. At this stage they are described as tawny ports.

VINTAGE PORT is produced from wine of a single year which is aged in wood for two years, then bottled and further aged for 20 years and more before it is ready for consumption. During the aging process it becomes more mellow and dry, acquiring a fine, delicate bouquet and superb body and color. It takes great care and an enormous amount of time to make a vintage port, not to mention the cooperation of nature: the right combination of elements must conspire to produce an exceptional wine in the first place. Accordingly, vintage ports are highly prized and quite expensive.

CRUSTED PORT is wine of no declared year, which is not quite up to vintage quality, but which is bottled in the same way and is of the same character as vintage port. Sometimes it is made up of a blend of vintage wines from different years.

TAWNY PORT is light in body and color and is made up of a blend of wines, aged in wood for up to 15 years.

RUBY PORT, the least expensive port, is a younger wine, aged in wood for a relatively short time. It is sweet and of a light red color, and has more kick.

SHERRY

Sherry is made in southern Spain in the province of Cadiz, a small district of which the town of *Jerez de la Frontera* is the center. The Cadiz district, some 60 miles north of Gilbraltar, produces all the genuine sherry in the world. The two main types of sherry are the Finos, which are pale and dry and serve as ideal appetizers, and the Olorosos — darker and stronger than the Finos, and more acceptable as dessert wines. These categories may be further sub-divided, for there are two types of Finos: the Finos proper, which are delicate, pale and dry, and the Amontillados, medium sherries that are amber-colored and dry, with a soft nut-like flavor. Also, there are several types of the more full-bodied Olorosos, ranging from dry and dark golden to quite sweet, with a rich mahogany color. A Cream sherry, for example, is a full Oloroso.

After fermentation, the cellarer inspects the casks of wine and makes an initial classification of the contents of each. Some will be designated as suitable for Finos, others will be marked for Olorosos. The next stage involves "fortifying" the wine, usually with grape brandy. The exact amount added depends upon the individual wine's classification. The brandy arrests fermentation so that some of the wine's natural grape sugar is retained.

The aging process (during which sherry actually increases in alcoholic strength) is very important to the development of a true sherry. Also important is the matter of successful blending. Sherries are blended by means of what is known in the industry as the "solera system." This is an extremely delicate process requiring much experience and skill. Various wines to be blended are drawn from a series of casks, laid down over the years in tiers. The amount of wine taken from the first tier (composed of the oldest casks) is continually replaced with similar, slightly younger wine taken from the next row. Wine can travel for several years through this line of tiers, gradually acquiring rich flavor and color before being bottled. Through this system, a constant blending process can be maintained, and a consistent product is virtually guaranteed.

MADEIRA

Off the coast of Africa, in the Atlantic, lies the mountainous and romantic little Portuguese island of Madeira. Madeira is famous as a port of call for traders from the East and West. It is also famous for delicious wines that are among the most long-lived in the world.

Madeira is a fortified white wine, the spirit being added after all natural fermentation is complete. The wine differs in character from all other fortified wines because of the peculiarities of the Madeiran soil and climate and because of the manner in which it is made and matured. No other wine, for example, is "cooked" in hot houses as Madeira is. After maturing in this way the wine is allowed to rest, then it is fortified, blended and matured. Madeira wine is shipped in four distinct types: Malmsey, which is the sweetest and richest: Bual, which is a golden, medium-sweet wine; Verdelho, a semi-dry wine; and Sercial, which is a very fine dry wine, amber in color. The drier wines are chilled and sipped as apéritifs; the rich ones, served at room temperature, are best after dinner, or with dessert. All of these wines are fragrant and full-bodied.

PUNCHES AND OTHER DRINKS

PUNCHES

In the world of parties and entertaining there is nothing as universally acceptable as a good punch. Many punches can be made for individual serving and are not very complicated to prepare. Mostly, however, punches are made in quantity and are served from fancy china, glass or silver bowls. Below are a few basic rules and hints that should help make any punch you prepare a smashing success.

1 A summery punch may not be popular on a cool autumn evening: be sure to choose a punch recipe that is appropriate for the occasion, the season and the hour at which the festivities are to be held.

2 See that you have all the ingredients you'll need, and prepare a batch of the central, non-perishable ingredients in advance. Before refrigerating, let stand at room temperature for a while to allow flavors to blend. Then, to be safe, combine some of this mixture with the last-minute ingredients and do a taste-test.

3 If you're making a cold punch, ingredients should be chilled thoroughly before being put in the punch bowl. Mix up several pitchers of the basic mix and have on hand all last-minute additions. Keep everything in a cool place so that you can prepare fresh batches of punch in minutes.

4 The punch bowl itself: pack it with ice, or set it in the refrigerator to chill before pouring in ingredients. Hot punches should be served warm and preferably in a metal bowl.

5 Ice is important. It should be clean and clear, and a solid block of it, placed in the bottom of your punch bowl, is better than cubes. (There will be less dilution of the punch over the course of the party.)

6 One or two tips on ingredients: use freshly-squeezed *fruit juices* where possible; *sugar syrup*, if needed, blends better than plain sugar; *cucumber peel* adds a delicate flavor to wine punches, provided the peel is removed and discarded after a few minutes; *spices* tied up in a small bag and dunked in the punch can contribute interesting flavor.

7 Don't fill your punch so full with slices and chunks of fruit that it resembles a fruit salad.

BEER

From evidence gathered by excavators and archeologists we know that beer has been brewed for centuries, in every part of the world. Originally, it was made by the priests of ancient civilizations as a religious offering to the gods of fertility; today, beer is quaffed for sheer enjoyment, pleasure and refreshment.

ALE A full-bodied malt brew with a pronounced hop flavor. The main difference between ale and beer is that ale is fermented at a higher temperature than beer, using a particular strain of yeast which remains at the top of the brew during fermentation.

LAGER Lager beer, with its light, clean color and taste, is the most popular kind of beer consumed in North America.

PORTER This type of English ale — so-named because London porters liked to drink it — is darker, richer and sweeter than lager; yet not as strongly flavored with hops as its cousin, stout.

STOUT A version of porter, and an ale so dark it's almost black in color. Stout has a strong hop character and strong malt taste.

OTHER DRINKS

CIDER Made from the fermented juice of apples, this "apple wine" comes in many forms — still, sparkling, mild, strong, dry or sweet. Cider is a popular ingredient in many punches and cups.

EGGNOG The traditional drink of the Christmas holiday season is eggnog, a creamy mixture of liquor, sugar, milk and beaten eggs, topped off with grated nutmeg. Non-alcoholic versions are popular too.

KIR Canon Kir, one-time mayor of Dijon, invented this drink in which Crème de Cassis (a blackcurrant liqueur) and chilled Chablis are mixed together (5 parts wine to one part Cassis) with delicious results.

WASSAIL An Old English drink, usually served piping hot, traditionally consisting of spiced wine, cider or ale and various other ingredients.

MIXES GARNISHES AND TRIMMINGS

There is more to a cocktail than just alcohol: mixes, trimmings and special flavoring agents are ingredients that can magically smooth out or enhance the flavor of raw liquor, sweeten it or make it bitter, add richness, tartness and texture, and contribute flavor, color and aroma. Mint, spices, fruit slices and peels, berries, olives and other garnishes, plus ingredients such as sugar and cream, syrups, eggs, juices and liqueurs, can transform the most ordinary glass of chilled liquor into an inspirational delight.

JUICES AND SYRUPS

As far as fruit juices go, there is one firm rule: freshly-squeezed juice is best, especially when lemon, lime or orange juice is called for. Canned, frozen or bottled varieties should be used only as a last resort. The two possible exceptions to this rule are grapefruit juice, which is better canned (be sure it's unsweetened), and pineapple juice, which is fine in its frozen, concentrated form. Fruit juices most commonly used in preparing drinks are: apple, cranberry, grape, grapefruit, lemon, lime, orange, pineapple and tomato juice. *Rose's Lime Juice* is a well-known mix which is actually a lime syrup. As such, it is not a substitute for fresh lime juice. *Passion Fruit Juice* is a tart tropical nectar used in a number of rum drinks, as well as in punches and cups. As for syrups, they add color and flavor to mixed drinks. The thing to remember is that they tend to be heavy and sweet and so should be used sparingly, measured by drops and dashes.

CASSIS A sweet, colorful, non-alcoholic syrup made from blackcurrants. It blends well with gin and other fruit flavors, and is absolutely essential if your guest asks for a kir. The liqueur Crème de Cassis is an alcoholic version of this syrup.

CURRANT SYRUP A red flavoring agent made from red currants.

FALERNUM Almonds and spices go into making this West Indian syrup.

GRENADINE Bright red, non-alcoholic syrup made from pomegranate pulp. Grenadine has a longer shelf life than many of the other syrups.

HONEY; MAPLE SYRUP A few drinks may call for either of these sweeteners.

ORANGE FLOWER WATER   Flavoring agent with a delicate taste of orange blossom.

ORGEAT   Bittersweet, non-alcoholic almond syrup from France, used for flavoring.

PAPAYA SYRUP   Tropical juice used in some rum drinks.

RASPBERRY SYRUP   A sweetener similar to Grenadine, but not as tart.

STRAWBERRY SYRUP   Another brilliant red sweetener.

SUGAR SYRUP   As an alternative to granulated sugar (which doesn't dissolve easily in alcohol), prepare a batch of sugar syrup with which to sweeten mixed drinks: Add 1 cup of sugar to 1 cup of cold water in a saucepan. Heat to a boil and simmer for a few minutes. Then cool and bottle the mixture. Sugar syrup will keep for a long time, stored at room temperature.

MINERAL WATERS AND OTHER MIXERS

Tap water that tastes of chlorine and other chemicals can ruin a drink, and so can ice cubes made from such water. The best way to avoid the problem is to use bottled spring water, also known as mineral water. Spring waters can be either still or aerated: those that bubble naturally have acquired carbonic acid on their way to the earth's surface, while others are artificially carbonated at the time of bottling. In addition to these natural waters, carbonated beverages such as Coca-Cola, 7-Up, tonic water and ginger ale are used extensively to add sparkle to many mixed drinks.

APOLLINARIS   Refreshing, sparkling mineral water from Germany.

BITTER LEMON   A soft drink with an unsweetened lemon taste, often used in gin drinks.

CLUB SODA   An indispensable sparkling water that adds zing to many mixed drinks. Buy small bottles for individual drinks; for parties stock up with the more economical large-size bottles.

COCA-COLA   Especially popular in rum concoctions, but it mixes well with many other liquors. Coke is made from a basic syrup (the formula is a secret) with sugar, water and carbon dioxide added.

EVIAN   A sweet, clean-tasting still water from France.

GINGER ALE   Avoid brands that are heavy and syrupy. A really dry, pale ginger ale with plenty of fizz is what's needed for mixing drinks.

PERRIER   From France — an effervescent water with a light, fresh taste.

QUININE   "Tonic" water, an important ingredient in many mixed drinks, is especially linked with gin (as in gin-and-tonic). It has quite a distinctive bitter-sweet flavor.

7-UP   A light, carbonated lemon-lime soft drink that blends well with many liquors.

TONIC   Same as quinine.

A word or two about packaged cocktail mixes. There are times when these can come in handy: A **Bloody Mary mix** (pre-mixed tomato juice and spices) or **Pina Colada mix** (pineapple and cream of coconut syrup combined) or some variety of **sweet and sour mix** (reconstituted lemon juice plus sugar) may prove to be a convenient time-saver and indeed, such mixes are often stocked in home bars. But the fact is, a drink made this way will simply not measure up to a cocktail that has been carefully prepared using fresh ingredients. If you do intend to buy packaged drink mixes, it's a good idea to shop around first, comparing brands for flavor and value.

BITTERS

Bitters, an essential ingredient in many mixed drinks, can be relied upon to freshen and add tang to a sweet drink, or to make a harsh drink taste smoother. And there are some kinds, diluted with water or sweetened with a little fruit syrup, that are delicious on their own. Most bitters are concocted from recipes that originated in the nineteenth century. Although the specific ingredients used are the secret of individual bitters houses, the method of production is well known: herbs, roots, seeds, spices and fruits are steeped in alcohol. The resulting spirit, infused with flavor, is sweetened, colored and eventually bottled.

ABBOT'S BITTERS   An American bitters made in Baltimore, Maryland.

ANGOSTURA BITTERS   The original formula was developed for medicinal purposes by Dr. Siegert in 1824, while Siegert was stationed in the town of Angostura, Venezuela. Today, the company he founded conducts a thriving business from its headquarters in Port-of-Spain, Trinidad.

AMER PICON   A popular French bitters often mixed with water and a dash of grenadine, and served as an apéritif. Picon also goes well with sweet Vermouth.

BOONEKAMP BITTERS   Dutch bitters from Bols of Holland.

CAMPARI BITTERS   Best-selling bitters from Italy — the Campari empire is based in Milan. The taste is uniquely bittersweet; and the color is a clear red. Campari teamed with soda and a slice of orange is an immensely popular, refreshing drink. Or Campari can be enjoyed in cocktails such as the Negroni and the Americano.

FERNET BRANCA   An Italian bitters, purportedly good for hangovers.

ORANGE BITTERS   Best used as a flavoring essence. Various brands of orange bitters are available.

PEYCHAUD'S BITTERS   Similar in some respects to Angostura bitters. Peychaud's is manufactured in New Orleans and is a crucial ingredient in the Sazerac cocktail.

GARNISHES ETC.

The following is a checklist of the other odds and ends you'll need in order to prepare and dress up your drinks.

Almonds	Cream	Nutmeg
Allspice	Cucumber	Olives
Berries	Eggs	Onions
Butter	Ginger	Oranges
Celery sticks	Lemon	Pineapple
Cinnamon sticks	Lime	Salt
Cloves	Milk	Tabasco sauce
Coconut	Mint	Worcestershire sauce

HINTS AND TIPS ON MIXING

MIXING DRINKS

BUY THE BEST   A cocktail can only be as good as the ingredients in it. Whatever you're using — whether liquor, liqueurs, juices or mix — it should always be of good quality. Use the less costly ingredients first in case of a mistake. It will be much less expensive to discard and start again.

MEASURING   Whether you follow recipes carefully and measure precisely the ingredients used or alter proportions of ingredients and adapt recipes to your own taste, try to stick to your measurements with reasonable accuracy to ensure consistency in the drinks you prepare. Where recipes call for only a dash of a liquid, use a special dash dropper for proper measurement every time.

CLEANING GLASSES   Glasses should always be sparking clean. Use one towel for wiping, and another for polishing; and always handle the glasses by the base or stem. Beer glasses should be washed with water and salt, never soap. Soap leaves a film inside the glass that will make beer taste flat.

CHILLING GLASSES   All cocktail glasses should be well chilled to keep their contents fresh and more appealing. If possible, chill the glasses in the refrigerator. Or, before mixing the drinks, fill the glasses with crushed ice. (Remember to discard the ice before pouring the drink).

FROSTING GLASSES   To give glasses a frosted, ice-cold look, dip them in water and put them in the freezer for a couple of hours.

SUGAR-RIMMED GLASSES   Sugar-frosted glasses are prepared by (1) rubbing the rim of a chilled glass with a wedge of lemon or orange — or moistening it with a liqueur or syrup — and (2) dipping the rim in sugar, coating it thoroughly. Sugar-rimmed glasses may then be stored in the refrigerator until needed.

ICE   Cocktails should be served ice cold. Always use ice that is fresh, clean, dry and very hard. (Ice that has absorbed odors from the refrigerator or that tastes of chlorine is no good). When emptying ice trays don't run water over them. The ice cubes may come out more easily this way, but they will inevitably clump together in the ice bucket or in glasses. Finally, cubes of ice belong in stirred drinks; cracked or shaved ice in drinks that are shaken. Do use plenty of ice; the more ice, the less dilution and the faster your drink will become chilled.

STIRRING   Some cocktails and drinks (martinis, manhattans etc.) are made with clear liquors and are supposed to look clear. Since shaking them will give them a cloudy appearance, such drinks should be stirred briskly, long enough to mix, but not too long or the drink will be diluted by melted ice. Any drink containing a carbonated mix must be stirred gently and very briefly, or else the fizzy sparkle will dissipate.

SHAKING   Drinks to be shaken are generally those containing sugar, fruit juices, eggs, cream or other ingredients difficult to blend. Use a bartender's shaker, which consists of two containers: the ingredients go in one and the ice in the other. Put the ice in first and the liquor in last, adding the other ingredients in between. This way, the ice cools all the ingredients that follow, and the measure of liquor, added last, is in less danger of being inadvertently doubled or forgotten. Leave enough room in the shaker to allow the ingredients to be tossed and, finally, shake firmly so that the drink comes out creamy. Mixing in an electric blender gives the same effect as shaking. Never shake a drink containing an effervescent liquid.

STRAINING   Strain all cocktails before serving to prevent bits of ice from getting into the glass.

POURING   Don't fill glasses so full that the drink sloshes over the rim. Leave at least 1/4 inch of space at the top — more if fruit garnishes are going to be added. Sometimes you will have prepared more than one serving of the same cocktail in a mixing glass or cocktail shaker. Before pouring, be sure to set your glasses in a row on the bar with their edges touching. Then pour each drink halfway, and go back and level off. Pouring this way will ensure consistency in each drink: you won't get the top layer in the first glass and heavier liquid in the others. Also, when you make too much and leave some of the drink in the shaker, always be sure to remove any ice that remains. Otherwise it will produce a watery second helping.

EYE APPEAL   Try to make your drinks *look* attractive and delicious. Eye appeal can be as important as taste.

FRESH FRUIT   Use fresh, unblemished fruit if possible. Lemons, limes and oranges are essential for juice, slices, wedges, wheels, peels and twists. To get the most juice out of citrus fruits, soak them in hot water, then roll them back and forth several times on the counter, pushing down with the palm of your hand. Do not cut orange or lemon peel too thin or it will curl and droop: use a sharp paring knife and cut 3/8 inch strips of peel off the fruit lengthwise, making sure that none of the white layer under the skin is included. Only a little peel, twisted over the rim of the glass, is needed for each drink. Oranges slices should always be halved when used as a garnish. A wedge of lemon or lime is obtained by quartering the fruit lengthwise. It may be divided again, lengthwise, if quarter sections are too large.

FLOATING LIQUEURS   The easiest way to float liqueurs on top of one another is to pour them, in any sequence, into a glass and put the glass in the refrigerator. In time, each liqueur will find its own weight level and the drink will have a layered look. A quicker method is to pour each liqueur, in order, (the densest and heaviest first) over the back of a bar spoon held inside a glass, or down the side of a mixing rod held in the glass. Pour slowly: the spoon will check the fall of the liquid and allow it to settle on top of the other liqueurs.

FLAMING LIQUOR   To flame liquor in a drink, pre-warm the spirit first. Set just a small amount on fire, and then pour this flaming liquid into the rest of the liquor for the full effect.

EGGS, MILK   Hot wines or hot liquor to be used in punches or mulled drinks must be poured gradually, and stirred briskly, into any mixture containing eggs or milk — otherwise, eggs will 'cook' and milk may curdle.

and SUGAR   Always use the finest granulated sugar except for the few drinks that call for lump sugar. Confectioners' powdered sugar blends quickly and may also be used. Sugar syrup (simple syrup) is easy to make and keeps indefinitely. It requires no stirring or mixing to dissolve and can save time preparing drinks. Recipe for sugar syrup: Dissolve 1 cup of granulated sugar in a cup of boiling water and simmer for about 2 minutes, stirring constantly. Allow to cool, then bottle. When mixing drinks, substitute equal amounts of sugar syrup for sugar.

BAR EQUIPMENT

There is practically no limit to the variety of equipment the really serious-minded bartender can assemble within arms' reach. However, too much equipment and too many tools tend to complicate rather than simplify the art of mixing. There is no doubt that practice makes perfect — and no amount of costly equipment can replace experience. Many bartenders religiously rely on a measuring glass to measure liquor, others simply rely on their experienced eye. The tools of the trade that you use repeatedly will evolve from your own style and technique . . . there is no right or wrong. The following list includes a few reminders that are found in most bars.

Bar muddler, for muddling sugar, mint, etc.

Bar spoon, long-handled, for stirring drinks. It measures one teaspoon.

Blender, not essential, but a good idea if you're making drinks such as Margaritas and Brandy Alexanders.

Coasters, so your guests have something to set their drinks on.

Cocktail shakers, consisting of 2 containers — one for ice, the other for the drink ingredients. One size holds about a pint; larger sizes are available. A Boston-type cocktail shaker holds approximately one quart and is great for those drinks (eggnogs, flips, sours etc.) that need a lot of shaking space.

Corkscrew, can and bottle opener. Check out different styles and buy whatever ones are sturdy, efficient and comfortable to use.

Cutting board, on which to slice fruits.

Ice bucket, to cut down on trips to the freezer.

Ice crusher, not an essential item: wrap cubes in a heavy cloth and pound with a mallet.

Lemon squeezer, an indispensable item for extracting juice from oranges, lemons and limes.

Measuring equipment, such as a set of measuring spoons and a double-ended measuring glass (with or without a handle). One end holds a jigger (1 1/2 oz.) and the other holds a pony (1 oz.).

Mixing glass, large, in which to stir drinks that are not shaken.

Paring knife, of good quality, for slicing fruit.

Pitcher, to hold water.

Strainer, made of metal, with a coil-spring rim that adjusts to fit any shaker or mixing glass. Place over the mixing cup and strain drink into the glass.

Swizzle sticks & straws, for stirring any drink served over ice.

Tongs, with which to pick up ice.

Toothpicks, for easy handling of olives, onions and cut-up fruit.

Towels, for keeping the bar counter clean and dry.

Tray, to hold mixings and garnishes.

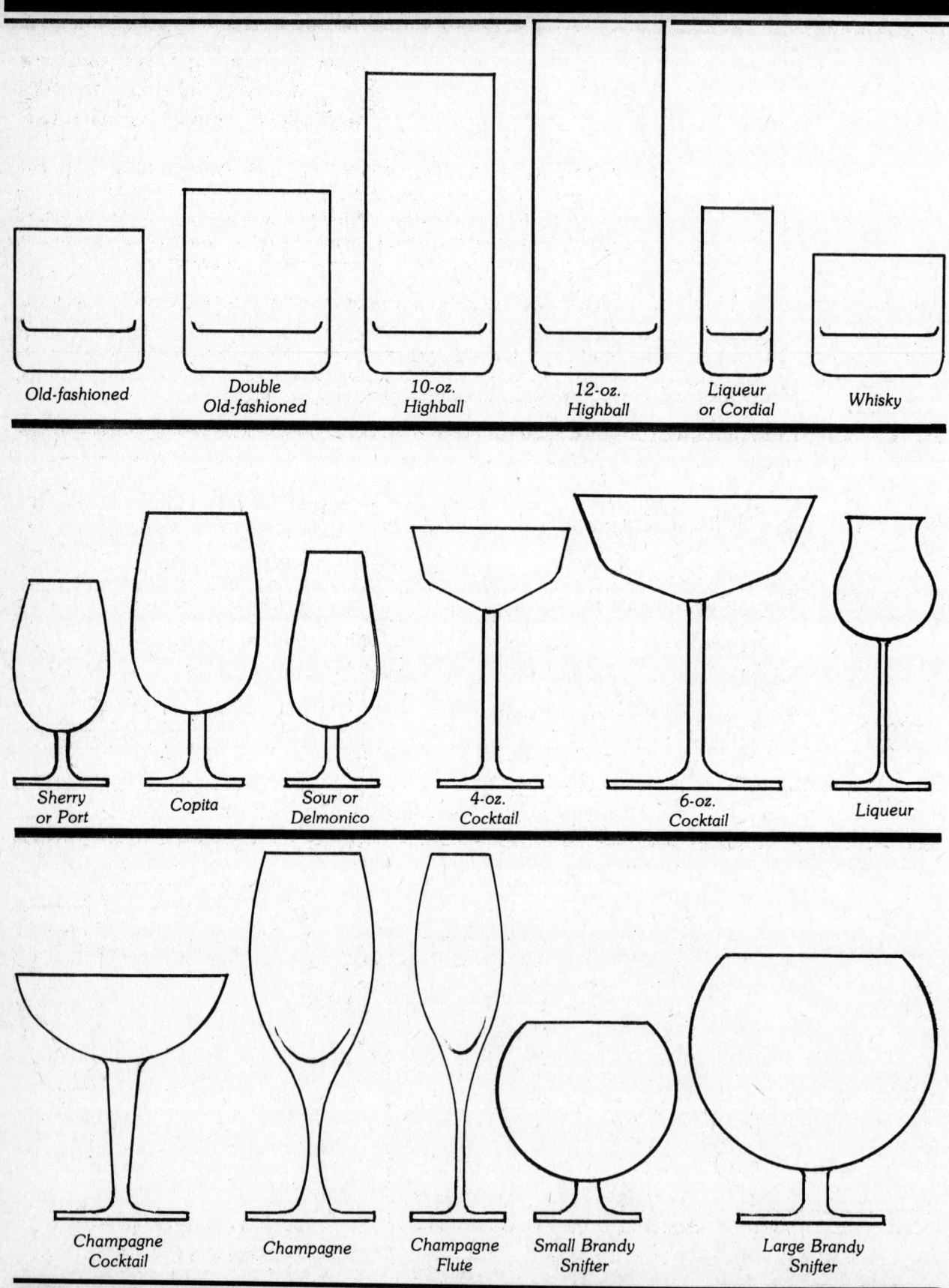

Old-fashioned Double
Old-fashioned 10-oz.
Highball 12-oz.
Highball Liqueur
or Cordial Whisky

Sherry
or Port Copita Sour or
Delmonico 4-oz.
Cocktail 6-oz.
Cocktail Liqueur

Champagne
Cocktail Champagne Champagne
Flute Small Brandy
Snifter Large Brandy
Snifter

GLASSES

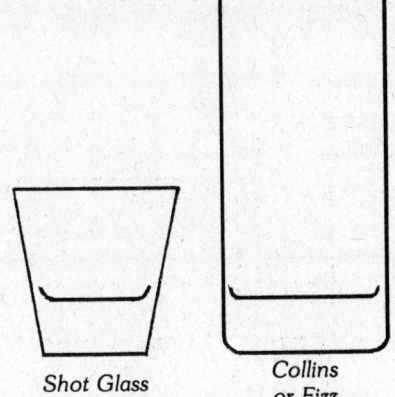

Glasses come in many different styles, shapes and sizes. They can be plain or exquisite, handsome or delicate, made of crystal or of pressed glass — as long as they are clear (avoid colored or tinted glass) and sparkling clean: wash in warm soapy water, rinse in scalding-hot water, dry, and polish to a gleaming shine.

Certain drinks are customarily served in certain shapes of glasses. Even if you don't own an infinite variety of glassware, be sure to have at least two basic shapes — tumblers and stemware — on hand. You can add the more specialized glasses (snifters, goblets, liqueur glasses) to your collection gradually.

Shot Glass

Collins or Fizz

Cordial or Pony

Martini

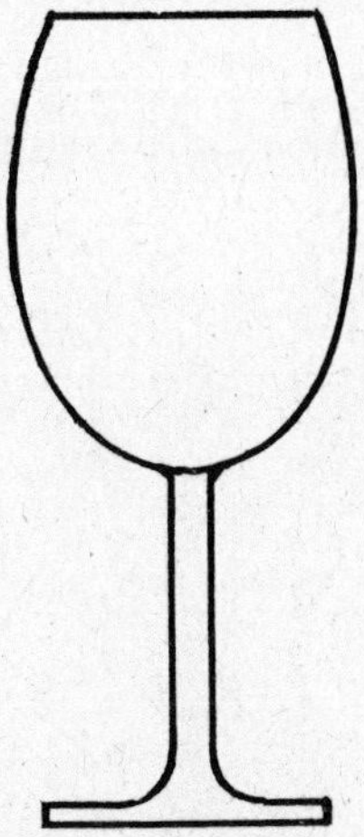

Tulip Wine Glass

Red Wine Glass

Goblet

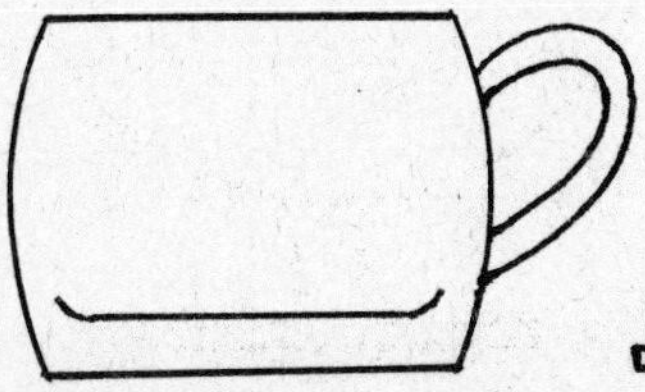

Punch Cup

Pilsner

Glass Mug

Tankard or Stein

COCKTAILS

A & A COCKTAIL

1 dash Apricot-flavored Brandy
1 oz. Apple Brandy
1 oz. Dry Vermouth
1 oz. Sweet Vermouth

Stir with ice and strain into a cocktail glass.

ABBEY COCKTAIL NO. 1

1½ oz. Gin
¼ oz. Lillet
¾ oz. Orange Juice
1 dash Angostura Bitters

Stir with ice and strain into a cocktail glass. Serve with a cherry or a twist of orange peel.

ABBEY COCKTAIL NO. 2

2 oz. Gin
1 oz. Orange Juice
1 dash Angostura Bitters
1 dash Sweet Vermouth
1 Maraschino Cherry

Shake with ice and strain into a cocktail glass.

ABERDEEN ANGUS

2 oz. Scotch
1 oz. Drambuie
1 tbsp. Honey
2 tsp. Lime Juice

Stir the Scotch and the honey in a mug until smooth. Add lime juice. Warm the Drambuie over a low flame. Ignite and add to other ingredients. Stir and serve immediately.

ABSINTHE AMERICAN

1 oz. Pernod
1 oz. Water
Sugar to taste

Shake with ice and strain into a cocktail glass.

ABSINTHE AND EGG

1½ oz. Pernod
1 Egg White
½ oz. Gin
Sugar to taste

Shake with ice and strain into a cocktail glass.

ABSINTHE COCKTAIL NO. 1

1½ oz. Pernod
2 tbsp. Water
1½ tsp. Anisette
1 dash Orange Bitters

Shake with ice and strain into a cocktail glass.

ABSINTHE COCKTAIL NO. 2

1 oz. Pernod
1 dash Orgeat
1 dash Anisette
1 dash Angostura Bitters

Shake with ice and strain into a cocktail glass. Serve with a lemon twist and a water chaser.

ABSINTHE DRIP COCKTAIL

Pour 1½ oz. Pernod into an Old-fashioned glass. Place a cube of sugar in a silver tea strainer. Pack the strainer with cracked ice and pour in enough cold water to fill. When water has dripped through into the glass, the drink is ready.

ABSINTHE FRAPPE

1 tsp. Benedictine
1½ oz. Pernod

Shake with ice and strain into an Old-fashioned glass. Fill with soda.

ABSINTHE FRENCH

Half fill an Old-fashioned glass with shaved ice. Place a sugar cube on top of ice. Drip 2 oz. of Pernod slowly through sugar and ice. Serve with a lemon twist and straws.

ABSINTHE FROZEN

¾ oz. Pernod
1 tsp. Sugar Syrup

Shake with ice and strain into a highball glass. Fill with soda.

ABSINTHE ITALIAN

1½ oz. Pernod
¾ oz. Anisette
2 dashes Maraschino Liqueur
¼ oz. Water

Shake with ice and strain into a cocktail glass.

ABSINTHE MARTINI

2 oz. Gin
1 oz. Dry Vermouth
1 tbsp. Pernod

Stir with ice and strain into a cocktail glass.

Here's to you, as good as you are,
And here's to me, as bad as I am;
But as good as you are, and as bad as I am,
I am as good as you are, as bad as I am.
— An Old Scotch Toast

ABSINTHE NEW ORLEANS

1½ oz. Whisky
1 dash Angostura Bitters
1 dash Orange Bitters
1 dash Anisette
½ lump Sugar
2 dashes Pernod

Shake with ice and strain into a highball glass. Serve with a lemon twist.

ABSINTHE SPECIAL

1	oz. Pernod
¼	oz. Anisette
¼	oz. Gin
1	dash Orange Bitters

Shake with ice and strain into a cocktail glass. Serve with a water chaser.

ABSINTHE SPECIAL COCKTAIL

1½	oz. Pernod
1	oz. Water
¼	tsp. Powdered Sugar
1	dash Orange Bitters

Shake with ice and strain into a cocktail glass.

ABSINTHE SUISSESSE

| 1½ | oz. Pernod |
| 1 | Egg White |

Several drops of Anisette, White Creme de Menthe and Orange Flower Water

Shake with ice and strain into a cocktail glass.

ACACIA

1	oz. Gin
½	oz. Benedictine
1	tsp. Kirschwasser

Shake with ice and strain into a cocktail glass.

ACAPULCO

1½	oz. Light Rum
1	tbsp. Lime Juice
1½	tsp. Triple Sec or Orange Curacao
1	tsp. Sugar
1	tsp. Egg White

Combine and shake all ingredients with ice and strain into an Old-fashioned glass over ice cubes. Add a sprig of mint.

ACE

¾	oz. Gin
¼	oz. Grenadine
¼	oz. Cream
½	Egg White

Shake with ice and strain into a cocktail glass. Sprinkle nutmeg on top.

ADAM AND EVE

1	oz. Forbidden Fruit
1	oz. Gin
1	oz. Brandy
1	dash Lemon Juice

Shake with ice and strain into a cocktail glass.

ADAM AND EVE OLD-FASHIONED

1	lump Sugar
1	dash Bitters
2	oz. Whisky
½	oz. Galliano

Place sugar and Bitters in Old-fashioned glass. Add enough soda to cover sugar. Stir well. Add 3 ice cubes. Pour Whisky over this. Float ½ oz. Galliano on top and serve.

ADDINGTON

| 1½ | oz. Sweet Vermouth |
| 1½ | oz. Dry Vermouth |

Stir with ice and strain into a highball glass. Fill with soda. Serve with a lemon twist.

ADDISON

| 1 | oz. Gin |
| 1½ | oz. Sweet Vermouth |

Stir with ice and strain into a cocktail glass. Serve with a twist of orange peel.

ADELLE SPECIAL

| ½ | oz. Orange Curacao |
| 1½ | oz. Scotch |

Mix in an Old-fashioned glass. Fill with crushed ice.

ADIOS AMIGOS

1	oz. Light Rum
½	oz. Dry Vermouth
½	oz. Brandy
½	oz. Gin
¾	oz. Lime Juice

Shake with ice and strain into a cocktail glass.

ADMIRAL COCKTAIL NO. 1

1½	oz. Gin
1	oz. Cherry Cordial
½	oz. Lime Juice

Sugar to taste

Shake with ice and strain into a cocktail glass.

There may be a toast I'd like to say,
If I could only think it;
So fill your glass to anything,
And, thank the Lord, I'll drink it.

ADMIRAL COCKTAIL NO. 2

1½	oz. Bourbon
½	oz. Dry Vermouth
¾	oz. Lemon Juice

Shake with ice and strain into a cocktail glass.

ADMIRAL HIGHBALL

1½	oz. Whisky
1½	oz. Tokay Wine
2	dashes Pineapple Juice
2	dashes Lemon Juice

Stir with ice and strain into a highball glass. Add an ice cube and fill with soda.

ADONIS COCKTAIL

1   dash Orange Bitters
¾   oz. Sweet Vermouth
1½   oz. Dry Sherry

Stir with ice and strain into a cocktail glass.

AFFINITY COCKTAIL NO. 1

¾   oz. Dry Vermouth
¾   oz. Sweet Vermouth
¾   oz. Scotch
2   dashes Orange Bitters (or Angostura)

Stir with ice and strain into a cocktail glass. Add a lemon twist and cherry.

AFFINITY COCKTAIL NO. 2

1   oz. Dry Vermouth
1   oz. Sweet Vermouth
½   oz. Creme d'Yvette

Stir with ice and strain into a cocktail glass.

AFTER DINNER COCKTAIL NO. 1

1   oz. Apricot-flavored Brandy
1   oz. Triple Sec or Orange Curacao
Juice 1 Lime

Shake with ice and strain into a cocktail glass. Leave lime in glass.

AFTER DINNER COCKTAIL NO. 2

1   oz. Prunelle Liqueur
1   oz. Cherry Liqueur
1   tsp. Lemon Juice

Shake with ice and strain into a sherry glass.

AFTER DINNER SPECIAL NO. 1

¾   oz. Lime Juice
¾   oz. Cherry-flavored Brandy
1½   oz. Swedish Punch

Shake with ice and strain into a cocktail glass.

AFTER DINNER SPECIAL NO. 2

⅓   oz. Benedictine
⅓   oz. Cointreau
⅓   oz. Yellow Chartreuse

Pour carefully, in order given, into a pony glass so that each ingredient floats on the preceding one without mixing.

> Here's to the maiden of
>   bashful fifteen;
> Here's to the widow of fifty;
> Here's to the flaunting
>   extravagant queen;
> And here's to the housewife
>   that's thrifty.
> Let the toast pass,
> Drink to the lass,
> I'll warrant she'll prove an
>   excuse for the glass.
>   — Sheridan

AFTER SUPPER COCKTAIL

1   oz. Apricot-flavored Brandy
1   oz. Triple Sec or Orange Curacao
½   tsp. Lemon Juice

Shake with ice and strain into a cocktail glass.

AGGRAVATION

1   oz. Kahlua
1   oz. Scotch

Mix in a highball glass. Fill with milk and ice.

AGONIE

¾   oz. Lemon Juice
1½   oz. Gin
¼   oz. Rum
½   tsp. Sugar

Shake with ice and strain into a cocktail glass.

AINSWORTH COCKTAIL

1¾   oz. Gin
¾   oz. Dry Vermouth

Stir with ice and strain into a cocktail glass.

AIR MAIL

¾   oz. Lime Juice
1   tsp. Honey
1½   oz. Gold Rum

Shake and strain into a highball glass. Fill with Champagne.

A.J.

1½   oz. Applejack
1   oz. Grapefruit Juice

Shake with ice and strain into a cocktail glass.

ALABAMA COCKTAIL

1   tbsp. Lemon Juice
½   tsp. Powdered Sugar
1½   oz. Brandy
1   tsp. Triple Sec or Orange Curacao

Shake with ice and strain into a cocktail glass. Serve with a twist of orange peel.

ALABAMA FIZZ

Juice ½ Lemon
1   tsp. Powdered Sugar
2   oz. Gin

Shake with cracked ice and strain into a highball glass over two ice cubes. Fill with soda. Add two sprigs of fresh mint.

ALABAZAM

2	oz. Cognac
2	tsp. Sugar Syrup
1	tbsp. Curacao
1	tsp. Lemon Juice
2	dashes Orange Bitters

Shake with ice and strain into a cocktail glass.

A LA DONNA

1½	oz. Rum
1½	oz. Orange Juice
1½	oz. Grapefruit Juice

Blend with ice and strain into a double Old-fashioned glass. Fill with crushed ice.

A LA FRANCAISE

Pour 1½ oz. Pernod into a highball glass. Fill with cold water.

ALASKA COCKTAIL

2	dashes Orange Bitters
1½	oz. Gin
¾	oz. Yellow Chartreuse

Stir with ice and strain into a cocktail glass. Serve with a lemon twist.

ALBEMARLE FIZZ

	Juice ½ Lemon
1	tsp. Powdered Sugar
2	oz. Gin

Shake with ice and strain into a highball glass over two ice cubes. Fill with soda. Add one tsp. raspberry syrup.

ALBERTINE

¾	oz. Cointreau
¾	oz. Yellow Chartreuse
¾	oz. Kirschwasser
1	dash Maraschino Liqueur

Shake with ice and strain into a cocktail glass.

ALBERTI'S NIGHT COCKTAIL

1¾	oz. Whisky
¾	oz. Strega
1	dash Orange Bitters

Stir with ice and strain into a cocktail glass.

ALE FLIP

2	oz. Ale
¾	tsp. Sugar
1	Egg

Shake with ice and strain into a cocktail glass. Sprinkle nutmeg on top.

ALEJANDRA

¾	oz. Kahlua
¾	oz. Brandy
1	oz. Cream

Shake with ice and strain into a cocktail glass. Sprinkle nutmeg on top.

ALE SANGAREE

| ½ | tsp. Sugar |
| | Ale |

In a double Old-fashioned glass, dissolve sugar in a little water. Fill with chilled Ale and add several ice cubes. Sprinkle nutmeg on top.

> Drink, for you know not
> When you came, nor why;
> Drink, for you know not why
> You go, nor whence.
> — *Omar Khayyam*

ALEXANDER COCKTAIL NO. 1

1	oz. Gin
1	oz. White Creme de Cacao
1	oz. Sweet Cream

Shake with ice and strain into a cocktail glass. Sprinkle nutmeg on top.

ALEXANDER COCKTAIL NO. 2

1	oz. White Creme de Cacao
1	oz. Brandy
1	oz. Sweet Cream

Shake with ice and strain into a cocktail glass. Sprinkle nutmeg on top.

ALEXANDER'S SISTER COCKTAIL

1	oz. Gin
1	oz. Green Creme de Menthe
1	oz. Sweet Cream

Shake with ice and strain into a cocktail glass. Sprinkle nutmeg on top.

ALEXANDER WITH PRUNELLE

1½	oz. Gin
1	oz. Prunelle Liqueur
1	oz. Cream

Shake with ice and strain into a cocktail glass. Dust with cinnamon.

ALEXANDER YOUNG

½	oz. Pineapple Juice
½	oz. Orange Juice
½	oz. Lemon Juice
1½	oz. Bourbon
1	dash Grenadine
1	dash Angostura Bitters

Shake with ice and strain into a cocktail glass.

ALEXANDRA

1	oz. Cream
1	oz. Gin
1	oz. Dark Creme de Cacao

Shake with ice and strain into a cocktail glass.

ALFIE COCKTAIL

1½ oz. Lemon Vodka
1 tbsp. Pineapple Juice
1 dash Triple Sec or Orange Curacao

Shake with ice and strain into a cocktail glass.

ALFONSO COCKTAIL

1 cube Sugar
1 dash Angostura Bitters
1 cube Ice
1 oz. Dubonnet
4 oz. chilled Champagne

Put the sugar in a champagne glass and sprinkle it with the Bitters. Add ice cube and Dubonnet and fill with Champagne. Drop in a twist of lemon peel.

ALFONSO SPECIAL

1 oz. Gin
¼ oz. Sweet Vermouth
1 oz. Dry Vermouth
½ oz. Grand Marnier
1 dash Bitters

Stir with ice and strain into a cocktail glass.

ALGONQUIN

¾ oz. Pineapple Juice
¾ oz. Dry Vermouth
1½ oz. Rye Whisky

Shake with ice and strain into a cocktail glass.

ALGONQUIN BAR PUNCH

½ tsp. Sugar
1½ oz. Lemon Juice
1½ oz. Sloe Gin
½ oz. Jamaica Rum

Mix in a Collins glass. Fill with crushed ice. Float raspberry syrup. Garnish with fruit.

ALHAMBRA ROYAL

Pour 1 oz. Cognac into a cup. Fill with hot chocolate. Add a lemon wedge.

ALICE

1 oz. Scotch Whisky
1 oz. Kummel
1 oz. Sweet Vermouth

Stir with ice and strain into a cocktail glass.

ALICE MINE NO. 1

½ oz. Dry Vermouth
4 dashes Sweet Vermouth
1 oz. Grand Marnier
½ oz. Gin
1 dash Angostura Bitters

Stir with ice and strain into a cocktail glass.

ALICE MINE NO. 2

¾ oz. Bourbon
¾ oz. Kummel
¾ oz. Sweet Vermouth

Stir with ice and strain into a cocktail glass.

ALLEGHENY

1 oz. Bourbon
1 oz. Dry Vermouth
1½ tsp. Blackberry-flavored Brandy
1½ tsp. Lemon Juice

Shake with ice and strain into a cocktail glass. Add a twist of lemon peel on top.

ALLEN COCKTAIL

1½ tsp. Lemon Juice
¾ oz. Maraschino Liqueur
1½ oz. Gin

Shake with ice and strain into a cocktail glass.

ALLIES COCKTAIL

1 oz. Dry Vermouth
1 oz. Gin
½ tsp. Kummel

Stir with ice and strain into a cocktail glass.

ALLIGATOR

1 oz. Orgeat
1½ oz. Gin
1 dash Eau de Malisse

Shake with ice and strain into a cocktail glass.

AL LONG'S SPECIAL HOT TODDY

2 oz. Drambuie
2 oz. Scotch
1 oz. Raspberry Syrup
1 tbsp. Lime Juice
3 oz. Water

Combine in a saucepan and bring to a boil. Serve hot in a mug.

Drink ye to her that each loves best,
And, if you nurse a flame,
That's told but to her mutual breast,
We will not ask her name.
— *Thomas Campbell*

ALL WHITE FRAPPE

1 oz. Anisette
1 oz. Light Creme de Cacao
½ oz. White Creme de Menthe
¼ oz. Lemon Juice

Stir with ice and strain into a saucer champagne glass. Fill with crushed ice.

ALMERIA

1½ oz. Rum
1 oz. Coffee-flavored Brandy
1 Egg White

Shake all ingredients with cracked ice and strain into a cocktail glass.

ALMOND COCKTAIL

2   oz. Gin
1   oz. Dry Vermouth
1   pair of Almonds, peeled
1   crushed Peach Kernel
½   tsp. Powdered Sugar
1   tsp. Kirsch
1   tsp. Peach-flavored Brandy

Warm the Gin; add the almonds, sugar and peach kernel. Allow to cool; add the remaining ingredients and stir. Strain into an Old-fashioned glass and add ice.

ALPHONSE

Fill a pony glass with Dark Creme de Cacao. Float cream on top.

ALPINE GLOW

1   tsp. Cointreau
½   oz. Lemon Juice
1   oz. Cognac
1   oz. Rum
2   dashes Grenadine

Shake with ice and strain into a cocktail glass.

ALSACE LORRAINE COCKTAIL

¾   oz. Kirschwasser
¾   oz. Anisette

Pour into a pony glass. Serve with a water chaser.

A LULU

1   oz. Light Puerto Rican Rum
½   oz. Creme de Noyaux
1   oz. Orange Juice
½   oz. Passion Fruit Mix
½   oz. Galliano

Shake with ice and strain into an Old-fashioned glass. Fill with ice cubes.

AMABILE BEONE

1½ oz. Green Creme de Menthe
¾   oz. Drambuie

Shake with ice and strain into a cocktail glass coated with Pernod and rimmed with sugar.

> Here's to the woman with face so fair,
> Framed in a wreath of beautiful hair.
> Pretty red lips as soft as a rose —
> How many have kissed them, God only knows.

AMARANTH

1½ oz. Rye
2   dashes Bitters
1   tsp. Sugar

Mix in a highball glass. Fill with soda and ice.

AMARETTO CAFE

Add 1 oz. of Amaretto to a cup of black coffee.

AMAROSA

1   oz. Gin
1   oz. Amarosa
1   oz. Cherry Liqueur

Shake with ice and strain into a cocktail glass.

AMBASSADOR

2   oz. Tequila
Orange Juice

Pour the Tequila into an Old-fashioned glass. Add ice and orange juice. Sweeten to taste.

AMBER CLOUD

1½ oz. Cognac
2   tbsp. Galliano

Shake with ice and pour over crushed ice in a cocktail glass.

AMBER DAWN COCKTAIL

1   oz. Jamaica Rum
1   oz. Orange Juice
1   dash Curacao
1   dash Water

Shake with ice and strain into a cocktail glass.

AMBER DREAM COCKTAIL

1½ oz. Gin
1   tbsp. Chartreuse
1   oz. Sweet Vermouth
1   dash Orange Bitters

Shake with ice and strain into a cocktail glass.

AMBROSIA NO. 1

1   oz. Applejack
1   oz. Brandy
1   dash Triple Sec or Orange Curacao
Juice 1 Lemon
Champagne

Shake all ingredients except Champagne. Pour contents into a highball glass with cubed ice. Fill glass with Champagne.

AMBROSIA NO. 2

1   oz. Galliano
½   oz. Orange Juice
½   oz. Cream
½   oz. Gin
1   tsp. grated Coconut

Blend with ice and strain into a cocktail glass.

AMERICANA

½   tsp. Sugar
1   dash Bitters
¼   oz. 100-proof Bourbon

Pour into a champagne glass. Fill with Champagne and add a peach slice.

AMERICAN BEAUTY COCKTAIL NO. 1

1   tbsp. Orange Juice
1   tbsp. Grenadine
½   oz. Dry Vermouth
½   oz. Brandy
¼   tsp. White Creme de Menthe

Shake with ice and strain into a cocktail glass and top with a little Port.

AMERICAN BEAUTY COCKTAIL NO. 2

Pour 1 oz. Muscatel into a champagne glass. Fill with chilled Champagne and serve with 1 large grape.

AMERICAN FIZZ

1½   oz. Gin
1½   oz. Brandy
½   oz. Grenadine
Juice of ½ Lemon

Shake with ice and strain into a highball glass.

> Don't ask me to give you a
> toast from my head,
> For straightway its warmth
> will depart;
> But here's to our friendship
> — I pledge you instead,
> 'Tis a toast that was made
> in my heart.

AMERICAN FLYER

1½   oz. Rum
1½   tsp. Lime Juice
1   pinch Sugar

Shake with ice and strain into a Sour glass. Fill with Champagne.

AMERICAN GLORY COCKTAIL

2   oz. chilled Champagne
1   oz. Orange Juice

Serve in an Old-fashioned glass. Stir gently and fill with soda. Serve with a straw.

AMERICAN GROG

1   lump Sugar
1½   oz. Rum
Juice ¼ Lemon

Pour ingredients into a whisky glass and fill with hot water. Stir. (Rye or Bourbon may be used in place of Rum.) Add a lemon wedge.

AMERICAN LEGION MARGUERITA

2   oz. Tequila
1   oz. Cointreau
½   oz. Lemon Juice
½   oz. Lime Juice

Shake with ice and strain into a salt-rimmed cocktail glass.

AMERICANO

3   oz. Sweet Vermouth
1½   oz. Campari

Mix in a large cocktail glass. Add ice cubes and a lemon twist. Fill with soda.

AMERICANO COOLER

3   oz. Sweet Vermouth
2   oz. Campari
2   cubes Ice

Put Sweet Vermouth and Campari in a Collins glass. Add ice cubes and a twist of lemon. Fill with chilled soda.

AMERICAN PUNCH NO. 1

¾   oz. Dry Vermouth
¾   oz. Brandy
½   tsp. Sugar
1½   oz. Orange Juice

Shake with ice and strain into a Collins glass. Fill with crushed ice. Float ½ oz. White Creme de Menthe on top.

AMERICAN PUNCH NO. 2

½   oz. Grenadine
½   tsp. Sugar
2   oz. Lemon Juice
1   dash Soda

Stir gently in a Collins glass. Fill with cracked ice. Float 1½ oz. White Creme de Menthe and 1 oz. Creme d'Yvette on top.

AMERICAN ROSE

1½   oz. Brandy
1   tsp. Grenadine
1   dash Pernod
½   ripe Peach, mashed

Shake with ice and strain into a Collins glass. Fill with chilled Champagne.

AMER PICON COCKTAIL

1   tsp. Grenadine
1½   oz. Amer Picon
Juice 1 Lime

Shake with ice and strain into a cocktail glass.

AMER PICON COOLER

½   oz. Lemon Juice
¼   tsp. Sugar
1   oz. Gin
1½   oz. Amer Picon

Shake with ice and strain into a Collins glass. Fill with soda and ice.

AMER PICON FIZZ

1   Egg White
½   oz. Grenadine
2   oz. Amer Picon

Shake with ice and strain into a Collins glass. Fill with soda and ice. Stir gently.

AMER PICON HIGHBALL

Pour 2 oz. Amer Picon and ¾ oz. Grenadine into a highball glass. Fill with ice and soda and stir gently.

AMONTILLADO COCKTAIL

1 oz. Amontillado
1 oz. Dubonnet

Pour into a saucer champagne glass; stir gently. Touch up with a twist of lemon and add ice.

AMOUR COCKTAIL

2 dashes Orange Bitters
1½ oz. Sherry
1½ oz. Dry Vermouth

Stir with ice and strain into a cocktail glass. Serve with a lemon twist.

AMSTERDAM COCKTAIL

1 oz. Holland Gin
½ oz. Orange Juice
½ oz. Cointreau
4 dashes Orange Bitters

Shake with ice and strain into a cocktail glass.

ANCHORS AWEIGH

1 oz. Bourbon
2 tbsp. Heavy Cream
2 tsp. each Triple Sec, Peach-flavored Brandy and Maraschino Liqueur
A few drops Cherry Juice

Shake with ice and strain into a cocktail glass.

ANDALUSIA

1½ oz. Dry Sherry
½ oz. Brandy
½ oz. Rum

Stir with ice and strain into a cocktail glass.

ANGEL

⅓ oz. Raspberry Syrup or Grenadine
⅓ oz. Maraschino Liqueur
⅓ oz. Creme de Violette

Pour carefully, in order given, into a pony glass so that each ingredient floats on the preceding one without mixing.

Here's to mine and here's to thine!
Now's the time to clink it!
Here's a flagon of old wine
And here we are to drink it.

ANGELES COCKTAIL

1½ oz. Gin
1 dash Pernod
3 dashes Grenadine
1 tsp. Lime Juice
½ White of 1 Egg

Shake with ice and strain into a cocktail glass. Sprinkle nutmeg on top.

ANGEL FACE NO. 1

1 oz. Gin
½ oz. Apricot-flavored Brandy
½ oz. Apple Brandy

Shake with ice and strain into a cocktail glass.

ANGEL FACE NO. 2

¾ oz. Creme de Cacao
¾ oz. Prunelle Liqueur

Pour carefully, in order given, into a pony glass so that each ingredient floats on the preceding one without mixing.

ANGELIC

1 oz. Cream
1 oz. Bourbon
1 oz. Light Creme de Cacao
¼ oz. Grenadine

Shake with ice and strain into a cocktail glass.

ANGELIQUE

1 oz. Ouzo
1 oz. Advokaat
1 oz. Strega
1 oz. fresh Cream
1 oz. Orange Juice

Shake with ice and strain into a fizz glass. Serve with a cherry.

ANGELINO

1 oz. Scotch
1 oz. Inca Pisco
¾ oz. Galliano

Shake with ice and strain into a cocktail glass. Serve with a cherry.

ANGEL'S BLUSH

¼ oz. Maraschino Liqueur
¼ oz. Creme d'Yvette
¼ oz. Benedictine
¼ oz. Cream

Pour ingredients carefully, in order given, so that they do not mix. Use a pony glass.

ANGEL'S DELIGHT

1½ tsp. Grenadine
1½ tsp. Triple Sec or Orange Curacao
1½ tsp. Creme d'Yvette
1½ tsp. Sweet Cream

Pour carefully, in order given, into a pony glass so that each ingredient floats on the preceding one without mixing.

ANGEL'S DREAM COCKTAIL

⅓ oz. Maraschino Liqueur
⅓ oz. Sweet Cream
⅓ oz. Creme d'Yvette

Pour carefully, in order given, into a pony glass so that each ingredient floats on the preceding one without mixing.

ANGEL'S KISS NO. 1

¾ oz. Apricot Liqueur
¼ oz. Thick Cream floated on top

Pour carefully, in order given, into a pony glass so that each ingredient floats on the preceding one without mixing.

ANGEL'S KISS NO. 2

¼ oz. Creme de Cacao
¼ oz. Creme de Violette
¼ oz. Prunelle Liqueur
¼ oz. fresh Cream

Pour carefully, in order given, into a pony glass so that each ingredient floats on the preceding one without mixing.

> May we breakfast with Health — dine with Friendship — crack a bottle with Mirth — and sup with the goddess of Contentment.

ANGEL'S KISS NO. 3

1/6 Maraschino Liqueur
1/6 Parfait Amour
1/6 Yellow Chartreuse
1/6 Benedictine
1/6 Cognac
1/6 fresh Cream

Pour carefully, in order given, into a pony glass so that each ingredient floats on the preceding one without mixing.

ANGEL'S KISS NO. 4

¼ Dark Creme de Cacao
¼ Creme d'Yvette
¼ Brandy
¼ Cream

Pour carefully, in order given, into a pony glass so that each ingredient floats on the preceding one without mixing.

ANGEL'S LIPS COCKTAIL

⅔ oz. Benedictine
⅓ oz. Sweet Cream

Pour carefully, in order given, into a pony glass so that each ingredient floats on the preceding one without mixing.

ANGEL'S TIP NO. 1

¾ oz. White Creme de Cacao
¼ oz. Sweet Cream

Float cream and insert toothpick in cherry and put on top to bridge glass. Use a pony glass.

ANGEL'S TIP NO. 2

¾ oz. Maraschino Liqueur
¼ oz. Whipped Cream

Serve in a pony glass with a cherry on top.

ANGEL'S WING NO. 1

¼ oz. White Creme de Cacao
¼ oz. Brandy
½ tbsp. Sweet Cream

Pour ingredients carefully, in order given, so that they do not mix. Use a pony glass.

ANGEL'S WING NO. 2

¾ oz. Dark Creme de Cacao
¾ oz. Prunelle Liqueur

Pour ingredients carefully, in order given, so that they do not mix. Use a pony glass.

ANGEL'S WING NO. 3

½ oz. Creme de Violette
½ oz. Raspberry Syrup
½ oz. Maraschino Liqueur

Pour ingredients carefully, in order given, so that they do not mix. Use a pony glass.

ANGEL'S WING NO. 4

½ oz. Cherry Liqueur
½ oz. Maraschino Liqueur
½ oz. Parfait Amour

Pour ingredients carefully, in order given, so that they do not mix. Use a pony glass.

ANGLER'S COCKTAIL

2 dashes Angostura Bitters
3 dashes Orange Bitters
1½ oz. Gin
1 dash Grenadine

Shake with cracked ice and pour into an Old-fashioned glass over ice cubes. (Cointreau may be used in place of Grenadine.)

ANGOSTURA FIZZ

1 oz. Angostura Bitters
1½ oz. Lime Juice
1 Egg White
½ oz. Cream
¼ oz. Grenadine

Shake with ice and strain into a Collins glass. Fill with soda and ice. Add a pineapple spear and a grated lemon peel.

ANGOSTURA HIGHBALL

Pour 1 oz. Angostura Bitters into a highball glass. Fill with ginger ale. Add ice cubes and serve with a lemon twist.

ANIS DEL OSO

| 1½ | oz. Anis Del Oso |
| 1½ | oz. Grenadine |

Mix in a Collins glass and fill with soda and ice.

ANISETTE MAN

1	oz. Bourbon
1	oz. Sweet Vermouth
½	oz. Anisette

Stir with ice and strain into a cocktail glass.

ANISETTE COCKTAIL NO. 1

1	oz. Gin
½	oz. Anisette
½	oz. Sweet Cream
½	White of 1 Egg

Shake with ice and strain into a cocktail glass. Sprinkle nutmeg on top.

ANISETTE COCKTAIL NO. 2

1	oz. Anisette
½	oz. Benedictine
1	dash Angostura Bitters

Shake with ice and strain into a highball glass. Add ice cubes and water.

ANKLE BREAKER

1½	oz. Cherry-flavored Brandy
1	oz. Lime Juice
1	oz. 151-proof Rum
2	tsp. Sugar Syrup

Shake with ice and strain into an Old-fashioned glass.

Here's to beefsteak when
you're hungry,
Whisky when you're dry,
All the girls you ever want
And heaven when you die.

ANNE

1½	oz. Apple Brandy
¾	oz. Cointreau
¾	oz. Dubonnet
1-2	dashes Angostura Bitters

Mix without ice and pour over ice in an Old-fashioned glass. Decorate with one red and one green cherry, a slice of orange and a slice of lime.

ANNOUNCER COCKTAIL

½	oz. Lemon Juice
¼	oz. Cointreau
¾	oz. Gin
¾	oz. Cognac Brandy

Shake with ice and strain into a cocktail glass.

ANN SHERIDAN

¾	oz. Lime Juice
1½	oz. Light Rum
½	oz. Orange Curacao

Shake with ice and strain into a cocktail glass.

ANTE NO. 1

1	oz. Apple Brandy
½	oz. Triple Sec or Orange Curacao
1	oz. Dubonnet

Stir with ice and strain into a cocktail glass.

ANTE NO. 2

1½	oz. Calvados
½	oz. Cointreau
½	oz. Pernod

Stir with ice and strain into a cocktail glass.

ANTOINE SPECIAL

| 1½ | oz. Dubonnet |
| 1½ | oz. Dry Vermouth |

Float Vermouth on top of chilled Dubonnet in a wine glass.

ANTONIO

1	oz. Gin
1	oz. Brandy
¼	oz. Maraschino Liqueur
¼	oz. White Creme de Menthe

Shake with ice and strain into a cocktail glass.

ANTS IN THE PANTS

1	oz. Gin
½	oz. Grand Marnier
½	oz. Sweet Vermouth
1	dash Lemon Juice

Shake with ice and strain into a cocktail glass.

APACHE

1	oz. Gin
1	oz. Dry Vermouth
1	dash Onion Juice
½	oz. Orange Curacao

Stir with ice and strain into a cocktail glass.

APERITIF CHAMPAGNE COOLER

¼	tsp. Sugar
1	dash Lemon Juice
1	dash Bitters
1	oz. Brandy
3	oz. chilled extra dry Champagne

Stir gently with ice and strain into a champagne glass.

APOLLO 8

½	oz. Galliano
¼	oz. Blue Curacao
¼	oz. Tequila

Mix in a pony glass and float cream on top.

APOLLO MOON MAIDEN

1	oz.	Galliano
1	oz.	Brandy
1½	oz.	Cream
3	drops	Vanilla Extract

Shake with ice and strain into a cocktail glass. Add a slice of lime.

APPARENT

1	oz.	Gin
1	oz.	Dubonnet
¼	oz.	Pernod

Stir with ice and strain into a cocktail glass.

APPENDECTOMY

1½	oz.	Gin
½	oz.	Lime Juice
½		Egg White
¼	oz.	Grand Marnier

Shake with ice and strain into a cocktail glass.

APPENDICITIS

1½	oz.	Gin
½	oz.	Lime Juice
½		Egg White
¼	oz.	Orange Curacao

Shake with ice and strain into a cocktail glass.

APPETIZER NO. 1

1½	oz.	Dubonnet
1½	oz.	Orange Juice

Shake with ice and strain into a cocktail glass.

APPETIZER NO. 2

1	oz.	Gin
1	oz.	Dubonnet
¾	oz.	Orange Juice
1	dash	Angostura Bitters

Shake with ice and strain into a cocktail glass.

APPETIZER NO. 3

2¼	oz.	Rye Whisky
¼	oz.	Orange Curacao
2	dashes	Peychaud's Bitters

Shake with ice and strain into a cocktail glass. Serve with lemon and orange twists.

APPLE & GINGER COCKTAIL

1¼	oz.	Applejack
¾	oz.	Ginger-flavored Brandy
½	oz.	Lime Juice
½	tsp.	Sugar

Shake with ice and strain into a cocktail glass.

APPLE-BERRY CLARET

4	oz.	Cranberry-Apple Drink
4	oz.	Claret
Crushed Ice		
Sprigs of Mint		

Mix Cranberry-Apple drink and Claret. Fill a Collins glass half full with crushed ice. Pour wine over ice. Serve with a mint sprig.

APPLE BLOSSOM COCKTAIL NO. 1

1½	oz.	Applejack
1½	oz.	Sweet Vermouth
2	dashes	Grenadine
2	dashes	Pineapple Juice

Shake with ice and strain into a cocktail glass.

APPLE BLOSSOM COCKTAIL NO. 2

1½	oz.	Applejack
¾	oz.	Apple Juice
½	oz.	Lime Juice
¼	oz.	Maple Syrup

Shake with ice and strain into a cocktail glass. Serve with a lemon wedge.

APPLE BLOW FIZZ

Juice ½ Lemon		
1		Egg White
1	tsp.	Powdered Sugar
2	oz.	Apple Brandy

Shake with ice and strain into a highball glass with two ice cubes. Fill with soda.

APPLE BLUSH

4	oz.	Apple Juice
4	oz.	Ruby Chablis
Ice Cubes		
Lemon		

Pour apple juice and Chablis into a Collins glass. Stir. Add ice cubes, a squeeze of lemon juice and a twist of lemon peel.

APPLE BRANDY COCKTAIL

1½	oz.	Apple Brandy
1	tsp.	Grenadine
1	tsp.	Lemon Juice

Shake with ice and strain into a cocktail glass.

APPLE BRANDY COOLER

1½	oz.	Brandy
¾	oz.	Rum
3	oz.	Apple Juice

Shake with ice and strain into a Collins glass. Fill with ice. Float ¼ oz. Jamaica Rum on top. Serve with a lime wheel.

APPLE BRANDY HIGHBALL

2	oz.	Apple Brandy

Pour over ice cubes in a highball glass. Fill with ginger ale or soda. Add a twist of lemon peel, if desired, and stir.

APPLE BRANDY RICKEY

Juice ½ Lime
1½ oz. Apple Brandy

Fill a highball glass with soda and ice cubes. Leave lime in glass. Stir.

APPLE BRANDY SOUR

Juice ½ Lemon
½   tsp. Powdered Sugar
2   oz. Apple Brandy

Shake with ice and strain into a Sour glass. Decorate with a half slice of lemon and a cherry.

APPLE BUCK

1½ oz. Applejack
¼   oz. Lemon Juice

Mix in a highball glass. Fill with ginger ale and ice. Add a lemon twist.

APPLE BYRRH

1   oz. Calvados or Apple Brandy
¾   oz. Byrrh
½   oz. Dry Vermouth
2   dashes Lemon Juice

Stir with ice and strain into a cocktail glass. Serve with a lemon twist.

APPLECAR

1   oz. Applejack
1   oz. Triple Sec or Orange Curacao
1   oz. Lemon Juice

Shake with ice and strain into a cocktail glass.

APPLE COCKTAIL NO. 1

2   oz. Brandy
1   oz. Apple Brandy

Shake with ice and strain into a cocktail glass.

APPLE COCKTAIL NO. 2

1   oz. Calvados or Apple Brandy
½   oz. Brandy
½   oz. Gin
1   oz. Sweet Cider

Shake with ice and strain into a cocktail glass.

APPLE DANDY

Pour 1½ oz. Vodka into a highball glass and fill with ice and apple juice.

APPLE DUBONNET

1½ oz. Calvados
1½ oz. Dubonnet

Shake with ice and strain into a cocktail glass. Add ice and top with a slice of lemon.

APPLE GINGER FIX

¾   oz. Applejack
¾   oz. Ginger-flavored Brandy
½   oz. Lemon Juice
½   tsp. Sugar dissolved in a splash of water

Mix in a highball glass. Fill with crushed ice and add a lemon wedge.

APPLE GINGER SANGAREE

¼   tsp. Sugar
1½ oz. Apple Brandy
2   oz. Green Ginger Wine

Mix in a double Old-fashioned glass. Fill with ice and add a lemon wedge. Sprinkle nutmeg on top.

APPLEHAWK

1¼ oz. Applejack
1¼ oz. Grapefruit Juice
¼   tsp. Sugar

Shake with ice and strain into a cocktail glass.

APPLEJACK NO. 1

1½ oz. Applejack
1   tsp. Sugar Syrup
2   dashes Orange Bitters
1   dash Angostura Bitters

Stir with ice and strain into a cocktail glass.

APPLEJACK NO. 2

1½ oz. Calvados or Applejack
½   oz. Sweet Vermouth
1   dash Angostura Bitters

Stir with ice and strain into a cocktail glass.

APPLEJACK NO. 3

1½ oz. Applejack
½   oz. Lemon Juice
¼   oz. Grenadine

Shake with ice and strain into a cocktail glass.

APPLEJACK NO. 4

1½ oz. Applejack
1½ oz. Sweet Vermouth

Stir with ice and strain into a cocktail glass.

APPLEJACK ALGONQUIN

1½ oz. Applejack
1   lump Sugar
1   piece of Baked Apple

Mix in an Old-fashioned glass and fill with hot water. Sprinkle nutmeg on top.

APPLEJACK COLLINS

1½ oz. Applejack
1   tsp. Powdered Sugar
1   oz. Lemon Juice
2   dashes Orange Bitters

Shake with ice and strain into a Collins glass. Fill with crushed ice. Add soda and serve with a lemon wedge.

APPLEJACK COOLER

1 oz. Lemon Juice
1½ oz. Applejack
1 tsp. Sugar

Shake with ice and strain into a Collins glass. Add ice cubes and soda. Float ¼ oz. Brandy and ¼ oz. Grenadine on top.

APPLEJACK DAISY NO. 1

1 oz. Lemon Juice
½ tsp. Powdered Sugar
¾ oz. Grenadine
1½ oz. Applejack

Half fill a highball glass with finely cracked ice. Stir until glass is frosted. Pour ingredients over ice. Fill with soda water. Decorate with a sprig of fresh mint, a slice of lemon and a slice of orange.

APPLEJACK DAISY NO. 2

1½ oz. Applejack
1 oz. Brandy
1½ oz. Lemon Juice
1 tsp. Sugar
½ oz. Grenadine

Shake with ice and strain into a large cocktail glass. Serve with a lemon wedge and a cherry.

APPLEJACK DAISY NO. 3

1 oz. Applejack
1 oz. Gin
½ oz. Lemon Juice
¼ oz. Grenadine

Shake with ice and strain into a cocktail glass.

Here's a toast to the hostess,
a toast to the host;
May we never meet again
  ere we give up the ghost.

APPLEJACK FLIP

4 oz. Applejack
1 whole Egg
2 tsp. Sugar
½ cup crushed Ice
Nutmeg

Put all ingredients except the nutmeg into an electric blender and blend on high speed for 30 seconds. Pour into 6 oz. stemmed glasses and grate a little nutmeg on top.

APPLEJACK MAN

1¾ oz. Applejack
¾ oz. Sweet Vermouth
1 dash Orange Bitters

Stir with ice and strain into a cocktail glass. Serve with a cherry.

APPLEJACK OLD-FASHIONED

1 cube Sugar
1 dash Angostura Bitters
1 dash Club Soda
1½ oz. Applejack
½ cup cracked Ice

Muddle the sugar and bitters in an Old-fashioned glass with the soda. Pour in the Applejack, add the ice and stir. Serve with a lemon twist.

APPLEJACK PUNCH

1½ oz. Applejack
¼ oz. Grenadine
¾ oz. Orange Juice

Mix in a Collins glass. Fill with ginger ale and ice. Garnish with fruit.

APPLEJACK RABBIT

1½ oz. Applejack or Apple Brandy
½ oz. Lemon Juice
½ oz. Orange Juice
Maple Syrup to taste

Shake with ice and strain into a cocktail glass.

APPLEJACK RICKEY

1½ oz. Applejack
¼ oz. Brandy
¼ oz. Grenadine
¾ oz. Lime Juice

Mix in a highball glass. Fill with soda and ice.

APPLEJACK SMASH

1½ oz. Applejack
2 tsp. Water
½ tsp. Sugar
3 sprigs fresh Mint

Muddle sugar and water in an Old-fashioned glass, with mint. Add Applejack and cracked ice.

APPLEJACK SOUR NO. 1

1½ oz. Applejack
1 oz. Lemon Juice
1 tsp. Sugar

Shake with ice and strain into a Sour glass. Serve with a lemon wedge and a cherry.

APPLEJACK SOUR NO. 2

1½ oz. Applejack
½ oz. Lemon Juice
½ oz. Lime Juice
½ tsp. Sugar
¼ oz. Grenadine

Shake with ice and strain into a Sour glass. Serve with a lemon wedge and a cherry.

APPLEJACK TODDY

1 lump Sugar
3 tsp. Water
2 oz. Applejack

Put the sugar in an Old-fashioned glass and dissolve in the water. Add Applejack, ice and a dash of nutmeg. Serve with a teaspoon.

APPLE KNOCKER

2½ oz. Applejack
½ oz. Sweet Vermouth
3 oz. Orange Juice
½ oz. Lemon Juice
1 tsp. Sugar

Shake with ice and strain into a Collins glass.

Here's to the four hinges of
friendship,
Swearing, Lying, Stealing
and Drinking.
When you swear, swear by
your country;
When you lie, lie for a pretty
woman;
When you steal, steal away
from bad company;
And when you drink, drink
with me.
— *Gus Melbourne*

APPLE LILLET

1½ oz. Calvados
1½ oz. Lillet

Shake with ice and strain into a cocktail glass. Add ice and top with an orange slice.

APPLE PIE COCKTAIL

¾ oz. Rum
¾ oz. Sweet Vermouth
1 tsp. Apricot-flavored Brandy
½ tsp. Grenadine
1 tsp. Lemon Juice

Shake with ice and strain into a cocktail glass.

APPLE RUM RICKEY

¾ oz. Applejack
¾ oz. Rum
¼ Lime

Pour applejack and rum into a highball glass over ice cubes. Fill with soda. Squeeze in the juice from the lime and drop lime wedge into the glass. Stir.

APPLE SMILE

1½ oz. Gin
1 tbsp. Apple Brandy
2 tsp. Lime Juice
A few drops Grenadine

Shake with ice and strain into a cocktail glass. Add ice.

APPLE SWIZZLE

1 oz. Lime Juice
1 oz. Apple Brandy
¾ oz. Rum
5 dashes Angostura Bitters
1 tsp. Sugar

Mix in a highball glass. Fill with shaved ice and swizzle until glass frosts.

APPLE TODDY (Hot) NO. 1

Place ¼ Baked Apple in an Old-fashioned glass with 1 tsp. powdered sugar. Add 2 oz. Calvados or Applejack. Fill the glass with hot Apple Cider and sprinkle nutmeg on top.

APPLE TODDY (Hot) NO. 2

½ tsp. Powdered Sugar
1½ oz. Applejack

Mix in an Old-fashioned glass. Fill with hot Apple Cider. Sprinkle nutmeg on top.

APPLE TREE

1½ oz. Applejack
1½ oz. Sweet Cider or Apple Juice
1 dash Dry Vermouth

Mix in an Old-fashioned glass. Serve with a lemon twist.

APPROVE NO. 1

2 oz. Rye
½ oz. Orange Curacao
1 dash Angostura Bitters

Shake with ice and strain into a cocktail glass. Add a twist of lemon.

APPROVE NO. 2

¼ Baked Apple in glass
½ tsp. Sugar
1½ oz. Applejack

Shake with ice and strain into a cocktail glass. Fill with boiling water. Sprinkle nutmeg on top.

APRICOT

2 oz. Apricot-flavored Brandy
1 oz. Orange Juice
1 oz. Lemon Juice
A few drops of Gin

Shake with ice and strain into an Old-fashioned glass. Add ice.

APRICOT ANISE COLLINS

1½ oz. Gin
½ oz. Apricot-flavored Brandy
1½ tsp. Anisette
1 tbsp. Lemon Juice

Shake with ice and strain into a Collins glass over ice cubes. Fill with soda and stir lightly. Garnish with a slice of lemon.

APRICOT BRANDY

2 oz. Apricot-flavored Brandy
Several drops Grenadine
Soda

Stir with ice and strain into a cocktail glass. Fill with soda. Serve with a lemon twist and an orange peel. Top with fruit slices.

APRICOT BRANDY RICKEY

Juice ½ Lime
2 oz. Apricot-flavored Brandy

Pour into a highball glass over ice cubes and fill with soda. Drop rind of lime into glass. Stir.

APRICOT COCKTAIL

Juice ¼ Lemon
Juice ¼ Orange
1½ oz. Apricot-flavored Brandy
1 tsp. Gin

Shake with ice and strain into a cocktail glass.

APRICOT COOLER

1 cup crushed Ice
2 oz. Apricot-flavored Brandy
2 dashes Grenadine

Put the ice in a highball glass; add the Brandy and Grenadine and stir. Fill with soda or ginger ale and decorate with fruit peel.

APRICOT FIZZ

Juice ½ Lemon
Juice ½ Lime
1 tsp. Powdered Sugar
2 oz. Apricot-flavored Brandy

Shake with cracked ice and strain into a highball glass with 2 ice cubes. Fill with soda.

APRICOT LADY

1¼ oz. Rum
1 oz. Apricot-flavored Brandy
½ tsp. Triple Sec or Orange Curacao
1 tbsp. Lime Juice
1 tsp. Egg White

Shake all ingredients with ice and strain into an Old-fashioned glass over ice cubes. Add an orange slice.

APRICOT NOG

4 oz. White Rum
4 oz. Heavy Cream
4 oz. Apricot Nectar
2 oz. Apricot-flavored Brandy
1 Egg, well beaten
4 oz. crushed Ice

Blend at a high speed until smooth. Serve in mugs. Sprinkle nutmeg on top.

APRICOT PIE

1 oz. White Rum
1 oz. Sweet Vermouth
¼ oz. Apricot-flavored Brandy
½ tsp. Lemon Juice
Several drops Grenadine

Shake with ice and strain into a cocktail glass. Add ice and an orange twist.

AQUARIUS

1½ oz. Whisky
½ oz. Blackberry-flavored Brandy
1 oz. Cranberry Juice

Shake with ice and strain into an Old-fashioned glass on the rocks.

AQUAVIT FIZZ

1 oz. Lemon Juice
½ Egg White
½ tsp. Sugar
¼ oz. Cherry Heering
1½ oz. Aquavit

Shake with ice and strain into a Collins glass. Fill with soda and ice. Serve with a lemon twist.

> May all your troubles be little ones;
> May all your troubles be small;
> May all your troubles be light as bubbles;
> May you have no troubles at all.

AQUAVIT HIGHBALL

1½ oz. Aquavit

Pour into a highball glass. Fill with ginger ale and ice. Serve with a lemon twist.

AQUAVIT RICKEY

1½ oz. Aquavit
¼ oz. Lime Juice

Mix in a highball glass and fill with soda and ice. Drop in the lime shell; float 1 dash Kummel on top.

AQUEDUCT

1½ oz. Vodka
1½ tsp. Curacao
1½ tsp. Apricot-flavored Brandy
1 tbsp. Lime Juice

Combine and shake all ingredients and strain into a cocktail glass. Add a twist of orange peel.

ARAWAK

1½ oz. Jamaica Rum
1½ oz. Cream Sherry
1 dash Angostura Bitters

Stir with ice and strain into a cocktail glass.

ARCHBISHOP PUNCH

2 oz. Port
2 oz. Water
1 oz. Lime Juice
½ tsp. Sugar
½ oz. Jamaica Rum

Mix in a highball glass. Fill with ice.

ARGENTINA COCKTAIL

1 oz. Gin
1 oz. Dry Vermouth
¼ oz. Cointreau
¼ oz. Benedictine
1 dash Orange Bitters
1 dash Angostura Bitters

Stir with ice and strain into a cocktail glass.

ARGENTINE JULEP

1 oz. Orange Juice
1 oz. Pineapple Juice
1 oz. Spanish Brandy
1 oz. Claret
¼ oz. Cointreau

Mix in a Collins glass. Fill with shaved ice. Serve with an orange slice and mint sprig.

ARISE MY LOVE

1 tsp. Green Creme de Menthe
Chilled Champagne

Put Creme de Menthe into a champagne glass. Fill with Champagne.

ARMOUR

1½ oz. Sherry
1½ oz. Dry Vermouth
1 dash Orange Bitters

Stir with ice and strain into a cocktail glass.

ARMY COCKTAIL

2 oz. Gin
½ oz. Sweet Vermouth

Stir with ice and strain into a cocktail glass. Serve with a twist of orange peel.

ARRACK COOLER

1½ oz. Arrack
½ tsp. Sugar
½ oz. Rum
¼ oz. Lemon Juice

Mix in a highball glass. Fill with ice. Add soda or champagne.

ARRACK PUNCH

1 oz. Orange Juice
1 oz. Lemon Juice
1 tsp. Sugar
1½ oz. Arrack

Mix in a cup. Fill with boiling water. Stir. Dunk a tea bag to taste.

ARROWHEAD

1 Egg White
1 oz. Whisky
¼ oz. Sweet Vermouth
¼ oz. Dry Vermouth
½ oz. Lemon Juice

Shake with ice and strain into a cocktail glass.

ARSENIC & OLD LACE

1½ oz. Gin
½ oz. Pernod
¼ oz. Dry Vermouth
½ oz. Creme de Violette

Stir with ice and strain into a cocktail glass.

ARTILLERY

1½ oz. Gin
1½ tsp. Sweet Vermouth
2 dashes Angostura Bitters

Stir with ice and strain into a cocktail glass.

ARTILLERY PUNCH

1 quart Rye Whisky
1 pint Dark Rum
½ pint Gin
½ pint Brandy
3 oz. Benedictine
1 bottle dry Red Wine
2 cups Orange Juice
1 cup Lemon Juice
1 quart strong black Tea
1 large block Ice
Sugar Syrup (optional)
Twist Lemon Peel

Combine all ingredients, except sugar syrup and lemon peel, in a large punch bowl with a block of ice. Stir gently and add a little sugar syrup. Decorate with lemon peel twists. Serve in 4-oz. punch glasses. Makes about 36 servings. For a more flavorful punch, make the block of ice from the tea. This will reduce the servings to about 28.

ARTIST'S SPECIAL

1 oz. Whisky
1 oz. Sherry
½ oz. Lemon Juice
½ oz. Sugar Syrup
¼ oz. Grenadine

Stir with ice and strain into a cocktail glass.

ASTRONAUT

1½ oz. Jamaica Rum
1½ oz. Vodka
1½ tsp. Lemon Juice
A few drops Passion Fruit Juice

Shake with ice and strain into an Old-fashioned glass. Add ice.

ASYLUM COCKTAIL

Fill an Old-fashioned glass with ice; add 1 oz. Gin and 1 oz. Pernod. Float Grenadine on top.

ATLANTA BELLE

1 oz. Early Times
¾ oz. Green Creme de Menthe
¾ oz. Light Creme de Cacao
1 oz. Cream

Blend with ice and strain into a Sour glass.

ATLAS COCKTAIL

1 dash Angostura Bitters
½ oz. Cointreau
1 oz. Demerara Rum
1 oz. Calvados

Shake with ice and strain into a cocktail glass.

ATTA BOY

2 oz. Gin
½ oz. Dry Vermouth
2 dashes Grenadine

Stir with ice and strain into a cocktail glass.

ATTENTION

¾ oz. Gin
¾ oz. Pernod
¾ oz. Dry Vermouth
¾ oz. Creme de Violette
2 dashes Orange Bitters

Stir with ice and strain into a cocktail glass.

ATTY COCKTAIL

½ oz. Dry Vermouth
3 dashes Pernod
2 oz. Gin
3 dashes Creme de Violette

Shake with ice and strain into a cocktail glass. Serve with a lemon twist.

AUBURN

1 oz. Orange Juice
½ oz. Galliano
¼ oz. Creme de Cassis
1 oz. Vodka

Shake with ice and strain into a cocktail glass.

AULD MAN'S MILK

1½ oz. Scotch
½ tsp. Sugar
1 Egg

Shake with ice and strain into a highball glass.

AULD MAN'S MILK PUNCH

6 large Eggs, separated
½ pound superfine Sugar
1 quart half-and-half Cream
1 pint Scotch Whisky

Beat egg yolks until thick and lemon-colored. Add sugar and cream and stir until sugar dissolves. Slowly stir in the Scotch. Beat egg whites until light and frothy, and fold into the whisky mixture. Grate a little nutmeg over the punch and serve in 4-oz. punch glasses. Makes about 16 servings.

AUNT AGATHA

2 cubes Ice
2 oz. Light Rum
3-4 oz. Orange Juice, chilled
1 dash Angostura Bitters

Put the ice cubes in an Old-fashioned glass, add the Rum and orange juice and stir gently. Add the Bitters and serve with an orange slice.

AUNT JEMIMA

½ oz. Brandy
½ oz. White Creme de Cacao
½ oz. Benedictine

Pour carefully, in order given, into a pony glass so that ingredients do not mix.

AUTOMOBILE

1 oz. Scotch Whisky
1 oz. Gin
1 oz. Sweet Vermouth
1 dash Orange Bitters

Stir with ice and strain into a cocktail glass.

AUTUMN LEAF

1 oz. Arrack
1 oz. Creme de Cacao
1 oz. Danziger Goldwasser

Stir with ice and strain into a cocktail glass.

AVIATION COCKTAIL NO. 1

½ oz. Lemon Juice
1½ oz. Gin
¼ oz. Maraschino Liqueur
¼ oz. Apricot-flavored Brandy

Shake with ice and strain into a cocktail glass.

AVIATION COCKTAIL NO. 2

1½ oz. Bourbon
1½ oz. Grape Juice

Stir with ice and strain into a cocktail glass.

AVIATOR COCKTAIL

¾ oz. Dubonnet
¾ oz. Sherry

Shake with ice and strain into a cocktail glass. Serve with a lemon twist.

AZIZ FIZZ

1 Egg White
½ tsp. Sugar
2 oz. Lemon Juice
2 oz. Gin

Shake with ice and strain into a cocktail glass. Fill with soda and ice. Add a dash of Orange Flower Water.

B & B

½ oz. Benedictine
½ oz. Brandy

Use a cordial glass and carefully float the Brandy on top of the Benedictine.

B & B COLLINS

1½ oz. Cognac
1 oz. Lemon Juice
1 tsp. Sugar

Shake with ice and strain into a Collins glass. Fill with soda and ice. Float Benedictine on top. Serve with a lemon wedge.

BABBIE'S SPECIAL COCKTAIL

1 tbsp. Sweet Cream
1½ oz. Apricot-flavored Brandy
¼ tsp. Gin

Shake with ice and strain into a cocktail glass.

BABY FINGERS COCKTAIL

1½ oz. Sloe Gin
¾ oz. Gin
2 dashes Angostura Bitters

Shake with ice and strain into a cocktail glass.

BABY KITTY COCKTAIL

⅓   oz. Anisette
⅓   oz. Creme de Violette
⅓   oz. Cream

Pour carefully, in order given, into a pony glass so that each ingredient floats on the preceding one without mixing. Top with a cherry.

BACARDI-ABSINTHE

¾   oz. Maraschino Liqueur
1½   oz. Light Bacardi Rum
¼   oz. Pernod

Mix in a Collins glass. Fill with Champagne and ice. Serve with straws.

BACARDI-BLOSSOM COCKTAIL

½   oz. Orange Juice
½   tsp. Lemon Juice
½   tsp. Sugar
2   oz. Bacardi Rum

Shake with ice and strain into a cocktail glass. Sprinkle nutmeg on top.

BACARDI BUCK COCKTAIL

1½   oz. Bacardi Rum
¾   oz. Cointreau
2   tsp. Lemon Juice
2   tsp. Sugar Syrup

Shake with ice and strain into a highball glass. Fill with lime rickey.

BACARDI COCKTAIL NO. 1

Juice ½ Lime
1½   oz. Bacardi Rum
½   tsp. Grenadine
1   dash Egg White
1   Maraschino Cherry

Shake with ice and strain into a cocktail glass. Serve with a cherry.

BACARDI COCKTAIL NO. 2

Juice 1 Lime
½   tsp. Sugar
1½   oz. Bacardi Rum
¾   oz. Pineapple Juice

Serve in a champagne glass with shaved ice.

BACARDI COLLINS

1   oz. Lime Juice
1   tsp. Sugar
1½   oz. Light Bacardi Rum

Shake with ice and strain into a Collins glass. Fill with soda and ice.

BACARDI DRY

2   oz. Light Bacardi Rum
½   oz. Dry Vermouth

Stir with ice and strain into a cocktail glass.

BACARDIDUB

1½   oz. Light Bacardi Rum
¾   oz. Dubonnet
¼   oz. Grenadine

Stir with ice and strain into a cocktail glass.

BACARDI DUBONNET

¾   oz. Bacardi Rum
¾   oz. Dubonnet
1   tsp. Grenadine
1   tsp. Lime Juice

Stir with ice and strain into a cocktail glass.

BACARDI FIZZ

2   oz. Bacardi Rum
1   tsp. Sugar
2   oz. Lemon Juice

Shake with ice and strain into a highball glass. Fill with soda and ice. (Gin, Whisky, or Brandy can be used instead of Rum.)

BACARDI GROG

1½   oz. Bacardi Rum
1   tsp. Sugar Syrup
¾   oz. hot Tea

Stir well in a punch cup. Fill with hot water. Grate nutmeg over top. Serve with a spoon.

BACARDI HIGHBALL

1½   oz. Bacardi Rum

Pour into a highball glass. Fill with ginger ale or soda. Add ice and serve with a lemon twist.

BACARDI PEACH COCKTAIL

1   oz. Bacardi Rum
1   tsp. Lemon Juice
1   oz. Peach-flavored Brandy
1   tsp. Sugar Syrup
1   sprig Mint

Shake and strain into a cocktail glass.

BACARDI PUNCH NO. 1

1½   oz. Bacardi Rum
¾   oz. Curacao
¾   oz. Pineapple Juice
¾   oz. Grenadine
½   oz. Lemon Juice

Stir in a highball glass. Fill with ice. Add orange slices.

BACARDI PUNCH NO. 2

1½   oz. Bacardi Rum
½   oz. Lemon Juice
½   oz. Cointreau
½   oz. Sugar Syrup

Shake with ice and strain into a highball glass. Fill with soda and ice. Serve with an orange slice.

BACARDI PUNCH NO. 3

2½ oz. Light Bacardi Rum
¾ oz. Grenadine

Mix in a Collins glass. Fill with shaved ice. Stir and top with soda.

BACARDI RICKEY NO. 1

1 oz. Rum
1 oz. Benedictine
½ tsp. Grenadine
½ tsp. Lemon Juice

Stir with ice and strain into a highball glass. Fill with soda and ice. Garnish with fruit.

BACARDI RICKEY NO. 2

1½ oz. Rum
1½ tsp. Lemon Juice
1½ tsp. Maraschino Liqueur

Stir with ice and strain into a highball glass. Fill with soda and ice. Garnish with fruit.

BACARDI SILVER

½ oz. Pineapple Juice
¼ oz. Lemon Juice
1 oz. Light Bacardi Rum
½ oz. Gin
½ Egg White

Shake with ice and strain into a cocktail glass. Serve with a cherry.

BACARDI SPECIAL

1½ oz. Light Rum
¾ oz. Gin
½ oz. Grenadine
1 oz. Lime Juice

Shake with ice and strain into a cocktail glass. (Dark Rum may be used instead of Light Rum.)

BACARDI SWEET

2 oz. Light Bacardi Rum
½ oz. Sweet Vermouth

Stir with ice and strain into a cocktail glass.

BACARDI VERMOUTH

1½ oz. Bacardi Rum
1½ oz. Vermouth

Shake with ice and strain into a cocktail glass.

BACHELOR'S BAIT COCKTAIL

1½ oz. Gin
1 Egg White
1 dash Orange Bitters
½ tsp. Grenadine

Shake with ice and strain into a cocktail glass.

BAHIA COCKTAIL

1 oz. Dry Vermouth
1 oz. Dry Sherry
¼ oz. Pernod
1 dash Angostura Bitters

Stir with ice and strain into a cocktail glass. Serve with a lemon twist.

BAIRN

2 oz. Scotch
½ oz. Cointreau
1 dash Orange Bitters

Stir with ice and strain into a cocktail glass.

BALALAIKA

1 oz. Vodka
1 oz. Lemon Juice
½ oz. Cointreau

Shake with ice and strain into a cocktail glass.

BALD HEAD

1 oz. Gin
¾ oz. Dry Vermouth
¾ oz. Sweet Vermouth
1 dash Pernod

Stir with ice and strain into a cocktail glass. Serve with a lemon twist.

BALI HAI

1 oz. Light Rum
½ oz. Okolehao
2 oz. Tom Collins Mix
3 oz. Lime Juice
2 oz. Champagne

Fill a Collins glass three-quarters full with crushed ice. Pour in the Rum, Okolehao, Tom Collins mix and lime juice and stir. Top with Champagne.

BALI HI

¼ oz. Orange Curacao
¼ oz. Mandarin Liqueur
1 oz. Advokaat

Mix in a highball glass. Top with Fanta and stir. Garnish with a slice of orange or a cherry and serve.

BALI PUNCH

1 oz. Lime Juice
1 tsp. Sugar
1½ oz. Rum
½ oz. Passion Fruit

Shake with ice and strain into a highball glass. Fill with crushed ice and garnish with fruit.

BALLANTINE COCKTAIL

2 dashes Orange Bitters
¾ oz. Dry Vermouth
1½ oz. Gin
1 dash Pernod

Shake with ice and strain into a cocktail glass.

BALM COCKTAIL

¼ oz. Orange Juice
¼ oz. Cointreau
2 oz. Sherry
1 dash Orange Bitters
2 dashes Jamaica Rum

Shake with ice and strain into a cocktail glass. Serve with an olive.

BALTIMORE BANG

1½ oz. Early Times
½ oz. Apricot-flavored Brandy
1 oz. Lemon Juice
½ tsp. Sugar

Blend with ice and strain into a cocktail glass. Serve with an orange slice and a cherry.

BALTIMORE BRACER COCKTAIL NO. 1

1 oz. Anisette
1 oz. Brandy
1 Egg White

Shake with ice and strain into a cocktail glass.

BALTIMORE BRACER COCKTAIL NO. 2

¾ oz. Cognac
½ oz. Madeira
2 tsp. Sugar Syrup
3 oz. Milk
1 Egg
1 tsp. Rum

Shake with ice and strain into a highball glass. Sprinkle nutmeg on top.

BALTIMORE EGGNOG NO. 1

1 Egg
1 tsp. Powdered Sugar
1 oz. Brandy
1 oz. Jamaica Rum
1 oz. Madeira
¾ cup Milk

Shake with ice and strain into a Collins glass. Dust with nutmeg.

BALTIMORE EGGNOG NO. 2

1 oz. Bourbon
1 oz. Madeira Wine
2 oz. Milk
½ tsp. Sugar

Shake with ice and strain into a Collins glass. Dust with nutmeg.

BAMBOO COCKTAIL

1½ oz. Dry Sherry
¾ oz. Dry Vermouth
1 dash Orange Bitters

Stir with ice and strain into a cocktail glass.

BANANA BIRD

1 oz. Bourbon
1 oz. Heavy Cream
2 tsp. Creme de Bananes
2 tsp. Triple Sec or Orange Curacao

Shake with ice and strain into a Sour glass.

BANANA CHARTREUSE

4 Bananas, barely ripe
4 oz. Yellow Chartreuse
Butter
Ground Ginger

Peel the bananas. Slice them into quarters, first lengthwise, then in half. Sauté the banana slices in a generous amount of butter, sprinkle with ginger and pour the Chartreuse over them. Ignite, burn for no more than sixty seconds and serve at once.

> A drink, my lass, in a deep
>   clear glass
> Just properly tempered by
>   ice,
> And here's to the lips mine
>   last have kissed;
> And if they were thine,
>   here's twice.

BANANA COCKTAIL

1¼ oz. Vodka
1 tsp. Banana Liqueur

Combine the Vodka and Banana Liqueur with ice, shake well and strain into a highball glass. Squeeze in juice from half a lime and drop in the peel. Add ice and fill with soda. Stir gently and top with sprigs of mint.

BANANA COW NO. 1

3 oz. Milk
1½ oz. Rum
½ tsp. Sugar
1 crushed, ripe Banana

Blend with ice and strain into a cocktail glass.

BANANA COW NO. 2

3 oz. Milk
1 Banana
1 dash Angostura Bitters
1 dash Vanilla
1 tsp. Sugar
1½ oz. Rum

Blend with ice and strain into a Collins glass.

BANANA DAIQUIRI-FROZEN

Fill blender ⅔ full with crushed ice. Add 1 oz. lime juice and ½ a crushed, ripe banana. Blend to a snow cone consistency. Pour into a large cocktail glass. Top with Light and Dark Rum. Add a dash of Grenadine and serve with a cherry.

BANANA DAIQUIRI NO. 1

2 oz. Light Rum
½ oz. Banana Liqueur
½ oz. Lime Juice
½ small Banana, peeled and coarsely chopped

Blend with ice and strain into a large cocktail glass.

BANANA DAIQUIRI NO. 2

1	oz. Lime Juice
1½	oz. Rum
½	tsp. Sugar
½	oz. Banana Liqueur

Shake with ice and strain into a cocktail glass.

BANANA DAIQUIRI NO. 3

1	oz. Lime Juice
1	slice fresh Banana
1	tsp. Sugar
½	oz. Maraschino Liqueur
1½	oz. Rum

Shake with ice and strain into a cocktail glass.

BANANA ITALIANO

1	oz. Cream
1	oz. Galliano
½	oz. Creme de Bananes

Shake with ice and strain into a cocktail glass.

BANANA MANGO

1½	oz. White Rum
½	oz. Mango Nectar
¾	tsp. Banana Liqueur
2	tsp. Lime Juice
1	Mango slice

Shake with ice and strain into an Old-fashioned glass. Add ice. Top with a mango slice.

BANANA PUNCH

2	oz. Vodka
1½	tsp. Apricot-flavored Brandy
Juice ½ Lime	

Pour into a Collins glass filled with crushed ice. Add soda and top with slices of banana and sprigs of mint.

BANANA PUNCH FRAPPE

½	oz. Banana Liqueur
1	oz. Rum
¾	oz. Orange Juice

Shake and strain over crushed ice in a cocktail glass.

BANANA RUM FRAPPE

½	oz. White Rum
½	oz. Banana Liqueur
½	oz. Orange Juice

Mix and pour over crushed ice in a cocktail glass.

BANANA SQUASH

4	oz. White Rum
3	tsp. Lime Juice
2	brown Bananas, sliced
6	oz. crushed Ice

Soak the banana slices with the Rum for several hours. Blend with the lime juice and ice at a high speed for 15 seconds and pour into a Collins glass.

BANANA WINE SHAKE

½	large Banana
3	oz. Milk
5	oz. Vanilla Ice Cream
1½	oz. Dry Sherry
Pinch of Nutmeg	
Pinch of Salt	

Blend until smooth and foamy. Pour into a Collins glass.

BANMAN

½	oz. Lime Juice
1½	oz. Rum
¼	oz. Banana Liqueur
½	oz. Mango Liqueur

Shake with ice and strain into a cocktail glass. Serve with a mango slice.

BANSET

| ¾ | oz. Creme de Bananes |
| ¾ | oz. Anisette |

Mix in an Old-fashioned glass.

BANSHEE

1	oz. Creme de Bananes
½	oz. White Creme de Cacao
½	oz. Sweet Cream

Shake with ice and strain into a cocktail glass.

BARBADOS COCKTAIL

1	oz. Falernum
1½	oz. Barbados Rum
Juice ½ Lime	

Shake with ice and strain into a cocktail glass.

BARBADOS RUM SWIZZLE

Juice ½ Lime	
2	oz. Barbados Rum
1	dash Bitters
½	tsp. Sugar

Fill a Collins glass with shaved ice. Squeeze lime and leave shell in glass. Add other ingredients and swizzle.

> Here's a toast to all who are here,
> No matter where you are from;
> May the best day you have ever seen
> Be worse than your worst to come.

BARBARA COCKTAIL NO. 1

1½	oz. Sweet Cream
¾	oz. Creme de Cacao
1½	oz. Vodka

Shake with ice and strain into a cocktail glass.

BARBARA COCKTAIL NO. 2

1½ oz. Whisky
1 oz. Grapefruit Juice
2 dashes Apricot Liqueur
1 dash Sugar Syrup

Shake with ice and strain into a cocktail glass.

BARBARA EAST

1 oz. Bourbon
¾ oz. Grapefruit Juice
½ oz. Apricot-flavored Brandy
¼ tsp. Sugar

Shake with ice and strain into a cocktail glass.

BARBARA WEST

1 oz. Gin
1 oz. Sherry
½ oz. Lemon Juice
1 dash Angostura Bitters

Stir with ice and strain into a cocktail glass.

BARBARESQUE

1½ oz. Rum
¾ oz. Lemon Juice
½ oz. Cointreau

Shake with ice and strain into a cocktail glass.

BARBARY COAST COCKTAIL

½ oz. Gin
½ oz. Rum
½ oz. Creme de Cacao
½ oz. Scotch Whisky
½ oz. Sweet Cream

Shake with ice and strain into a cocktail glass.

> Welcome be ye that are here,
> Welcome all, and make good cheer,
> Welcome all, another year.

BARBARY COAST HIGHBALL

1 oz. Bourbon
½ oz. Light Creme de Cacao
½ oz. Gin
½ oz. Cream

Mix in a highball glass. Fill with soda and ice.

BARBOTAGE OF CHAMPAGNE

1 dash Angostura Bitters
1 tsp. Sugar
1 tsp. Lemon Juice
6 oz. chilled Champagne

Half fill a large goblet with crushed ice. Add Angostura Bitters, sugar, lemon juice and fill up with champagne. Garnish with an orange peel.

BAR-B-Q ACCOMPANIMENT

2 oz. Orgeat Syrup
2 dashes Lemon Juice
6 oz. Dry Sherry
1 oz. Burgundy
Cracked Ice
Fresh Fruit

Pour Orgeat Syrup and Lemon Juice into a Collins glass. Fill with cracked ice. Add Sherry and stir. Garnish with fruit. Float Burgundy.

BARCELONA FIZZ

1½ oz. Gin
1 oz. Sherry
¼ oz. Lime Juice
¼ tsp. Sugar

Mix in a highball glass. Fill with soda and ice.

BARKING DOG

¾ oz. Gin
¾ oz. Dry Vermouth
¾ oz. Sweet Vermouth
2 dashes Calisay

Shake with ice and strain into a cocktail glass.

BARNACLE BILL COCKTAIL NO. 1

¾ oz. Chartreuse
¾ oz. Parfait Amour
¾ oz. Pernod

Shake with ice and strain into a cocktail glass.

BARNACLE BILL COCKTAIL NO. 2

1½ oz. Vodka
1½ oz. Tomato Juice
1 dash Salt
1 dash Worcestershire Sauce
1 dash Tabasco Sauce
1½ oz. Clam Juice
1 tsp. Lemon Juice

Shake with ice and strain into a Sour glass.

BARNEY BARNATO

1 oz. Brandy
1 oz. Dubonnet
1 dash Angostura Bitters
1 dash Curacao

Stir with ice and strain into a cocktail glass.

BARNEY FRENCH NO. 1

2 oz. Whisky
2 dashes Peychaud's Bitters

In an Old-fashioned glass muddle Bitters, an orange slice and a twist of lemon peel with 1 or 2 ice cubes. Add Whisky.

BARNEY FRENCH NO. 2

1½ oz. Bourbon
½ oz. Pernod
2 dashes Peychaud's Bitters

Place 4 slices of orange, 1 lemon twist, Bitters and 1-2 ice cubes in an Old-fashioned glass and muddle well. Add Pernod and Bourbon. Fill with ice.

BARNUM

1½ oz. Gin
½ oz. Apricot-flavored Brandy
2 dashes Angostura Bitters
1 dash Lemon Juice

Shake with ice and strain into a cocktail glass.

BARON COCKTAIL

½ oz. Dry Vermouth
1½ oz. Gin
1½ tsp. Triple Sec or Orange Curacao
½ tsp. Sweet Vermouth

Stir with ice and strain into a cocktail glass. Add a twist of lemon peel.

BARONET

1½ oz. Lochan Ora
1½ oz. Chivas Regal

Mix in an Old-fashioned glass.

BARRACUDA

1 oz. Pineapple Juice
½ oz. Galliano
1 oz. Gold Rum
¼ oz. Lime Juice
¼ tsp. Sugar

Shake with ice and strain into a large cocktail glass. Fill with Champagne. Serve with a cherry and a lime wheel.

BARRY

1½ oz. Gin
¾ oz. Sweet Vermouth
1 dash Angostura Bitters

Stir with ice and strain into a cocktail glass. Float White Creme de Menthe on top. Serve with a lemon twist.

BARTON SPECIAL

½ oz. Applejack
¼ oz. Scotch Whisky
¼ oz. Gin

Shake with ice and strain into an Old-fashioned glass over ice cubes.

BATH CURE

1 oz. Lemon Juice
1 oz. Pineapple Juice
½ oz. Grenadine
1½ oz. Jamaica Rum
1 oz. Light Rum
1 oz. Vodka
1½ oz. Brandy
1 oz. 151-proof Rum

Blend with ice and strain into a Collins glass.

BATIDO DE PINA

2-3 oz. Light Rum
⅔ fresh Pineapple, coarsely chopped
½ cup crushed Ice
Sugar to taste

Combine the Rum, pineapple and sugar in an electric blender and blend on high speed until smooth. Put the ice into a goblet and add liquor. Decorate with a fresh mint sprig.

BATISTE

1½ oz. Rum
¾ oz. Grand Marnier

Mix in an Old-fashioned glass. Serve on the rocks.

BATTERY CHARGER COCKTAIL

1 tbsp. Grenadine
1½ oz. Pernod

Stir with ice and strain into a cocktail glass. Fill with soda and ice.

BAYARD BEAUTY FIZZ

¼ oz. Raspberry Syrup
¼ oz. Maraschino Liqueur
½ oz. Lemon Juice
1½ oz. Gin

Shake with ice and strain into a Collins glass. Fill with soda and ice.

BAYOU

1½ oz. Brandy
¼ oz. Peach-flavored Brandy
½ oz. Mango Nectar
¼ oz. Lime Juice

Shake with ice and strain into a cocktail glass. Serve with a peach slice.

BEACHCOMBER

1½ oz. Rum
½ oz. Lime Juice
½ oz. Triple Sec or Orange Curacao
1 dash Maraschino Liqueur

Shake with cracked ice and strain into a cocktail glass rimmed with lime juice and sugar.

BEACHCOMBER'S BRACER

1 oz. White Rum
1 tbsp. Orange Curacao
1 tbsp. Bourbon
1 tsp. Powdered Sugar
A few dashes of Angostura Bitters
Lemon Juice

Dissolve the sugar with a few drops of lemon juice in a mug; add the remaining ingredients. Fill the mug with boiling water and stir well.

BEACHCOMBER'S GOLD

1½ oz. Rum
½ oz. Dry Vermouth
½ oz. Sweet Vermouth

Stir with ice and strain into a cocktail glass.

BEADLESTONE COCKTAIL

1½ oz. Dry Vermouth
1½ oz. Scotch Whisky

Stir with ice and strain into a cocktail glass.

BEADLETOWN SPECIAL

1½ oz. Scotch
½ oz. Dry Sherry
½ oz. Benedictine

Stir with ice and strain into a cocktail glass. Serve with a lemon twist.

BEALS COCKTAIL

1½ oz. Scotch Whisky
½ oz. Dry Vermouth
½ oz. Sweet Vermouth

Stir with ice and strain into a cocktail glass.

BEANO

1 oz. Cognac
¾ oz. Galliano
¾ oz. Tia Maria

Shake with ice and strain into a cocktail glass.

BEAT THE HEAT

Cracked Ice
4 oz. Ruby Port
4 oz. Ginger Ale, chilled

Fill a Collins glass half full with cracked ice. Pour in Wine and ginger ale. Stir well.

BEAU BRUMMEL COCKTAIL

1½ oz. Whisky
1 oz. Orange Juice
2 dashes Prunelle Liqueur
½ tsp. Sugar Syrup

Stir with ice and strain into a cocktail glass.

BEAUTY SPOT COCKTAIL NO. 1

1 tsp. Orange Juice
½ oz. Sweet Vermouth
½ oz. Dry Vermouth
1 oz. Gin

Shake with ice and strain into a cocktail glass, with a dash of Grenadine in bottom of glass.

BEAUTY SPOT COCKTAIL NO. 2

1½ oz. Gin
1 Egg White
1 oz. Cream
½ oz. Grenadine

Shake with ice and strain into a cocktail glass. Serve with a cherry.

BEAUX ARTS COCKTAIL

1 oz. Gin
½ oz. Sweet Vermouth
½ oz. Pineapple Juice
½ oz. Dry Vermouth
1 dash Anisette
½ oz. Orange Juice

Shake with ice and strain into a cocktail glass.

BEBBO COCKTAIL

1 oz. Lemon Juice
½ oz. Orange Juice
½ oz. Honey
1½ oz. Gin

Shake with ice and strain into a cocktail glass.

BECK

1½ oz. Gin
½ oz. Dry Vermouth
½ oz. Sweet Vermouth
1 dash Anisette

Stir with ice and strain into a cocktail glass.

BEE BEE NO. 1

1½ oz. Bourbon
½ oz. Honey
Lemon Twists
Orange Peels

Muddle several lemon twists and orange peels in an Old-fashioned glass and add Bourbon and honey. Fill with ice.

BEE BEE NO. 2

Bourbon
Honey
Skins of 2 Oranges, 3 Lemons and 4 Limes

Dice fruit skins and place in the coffee receptacle of a percolator. Pour several teaspoons of honey over the skins and percolate in Bourbon. Serve hot.

BEEF AND BULL

2 oz. Beef Bouillon
1 oz. Bourbon
A pinch Salt

Shake with ice and strain into an Old-fashioned glass. Garnish with cucumber slices.

BEEHIVE

1½ oz. Bourbon
1½ oz. Grapefruit Juice
1 tsp. Honey

Shake with ice and strain into a cocktail glass.

BEEN BEE

1½ oz. Brandy
1 oz. Benedictine

Stir with ice and strain into a cocktail glass.

BEER BUSTER

1½ oz. 100-proof Vodka
2 dashes Tabasco Sauce
Fill glass with ice cold Beer

Mix in a Collins glass.

BEER PANACHE

10 oz. Beer
12 oz. Lime Soda
2 tbsp. Sugar
1 tsp. Lime Juice

Mix in a pitcher with ice.

BEE'S KISS

1½ oz. Light Rum
1 tsp. Honey
1 tsp. Heavy Cream

Shake with ice and strain into a cocktail glass.

BEE'S KNEES NO. 1

1½ oz. Gin
½ oz. Honey
1 tbsp. Lemon Juice

Shake with ice and strain into a cocktail glass.

BEE'S KNEES NO. 2

1½ oz. Applejack
1 oz. Lemon Juice
½ oz. Honey

Shake with ice and strain into a cocktail glass.

BEE'S KNEES NO. 3

1½ oz. Rum
½ oz. Orange Juice
½ oz. Lime Juice
½ oz. Honey
2 dashes Orange Bitters

Shake with ice and strain into a cocktail glass. Serve with a twist of orange peel.

BEFORE "S" COCKTAIL

1½ oz. Pernod
Chilled Champagne

Put Pernod in a champagne glass, filled with chilled Champagne.

BEL-AIRE

1½ oz. Gin
¾ oz. Sweet Vermouth
¼ oz. Orange Curacao

Stir with ice and strain into a cocktail glass.

BELL OF CAMILLE

1½ oz. Bourbon
1 oz. Campari

Stir with ice and strain into a cocktail glass.

BELMONT

2 oz. Gin
½ oz. Grenadine or Raspberry Syrup
¾ oz. Heavy Cream

Shake with ice and strain into a cocktail glass.

BELOTE

1 oz. Orange Juice
1 oz. Calvados or Apple Brandy
¼ oz. Anisette
½ oz. Grenadine

Shake with ice and strain into a cocktail glass.

BENEDICT

1 oz. Scotch
½ oz. Benedictine

Mix in a highball glass. Fill with ginger ale and ice.

BENEDICT ARNOLD

1½ oz. Scotch
½ oz. Benedictine

Mix in an Old-fashioned glass. Serve on the rocks.

> I'm as dear to you as he,
> He's as dear to me as thee,
> You're as dear to him as me;
> Here's to "Three's good company."

BENEDICTINE COCKTAIL NO. 1

Cut Lemon
Sugar
Maraschino Cherry
3 oz. Benedictine
1 dash Angostura Bitters

Rub the rim of a cocktail glass with lemon and then dip it in sugar. Put a cherry in the bottom of the glass. Combine the Benedictine, Bitters and ice in a cocktail shaker and shake lightly. Pour into the prepared glass.

BENEDICTINE COCKTAIL NO. 2

½ oz. Benedictine
½ oz. Lemon Juice
1½ oz. Cognac Brandy

Shake with ice and strain into a cocktail glass.

BENEDICTINE FRAPPE

Fill a pony glass ⅔ full of ice. Fill with Benedictine. Garnish with an orange slice and a cherry. Serve with a straw.

BEN HURTZ COCKTAIL

1 oz. Rum
½ oz. Strega
Orange Juice

Pour Rum into a Collins glass. Fill the glass with orange juice and ice and float Strega on top. Serve with a cherry and a lime wheel.

BENNETT

2 oz. Gin
2 tbsp. Lime Juice
1 tsp. Sugar
2 dashes Angostura or Orange Bitters

Shake with ice and strain into a cocktail glass.

BENTLY COCKTAIL

1½ oz. Calvados or Applejack
1½ oz. Dubonnet

Shake with ice and strain into a cocktail glass.

BENTOTE

1 oz. Cognac
¾ oz. Orange Curacao
¾ oz. Orange Juice

Shake with ice and strain into a cocktail glass.

BERLIN BINGE

½ oz. Bourbon
½ oz. Gin
½ oz. Cognac
½ oz. Vodka

Shake with ice and strain into a cocktail glass.

BERLINER

1½ oz. Gin
½ oz. Dry Vermouth
¼ oz. Kummel
½ oz. Lemon Juice

Stir with ice and strain into a cocktail glass.

BERMUDA BOUQUET

½ oz. Orange Juice
1 oz. Lemon Juice
1 tsp. Powdered Sugar
1½ oz. Gin
1 oz. Apricot-flavored Brandy
1 tsp. Grenadine
½ tsp. Curacao

Shake with ice and strain into a highball glass.

BERMUDA HIGHBALL

¾ oz. Gin
¾ oz. Brandy
¾ oz. Dry Vermouth

Put ice cubes, Gin, Brandy and Dry Vermouth in a highball glass and fill with ginger ale or soda.

BERMUDA ROSE

1½ oz. Gin
1 dash Grenadine
1 dash Apricot-flavored Brandy
1 tbsp. Lime or Lemon Juice

Shake with ice and strain into a cocktail glass.

> The world is gay and colorful
> And life itself is new;
> I am very grateful for
> The friend I found in you.

BERRYADE

Muddle various berries in an Old-fashioned glass. Add 1 tsp. sugar, 1½ oz. Port and fill with hot water.

BERRY COCKTAIL NO. 1

½ oz. Orange Juice
½ oz. Pineapple Juice
1½ oz. Rum
1 dash Grenadine

Shake with ice and strain into a cocktail glass.

BERRY COCKTAIL NO. 2

1½ oz. Gin
½ oz. Dry Vermouth
½ oz. Sweet Vermouth
½ oz. Mandarin Liqueur

Stir with ice and strain into a cocktail glass.

BERRY WALL

1½ oz. Gin
1½ oz. Sweet Vermouth
½ oz. Curacao

Stir with ice and strain into a cocktail glass. Serve with a cherry.

BESSIE AND JESSIE

2 oz. American Blended Whisky
6 oz. Milk
1 oz. Advokaat

Shake the first two ingredients with ice and strain into a highball glass. Float Advokaat on top.

BEST HOME-MADE

1½ oz. Gin
1 oz. Orange Juice

Shake with ice and strain into a cocktail glass.

BETSY ROSS

1½ oz. Brandy
1½ oz. Port
1 dash Curacao
2 dashes Angostura Bitters
1 Egg Yolk
1 tsp. Sugar

Shake with ice and strain into a large cocktail glass. Sprinkle nutmeg on top.

BETTY COCKTAIL NO. 1

¾ oz. Gin
¾ oz. Cointreau
¾ oz. Rum

Shake with ice and strain into a cocktail glass.

BETTY COCKTAIL NO. 2

1½ oz. Gin
½ oz. Swedish Punch
½ Lemon

Fill a cocktail glass with crushed ice. Pour in the Gin and Swedish Punch. Squeeze in lemon juice and drop in the peel. Stir well.

BETTY JAMES

1 oz. Gin
½ oz. Lemon Juice
¼ oz. Maraschino Liqueur
1 dash Bitters

Shake with ice and strain into a cocktail glass.

BETWEEN-THE-SHEETS COCKTAIL

Juice ¼ Lemon
½ oz. Brandy
½ oz. Triple Sec or Cointreau
½ oz. Light Rum

Shake with ice and strain into a cocktail glass.

BIANCO

1½ oz. Bourbon
½ oz. Dry Vermouth
1 dash Angostura Bitters

Stir with ice and strain into a cocktail glass. Serve with a lemon twist.

BIARRITY

1 oz. Calvados or Applejack
1 oz. Rum
1 oz. Izarra

Stir with ice and strain into a cocktail glass.

BICH'S SPECIAL

2 oz. Gin
1 oz. Lillet
1 dash Angostura Bitters

Shake with ice and strain into a cocktail glass.

> Fill the goblet again; for I never before
> Felt the glow which now gladdens my heart to its core.
> Let us drink; who would not? since through life's varied round
> In the goblet alone no deception is found.
> — *Byron*

BIDOU

1½ oz. Gin
½ oz. Dry Vermouth
½ oz. Peach-flavored Brandy

Stir with ice and strain into a cocktail glass.

BIFFY COCKTAIL

Juice ½ Lemon
1 tbsp. Swedish Punch
1½ oz. Gin

Shake with ice and strain into a cocktail glass.

BIG APPLE

1 oz. Apple Brandy
3 oz. Apple Juice
3 tbsp. Baked Apple
A pinch of Ground Ginger

Heat the juice and the ginger; simmer for a few minutes. Warm a glass tumbler; add the baked apple. Pour the Apple Brandy into a ladle; ignite and pour over the baked apple. Put out the fire with the warm, spiced juice. Stir gently. Serve warm with a spoon.

BIG BAD WOLF COCKTAIL

½ oz. Orange Juice
1 oz. Brandy
1 tsp. Grenadine
1 Egg Yolk

Shake with ice and strain into a cocktail glass.

BIG BOY

1½ oz. Brandy
¾ oz. Cointreau
¾ oz. Sirop de Citron

Shake with ice and strain into a cocktail glass.

BIG JOHN'S SPECIAL

2 oz. Grapefruit Juice
2 tbsp. Gin
1 tbsp. Vodka
1 tbsp. Orange Juice
1 slice Orange, cut into small pieces
2 oz. crushed Ice
A few drops Orange Flower Water
A few Maraschino Cherries
A few drops Cherry Juice

Blend at a high speed until smooth. Serve unstrained.

BIJOU COCKTAIL NO. 1

¾ oz. Gin
¾ oz. Green Chartreuse
¾ oz. Sweet Vermouth
1 dash Orange Bitters

Stir with ice and strain into a cocktail glass. Add a cherry on top.

BIJOU COCKTAIL NO. 2

1½ oz. Gin
½ oz. Dry Vermouth
½ oz. Orange Curacao
1 dash Orange Bitters

Stir with ice and strain into a cocktail glass. Serve with a lemon twist.

BILL LYKEN'S DELIGHT NO. 1

1½ oz. Gin
1½ oz. Sweet Vermouth
4 dashes Curacao

Stir with ice and strain into a cocktail glass. Serve with a lemon and an orange twist.

BILL LYKEN'S DELIGHT NO. 2

1½ oz. Gin
½   oz. Dry Vermouth
½   oz. Sweet Vermouth

Stir with ice and strain into a cocktail glass. Serve with a lemon and orange twist.

BILL ORR

1½ oz. Scotch
1   oz. Orange Juice
1   dash Orange Bitters

Shake with ice and strain into a cocktail glass.

BILLY TAYLOR

Juice ½ Lime
2   oz. Gin

Fill a Collins glass with soda and ice cubes. Stir.

BIMBO PUNCH

6   large Lemons, thinly sliced
1½ quarts Brandy
1   pound lump Sugar
1   large block of Ice
Orange and Lemon slices

Steep lemon slices in Brandy for 8 hours. Strain the Brandy. Dissolve the lump sugar in boiling water, cool, and add to the Brandy. Chill. Put the ice in a punch bowl and pour the liquor over it. Decorate with orange and lemon slices. Serve in 4-oz. punch glasses. Makes 16 servings.

BIM COCKTAIL

1½ oz. Rum
1   tsp. Curacao
1   tsp. Grenadine
1   tsp. Pineapple Juice
1   tsp. Orange Juice

Shake with ice and strain into a cocktail glass.

BIMINI COOLER

1   oz. Light Creme de Cacao
1   oz. Gin
1   oz. Cream

Mix in a Collins glass. Fill with soda and ice.

BIRD COCKTAIL

1½ oz. Cognac
½   oz. Triple Sec

Fill an Old-fashioned glass with crushed ice. Add Cognac and Triple Sec. Serve with an orange twist.

BIRDIE

1½ oz. Rum
¼   oz. Orange Curacao
¼   oz. Pineapple Juice
¼   oz. Orange Juice
¼   oz. Grenadine

Shake with ice and strain into a cocktail glass.

BIRD-OF-PARADISE FIZZ

Juice ½ Lemon
1   tsp. Powdered Sugar
1   Egg White
1   tsp. Grenadine
2   oz. Gin

Shake with ice and strain into a highball glass over two ice cubes. Fill with soda.

BIRIBIE

1   oz. Gin
1   oz. Dubonnet
½   oz. Grand Marnier

Stir with ice and strain into a cocktail glass.

> Here, with a cup that's stored unto the brim,
> We drink this health to you.
> — *Shakespeare*

BISCAYNE

1   oz. Gin
½   oz. Rum
½   oz. Forbidden Fruit
¾   oz. Lime Juice

Shake with ice and strain into a cocktail glass. Serve with a lime wedge.

BISHOP NO. 1

1½ oz. Bourbon
¾   oz. Sweet Vermouth
1   oz. Orange Juice
1   dash Yellow Chartreuse

Shake with ice and strain into a cocktail glass.

BISHOP NO. 2

1½ oz. Rum
¾   oz. Claret
1   oz. Lime Juice
1   tsp. Sugar

Shake with ice and strain into a cocktail glass.

BISHOP COOLER NO. 1

¾   oz. Orange Juice
½   oz. Lemon Juice
½   tsp. Sugar

Shake with ice and strain into a highball glass. Fill with burgundy and ice. Serve with a fruit garnish.

BISHOP COOLER NO. 2

1   oz. Dark Rum
1   oz. Orange Juice
½   oz. Lemon Juice
½   tsp. Sugar
2   dashes Angostura Bitters

Mix in a Collins glass. Fill with burgundy and crushed ice.

BISHOP POKER COCKTAIL

1 oz. Dry Vermouth
1 oz. Sweet Vermouth
1 oz. Gin
1 dash Amer Picon Bitters

Shake with ice and strain into a cocktail glass.

BISHOP'S COCKTAIL

2 oz. Gin
2 oz. Ginger Wine

Stir with ice and strain into a cocktail glass.

BISMARCK FIZZ (SLOE GIN FIZZ)

3 oz. Sloe Gin
2 oz. Lemon Juice

Shake with ice and strain into a highball glass. Fill with soda.

BITER COCKTAIL

1½ oz. Gin
¼ oz. Yellow Chartreuse
½ oz. Pernod
¾ oz. Lemon Juice

Shake with ice and strain into a cocktail glass.

BITTER

1½ oz. Gin
¾ oz. Lemon Juice
¾ oz. Green Chartreuse
1 dash Pernod
Sugar to taste

Shake with ice and strain into a cocktail glass.

BITTER APPLE

1½ oz. Applejack
2 dashes Angostura Bitters

Fill an Old-fashioned glass with ice cubes. Add Applejack, Bitters and a squirt of soda. Serve with a lemon twist.

BITTER BANANA COOLER

1½ oz. Rum
¼ of ripe Banana
¾ oz. Pineapple Juice
½ oz. Lemon Juice
2 dashes Peychaud's Bitters

Shake with ice and strain into a Collins glass. Fill with ice and bitter lemon soda.

BITTER BOURBON LEMONADE

1½ oz. Bourbon
1 oz. Lemon Juice
½ oz. Lime Juice
¼ oz. Grenadine
1 tsp. Sugar

Shake with ice and strain into a Collins glass. Fill with ice and bitter lemon soda. Serve with a lemon twist.

BITTER BRANSHER

1 oz. Brandy
1 oz. Cream Sherry
¼ oz. Lemon Juice
½ oz. Cherry Heering

Shake with ice and strain into a Collins glass. Fill with ice and bitter lemon soda. Serve with a lemon twist.

BITTER LEMON COOLER

1½ oz. Dry Vermouth
1 oz. Gin
1 tsp. Lemon Juice
1 tsp. Raspberry Syrup

Shake with ice and strain into a cocktail glass. Fill with ice and lemon soda. Add a twist of lemon; stir.

BITTER ORANGE COOLER

2 oz. Orange Juice
1½ oz. Sweet Vermouth
½ oz. Lemon Juice
½ oz. Cherry Heering

Shake with ice and strain into a Collins glass. Fill with ice and bitter orange soda. Serve with an orange slice.

BITTERS HIGHBALL

¾ oz. Bitters
Ginger Ale or Soda

Fill a highball glass with Bitters, ice cubes and ginger ale or soda. Add a twist of lemon peel, if desired, and stir.

BITTERSWEET

1½ oz. Sweet Vermouth
1½ oz. Dry Vermouth
1 dash Angostura Bitters
1 dash Orange Bitters

Stir with ice and strain into a cocktail glass. Serve with a twist of orange peel.

BIZZY IZZY HIGHBALL

1 oz. Bourbon
1 oz. Sherry
1 dash Lemon Juice

Mix in a highball glass. Fill with soda and ice.

BLACK BEAUTY

3 oz. Blackberry Liqueur
1 tbsp. Lime Juice

Shake with ice and strain into a champagne glass.

BLACKBERRY COOLER

1½ oz. Blackberry-flavored Brandy
½   oz. Lemon Juice

Mix in a Collins glass. Fill with soda and ice. Serve with a lemon wedge and a cherry.

BLACKBERRY DEMI TASSE

Heat (do not boil):

1   oz. Blackberry Liqueur
1   tbsp. Blackberry Jelly
½   oz. Cognac
½   oz. Water
¼   oz. Lemon Juice

Pour into a cup. Serve with a lemon wedge.

BLACKBERRY FLIP

2   oz. Blackberry-flavored Brandy
1   Egg
1   tsp. Powdered Sugar

Shake with ice and strain into a cocktail glass. Sprinkle nutmeg on top.

BLACKBERRY JULEP

2   oz. Blackberry-flavored Brandy
4   sprigs fresh Mint
1   lump Sugar

Fill a Collins glass with crushed ice and set it aside. In an Old-fashioned glass, crush the sugar. Add mint leaves and bruise lightly. Add Blackberry-flavored Brandy and mix together. Pour over crushed ice in Collins glass. Stir until outside of glass is frosted. Add a sprig of mint and dust with powdered sugar.

BLACK DAIQUIRI

1½ oz. Jamaica Rum
2   tsp. Lime Juice
1   tsp. Honey

Shake with ice and strain into a cocktail glass.

BLACK DEVIL

2   oz. Rum
½   oz. Dry Vermouth

Stir with cracked ice and strain into a cocktail glass. Add a black olive.

BLACK EYE

1½ oz. Vodka
2   tsp. Blackberry-flavored Brandy
2   tbsp. Lime Juice

Shake with ice and strain into a cocktail glass. Decorate with a slice of lime.

BLACK HAWK COCKTAIL

1¼ oz. Rye or Bourbon Whisky
1¼ oz. Sloe Gin

Stir with ice and strain into a cocktail glass. Serve with a cherry. (½ oz. lemon juice is optional)

BLACKJACK NO. 1

1   oz. Kirschwasser
½   oz. Brandy
1   oz. Coffee

Shake with cracked ice and strain into an Old-fashioned glass over ice cubes.

BLACKJACK NO. 2

1½ oz. Gin
½   oz. Creme de Cassis
½   oz. Kirschwasser

Shake with cracked ice and strain into an Old-fashioned glass over ice cubes.

BLACK MAGIC

1½ oz. Vodka
¾   oz. Coffee Liqueur
1   dash Lemon Juice

Stir and serve in an Old-fashioned glass over ice cubes and add a twist of lemon peel.

BLACK MARIA

2   oz. Coffee-flavored Brandy
2   oz. Rum
4   oz. strong black Coffee
2   tsp. Sugar

Stir ingredients in a Brandy snifter and add cracked ice.

BLACKOUT

1   oz. Lime Juice
1½ oz. Gin
¾   oz. Blackberry-flavored Brandy

Shake with ice and strain into a cocktail glass.

BLACK PEARL NO. 1

¾   oz. Tia Maria
¾   oz. Cognac

Pour into a champagne glass. Fill with Champagne. Serve with a black cherry.

BLACK PEARL NO. 2

1½ oz. Gold Rum
1   tsp. Apricot-flavored Brandy
2   tsp. Pineapple Juice
1   tsp. Jamaica Rum

Shake with ice and strain into a cocktail glass.

BLACK POWER

2   oz. Marsala (dessert wine)
Coca-Cola
Slice Lemon

Mix Marsala and Coca-Cola and pour over ice cubes in an Old-fashioned glass. Serve with a lemon twist.

BLACK ROSE

1½ oz. Rum
2 cubes Ice
Black Coffee, cold

Put Rum and ice cubes in a tumbler or highball glass and fill with cold, black coffee. Stir and serve.

BLACK RUSSIAN

1½ oz. Vodka
¾ oz. Coffee-flavored Brandy or Kahlua

Pour over ice cubes in a large cocktail glass.

BLACK STRIPE NO. 1

2 oz. Dark Rum
1 tbsp. Molasses
1 cup crushed Ice

Shake with ice and strain into a cocktail glass.

BLACK STRIPE NO. 2

1 tsp. Molasses or Honey
3 oz. Dark Rum
Twist Lemon Peel

Put the molasses, Rum and lemon peel in an 8 oz. mug and fill with boiling water. Stir.

BLACKTHORNE COCKTAIL NO. 1

1½ oz. Gin
½ oz. Dubonnet
½ oz. Kirschwasser

Shake with ice and strain into a cocktail glass.

BLACKTHORNE COCKTAIL NO. 2

1½ oz. Sloe Gin
1½ oz. Sweet Vermouth
2 dashes Orange Bitters

Shake with ice and strain into a cocktail glass. Serve with a lemon twist and a cherry.

BLACKTHORNE COCKTAIL NO. 3

2 dashes Angostura Bitters
½ oz. Pernod
1 oz. Irish Whisky
1 oz. Dry Vermouth

Shake with ice and strain into a cocktail glass.

BLACKTHORNE COCKTAIL NO. 4

1½ oz. Sloe Gin
1 oz. Dry Vermouth
1 oz. Sweet Vermouth
1 dash Orange Bitters
1 dash Angostura Bitters

Stir with ice and strain into a cocktail glass. Serve with a lemon twist and a cherry.

BLACKTHORNE COCKTAIL NO. 5

1 oz. Irish Whisky
1 oz. Dry Vermouth
3 dashes Pernod
3 dashes Angostura Bitters

Shake with ice and strain into a cocktail glass.

BLACKTHORNE COCKTAIL NO. 6

1½ oz. Sloe Gin
1 oz. Sweet Vermouth

Stir with ice and strain into a cocktail glass. Add a twist of lemon peel.

BLACK VELVET

5 oz. chilled Stout
5 oz. chilled Champagne

Pour very carefully, in order given, into a champagne glass so that the Stout and Champagne don't mix.

BLACK WATCH

1½ oz. Scotch
¾ oz. Kahlua

Fill an Old-fashioned glass with ice. Add Scotch and Kahlua and serve with a lemon twist. (Squirt of soda optional.)

BLANCHE

1 oz. Anisette
1 oz. Triple Sec
½ oz. White Curacao

Shake with cracked ice and strain into a cocktail glass.

BLARNY COCKTAIL

1 oz. Sweet Vermouth
1½ oz. Irish Whisky

Stir with ice and strain into a cocktail glass.

BLARNY STONE COCKTAIL

2 oz. Irish Whisky
½ tsp. Pernod
½ tsp. Triple Sec or Orange Curacao
¼ tsp. Maraschino Liqueur
1 dash Bitters

Shake with ice and strain into a cocktail glass. Add a twist of orange peel and an olive.

BLENDED COMFORT

1 oz. Orange Juice
1½ oz. Lemon Juice
½ oz. Dry Vermouth
½ ripe Peach, diced and crushed
¾ oz. Southern Comfort
1½ oz. Blended Whisky

Shake with ice and strain into a Collins glass. Fill with ice.

BLENHEIM

1	oz. Apple Brandy
½	oz. Apricot-flavored Brandy
¾	oz. Lemon Juice
¼	oz. Grenadine
1	dash Orange Bitters

Shake with ice and strain into a cocktail glass.

BLENTON

2	oz. Gin
1	oz. Dry Vermouth
1	dash Angostura Bitters

Stir with ice and strain into a cocktail glass. Serve with a lemon twist and a cherry.

BLIMEY

1	cube Sugar
2	dashes Aromatic Bitters

Chilled Dry Champagne

Splash Bitters on the sugar cube in a highball glass. Muddle well. Add an orange twist and ice cube. Fill with chilled Champagne. Stir gently.

BLINKER

1½	oz. Rye Whisky
2	oz. Grapefruit Juice
¾	oz. Grenadine

Shake with ice and strain into a cocktail glass.

BLISTER

1	oz. Gin
¾	oz. Lemon Juice
½	oz. Creme de Noyaux
½	tsp. Sugar

Shake with ice and strain into a cocktail glass.

BLIZZARD

3	oz. Bourbon
1	oz. Cranberry Juice
1	tbsp. Lemon Juice
2	tbsp. Sugar Syrup
4	oz. crushed Ice

Blend until the drink is thick. Serve in a highball glass.

BLOCK AND FALL

¾	oz. Brandy
¾	oz. Cointreau
½	oz. Calvados or Apple Brandy
½	oz. Pernod

Shake with ice and strain into a cocktail glass.

BLONDE COCKTAIL

1½	oz. Apple Brandy
¾	oz. Light Dubonnet
¾	oz. Dry Vermouth

Stir with ice and strain into a cocktail glass.

> Let's drink to our friend and host. May his generous heart, like his good wine, only grow mellower with the years.

BLOOD-AND-SAND COCKTAIL

1	tbsp. Orange Juice
½	oz. Scotch Whisky
½	oz. Cherry-flavored Brandy
½	oz. Sweet Vermouth

Shake with ice and strain into a cocktail glass.

BLOOD BRONX COCKTAIL

1½	oz. Gin
1½	tsp. Dry Vermouth

Juice ¼ Blood Orange

Shake with ice and strain into a cocktail glass.

BLOODHOUND COCKTAIL NO. 1

½	oz. Dry Vermouth
½	oz. Sweet Vermouth
1	oz. Gin

Shake with ice and strain into a cocktail glass. Decorate with two or three crushed strawberries.

BLOODHOUND COCKTAIL NO. 2

1½	oz. Vodka
3	oz. Tomato Juice
½	oz. Sherry

Mix in a highball glass. Fill with ice.

BLOOD TRANSFUSER COCKTAIL

1	oz. Grape Juice
1	oz. Bourbon

Stir with ice and strain into a cocktail glass.

BLOODY BLOODY MARY COCKTAIL

1½	oz. Vodka
3	oz. Tomato Juice
½	tsp. Worcestershire Sauce
¼	tsp. Sugar

Juice of ½ Lemon
Pinch of Salt, Pepper and Celery Salt

Shake well with ice and strain into a salt-rimmed double Old-fashioned glass. Fill with tomato juice and ice. Garnish with a fresh mint sprig.

> I wish you all the joy that you can wish.
> — *Shakespeare*

BLOODY BULLSHOT

1½ oz. Vodka
1½ oz. Tomato Juice
1½ oz. Beef Bouillon, chilled
1 tsp. Lemon Juice
1 dash Salt
1 dash Worcestershire Sauce
1 dash Tabasco

Shake with ice and strain into a Sour glass.

BLOODY MARIA

1 oz. Tequila
2 oz. Tomato Juice
1 dash Lemon Juice
1 dash Tabasco Sauce
1 dash Celery Salt
1 dash Worcestershire Sauce,
Salt and freshly ground
Pepper to taste

Shake all ingredients with cracked ice. Strain into an Old-fashioned glass over ice cubes. Add a slice of lemon.

BLOODY MARIANA

2 oz. Vodka
6 oz. V-8 Vegetable Juice
1 tsp. Lime Juice
A few drops Tabasco Sauce
A few drops Worcestershire Sauce
A pinch of White Pepper
A pinch of Celery Salt
A pinch of Oregano

Shake with ice and strain into a Collins glass. Add ice.

BLOODY MARY

1½ oz. Vodka
3 oz. Tomato Juice
1 dash Lemon Juice
½ tsp. Worcestershire Sauce
2 or 3 drops Tabasco Sauce
Pepper and Salt

Shake with ice and strain into an Old-fashioned glass over ice cubes. A wedge of lime may be added. (White Rum, Gin or Tequila can be substituted for Vodka.)

BLOSSOM NO. 1

½ oz. Pineapple Juice
½ oz. Lime Juice
2 oz. Rum

Shake with ice and strain into a cocktail glass.

BLOSSOM NO. 2

1 oz. Gin
1 oz. Orange Juice
½ oz. Grenadine
½ Egg White
1 dash Orange Bitters

Shake with ice and strain into a cocktail glass.

BLOWTORCH

1½ oz. Southern Comfort
1½ oz. Gin
1½ oz. Triple Sec or Orange Curacao
3 oz. Orange Juice
½ oz. Grenadine

Shake with ice and strain into a Collins glass.

BLOW UP

1 oz. Rum
1 oz. Yellow Chartreuse
½ oz. Parfait Amour
5 drops Grenadine
5 drops Creme de Menthe

Half fill a mixing glass with cracked ice. Add Rum, Chartreuse and Parfait Amour. Stir and strain into 5 oz. champagne glass. Add Grenadine and Creme de Menthe and serve.

BLUE ANGEL

½ oz. Blue Curacao
½ oz. Parfait Amour
½ oz. Brandy
½ oz. Lemon Juice
½ oz. Cream

Shake with ice and strain into a cocktail glass.

BLUE BELL

1½ oz. Whisky
1 tbsp. Dry Vermouth
1-2 dashes Angostura Bitters

Shake with ice and strain into a cocktail glass.

BLUEBERRY RUM FIZZ

2½ oz. Rum
¼ oz. Triple Sec or Orange Curacao
½ oz. Blueberry Syrup
¾ oz. Lemon Juice

Shake with ice and strain into a Collins glass. Fill with soda and ice. Add blueberries and a lemon wedge.

BLUE BIRD

1½ oz. Gin
½ oz. Triple Sec or Orange Curacao
1 dash Bitters

Stir with ice cubes and strain into a cocktail glass. Add a twist of lemon peel and a cherry.

To the sun that warmed the vineyard,
To the juice that turned to wine,
To the host that cracked the bottle
And made it yours and mine.

BLUE BLAZER

2 large mugs with handles
3 oz. Scotch or other whisky
3 oz. boiling Water
1 tsp. Sugar
1 twist Lemon Peel

Put the Scotch in one mug and the boiling water in the other. Ignite the whisky and, while it is blazing, pour it and the water back and forth from one mug to the other. Properly done, this looks like a stream of fire. Add the sugar and serve with a twist of lemon peel in a warmed mug.

BLUE BOY

1½ oz. Rum
¾ oz. Sweet Vermouth
1 dash Angostura Bitters
1 dash Orange Bitters

Stir with ice and strain into a cocktail glass.

BLUE DEVIL

1½ oz. Gin
¾ oz. Maraschino Liqueur
¾ oz. Lime or Lemon Juice
½ tsp. Creme d'Yvette or dash of blue vegetable coloring

Shake with ice and strain into a cocktail glass.

BLUE FLYER

1 oz. Gin
¾ oz. Lime Juice
½ oz. Blue Curacao

Shake with ice and strain into a cocktail glass.

BLUE HAWAII NO. 1

2 oz. Lime Juice
2 oz. Vodka
1½ oz. Blue Curacao

Shake with ice and strain into a double Old-fashioned glass. Fill with ice. Float ½ oz. Galliano on top. Serve with a cherry and a pineapple spear.

BLUE HAWAII NO. 2

1½ oz. Vodka
1½ oz. Pineapple Juice
1½ oz. Coconut Cream
¾ oz. Blue Curacao

Shake with ice and strain into a double Old-fashioned glass.

> Quiet days, fair issue and long life.
> — *Shakespeare*

BLUE HAWAII NO. 3

1½ oz. Lemon Juice
1 tsp. Sugar
1½ oz. Vodka

Shake with ice and strain into a double Old-fashioned glass. Fill with soda and ice.

BLUE HAZE

1 oz. Rum
½ oz. Dry Vermouth
½ oz. Parfait Amour
½ oz. Cointreau
½ oz. Blue Curacao

Stir all ingredients except Curacao and strain. Add Curacao.

BLUE HEAVEN HIGHBALL

1 dash Pernod
1½ oz. Scotch Whisky
Juice ½ Lime

Shake with ice and strain into a highball glass. Fill with ginger ale and ice.

BLUE HORN

½ oz. Pernod
½ oz. Blue Curacao
1 oz. Rum
1 dash Lemon Juice
Bitter Lemon

Pour Pernod, Curacao, Rum and lemon juice in a 10 oz. highball glass. Top up with bitter lemon and serve.

BLUE MONDAY COCKTAIL

1½ oz. Vodka
¾ oz. Triple Sec or Orange Curacao
1 dash Blue Curacao

Stir with ice and strain into a cocktail glass.

BLUE MOON NO. 1

2 oz. Gin
½ oz. Creme d'Yvette

Stir with ice and strain into a cocktail glass.

BLUE MOON NO. 2

1½ oz. Gin
1 Egg White
¾ oz. Lemon Juice
¼ oz. Creme d'Yvette

Shake with ice and strain into a cocktail glass.

BLUE MOON NO. 3

¼ oz. Creme d'Yvette
1½ oz. Gin
1 oz. Dry Vermouth
1 dash Orange Bitters

Stir with ice and strain into a cocktail glass.

BLUE MOON NO. 4

¾ oz. Benedictine
¾ oz. Rye Whisky
¾ oz. Ginger Ale

Stir gently with crushed ice and strain into a cocktail glass.

BLUE MOUNTAIN

1½ oz. Dark Rum
¾ oz. Vodka
¾ oz. Tia Maria
2 tbsp. Orange Juice

Shake with ice and strain into a large cocktail glass.

BLUE NEGLIGEE

¾ oz. Ouzo
¾ oz. Parfait Amour
¾ oz. Green Chartreuse

Shake with ice and strain into a cocktail glass. Serve with a cherry.

BLUE PACIFIC

3	oz. Gin
1-2	dashes Vodka
1-2	dashes blue Food Coloring
A few drops of Dry Vermouth

Stir without ice until blended. Pour out over ice in a cocktail glass. Decorate with a black olive.

BLUE SHARK

1½	oz. Tequila
1½	oz. Vodka
1-2	dashes blue Food Coloring

Shake with ice and strain into a cocktail glass. Add ice.

BLUE SPECIAL

| 1 | oz. Cognac |
| 1 | oz. Pineapple Juice |

Shake with ice and strain into a highball glass. Fill with ice and Champagne.

BLUE TAIL FLY

1½	oz. Blue Curacao
1	tbsp. White Creme de Cacao
1	tbsp. Light Cream

Shake with ice and strain into a cocktail glass. Add ice.

BLUE TRAIN NO. 1

1½	oz. Gin
¾	oz. Cointreau
¾	oz. Lime Juice
½	tsp. Creme d'Yvette
1	dash blue Food Coloring

Shake with ice and strain into a cocktail glass.

BLUE TRAIN NO. 2

½	cup crushed Ice
2	oz. Brandy
2	oz. Pineapple Juice

Shake with ice and strain into a Collins glass. Fill with champagne.

BOA CONSTRICTOR

Fill an Old-fashioned glass with ice. Pour 2 oz. Blackberry-flavored Brandy over ice. Sprinkle nutmeg on top.

BOBBY BURNS COCKTAIL

1½	oz. Sweet Vermouth
1½	oz. Scotch Whisky
1¼	tsp. Benedictine

Stir with ice and strain into a cocktail glass. Add a twist of lemon peel.

BOB DANBY

| 2 | oz. Dubonnet. |
| 1 | oz. Brandy |

Stir with ice and strain into a cocktail glass.

BOCCIE BALL

| 1½ | oz. Amaretto |
| 1½ | oz. Orange Juice |

Pour into a highball glass. Fill with soda and ice.

BOGEY

1	oz. Gin
1	oz. Dry Vermouth
¼	oz. Bourbon
¼	oz. Pernod
1	dash Lemon Juice

Stir with ice and strain into a cocktail glass.

BOILERMAKER

| 2 | oz. Blended Whisky |
| 8 | oz. chilled Beer |

Serve the Whisky straight and follow with a Beer chaser, or combine the ingredients in a highball glass, pouring the whisky into the Beer without stirring. (Scotch Whisky may be used for this drink instead of Blended Whisky.)

BOLAND PUNCH

1	lump Sugar
6	oz. boiling Water
3	oz. Scotch Whisky
½	oz. Ginger Ale

Stir gently in a goblet and serve.

> To Our Hosts: Happiness, health and prosperity.

BOLERO COCKTAIL

1½	oz. Rum
¾	oz. Apple Brandy
¼	tsp. Sweet Vermouth

Stir with ice and strain into a cocktail glass.

BOLO

3	oz. Light Rum
1½	tbsp. Lime Juice
2	tbsp. Orange Juice
1	tsp. Sugar

Shake with ice and strain into a cocktail glass.

BOMB

1½	oz. Sherry
½	oz. Cointreau
¾	oz. Orange Juice
1	dash Orange Bitters
1	dash Pimento Dram

Shake with ice and strain into a cocktail glass.

BOMBAY COCKTAIL NO. 1

½	oz. Dry Vermouth
½	oz. Sweet Vermouth
1	oz. Brandy
¼	tsp. Pernod
½	tsp. Triple Sec or Orange Curacao

Stir with ice and strain into a cocktail glass.

BOMBAY COCKTAIL NO. 2

2   oz. Swedish Punch
¾   oz. Lemon Juice

Shake with ice and strain into a cocktail glass.

BOMBER

1½   oz. Cognac
1   oz. Vodka
¼   oz. Cointreau
¼   oz. Anisette

Stir with ice and strain into a cocktail glass.

BOMBO

2   oz. Rum

Pour into an Old-fashioned glass. Fill glass with water and ice. Serve with 2 sticks of sugar cane.

BONANZA COCKTAIL

1   oz. Brandy
1½   oz. Sherry

Stir in highball glass. Fill with Riesling Wine and ice.

BON APPETIT

1   oz. Gin
¾   oz. Dubonnet
1½   oz. Orange Juice
2   dashes Angostura Bitters

Shake with ice and strain into a cocktail glass.

BONBINI

1   oz. Light Rum
1   oz. Orange Curacao
¼   oz. Lime Juice
¼   oz. Pineapple Juice

Shake with ice and strain into a cocktail glass.

BOND 7 and JAMES

2   oz. BOND 7
1   dash Sweet Vermouth

Mix in a highball glass. Fill with soda and ice. Garnish with a twist of orange peel and a cherry.

BONNIE PRINCE

1½   oz. Gin
½   oz. Lillet
½   oz. Drambuie

Stir with ice and strain into a cocktail glass.

BONNIE PRINCE CHARLIE COCKTAIL

½   oz. Drambuie
1   oz. Cognac
1   oz. Lime

Shake with ice and strain into a cocktail glass.

BON SOIR HIGHBALL

1   oz. Benedictine
1   oz. Creme de Violette

Stir in a highball glass. Fill with ginger ale and ice.

BONSONI

3   oz. Sweet Vermouth
1   oz. Fernet Branca

Stir with ice and strain into a cocktail glass.

BOOMERANG NO. 1

1   oz. Dry Vermouth
1½   oz. Gin
1   dash Bitters
1   dash Maraschino Liqueur

Stir with ice cubes and strain into a cocktail glass. Add a twist of lemon peel.

BOOMERANG NO. 2

¾   oz. Passion Fruit Syrup
¾   oz. Gin
¾   oz. Rum
1   dash Lemon Juice
1   dash Orange Bitters

Shake with ice and strain into a cocktail glass.

BOOMERANG NO. 3

1   oz. Rye Whisky
¾   oz. Dry Vermouth
¾   oz. Swedish Punch
1   dash Angostura Bitters
2   dashes Lemon Juice

Shake with ice and strain into a cocktail glass.

BOOSTER

2-3   oz. Brandy
½   oz. Curacao
1   Egg White

Shake with ice and strain into a cocktail glass. Sprinkle nutmeg on top.

BOOTLEG FIZZ

1½   oz. Gin
1   oz. Lemon Juice
1   tsp. Sugar
1   Egg White

Shake with ice and strain into a Collins glass. Fill with soda. Serve with a mint sprig.

BORDEN CHASE

2   oz. Scotch
½   oz. Sweet Vermouth
¼   oz. Pernod
1   dash Orange Bitters

Stir with ice and strain into a cocktail glass.

BORDEVER

| 2 | oz. Bourbon |
| ½ | oz. Ginger Ale |

Stir with ice and strain into a cocktail glass. Serve with a lemon twist.

BORINQUEN

1½	oz. Rum
1	tbsp. Passion Fruit Syrup
1	oz. Lime Juice
1	oz. Orange Juice
1	tsp. 151-proof Rum

Put half a cup of crushed ice into a blender. Add all ingredients and blend at a low speed. Pour into an Old-fashioned glass.

BOSCOE

| 1½ | oz. Tequila |
| ¾ | oz. Kahlua |

Mix in a Collins glass. Fill with ice and half & half cream

BOSOM CARESSER NO. 1

1	oz. Brandy
1	oz. Madeira Wine
½	oz. Triple Sec or Orange Curacao

Stir with ice and strain into a cocktail glass.

BOSOM CARESSER NO. 2

1½	oz. Brandy
½	oz. Curacao
1	Egg Yolk
1	tsp. Grenadine

Shake with ice and strain into a cocktail glass.

BOSS

| 1½ | oz. Bourbon |
| ½ | oz. Amaretto |

Fill an Old-fashioned glass with ice and add ingredients.

BOSSA NOVA SPECIAL

1	oz. Galliano
1	oz. Rum
¼	oz. Apricot-flavored Brandy
2	oz. Pineapple Juice
½	Egg White
¼	oz. Lemon Juice

Shake with ice and strain into a Collins glass. Add ice. Garnish with fruit.

BOSTON BOURBON MARY

1½	oz. Early Times
	Tomato Juice
	Worcestershire Sauce
	Tabasco Sauce

Pour Early Times into a Collins glass. Fill with tomato juice. Add ice, Worcestershire Sauce and Tabasco to taste. Garnish with a lime wheel.

BOSTON BULLET

| 2 | oz. Gin |
| ½ | oz. Dry Vermouth |

Stir with ice and strain into a cocktail glass. Serve with an almond-stuffed olive.

BOSTON CLUB COCKTAIL

1½	oz. Gin
½	oz. Sweet Vermouth
1	oz. Lime Juice

Shake with ice and strain into a cocktail glass.

BOSTON COCKTAIL

¾	oz. Gin
¾	oz. Apricot-flavored Brandy
1½	tsp. Grenadine
	Juice ¼ Lemon

Shake with ice and strain into a cocktail glass.

> We come into this world all
> naked and bare,
> We go through this world
> full of sorrow and care,
> We go out of this world, we
> know not where,
> But if we're good fellows
> here, we'll be thorough-
> breds there.

BOSTON COOLER

2	oz. Rum
2	oz. Soda
1	tsp. Sugar
	Juice ½ Lemon

In a Collins glass, stir together lemon juice, sugar and soda. Then fill glass with cracked ice and add Rum. Fill with soda or ginger ale and stir again. Add a twist of orange or lemon peel.

BOSTON EGGNOG

1	Egg Yolk and
¾	tsp. Sugar, beaten together
½	oz. Brandy
¼	oz. Jamaica Rum
4	oz. Madeira wine

Shake with ice and strain into a Collins glass. Dust with nutmeg.

BOSTON FLIP

1½	oz. Rye Whisky
1½	oz. Madeira Wine
1	tsp. Sugar
1	whole Egg

Shake with ice and strain into a cocktail glass. Sprinkle nutmeg on top.

BOSTON GOLD

1	oz. Vodka
½	oz. Creme de Bananes
	Orange Juice

Pour Vodka and Banana Liqueur over ice cubes in a highball glass. Fill with orange juice and stir.

BOSTONIAN COCKTAIL

1½ oz. Gin
¼ oz. Sweet Vermouth
¼ oz. Orange Juice
¼ oz. Lemon Juice
½ oz. Sugar Syrup
3 sprigs Mint

Crush mint with fruit juices and syrup. Add Gin and shake with ice. Serve in a cocktail glass.

BOSTON SIDECAR COCKTAIL

¾ oz. Brandy
¾ oz. Rum
¾ oz. Triple Sec or Orange Curacao
Juice ½ Lime

Shake with ice and strain into a cocktail glass.

BOSTON SOUR

Juice ½ Lemon
1 tsp. Powdered Sugar
2 oz. Rye Whisky
1 Egg White

Shake with ice and strain into a Sour glass. Add a slice of lemon and a cherry.

BOULEVARD COCKTAIL NO. 1

1½ oz. Gin
¾ oz. Sweet Vermouth
¾ oz. Orange Juice

Shake with ice and strain into a cocktail glass.

BOULEVARD COCKTAIL NO. 2

1 oz. Sweet Vermouth
1 oz. Pernod
2 dashes Angostura Bitters

Shake with ice and strain into a cocktail glass. Serve with a lemon twist.

BOURBON AND EGG (for hangovers)

Break a raw egg into a glass. Add Bourbon. Stir and drink.

BOURBON AND ICED TEA

2 oz. Bourbon
Iced Tea
Sugar

Pour Bourbon into a Collins glass. Fill with iced tea and add sugar to taste. Add ice and serve with a lemon twist.

BOURBON COLLINS

1 oz. Lemon Juice
1½ oz. Bourbon
½ tsp. Sugar
1 dash Peychaud's Bitters

Shake with ice and strain into a Collins glass. Fill with soda and ice. Serve with a lemon twist.

BOURBON CREAM

2 oz. Bourbon
1 oz. Cream

Shake with ice and strain into a cocktail glass.

BOURBON DAISY

1½ oz. Bourbon
1 oz. Lemon Juice
½ oz. Grenadine
½ oz. Southern Comfort

Shake with ice and strain into a large cocktail glass. Fill with soda. Serve with an orange slice and a cherry.

> Mingle with the friendly bowl
> The feast of reason and the flow of soul.
> — Alexander Pope

BOURBON EGGNOG

1 Egg
½ tsp. Sugar
1½ oz. Bourbon
½ oz. Rum
½ oz. Cream

Shake with ice and strain into a highball glass. Add ice and sprinkle nutmeg on top.

BOURBON FRUIT

Drop one slice each of lime, lemon and orange into an Old-fashioned glass, over ice. Fill with Bourbon.

BOURBON HIGHBALL

2 oz. Bourbon
Ginger Ale or Soda

Fill a highball glass with ice cubes, Bourbon and ginger ale or soda. Add a twist of lemon peel, if desired, and stir.

BOURBON LANCER

1½ oz. Bourbon
½ tsp. Sugar
1 dash Angostura Bitters
Several cubes Ice

Mix in a Collins glass. Fill with Champagne. Serve with a lemon twist.

BOURBONNAISE

1½ oz. Bourbon
½ oz. Dry Vermouth
½ oz. Creme de Cassis
1 dash Lemon Juice

Stir with ice and strain into a cocktail glass.

BOURBON OLD-FASHIONED

1   lump Sugar
1   dash Bitters
2   oz. Bourbon

Place sugar in an Old-fashioned glass and sprinkle with Bitters. Add Bourbon and ice cubes. Serve with a twist of lemon, an orange slice and a maraschino cherry.

BOURBON SHAKE

2   tsp. Sugar Syrup
3   tsp. Lemon Juice
3   oz. Bourbon

Mix ingredients with shaved ice and strain into a cocktail glass. Garnish with mint leaves.

BOURBON SLOE GIN FIX

½   tsp. Sugar dissolved in
½   oz. Water
1½ oz. Bourbon
½   oz. Sloe Gin
½   oz. Lemon Juice

Mix in a highball glass. Fill with crushed ice and stir. Serve with a lemon wedge and a cherry.

BOURBON SOUR

1½ oz. Lemon Juice
¾   tsp. Sugar
1½ oz. Bourbon

Shake with ice and strain into a Sour glass. Serve with an orange or lemon slice and a cherry.

BOURBON SQUASH

1   oz. Lemon Juice
1½ oz. Orange Juice
1   tsp. Sugar
2   oz. Bourbon

Mix in a Collins glass. Fill with tightly-packed shaved ice. Serve with straws.

BOXCAR

1   oz. Lime Juice
1   Egg White
½   oz. Cointreau
1½ oz. Gin
¼   oz. Grenadine

Shake with ice and strain into a cocktail glass.

BRACER COCKTAIL

1¼ oz. Pernod
1¼ oz. Sweet Vermouth
2   drops Angostura Bitters

Stir with ice and strain into a cocktail glass. Serve with a lemon twist.

> Here's to our friends in adversity, and may we never be in the same fix.

BRACER HIGHBALL

1½ oz. Brandy
¼   oz. Anisette
1   dash Angostura Bitters
½   tsp. Sugar
½   oz. Lemon Juice
1   Egg

Shake with ice and strain into a highball glass. Fill with soda and ice.

BRAIN DUSTER

1¼ oz. Cognac
1¼ oz. Pernod
1   dash Angostura Bitters

Stir with ice and strain into a cocktail glass.

BRAINSTORM COCKTAIL

2   oz. Irish Whisky
¼   oz. Benedictine
½   oz. Dry Vermouth

Stir with ice and strain into a cocktail glass. Serve with a twist of orange peel.

BRANDIED APRICOT

1   oz. Lemon Juice
1½ oz. Brandy
½   oz. Apricot-flavored Brandy

Shake with ice and strain into a sugar-rimmed cocktail glass. Serve with a twist of orange peel.

BRANDIED APRICOT FLIP

1   Egg
1   tsp. Sugar
1½ oz. Brandy
½   oz. Apricot-flavored Brandy

Shake with ice and strain into a cocktail glass. Dust with nutmeg.

BRANDIED BANANA COLLINS

1½ oz. Brandy
1   oz. Creme de Bananes
1   oz. Lemon Juice

Shake with ice and strain into a Collins glass. Fill with crushed ice. Serve with a lemon wedge and a slice of banana.

BRANDIED CORDIAL

½   oz. Lemon Juice
1½ oz. Brandy
½   oz. Cordial Medoc

Shake with ice and strain into a cocktail glass. Serve with a twist of orange peel.

BRANDIED GINGER

1½ oz. Brandy
½   oz. Ginger-flavored Brandy
¼   oz. Lime Juice
¼   oz. Orange Juice

Shake with ice and strain into a cocktail glass.

BRANDIED MADEIRA

1 oz. Brandy
1 oz. Madeira Wine
½ oz. Dry Vermouth

Stir with cracked ice and strain into an Old-fashioned glass over ice cubes. Add a twist of lemon peel.

BRANDIED PEACH FIZZ

1½ oz. Brandy
½ oz. Peach-flavored Brandy
½ oz. Lemon Juice
½ tsp. Sugar
¼ oz. Banana Liqueur

Shake with ice and strain into a Collins glass. Fill with crushed ice and soda. Serve with a peach slice.

BRANDIED PEACH SLING

1½ oz. Brandy
½ oz. Peach-flavored Brandy
1 oz. Lemon Juice
1 tsp. Sugar

Shake with ice and strain into a cocktail glass. Fill with crushed ice and soda. Serve with a lemon twist.

BRANDIED PORT

1 oz. Brandy
1 oz. Tawny Port
1 tbsp. Lemon Juice
1 tsp. Maraschino Liqueur

Shake all ingredients and strain into an Old-fashioned glass with ice cubes. Add a slice of orange.

BRANDT

2 oz. Brandy
½ oz. White Creme de Menthe
2 dashes Bitters

Stir with ice and strain into a cocktail glass. Serve with a lemon twist.

BRANDY ALEXANDER

¾ oz. Brandy
¾ oz. Creme de Cacao
¾ oz. fresh Cream

Shake with ice and strain into a cocktail glass. Sprinkle nutmeg on top.

BRANDYAMER

2 oz. Brandy
½ oz. Amer Picon

Stir with ice and strain into a cocktail glass. Serve with a lemon twist and a piece of orange peel.

BRANDY AND SODA

Pour 2 oz. Brandy into a Collins glass with ice cubes. Add soda.

BRANDY APRICOT FRAPPE

¾ oz. Brandy
¼ oz. Creme de Noyaux
½ oz. Apricot-flavored Brandy

Pack a cocktail glass with crushed ice. Pour ingredients over the ice (ingredients may be pre-mixed).

There is so much good in the worst of us,
And so much bad in the best of us,
That it hardly becomes any of us
To talk about the rest of us.

BRANDY BERRY FIX

1 tsp. Sugar dissolved in water
2 oz. Brandy
¼ oz. Strawberry Liqueur
¾ oz. Lemon Juice

Mix in a highball glass. Fill with crushed ice. Serve with a lemon wedge.

BRANDY BLAZER

1 lump Sugar
1 piece Orange Peel
1 piece Lemon Peel
2 oz. Brandy

Combine ingredients in an Old-fashioned cocktail glass. Light the liquid with a match, stir with a long spoon for a few seconds and strain into a whisky glass.

BRANDY BUCK

1½ oz. Brandy
½ oz. Lemon Juice

Pour into a highball glass. Fill with ice and ginger ale. Serve with a lemon twist.

BRANDY CASSIS

1½ oz. Brandy
1 oz. Lemon Juice
1 dash Creme de Cassis

Shake with ice and strain into a cocktail glass. Serve with a lemon twist.

BRANDY CHAMPERELLE NO. 1

1 oz. Orange Curacao
1 oz. Cognac Brandy
3 drops Angostura Bitters

Stir with ice and strain into a cocktail glass.

BRANDY CHAMPERELLE NO. 2

¾ oz. Orange Curacao
¾ oz. Brandy
½ oz. Yellow Chartreuse
½ oz. Anisette

Stir with ice and strain into a cocktail glass.

BRANDY COBBLER

2-3 oz. Brandy
1 tsp. Curacao
½ tsp. Sugar

Fill a 10 oz. goblet three-quarters full with crushed ice. Add Brandy, Curacao and sugar. Stir. Garnish with an orange slice and a pineapple stick.

BRANDY COCKTAIL NO. 1

2 oz. Brandy
¼ tsp. Sugar Syrup
2 dashes Bitters

Stir with ice and strain into a cocktail glass. Serve with a lemon twist.

BRANDY COCKTAIL NO. 2

2 oz. Cognac
½ oz. Gomme Syrup
2 drops Angostura Bitters

Stir with ice and strain into a cocktail glass.

BRANDY COCKTAIL NO. 3

2 oz. Brandy
½ oz. Dry Vermouth
1 dash Orange Bitters

Stir with ice and strain into a cocktail glass. Serve with a lemon twist.

BRANDY COLLINS

Juice ½ Lemon
1 tsp. Powdered Sugar
2 oz. Brandy

Shake with ice and strain into a Collins glass. Fill with soda and ice. Decorate with a cherry and a slice of orange or lemon. Serve with straws.

BRANDY COOLER

2½ oz. Brandy
Ginger Ale

Fill a Collins glass with ice and add Brandy. Fill with ginger ale and garnish with a twist of lemon peel.

> Not the laurel — but the race;
> Not the quarry — but the chase;
> Not the dice — but the play;
> May I, Lord, enjoy alway.

BRANDY CRUSTA COCKTAIL

Moisten the edge of a cocktail glass with lemon and dip into sugar. Cut the rind of half a lemon in a twist and place in the glass.

1 tsp. Maraschino Liqueur
1 dash Bitters
1 tsp. Lemon Juice
½ oz. Triple Sec or Orange Curacao
2 oz. Brandy

Stir above ingredients with ice and strain into sugar-rimmed glass. Add a slice of orange.

BRANDY DAISY

Juice ½ Lemon
½ tsp. Powdered Sugar
1 tsp. Raspberry Syrup or Grenadine
2 oz. Brandy

Shake with ice and strain into a stein or 8 oz. metal cup. Add cubes of ice and decorate with fruit.

BRANDY EGGNOG NO. 1

1 Whole Egg
1 tsp. Powdered Sugar
2 oz. Brandy

Shake with ice and strain into a Collins glass. Fill the glass with milk. Sprinkle nutmeg on top.

BRANDY EGGNOG NO. 2

2 oz. Brandy
4 oz. Milk
2 tsp. Sugar Syrup
1 oz. Jamaica Rum
1 whole Egg

Shake with ice and strain into a Collins glass. Sprinkle nutmeg on top.

BRANDY FANCY

2 oz. Brandy
¼ oz. Maraschino Liqueur
1 dash Orange Bitters
1 dash Angostura Bitters

Stir with ice and strain into a cocktail glass.

BRANDY FINO

1½ oz. Brandy
½ oz. Dry Sherry
½ oz. Drambuie

Stir with ice and strain into a cocktail glass. Serve with a lemon twist and an orange peel.

BRANDY FIX NO. 1

1½ oz. Brandy
1 oz. Cherry-flavored Brandy
1 tsp. Sugar
1 tsp. Water

Stir with ice and strain into a highball glass. Serve with a lemon twist. (Rum, Gin and Whisky Fixes are made as above—Omit Brandy and Cherry-flavored Brandy)

BRANDY FIX NO. 2

2½ oz. Brandy
1½ oz. Lemon Juice
1 tsp. Sugar

Pour lemon juice and sugar syrup into a highball glass. Fill with shaved ice. Add Brandy. Serve with a lemon wedge.

BRANDY FIZZ

Juice ½ Lemon
1   tsp. Powdered Sugar
2   oz. Brandy

Shake with ice and strain into a highball glass over two ice cubes. Fill with soda.

BRANDY FLIP

1   whole Egg
1   tsp. Powdered Sugar
1½ oz. Brandy
2   tsp. Sweet Cream (if desired)

Shake with ice and strain into a flip glass. Sprinkle nutmeg on top. (Any of the Fruit Brandies, Rum, Sherry or Whisky may be substituted for the Brandy in this recipe.)

BRANDY FLOAT

Chilled Club Soda
2½ oz. Brandy

Put ice cubes in an Old-fashioned glass and fill two-thirds full with soda. Float the Brandy carefully on top so that it does not mix. (Rum or Whisky may be substituted for the Brandy.)

BRANDY GOMME

3   dashes Gomme Syrup
2   dashes Curacao
1½ oz. Cognac Brandy

Stir with ice and strain into a cocktail glass. Serve with a lemon twist.

BRANDY GUMP COCKTAIL

1½ oz. Brandy
½   tsp. Grenadine
Juice ½ Lemon

Shake with ice and strain into a cocktail glass.

BRANDY HIGHBALL NO. 1

In a highball glass pour 2 oz. Brandy over ice cubes and fill with ginger ale or soda. Add a twist of lemon peel, if desired, and stir gently.

BRANDY HIGHBALL NO. 2

1½ oz. Brandy
¼   oz. Pernod
1   dash Lemon Juice

Pour into a highball glass. Fill with soda and ice.

BRANDY HOT

In an Old-fashioned glass dissolve ½ tsp. of sugar. Add 2 oz. Brandy. Flame. Serve with an orange peel.

BRANDY JULEP

2½ oz. Brandy
1   tsp. Sugar
Fresh Mint

Put sugar, Brandy and 5 or 6 leaves of fresh mint into a Collins glass. Fill glass with finely shaved ice and stir, being careful not to bruise the leaves, until mint rises to top. Decorate with a slice of pineapple, orange or lemon and a cherry.

> Merry met, and merry part, I drink to thee with all my heart.

BRANDY LIME AND SODA

1½ oz. Brandy
½   oz. Lime Juice
Soda

Top Brandy and lime juice with soda and ice. Serve in a Collins glass and garnish with a slice of lemon.

BRANDY MANHATTAN

2   oz. Brandy
½   oz. Sweet Vermouth
1   dash Bitters

Stir with ice and strain into a cocktail glass. Serve with a cherry.

BRANDY MELBA

1½ oz. Brandy
¼   oz. Peach-flavored Brandy
¼   oz. Grenadine
½   oz. Lemon Juice
1   dash Orange Bitters

Shake with ice and strain into a cocktail glass.

BRANDY MILK PUNCH

1   tsp. Powdered Sugar
2   oz. Brandy
1   cup Milk

Shake with ice and strain into a Collins glass. Sprinkle nutmeg on top.

BRANDY MINT FIZZ

1½ oz. Brandy
¼   oz. White Creme de Menthe
¼   oz. Light Creme de Cacao
¾   oz. Lemon Juice
½   tsp. Sugar

Shake with ice and strain into a Collins glass. Fill with crushed ice. Serve with a mint sprig.

BRANDY OLD-FASHIONED

1   cube Sugar
1   dash Angostura Bitters
2-3 oz. Brandy

Put the sugar cube in an Old-fashioned glass and sprinkle with Bitters. Add a lemon peel and ice cubes. Pour in the Brandy and stir.

BRANDY PUFF

2-3 oz. Brandy
2-3 oz. Milk
Chilled Soda

Put ice cubes in a small tumbler, add the Brandy and milk and fill up with soda. Stir gently.

BRANDY PUNCH NO. 1

Juice ½ Lemon
½ tsp. Sugar
1 oz. Water
2 oz. Brandy

Shake with ice and strain into a highball glass.

BRANDY PUNCH NO. 2

2 oz. Brandy
¼ oz. Orange Curacao
¼ oz. Rum
½ tsp. Sugar

Mix in a highball glass. Fill with soda and ice.

BRANDY RICKEY

1½ oz. Brandy
½ tsp. Maraschino Liqueur
½ tsp. Rum
½ tsp. Lemon Juice

Stir with ice and strain into a cocktail glass. Add soda to fill. Garnish with fruit.

BRANDY SANGAREE

1 tbsp. Port
2 oz. Brandy
½ tsp. Powdered Sugar
Soda

Dissolve sugar in 1 tsp. of water and add Brandy. Pour into a highball glass over ice cubes. Fill with soda and stir. Float Port on top. Dust with nutmeg.

BRANDY SCAFFA NO. 1

⅓ oz. Maraschino Liqueur
⅓ oz. Green Chartreuse
⅓ oz. Cognac

Pour carefully, in order given, into a pony glass so that each ingredient floats on the preceding one without mixing.

BRANDY SCAFFA NO. 2

1 dash Angostura Bitters
¾ oz. Maraschino Liqueur
1½ oz. Brandy

Stir with ice and strain into a cocktail glass.

BRANDY SLING

2 oz. Brandy
1 tsp. Powdered Sugar
Juice ½ Lemon

Dissolve sugar in lemon juice and a tsp. of water. Add Brandy. Serve in a large cocktail glass with ice cubes and a twist of lemon peel.

BRANDY SMASH

2 oz. Brandy
1 oz. Soda
1 lump Sugar
4 sprigs of Mint

In an Old-fashioned glass, mix sugar with soda and mint. Add Brandy and ice cubes and stir. Decorate with a slice of orange and a cherry. Serve with a lemon twist. (1 dash of Benedictine may be added to taste.)

BRANDY SOUR

Juice ½ Lemon
½ tsp. Powdered Sugar
2 oz. Brandy

Shake with ice and strain into a Sour glass. Decorate with a half slice of lemon and a cherry.

BRANDY SPECIAL

2 oz. Brandy
¼ oz. Orange Curacao
2 dashes Bitters

Stir with ice and strain into a cocktail glass. Serve with a lemon twist.

BRANDY SQUIRT

1½ oz. Brandy
1 tbsp. Powdered Sugar
1 tsp. Raspberry Syrup or Grenadine

Shake with ice and strain into a highball glass. Fill with Soda. Decorate with a stick of pineapple and strawberries.

BRANDY SWIZZLE

1½ oz. Lime Juice
1 tsp. Sugar
2 oz. Soda
2 dashes Bitters
2 oz. Brandy

Pour lime juice and sugar into a Collins glass. Fill with ice and stir thoroughly. Add Bitters and Brandy. Fill with soda and stir. Garnish with fruit.

BRANDY TODDY

½ tsp. Sugar dissolved in
1 tsp. Water
2 oz. Brandy
1 cube Ice

Mix ingredients in an Old-fashioned glass and serve with a twist of lemon peel on top.

BRANDY TODDY (HOT)

2 oz. Brandy
1 lump Sugar

Put sugar into a whisky glass and fill two-thirds with boiling water. Add Brandy. Stir and decorate with a slice of lemon. Sprinkle nutmeg on top.

BRANDY VERMOUTH COCKTAIL

½ oz. Sweet Vermouth
2 oz. Brandy
1 dash Bitters

Stir with ice and strain into a cocktail glass.

BRANDY ZOOM

2 oz. Brandy
¼ oz. Cream
1 tsp. Honey

Dissolve honey with hot water. Place in a shaker with the cream and Brandy. Shake and strain into a cocktail glass.

BRANTINI

1½ oz. Brandy
1 oz. Gin
1 dash Dry Vermouth

Stir with ice and strain into an Old-fashioned glass. Add ice. Serve with a lemon twist.

BRAVE BULL

1½ oz. Tequila
¾ oz. Kahlua

Fill an Old-fashioned glass with ice and add Tequila and Kahlua.

BRAZIL COCKTAIL

1½ oz. Dry Vermouth
1½ oz. Dry Sherry
1 dash Bitters
¼ tsp. Pernod

Stir with ice and strain into a cocktail glass.

BREAKFAST

2 oz. Gin
1 oz. Grenadine
1 Egg White

Shake with ice and strain into a cocktail glass.

BREAKFAST EGGNOG

1 whole Egg
½ oz. Triple Sec or Orange Curacao
2 oz. Apricot-flavored Brandy
6 oz. Milk

Shake with ice and strain into a Collins glass. Sprinkle nutmeg on top.

> Here's to man — something a beautiful woman fascinates, a clever woman interests and a sympathetic woman gets.

BREATHALISER BUSTER

¾ oz. Creme de Menthe
¾ oz. Cointreau
¾ oz. Vodka

Shake with ice and strain into a cocktail glass.

BRECK AND BRACE

Pour 1 oz. Cognac into a highball glass. Fill with Champagne. Add ice and stir. Serve with a lemon twist.

BRETT'S OWN

1¼ oz. Pernod
1¼ oz. Sweet Vermouth

Stir with ice and strain into a cocktail glass.

BRIGHTON PUNCH

¾ oz. Bourbon Whisky
¾ oz. Brandy
¾ oz. Benedictine
Juice ½ Orange
Juice ½ Lemon

Shake with ice and pour into a Collins glass nearly filled with shaved ice. Then fill with soda and stir gently. Decorate with orange and lemon slices and serve with a straw.

BRITTANY

¼ oz. Orange Juice
¼ oz. Lemon Juice
½ oz. Amer Picon
1½ oz. Gin

Stir with ice and strain into a cocktail glass. Serve with a twist of orange peel.

BROADMOOR COOLER

1½ oz. Rum
¼ oz. Green Creme de Menthe
¾ oz. Lime Juice

Mix in a Collins glass. Fill with ice and 7-Up. Serve with a mint sprig.

BROADWAY SMILE

⅓ oz. Creme de Cassis
⅓ oz. Swedish Punch
⅓ oz. Cointreau

Pour carefully, in order given, into a pony glass so that each ingredient floats on the preceding one without mixing.

BROADWAY SPECIAL

1 oz. Gin
½ oz. Sweet Vermouth
¼ oz. Grenadine
¼ oz. Pineapple Juice
½ Egg White

Shake with ice and strain into a cocktail glass. Dust with nutmeg.

BROKEN LEG

1 oz. Bourbon
2½ oz. hot Apple Juice

Mix in a highball glass. Add raisins and cinnamon and serve with a lemon wedge.

BROKEN SPUR NO. 1

3 oz. White Port
½ oz. Gin
½ oz. Sweet Vermouth
1 Egg Yolk
1 tsp. Anisette

Shake with ice and strain into a large cocktail glass.

BROKEN SPUR NO. 2

1½ oz. Port
¾ oz. Sweet Vermouth
¼ oz. Orange Curacao

Stir with ice and strain into a cocktail glass.

BROKER COCKTAIL

1 oz. White Port
½ oz. Sweet Vermouth
½ oz. Gin
1 dash Anisette
½ Yolk of 1 Egg

Shake with ice and strain into a cocktail glass.

BRONX COCKTAIL

1 oz. Gin
½ oz. Dry Vermouth
½ oz. Sweet Vermouth
Juice ¼ Orange

Shake with ice and strain into a cocktail glass. Serve with an orange slice.

BRONX COCKTAIL (DRY)

1 oz. Gin
1 oz. Dry Vermouth
Juice ¼ Orange

Shake with ice and strain into a cocktail glass. Serve with an orange slice.

BRONX DISCOTHEQUE

½ oz. Galliano
1 oz. Gin
¼ oz. Sweet Vermouth
¼ oz. Dry Vermouth
¾ oz. Orange Juice

Stir with ice and strain into a cocktail glass.

BRONX GOLDEN COCKTAIL

1 oz. Gin
½ oz. Sweet Vermouth
½ oz. Dry Vermouth
1 oz. Orange Juice
1 Egg Yolk

Shake with ice and strain into a cocktail glass. Serve with an orange slice.

BRONX PINEAPPLE COCKTAIL

1½ oz. Gin
½ oz. Sweet Vermouth
½ oz. Dry Vermouth
½ oz. Pineapple Juice

Shake with ice and strain into a cocktail glass.

BRONX SILVER COCKTAIL

Juice ½ Orange
1 Egg White
½ oz. Dry Vermouth
1 oz. Gin

Shake with ice and strain into a flip glass.

BRONX TERRACE COCKTAIL

1½ oz. Gin
1½ oz. Dry Vermouth
Juice ½ Lime

Shake with ice and strain into a cocktail glass. Serve with a cherry.

BROOKLYN COCKTAIL

¼ oz. Amer Picon
¼ oz. Maraschino Liqueur
1½ oz. Whisky
½ oz. Dry Vermouth

Shake with ice and strain into a cocktail glass.

BROOKLYNITE

2 oz. Jamaica Rum
½ oz. Honey
½ oz. Lime Juice
1 dash Angostura Bitters

Shake with ice and strain into a cocktail glass.

BROUSSARD'S ORANGE BRULOT

Pour Brandy into ½ orange shell. Add 1 sugar lump. Flame and serve.

BROWN COCKTAIL NO. 1

2 dashes Orange Bitters
1 oz. Dry Vermouth
1½ oz. Whisky

Shake with ice and strain into a cocktail glass.

BROWN COCKTAIL NO. 2

¾ oz. Gin
¾ oz. Rum
¾ oz. Dry Vermouth

Stir with ice and strain into a cocktail glass.

BROWN COW

Crushed Ice
3 oz. cold Milk
1 oz. Creme de Cafe

Pour cold milk and Creme de Cafe over crushed ice in a highball glass. Stir lightly.

BROWN DERBY NO. 1

1 oz. Lime Juice
1½ oz. Dark Rum
1 tsp. Maple Syrup

Shake with ice and strain into a cocktail glass.

BROWN DERBY NO. 2

1½ oz. Bourbon
¾ oz. Grapefruit Juice
1 tsp. Honey

Shake with ice and strain into a cocktail glass.

BROWN HAMMER

1 oz. Cream
1 oz. White Orange-flavored Liqueur
1 tsp. Creme de Cafe

Shake with ice and strain into a cocktail glass. Add an ice cube.

BROWN SHAKE

1½ oz. Orange Curacao
2 dashes Angostura Bitters
¾ oz. Lemon Juice

Shake with ice and strain into a cocktail glass.

BROWN UNIVERSITY

1¼ oz. Bourbon
1¼ oz. Dry Vermouth
1 dash Orange Bitters

Stir with ice and strain into a cocktail glass.

BRUNELLE

1 oz. Pernod
3 oz. Lemon Juice
1½ tsp. Sugar

Shake with ice and strain into a cocktail glass.

BRUNETTE

¾ oz. Kahlua
¾ oz. Bourbon
¾ oz. Cream
¼ tsp. Sugar

Shake with ice and strain into a cocktail glass.

BRUNSWICK SOUR

1½ oz. Light Rum
¾ oz. Lime Juice
1 tsp. Sugar

Shake with ice and strain into a Sour glass. Float Claret on top.

BRUT COCKTAIL

1½ oz. Dry Vermouth
¾ oz. Amer Picon
2 dashes Orange Bitters
3 drops Angostura Bitters

Stir with ice and strain into a cocktail glass. Serve with a lemon twist.

BUBY

2 oz. Gin
2 oz. Lemon Juice
1 tsp. Grenadine

Shake with ice and strain into a cocktail glass.

> To you, and yours, and theirs, and mine,
> I pledge with you, their health in wine.

BUCKAROO

1½ oz. Bourbon
2 dashes Angostura Bitters

Mix in a Collins glass. Fill with ice and Coca-Cola.

BUCK JONES

1½ oz. Rum
1 oz. Sweet Sherry
Juice ½ Lime

Pour ingredients into a highball glass over ice cubes and stir. Fill with ginger ale.

BUCKS FIZZ NO. 1

1½ oz. Gin
½ tsp. Sugar
2 oz. Orange Juice

Shake with ice and strain into a highball glass. Fill with chilled Champagne.

BUCKS FIZZ NO. 2

3 oz. fresh Orange Juice
8 oz. chilled Champagne

Pour orange juice into a 12 oz. Collins glass. Add the Champagne and stir gently to mix.

BUD'S SPECIAL COCKTAIL

1 dash Angostura Bitters
¾ oz. Sweet Cream
2 oz. Cointreau

Stir with ice and strain into a cocktail glass.

BUENOS DIAS

2 oz. Calisay
2 oz. Sweet Vermouth
3 dashes Simple Syrup

Stir with ice and strain into a cocktail glass.

BUGHOUSE

1½ oz. Cognac
¾ oz. Sweet Vermouth
¼ oz. Pernod

Stir with ice and strain into a cocktail glass.

BUILDER UPPER

1½ oz. Cognac
1 oz. Benedictine

Fill a Collins glass with crushed ice. Add Cognac and Benedictine. Fill with soda. Serve with a twist of lemon peel.

BULLDOG NO. 1

1½ oz. Cherry-flavored Brandy
¾ oz. Light Rum
1½ tbsp. Lime Juice

Shake with ice and strain into a cocktail glass.

BULLDOG NO. 2

1½ oz. Cherry-flavored Brandy
¾ oz. Gin
Juice ½ Lime

Shake with ice and strain into a cocktail glass.

BULLDOG COOLER

2 oz. Gin
¼ tsp. Sugar
¼ oz. Lemon Juice

Stir with ice and strain into a highball glass. Add soda (or ginger ale) and ice.

BULLDOG HIGHBALL

Juice ½ Orange
2 oz. Gin

Pour into a highball glass over ice cubes. Fill with ginger ale and stir.

BULLDOZER

1½ oz. Vodka

Pour into a highball glass. Fill with ice and beef bouillon.

BULLFROG

Pour 2 oz. Vodka into a Collins glass. Fill with ice and lime soda.

BULL'S EYE

1 oz. Brandy
2 oz. Hard Cider

Pour into a highball glass over ice cubes and fill with ginger ale. Stir.

BULLSHOT NO. 1

1-2 oz. Gin
3 oz. chilled Beef Bouillon

Put ice cubes in an Old-fashioned glass. Add Gin and bouillon and stir gently. (Vodka may be used instead of Gin.)

BULLSHOT NO. 2

1 cube Beef Stock
2 oz. hot Water
¼ tbsp. Celery Salt or Salt
¼ oz. Lemon Juice
1¼ oz. Vodka

Dissolve stock cube in hot water. Add salt, lemon juice and Vodka. Stir vigorously. Serve on the rocks in an Old-fashioned glass with a lemon peel garnish. (Rum can be substituted for Vodka in the above recipe.)

BULL'S MILK NO. 1

1 tsp. Powdered Sugar
1 oz. Rum
1½ oz. Brandy
1 cup Milk

Shake with ice and strain into a Collins glass. Sprinkle nutmeg and a pinch of cinnamon on top.

BULL'S MILK NO. 2

2 oz. Brandy
2 oz. Milk
¼ tsp. Powdered Sugar

Mix in a highball glass. Sprinkle nutmeg on top.

BUMBLE BEE STINGER

¾ oz. Galliano
1½ oz. Brandy
½ oz. Pernod

Shake with ice and strain into a cocktail glass.

BUMPER COCKTAIL

1½ oz. Jamaica Rum
½ oz. Gin
½ oz. Lemon Juice

Stir with ice and strain into a cocktail glass. Serve with a lemon twist.

BUNNY BONANZA

1 oz. Tequila
¾ oz. Applejack
½ oz. Lemon Juice
¼ oz. Orange Curacao
½ tsp. Sugar

Shake with ice and strain into a cocktail glass.

BUNNY HUG OR EARTHQUAKE

¾ oz. Gin
¾ oz. Whisky
¾ oz. Pernod

Shake with ice and strain into a cocktail glass.

BUNNY HUG COCKTAIL NO. 2

¾ oz. Gin
¾ oz. Scotch Whisky
¾ oz. Pernod
1 dash Anisette

Shake with ice and strain into a cocktail glass.

BUNNY MOTHER

1½ oz. Vodka
1 oz. Orange Juice
1 oz. Lemon Juice
1 tsp. Sugar
¼ oz. Grenadine
¼ oz. Cointreau

Shake with ice and strain into a Collins glass. Fill with crushed ice. Serve with an orange slice and a cherry.

BURGUNDY A GO-GO

Juice ½ Lemon
2 tsp. Powdered Sugar
1 drop Rum Extract
6 oz. Burgundy
Fruit

Place first four ingredients in a tall glass. Stir. Add ice cubes. Garnish with fruit.

BURGUNDY BISHOP

Juice ¼ Lemon
1 tsp. Powdered Sugar
1 oz. Rum

Shake with ice and strain into a highball glass over ice cubes. Fill with Burgundy Wine and stir. Decorate with fruits.

BURGUNDY FLIP

1 Egg
½ tsp. Sugar
2 oz. Burgundy
½ cup crushed Ice

Blend with ice and strain into a highball glass. Sprinkle nutmeg on top.

BURNT BRANDY AND PEACH COCKTAIL

1½ oz. Cognac
2 lumps Sugar

Flame Brandy with the sugar in a saucer. Place 2-3 pieces of fresh peach in a cocktail glass. Pour in the burnt liquid and serve.

BURROUGH'S OLD-FASHIONED

1 lump Sugar dissolved in Water
2 dashes Angostura Bitters
1½ oz. Bourbon

Mix the first two ingredients in an Old-fashioned glass. Fill with ice and add the Bourbon.

> Here's to a long life and a merry one,
> A quick death and an easy one,
> A full bottle and another one.

BUSHRANGER

1½ oz. Rum
1 oz. Dubonnet
1 dash Bitters

Stir with ice and strain into a cocktail glass.

BUSTANBY

2 oz. White Creme de Menthe
¼ tsp. Sugar
1 dash Orange Bitters
1 dash Angostura Bitters
1 dash Orange Juice

Shake with ice and strain into a cocktail glass.

BUSTER

2 oz. Rum
½ oz. Pernod

Stir with ice and strain into a cocktail glass.

BUSTER BROWN

1½ oz. Bourbon
¼ tsp. Sugar
½ oz. Lemon Juice
1 dash Orange Bitters

Shake with ice and strain into a cocktail glass.

BUTTERED APPLE GROG

Place a piece of Baked Apple in a preheated Old-fashioned glass.

Add: 1 oz. Apple Brandy
     1 oz. Dry Vermouth
     2 oz. Apple Juice (preheated to a boil)
Add: Sugar and ½ a pat of Butter to taste

BUTTERED BOURGIN

1½ oz. Bourbon
1 oz. Ginger-flavored Brandy
½ pat Butter

Mix in a mug. Add 6 oz. heated apple juice. Dust with cinnamon.

BUTTERFLY

¾ oz. Dry Vermouth
¾ oz. Sweet Vermouth
½ oz. Dubonnet
½ oz. Orange Juice

Shake with ice and strain into a cocktail glass.

BUTTERFLY MILK PUNCH

2 oz. Cognac
1 dash Angostura Bitters
1 oz. Dark Creme de Cacao
3 oz. Milk
½ tsp. Sugar

Shake with ice and strain into a highball glass. Dust with nutmeg.

BUTTON HOOK COCKTAIL

½ oz. White Creme de Menthe
½ oz. Apricot-flavored Brandy
½ oz. Pernod
½ oz. Brandy

Stir with ice and strain into a cocktail glass.

B.V.D. NO. 1

2 oz. Apple Brandy
½ oz. Sweet Vermouth

Stir with ice and strain into a cocktail glass. Serve with a lemon twist.

B.V.D. NO. 2

¾ oz. Gin
¾ oz. Rum
¾ oz. Dry Vermouth

Stir with ice and strain into a cocktail glass.

B.V.D. NO. 3

¾ oz. Rum
¾ oz. Dubonnet
¾ oz. Dry Vermouth

Stir with ice and strain into a cocktail glass.

BYCULLA

1 oz. Sherry
1 oz. Port
1 oz. Curacao
1 oz. Ginger Wine

Stir with ice and strain into a cocktail glass.

BYRRH

1 oz. Byrrh
1 oz. Rye Whisky
1 oz. Dry Vermouth

Stir with ice and strain into a cocktail glass.

BYRRH BRANDY

¾ oz. Byrrh
1 oz. Cognac
¾ oz. Dry Vermouth

Stir with ice and strain into a cocktail glass.

BYRRH CASSIS

2 cubes Ice
3 oz. Byrrh
2 tsp. Creme de Cassis
Soda

Place ice cubes in a Collins glass. Add Byrrh and Creme de Cassis and fill with soda. Stir lightly.

BYRRH CASSIS COOLER

2 oz. Byrrh
½ oz. Creme de Cassis

Mix in a Collins glass. Fill with soda and ice. Serve with a lemon wedge.

BYRRH FRAPPE

2 oz. Byrrh

Pour Byrrh into a cocktail glass filled with cracked ice. Serve with a lemon twist.

BYRRH FREEZE

2 oz. Byrrh
½ oz. Lemon Cordial
1 Maraschino Cherry

Pour Byrrh and Cordial into a glass. Top with soda and garnish with a slice of lemon and a cherry. Serve in a highball glass with ice.

BYRRH SPECIAL

1½ oz. Byrrh
1½ oz. Gin

Stir with ice and strain into a cocktail glass.

CABARET COCKTAIL NO. 1

1½ oz. Gin
2 dashes Bitters
½ tsp. Dry Vermouth
¼ tsp. Benedictine

Stir with ice and strain into a cocktail glass. Serve with a cherry.

CABARET COCKTAIL NO. 2

1 oz. Gin
1 oz. Dubonnet
¼ oz. Pernod
1 dash Angostura Bitters

Stir with ice and strain into a cocktail glass. Serve with a cherry.

CABLEGRAM HIGHBALL

Juice ½ Lemon
1 tsp. Powdered Sugar
2 oz. Rye or Bourbon

Stir with ice cubes in a highball glass and fill with ginger ale.

CACTUS BANGER

1½ oz. Tequila
½ oz. Galliano

Pour Tequila into a Collins glass. Fill with ice and orange juice. Float Galliano on top.

CADIZ

¾ oz. Dry Sherry
¾ oz. Blackberry-flavored Brandy
½ oz. Triple Sec or Orange Curacao
1 tbsp. Sweet Cream

Shake with ice and strain into an Old-fashioned glass over ice cubes.

CAFE AUX COGNACS

4 oz. strong hot Coffee
1 oz. Brandy

Rub the rim of a heavy 6 oz. goblet with lemon and then dip it in sugar. Fill the glass three-quarters full with hot coffee and float the brandy on top. Light the Brandy and serve.

Here's to bachelors, created by God for the consolation of widows and the hope of maidens.

CAFE BRULOT COCKTAIL NO. 1

Fill a cocktail glass, rimmed with sugar, with hot black coffee. Float 1½ oz. Cognac on top. Flame the Cognac and serve.

CAFE BRULOT COCKTAIL NO. 2

1½ oz. Brandy
1 lump Sugar
1 stick Cinnamon
1 Vanilla Bean

Mix sugar, cinnamon and vanilla bean in a cup. Add an orange peel and a lemon twist. Fill with hot black coffee. Float the Brandy on top, flame and serve.

CAFE CACAO

1½ oz. Dark Creme de Cacao
4 oz. Iced Coffee

Stir gently in an Old-fashioned glass.

CAFE CHARENTAIS

1 demitasse strong hot Coffee
1 oz. Brandy
1 tbsp. Whipped Cream
Sugar to taste

Sweeten the coffee to taste, add the Brandy and top with whipped cream.

CAFE COCKTAIL

½ oz. Dark Creme de Cacao
1½ oz. Cognac
2 oz. Black Coffee
½ tsp. Sugar

Shake with ice and strain into a cocktail glass. Serve with a lemon twist.

CAFE CURACAO

1 oz. Orange Curacao
1 oz. Kahlua

Mix in an Old-fashioned glass. Serve with a twist of orange peel.

CAFE DE PARIS COCKTAIL

1 Egg White
1 tsp. Pernod
1 tsp. Sweet Cream
1½ oz. Gin

Shake with ice and strain into a cocktail glass.

CAFE DIABLE

Sprinkle Allspice
Grated Orange Peel
1 Cinnamon stick
1 oz. Cognac
¾ oz. Grand Marnier
½ oz. Sambuca
½ tsp. Sugar

Put all ingredients into a cup and fill with hot black coffee. Strain into a fresh, preheated cup. Float additional Cognac. Flame and serve.

CAFE FLORIDE

1 demitasse strong hot Coffee
Sugar to taste
Orange Peel soaked in Orange Liqueur
1 tbsp. Whipped Cream

Sweeten the coffee to taste, add orange peel and top with whipped cream.

CAFE GALLIANO

¾ oz. Galliano
1 oz. Brandy
1 oz. cold black Coffee

Shake with ice and strain into a cocktail glass. Float cream on top.

CAFE GROGG

1½ oz. Jamaica Rum
¼ oz. Brandy
1 lump Sugar
Coffee

Pour Rum into a cup and add sugar, a lemon wedge and Brandy. Fill with soda and serve.

CAFE JAMAIQUE

1 demitasse strong hot Coffee
Sugar to taste
1 oz. Jamaica Rum
1 tbsp. Whipped Cream

Sweeten coffee to taste. Add the Rum and top with whipped cream.

CAFE KIRSCH NO. 1

1½ oz. Kirsch
1 tsp. Sugar
3 oz. cold black Coffee
1 Egg White

Shake with ice and strain into a cocktail glass.

CAFE KIRSCH NO. 2

¾ oz. Cognac
¾ oz. Kirschwasser
1½ oz. cold black Coffee

Shake with ice and strain into a cocktail glass. May be served hot or cold.

CAFE LIEGEOISE

4 oz. strong Coffee, chilled
4 oz. Vanilla Ice Cream
1 oz. Brandy

Blend until smooth and serve in a large stemmed goblet.

CAFE PUCCI

¾ oz. Trinidad Rum
¾ oz. Amaretto

Pour into a cup or mug. Fill with hot coffee and top with whipped cream.

CAFE ROYALE NO. 1

Place 1 lump of sugar into a cup. Pour ½ oz. Yellow Chartreuse over sugar. Add hot coffee and stir.

CAFE ROYALE NO. 2

Put a cube of sugar, well soaked with Brandy, in a teaspoon; hold so that it will rest on top of one cup of hot black coffee and ignite. Hold until flame burns out. Drop contents in coffee.

CAFE SHAKE COCKTAIL

1   oz. Creme de Cafe
Chocolate Syrup
Vanilla Ice Cream

Add Creme de Cafe to the chocolate syrup and vanilla ice cream. Blend. Serve in a cocktail glass.

CALEDONIA

1   oz. Creme de Cacao
1   oz. Brandy
1   oz. Milk or Cream
1   Egg Yolk

Shake with ice and strain into an Old-fashioned glass over ice cubes. Sprinkle cinnamon on top.

CALIENTE COCKTAIL NO. 1

1   oz. Gin
¼   oz. Lemon Juice
½   tsp. Sugar
½   oz. Sweet Cream
½   White of 1 Egg

Shake with ice and strain into a cocktail glass. Sprinkle nutmeg on top.

CALIENTE COCKTAIL NO. 2

2   oz. Gin
1   oz. Lime Juice
1   dash Angostura Bitters
½   tsp. Sugar

Shake with ice and strain into a cocktail glass.

CALIFORNIA CHAMPAGNE FIZZ

Juice 1 Lime
1   tsp. Sugar
Extra Dry Champagne, chilled

Place ice cubes in a Collins glass. Add lime juice and sugar. Fill with Champagne.

CALIFORNIA EGGNOG

¾   oz. Bourbon
¾   oz. Brandy
¾   oz. Rum
1   Egg
1   oz. Cream

Shake with ice and strain into a Collins glass. Sprinkle nutmeg on top.

CALIFORNIA LEMONADE

Juice 1 Lemon
Juice 1 Lime
1   tbsp. Powdered Sugar
2   oz. Rye or Bourbon
¼   tsp. Grenadine

Shake with ice and strain into a Collins glass over shaved ice. Fill with soda and decorate with slices of orange and lemon and a cherry. Serve with straws.

CALIFORNIAN NO. 1

4   oz. Brandy
1   oz. Dry Vermouth
1   oz. Port

Stir with ice and strain into a cocktail glass.

CALIFORNIAN NO. 2

1½   oz. Sweet Vermouth
1   oz. Blended Whisky
2   oz. Orange Juice
¼   oz. Orgeat

Shake with ice and strain into a cocktail glass.

CALIFORNIA SPRITZER

6   oz. Vin Rose, chilled
3   oz. chilled Soda

Mix and pour over ice cubes in a Collins glass.

CALIFORNIA SUNSHINE

3   oz. Orange Juice

Pour into a highball glass. Fill with Champagne and ice.

CALISAY

1½   oz. Calisay
1½   oz. Sweet Vermouth
3   dashes Sugar

Stir with ice and strain into a cocktail glass.

CALISAYA COCKTAIL

1½   oz. Bourbon
1   oz. Calisay

Stir with ice and strain into a cocktail glass. Serve with a lemon twist.

CALM VOYAGE

½   oz. Strega or Galliano
½   oz. Rum
1   tbsp. Passion Fruit Syrup
2   tsp. Lemon Juice
½   Egg White

Put all ingredients in a blender with half a cup of crushed ice. Blend at low speed and pour into a champagne glass.

CALVADOS COCKTAIL NO. 1

1½   oz. Calvados
2   dashes Curacao
2   dashes Sugar Syrup

Shake with ice and strain into a cocktail glass.

CALVADOS COCKTAIL NO. 2

1½ oz. Calvados
1 oz. Orange Juice
¼ oz. Cointreau
1 dash Orange Bitters

Shake with ice and strain into a cocktail glass.

CALVADOS FIZZ

2 oz. Calvados
½ oz. Lemon Juice
½ Egg White
¼ oz. Cream
½ tsp. Sugar

Shake with ice and strain into a Collins glass. Fill with soda and ice. Serve with a lemon slice and a cherry.

CALVADOS SOUR

1½ oz. Calvados
1 oz. Lemon Juice
1 tsp. Sugar

Shake with ice and strain into a Sour glass. Serve with a lemon wedge and a cherry.

CALYPSO COCKTAIL

1 oz. Dry Vermouth
¾ oz. Strega
¾ oz. Rum

Stir with ice and strain into a cocktail glass.

CALYPSO COFFEE

1 tsp. Brown Sugar
1½ oz. Rum

Pour into a fizz glass. Fill with hot black coffee. Top with whipped cream.

CALYPSO COOLER

2½ oz. Rum
1 oz. Pineapple Juice
½ oz. Lime Juice
½ tsp. Sugar

Shake with ice and strain into a Collins glass. Fill with soda. Serve with a pineapple spear and a lime wheel.

CAMEL JUICE

½ oz. Galliano
½ oz. Kahlua
½ oz. Brandy
½ oz. Rum
1 oz. cold black Coffee

Shake with ice and strain into a cocktail glass.

CAMERON'S

1½ oz. Scotch
¾ oz. Lime Juice
¼ oz. Orgeat

Shake with ice and strain into a cocktail glass.

CAMERON'S KICK COCKTAIL

¾ oz. Scotch Whisky
¾ oz. Irish Whisky
2 dashes Orange Bitters or ½ tbsp. Orgeat Syrup
Juice ¼ Lemon

Shake with ice and strain into a cocktail glass.

CAMPARINETE

1 oz. Gin
¾ oz. Sweet Vermouth
¾ oz. Campari

Stir with ice and strain into a cocktail glass.

CAMPDEN

1½ oz. Gin
¾ oz. Cointreau
¾ oz. Lillet

Shake with ice and strain into a cocktail glass. Serve with a cherry.

A health to you
And wealth to you
And the best that life can give to you.
May fortune still be kind to you
And Happiness be true to you
And Life be long and good to you —
Is the toast of all your friends to you.

CAMPEXPORT

¾ oz. Gin
¾ oz. Campari
¾ oz. Dry Vermouth
¾ oz. Cordial Campari

Stir with ice and strain into a cocktail glass. Serve with a cherry.

CANADIAN NO. 1

1½ oz. Curacao
3 dashes Jamaica Rum
1 tsp. Sugar
2 tbsp. Lemon Juice

Shake with ice and strain into a cocktail glass.

CANADIAN NO. 2

1½ oz. Rye Whisky
½ oz. Lemon Juice
½ oz. Orange Curacao
½ tsp. Sugar
2 dashes Orange Bitters

Shake with ice and strain into a cocktail glass.

CANADIAN NO. 3

2 oz. Rye Whisky
½ oz. Sweet Vermouth
¼ oz. Orange Curacao
1 dash Angostura Bitters

Shake with ice and strain into a cocktail glass. Serve with an orange slice.

CANADIAN AND CAMPARI

1 oz. Canadian Whisky
1 oz. Dry Vermouth
2 tsp. Campari

Shake with ice and strain into a cocktail glass. Add a twist of lemon.

CANADIAN APPLE

1½ oz. Canadian Whisky
½ oz. Calvados or Apple Brandy
½ oz. Lemon Juice
½ tsp. Sugar

Shake with ice and strain into a cocktail glass. Dust with cinnamon.

CANADIAN BLACK FIX

½ tsp. Sugar dissolved in water
1½ oz. Canadian Whisky
½ oz. Blackberry-flavored Brandy
½ oz. Lemon Juice

Mix in a highball glass. Fill glass with crushed ice and stir. Serve with a lemon wedge and a berry.

CANADIAN CHERRY

1½ oz. Rye Whisky
½ oz. Cherry-flavored Brandy
1½ tsp. Lemon Juice
1½ tsp. Orange Juice

Shake all ingredients and strain into an Old-fashioned glass over ice cubes. Moisten the rim of the glass with Cherry Brandy and coat it with sugar.

CANADIAN DAISY

2 oz. Canadian Whisky
1 oz. Lemon Juice
½ oz. Grenadine (Raspberry Syrup)

Shake with ice and strain into a large cocktail glass. Add a squirt of soda and berries and float ¼ oz. Metaxa on top.

CANADIAN GRENADIER

1½ oz. Canadian Whisky
1 small scoop Lemon Sherbet

Put into a highball glass. Fill with ginger ale. Float ¼ oz. Grenadine on top.

CANADIAN OLD-FASHIONED

¼ oz. Orange Curacao
1 dash Angostura Bitters
¼ oz. Lemon Juice
1½ oz. Canadian Whisky

Mix in an Old-fashioned glass. Fill with ice cubes. Serve with a lemon twist and an orange peel.

CANADIAN PINE

½ oz. Canadian Whisky
½ oz. Pineapple Juice
½ oz. Lemon Juice
¼ oz. Maraschino Liqueur

Shake with ice and strain into a cocktail glass.

CANADIAN PINEAPPLE

1½ oz. Rye Whisky
1 tsp. Pineapple Juice
1 tbsp. Lemon Juice
½ tsp. Maraschino Liqueur

Shake with ice and strain into an Old-fashioned glass over ice cubes. Serve with a pineapple stick.

CANADIAN STAVE

1½ oz. Canadian Whisky
1 oz. Dubonnet
½ Egg White
1 dash Angostura Bitters
¼ oz. Lemon Juice

Shake with ice and strain into a cocktail glass.

CANADO SALUDO

1½ oz. Rum
1 oz. Orange Juice
1 oz. Pineapple Juice
5 dashes Lemon Juice
5 dashes Grenadine
5 dashes Angostura

Serve over ice cubes in a 6 oz. glass with pineapple slices, an orange slice and a cherry.

CANAL STREET DAISY

Juice ¼ Lemon
Juice ¼ Orange
1 oz. Rye Whisky

Pour all ingredients into a Collins glass over ice cubes. Add soda and an orange slice.

CANASTA

1 oz. Lemon Juice
2 oz. Southern Comfort

Shake with ice and strain into a cocktail glass.

CANCAMP

1½ oz. Canadian Whisky
½ oz. Campari
½ oz. Dry Vermouth

Stir with ice and strain into a cocktail glass. Serve with a lemon twist.

CAN CAN

1 oz. Vodka

Pour into a champagne glass. Fill with cold Champagne. Serve with a lemon twist.

CANDY

1 oz. Galliano
1 oz. Brandy
¼ oz. Maraschino Liqueur
2 scoops Orange Sherbet

Blend with ice and strain into a cocktail glass.

CANTON

1½ oz. Jamaica Rum
¼ oz. Maraschino Liqueur
¼ oz. Orange Curacao
1 dash Grenadine

Stir with ice and strain into a cocktail glass. Serve with a cherry and a piece of orange peel.

CANVAS BACK

1 oz. Bourbon
½ oz. Sweet Vermouth
¼ oz. Gin
¼ oz. Orange Curacao
1 dash Angostura Bitters
1 dash Lemon Juice

Stir with ice and strain into a cocktail glass. Serve with a lemon twist.

CAPACIOUS

1 tsp. Lemon Juice
1 tsp. Simple Syrup
1 dash Aromatic Bitters
Extra Dry Champagne, chilled

Fill a Collins glass half full of crushed ice. Add lemon juice, syrup and bitters. Fill with chilled Champagne. Serve with a twist of orange peel.

CAPE COCKTAIL

1½ oz. Gin
½ oz. Dubonnet
½ oz. Orange Juice

Shake with ice and strain into a cocktail glass. Serve with a cherry.

CAPE CODDER

1½ oz. Vodka or Rum
3 oz. Cranberry Juice
Juice ½ Lime (if desired)

Serve on the rocks in an Old-fashioned glass or highball glass with cubes of ice and soda. Stir.

CAPETOWN

1½ oz. Rye Whisky
1½ oz. Dubonnet
3 dashes Curacao
1 dash Angostura Bitters

Stir with ice and strain into a cocktail glass. Serve with a lemon twist.

CAPPUCINO COCKTAIL

¾ oz. Coffee-flavored Brandy
¾ oz. Vodka
¾ oz. Sweet Cream

Shake with ice and strain into a cocktail glass.

CAPPUCCINO COFFEE

½ oz. Dark Creme de Cacao
¼ oz. Rum
¼ oz. Brandy

Pour into a cup and fill with hot black coffee. Add ¼ oz. Cream and ½ oz. Galliano. Top with whipped cream.

CAPRI NO. 1

1½ oz. White Creme de Cacao
2 tbsp. Blue Curacao
1 tbsp. Green Creme de Menthe

Shake with ice and strain into a cocktail glass. Add ice.

CAPRI NO. 2

¾ oz. White Creme de Cacao
¾ oz. Creme de Bananes
¾ oz. Sweet Cream

Shake with ice and strain into an Old-fashioned glass over ice cubes.

CAPRICE

2 oz. Gin
1 oz. Sweet Vermouth
1 oz. Campari

Shake with ice and strain into a Martini glass.

CAPRICE COCKTAIL

1½ oz. Gin
½ oz. Dry Vermouth
½ oz. Benedictine
2 dashes Orange Bitters

Shake with ice and strain into a cocktail glass. Serve with an olive.

CAPTAIN KIDD

1½ oz. Jamaica Rum
½ oz. Dry Sherry
½ oz. Scotch
1 dash Orange Bitters

Stir with ice and strain into a cocktail glass.

CAPTAIN'S BLOOD

1½ oz. Jamaica Rum
1 oz. Lime Juice
½ tsp. Sugar
¼ oz. Falernum
1 dash Angostura Bitters

Shake with ice and strain into a cocktail glass.

> Pretend we've known you all along,
> That you're an old-time friend.
> Perhaps before the evening is o'er,
> The make-believe will end.

CARABINI

1 oz. Galliano
1½ oz. Lime Juice
1½ oz. Orange Juice
¾ oz. Creme de Noyaux

Shake with ice and strain into a cocktail glass.

CARACAS

½ oz. Sweet Cream
½ oz. Creme de Cacao
2 oz. Bourbon

Stir with ice and strain into a cocktail glass.

CARA SPOSA NO. 1

1   oz. Tia Maria
1   oz. Curacao
½   Heavy Cream
3   oz. crushed Ice

Blend at a low speed for 15 seconds. Strain into an Old-fashioned glass.

CARA SPOSA NO. 2

1   oz. Coffee-flavored Brandy
1   oz. Triple Sec or Orange Curacao
½   oz. Sweet Cream

Shake with ice and strain into a cocktail glass.

CARDINAL

1   oz. Gin
¾   oz. Campari
¾   oz. Dry Vermouth

Stir with ice and strain into a cocktail glass. Serve with a lemon twist.

CARDINAL'S COCKTAIL

1½   oz. Rum
1   oz. Lime Juice
¼   oz. Grenadine
¼   oz. Triple Sec or Orange Curacao
¼   oz. Orgeat

Shake with ice and strain into a cocktail glass.

CARIB

¾   oz. Rum
¾   oz. Gin
1   oz. Lemon Juice
1   tsp. Sugar

Shake with ice and strain into a cocktail glass.

CARIBBEAN

1   oz. Galliano
1   oz. Rum
1   oz. Orange Juice
1   oz. Lime Juice

Shake with ice and strain into a Collins glass. Fill with soda and ice. Serve with an orange slice and a cherry.

CARIBBEAN CAPER

1½   oz. Jamaica Rum
1½   oz. Coconut Milk

Pour into a highball glass. Fill with soda and ice.

CARIBBEAN CHAMPAGNE

½   tsp. Rum
½   tsp. Creme de Bananes
Chilled Champagne

Pour Rum and Banana Liqueur into a champagne glass. Fill with Champagne and stir lightly. Add a slice of banana.

CARIBBEAN COCKTAIL

2   oz. White Rum
8   oz. Pineapple Juice
2   tbsp. Lime Juice
1   oz. Sugar Syrup
1-2   dashes Orange Bitters

Shake with ice and strain into a Collins glass. Fill with soda and ice.

CARIBBEAN HOT SWIZZLE

1   tsp. Sugar
1½   oz. Jamaica Rum
¾   oz. Lime Juice
Leave ½ lime shell in glass

Mix in a highball glass. Fill with hot water and stir.

CARIBBEAN JOY

1½   oz. Scotch
1   oz. Lime Juice
½   oz. Cointreau
½   tsp. Sugar

Shake with ice and strain into a cocktail glass.

CARIBE COCKTAIL

1½   oz. Light Rum
1   oz. Pineapple Juice
¾   oz. Lemon Juice

Shake with ice and strain into a cocktail glass.

CARIBE WELCOME

1   oz. Rum
1   oz. Apricot-flavored Brandy
1   oz. Coconut Cream
1   oz. Pineapple Juice

Shake with ice and strain into a cocktail glass.

CARIOCA

Juice ½ Lime
1½   oz. Rum
½   tsp. Sugar
1   dash Maraschino Liqueur

Shake with ice and strain into a cocktail glass.

CARIOCA COLLINS

Juice ½ Lime
¼   tsp. Powdered Sugar
1½   oz. Rum

Shake with ice and strain into a Collins glass. Add an ice cube and fill with soda.

Here's to you and here's to me,
Here's to what we used to be;
Here's to what we might have been,
And here's to what we'll be again.

CARIOCA COOLER

1½ oz. White Rum
1   oz. Honey
1   oz. Lime Juice
2   tsp. Mandarin Liqueur
2   oz. crushed Ice

Blend at a high speed for 10 seconds. Strain into a highball glass filled with crushed ice. Top with a lime wheel.

CARIOCA EGGNOG

1   Egg
1   tbsp. Powdered Sugar
1½ oz. Rum
1   glass Milk

Break the egg into a shaker. Add ice and other ingredients. Shake well and strain into a tall highball glass. Sprinkle nutmeg on top.

CARLTON

3   oz. Orange Juice
2   tbsp. Grand Marnier
1   Egg White
A few drops of Peach Bitters

Shake with ice and strain into a champagne glass. Add Champagne and stir gently. Decorate with a cherry.

CARLTON COCKTAIL

1   oz. Rye or Bourbon
½   oz. Orange Juice
½   oz. Cointreau

Shake with ice and strain into a cocktail glass.

CARLTON SPECIAL

¾   oz. Benedictine
¾   oz. Orange Bitters
¾   oz. Creme de Cacao

Shake with ice and strain into a cocktail glass.

CAROLINA

3   oz. Centenario or Aged Tequila
1   oz. Heavy Cream
1½ tsp. Grenadine
1   Egg White
Several drops Vanilla Extract

Shake with ice and strain into an Old-fashioned glass. Dust with cinnamon. Top with a cherry.

CARROL COCKTAIL

1½ oz. Brandy
¾   oz. Sweet Vermouth

Stir with ice and strain into a cocktail glass. Serve with a cherry.

CARTHUSIAN COOLER

1   oz. Yellow Chartreuse
1   oz. Bourbon

Mix in a highball glass. Fill with soda and ice.

CARUSO

1½ oz. Gin
1   oz. Dry Vermouth
½   oz. Green Creme de Menthe

Stir with ice and strain into a cocktail glass.

> To the men I've loved,
> To the men I've kissed;
> My heartfelt apologies
> To the men I've missed.

CASA BLANCA

2   oz. Rum
1½ tsp. Lime Juice
1½ tsp. Triple Sec or Orange Curacao
1½ tsp. Maraschino Liqueur

Shake with ice and strain into a cocktail glass.

CASA BLANCA SPECIAL

2   oz. Dark Rum
3   tsp. Sugar Syrup
3   tsp. Lime Juice
1   tsp. each of Cointreau, Cherry-flavored Brandy and Grenadine
1-2 dashes Angostura Bitters

Shake with ice and strain into an Old-fashioned glass. Serve with an orange slice and a cherry.

CASEY'S CANNONBALL

1½ oz. Okolehao
1   dash Curacao

Put ice cubes into a goblet or an Old-fashioned glass and add the Okolehao and Curacao. Stir lightly and garnish with an olive.

CASINO COCKTAIL NO. 1

2   dashes Orange Bitters
¼   tsp. Maraschino Liqueur
¼   tsp. Lemon Juice
2   oz. Gin

Shake with ice and strain into a cocktail glass. Serve with a cherry.

CASINO COCKTAIL NO. 2

½   oz. Gin
½   oz. Apple Brandy
¼   oz. Plum Brandy
¼   oz. Sweet Vermouth
1   dash Cointreau

Shake with ice and strain into a cocktail glass.

CASON COCKTAIL

¼ oz. Grenadine
¼ oz. Swedish Punch
¼ oz. Calvados
¼ oz. Lemon Juice
1 oz. Gin

Shake with ice and strain into a cocktail glass.

CASSISCO

1½ oz. Brandy
1 tbsp. Creme de Cassis

Place 2 ice cubes into a highball glass and add Creme de Cassis and Brandy. Fill with soda and serve.

CASSIS COCKTAIL

1 oz. Whisky
½ oz. Dry Vermouth
2 tsp. Creme de Cassis

Shake with ice and strain into a cocktail glass. Serve with a cherry.

CASSIS KIRSCH HIGHBALL

1½ oz. Creme de Cassis
1 oz. Kirschwasser

Pour into a highball glass. Fill with soda and ice. Stir briskly.

CASSISMAN

1½ oz. Bourbon
½ oz. Dry Vermouth
½ oz. Creme de Cassis

Stir with ice and strain into a cocktail glass.

CASSISODA

1½ oz. Creme de Cassis
1 dash Angostura Bitters

Mix in a highball glass. Fill with soda and ice.

CASTLE DIP COCKTAIL

1 oz. Apple Jack
1 oz. White Creme de Menthe
3 dashes Pernod

Shake with ice and strain into a cocktail glass.

> Here's to us that are here, to you that are there, and the rest of us everywhere.
> — Rudyard Kipling

CASTLE SPECIAL

2 oz. Dark Rum
1½ tsp. Lime Juice
A few drops of Curacao
A few drops of Rock Candy Syrup

Shake with ice and strain into a cocktail glass. Add ice. Decorate with mint leaves.

CATALINA AT 5 O'CLOCK

2 tbsp. Pineapple Juice
2 tbsp. Orange Juice
2 tbsp. White Orange-flavored Liqueur
2 tbsp. Brandy
2 tbsp. Zinfandel
½ tsp. Sugar

Pour first five ingredients into a Collins glass. Add cracked ice and stir well. Add a sprinkling of sugar. Garnish with a mint sprig and an orange wheel.

CATAMARAN

2 oz. Pineapple Juice
1 oz. Lemon Juice
½ tsp. Sugar
1 oz. Vodka
1 oz. Gold Rum
1 dash Grenadine

Blend with ice and strain into a Collins glass. Garnish with fruit.

CATERPILLAR NO. 1

1½ oz. Whisky
½ oz. Grape Juice
1 dash Angostura

Shake with ice and strain into a cocktail glass.

CATERPILLAR NO. 2

1½ oz. Bourbon
¾ oz. Grape Juice
1 dash Angostura Bitters

Shake with ice and strain into a cocktail glass.

CAT'S EYE

1½ oz. Gin
½ oz. Dry Vermouth
¼ oz. Kirsch
¼ oz. Cointreau
1 dash Lemon Juice

Stir with ice and strain into a cocktail glass.

CAUCASIAN

2 oz. Vodka
½ oz. Cointreau
1 dash Blue Vegetable Coloring
or
½ oz. Blue Curacao in place of Cointreau

Stir with ice and strain into a cocktail glass.

CAVALIER

1 oz. Galliano
½ oz. Tequila
1 oz. Orange Juice
½ oz. Cream

Shake with ice and strain into a cocktail glass.

> I thank you for your welcome which was cordial, And your cordial which was welcome.

CECIL PICK-ME-UP

2-3 oz. Brandy
1 tsp. Sugar
1 Egg Yolk

Shake with ice and strain into a cocktail glass. Fill with chilled Champagne.

CEMENT BOOT

1/5 oz. Creme de Cassis
1/5 oz. Light Creme de Cacao
1/5 oz. Green Creme de Menthe
1/5 oz. Tia Maria
1/5 oz. Cognac

Pour carefully, in order given, into a pony glass so that each ingredient floats on the preceding one without mixing.

CEON DE PAU COCKTAIL

1 oz. Dry Vermouth
¾ oz. Gin
½ oz. Armagnac
1 dash Izarra

Stir with ice and strain into a cocktail glass.

CE SOIR OU JAMAIS (TONIGHT OR NEVER)

1 oz. Gin
1 oz. Dry Vermouth
½ oz. Cognac

Stir with ice and strain into a cocktail glass.

C'EST VERT, MAIS JUSTE (GREEN BUT RIGHT)

1 oz. Gin
¾ oz. Green Creme de Menthe
¾ oz. Cognac
1 dash Bitters

Shake with ice and strain into a cocktail glass.

CEYLON

1 oz. Brandy
1 oz. Dry Sherry
½ oz. Triple Sec
¾ oz. Dry Vermouth
½ oz. Lemon Juice

Shake with ice and strain into a cocktail glass. Dust with cinnamon.

C.F.H.

1½ oz. Gin
½ oz. Calvados or Apple Brandy
½ oz. Swedish Punch
½ oz. Grenadine
½ oz. Lemon Juice

Shake with ice and strain into a cocktail glass.

CHABLIS AND BITTERS

1 dash Bitters
3 oz. chilled Chablis

Put Bitters into a pre-chilled cocktail glass. Add chilled Chablis. Serve with a lemon twist.

CHABLIS COOLER NO. 1

½ oz. Lemon Juice
½ oz. Grenadine
1 oz. Vodka

Mix in a Collins glass. Fill with Chablis and ice.

I have known many,
Liked a few,
Loved one —
Here's to you.

CHABLIS COOLER NO. 2

Fill a Collins glass with Chablis and ice. Add 1 dash lemon juice, 1 dash Falernum and a squirt of soda.

CHABLIS FIZZ

1 Egg White
1 tsp. Powdered Sugar
3 dashes Orange Bitters
2 oz. Grapefruit Juice
4 oz. Chablis

Shake with ice and strain into a Collins glass. Fill with soda.

CHAMPAGNE BAYOU

2 oz. Gin
2 tsp. Sugar Syrup
1 tsp. Lemon Juice

Shake with ice and strain into a cocktail glass. Fill with Champagne. (Flavored Brandies can be used instead of Gin.)

CHAMPAGNE BUCK

½ oz. Gin
¼ oz. Cherry-flavored Brandy
¼ oz. Orange Juice

Mix in a highball glass. Fill with chilled Champagne. Serve with a twist of orange peel.

CHAMPAGNE CASSIS HIGHBALL

3-4 cubes Ice
1 dash Creme de Cassis
2 dashes Kirsch
6 oz. chilled Champagne

Place ice cubes in a highball glass, add the Creme de Cassis and Kirsch, and fill with Champagne.

CHAMPAGNE COBBLER NO. 1

½ tsp. Lemon Juice
½ tsp. Curacao
Chilled Champagne

Fill a 10 oz. goblet two-thirds full with crushed ice. Add lemon juice and Curacao, stir and add an orange slice and a pineapple stick. Fill with Champagne.

CHAMPAGNE COBBLER NO. 2

1 oz. Brandy
1 oz. Curacao
1 tsp. Lemon Juice

Stir with ice and strain into a high-ball glass. Fill with crushed ice and Champagne. Garnish with fruit.

CHAMPAGNE COCKTAIL NO. 1

½ tsp. Sugar
1 dash Bitters
Champagne, well chilled

Put sugar in a champagne glass. Add Bitters and a twist of orange or lemon peel. Fill with well-chilled Champagne. Stir lightly.

> Here's a health to all those
> that we love,
> Here's a health to all those
> that love us.
> Here's a health to all those
> that love them that love
> those
> That love them that love
> those that love us.

CHAMPAGNE COCKTAIL NO. 2

1 oz. Southern Comfort
1 dash Angostura Bitters
4 oz. chilled Champagne

Pour the Southern Comfort into a champagne glass, add Bitters and Champagne. Serve with a lemon twist.

CHAMPAGNE COCKTAIL NO. 3

1 oz. Brandy
4 oz. chilled Champagne

Pour Brandy into a champagne glass, fill with Champagne. Serve with a twist of orange peel.

CHAMPAGNE COCKTAIL NO. 4

1 lump Sugar
2-3 dashes Angostura Bitters
1 oz. Cognac
4 oz. chilled Champagne

Place the sugar in a champagne glass and moisten thoroughly with Bitters. Add the Cognac and pour on the Champagne. (This cocktail is sometimes called an Ambrosia.)

CHAMPAGNE COCKTAIL NO. 5

2 small cubes Sugar
1 oz. Benedictine
1 oz. Creme de Cacao
4 oz. Champagne

Soak one cube of sugar in Benedictine and the other in Creme de Cacao and place them in the bottom of a champagne flute. Fill with chilled Champagne.

CHAMPAGNE COOLER

1 oz. Brandy
1 oz. Cointreau
6 oz. chilled Champagne
Mint sprigs

Half fill a 12 oz. highball glass with crushed ice. Pour in Brandy and Cointreau and fill with Champagne. Garnish with mint.

CHAMPAGNE DE MENTHE

1 tsp. Creme de Menthe
Dry Champagne, chilled

Put Creme de Menthe in a frosted champagne glass. Fill with chilled Champagne.

CHAMPAGNE DU MARCO

2 oz. Vanilla Ice Cream
1 tsp. Maraschino Liqueur
1 tsp. Orange Curacao
1 tsp. Cognac

Blend and pour into a highball glass. Fill with chilled Champagne. Garnish with fruit.

CHAMPAGNE FIZZ

2 oz. Orange Juice
Chilled Champagne

Pour orange juice into a highball glass. Add ice and fill with Champagne.

CHAMPAGNE FLIP

1 Egg Yolk
½ tsp. Sugar
3 oz. Champagne

Shake with ice and strain into a Sour glass. Float ¼ oz. Brandy on top.

CHAMPAGNE FRAISE

¼ oz. Raspberry Syrup or Grenadine
½ oz. Creme de Kirsch

Pour into a champagne glass. Fill with Champagne and serve with a strawberry.

CHAMPAGNE JULEP

4 sprigs of Mint
1 cube Sugar
2 oz. chilled Dry Champagne
2 oz. Brandy

Place mint sprigs and sugar cube in a Collins glass. Add a dash of water and crush ingredients. Fill the glass half full of cracked ice. Pour in Brandy. Fill with chilled Champagne. Garnish with a mint sprig. Serve with straws.

CHAMPAGNE LANCER

1   tsp. Sugar
3   dashes Bitters
2   oz. Brandy
Champagne, chilled

Place sugar, Bitters and Brandy in a Collins glass. Stir and add ice cubes. Fill with Champagne. Serve with a lemon twist.

CHAMPAGNE MANHATTAN

1   oz. Blended Whisky
¼   oz. Sweet Vermouth
1   dash Bitters

Stir with ice and strain into a cocktail glass. Fill with Champagne. Serve with a cherry.

CHAMPAGNE NORMANDE

1   oz. Calvados
1   dash Angostura Bitters
½   tsp. Sugar

Stir with ice and strain into a cocktail glass. Fill with Champagne.

CHAMPAGNE NUT

½   oz. Creme de Noyaux
½   oz. Creme de Cacao

Shake with ice and strain into a cocktail glass. Fill with Champagne. Garnish with an almond.

CHAMPAGNE OLD-FASHIONED

½   oz. Grand Marnier
1   dash Orange Bitters

Pour into an Old-fashioned glass, Fill with Champagne and ice. Serve with a cherry and an orange slice.

CHAMPAGNE PEACH DELIGHT

2   ripe Peach Slices
1   dash Pernod
1   tsp. Grenadine
1½   oz. Brandy
Crushed Ice
Extra Dry Champagne, chilled

Mash peach slices and shake with other ingredients (except Champagne). Strain into a Collins glass. Fill with Champagne.

CHAMPAGNE POLONAISE

½   oz. Blackberry-flavored Brandy
¼   oz. Cognac

Pour into a champagne glass. Fill with Champagne.

CHAMPAGNE PUNCH

1   oz. Orange Curacao
½   tsp. Sugar
½   oz. Lemon Juice

Mix in a highball glass. Fill with crushed ice and Champagne. (Any liqueur substitution may be made.)

CHAMPAGNE PUNCH

3   cups Lemon Juice
1   cup superfine Sugar
1   large block Ice
½   pint Maraschino Syrup
1   pint Curacao
1   pint Brandy
2   quarts Champagne
1   quart Club Soda
Fruits in season

Combine the lemon juice and sugar and stir until the sugar is dissolved. Place the ice in a punch bowl, add the sweetened lemon juice, the Maraschino, Curacao and Brandy. Pour in Champagne and club soda and stir gently. Decorate with fruits in season and serve in 4-oz. punch glasses. Makes about 40 servings.

CHAMPAGNE ST. MORITZ

1   tbsp. Gin
1   tbsp. Apricot-flavored Brandy
1   tbsp. Orange Juice

Shake with ice and strain into a champagne glass. Fill with Champagne and stir.

CHAMPAGNE SOUR

½   oz. Lemon Juice
½   tsp. Sugar

Mix in a Sour glass and fill with chilled Champagne. Serve with a lemon slice and a cherry.

CHAMPAGNE SUPREME COCKTAIL

2   dashes Orange-flavored Liqueur
2   dashes Aromatic Bitters
1½   oz. Brandy
Extra Dry Champagne, chilled

Pour first three ingredients into a mixing glass and stir gently with cracked ice. Strain into a chilled champagne glass and fill with chilled Champagne. Serve with a lemon twist.

CHAMPAGNE TANGO

1   oz. Tangerine-flavored Wine
3   oz. Brut Champagne, chilled

Pour the tangerine-flavored Wine and the Champagne into a pre-chilled champagne glass. Stir gently. Garnish with a tangerine or orange slice.

Here's a toast to the host
who carved the roast;
And a toast to the hostess —
may she never ''roast'' us.

CHAMPAGNE VELVET

Half fill a Collins glass with Stout and fill the other half with chilled Champagne.

CHAMPAGNE WHEEL

½ tsp. Lemon Juice
½ tsp. Orange-flavored Liqueur
Orange Wheel
Small Pineapple Stick
Extra Dry Champagne, well chilled

Fill a Collins glass two-thirds full with cracked ice. Add lemon juice and liqueur. Add the orange wheel and pineapple stick. Fill with Champagne. Stir gently. Serve with straws.

CHAMPERELLE

¼ oz. Orange Curacao
¼ oz. Anisette
¼ oz. Green Chartreuse
¼ oz. Cognac

Pour carefully, in order given, into a pony glass so that each ingredient floats on the preceding one without mixing.

CHAMPS ELYSEES COCKTAIL

1 oz. Brandy
½ oz. Yellow Chartreuse
½ tsp. Powdered Sugar
1 dash Bitters
Juice ¼ Lemon

Shake with ice and strain into a cocktail glass.

> Let us have wine and women, mirth and laughter,
> Sermons and soda-water the day after.
> — Byron

CHANCELLOR COCKTAIL

1¾ oz. Scotch
½ oz. Dry Vermouth
½ oz. Port
1 dash Peychaud's Bitters

Stir with ice and strain into a cocktail glass.

CHANGE OF PACE

(Note: Use any proportions to please yourself.)

Iced Tea
Fresh Orange Juice
Fresh Lime Juice
Sherry or Sauterne
Sugar to taste

Stir and pour over crushed ice in a Collins glass.

CHANTICLEER

2 oz. Gin
1¼ oz. Lemon Juice
½ oz. Grenadine
1 Egg White

Shake with ice and strain into a cocktail glass.

CHAPALA

1½ oz. Tequila
1 tbsp. Orange Juice
1 tbsp. Lemon Juice
1 dash Orange Flower Water
2 tsp. Grenadine

Shake with ice and strain into an Old-fashioned glass over ice cubes. Add a slice of orange.

CHAPARRA

1¼ oz. Rum
1¼ oz. Sweet Vermouth

Stir with ice and strain into a cocktail glass. Serve with a lemon twist.

CHAPEL HILL NO. 1

1½ oz. Bourbon Whisky
½ oz. Triple Sec or Orange Curacao
1 tbsp. Lemon Juice

Shake with ice and strain into a cocktail glass. Add a twist of orange peel.

CHAPEL HILL NO. 2

1 oz. Blackberry-flavored Brandy
½ oz. Orange Curacao
¾ oz. Lemon Juice

Shake with ice and strain into a cocktail glass. Serve with a lemon twist.

CHAPPELLE

2 slices fresh Pineapple
1 oz. Gin
1 oz. Sweet Vermouth
2 tbsp. Lime Juice

Muddle the pineapple in a cocktail shaker. Add the remaining ingredients and shake vigorously. Strain into a cocktail glass.

CHARLES

1½ oz. Brandy
1½ oz. Sweet Vermouth
1 dash Angostura or Orange Bitters

Stir with ice and strain into a cocktail glass.

CHARLESTON COCKTAIL NO. 1

¾ oz. Rum
¾ oz. Dubonnet
¾ oz. Gin

Shake with ice and strain into a cocktail glass.

CHARLESTON COCKTAIL NO. 2

½ oz. Gin
½ oz. Kirschwasser
½ oz. Dry Vermouth
½ oz. Sweet Vermouth
½ oz. Maraschino Liqueur
½ oz. Orange Curacao

Shake with ice and strain into a cocktail glass. Serve with a lemon twist.

CHARLEY COLLINS

¾ oz. Lime Juice
½ tsp. Sugar
1½ oz. Rum

Mix in a highball glass. Fill with soda and ice.

CHARLEY GOODLEG

¾ oz. Galliano
1½ oz. Tequila

Pour Tequila into a Collins glass and fill with orange juice and ice. Float Galliano on top. (This drink is sometimes called a Tequila Banger.)

CHARLEY PIE

1 oz. Gin
¾ oz. Sweet Vermouth
½ oz. Campari

Stir with ice and strain into a cocktail glass.

CHARLEY PUNCH

1½ oz. Vermouth
1½ oz. New England Rum
1 dash Orange Bitters
3 dashes Gum Syrup

Stir with ice and strain into a highball glass. Add the juice of half a lemon and serve with a slice of fresh peach.

CHARLIE CHAPLIN

1 oz. Sloe Gin
1 oz. Apricot-flavored Brandy
1 oz. Lemon Juice

Shake with ice and strain into an Old-fashioned glass over ice cubes.

> Here's health to the girl who will drink when she can
> Here's health to the girl who will rush the tin can
> And health to the girl who can dance the can can
> 'Tis the canny toast of an uncanny man.

CHARLIE LINDBERGH

1½ oz. Gin
1½ oz. Lillet
2 dashes Apricot-flavored Brandy
2 dashes Orange Juice

Stir with ice and strain into a cocktail glass. Serve with a lemon twist.

CHARLIE O COCKTAIL

1½ oz. Gin
½ oz. Dry Vermouth
¼ oz. Cointreau
¼ oz. Grand Marnier

Shake with ice and strain into a cocktail glass. Serve with a lemon twist.

CHARME DE PARIS

1 oz. Gin
1 oz. Sweet Vermouth
¼ oz. Anisette
½ oz. Rum

Stir with ice and strain into a cocktail glass.

CHARTREUSE CHAMPAGNE

½ oz. Green Chartreuse
½ oz. Cognac

Pour into a champagne glass. Fill with Champagne. Serve with a lemon twist.

CHARTREUSE COCKTAIL

1 oz. Bourbon
¾ oz. Yellow Chartreuse
¾ oz. Dry Vermouth

Stir with ice and strain into a cocktail glass. Serve with a cherry.

CHARTREUSECO FRAPPE

Pack a cocktail glass with crushed ice and over the ice pour:

1 oz. Yellow Chartreuse and
1 oz. Cognac

Serve with short straws.

CHARTREUSE COGNAC FRAPPE

1 tbsp. Yellow Chartreuse
1 tbsp. Cognac

Shake with ice and strain over crushed ice into a cocktail glass. Fill with lemon soda.

CHARTREUSE COOLER

1 oz. Green Chartreuse
3 oz. Orange Juice
½ oz. Lime Juice

Mix in a Collins glass. Fill with soda and ice. Serve with an orange slice.

CHATEAU D'ISSOGNE

1½ oz. Bourbon
1½ oz. Sweet Vermouth
1 tbsp. Aquavit
A few drops of Campari

Shake with ice and strain into a cocktail glass.

CHATHAM

1½ oz. Gin
½ oz. Ginger-flavored Brandy
½ oz. Lemon Juice

Shake with ice and strain into a cocktail glass.

CHATTERLEY

1½ oz. Gin
¾ oz. Dry Vermouth
½ oz. Orange Juice
½ oz. Curacao

Shake with ice and strain into a cocktail glass.

CHAUNCEY

¾ oz. Rye
¾ oz. Gin
½ oz. Sweet Vermouth
½ oz. Brandy
1 dash Orange Bitters

Stir with ice and strain into a cocktail glass.

CHEERIO COCKTAIL

1 oz. Bourbon
1 oz. Curacao
¼ oz. Maraschino Liqueur

Stir with ice and strain into a cocktail glass.

CHEERY CHERRY COCKTAIL

Juice 1 Lime
1½ oz. Brandy
1½ oz. Cherry Wine

Shake with ice and strain into a cocktail glass.

CHELSEA SIDECAR COCKTAIL

Juice ¼ Lemon
¾ oz. Triple Sec or Orange Curacao
¾ oz. Gin

Shake with ice and strain into a cocktail glass.

CHERIE

Juice 1 Lime
½ oz. Triple Sec or Orange Curacao
1 oz. Rum
½ oz. Cherry-flavored Brandy

Shake with ice and strain into a cocktail glass. Serve with a cherry.

CHERRY BANANA

1 oz. Cream
1 oz. Cheri-Suisse
½ oz. Creme de Bananes

Shake with ice and strain into a cocktail glass.

> The man that drinks hot
>   whisky punch,
> And goes to bed right
>   mellow,
> Lives as he ought to live
> And dies a jolly good fellow.

CHERRY BLOSSOM COCKTAIL NO. 1

1½ oz. Brandy
½ oz. Cherry-flavored Brandy
1½ tsp. Triple Sec or Orange Curacao
1½ tsp. Grenadine
2 tsp. Lemon Juice

Prepare a cocktail glass by moistening the rim with Cherry Liqueur and dipping it into sugar. Shake the above ingredients with ice and strain into the glass. Serve with a maraschino cherry.

CHERRY BLOSSOM COCKTAIL NO. 2

1½ oz. Gin
¼ oz. Raspberry Syrup
¼ oz. Orange Bitters
½ Egg White

Shake with ice and strain into a cocktail glass. Sprinkle nutmeg on top.

CHERRY CHAMPAGNE

½ oz. Cherry Heering

Pour into a champagne glass. Fill with Champagne and serve with a cherry.

CHERRY COBBLER

½ oz. Cherry Heering
½ oz. Lemon Juice
2 tsp. Creme de Cassis
1½ oz. Gin
½ tsp. Sugar

Mix in a cup. Fill the glass with shaved ice. Serve with a lemon wedge and a cherry.

CHERRY COCKTAIL

1¼ oz. Cherry Liqueur
1 oz. Dry Vermouth
1 dash Orange Bitters

Shake with ice and strain into a cocktail glass. Serve with a cherry.

CHERRY COOLER

2 oz. Cherry Vodka
Cola

Pour Cherry Vodka into a Collins glass over ice cubes. Fill with Cola, add a slice of lemon and stir.

CHERRY DAIQUIRI

1½	oz.	Rum
¾	oz.	Lime Juice
½	oz.	Cherry Liqueur
¼	oz.	Kirsch

Shake with ice and strain into a cocktail glass.

CHERRY DUBONNET HIGHBALL

2	tsp.	Lemon Juice
1	oz.	Orange Juice
2	tsp.	Cherry-flavored Brandy
3	oz.	Dubonnet

Stir with ice and strain into a highball glass. Fill with chilled soda.

CHERRY FIZZ

Juice ½ Lemon
2   oz. Cherry-flavored Brandy

Shake with ice and strain into a highball glass with two ice cubes. Fill with soda and decorate with a cherry.

CHERRY FLIP

1		Whole Egg
1	tsp.	Powdered Sugar
1½	oz.	Cherry-flavored Brandy
2	tsp.	Sweet Cream (if desired)

Shake with ice and strain into a flip glass. Sprinkle nutmeg on top.

CHERRY GINGER FRAPPE

Pack a cocktail glass with crushed ice and pour over the ice:

1	oz.	Cherry Liqueur
½	oz.	Ginger-flavored Brandy and
¼	oz.	Kirsch

Serve with a cherry.

CHERRY JULEP

1½	oz.	Gin
1	oz.	Cherry-flavored Brandy
½	oz.	Sloe Gin
1¼	oz.	Lemon Juice
1	tsp.	Sugar

Mix in a Collins glass. Fill glass with crushed ice. Add mint sprigs and soda to taste.

CHERRY MIXTURE

1½	oz.	Sweet Vermouth
1½	oz.	Dry Vermouth
1	dash	Maraschino Liqueur
1	dash	Angostura Bitters

Stir with ice and strain into a cocktail glass. Serve with a cherry.

CHERRY RUM

1¼	oz.	Rum
1½	tsp.	Cherry-flavored Brandy
1	tbsp.	Sweet Cream

Shake with ice and strain into a cocktail glass.

CHERRY RUM FIX

½	tsp.	Sugar dissolved in water
1½	oz.	Rum
½	oz.	Cherry Liqueur
½	oz.	Lemon Juice

Mix in a highball glass. Fill glass with crushed ice. Stir until glass frosts. Serve with a cherry and a lemon twist.

CHERRY RUM FIZZ

1¼	oz.	Lemon Juice
1	tsp.	Sugar
½	oz.	Cherry-flavored Brandy
1½	oz.	Rum

Shake with ice and strain into a Collins glass. Fill with soda and ice.

CHERRY SLING NO. 1

2	oz.	Cherry-flavored Brandy

Juice ½ Lemon
Sugar to taste

Serve in an Old-fashioned glass with ice cubes and stir. Add a twist of lemon peel.

CHERRY SLING NO. 2

1	oz.	Gin
¾	oz.	Cherry Heering
1	oz.	Lime Juice

Shake with ice and strain into a highball glass. Add soda to taste.

CHERRY VODKA

1½	oz.	Vodka
¾	oz.	Cherry-flavored Brandy
1	oz.	Lemon Juice

Shake with ice and strain into a cocktail glass.

CHERRY WINE COCKTAIL

¾	oz.	Danish Cherry Wine
¾	oz.	Vodka

Juice ½ Lime

Shake with ice and strain into a cocktail glass.

> Candy is dandy,
> But liquor is quicker.
> — Ogden Nash

CHEVALIER COCKTAIL

1	oz.	Brandy
1	dash	Angostura Bitters
½	oz.	Cointreau
1	oz.	Lemon Juice
2	tsp.	Sugar Syrup

Shake with ice and strain into a cocktail glass.

CHEVONEY

1	oz. Galliano
½	oz. Grand Marnier
½	oz. Vodka
1	scoop Vanilla Ice Cream

Blend with ice and strain into a Collins glass.

CHIANTI BREEZE

| 6 | oz. Chianti |

Fruit-flavored Soda (your choice), chilled

Pour Chianti over cracked ice in a Collins glass. Fill with soda.

CHICAGO

| 1½ | oz. Brandy |
| 1-2 | dashes Angostura Bitters |

A few drops Curacao
Powdered Sugar

Shake with ice and strain into a sugar-rimmed brandy glass. Fill with Champagne.

CHICAGO BOMB

2	oz. Vanilla Ice Cream
1	tsp. White Creme de Cacao
1	tsp. Green Creme de Menthe

Blend with ice at a high speed for a few seconds and strain into a cocktail glass.

CHICAGO COCKTAIL

2	oz. Brandy
1	dash Bitters
¼	tsp. Triple Sec or Orange Curacao

Prepare an Old-fashioned glass by rubbing a slice of lemon around the rim and dipping rim in sugar. Stir above ingredients with ice and strain into the prepared glass.

CHICAGO FIZZ

Juice ½ Lemon	
1	tsp. Powdered Sugar
1	Egg White
1	oz. Port
1	oz. Jamaica Rum

Shake with ice and strain into a highball glass over two cubes of ice. Fill with soda and stir.

CHICAGO MANHATTAN

2	oz. Early Times
½	oz. Sweet Vermouth
1	dash Bitters

Stir with ice and strain into a cocktail glass. Serve with a cherry.

CHICAGO MARTINI

| 2 | oz. Gin |
| ½ | oz. Scotch |

Stir with ice and strain into a cocktail glass. Serve with an olive.

CHI CHI

2	oz. Pineapple Juice
2	oz. Coconut Cream
1½	oz. Vodka
1	tsp. Coconut Snow (optional)

Blend with ice and strain into a Collins glass. Fill with crushed ice. Serve with a pineapple spear and a cherry.

CHIEF'S CALABASH

1	cup crushed Ice
2	oz. Okolehao
3	oz. Coconut Milk
1	tbsp. Orgeat Syrup

Blend with ice and strain into a double Old-fashioned glass. Serve with a pineapple stick.

CHILLED IRISH COFFEE

1	cup freshly brewed Coffee
¼	cup Heavy Cream
1	tsp. Sugar
2	tbsp. Whipped Cream
3	cubes Ice
2	oz. Irish Whisky

Nutmeg or Cinnamon

Combine coffee, cream and sugar, stir to dissolve the sugar and chill thoroughly. Put 1 tbsp. of whipped cream in a 14 oz. highball glass, fill with the coffee mixture, add ice cubes and Whisky. Top with the remaining tbsp. of whipped cream and dust with grated nutmeg or ground cinnamon. (Iced Irish: Use iced instead of hot coffee, and omit the heavy cream, ice cubes, nutmeg or cinnamon.)

CHILLY WILLY

1	Egg Yolk
1	tsp. Sugar
1	oz. Orange-flavored Liqueur
4	oz. Chianti

Mix egg yolk and sugar in small saucepan. Add Liqueur and Chianti. Heat well, stirring constantly. Serve in a preheated mug. Float a lemon wheel on top. Dust with cinnamon.

CHINA

2	oz. Golden Rum
½	oz. Orange Curacao
¼	oz. Grenadine
¼	oz. Passion Fruit Syrup
1	dash Angostura Bitters

Stir with ice and strain into a cocktail glass.

CHINA CLIPPER

1½	oz. Yellow Gin
½	oz. Dry Vermouth
1	dash Grapefruit Juice
2	dashes Orange Bitters

Stir with ice and strain into a cocktail glass. Serve with a lime garnish.

CHINATOWN

1	oz. Gin
¾	oz. Dry Vermouth
¾	oz. Sweet Vermouth
¼	oz. Brandy

Stir with ice and strain into a cocktail glass.

CHINESE COCKTAIL

1	tbsp. Grenadine
1½	oz. Jamaica Rum
1	dash Bitters
1	tsp. Maraschino Liqueur
1	tsp. Triple Sec or Orange Curacao

Shake with ice and strain into a cocktail glass.

CHIQUITA

1½	oz. Vodka
½	oz. Banana Liqueur
½	slice Banana
½	oz. Lime Juice
½	tsp. Sugar

Blend with ice and strain into a cocktail glass.

CHIQUITA PUNCH

1½	oz. Banana Liqueur
1½	oz. Orange Juice
1½	oz. Cream
½	oz. Grenadine

Blend with ice and strain into a highball glass. Serve with a banana slice and a cherry.

CHOCOLATE COCKTAIL NO. 1

1½	oz. Port
1½	tsp. Yellow Chartreuse
1	Egg Yolk
1	tsp. Powdered Sugar or
1	tsp. Chocolate, crushed

Shake with ice and strain into a flip glass.

CHOCOLATE COCKTAIL NO. 2

1	Egg Yolk
1	tsp. Sugar
1	oz. Yellow Chartreuse
1	oz. Maraschino Liqueur

Shake with ice and strain into a cocktail glass.

CHOCOLATE DAISY

Juice ½ Lemon	
½	tsp. Powdered Sugar
1	tsp. Raspberry Syrup or Grenadine
1½	oz. Brandy
1½	oz. Port

Shake with ice and strain into a stein or metal cup. Add ice cubes and decorate with fruit.

> Be merry while you can to-day,
> There may be no to-morrow.
> No man so sad who cannot find
> In ale a balm for sorrow.

CHOCOLATE FLIP NO. 1

1	Egg
1	tsp. Powdered Sugar
¾	oz. Sloe Gin
¾	oz. Brandy
2	tsp. Sweet Cream (if desired)

Shake with ice and strain into a flip glass. Sprinkle nutmeg on top.

CHOCOLATE FLIP NO. 2

1½	oz. Port
¼	oz. Yellow Chartreuse
1	Egg
1	tsp. crushed Chocolate or Sugar to taste

Shake with ice and strain into a cocktail glass.

CHOCOLATE ORANGE FRAPPE

1	oz. Creme de Cacao
1	oz. Orange Juice
¼	oz. Galliano

Fill a cocktail glass with crushed ice. Mix ingredients together and pour over ice in the cocktail glass.

CHOCOLATE PEPPERMINT

| 1½ | oz. Scotch Whisky |
| 1 | oz. Chocolate Peppermint Liqueur |

Shake with ice and strain into a cocktail glass.

CHOCOLATE RUM

1	oz. Rum
½	oz. Creme de Cacao
½	oz. White Creme de Menthe
1	tbsp. Sweet Cream
1	tsp. 151-proof Rum

Shake with ice and strain into an Old-fashioned glass over ice cubes.

CHOCOLATE SOLDIER COCKTAIL

Juice ½ Lime	
¾	oz. Dubonnet
1½	oz. Gin

Shake with ice and strain into a cocktail glass.

CHOCOLATE SUPREME

1	Egg Yolk
1	tsp. Chocolate, crushed
¾	oz. Yellow Chartreuse
2½	oz. Port

Shake with ice and strain into a large cocktail glass. Add ice.

CHOKER COCKTAIL

2 oz. Scotch Whisky
1 oz. Pernod
1 dash Angostura Bitters

Shake with ice and strain into a cocktail glass.

CHORUS LADY

¾ oz. Gin
¾ oz. Dry Vermouth
¾ oz. Sweet Vermouth
¾ oz. Orange Juice

Stir with ice and strain into a cocktail glass. Serve with an orange slice and a cherry.

CHRISTOPHE

1½ oz. Haitian Rum
¾ oz. Gin
¼ tsp. Sugar

Stir with ice and strain into a cocktail glass. Serve with a lime wedge.

CHRISTOPHER'S MOTHER

2 oz. Gin
2 tsp. Orange Juice
1 tsp. Lemon Juice
A few drops of Whisky

Shake with ice and strain into a fizz glass. Add ice.

CHRYSANTHEMUM

1½ oz. Dry Vermouth
1½ oz. Benedictine
3 dashes Pernod

Stir with ice and strain into a cocktail glass. Serve with a twist of orange peel.

CHURCHILL

1½ oz. Scotch
½ oz. Cointreau
½ oz. Sweet Vermouth
¼ oz. Lime Juice

Stir with ice and strain into a cocktail glass.

CHURCH PARADE

2 oz. Gin
1 oz. Dry Vermouth
1 dash Curacao
½ oz. Orange Juice

Stir with ice and strain into a cocktail glass. Serve with a cherry.

CIDER EGGNOG

1 Egg
1 tsp. Powdered Sugar
½ cup Milk

Shake with ice and strain into a Collins glass. Then fill the glass with sweet cider and stir. Sprinkle nutmeg on top.

CIDER FIZZ

1 oz. Gold Rum
¼ oz. Lemon Juice
¼ tsp. Sugar
2 oz. Apple Cider

Shake with ice and strain into a highball glass. Fill with soda or ginger ale and ice.

CIDER NECTAR HIGHBALL

½ oz. Brandy
½ oz. Lemon Juice
½ tsp. Sugar Syrup

Stir with ice and strain into a highball glass. Fill with ice and cider.

CIDER SMASH

2 oz. Brandy
1 tbsp. Powdered Sugar
Pineapple Chunks
Lemon Slices
Cider

Dissolve the sugar with Brandy in a highball glass. Add fruit slices plus plenty of crushed ice. Fill with cider and stir gently.

CIGALON

1½ oz. Rum
1 oz. Sweet Vermouth
¼ oz. Maraschino Liqueur
1 dash Orange Bitters

Stir with ice and strain into a cocktail glass.

CINCINNATI

Fill a highball glass half full with Beer. Fill up with chilled soda and serve.

CINZANO

3 oz. Cinzano Vermouth
2 dashes Orange Bitters
2 dashes Angostura Bitters

Stir with ice and strain into a cocktail glass. Serve with a twist of orange peel.

CIRCUS RICKEY

Juice ½ Lime
1 cube Ice
½ tsp. Grenadine
1½ oz. Gin

Fill an 8 oz. highball glass with soda and stir. Leave lime in glass.

CITRIC FRAPPE

Juice ½ Lemon
1 tbsp. Sugar
4 oz. Orange Juice
4 oz. Tokay

Combine ingredients. Stir until sugar is dissolved. Fill a Collins glass half full with crushed ice. Pour mixture over ice.

CITY SLICKER

2 oz. Brandy
1 oz. Curacao
1 dash Pernod

Shake with ice and strain into a cocktail glass.

CLAMATO COCKTAIL

1½	oz. Vodka
1	oz. Clam Juice
3	oz. Tomato Juice

Shake with ice, strain and serve over ice cubes in a large Old-fashioned glass.

CLAM JUICE COCKTAIL

1	tsp. Catsup
1	pinch Celery Salt
1	dash Tabasco Sauce
4	oz. Clam Juice
1½	oz. Vodka

Shake with ice and strain into a double Old-fashioned glass.

CLARET COBBLER

1	dash Maraschino Liqueur
1	tsp. Sugar
1	tsp. Lemon Juice
4	oz. Claret

Half fill a Collins glass with crushed ice; add Maraschino Liqueur, sugar and lemon juice and stir. Pour in the Claret. Decorate with orange and pineapple garnish.

CLARET COCKTAIL

1	oz. Dry Red Wine
1	oz. Brandy
¼	oz. Orange Curacao
¼	oz. Lemon Juice
1	dash Anisette

Stir with ice and strain into a cocktail glass. Serve with a twist of orange peel.

CLARET COOLER

4	oz. Red Wine
½	oz. Brandy
½	oz. Lemon Juice

Mix in a Collins glass. Fill with soda and ice. Float ½ oz. Grenadine or Orange Curacao on top. Serve with a lemon twist and an orange peel.

CLARET FLIP

2	oz. Claret
1	Egg
1	tsp. Sugar
1	dash Angostura Bitters

Shake with ice and strain into a flip glass. Sprinkle nutmeg on top.

CLARET LEMONADE

4	tbsp. Lemon Juice
2	tsp. Sugar
6	oz. crushed Ice
8	oz. chilled Claret or other Dry Red Wine

Combine lemon juice and sugar in a Collins glass and stir until sugar is dissolved. Add ice, pour in Claret and garnish with a lemon slice. Serve with a straw.

CLARET PUNCH

| 1½ | oz. Lemon Juice |
| ½ | tsp. Sugar |

Mix in a highball glass. Fill with crushed ice and Claret. Garnish with fruit and a mint sprig. Serve with a straw.

CLARET RUM COOLER

3	oz. Claret
1	oz. Rum
½	oz. Falernum

Mix in a Collins glass. Fill with soda and ice.

> Old wood to burn,
> Old books to read,
> Old wine to drink,
> Old friends to trust.
> — Francis Bacon

CLARET SANGAREE

| ¾ | oz. Brandy |
| ½ | tsp. Sugar |

Mix in a cup. Fill with ice and Claret. Sprinkle nutmeg on top.

CLARET SPRITZER

| 2 | oz. Claret |
| 4 | oz. chilled Soda |

Fill a Collins glass with ice cubes. Pour in Wine and soda. Garnish with an orange wheel.

CLARIDGE COCKTAIL

¾	oz. Gin
¾	oz. Dry Vermouth
1	tbsp. Apricot-flavored Brandy
1	tbsp. Triple Sec or Orange Curacao

Stir with ice and strain into a cocktail glass.

CLASSIC COCKTAIL

Juice	¼ Lemon
1½	tsp. Curacao
1½	tsp. Maraschino Liqueur
1	oz. Brandy

Prepare the rim of an Old-fashioned glass by rubbing with lemon and dipping into sugar. Shake ingredients with ice and strain into prepared glass.

CLAYTON'S SPECIAL

1½	oz. Light Rum
¾	oz. Cola
¾	oz. Sirop de Citron

Shake with ice and strain into a cocktail glass.

CLIMAX

1	Egg White
1½	oz. Applejack
¼	oz. Grenadine
½	oz. Lemon Juice
¼	oz. Dry Vermouth
½	tsp. Sugar

Shake with ice and strain into a cocktail glass. Sprinkle nutmeg on top.

CLIQUET

1½ oz. Bourbon
2 oz. Orange Juice
½ oz. Rum

Shake with ice and strain into a cocktail glass.

CLOAK AND DAGGER

Fill a highball glass with ice cubes. Add 2 oz. of Jamaica Rum and fill with Cola. Add a generous twist of orange peel and a dash of orange bitters.

CLOISTER

1½ oz. Gin
½ oz. Grapefruit Juice
¼ oz. Lemon Juice
¼ oz. Yellow Chartreuse

Shake with ice and strain into a cocktail glass.

CLOUDY SKY RICKEY

1½ oz. Sloe Gin
½ oz. Lime Juice
¼ oz. Grenadine

Mix in a highball glass. Fill with soda and ice. Serve with a piece of lime shell.

CLOUDY WITH SHOWERS

1 oz. Gin
¾ oz. Sweet Vermouth
¾ oz. Orange Juice
¼ oz. Orange Curacao

Shake with ice and strain into a cocktail glass.

CLOVE COCKTAIL

1 oz. Sweet Vermouth
½ oz. Sloe Gin
½ oz. Muscatel

Stir with ice and strain into a cocktail glass.

CLOVER CLUB COCKTAIL

Juice ½ Lemon
2 tsp. Grenadine
1 Egg White
1½ oz. Gin

Shake with ice and strain into a cocktail glass.

CLOVER CLUB ROYAL

1 oz. Lemon Juice
½ oz. Grenadine
1 Egg Yolk
1½ oz. Gin
½ tsp. Sugar

Shake with ice and strain into a cocktail glass.

CLOVER LEAF COCKTAIL

Juice 1 Lime
2 tsp. Grenadine
1 Egg White
1½ oz. Gin

Shake with ice and strain into a cocktail glass. Serve with a mint leaf on top.

CLUB COCKTAIL NO. 1

1½ oz. Gin
¾ oz. Sweet Vermouth
¼ oz. Yellow Chartreuse

Stir with ice and strain into a cocktail glass. Add a cherry or an olive.

CLUB COCKTAIL NO. 2

1½ oz. Brandy
1 dash Orange Bitters
¼ oz. Maraschino Liqueur
¼ oz. Pineapple Syrup

Stir with ice and strain into a cocktail glass.

CLUB COCKTAIL NO. 3

1 tsp. Sugar
2 dashes Angostura Bitters

Mix in a highball glass. Fill with soda and ice.

CLUB FORREST

1 Egg Yolk
½ tsp. Sugar
¾ oz. Port

Shake with ice and strain into a cocktail glass.

CLUB KAHLUA

1½ oz. Kahlua

Pour into a Collins glass. Fill with soda and ice.

CLUB MARTINI

1½ oz. Gin
2 tsp. Sweet Vermouth

Shake with ice and strain into a Martini glass. Serve straight up with an olive.

COBRA

1½ oz. Sloe Gin

Pour into a Collins glass. Fill with ice and orange juice.

COCICE

1½ oz. White Rum
1   oz. Coconut Milk
1   tsp. Sugar Syrup
6   oz. crushed Ice

Blend at a high speed for 25 seconds. Pour into a highball glass.

COCKNEY

¾   oz. Gin
¾   oz. Champagne
¾   oz. Lemon Juice
½   tsp. Sugar

Stir with ice and strain into a cocktail glass.

COCKTAIL A LA NOIX DE COCO

1½ oz. Brandy
1½ oz. Madeira Wine
2   dashes Angostura Bitters
3   oz. Coconut Milk

Shake with ice and strain into a Collins glass.

COCKTAIL MAISON

1   oz. Gin
¾   oz. Dry Vermouth
¾   oz. Creme de Cassis

Stir with ice and strain into a cocktail glass.

COCKTAIL PUNCH

1   oz. Sherry
1   oz. Brandy
1   oz. Sauterne

Mix in a Collins glass. Fill with ice and Champagne.

COCOA RICKEY

Place a scoop of vanilla Ice Cream in a large highball glass. Add 1½ oz. Creme de Cacao, 1 oz. milk and fill with soda. Stir and add sugar to taste.

COCO LOCO (CRAZY COCONUT)

Fresh green Coconut
2   oz. Tequila

Cut the top off a green coconut with a large knife and pour in the Tequila. Sip through a straw. If the coconut has abundant liquid, add more Tequila. (Gin, Rum, or Vodka may be substituted for Tequila.)

> I have eaten your bread and salt,
> I have drunk your water and wine;
> The deaths ye died I have watched beside
> And the lives ye lived were mine.
>
> — *Rudyard Kipling*

COCOMACOQUE

Juice ½ Lemon
2   oz. Pineapple Juice
2   oz. Orange Juice
1½ oz. Rum
2   oz. Burgundy

Shake all ingredients except wine. Pour into a Collins glass over ice cubes and top with Wine. Add a pineapple stick.

COCONUT GIN

1½ oz. Gin
½   oz. Lemon Juice
¼   oz. Maraschino Syrup
¼   oz. Coconut Cream

Shake with ice and strain into a cocktail glass.

COCONUT GROVE

¾   oz. Gin
¾   oz. Dry Vermouth
¾   oz. Sweet Vermouth

Stir with ice and strain into a cocktail glass.

COCONUT GROVE COOLER

1½ oz. Bourbon
2   tsp. each of Orange Juice, Lemon Juice, Orange Curacao, Grenadine, and Pineapple Juice
1   tsp. Passionola

Shake with ice and strain over crushed ice into a Collins glass. Decorate with orange and pineapple slices, a cherry and a mint sprig.

COCONUT PUNCH

1½ oz. Demerara 151-proof Rum
2   oz. Coconut Milk
½   oz. Lemon Juice
½   tsp. Sugar

Shake with ice and strain into a Collins glass.

COCONUT TEQUILA

1½ oz. Tequila
½   oz. Coconut Cream
½   oz. Lemon Juice
¼   oz. Maraschino Liqueur

Shake with ice and strain into a cocktail glass.

COCTEL VERACRUZANA

1½ oz. Dark Rum
1   oz. Dry Vermouth
1   oz. Pineapple Juice

Shake with ice and strain into a cocktail glass.

COEXISTENCE COLLINS

1½ oz. Vodka
½   oz. Lemon Juice
½   tsp. Sugar
¼   oz. Kummel

Shake with ice and strain into a Collins glass. Fill with soda and ice. Serve with a lemon twist.

COFFEE ALEXANDER

1 oz. Brandy
1 oz. Coffee Liqueur
1 oz. Cream

Shake with ice and strain into a cocktail glass.

COFFEE BLAZER

1 tbsp. Coffee Liqueur
1 tbsp. Cognac
Sugar
Lemon slice
Hot Coffee
Whipped Cream

Warm the Coffee Liqueur and Cognac over a low flame. Line the rim of an Old-fashioned glass with the juice of the lemon slice; press the rim in sugar, and drop the lemon slice in the glass. Warm the glass to melt the sugar, pour in the warmed liquor and ignite. Pour in the coffee and stir well. Garnish with whipped cream.

COFFEE COBBLER

1½ oz. Brandy
¾ oz. Port

Stir with ice and strain into a highball glass. Fill with shaved ice.

COFFEE COCKTAIL NO. 1

1 Egg
1 tsp. Powdered Sugar
1 oz. Port
1 oz. Brandy

Shake with ice and strain into a flip glass. Sprinkle nutmeg on top.

COFFEE COCKTAIL NO. 2

¾ oz. Apple Brandy
1 Egg Yolk
¾ oz. Port

Shake with ice and strain into a cocktail glass. Sprinkle nutmeg on top.

COFFEE COCKTAIL NO. 3

1 oz. Brandy
1 oz. Coffee
½ oz. Cointreau

Shake with ice and strain into a cocktail glass.

COFFEE COCKTAIL NO. 4

1½ oz. Brandy
¾ oz. Port
¼ oz. Orange Curacao
1 Egg Yolk
½ tsp. Sugar

Shake with ice and strain into a cocktail glass. Sprinkle nutmeg on top.

COFFEE COOLER NO. 1

Freeze coffee in an ice cube tray. Fill a highball glass with crushed coffee cubes. Pour Galliano over cubes. Serve with a lemon twist.

COFFEE COOLER NO. 2

1½ oz. Vodka
1 oz. Cream
1 oz. Coffee Liqueur
1 tsp. Sugar
4 oz. cold black Coffee
1 small scoop Coffee Ice Cream

Shake with ice and strain into a Collins glass.

COFFEE DELIGHT

½ oz. Brandy
½ oz. Cream Sherry
3 tbsp. Chocolate Ice Cream
Strong Coffee

Put Brandy, Sherry and chocolate ice cream into a preheated mug. Fill with hot coffee.

COFFEE EGGNOG

1 Egg
1½ oz. Coffee Liqueur
½ tsp. Sugar
3 oz. Milk
1 oz. Coffee

Shake with ice and strain into a Collins glass. Fill with ice. Sprinkle nutmeg on top.

COFFEE FILLIP (Iced)

8 oz. Iced Coffee
1½ oz. Tia Maria

Mix in a Collins glass. Fill with ice and stir.

COFFEE FLIP

1 Egg
1 tsp. Powdered Sugar
1 oz. Coffee-flavored Brandy
1 oz. Port
2 tsp. Sweet Cream (if desired)

Shake with ice and strain into a flip glass. Sprinkle nutmeg on top.

COFFEE GRAND

¾ oz. Grand Marnier
¾ oz. Coffee Liqueur
¾ oz. Orange Juice

Pour over crushed ice into a cocktail glass. Serve with an orange slice.

COFFEE GRASSHOPPER

¾ oz. Coffee-flavored Brandy
¾ oz. White Creme de Menthe
¾ oz. Sweet Cream

Shake with ice and strain into an Old-fashioned glass over ice cubes.

COFFEE KIRSCH

1 oz. Kirsch
1 Egg White
4 oz. Coffee
A pinch of Sugar

Shake with ice and strain into an Old-fashioned glass. Add ice.

COFFEE MERGER

1 oz. Brandy
1 oz. Cointreau
1 oz. strong chilled black Coffee

Shake with ice and strain into a cocktail glass.

COFFEE NERO

1 oz. Galliano
Hot Coffee
Whipped Cream

Coat the inside rim of a fizz glass with sugar and pour in the Galliano; flame, and rotate the glass until the sugar coating is brown. Add hot coffee and top with whipped cream.

COFFEE ROIANO

1½ oz. Roiano
2 tsp. Coffee Liqueur
2 tsp. Cream
3 oz. crushed Ice

Blend at a low speed for 15 seconds. Strain into an Old-fashioned glass.

COFFEE ROY

¾ oz. Roiano
¾ oz. Coffee Liqueur
¾ oz. Cream

Shake with ice and strain into a cocktail glass.

COFFEE ROYALE

¾ oz. Metaxa
¾ oz. Galliano

Pour into a fizz glass. Fill with hot black coffee.

COFFEE SOUR

1½ oz. Coffee-flavored Brandy
1 oz. Lemon Juice
1 tsp. Powdered Sugar
½ Egg White

Shake with ice and strain into a Sour glass.

COGNAC COCKTAIL

1 oz. Brandy
1 oz. Lemon Juice
½ oz. Cointreau
1 dash Orange Bitters

Stir with ice and strain into a cocktail glass. Serve with a lemon twist.

COGNAC COUPLING

2 oz. Brandy
1 oz. Port
½ oz. Pernod
1 tsp. Lemon Juice

Shake with ice and strain into an Old-fashioned glass over ice cubes.

COGNAC HIGHBALL

2 oz. Cognac or Brandy

Pour into a highball glass over ice cubes and fill with ginger ale or soda. Add a twist of lemon peel, if desired, and stir.

COGNAC MINT FRAPPE

1 oz. Cognac
¾ oz. White Creme de Menthe

Pour over crushed ice into a cocktail glass. Serve with a mint sprig.

COGNAC WITH CASSIS

2-3 cubes Ice
2 oz. Cognac
1 tsp. Creme de Cassis

Put ice cubes into an Old-fashioned glass and pour in the Cognac. Add Creme de Cassis and stir lightly.

COINTREAU COCKTAIL

¾ oz. Gin
¾ oz. Rum
¾ oz. Cointreau

Shake with ice and strain into a cocktail glass.

COKE AND DAGGER

2 oz. Jamaica Rum
1-2 drops Orange Bitters
Coca-Cola

Stir with ice and strain into a cup. Fill with ice and Cola. Stir gently and serve with an orange twist.

COLA ABSENT

1 oz. Pernod

Pour into a highball glass. Fill with cola and ice.

COLA COCKTAIL

1 oz. Gin
1 oz. Orange Curacao
1 dash Orange Bitters

Stir with ice and strain into a cocktail glass.

COLA TONIC COCKTAIL

1 oz. Gin
2 oz. Orange Curacao
2 dashes Orange Bitters

Shake with ice and strain into a cocktail glass.

COLD DECK COCKTAIL

½ tsp. White Creme de Menthe
½ oz. Sweet Vermouth
1 oz. Brandy

Stir with ice and strain into a cocktail glass.

COLD IRISH COFFEE

1½ oz. Irish Whisky
½ oz. Irish Mist

Mix in a Collins glass. Fill with ice and coffee soda (or cold coffee and soda). Top with whipped cream. Float Dark Creme de Cacao on top.

COLD TODDY

½ tsp. Sugar dissolved in
½ oz. Lemon Juice
1½ oz. Bourbon (or other whisky)

Mix in an Old-fashioned glass. Fill with ice and water. Add a cinnamon stick and sprinkle nutmeg on top.

COLD WINE FLIP

3 oz. Claret, Burgundy or Sherry
1 Egg
1 tsp. Powdered Sugar

Shake with ice and strain into a flip glass. Sprinkle nutmeg on top.

COLONEL APPLETON COCKTAIL

1 oz. Brandy
¾ oz. Rum
½ oz. White Creme de Menthe

Shake with ice and strain into a cocktail glass. Serve with a mint sprig.

> May you always be happy
> And live at your ease,
> Get a kind husband
> And do as you please.

COLONEL BATISTA

1½ oz. Rum
1 oz. Lemon Juice
1 tsp. Sugar
½ oz. Dry Vermouth

Shake with ice and strain into a cocktail glass.

COLONEL COCKTAIL

2 oz. Bourbon
½ oz. Apricot-flavored Brandy
½ oz. Grapefruit Juice
¼ tsp. Sugar

Stir with ice and strain into a cocktail glass. Serve with a lemon twist.

COLONEL'S BIG ONE

1 oz. Cointreau
1 oz. Gin
Juice ½ Lime

Mix in a Collins glass, leaving the lime shell in the bottom. Fill with ice and Champagne.

COLONIAL COCKTAIL

½ oz. Grapefruit Juice
1 tsp. Maraschino Liqueur
1½ oz. Gin

Shake with ice and strain into a cocktail glass. Serve with an olive.

COLONY

1 oz. Gin
¾ oz. Dry Vermouth
1 dash Orange Bitters
½ oz. Liqueur d'Or

Stir with ice and strain into a cocktail glass.

COLORADO

¾ oz. Cherry-flavored Brandy
1 oz. Cream
¾ oz. Kirschwasser

Shake with ice and strain into a cocktail glass.

COLUMBIA

1½ oz. Light Rum
½ oz. Raspberry Syrup or Grenadine
½ oz. Lemon Juice

Shake with ice and strain into a cocktail glass.

COLUMBIA COLLINS

1½ oz. Rum
½ tsp. Brown Sugar
½ oz. Lemon Juice

Mix in a Collins glass. Fill glass with ice and grapefruit juice. Serve with a mint sprig, an orange slice and a lemon wedge.

COLUMBIA SKIN

1 tbsp. Water
2 cubes Sugar
2 tbsp. Lemon Juice
1 tsp. Curacao
3 oz. Rum

Combine all ingredients in a small, heavy saucepan and heat until the contents foam. Do not boil. Serve in a warmed fizz glass. (Brandy, Gin or Whisky may be used instead of Rum.)

COMBO

2½ oz. Dry Vermouth
1 tsp. Brandy
½ tsp. Triple Sec or Orange Curacao
½ tsp. Powdered Sugar
1 dash Bitters

Shake with ice and strain into an Old-fashioned glass over ice cubes.

COME AGAIN

2 oz. Gin
2 dashes Peach Bitters
2 sprigs fresh Mint

Shake with shaved ice and strain into a cocktail glass.

COMFORTABLE BANG

1½ oz. Vodka

Pour into a Collins glass. Fill with ice and orange juice. Float ½ oz. Southern Comfort on top.

COMFORTABLE SCREW

1½ oz. Southern Comfort

Pour into a Collins glass. Fill with ice and orange juice.

COMFORTER

1½ oz. Scotch
½   oz. Lemon Juice
¼   tsp. Sugar
¼   oz. Cointreau

Shake with ice and strain into a cocktail glass.

COMMANDO

½   oz. Cointreau
1   oz. Lime Juice
2   oz. Bourbon
½   oz. Pernod

Stir with ice and strain into a cocktail glass.

COMMERCIAL CLUB GIN OLD-FASHIONED

1½ oz. Gin
2   dashes Grenadine
1   dash Bitters
½   oz. Coconut Cream
¼   oz. Orange Curacao

Shake with ice and strain into an Old-fashioned glass.

COMMODORE COCKTAIL NO. 1

½   tsp. Sugar
1   dash Lemon Juice
1   Egg White
1½ oz. Rum
1   dash Grenadine

Shake with ice and strain into a cocktail glass.

COMMODORE COCKTAIL NO. 2

Juice ½ Lime or ¼ Lemon
1   tsp. Powdered Sugar
2   dashes Orange Bitters
1½ oz. Whisky

Shake with ice and strain into a cocktail glass.

COMMODORE COCKTAIL NO. 3

1   oz. Lemon Juice
1   oz. Bourbon
1   oz. Creme de Cacao
1   dash Grenadine

Shake with ice and strain into a cocktail glass.

COMMODORE COCKTAIL NO. 4

1½ oz. Rye Whisky
½   oz. Lime Juice
¼   oz. Orange Juice
½   oz. Strawberry Liqueur
1   dash Orange Bitters

Shake with ice and strain into a cocktail glass.

COMMODORE PERRY

1½ oz. Rum
1   Egg White
¼   oz. Grenadine
½   oz. Lemon Juice
½   tsp. Sugar

Shake with ice and strain into a cocktail glass.

COMMONWEAL

1   oz. Scotch
½   oz. Lemon Juice
½   oz. Ginger Wine
¼   oz. Maraschino Liqueur

Shake with ice and strain into a cocktail glass.

COMMONWEALTH

1¾ oz. Canadian Whisky
¼   oz. Lemon Juice
½   oz. Van der Hum Liqueur

Shake with ice and strain into a cocktail glass. Serve with a twist of orange peel.

CONCHITA

1   oz. Tequila
1   oz. Grapefruit Juice
A few drops of Lemon Juice

Shake with ice and strain into a cocktail glass. Add ice.

CONCH SHELL

4   oz. Rum
¾   oz. Lime Juice

Shake with ice and strain into an Old-fashioned glass.

CONDITIONER

1   oz. Rum
1   Egg Yolk
1   oz. Orange Curacao
½   oz. Pernod

Shake with ice and strain into a cocktail glass.

CONFIDENTIAL COCKTAIL

¾   oz. Gin
¾   oz. Dry Vermouth
½   oz. Strega
½   oz. Cherry-flavored Brandy

Stir with ice and strain into a cocktail glass.

CONGO

2   oz. Rum
1   tsp. Powdered Coconut

Shake with ice and strain into a cocktail glass. Sprinkle nutmeg on top.

CONNECTICUT BULLFROG

1   oz. Gin
½   oz. New England Rum
½   oz. Lemon Juice
½   oz. Maple Syrup

Strain over packed ice into a cocktail glass.

CONSOLATION

1½ oz. Gin
½ oz. White Creme de Menthe
1 dash Angostura Bitters
½ oz. Lemon Juice

Shake with ice and strain into a cocktail glass.

CONSTELLATION

¾ oz. Dark Rum
¾ oz. Sweet Vermouth
¾ oz. Ginger Wine
1 dash Lime Juice
1 dash Angostura Bitters

Shake with ice and strain into a cocktail glass.

CONTINENTAL

1¾ oz. Rum
1 tbsp. Lime Juice
1½ tsp. Green Creme de Menthe
½ tsp. Powdered Sugar

Shake with ice and strain into a cocktail glass. Add a twist of lemon peel.

CONTINENTAL HIGHBALL

1½ oz. Pernod
½ tsp. Sugar

Stir with ice and strain into a highball glass. Fill with soda and ice.

CONTINENTAL SOUR

1 Egg White
1¼ oz. Lemon Juice
1¼ oz. Rye Whisky
1 tsp. Sugar

Shake with ice and strain into a Sour glass. Serve with an orange slice and a cherry. Float ½ oz. Claret on top. (Egg white may be omitted and Bourbon may be used in place of Rye Whisky.)

COOCH BEHAR

2-3 cubes Ice
1½ oz. Vodka
3 oz. Tomato Juice

Put ice cubes in an Old-fashioned glass, add the Vodka and tomato juice and stir gently.

COOK'S TOWN

1 oz. Gin
1 oz. White Creme de Menthe
1 oz. Pineapple Juice

Shake with ice and strain into a cocktail glass.

COOL COLONEL

1½ oz. Bourbon
3 oz. Tea
¼ oz. Lemon Juice
¼ tsp. Sugar

Mix in a Collins glass. Fill with soda and ice. Float 1 oz. Southern Comfort on top.

COOL OF THE EVENING

½ oz. White Creme de Menthe
½ oz. Lemon Juice
1½ oz. Rum

Shake with ice and strain into a cocktail glass.

> Here's to hell!
> May the stay there
> Be as much fun as the way there!

COOPER'S RANCH PUNCH

2 oz. Rum
2 oz. Guava Juice
¼ oz. Grenadine
1 oz. Lime Juice
2 oz. Pineapple Juice

Mix in a Collins glass. Fill with soda and ice. Serve with a mint sprig.

COOPERSTOWN COCKTAIL

½ oz. Dry Vermouth
½ oz. Sweet Vermouth
1 oz. Gin

Shake with ice and strain into a cocktail glass. Add a sprig of mint.

COOW WOOW

2 oz. Rum
2 oz. Water

Mix in an Old-fashioned glass. Serve with a piece of ginger.

COPA DE ORO

1 oz. Gold Rum
3 tsp. Lime Juice
2 tsp. Sugar Syrup
A few drops of Maraschino Liqueur
3 oz. crushed Ice

Blend at a high speed for 10 seconds. Strain into a champagne cocktail glass. Float a few drops of Pernod on top.

COPENHAGEN NO. 1

1 oz. Gin
1 oz. Aquavit
½ oz. Dry Vermouth

Stir with ice and strain into a cocktail glass. Serve with an olive.

COPENHAGEN NO. 2

1½ oz. Aquavit
¾ oz. Lemon (or Lime) Juice
¾ oz. Triple Sec or Orange Curacao

Stir with ice and strain into a cocktail glass.

COPENHAGEN SPECIAL

1 oz. Aquavit
1 oz. Arrack Punch
1 oz. Lemon Juice

Shake with ice and strain into a cocktail glass.

COPPER MIST

1½ oz. Irish Mist Liqueur

Pour into a highball glass. Fill with crushed ice and lemon juice. Add sugar to taste.

CORAL COCKTAIL

1½ oz. Gin
½ oz. Sweet Vermouth
½ oz. 7 Fruits

Shake with ice and strain into a cocktail glass.

CORDIAL MEDOC COCKTAIL

1 oz. Gin
½ oz. Cordial Medoc
½ oz. Dry Vermouth
¼ oz. Lemon Juice

Stir with ice and strain into a cocktail glass.

CORDIAL MEDOC CUP

1 oz. Cordial Medoc
½ oz. Cognac
1 oz. Lemon Juice
½ tsp. Sugar

Mix in a Collins glass. Fill with ice and Champagne. Serve with an orange slice.

CORDIAL MEDOC SOUR NO. 1

1½ oz. Cordial Medoc
1 oz. Lemon Juice

Shake with ice and strain into a Sour glass. Serve with an orange slice and a cherry.

If you two like we two like
we two like you two,
Then "Here's to us four."
But if you two don't like
we two
Like we two like you two,
then
"Here's to us two and no
more!"

CORDIAL MEDOC SOUR NO. 2

1½ oz. Gin
½ oz. Cordial Medoc
½ oz. Lemon Juice

Shake with ice and strain into a Sour glass.

CORDOVA

2 oz. Gin
1 oz. Sweet Vermouth
1 dash Pernod
1 tsp. Cream

Shake with ice and strain into a cocktail glass.

CORKSCREW

1½ oz. Rum
½ oz. Dry Vermouth
½ oz. Peach-flavored Brandy

Shake with ice and strain into a cocktail glass.

CORNELL COCKTAIL NO. 1

½ tsp. Lemon Juice
1 tsp. Maraschino Liqueur
1 Egg White
1½ oz. Gin

Shake with ice and strain into a cocktail glass.

CORNELL COCKTAIL NO. 2

1¼ oz. Gin
1¼ oz. Dry Vermouth

Shake with ice and strain into a cocktail glass. Serve with a cherry.

CORNELL SPECIAL

½ oz. Lemon Juice
1 oz. Gin
¾ oz. Benedictine
¼ oz. Grenadine

Shake with ice and strain into a cocktail glass.

CORN PEPPER

1½ oz. Corn Whisky
½ oz. Cream
1 Egg White
½ oz. Grenadine

Shake with ice and strain into a Collins glass. Fill with soda and ice.

CORONATION COCKTAIL NO. 1

¾ oz. Sweet Vermouth
¾ oz. Dry Vermouth
¾ oz. Applejack
1 dash Peach Liqueur

Shake with ice and strain into a cocktail glass.

CORONATION COCKTAIL NO. 2

1½ oz. Sherry
1½ oz. Dry Vermouth
1 dash Maraschino Liqueur
2 dashes Orange Bitters

Shake with ice and strain into a cocktail glass.

CORONATION COCKTAIL NO. 3

1½ oz. Brandy
¾ oz. Curacao
1 dash Peach Bitters
1 dash White Creme de Menthe

Stir with ice and strain into a cocktail glass.

CORONATION COCKTAIL NO. 4

¾ oz. Gin
¾ oz. Dubonnet
¾ oz. Dry Vermouth

Stir with ice and strain into a cocktail glass.

CORONET

2 oz. Gin
¾ oz. Port

Shake with ice and strain into a cocktail glass. Serve with a lemon twist.

CORPSE REVIVER COCKTAIL NO. 1

½ oz. Sweet Vermouth
½ oz. Apple Brandy
1 oz. Brandy

Shake with ice and strain into a cocktail glass.

CORPSE REVIVER COCKTAIL NO. 2

¾ oz. Gin
¾ oz. Cointreau
¾ oz. Swedish Punch
¾ oz. Lemon Juice
1 dash Pernod

Shake with ice and strain into a cocktail glass. (Lillet may be used instead of Swedish Punch.)

CORPSE REVIVER COCKTAIL NO. 3

¾ oz. Lemon Juice
1½ oz. Pernod

Mix in a highball glass. Fill with ice and Champagne.

CORSON

1½ oz. Sherry
1½ oz. Gin
1 oz. Lemon Juice
A few drops of Sweet Vermouth, Dry Vermouth, Curacao, Cherry-flavored Brandy, and White Creme Cacao.

Shake with ice and strain into an Old-fashioned glass. Add ice.

CORVEE

2 oz. Southern Comfort
1 oz. Sloe Gin

Mix in a Collins glass. Fill with ice and lemon soda.

COSMOPOLITAN CLARET PUNCH

1½ oz. Brandy
1 tsp. Sugar
4 oz. Claret

Shake with ice and strain into an Old-fashioned glass. Serve with a fruit garnish.

COSSACK COOLER

1½ oz. Vodka

Pour into a Collins glass. Fill with ice, ginger ale, and dry cider. Serve with a lemon wedge and mint sprigs.

COSTA DEL SOL

2 oz. Gin
1 oz. Apricot-flavored Brandy
1 oz. Cointreau

Shake with ice and strain into an Old-fashioned glass.

COTA

1 oz. Gin
¾ oz. Hercules
¾ oz. Cointreau

Stir with ice and strain into a cocktail glass.

COTE D'AMERAND

1 oz. Gin
1 oz. Armagnac
1 oz. Izarra
1 dash Lemon Juice

Stir with ice and strain into a cocktail glass.

COTE D'AZUR COOLER

1 oz. Brandy
2 tsp. Lemon Juice
2 tsp. Pineapple Juice
A few drops of Maraschino Liqueur

Shake with ice and strain into a Collins glass.

COUCOU CUMBER

1½ oz. Vodka
2 tsp. Sugar Syrup
1 tsp. Pernod
1 large Cucumber

Combine everything except the cucumber with ice; shake well. Slice one end off the cucumber, use an apple corer on the other end to hollow out all the meat. Strain in the drink, add crushed ice to fill the cucumber and serve on a flat dish for support.

COUNT CURREY

1½ oz. Gin
1 tsp. Powdered Sugar

Shake with ice and strain into a champagne glass over ice cubes. Fill with chilled Champagne.

COUNTRY CLUB

4   oz. Dry Vermouth
¼   oz. Grenadine

Mix in a highball glass. Fill with soda and ice.

COUNTRY CLUB COOLER

2   oz. Dry Vermouth
½   tsp. Grenadine
Soda

Mix Grenadine and 2 oz. soda in a Collins glass. Add ice cubes and Vermouth. Fill the glass with soda or ginger ale and stir again. Add a twist of orange or lemon peel (or both) and dangle end over the rim of the glass.

COUNTRY COCKTAIL

¾   oz. Applejack
½   oz. Lemon Juice
½   Egg White
¾   oz. Port
½   tsp. Sugar Syrup

Shake with ice and strain into a cocktail glass.

COUNTRY GENTLEMAN COCKTAIL

1   oz. Applejack
½   oz. Curacao
½   oz. Lemon Juice
¼   tsp. Sugar Syrup

Shake with ice and strain into a cocktail glass.

COUNTRY LIFE

¾   oz. Jamaica Rum
¾   oz. Port
1½   oz. Bourbon Whisky
3   dashes Angostura Bitters
1   dash Orange Bitters

Shake with ice and strain into a cocktail glass.

COUP DE ROULES

1   oz. Gin
1   oz. Dry Vermouth
½   oz. Cointreau
½   oz. Cherry-flavored Brandy

Stir with ice and strain into a cocktail glass.

COWBOY COCKTAIL

1½   oz. Rye Whisky
1   tbsp. Sweet Cream

Shake with ice and strain into a cocktail glass.

CRANBERRY DELIGHT

1   oz. Galliano
1   oz. Vodka
1   oz. Cranberry Sauce

Shake with ice and strain into a cocktail glass.

CRANBERRY SHRUB

4   oz. Cranberry Juice cocktail, chilled
1½   oz. frozen Pineapple Juice concentrate
4   oz. Rosé, chilled

Mix and pour over ice cubes in a Collins glass.

CRAWL

1   oz. Cognac
½   oz. Rum
¼   oz. Orange Curacao
½   oz. Creme de Noyaux
1   dash Angostura Bitters

Stir with ice and strain into a cocktail glass. Serve with a lemon twist.

> A glass in the hand's worth two on the shelf —
> Tipple it down and refresh yourself!

CREAM DREAM

1   oz. Creme de Cafe
Heavy Cream
Maraschino Cherry

Pour Creme de Cafe into a pony glass. Place a teaspoon bottomside up on top of glass. Float some cream by pouring slowly over the rounded surface of the spoon. Garnish with a maraschino cherry speared on a toothpick.

CREAM FIZZ

Juice ½ Lemon
2   oz. Gin
½   tsp. Powdered Sugar
1   tsp. Fresh Cream

Shake with ice and strain into a highball glass. Fill with soda and ice.

CREAM GIN FIZZ

1½   oz. Gin
1½   oz. Milk
3   tsp. Sugar
4   tbsp. Lime Juice

Shake with ice and strain into a highball glass. Add soda to fill and stir quickly to make it foam up.

CREAM PUFF

2   oz. Rum
1   oz. Sweet Cream
½   tsp. Powdered Sugar

Shake with ice and strain into a highball glass over two cubes of ice. Fill with soda and stir.

CREAM PUNCH

2   oz. Cognac
¼   tsp. Sugar
2   oz. Cream
¼   oz. Lemon Juice
¼   oz. Rum

Shake with ice and strain into a highball glass. Fill with crushed ice. Sprinkle nutmeg on top.

CREAMSICLE

1¼ oz. Amaretto
1¼ oz. Triple Sec or Orange Curacao
2 oz. Cream

Shake with ice and strain into a highball glass. Fill with crushed ice.

CREAMY DRIVER

1½ oz. Vodka
1 Egg Yolk
4 oz. Orange Juice
½ tsp. Sugar

Shake with ice and strain into a Collins glass. Fill with crushed ice.

CREAMY ORANGE

1 oz. Orange Juice
1 oz. Cream Sherry
¾ oz. Brandy
1 tbsp. Sweet Cream

Shake with ice and strain into a cocktail glass.

CREAMY SCREWDRIVER

2 oz. Vodka
1 Egg Yolk
6 oz. Orange Juice
1 tsp. Sugar

Combine all ingredients with half a cup of crushed ice in a blender. Blend at a low speed and pour into a Collins glass with ice cubes.

CREME DE CAFE

1 oz. Coffee-flavored Brandy
½ oz. Rum
½ oz. Anisette
1 oz. Sweet Cream

Shake with ice and strain into an Old-fashioned glass over ice cubes.

CREME DE GIN COCKTAIL

1½ oz. Gin
½ oz. White Creme de Menthe
1 Egg White
2 tsp. Lemon Juice
2 tsp. Orange Juice

Shake with ice and strain into a cocktail glass.

CREME DE MENTHE FRAPPE

Fill a cocktail glass up to the brim with shaved ice. Add Green Creme de Menthe. Serve with two short straws.

CREOLE COCKTAIL NO. 1

1 oz. Whisky
1 oz. Sweet Vermouth
2 dashes Benedictine
2 dashes Amer Picon

Stir with ice and strain into a cocktail glass. Serve with a lemon twist.

CREOLE COCKTAIL NO. 2

1½ oz. Bourbon
¼ oz. Curacao
1 dash Angostura Bitters
1 dash Peychaud's Bitters

Stir with ice and strain into a cocktail glass previously coated with Pernod.

CREOLE COCKTAIL NO. 3

1 oz. Gin
1 oz. Sherry
1 oz. Lemon Juice

Shake with ice and strain into a cocktail glass.

CREOLE COCKTAIL NO. 4

1 dash Orange Bitters
¾ oz. Pernod
¾ oz. Sweet Vermouth

Shake with ice and strain into a cocktail glass.

CREOLE COCKTAIL NO. 5

1½ oz. Rum
1 dash Tabasco Sauce
1 tsp. Lemon Juice
Salt and Pepper

Shake with ice and strain into an Old-fashioned glass over ice cubes. Fill with cold beef bouillon and stir.

CREOLE FIZZ

1½ oz. Sloe Gin
½ oz. Cream
1 oz. Lemon Juice
1 Egg White
½ tsp. Sugar

Shake with ice and strain into a highball glass. Fill with soda and ice.

CREOLE LADY COCKTAIL

1½ oz. Bourbon Whisky
1½ oz. Madeira
1 tsp. Grenadine

Stir with ice and strain into a cocktail glass. Serve with one green and one red cherry.

CRIMSON COCKTAIL

2 oz. Gin
1 oz. Port
½ oz. Lemon Juice
1 tsp. Grenadine

Mix Gin, juice and Grenadine with ice and shake well. Strain into a highball glass. Add ice and float the Port on top.

CROCKER

1½　oz. Gin
½　oz. Sweet Vermouth
½　oz. Dry Vermouth

Stir with ice and strain into a cocktail glass.

CROISETTE

¾　oz. Cherry-flavored Brandy
¾　oz. Sweet Vermouth
¾　oz. Dry Vermouth
¼　oz. Kirschwasser

Stir with ice and strain into a cocktail glass. Serve with a cherry.

CROOK COCKTAIL

1　dash Orange Bitters
½　oz. Pernod
1½　oz. Sweet Vermouth

Shake with ice and strain into a cocktail glass.

CROTON

1½　oz. Bourbon
¾　oz. Sherry

Stir with ice and strain into a cocktail glass. Serve with a lemon twist.

> Ship me somewhere east of
>   Suez,
> Where the best is like the
>   worst;
> Where there aren't no ten
>   commandments,
> And a man can raise a thirst.
> — *Rudyard Kipling*

CROW

1½　oz. Whisky
¾　oz. Lemon Juice
1　dash Grenadine
½　tsp. Sugar

Stir with ice and strain into a cocktail glass.

CRUSTAS

Lemon
Sugar
Lemon or Orange twist
Maraschino Cherry
1　dash Angostura Bitters
1　tsp. Maraschino Liqueur
1　tsp. Lemon Juice
2-3　oz. Liquor (Brandy, Gin, Rum, Whisky)

Rub the rim of a 4-oz. cocktail glass with lemon and dip into sugar. Put the lemon or orange twist and cherry into the glass. Combine ice, bitters, lemon juice, maraschino and liquor in a mixing glass and stir. Strain into the prepared glass. Add a slice of orange.

CRUX COCKTAIL

½　oz. Lemon Juice
½　oz. Cointreau
½　oz. Dubonnet
½　oz. Cognac

Shake with ice and strain into a cocktail glass.

CRYSTAL BRONX

1½　oz. Dry Vermouth
1½　oz. Sweet Vermouth
Juice ¼ Orange

Pour into a large cocktail glass with ice and fill with soda.

CRYSTAL RUM FIZZ

1½　oz. Rum
1　Mint Life Saver

Mix in a highball glass. Fill with ginger ale and ice.

CRYSTAL SLIPPER COCKTAIL

½　oz. Creme d'Yvette
2　dashes Orange Bitters
1½　oz. Gin

Stir with ice and strain into a cocktail glass.

CUBAINE

1½　oz. Light Rum
½　oz. Orange Juice
½　oz. Lemon Juice
1　tsp. Sugar

Shake with ice and strain into a cocktail glass.

CUBA LIBRE

3　oz. Rum
1½　tbsp. Lime Juice
Chilled Cola

Put ice cubes in a highball glass, add the rum and lime juice, fill with Cola and garnish with a slice of lime.

CUBA LIBRE COCKTAIL

1　oz. Rum
½　oz. 151-proof Rum
1　oz. Cola
½　oz. Lime Juice
½　tsp. Sugar

Shake with ice and strain into a cocktail glass. Serve with a lime wheel.

CUBA LIBRE SUPREME

1½　oz. Southern Comfort

Pour into a Collins glass. Fill with ice and Cola. Add a slice of lime.

CUBAN BANGER

½　oz. Rum
¾　oz. Galliano
Orange Juice

Pour the Rum into a Collins glass, fill with orange juice and ice and float the Galliano on top.

CUBAN COCKTAIL NO. 1

Juice ½ Lime
½ tsp. Powdered Sugar
2 oz. Rum

Shake with ice and strain into a cocktail glass.

CUBAN COCKTAIL NO. 2

1½ oz. Light Rum
½ oz. Maraschino Liqueur
¼ oz. Grenadine
1 dash Orange Bitters
½ oz. Lemon Juice

Shake with ice and strain into a cocktail glass.

CUBAN COCKTAIL NO. 3

Juice ½ Lime or ¼ Lemon
½ oz. Apricot-flavored Brandy
1½ oz. Brandy
1 tsp. Rum

Shake with ice and strain into a cocktail glass.

CUBAN COCKTAIL NO. 4

1½ oz. Light Rum
½ oz. Sweet Vermouth
1 dash Angostura Bitters
½ oz. Orange Juice

Shake with ice and strain into a cocktail glass.

CUBAN COCKTAIL NO. 5

1 oz. Rum
1 oz. Apricot-flavored Brandy
½ oz. Lime Juice

Shake with ice and strain into a cocktail glass.

CUBAN COCKTAIL NO. 6

1 oz. Apricot-flavored Brandy
½ oz. Grenadine
¾ oz. Lime Juice
1 oz. Rum

Shake with ice and strain into a cocktail glass.

CUBAN COCKTAIL NO. 7

1½ oz. Light Rum
1½ oz. Pineapple Juice
¼ oz. Grenadine
¼ oz. Maraschino Liqueur

Shake with ice and strain into a cocktail glass.

CUBAN COOLER

3 oz. Rum
Ginger Ale

Put 3 or 4 ice cubes in a tall highball glass, add the Rum and fill with ginger ale. Garnish with lemon peel.

May her voyage through life be as happy and as free As the dancing waves on the deep blue sea.

CUBANO NO. 1

1½ oz. Gin
1½ oz. Dry Vermouth
¼ oz. Kummel
2 drops Pineapple Syrup

Shake with ice and strain into a cocktail glass.

CUBANO NO. 2

1½ oz. Rum
¼ oz. Pineapple Juice
¾ oz. Lime Juice
½ tsp. Sugar

Shake with ice and strain into a cocktail glass.

CUBAN PRESIDENTE

1½ oz. Rum
½ oz. Dry Vermouth
¼ oz. Orange Curacao
¼ oz. Grenadine

Shake with ice and strain into a cocktail glass. Serve with a lemon twist and a cherry.

CUBAN SCREW

1½ oz. Rum

Pour into a Collins glass. Fill with ice and orange juice.

CUBAN SPECIAL COCKTAIL

Juice ½ Lime
1 tbsp. Pineapple Juice
1 oz. Rum
½ tsp. Triple Sec or Orange Curacao

Shake with ice and strain into a cocktail glass. Decorate with a stick of pineapple and a cherry.

CUCUMBER NO. 1

1 oz. Gin
¾ oz. Green Creme de Menthe
1¼ oz. Cream

Shake with ice and strain into a cocktail glass.

CUCUMBER NO. 2

¾ oz. Green Creme de Menthe

Pour into a pony glass. Float ¼ oz. cream on top.

CUCUMBER NO. 3

¾ oz. Green Creme de Menthe
¼ oz. Dark Creme de Cacao

Shake with ice and strain into a cocktail glass.

CUCUMBER CHAMPAGNE

1 oz. Benedictine
½ oz. Lemon Juice

Mix in a Collins glass. Add a lemon twist. Fill with champagne and ice.

CULPRIT FEY

½ oz. Gin
½ oz. White Creme de Menthe
½ oz. Anisette
½ oz. Cointreau
¾ oz. Cream

Shake with ice and strain into a cocktail glass.

CULROSS

¾ oz. Apricot-flavored Brandy
¾ oz. Lillet
¾ oz. Light Rum
1 tbsp. Lemon Juice

Stir with ice and strain into a cocktail glass.

CUPID COCKTAIL

1½ oz. Sherry
1 Egg
1 tsp. Powdered Sugar
1 dash Pepper

Shake with ice and strain into a cocktail glass.

CURACAO COCKTAIL NO. 1

1 oz. Bourbon
1 oz. Curacao
½ oz. Lemon Juice

Shake with ice and strain into a cocktail glass.

> If wine tells truth, and so
> have said the wise,
> It makes me laugh to think
> how brandy lies.
> — *Oliver Wendell Holmes*

CURACAO COCKTAIL NO. 2

¾ oz. Gin
¾ oz. Brandy
1 oz. Orange Curacao
1 oz. Orange Juice
1 dash Orange Bitters

Shake with ice and strain into a cocktail glass.

CURACAO COOLER

½ oz. Lime Juice
½ oz. Lemon Juice
1 oz. Vodka
1 oz. Blue Curacao

Mix in a Collins glass. Fill with ice, orange juice and soda.

CURACAO PUNCH

1 oz. Lemon Juice
1½ oz. Orange Curacao
1 oz. Brandy

Mix in a highball glass. Fill with crushed ice. Garnish with fruit. Serve with straws.

CURRIER

1½ oz. Blended Whisky
½ oz. Kummel
¼ oz. Lime Juice
¼ oz. Rose's Lime Juice

Shake with ice and strain into a cocktail glass. Serve with a lime wheel.

CUTEST ONE

1¼ oz. Gin
1¼ oz. Sherry

Stir with ice and strain into a cocktail glass. Serve with a cherry.

DA'BARRY

1¾ oz. Rye Whisky
¾ oz. Dubonnet
1 dash Orange Bitters

Stir with ice and strain into a cocktail glass. Serve with a cherry.

DAFFODIL

1 oz. Apple Brandy
1 oz. White Port
2 tsp. Apricot-flavored Brandy
2 tsp. Lemon Juice

Shake with ice and strain into a cocktail glass. Divide several gumdrops and spear them with toothpicks. Bridge the glass with speared gumdrops.

DAIQUIRI COCKTAIL

Juice 1 Lime
1 tsp. Powdered Sugar
1½ oz. Light Rum

Shake with ice and strain into a cocktail glass.

DAISY NO. 1

1 dash Grenadine
½ oz. Lemon or Lime Juice
2 oz. Whisky (or Applejack, Brandy, or Rum)

Mix and pour into a goblet filled with shaved ice. Stir until outside of the glass becomes frosted. Float 1-2 tbsp. Yellow Chartreuse on top. Decorate with fruit. Serve with straws.

DAISY NO. 2

2 oz. Tequila
2 tsp. Lemon Juice
2 tsp. Grenadine
2 tsp. Club Soda

Shake with ice and strain into an Old-fashioned glass. Add ice.

DALLAS TEXAN

1½ oz. Early Times
½ oz. Apricot-flavored Brandy
½ oz. Grenadine
½ oz. Lime Juice

Shake with ice and strain into a highball glass. Fill with ice and stir. Serve with a green cherry and a squeeze of lime.

DAMN-THE-WEATHER COCKTAIL

1 tsp. Triple Sec or Orange Curacao
1 tbsp. Orange Juice
1 tbsp. Sweet Vermouth
1 oz. Gin

Shake with ice and strain into a cocktail glass.

DANCING LEPRECHAUN

1½ oz. Irish Whisky
1½ oz. Lemon Juice

Shake with ice and strain into a Collins glass. Add ice and fill with equal parts of soda and ginger ale; stir gently. Serve with a lemon twist.

DANDY COCKTAIL

1 oz. Whisky
1 oz. Dubonnet
1 dash Angostura Bitters
3 dashes Cointreau

Shake with ice and strain into a cocktail glass. Garnish with a lemon and an orange peel.

DANIEL DE ORO

Orange Juice
1 oz. Tequila
½ tsp. Creme Damiana

Pour the Tequila into a highball glass; add ice and fill with orange juice. Top off with the Creme Damiana.

DANISH BULL

Use an Old-fashioned glass filled with ice and rimmed with salt.

Add: 1½ oz. Aquavit
1 dash Celery Salt

Fill with beef bouillon (pepper, Tabasco and Worcestershire sauce are optional). Serve with a squeeze of lime.

DANISH GIN FIZZ

1½ oz. Gin
½ oz. Cherry Heering
¼ oz. Kirschwasser
½ oz. Lime Juice
1 tsp. Sugar

Shake with ice and strain into a Collins glass. Fill with soda and ice. Serve with a cherry and a lime wheel.

DANISH MARY NO. 1

Fill a double Old-fashioned glass with ice.

Add: 1½ oz. Aquavit

Fill glass with Mary Mix.

DANISH MARY NO. 2

Use pepper, salt, celery salt, Worcestershire sauce and tomato juice in place of Mary Mix.

DANISH TODDY

1½ oz. Aquavit
½ oz. Lemon Juice
½ oz. Cherry Heering

Mix in a preheated Old-fashioned glass. Fill with hot water, add a cinnamon stick and sprinkle nutmeg on top.

DANNY'S SPECIAL

1 oz. Bourbon
1 oz. Lemon Juice
½ oz. Grand Marnier
½ oz. Cointreau

Shake with ice and strain into a cocktail glass.

DARB COCKTAIL

1 tsp. Lemon Juice
¾ oz. Dry Vermouth
¾ oz. Gin
¾ oz. Apricot-flavored Brandy

Shake with ice and strain into a cocktail glass.

DARBY

1½ oz. Gin
½ oz. Lime Juice
½ oz. Grapefruit Juice
1 tsp. Powdered Sugar

Shake with ice and strain into a large cocktail glass. Top with a squirt of soda and add a cherry.

DAREDEVIL COCKTAIL

1¼ oz. Port
1 Egg
1 dash Angostura Bitters

Shake with ice and strain into a cocktail glass.

DAREDEVIL FLIP

1 oz. Port
1 Egg
1 dash Angostura Bitters
½ tsp. Sugar

Shake with ice and strain into a flip glass.

> Here's to one and only one,
> And may that one be he
> Who loves but one and only one, —
> And may that one be me.

DAVIS

1½ oz. Dark Rum
1½ oz. Dry Vermouth
2 dashes Raspberry Syrup
3 tbsp. Lime Juice

Shake with ice and strain into a cocktail glass.

DAVIS BRANDY

2 oz. Brandy
1 oz. Dry Vermouth
4 dashes Grenadine
1 dash Angostura Bitters

Stir with ice and strain into a cocktail glass.

DAVIS COCKTAIL

½ oz. Jamaica Rum
1½ oz. Dry Vermouth
½ oz. Lime Juice
1 dash Grenadine

Shake with ice and strain into a cocktail glass.

DEATH IN THE AFTERNOON

1½ oz. Pernod

Pour into a champagne glass. Fill the glass with Champagne.

DEAUVILLE COCKTAIL

Juice ¼ Lemon
½ oz. Brandy
½ oz. Apple Brandy
½ oz. Cointreau

Shake with ice and strain into a cocktail glass.

DECEIVER

1½ oz. Gin
¾ oz. Green Chartreuse
¼ oz. White Creme de Menthe

Stir with ice and strain into a cocktail glass.

> The glasses fill with
>   generous juice,
> As generous as your mind;
> And pledge me in your
>   generous toast
> The whole of human kind.
> — *Daniel O'Connell*

DECH GERARD'S COCKTAIL

1½ oz. Gin
½ oz. Pineapple Juice
½ oz. Dry Vermouth

Shake with ice and strain into a cocktail glass.

DEEP PURPLE PUNCH

1 oz. Grape Juice
1 oz. Passion Fruit
½ oz. Lime Juice
1½ oz. Rum

Shake with ice and strain into a Collins glass. Fill with shaved ice. Serve with straws.

DEEP SEA COCKTAIL

1 oz. Dry Vermouth
¼ tsp. Pernod
1 dash Orange Bitters
1 oz. Gin

Stir with ice and strain into a cocktail glass.

DELIGHTFUL ZIN CUP

1 cup hot Tea
1 tsp. Sugar
1½ oz. California Zinfandel

Pour the hot tea into a preheated mug. Add sugar. Stir and add the wine (Zinfandel). Float a lemon wheel on top.

DELMONICO NO. 1

¾ oz. Gin
½ oz. Dry Vermouth
½ oz. Sweet Vermouth
½ oz. Brandy

Stir with ice and strain into a cocktail glass. Serve with a lemon twist.

DELMONICO NO. 2

1 dash Orange Bitters
1 oz. Dry Vermouth
1½ oz. Gin

Stir with ice and strain into a cocktail glass. Serve with a lemon twist.

DEL MONTE

1½ oz. Rum
¼ oz. Grenadine
¾ oz. Lemon Juice

Shake with ice and strain into a cocktail glass.

DELTA

1½ oz. Rye or Bourbon Whisky
½ oz. Southern Comfort
½ oz. Lime Juice
¼ tsp. Sugar

Shake with ice and strain into a cocktail glass. Garnish with a peach slice and a lime wedge.

DELUXE SHERRY COBBLER

3 oz. Cream Sherry
1 tsp. Sugar
1 dash Grenadine
Chilled Soda

Combine Sherry and sugar in a Collins glass. Stir well. Add cracked ice and fill with chilled soda. Stir gently and add a dash of Grenadine. Garnish with fresh fruit. Serve with straws.

DELYS COCKTAIL

1 oz. Gin
1 oz. Creme de Menthe
1 oz. Creme de Violette

Shake with ice and strain into a cocktail glass.

DEMEANOR COCKTAIL

1 dash Orange Bitters
¾ oz. Gin
¾ oz. Sweet Vermouth
2 dashes Creme de Violette

Stir with ice and strain into a cocktail glass.

DEMI PANACHE

½   Beer
½   Lemonade

Mix in a Collins glass.

DE MON CURE

¾   oz. Lemon Juice
¾   oz. Cognac
¾   oz. Light Rum
¾   oz. Calvados or Apple Brandy

Shake with ice and strain into a cocktail glass.

DEMPSEY COCKTAIL

1   oz. Gin
1   oz. Apple Brandy
½   tsp. Pernod
½   tsp. Grenadine

Stir with ice and strain into a cocktail glass.

DENVER MINT

1½   oz. Early Times
½   oz. White Creme de Menthe
¾   oz. Lime Juice
½   tsp. Sugar

Shake with ice and strain into a highball glass. Fill with soda and ice. Add an orange slice and serve with straws.

DEPTH BOMB

1   oz. Apple Brandy
1   oz. Brandy
1   dash Lemon Juice
1   dash Grenadine

Shake with ice and strain into an Old-fashioned glass over ice cubes.

DEPTH CHARGE COCKTAIL

½   tsp. Pernod
1   oz. Lillet
2   oz. Gin

Shake with ice and strain into a cocktail glass. Serve with a twist of orange peel.

DERBY NO. 1

1½   oz. Gin
2   dashes Peach Bitters
2   Mint sprigs

Shake with ice and strain into a cocktail glass. Garnish with mint sprigs.

DERBY NO. 2

1   oz. Whisky
½   oz. Sweet Vermouth
½   oz. White Curacao
1½   tbsp. Lime Juice

Shake with ice and strain into a cocktail glass. Garnish with a mint leaf.

DERBY DAIQUIRI

1½   oz. Rum
1   oz. Orange Juice
1   tbsp. Lime Juice
1   tsp. Sugar

Combine all ingredients with half a cup of shaved ice in a blender. Blend at a low speed. Pour into a champagne glass.

DERBY FIZZ

Juice ½ Lemon
1   tsp. Powdered Sugar
1   Egg
2   oz. Scotch Whisky
1   tsp. Triple Sec or Orange Curacao

Shake with ice and strain into a highball glass. Add two ice cubes, fill with soda and stir.

DERBY RUM FIX

2   oz. White Rum
2   tsp. Lime Juice
1½   tsp. Sugar Syrup
1   oz. Orange Juice

Stir without ice and strain over crushed ice in a highball glass. Decorate with an orange slice and a cherry.

DE RIGUEUR

1   oz. Whisky
½   oz. Grapefruit Juice
½   oz. Honey

Shake with ice and strain into a cocktail glass.

DERNIER ROUND

1½   oz. Gin
½   oz. Dry Vermouth
¼   oz. Cognac
¼   oz. Cointreau
1   dash Angostura Bitters

Stir with ice and strain into a cocktail glass.

To the old, long life and
   treasure;
To the young, all health and
   pleasure.
— Ben Jonson

DESERT COOLER

1½   oz. Gin
¾   oz. Cherry-flavored Brandy
2½   oz. Orange Juice

Shake with ice and strain into a Collins glass. Fill with soda and ice.

DESERT DREAM

¾   oz. Gin
¾   oz. Sweet Vermouth
¾   oz. Creme de Cacao
1   Egg White

Shake with ice and strain into a cocktail glass. Sprinkle nutmeg on top.

DESERT HEALER COCKTAIL

Juice 1 Orange
1½   oz. Gin
¾   oz. Cherry-flavored Brandy

Shake with ice and strain into a Collins glass. Fill with ice and ginger beer.

DESHLER COCKTAIL

¾   oz. Canadian Whisky
¾   oz. Dubonnet
2   dashes Cointreau
2   dashes Bitters

Shake with ice and strain into a cocktail glass. Serve with a lemon twist and a twist of orange peel.

DESSALINES

1   oz. Haitian Rum
½   oz. Clairin
½   oz. Whisky
½   oz. Lime Juice
½   tsp. Sugar

Shake with ice and strain into a cocktail glass.

DESTINY

1   oz. Gin
¾   oz. Sweet Vermouth
¾   oz. Pernod

Stir with ice and strain into a cocktail glass.

DEVIL COCKTAIL

1   oz. Brandy
1   oz. Creme de Menthe
1   pinch Red Pepper

Shake with ice and strain into a cocktail glass. Sprinkle red pepper on top.

DEVILISH DELIGHT

1   dash Aromatic Bitters
1   tbsp. White Orange-flavored Liqueur
1   tbsp. Cherry-flavored Brandy
Extra Dry Champagne, chilled

Fill a Collins glass with ice cubes. Add the first three ingredients. Fill with Champagne and stir gently.

> Since man is dust it would be fine
> To freshen him up with sparkling wine.

DEVIL'S COCKTAIL

½   tsp. Lemon Juice
1½   oz. Port
1½   oz. Dry Vermouth

Stir with ice and strain into a cocktail glass.

DEVIL'S LEAP

1   oz. Rum
1   oz. Swedish Punch
1   oz. Applejack

Stir with ice and strain into a cocktail glass.

DEVIL'S TAIL

1½   oz. Rum
1   oz. Vodka
1   tbsp. Lime Juice
1½   tsp. Grenadine
1½   tsp. Apricot-flavored Brandy

Combine all ingredients with half a cup of crushed ice in a blender. Blend at a low speed and pour into a champagne glass. Add a twist of lime peel.

DEWEY

1¼   oz. Gin
1¼   oz. Dry Vermouth
1   dash Orange Bitters

Stir with ice and strain into a cocktail glass.

D.F.

1½   oz. Gin
1½   oz. unsweetened Grapefruit Juice
Grenadine to taste

Stir with ice and strain into a cocktail glass.

DIABOLA COCKTAIL

2   oz. Dubonnet
1   oz. Gin
2   dashes Orgeat Syrup

Shake with ice and strain into a cocktail glass.

DIABOLO

1½   oz. Dry White Port
1   oz. Vermouth
A few drops Lemon Juice

Shake with ice and strain into a cocktail glass.

DIAMOND COCKTAIL

1   oz. Lime Juice
1   oz. Lemon Juice
1½   oz. Gin
¾   oz. Grenadine

Shake with ice and strain into a large cocktail glass. Fill with Champagne. Add sugar to taste.

DIAMOND FIZZ

Juice ½ Lemon
1   tsp. Powdered Sugar
2   oz. Gin

Shake with ice and strain into a highball glass. Add two cubes of ice, fill with Champagne and stir.

DIAMOND HEAD

1   oz. Lemon Juice
¾   oz. Apricot-flavored Brandy
1   oz. Gin

Shake with ice and strain into a fizz glass. Fill with pineapple juice and stir. Serve with a pineapple stick.

DIANA COCKTAIL

Fill a cocktail glass with ice, then fill three-quarters full with White Creme de Menthe and float Brandy on top.

DICK, JR. COCKTAIL

Juice 1 Lime
½   oz. Dry Vermouth
¾   oz. Gin
½   oz. Apricot-flavored Brandy

Shake with ice and strain into a cocktail glass.

DIKI-DIKI COCKTAIL NO. 1

½ oz. Grapefruit Juice
½ oz. Swedish Punch
2 oz. Calvados

Shake with ice and strain into a cocktail glass.

DIKI-DIKI COCKTAIL NO. 2

1 oz. Calvados
½ oz. Caloric Punch
½ oz. Grapefruit Juice

Shake with ice and strain into a cocktail glass.

DINAH COCKTAIL

Juice ¼ Lemon
½ tsp. Powdered Sugar
1½ oz. Rye Whisky

Shake with ice and strain into a cocktail glass. Serve with a mint sprig.

DINERFLO

1½ oz. Southern Comfort
¾ oz. Dry Vermouth
1 dash Cointreau

Stir with ice and strain into a cocktail glass. Serve with a lemon twist.

DINERMITE

¼ oz. Sherry
1 oz. Vodka or Gin

Serve over the rocks with soda. Serve with a lemon twist.

DINERMO

1½ oz. Vodka
3 drops Cointreau

Pour into a champagne glass. Add ice and fill with Champagne. Top with an orange slice.

DINK'S SURPRISE

3 dashes Orange-flavored Liqueur
½ cup Brut Champagne, chilled

Dash the Liqueur in a champagne glass. Fill with chilled Champagne. Serve with a twist of orange peel.

DIPLOMAT COCKTAIL

1½ oz. Dry Vermouth
½ oz. Sweet Vermouth
2 dashes Bitters
½ tsp. Maraschino Liqueur

Stir with ice and strain into a cocktail glass. Serve with a lemon wedge and a cherry.

DIPLOMAT SPECIAL

2 oz. Scotch
1 tbsp. Dry Vermouth
Several drops Pernod

Shake with ice and strain into a Martini glass.

DIRTY DOG

1½ oz. Brandy

Pour into a Collins glass and fill with ice and grapefruit juice. (Optional: Float ½ oz. Kahlua on top.)

DIRTY MOTHER NO. 1

1 oz. Brandy
1 oz. Kahlua

Mix in a Collins glass. Fill with ice. Float cream on top.

DIRTY MOTHER NO. 2

1 oz. Brandy
1 oz. Kahlua

Mix in an Old-fashioned glass. Fill with ice.

DIXIE COCKTAIL

Juice ¼ Orange
1 tbsp. Pernod
½ oz. Dry Vermouth
1 oz. Gin

Shake with ice and strain into a cocktail glass.

DIXIE JULEP

1 tsp. Powdered Sugar
2½ oz. Bourbon Whisky

Put sugar and Whisky into a Collins glass, fill with ice and stir gently until the glass is frosted. Decorate with mint sprigs. Serve with straws.

DIXIE PUNCH

½ oz. Gin
1 oz. Southern Comfort
¾ oz. Lime Juice
¼ oz. Grenadine
Piece of crushed Pineapple

Shake and pour over crushed ice in a Collins glass. Decorate with a pineapple spear and an orange slice.

DIXIE WHISKY COCKTAIL

½ tsp. Powdered Sugar
1 dash Bitters
¼ tsp. Triple Sec or Orange Curacao
½ tsp. White Creme de Menthe
2 oz. Rye or Bourbon Whisky

Shake with ice and strain into a cocktail glass.

DIZZY BLONDE

2 oz. Advokaat
1 oz. Pernod
1 Maraschino Cherry
Lemonade

Half fill a 10 oz. highball glass with cracked ice. Add Advokaat and Pernod. Top with lemonade. Place a slit cherry on the lip of the glass.

DIZZY COCKTAIL

1   oz. Whisky
1   oz. Sherry
1   oz. Pineapple Juice
2   dashes Lemon Juice

Shake with ice and strain into a cocktail glass.

DIZZY IZZY

¾   oz. Bourbon
¾   oz. Sherry
½   oz. Pineapple Juice
½   oz. Lemon Juice

Shake with ice and strain into a cocktail glass.

DOBBS

1½   oz. White Creme de Menthe
2   dashes Fernet Branca

Fill an Old-fashioned glass with crushed ice and add both ingredients.

DO BE CAREFUL

1   oz. Gin
¾   oz. Cointreau
½   oz. Lemon Juice
¼   oz. Grenadine

Shake with ice and strain into a cocktail glass.

DOCTOR

1½   oz. Swedish Punch
3   tbsp. Lime Juice

Stir with ice and strain into a cocktail glass.

DOCTOR COOK

¾   oz. Gin
1   tbsp. Lemon Juice
1   dash Maraschino Liqueur
1   Egg White

Shake with ice and strain into a wine glass.

DOCTOR FINK

1½   oz. Gin
1   oz. Pernod
½   oz. Lemon Juice

Shake with ice and strain into a highball glass. Fill with soda and ice. Add sugar to taste.

DOCTOR FUNK

1   small Lime (juice and shell)
3   oz. Dark Rum
1   tsp. Pernod
1   tsp. Grenadine
1   tbsp. Lemon Juice
1   tsp. Sugar

Shake with ice and strain into a Collins glass. Fill with soda.

DOCTOR MONAHAN

2   oz. Gin
¼   oz. Pernod
1   dash Orange Bitters

Stir with ice and strain into a cocktail glass. Serve with a lemon twist.

DODGE SPECIAL

1½   oz. Gin
1½   oz. Cointreau
1   dash Grape Juice

Stir with ice and strain into a cocktail glass.

DODO COCKTAIL

1   oz. Gin
1   oz. Green Creme de Menthe
1   dash Lemon Juice

Shake with ice and strain into a cocktail glass.

DOG'S NOSE

Place 2-3 oz. Gin in a tall highball glass. Fill up with cold Beer or Stout.

DOLLY O'DARE

1½   oz. Gin
1½   oz. Dry Vermouth
½   oz. Apricot-flavored Brandy

Stir with ice and strain into a cocktail glass. Serve with a twist of orange peel.

DOLORES NO. 1

¾   oz. Cherry-flavored Brandy
¾   oz. Light Creme de Cacao
¾   oz. Spanish Brandy
1   Egg White

Stir with ice and strain into a cocktail glass.

DOLORES NO. 2

1   oz. Sherry
½   oz. Jamaica Rum
¼   oz. Dubonnet
¾   oz. Orange Juice

Shake with ice and strain into a cocktail glass.

D.O.M.

1½   oz. Gin
½   oz. Orange Juice
½   oz. Benedictine

Shake with ice and strain into a cocktail glass.

DONALD H.

1½   oz. Gin
¾   oz. Pernod
2   dashes Orange Bitters

Shake with ice and strain into a cocktail glass.

DON LUIS

¾   oz. Galliano
1½   oz. Vodka
¾   oz. Orange Juice
¼   oz. Kirsch

Shake with ice and strain into a cocktail glass.

DON'T GIVE UP THE SHIP

1½ oz. Gin
¼ oz. Fernet Branca
¼ oz. Orange Curacao
½ oz. Dubonnet

Shake with ice and strain into a cocktail glass.

DON'T GO NEAR THE WATER

1 oz. Brandy
½ oz. Curacao
½ oz. Maraschino Liqueur
½ oz. Lemon Juice

Shake with ice and strain into a cocktail glass.

> Here's to us all — God bless us every one.
> — *Dickens*

DOOLITTLE SPECIAL

1 tsp. Sugar
1 oz. Lemon Juice (and rind, muddled)
1½ oz. Whisky

Muddle the lemon on the bottom of an Old-fashioned glass. Add Whisky, sugar and ice. Stir.

DORADO COCKTAIL

2 oz. Tequila
1 tbsp. Honey
2 tbsp. Lemon Juice

Shake with ice and strain into a cocktail glass.

DORFLINGER COCKTAIL

1 dash Orange Bitters
½ oz. Pernod
1 oz. Gin

Shake with ice and strain into a cocktail glass.

DOROTHY'S DELIGHT COCKTAIL

1 oz. Dry Vermouth
2 oz. Gin

Shake with ice and strain into a cocktail glass. Serve with an orange slice and a lemon twist.

DOUBLE ARROW

½ oz. Light Curacao
½ oz. Creme d'Yvette
Float Cream

Pour carefully, in order given, into a pony glass so that each ingredient floats on the preceding one without mixing.

DOUBLE DERBY

2 oz. Bourbon
2 oz. cold Tea
2 oz. Claret
1 oz. Orange Juice
½ oz. Lime Juice
1 oz. Red Currant Syrup

Mix in a double Old-fashioned glass. Fill with ice and stir. Serve with an orange slice.

DOUBLE 0 7 (007)

1 oz. Vodka
1 oz. Brandy
1 oz. Bourbon

Mix in a Collins glass. Fill with ice and orange juice. Add a squirt of 7-Up. (½ oz. Ouzo, optional)

DOUBLE STANDARD SOUR

Juice ½ Lemon or 1 Lime
½ tsp. Powdered Sugar
¾ oz. Blended Whisky
¾ oz. Gin
½ tsp. Raspberry Syrup or Grenadine

Shake with ice and strain into a Sour glass. Serve with a lemon wedge and a cherry.

DOUBLE TROUBLE

2 oz. Brandy
1 oz. Dry Vermouth
½ tsp. Grenadine
1 dash Angostura Bitters

Shake with ice and strain into a cocktail glass.

DOUGLAS

2 oz. Gin
1 oz. Dry Vermouth

Stir with ice and strain into a cocktail glass. Serve with an orange or lemon twist.

DOUGLAS FAIRBANKS

Juice 1 Lime
2 oz. Gin
1 oz. Apricot-flavored Brandy
1 Egg White

Shake with ice and strain into a Collins glass. Fill with ice.

DOWN THE HATCH COCKTAIL

¾ tsp. Blackberry-flavored Brandy
2 dashes Orange Bitters
2 oz. Bourbon Whisky

Shake with ice and strain into a cocktail glass.

DREAM COCKTAIL NO. 1

¾ oz. Triple Sec or Orange Curacao
1½ oz. Brandy
¼ tsp. Anisette

Shake with ice and strain into a cocktail glass.

DREAM COCKTAIL NO. 2

1 oz. Gin
½ oz. Apricot-flavored Brandy
½ oz. Grenadine
1 dash Lemon Juice

Shake with ice and strain into a cocktail glass.

DRONDA

1¾ oz. Gin
¾ oz. Calisay

Stir with ice and strain into a cocktail glass.

DRY COLD DECK

1¾ oz. Brandy
½ oz. Dry Vermouth
¼ oz. White Creme de Menthe

Shake with ice and strain into a cocktail glass.

DRY MANHATTAN

1¾ oz. Bourbon or Rye
¾ oz. Dry Vermouth

Stir with ice and strain into a cocktail glass. Serve with an olive.

DRY MANHATTAN COOLER

2 oz. Whisky
1 oz. Dry Vermouth
2 oz. Orange Juice
½ oz. Lemon Juice
½ oz. Orgeat Syrup

Shake with ice and strain into a Collins glass. Fill with soda and ice. Serve with a cherry.

DRY MARTINI

2 oz. Gin
¼ oz. Dry Vermouth

Stir with ice and strain into a cocktail glass. Serve with a lemon twist or an olive.

DRY ROB ROY

1¾ oz. Scotch
¾ oz. Dry Vermouth

Stir with ice and strain into a cocktail glass. Serve with an olive.

DRY RYE

2 oz. Rye
½ oz. Bitters

Stir with ice and strain into a cocktail glass. Serve with an olive.

DRY VERMOUTH COBBLER

3 oz. Dry Vermouth
3 oz. Club Soda

Fill a highball glass three-quarters full with crushed ice; pour in Vermouth and soda. Garnish with lemon peel.

DU BARRY COCKTAIL

1 dash Bitters
¾ oz. Dry Vermouth
½ tsp. Pernod
1½ oz. Gin

Stir with ice and strain into a cocktail glass. Serve with an orange slice.

DUBONNET AND APPLE

1½ oz. Apple Brandy
1½ oz. White Dubonnet

Stir with ice and strain into a cocktail glass.

DUBONNET AND CHERRY

1 oz. Cherry-flavored Brandy
1½ oz. Dubonnet

Stir with ice and strain into a cocktail glass. Serve with a lemon twist.

DUBONNET APPETIZER

2 oz. Dubonnet
Juice 1 Orange

Shake with ice and strain into a cocktail glass.

> Drink today and drown all sorrow,
> You shall perhaps not do it tomorrow.
> Best while you have it use your breath —
> There is no drinking after death.

DUBONNET APPLE

1¼ oz. Dubonnet
1¼ oz. Calvados

Stir with ice and strain into a cocktail glass. Serve with an orange wedge or an apple wedge.

DUBONNET AT SIX

1 dash Aromatic Bitters
2 oz. Brandy
2 oz. Dubonnet

Stir with ice and strain into a cocktail glass.

DUBONNET BLONDE FIZZ

Juice ¼ Lemon
Juice ½ Orange
1 tsp. Brandy
2 oz. White Dubonnet

Shake with ice and strain into a highball glass. Fill with chilled soda. Stir gently.

DUBONNET BLONDE MARTINI

2 oz. White Dubonnet
2 oz. Dry Vermouth

Stir with ice and strain into a cocktail glass.

DUBONNET CHAMPAGNE COCKTAIL

1 dash Bitters
1 oz. Dubonnet, chilled
Dry Champagne, well chilled
Sugar cube

Put the sugar cube in a champagne glass and dash with Bitters. Add an ice cube and chilled Dubonnet. Stir lightly. Fill with well-chilled Champagne. Serve with a lemon twist.

DUBONNET COCKTAIL NO. 1

1½ oz. Dubonnet
¾ oz. Gin
1 dash Orange Bitters (if desired)

Stir with ice and strain into a cocktail glass. Serve with a lemon twist.

DUBONNET COCKTAIL NO. 2

¾ oz. Gin
¾ oz. Dubonnet
2 dashes Maraschino Liqueur
2 drops Dry Vermouth

Shake with ice and strain into a cocktail glass.

DUBONNET DELIGHT

Juice ¼ Lemon
3 oz. Dubonnet
Soda, chilled

Combine lemon juice and Dubonnet. Pour over ice cubes in a large cocktail glass. Fill with chilled soda.

> Drink, drink, drink!
> Drink to the girl of your heart;
> The wisest, the wittiest, the bravest, the prettiest,
> May you never be far apart.

DUBONNET FIZZ

Juice ½ Orange
Juice ¼ Lemon
1 tsp. Cherry-flavored Brandy
2 oz. Dubonnet

Shake with ice and strain into a highball glass. Add two cubes of ice, fill with soda and stir.

DUBONNET HIGHBALL

2 oz. Dubonnet
Ginger Ale or Soda

Pour Dubonnet into a highball glass with two ice cubes and fill with Ginger ale or soda. Add a twist of lemon peel, if desired, and stir.

DUBONNET MANHATTAN

1½ oz. Dubonnet
1½ oz. Whisky

Stir with ice and strain into a cocktail glass. Add ice and top with a cherry.

DUBONNET MARTINI

2 oz. Dubonnet
2 oz. Dry Vermouth

Combine ingredients and stir well. Strain into a cocktail glass.

DUBONNET PUNCH

6 Limes
1 bottle Dubonnet
1 pint Gin
1 quart chilled Club Soda
Crushed Ice
Mint leaves

Squeeze limes and reserve shells. Pour the lime juice, Dubonnet and Gin into a large glass pitcher; add lime shells and soda. To serve, pack Collins or highball glasses three-quarters full with crushed ice. Fill up with punch and decorate with mint leaves. Makes 15-20 servings.

DUBONNET SUPREME COCKTAIL

1 oz. Orange-flavored Liqueur
1 oz. Amer Picon
2 oz. Dubonnet

Stir with ice and strain into a cocktail glass.

DUBONNET WITH A SMILE

1 oz. Lime Juice
1 dash Maraschino Liqueur
¾ oz. Brandy
1 oz. Dubonnet

Stir with ice and strain into a cocktail glass.

DUBONNET WITH A TWIST

¾ oz. Sweet Vermouth
¾ oz. Dry Vermouth
2 oz. Dubonnet

Stir with ice and strain into a cocktail glass. Serve with a lemon twist.

DUCHESS NO. 1

1½ oz. Pernod
½ oz. Dry Vermouth
½ oz. Sweet Vermouth

Shake with ice and strain into a cocktail glass.

DUCHESS NO. 2

2 tbsp. Vanilla Ice Cream
2 dashes Orange-flavored Liqueur
2 dashes Maraschino Liqueur
2 dashes Brandy
6 oz. Extra Dry Champagne, well chilled
1 slice each Pineapple, Orange, Lemon
2 Cherries
2 Strawberries

Put the first four ingredients in a pre-chilled Collins glass. Fill with Champagne. Stir. Garnish with fruit.

DUCK UNDER

1 oz. Gin
1 oz. Cointreau
1 oz. Grape Juice

Shake with ice and strain into a cocktail glass.

DUKE COCKTAIL

½ oz. Triple Sec or Orange Curacao
1 tsp. Orange Juice
2 tsp. Lemon Juice
½ tsp. Maraschino Liqueur
1 Egg

Shake with ice and strain into a cocktail glass. Fill with chilled Champagne and stir.

DUKE OF MARLBOROUGH

1½ oz. Sherry
1½ oz. Sweet Vermouth
3 dashes Raspberry Syrup
3 tbsp. Lime Juice

Shake with ice and strain into a cocktail glass. Add ice.

DULCET

1 oz. Vodka
½ oz. Cream
½ oz. Anisette
½ oz. Apricot-flavored Brandy
¼ oz. Lemon Juice

Shake with ice and strain into a cocktail glass. Top off with a brandied apricot.

DUMB DENNY

1 oz. Galliano
½ oz. Lemon Juice
¼ oz. Gin
¼ oz. Grenadine
1 oz. Cream
1 dash Triple Sec

Shake with ice and strain into a cocktail glass.

DUNDEE

1 oz. Gin
½ oz. Scotch
½ oz. Drambuie
¼ oz. Lemon Juice

Shake with ice and strain into an Old-fashioned glass. Add ice and a lemon twist.

DUNHILL'S SPECIAL

1 oz. Gin
1 oz. Sherry
1 oz. Dry Vermouth
¼ oz. Orange Curacao
1 dash Pernod

Stir with ice and strain into a cocktail glass. Serve with an olive.

DUNK COCKTAIL

⅓ oz. Galliano
1 oz. Gin
¼ oz. Blue Curacao
⅔ oz. Dry Vermouth

Stir with ice and strain into a cocktail glass. Serve with a cherry.

> Here is a riddle most
>   abstruse:
> Canst read the answer right?
> Why is it that my tongue
>   grows loose
> Only when I grow tight?

DUNLOP

1¾ oz. Rum
¾ oz. Sherry
1 dash Angostura Bitters

Shake with ice and strain into a cocktail glass.

DUPLEX

1¾ oz. Gin
¼ oz. Dry Vermouth
¼ oz. Sweet Vermouth
¼ oz. Lemon Juice
1 dash Orange Bitters

Shake with ice and strain into a cocktail glass.

DUPPY

1½ oz. Whisky
1 oz. Orange Curacao
Stir with a clove
2 dashes Orange Bitters

Stir with ice and strain into a cocktail glass.

DURANGO

1½ oz. Tequila
2 tbsp. Grapefruit Juice
1 tsp. Almond Extract
Mint sprigs

Shake with ice and strain into a double Old-fashioned glass. Add ice and fill with spring water. Garnish with mint leaves.

DURKEE HIGHBALL

1½ oz. Rum
¼ oz. Orange Curacao
¼ tsp. Sugar
½ oz. Lemon Juice

Mix in a highball glass. Fill with soda and ice.

DUSTY MARTINI

2¼ oz. Gin
¼ oz. Scotch

Stir with ice and strain into a cocktail glass. Serve with an olive.

DUTCH ALEXANDER

1 oz. Brandy
1 oz. Cream
1 oz. Vandermint

Shake with ice and strain into a cocktail glass.

DUTCH COFFEE

1½ oz. Vandermint

Pour into a fizz glass. Fill with hot coffee and top with whipped cream.

DUTCH GIRL

1½ oz. Brandy
¾ oz. Vandermint

Mix in an Old-fashioned glass. Fill with ice.

DUTCH TRADEWINDS

1½ oz. Gin
1 tbsp. Curacao
3 tbsp. Lemon Juice
1 Egg White
1 tsp. Sugar Syrup

Shake with ice and strain into a cocktail glass. Add ice.

DYSENTERY COCKTAIL NO. 1

1½ oz. Brandy
¾ oz. Port Wine
1½ oz. Blackberry-flavored Brandy
1 tsp. Sugar
¼ tsp. ground Nutmeg
¼ tsp. Jamaica Ginger

Put ingredients in a cocktail glass. Stir well, without ice.

DYSENTERY COCKTAIL NO. 2

1½ oz. Blackberry-flavored Brandy
1½ oz. Cognac Brandy
1 dash ground Nutmeg

Stir well, without ice. Use a cocktail glass.

EAGLE'S DREAM

½ oz. Lemon Juice
½ tsp. Sugar
1 Egg White
1½ oz. Gin
½ oz. Creme d'Yvette

Shake with ice and strain into a cocktail glass.

EARTHQUAKE NO. 1

1 oz. Gin
1 oz. Whisky
1 oz. Pernod

Shake with ice and strain into a cocktail glass.

EARTHQUAKE NO. 2

1½ oz. Tequila
1 tsp. Grenadine
2 Strawberries
1-2 dashes Orange Bitters
3 oz. crushed Ice

Blend at a high speed for 15 seconds. Serve with a lime slice and a strawberry.

EAST INDIA COCKTAIL NO. 1

1½ oz. Brandy
½ tsp. Pineapple Juice
½ tsp. Triple Sec or Red Curacao
1 tsp. Jamaica Rum
1 dash Bitters

Shake with ice and strain into a cocktail glass. Serve with a lemon twist and a cherry.

EAST INDIA COCKTAIL NO. 2

1½ oz. Dry Vermouth
1½ oz. Dry Sherry
1 dash Orange Bitters

Stir with ice and strain into a cocktail glass.

EAST INDIAN SPECIAL

1½ oz. Sherry
1½ oz. Dry Vermouth
1-2 dashes Orange Bitters

Shake with ice and strain into an Old-fashioned glass. Add ice.

EASY CHABLIS COOLER

1 tsp. Lemon Juice
Chablis

Fill a Collins glass half full with cracked ice. Add lemon juice and fill with Chablis. Serve with a lemon twist.

EASY LADY

1½ oz. Vodka
½ oz. Orange Curacao

Mix in an Old-fashioned glass. Fill with ice.

EASY LIFE

1½ oz. Vodka
½ oz. Brandy

Mix in an Old-fashioned glass. Add ice.

EASY MONEY

1 oz. Scotch Whisky
1 oz. Brandy

Mix in an Old-fashioned glass. Add ice.

EAU DU NIL COCKTAIL

1½ oz. Gin
½ oz. Whisky
¼ oz. Pernod
¼ oz. Grenadine

Shake with ice and strain into a cocktail glass.

ECLIPSE COCKTAIL

1 oz. Gin
2 oz. Sloe Gin
½ tsp. Lemon Juice

Into a cocktail glass, put enough Grenadine to cover a ripe olive. Mix the above ingredients with ice and pour carefully onto the Grenadine, without mixing. Serve with a twist of orange peel.

EDDIE BROWN

2 oz. Gin
1 oz. Lillet
2 dashes Apricot-flavored Brandy

Stir with ice and strain into a cocktail glass. Serve with a lemon twist.

EDIE CAFE

1½ oz. Galliano

Pour into an Old-fashioned glass. Fill with hot coffee and add ice.

EDITH DAY

1½ oz. Grapefruit Juice
1½ oz. Gin
1 Egg White
½ tsp. Sugar

Strain over crushed ice in a cocktail glass.

EDITOR'S CURSE

1 oz. Scotch
1 oz. Van der Hum
1 oz. Orange Juice

Shake with ice and strain into a cocktail glass.

EDWARD VIII COCKTAIL

1½ oz. Canadian Rye Whisky
1 dash Pernod
2 tsp. Sweet Vermouth
2 tsp. Water
1 piece Orange Peel

Mix in an Old-fashioned glass.

EGG AND WINE

1 Egg
1 oz. Sherry
1 tbsp. Sugar

Separate the egg. Beat the yolk with the sugar until creamy, add the Sherry and stir well. Beat the white until stiff. Fold the white with the Wine mixture and pour into a wine glass. Top with nutmeg.

EGG LEMONADE

1¼ oz. Brandy
2 tsp. Lemon Juice
1½ tsp. Sugar Syrup
1 Egg

Shake with ice and strain into a highball glass. Fill with soda and ice.

EGG MILK PUNCH

1 Egg
2 tsp. Powdered Sugar
1½ oz. Brandy
¾ oz. Rum
½ glass shaved Ice

Fill with milk. Shake well and strain into a punch cup. Sprinkle nutmeg on top.

EGGNOG

2-3 oz. Brandy or Light Rum
1 Egg
1 tbsp. Sugar
1 cup Milk
½ cup crushed Ice

Shake with ice and strain into a cocktail glass. Sprinkle nutmeg on top.

EGGNOG FOR ONE

1 Egg
2 tsp. Powdered Sugar
2 oz. Milk
4 oz. Rum
Few dashes Angostura Bitters

Heat the Rum, without boiling. Break the egg into a highball glass, add the sugar, Bitters and milk. Pour in the hot Rum and stir well. Serve hot.

EGGNOG TUACAN

1½ oz. Tuaca
3 oz. Milk
¼ tsp. Sugar

Shake with ice and strain into a highball glass. Add ice.

EGG SOUR

1 Egg
1 tsp. Powdered Sugar
2 oz. Brandy
¼ tsp. Triple Sec or Orange Curacao
Juice ½ Lemon

Shake with ice and strain into an Old-fashioned glass.

EGG SUISSESSE HIGHBALL

1 oz. Pernod
1 Egg White
½ oz. Orgeat Syrup

Shake with ice and strain into a highball glass. Fill with soda and ice.

EIGHT BALL

1 oz. Vodka
1 oz. Tia Maria

Mix in an Old-fashioned glass. Add ice.

EISENHOWER

1½ oz. Light Creme de Cacao
½ oz. Green Creme de Menthe

Mix in an Old-fashioned glass. Add ice.

EL DIABLO

½ Lime
1½ oz. Tequila
½ oz. Creme de Cassis
3-4 Ice cubes
Ginger Ale

Squeeze the juice of ½ a lime into a highball glass and then drop in the peel. Add Tequila, Cassis and ice cubes, fill with ginger ale and stir gently.

ELDORADO PUNCH

1 oz. Brandy
2 tsp. Powdered Sugar
½ oz. Jamaica Rum
½ oz. Bourbon Whisky

Shake with ice and strain into an Old-fashioned glass. Dress with fruits and add ice.

ELEGANT NO. 1

1¾ oz. Gin
½ oz. Dry Vermouth
¼ oz. Grand Marnier

Stir with ice and strain into a cocktail glass.

ELEGANT NO. 2

1½ oz. Bourbon
¼ oz. Maraschino Liqueur
¼ oz. Lemon Juice

Mix in an Old-fashioned glass. Fill with ice.

> Old friends are scarce,
> New friends are few;
> Here's hoping I've found
> One of each in you.

ELEPHANT'S EAR COCKTAIL

1 oz. Dry Vermouth
1 oz. Gin
1 oz. Dubonnet

Shake with ice and strain into a cocktail glass.

ELEPHANTS SOMETIMES FORGET

1 oz. Gin
¾ oz. Cherry-flavored Brandy
¾ oz. Lemon Juice
¼ oz. Dry Vermouth
1 dash Orange Bitters

Shake with ice and strain into a cocktail glass.

ELEPHANT WALK

1 oz. Gin
½ oz. Tequila
½ oz. fresh Orange Juice
1 dash Grenadine
1 dash Angostura Bitters
½ slice Orange
½ slice Lemon
2″ stick Cucumber

Fill an Old-fashioned glass with cracked ice. Add Gin, Tequila, orange juice, Grenadine and Bitters. Garnish with the orange, lemon and cucumber pieces. Serve with a swizzle stick.

ELK

1 oz. Gin
1 oz. Prunelle
2 dashes Dry Vermouth
3-4 cubes Ice

Shake with ice and strain into a cocktail glass.

ELK'S OWN COCKTAIL

1 Egg White
1½ oz. Rye or Bourbon Whisky
¾ oz. Port
1 tsp. Powdered Sugar
Juice ¼ Lemon

Shake with ice and strain into a cocktail glass. Add a strip of pineapple.

EL PRESIDENTE COCKTAIL NO. 1

1½ oz. Light Rum
½ oz. Curacao
½ oz. Dry Vermouth
1 dash Grenadine

Shake with ice and strain into a cocktail glass.

EL PRESIDENTE COCKTAIL NO. 2

Juice 1 Lime
1 tsp. Pineapple Juice
1 tsp. Grenadine
1½ oz. Dark Rum

Shake with ice and strain into a cocktail glass.

EL PRESIDENTE COCKTAIL NO. 3

¾ oz. Dry Vermouth
1½ oz. Dark Rum
1 dash Bitters

Stir with ice and strain into a cocktail glass.

EL PRESIDENTE COCKTAIL NO. 4

1½ oz. Gold Rum
¼ oz. Orange Curacao
½ oz. Dry Vermouth
¼ oz. Grenadine
¼ oz. Dark Rum
¼ oz. Lime Juice

Shake with ice and strain into a cocktail glass.

EMERALD

1 oz. Gin
¾ oz. Green Chartreuse
¾ oz. Sweet Vermouth
1 dash Orange Bitters

Stir with ice and strain into a cocktail glass. Serve with a cherry and a lemon twist.

EMERALD ISLE COCKTAIL

2 oz. Gin
1 tsp. Green Creme de Menthe
3 dashes Bitters

Stir with ice and strain into a cocktail glass.

EMERALD MIST

1½ oz. Irish Mist Liqueur
¾   oz. Blue Curacao

Shake with ice and strain into an Old-fashioned glass. Fill with ice.

EMERGENCY COCKTAIL

1   oz. Gin
1½ oz. Orange Juice

Shake with ice and strain into a cocktail glass. Sprinkle nutmeg on top.

EMERSON

1½ oz. Gin
1   oz. Sweet Vermouth
1   tsp. Maraschino Liqueur
Juice ½ Lime

Shake with ice and strain into a cocktail glass.

EMPIRE COCKTAIL

½   oz. Apricot-flavored Brandy
½   oz. Calvados
1   oz. Gin

Shake with ice and strain into a cocktail glass.

EMPIRE PEACH CUP PUNCH BOWL

2   large, ripe Peaches
2   bottles chilled Moselle
2   tbsp. superfine Sugar
1   bottle sparkling Moselle, chilled

Peel the peaches and drop them into a large glass pitcher or bowl. Add one of the bottles of Moselle and the sugar. Stir and refrigerate for half an hour. Add the second bottle of Moselle and the sparkling Moselle and serve immediately in wine glasses. Makes about 16 servings. To keep the bowl or pitcher cold, set it in a bed of crushed ice.

EMPIRE PUNCH

¼   oz. Benedictine
¼   oz. Orange Curacao
¼   oz. Brandy
3   oz. Claret

Mix in a Collins glass. Fill with ice and Champagne. Garnish with fruit.

ENGLISH BOLO

4   oz. Sherry
1½ oz. Lemon Juice
1   tsp. Sugar
1   Cinnamon stick

Muddle the sugar and the lemon juice with a cinnamon stick in an Old-fashioned glass. Add Sherry and stir.

ENGLISH COBBLER

½   oz. Lemon Juice
½   tsp. Sugar
1   oz. strong Tea
2   oz. Jamaica Rum

Mix in a highball glass, fill the glass with ice and garnish with berries. Serve with straws.

ENGLISH HIGHBALL

¾   oz. Gin
¾   oz. Brandy
¾   oz. Sweet Vermouth

Pour into highball glass over ice cubes and fill with ginger ale or soda. Add a lemon twist, if desired, and stir.

ENGLISH MULE

3   oz. Green Ginger Wine
1½ oz. Gin
2½ oz. Orange Juice

Mix in a Collins glass. Fill with soda and ice.

ENGLISH ROSE

1½ oz. Gin
¾   oz. Apricot-flavored Brandy
¾   oz. Dry Vermouth
1   tsp. Grenadine
¼   tsp. Lemon Juice

Prepare the rim of a cocktail glass by rubbing with lemon and dipping in sugar. Shake the above ingredients with ice and strain into the glass. Serve with a cherry.

E. NOS (OR ENOS)

1¾ oz. Gin
¾   oz. Dry Vermouth
¼   oz. Pernod

Stir with ice and strain into a cocktail glass. Serve with a cherry.

EPEE

2   oz. Cognac
½   oz. Sweet Vermouth

Stir with ice and strain into a cocktail glass.

EPICUREAN

½   oz. Kummel
¾   oz. Dry Vermouth
1½ oz. Cognac
1   dash Bitters

Stir with ice and strain into a cocktail glass.

ERIN COCKTAIL NO. 1

1¾ oz. Gin
¾   oz. Green Creme de Menthe

Stir with ice and strain into a cocktail glass. Add a green olive.

Drink to fair woman, who I think,
Is most entitled to it;
For if anything ever can drive me to drink
She certainly could do it.

ERIN COCKTAIL NO. 2

1½ oz. Gin
½ oz. Green Creme de Menthe
¼ oz. Lemon Juice
¼ oz. Orange Juice
1 Egg White

Shake with ice and strain into a cocktail glass. Add a green cherry and sprinkle nutmeg on top.

ERIN'S IRISH COCKTAIL

¼ oz. Green Creme de Menthe
2 tsp. Green Chartreuse
1½ oz. Irish Whisky

Shake with ice and strain into a cocktail glass.

ESKIMO

2 oz. Brandy
¼ oz. Maraschino Liqueur
¼ oz. Orange Curacao
1 oz. Vanilla Ice Cream

Shake with ice and strain into a large cocktail glass.

ETCHINGS

¾ oz. Brandy
¾ oz. Cherry-flavored Brandy
½ oz. Lemon Juice
¼ oz. Grenadine
¼ oz. Orange Curacao

Shake with ice and strain into a cocktail glass.

ETHEL COCKTAIL

1 oz. Apricot-flavored Brandy
1 oz. White Creme de Menthe
1 oz. Curacao

Shake with ice and strain into a cocktail glass.

ETHEL DUFFY COCKTAIL

¾ oz. Apricot-flavored Brandy
¾ oz. White Creme de Menthe
¾ oz. Triple Sec or Orange Curacao

Shake with ice and strain into a cocktail glass.

ETON (BLAZER) HIGHBALL

1 oz. Gin
½ oz. Kirschwasser
1 oz. Lemon Juice
½ tsp. Sugar

Shake with ice and strain into a highball glass. Fill with soda and ice.

EUREKA

1 oz. Gin
½ oz. Grenadine
½ oz. Lemon Juice
½ oz. Orange Juice

Shake with ice and strain into a cocktail glass.

EVANS

2 oz. Rye Whisky
¼ oz. Apricot-flavored Brandy
¼ oz. Orange Curacao

Stir with ice and strain into a cocktail glass.

EVE

Pink Champagne
Several drops of Pernod
1 tbsp. Cognac
2 tsp. Sugar
2 tsp. Curacao

Pour the Pernod drops into a wide champagne glass and turn the glass to coat its sides. Pour in Cognac. Soak the sugar with the Curacao until the sugar has dissolved, then add to the Cognac. Stir gently. Fill the glass with Champagne.

EVERGLADES SPECIAL

1 oz. White Rum
1 oz. White Creme de Cacao
1 oz. Light Cream
2 tsp. Coffee Liqueur

Shake with ice and strain into a cocktail glass. Fill with crushed ice.

EVERYBODY'S IRISH COCKTAIL

1 tsp. Green Creme de Menthe
1 tsp. Green Chartreuse
2 oz. Irish Whisky

Stir with ice and strain into a cocktail glass. Serve with a green olive.

EVERYBODY'S RUSH

1½ oz. Irish Whisky
1 tsp. Green Chartreuse
A few dashes Creme de Menthe

Shake with ice and strain into a cocktail glass. Add ice.

EVERYTHING BUT

¾ oz. Whisky
¾ oz. Gin
¾ oz. Lemon Juice
¾ oz. Orange Juice
1 tsp. Apricot-flavored Brandy
½ tsp. Powdered Sugar
1 Egg

Shake with ice and strain into a large cocktail glass.

EVE'S GARDEN

⅓ oz. Triple Sec or Orange Curacao
⅓ oz. Creme d'Yvette
⅓ oz. Apricot-flavored Brandy

Pour carefully, in order given, into a pony glass so that each ingredient floats on the preceding one without mixing. Float cream on top. Serve with a green cherry on a toothpick.

EWING

2¼ oz. Rye Whisky
¼ oz. Bitters

Stir with ice and strain into a cocktail glass.

EXORCIST

1½ oz. Tequila
¾ oz. Lime Juice
¾ oz. Blue Curacao

Shake with ice and strain into a cocktail glass

EXPORT CASSIS

2 oz. Dry Vermouth
1 oz. Creme de Cassis

Mix in a highball glass. Fill with soda and ice.

EXPOSITION COCKTAIL

1 oz. Sloe Gin
1 oz. Cherry-flavored Brandy
1 oz. Dry Vermouth

Shake with ice and strain into a cocktail glass.

EXPRESS COCKTAIL

1 dash Orange Bitters
1 oz. Sweet Vermouth
1¼ oz. Scotch Whisky

Shake with ice and strain into a cocktail glass.

EYE-IN-THE-GLASS

1 Egg Yolk
½ oz. Worcestershire Sauce
1½ oz. Port
Celery Salt
Black Pepper

Carefully place a whole egg yolk in a cocktail glass. Add the amount of black pepper desired, and Worcestershire sauce. Float the Port on top of the yolk. Sprinkle with celery salt —and swallow the drink without breaking the egg yolk.

EYE-OPENER COCKTAIL NO. 1

1 Egg Yolk
½ tsp. Powdered Sugar
1 tsp. Pernod
1 tsp. Triple Sec
1 tsp. White Creme de Cacao
2 oz. Light Rum

Shake with ice and strain into a flip glass.

> The man who drinks whisky
>   and water,
> Although he drinks early and
>   late,
> Will live to drink whisky
>   longer
> Than he who drinks whisky
>   straight.

EYE-OPENER COCKTAIL NO. 2

1 Egg Yolk
½ tsp. Powdered Sugar
1 tsp. Pernod
1 tsp. Curacao
1 tsp. Creme de Noyaux
2 oz. Dark Rum

Shake with ice and strain into a cocktail glass.

FAIR AND WARMER COCKTAIL NO. 1

¾ oz. Sweet Vermouth
1½ oz. Light Rum
½ tsp. Triple Sec

Stir with ice and strain into a cocktail glass. Serve with a lemon twist.

FAIR AND WARMER COCKTAIL NO. 2

¾ oz. Sloe Gin
¾ oz. Dubonnet
¾ oz. Sherry
¼ oz. Benedictine

Stir with ice and strain into a cocktail glass.

FAIRBANKS COCKTAIL NO. 1

¾ oz. Gin
¾ oz. Dry Vermouth
¾ oz. Apricot-flavored Brandy
1 dash Lemon Juice
1 dash Grenadine

Stir with ice and strain into a cocktail glass. Serve with a cherry.

FAIRBANKS COCKTAIL NO. 2

1¾ oz. Gin
¾ oz. Dry Vermouth
2 dashes Orange Bitters
2 dashes Creme de Noyaux

Stir with ice and strain into a cocktail glass. Serve with a cherry.

FAIR WEATHER

½ tsp. Sugar
1 dash Angostura Bitters
1 dash Orange Bitters
½ oz. Sweet Vermouth
1 oz. Apple Brandy

Mix in an Old-fashioned glass and add ice.

FAIRY BELLE COCKTAIL

1 Egg White
1 tsp. Grenadine
¾ oz. Apricot-flavored Brandy
1½ oz. Gin

Shake with ice and strain into a cocktail glass.

FALERNUM RUM COLLINS

1 tsp. Falernum
1½ oz. Barbados Rum
Juice ½ Lemon

Shake with ice and strain into a Collins glass. Fill with soda and ice.

FALERNUM TOM COLLINS

1 tsp. Falernum
1½ oz. Gin
Juice ½ Lemon

Shake with ice and strain into a Collins glass. Fill with soda and ice.

FALKLAND ISLAND WARMER

¼ oz. Lemon Juice
¼ tsp. Sugar
1 oz. Drambuie

Mix in an Old-fashioned glass. Fill with hot water.

FALLEN ANGEL COCKTAIL

Juice 1 Lime or ½ Lemon
1½ oz. Gin
1 dash Bitters
½ tsp. White Creme de Menthe

Shake with ice and strain into a cocktail glass. Serve with a cherry.

FALL RIVER

1 oz. Gin
1 oz. Brandy
¼ oz. White Creme de Menthe
¼ oz. Maraschino Liqueur

Stir with ice and strain into a cocktail glass.

> Here's to the girl who's
> bound to win,
> Her share at least of blisses,
> Who knows enough not to
> go in
> When it is raining kisses.

FANCIULLI

1 oz. Bourbon
½ oz. Sweet Vermouth
¼ oz. Fernet Branca

Pour over crushed ice in a cocktail glass.

FANCY BRANDY COCKTAIL

2 oz. Brandy
1 dash Bitters
¼ tsp. Triple Sec or Orange Curacao
¼ tsp. Powdered Sugar

Shake with ice and strain into a cocktail glass. Serve with a lemon twist. (Whisky or Gin may be substituted for Brandy.)

FANCY COCKTAIL NO. 1

2 oz. Bourbon
½ oz. Orange Curacao
2 dashes Angostura Bitters

Stir with ice and strain into a cocktail glass. Serve with a cherry and a lemon twist.

FANCY COCKTAIL NO. 2

1 oz. Cognac
1 dash Bitters

Stir with ice and strain into a sugar-rimmed cocktail glass. Fill with Champagne.

FANCY FREE

2 oz. Bourbon
½ oz. Maraschino Liqueur
1 dash Angostura Bitters
1 dash Orange Bitters

Stir with ice and strain into a cocktail glass.

FANCY GIN COCKTAIL

2 oz. Gin
½ oz. Orange Curacao
1 dash Bitters

Shake with ice and strain into a cocktail glass.

FANCY SLING

1 oz. Brandy
1 oz. Benedictine
1 oz. Pernod
½ oz. Lemon Juice
½ oz. Maraschino Liqueur

Shake with ice and strain into a Collins glass. Fill with ice water or soda. Sprinkle nutmeg on top.

FANCY SOUR

1 oz. Sweet Vermouth
1 dash Orange Bitters
1 dash Angostura Bitters
½ oz. Maraschino Liqueur
½ oz. Lemon Juice

Mix in an Old-fashioned glass. Fill with ice.

FANCY WHISKY COCKTAIL

2 oz. Whisky
½ oz. Orange Curacao
1 dash Bitters

Shake with ice and strain into a cocktail glass. Serve with a lemon twist.

FANDANGO COCKTAIL

1 oz. Gin
1 oz. Izarra
½ oz. Vodka

Stir with ice and strain into a cocktail glass.

FANS

1½ oz. Scotch Whisky
½ oz. Cointreau
½ oz. unsweetened Grapefruit Juice

Shake with ice and strain into a cocktail glass.

FAN TAN COCKTAIL

1½ oz. Ginger-flavored Brandy
½ oz. Lemon Juice
½ Egg White
1 dash Tabasco Sauce

Shake with ice and strain into a cocktail glass.

FANTASIA COCKTAIL

1 oz. Lime Juice
½ oz. Galliano
½ oz. Triple Sec or Orange Curacao
1½ oz. Early Times

Shake with ice and strain into a cocktail glass.

FANTASIO COCKTAIL

1 tsp. White Creme de Menthe
1 tsp. Maraschino Liqueur
1 oz. Brandy
¾ oz. Dry Vermouth

Stir with ice and strain into a cocktail glass. (Gin may be substituted for Dry Vermouth.)

FARE THEE WELL

1½ oz. Gin
½ oz. Dry Vermouth
1 dash Sweet Vermouth
1 dash Triple Sec or Orange Curacao

Shake with ice and strain into a cocktail glass.

FARMER'S COCKTAIL

1 oz. Gin
½ oz. Dry Vermouth
½ oz. Sweet Vermouth
2 dashes Bitters

Stir with ice and strain into a cocktail glass.

FASCINATION COCKTAIL

1 oz. Pernod
½ oz. Cointreau

Shake with ice and strain into a cocktail glass. Add a cube of ice and fill with soda.

FASCINATOR

1½ oz. Gin
½ oz. Dry Vermouth
¼ oz. Pernod

Shake with ice and strain into a cocktail glass. Serve with a mint sprig.

FAVORITE COCKTAIL NO. 1

¾ oz. Cognac
1¾ oz. Port

Stir with ice and strain into a cocktail glass.

FAVORITE COCKTAIL NO. 2

¾ oz. Apricot-flavored Brandy
¾ oz. Dry Vermouth
¾ oz. Gin
¼ tsp. Lemon Juice

Shake with ice and strain into a cocktail glass.

FEDORA PUNCH

1 oz. Lemon Juice
1 tsp. Sugar
1 oz. Cognac
½ oz. Jamaica Rum
½ oz. Bourbon
½ oz. Orange Curacao

Shake and pour over crushed ice in a highball glass. Garnish with fruit.

FEMINA COCKTAIL

1½ oz. Brandy
½ oz. Benedictine
½ oz. Orange Juice

Shake with ice and strain into a cocktail glass. Garnish with an orange slice.

FERNET BRANCA

2 oz. Gin
½ oz. Sweet Vermouth
½ oz. Fernet Branca
3-4 cubes Ice

Stir with ice and strain into a cocktail glass. Serve with a cherry.

FERNET COCKTAIL

1½ oz. Brandy
1½ oz. Fernet Branca
2 dashes Sugar Syrup
1 dash Angostura Bitters

Stir with ice and strain into a cocktail glass. Serve with a lemon twist.

FERN GULLY

1 oz. Light Rum
½ oz. Coconut Cream
¼ oz. Orange Juice
¼ oz. Orgeat
½ oz. Lime Juice
1 oz. Dark Rum

Blend with ice and strain into a cocktail glass.

FERN GULLY FIZZ

1 oz. Dark Jamaica Rum
1 oz. Rum
1 oz. Pineapple Juice
¾ oz. Lime Juice

Shake with ice and serve in a tall glass. Fill the glass with soda and add a pineapple stick and a lime wheel.

FESTIVAL COCKTAIL

¾   oz. Apricot-flavored Brandy
¾   oz. Creme de Cacao
¾   oz. Heavy Cream
1   tsp. Grenadine

Shake with ice and strain into a cocktail glass.

FIBBER McGEE

1½   oz. Gin
½   oz. Grapefruit Juice
½   oz. Sweet Vermouth
2   dashes Angostura Bitters

Stir with ice and strain into a cocktail glass.

FIFTH AVENUE NO. 1

½   oz. Creme de Cacao
½   oz. Apricot-flavored Brandy
1   tbsp. Sweet Cream

Pour carefully, in order given, into a parfait glass, so that each ingredient floats on the preceding one.

FIFTH AVENUE NO. 2

1½   oz. Gin
½   oz. Dry Vermouth
½   oz. Fernet Branca

Stir with ice and strain into a cocktail glass.

FIFTY-FIFTY COCKTAIL

1½   oz. Gin
1½   oz. Dry Vermouth

Stir with ice and strain into a cocktail glass.

FIG LEAF

1¼   oz. Sweet Vermouth
1   oz. Light Rum
1½   tbsp. Lime Juice
1   dash Angostura Bitters

Serve with a cherry. (Dry Vermouth may be substituted for Sweet Vermouth.)

FILMOGRAPH

1½   oz. Brandy
½   oz. Sirop de Citron
½   oz. Cola

Stir with ice and strain into a cocktail glass.

FIN DE SIECLE COCKTAIL

1½   oz. Gin
¾   oz. Sweet Vermouth
¼   oz. Amer Picon
1   dash Orange Bitters

Stir with ice and strain into a cocktail glass.

FINE-AND-DANDY COCKTAIL

Juice ¼ Lemon
½   oz. Triple Sec or Orange Curacao
1½   oz. Gin
1   dash Bitters

Shake with ice and strain into a cocktail glass. Serve with a cherry.

FINO

1¼   oz. Fino Sherry
1¼   oz. Sweet Vermouth

Stir with ice and strain into a cocktail glass. Serve with a lemon wedge.

FINO MARTINI

2   oz. Gin
2   tsp. Fino Sherry

Stir with ice and strain into a cocktail glass. Serve with a lemon twist.

FINO RICKEY

¾   oz. Fino Sherry
¾   oz. Gin

Stir in a highball glass. Fill with soda and ice. Add a squeeze of lime and leave the shell in the glass.

FIORD

1   oz. Brandy
½   oz. Aquavit
½   oz. Orange Juice
½   oz. Lime Juice
½   oz. Grenadine

Shake with ice and strain into a cocktail glass.

FIOUPE

1   oz. Brandy
1   oz. Sweet Vermouth
½   oz. Benedictine

Stir with ice and strain into a cocktail glass. Serve with a lemon twist and a cherry.

FIREMAN'S SOUR

Juice 2 Limes
½   tsp. Powdered Sugar
1   tbsp. Grenadine
2   oz. Light Rum

Shake with ice and strain into a Delmonico glass. Fill with soda. Decorate with a cherry and half a slice of lemon or a lime wheel.

FIREWORKS

¼   oz. Grenadine
¼   oz. Creme de Cassis
¼   oz. Apricot-flavored Brandy
¼   oz. Cointreau
¼   oz. Green Chartreuse
¼   oz. Cognac or other Brandy
¼   oz. Kirschwasser

Pour carefully, in the order given, into a 2 oz. liqueur glass.

FIRST REGIMENT PUNCH

¾   oz. Irish Whisky
¾   oz. Scotch Whisky
1   tsp. Powdered Sugar
3   dashes Lemon Juice
3   oz. Hot Water

Stir in a highball glass and serve.

162

FISHERMAN'S PLEASURE

½   oz. Lemon Juice
½   tsp. Sugar
2   tsp. Orange-flavored Liqueur
6   oz. Rhine Wine, chilled

Fill a Collins glass half full with cracked ice. Add lemon juice, sugar and liqueur. Fill with Wine. Stir. Garnish with slices of fresh fruit. Serve with straws.

FISH HOUSE PUNCH (INDIVIDUAL)

1   oz. Lemon Juice
½   tsp. Sugar
1   oz. Jamaica Rum
1   oz. Brandy
1   oz. Peach-flavored Brandy
1   oz. strong Tea

Mix in a Collins glass. Fill with soda and ice. Decorate with fruit.

FISH HOUSE PUNCH NO. 1

3   cups Lemon Juice
1   cup superfine Sugar
1   block Ice
1½ quarts Brandy
1   pint Peach-flavored Brandy
1   pint Rum
1   quart Club Soda
1   quart strong, cold, black Tea (optional)
Fruits in season

Put the lemon juice and sugar in a punch bowl and stir until sugar is dissolved. Add the large block of ice, both Brandies, Rum, club soda, tea (if desired) and stir well. Decorate with fruits in season. Serve in 4 oz. punch glasses. Serves approximately 34.

FISH HOUSE PUNCH NO. 2

3   6-oz. cans frozen concentrated Lemonade
2   bottles Dark Rum
2   bottles Golden Rum
2   bottles Brandy
1   cup Peach-flavored Brandy (optional)
1   block Tea Ice made from 1 qt. tea
3   quarts Water

Combine lemonade concentrate, Rums and Brandies. Allow to steep for about 2 hours at room temperature. When ready to serve, add tea ice and water and stir. Serve in punch glasses. Makes about 60 servings.

FISH HOUSE PUNCH NO. 3

1   cup Water
1½   cups superfine Sugar
3   cups Lemon Juice
3   pints dry White Wine
1   bottle Dark Rum
1   bottle Golden Rum
1   bottle Brandy
4   oz. Peach-flavored Brandy

Pour the water into a punch bowl, add sugar and lemon juice and stir until sugar is dissolved. Pour in Wine, both Rums, and the Brandies. Let the mixture stand at room temperature for a couple of hours and stir it occasionally. Just before serving, add a block of ice. Serve in 4 oz. punch glasses. Makes about 40 servings.

FITCHETTE

1¼   oz. Gin
¾   oz. Sweet Vermouth
½   oz. Benedictine
1   dash Orange Bitters

Shake with ice and strain into a cocktail glass. Add an olive.

FIVE FIFTEEN

1   oz. Dry Vermouth
1   oz. Orange Curacao
1   oz. Cream

Shake with ice and strain into a cocktail glass. Sprinkle nutmeg on top.

> Here's to the ships of our Navy,
> Here's to the ladies of our land,
> May the former be well rigged
> And the latter be well manned.

FIVE POUND NOTE

1½   oz. Lochan Ora
Bitter Lemon or Tonic, to taste
Squeeze of Lime

Stir with ice in a highball glass and serve.

FIX

2   tsp. Pineapple Syrup
½   oz. Lemon or Lime Juice
2   oz. Gin (or Applejack, Brandy, Rum or Whisky)
Float ½ oz. Green Chartreuse on top.

Mix in a Collins glass. Add ice. (Cointreau or Maraschino Liqueur may be substituted for pineapple syrup.)

FIZZ A LA VIOLETTE

2   oz. Gin
1   oz. Creme de Violette
1   Egg White
½   tsp. Sugar
½   oz. Cream
½   oz. Lime Juice
1   oz. Lemon Juice

Shake and pour into a tall glass. Fill with soda and ice.

FLAG

1 tsp. Creme d'Yvette
½ cup crushed Ice
1½ oz. Apricot-flavored Brandy
¼ oz. Curacao
1 oz. Claret (or other Dry Red Wine)

Put the Creme d'Yvette in a cocktail glass. Combine ice, Brandy and Curacao and shake vigorously. Carefully pour into the cocktail glass so as not to mix with the Creme d'Yvette. Top with the Claret, using a little more than an ounce if necessary.

FLAMBE

1 oz. Dry Vermouth
1 oz. Lemon Juice

Pack a cocktail glass with crushed ice and pour in Vermouth and lemon juice. Place a lemon wedge on top. Flame 1 oz. Galliano and pour over wedge.

FLAME THROWER

1½ oz. Vodka
¾ oz. Cherry Heering

Stir with ice and strain into an Old-fashioned glass.

FLAMING HOOKER

¾ oz. Drambuie
¼ oz. 151-proof Rum

Mix in a pony glass. Flame and serve.

FLAMING KAHLUA

¾ oz. Kahlua
¼ oz. Brandy

Mix in a pony glass. Flame and serve.

FLAMING PETER

1 oz. Vodka
1 oz. Cherry Heering
2 tsp. Dry Vermouth
2 tsp. Orange Juice

Shake with ice and strain into a cocktail glass.

FLAMING WITCH

1½ oz. Strega

Flame in a warmed snifter glass. Fill with 2 oz. hot Coffee or sip straight.

FLAMINGO COCKTAIL NO. 1

Juice ½ Lime
½ oz. Apricot-flavored Brandy
1½ oz. Gin
1 tsp. Grenadine

Shake with ice and strain into a cocktail glass.

FLAMINGO COCKTAIL NO. 2

1½ oz. Rum
1 dash Angostura Bitters

Mix in a Collins glass. Fill with 7-Up and ice and add a squeeze of lime.

FLANIGAN

1½ oz. Jamaica Rum
1 oz. Sweet Vermouth
1 dash Angostura Bitters
½ tsp. Sugar

Stir with ice and strain into a cocktail glass.

FLAPJACK

1¾ oz. Sherry
¾ oz. Cream
¼ tsp. Sugar

Shake with ice and strain into a cocktail glass.

FLASH

¾ oz. Cointreau
¾ oz. Kirschwasser
¾ oz. Benedictine
¾ oz. Maraschino Liqueur

Stir with ice and strain into a cocktail glass.

FLINTLOCK

1½ oz. Bourbon
½ oz. Apple Brandy
1 tsp. Lemon Juice
1-2 dashes White Creme de Menthe
Several drops Grenadine

Shake with ice and strain into a cocktail glass. Add ice.

FLOATER COCKTAIL

1½ oz. Imported Kummel
½ oz. Cognac Brandy

Fill a cocktail glass with shaved ice and add both ingredients.

FLOOR POLISH

1 oz. Gin
1 oz. Pineapple Juice
½ oz. Dry Vermouth
½ oz. Sweet Vermouth

Shake with ice and strain into a cocktail glass.

I wish thee health,
I wish thee wealth,
I wish thee gold in store,
I wish thee heaven upon earth —
What could I wish thee more?

FLORADORA

2 oz. Gin
2 oz. Lime Juice
1 tsp. Sugar Syrup
1 tbsp. Grenadine

Shake with ice and strain into a highball glass. Add soda.

FLORIDA NO. 1

½ oz. Gin
1½ tsp. Kirschwasser
1½ tsp. Triple Sec
1 oz. Orange Juice
1 tsp. Lemon Juice

Shake with ice and strain into a cocktail glass.

FLORIDA NO. 2

1½ oz. Grapefruit Juice
¾ oz. Galliano
1 oz. Gin
¼ oz. Campari

Shake with ice and strain into a cocktail glass. Add an orange slice.

FLORIDA NO. 3

1½ oz. Gin
1 oz. Orange Juice
½ tsp. Sugar

Shake with ice and strain into a cocktail glass.

Good company, good wine, good welcome — make good people.
— Shakespeare

FLORIDA PUNCH NO. 1

1 oz. Grapefruit Juice
1 oz. Orange Juice
1 oz. Dark Rum
½ oz. Brandy

Shake with ice and strain into a cocktail glass.

FLORIDA PUNCH NO. 2

2 oz. Bourbon
2 oz. Pineapple Juice
½ tsp. Sugar

Mix in a highball glass. Fill with soda and ice. Garnish with fruit.

FLORIDA SPECIAL NO. 1

1½ oz. Rum
¾ oz. Pineapple Juice
¼ oz. Dry Vermouth
¼ oz. Sweet Vermouth

Stir with ice and strain into a Collins glass.

FLORIDA SPECIAL NO. 2

2 oz. Gin
1¼ oz. Orange Juice

Mix in a Collins glass. Fill with crushed ice and ginger ale. Serve with a twist of orange peel.

FLORIDIAN NO. 1

1½ oz. Dry Vermouth
½ oz. Forbidden Fruit
¼ oz. Falernum
2 oz. Grapefruit
2 dashes Orange Bitters

Shake with ice and strain into a cocktail glass. Add a squeeze of lime.

FLORIDIAN NO. 2

1 oz. Gin
1 oz. Rum
1 oz. Orange Juice

Shake with ice and strain into a cocktail glass.

FLORIDIAN NO. 3

1½ oz. Rye Whisky
½ oz. Sweet Vermouth
¼ oz. Orange Curacao
¼ oz. Amer Picon
1 dash Bitters

Stir with ice and strain into a cocktail glass. Serve with a lemon twist.

FLORIDITA

1 oz. Lime Juice
2 oz. Rum
¼ oz. Grapefruit Juice
¼ oz. Maraschino Liqueur
½ tsp. Sugar

Shake with ice and strain into a cocktail glass.

FLU

3 oz. Rye Whisky
1 tsp. Ginger-flavored Brandy
1 tsp. Rock Candy Syrup
1 dash Jamaica Rum
Juice ¼ Lemon

Stir with ice and strain into a cocktail glass.

FLUFFY RUFFLES

1¼ oz. Rum
1¼ oz. Sweet Vermouth

Stir with ice and strain into a cocktail glass. Add a twist of lemon or lime.

FLYING DUTCHMAN NO. 1

2 oz. Gin
1 dash Triple Sec

Shake with ice and strain into an Old-fashioned glass over ice cubes.

FLYING DUTCHMAN NO. 2

Coat the inside of a cocktail glass with Orange Curacao, then add:

2½ oz. chilled Gin

FLYING FISH

1¾ oz. Gin
¾ oz. Orange Curacao
¼ oz. Maraschino Liqueur
1 dash Peach Bitters

(Cordial Medoc may be substituted for Curacao and Bitters.) Stir with ice and strain into a cocktail glass.

FLYING FORTRESS

1½ oz. Cognac
½ oz. Cointreau
½ oz. Anisette
1 oz. Vodka

Shake with ice and strain into a cocktail glass.

FLYING GRASSHOPPER COCKTAIL

¾ oz. Green Creme de Menthe
¾ oz. White Creme de Cacao
1 oz. Vodka

Stir with ice and strain into a cocktail glass.

FLYING HIGH

1½ oz. Gin
1 oz. Orange Juice
1 oz. Cherry Heering
¼ oz. Lemon Juice
1 dash Angostura Bitters
1 Egg White

Shake with ice and strain into a large cocktail glass.

FLYING SCOTCHMAN COCKTAIL

1 oz. Sweet Vermouth
1 oz. Scotch Whisky
1 dash Bitters
¼ tsp. Sugar Syrup

Stir with ice and strain into a cocktail glass.

FLYING TIGER COCKTAIL NO. 1

1¾ oz. Rum
½ oz. Gin
¼ oz. Grenadine
1 dash Bitters
¼ tsp. Sugar

Stir with ice and strain into a cocktail glass.

FLYING TIGER COCKTAIL NO. 2

¾ oz. Vodka
¾ oz. White Creme de Menthe
¾ oz. Galliano

Mix in an Old-fashioned glass.

FOAMY MARSALA

½ oz. Tea
2 tsp. Sugar
1 dash Cinnamon
1 dash Mace
6 oz. cold Water
4 oz. Vanilla Ice Cream, softened
2 oz. Marsala

Combine tea, sugar, cinnamon and mace in a mixing bowl. Blend in cold water. Beat in ice cream and Marsala until smooth and foamy. Pour into a Collins glass.

FOG CUTTER

1½ oz. Rum
½ oz. Brandy
½ oz. Gin
1 oz. Orange Juice
1½ oz. Lemon Juice
1½ tsp. Orgeat Syrup

Shake all ingredients and strain into a Collins glass over ice cubes. Top with a teaspoon of sweet Sherry.

FOGGY DAY

1½ oz. Gin
1 tsp. Pernod

Shake with ice and strain into an Old-fashioned glass. Rub a lemon slice around the rim of the glass, then drop it in. Add ice.

FOG HORN NO. 1

Juice ½ Lime
1½ oz. Gin

Pour the ingredients into a highball glass over ice cubes. Fill with ginger ale. Stir. Add a piece of lime.

FOG HORN NO. 2

½ oz. Lemon Juice
1½ oz. Gin

Pour into a highball glass over ice cubes. Fill with ginger beer.

FONTAINEBLEU SPECIAL

1 oz. Brandy
1 oz. Anisette
½ oz. Dry Vermouth

Shake with ice and strain into a cocktail glass.

FORESTER

1½ oz. Bourbon
½ oz. Lemon Juice
½ oz. Cherry Juice

Shake with ice and strain into a cocktail glass. Serve with a cherry.

FORT LAUDERDALE

1½ oz. Rum
½ oz. Sweet Vermouth
Juice ¼ Orange
Juice ¼ Lime

Shake with ice and strain into an Old-fashioned glass. Add a slice of orange.

FOR VISITING AUNTS

Iced Tea
Rum

Mix with ice in a Collins glass. Vary amount of Rum to taste.

FOUR FLUSH

1½ oz. Rum
½ oz. Swedish Punch
½ oz. Dry Vermouth
1 dash Grenadine or Sugar Syrup

Stir with ice and strain into a cocktail glass.

FOUR SECTORS

1   oz. Bourbon
1   oz. Vodka
1   oz. Grand Marnier
1   oz. unsweetened Lime Juice
2-3 dashes Angostura Bitters

Shake with ice and strain into an Old-fashioned glass. Garnish with slices of fruit, a slice of cucumber and a cherry.

FOURTH DEGREE NO. 1

¾   oz. Gin
¾   oz. Dry Vermouth
¾   oz. Sweet Vermouth
¼   oz. Pernod

Stir with ice and strain into a cocktail glass. Add a lemon twist and a cherry.

FOURTH DEGREE NO. 2

1¾ oz. Gin
¼   oz. Pernod
½   oz. Sweet Vermouth

Stir with ice and strain into a cocktail glass. Add a lemon twist and a cherry.

FOUR W

1½ oz. Jamaican or Cuban Rum
1½ oz. unsweetened Grapefruit Juice
1   dash Bitters
1   dash Maple Syrup

Shake with ice and strain into a cocktail glass.

FOXHOUND

1½ oz. Brandy
1½ oz. Cranberry Juice
¼   oz. Kummel
¼   oz. Lemon Juice

Shake with ice and strain into a cocktail glass.

FOX RIVER COCKTAIL

½   oz. Creme de Cacao
2   oz. Bourbon or Rye Whisky
4   dashes Bitters

Stir with ice and strain into a cocktail glass. Serve with a lemon twist.

FOX TROT

½   oz. Lemon or Lime Juice
1½ oz. Rum
½   oz. Orange Curacao

Shake with ice and strain into a cocktail glass.

> To our host, an excellent man;
> For is not man fairly judged by the company he keeps?

FRAISE FIZZ

1½ oz. Gin
1   oz. Chambery Fraise
½   oz. Lemon Juice
1   tsp. Sugar

Shake with ice and strain into a Collins glass. Fill with soda and ice and add a lemon twist. Top with a strawberry.

FRANCE FIZZ

1½ oz. Cognac
½   tsp. Pernod
½   tsp. Lemon Juice
½   tsp. Curacao
½   tsp. Grenadine

Shake with ice and strain into a highball glass. Fill with soda.

FRANCES ANN

1½ oz. Scotch Whisky
½   oz. Dry Vermouth
½   oz. Cherry Heering

Stir with ice and strain into a cocktail glass.

FRANCIS

1   oz. Gin
1   oz. Brandy
¼   oz. Dry Vermouth
¼   oz. Grand Marnier

Stir with ice and strain into a cocktail glass.

FRANGI PANGI

¾   oz. Galliano
1   oz. Rum
½   oz. Lime Juice
¼   tsp. Sugar
2   oz. Grape Juice

Shake with ice and strain into a large cocktail glass. Fill with crushed ice. Serve with an orange slice and a cherry.

FRANKENJACK COCKTAIL

1   oz. Gin
¾   oz. Dry Vermouth
½   oz. Apricot-flavored Brandy
1   tsp. Triple Sec or Orange Curacao

Stir with ice and strain into a cocktail glass. Serve with a cherry.

FRANKENSTEIN COCKTAIL

1   oz. Gin
1   oz. Dry Vermouth
½   oz. Apricot Liqueur
½   oz. Cointreau

Shake with ice and strain into a cocktail glass.

FRANKENSTEIN'S DELIGHT

2   cubes Ice
2   tsp. fresh Lemon Juice
1½   oz. Pernod
Extra Dry Champagne, chilled

Put ice cubes into a Collins glass. Add lemon juice and Pernod. Fill with Champagne and stir.

FRANK'S REFRESHER

1½ oz. Brandy
½ oz. Grenadine or Raspberry Syrup
Juice ½ Lemon

Mix with ice cubes in a highball glass. Fill with chilled Champagne and serve.

FRANK'S SPECIAL

1½ oz. Gin
¾ oz. Dry Vermouth
¼ oz. Peach-flavored Brandy

Stir with ice and strain into a cocktail glass.

FRANK'S SPECIAL FIZZ

1 oz. Lemon Juice
2 oz. Gin
½ tsp. Sugar
¼ Peach, crushed

Shake with ice and strain into a Collins glass. Add chilled Champagne or soda, and ice.

FRANK SULLIVAN

¾ oz. Brandy
¾ oz. Cointreau
¾ oz. Lillet
¾ oz. Lemon Juice

Shake with ice and strain into a cocktail glass.

FRAPPE WITH PERNOD

1½ oz. Pernod
½ oz. Anisette
2 dashes Angostura Bitters

Shake with ice and strain into a cocktail glass over crushed ice.

> Friendship's the wine of life.
> Let's drink of it and to it.

FREDDY FUDPUCKER

1½ oz. Tequila

Serve in a Collins glass. Fill with ice and orange juice. Float ¾ oz. Galliano on top.

FREDDY'S SPECIAL

1 oz. Cream
1 oz. Cognac
1 oz. Gin
1 oz. Galliano

Shake with ice and strain into a cocktail glass.

FREE SILVER

Juice ¼ Lemon
½ tsp. Powdered Sugar
1½ oz. Gin
½ oz. Dark Rum
1 tbsp. Milk

Shake with ice and strain into a Collins glass over ice cubes. Add soda.

FRENCH

1½ oz. Gin
¾ oz. Prunella
¼ oz. Kirschwasser
1 dash Grenadine

Shake with ice and strain into a cocktail glass.

FRENCH APPETIZER

1 tsp. Dry Vermouth
2-3 drops Pepsin
1-2 dashes Pernod

Stir with ice and strain into a highball glass. Fill with soda and ice.

FRENCH CHERRY

1½ oz. Dry Vermouth
½ oz. Creme de Kirsch

Mix in an Old-fashioned glass. Fill with crushed ice.

FRENCH CONNECTION

1½ oz. Cognac or Brandy
¾ oz. Amaretto

Mix in an Old-fashioned glass. Fill with crushed ice.

FRENCH CURACAO FRAPPE

½ oz. Pernod
½ oz. Orange Curacao
¼ oz. Lemon Juice
½ oz. Orange Juice

Stir without ice, then pour into a cocktail glass packed with crushed ice. Add an orange slice.

FRENCH EGGNOG

1½ oz. Brandy
2 dashes Rum
2 tsp. Sugar Syrup
2 Egg Yolks
3 oz. hot Milk

Beat egg with sugar syrup and a little hot milk. Then add Brandy, milk and Rum.

FRENCH FOAM

1 tsp. Sugar
1 dash Angostura Bitters
¼ oz. Brandy
¼ oz. Kirschwasser

Mix in a Collins glass. Fill with Champagne and float a small scoop of lemon sherbet on top.

FRENCH GREEN DRAGON

1½ oz. Cognac
1½ oz. Green Chartreuse

Shake with ice and strain into a cocktail glass. Add ice.

FRENCH GREENERY

1½   oz. Pernod
1½   oz. Green Creme de Menthe

Mix Pernod and Creme de Menthe and pour over ice cubes in an Old-fashioned glass. Add a sprig of mint for decoration.

FRENCH KISS

1½   oz. Gin
½   oz. Grand Marnier

Mix in an Old-fashioned glass. Fill with crushed ice.

FRENCH MAMMA

1½   oz. Brandy
½   oz. Creme de Cassis

Mix in an Old-fashioned glass. Fill with crushed ice.

FRENCH MANHATTAN

1¾   oz. Dubonnet
¾   oz. Dry Vermouth

Stir with ice and strain into a cocktail glass.

FRENCH ORANGE

1½   oz. Dry Vermouth
½   oz. Orange Curacao

Mix in an Old-fashioned glass and fill with crushed ice.

FRENCH RIVIERA

2   oz. Rye
1   oz. Apricot-flavored Brandy
1   tsp. Lemon Juice

Shake with ice and strain into a cocktail glass. Serve with a cherry.

FRENCH ROSE

1½   oz. Gin
½   oz. Cherry-flavored Brandy
½   oz. Cherry Liqueur

Stir with ice and strain into a cocktail glass.

FRENCH 75

1   oz. Lemon Juice
2   tsp. Sugar
2   oz. Gin

Stir in a Collins glass. Fill with ice and Champagne. Add a lemon wedge and an orange slice. Serve with straws.

FRENCH 95

Substitute Bourbon for the Gin in French 75

FRENCH 125

Substitute Brandy for the Gin in French 75

FRENCH TRI COLOR

⅓   oz. Grenadine
⅓   oz. Maraschino Liqueur
⅓   oz. Creme d'Yvette

Pour carefully, in order given, into a pony glass so that each ingredient floats on the preceding one without mixing.

FRENCH TWIST

1   scoop Vanilla Ice Cream
1   oz. Benedictine
½   oz. Pernod

Blend the ingredients and serve in a champagne glass.

FRENCH VERMOUTH AND CURACAO

2   oz. Dry Vermouth
1½   oz. Curacao
Soda

Pour the Vermouth into a highball glass and mix with Curacao. Add ice and fill with soda. Stir gently.

FRENCH VERMOUTH COCKTAIL

2   oz. Dry Vermouth
2   dashes Angostura Bitters
2   dashes Orange Bitters

Stir with ice and strain into a cocktail glass. Serve with a lemon twist and an olive.

FRENCH WENCH

2   oz. Dubonnet

Pour into a highball glass. Fill with ice and ginger ale. Add a squeeze of lime juice.

FRESCO

1   tsp. Sugar Syrup
½   oz. Lime Juice
2   oz. Rum
1   piece Pineapple, crushed

Shake with ice and strain into a frosted cocktail glass.

FRIGID QUACK

2   oz. frozen Raspberries, thawed
½   oz. fresh Lemon Juice
6   oz. Cold Duck, well chilled

Frost a tall glass by placing it in the freezer for 10-15 minutes. Press the thawed raspberries through a sieve. Add lemon juice. Mix with Cold Duck and serve in the frosted glass.

FRIGID WITCH

1½ oz. Strega

Pour into an Old-fashioned glass. Fill with crushed ice and add a squeeze of lime juice.

FRISCO

2 oz. Bourbon
½ oz. Benedictine

Stir with ice and strain into a cocktail glass. Serve with a lemon twist.

FRISCO CHAMPAGNE COCKTAIL

1 tsp. Grenadine
3 oz. Brandy
Juice ½ Lemon
Dry Champagne

Combine the first three ingredients and shake well. Strain into a champagne glass. Fill with well-chilled Champagne.

> Here's to good old whisky,
> So amber and so clear.
> 'Tis not so sweet as
> woman's lips
> But a damned sight more
> sincere.

FRISCO SOUR

2 oz. Whisky
1 tbsp. Lemon Juice
1 tbsp. Lime Juice
½ oz. Raspberry Syrup or Grenadine

Shake with ice and strain into a Sour or Delmonico glass. Fill with soda. Serve with a lemon wedge and a lime wheel.

FROBISHER

2 oz. Gin
1 dash Bitters

Mix in a Collins glass. Serve with a lemon twist.

FROSTBITE

1 oz. Tequila
2 oz. Heavy Cream
2 tsp. White Creme de Cacao
3 oz. crushed Ice

Blend at a low speed for 15 seconds. Strain and serve straight up in an Old-fashioned glass.

FROST GOLD

1 oz. Orange Juice, chilled
3 oz. Chablis, chilled
1 slice Orange

Stir with ice and strain into a Collins glass. Serve with an orange slice.

FROSTY COFFEE ROYALE

1½ tsp. Instant Coffee
1½ oz. Brandy
Whipped Cream
Chocolate Curls

In a Collins glass, dissolve the instant coffee in warm water. Add Brandy and fill with ice and water. Top with whipped cream and chocolate curls. Serve with a cinnamon stick.

FROSTY DAWN

1½ oz. Rum
1 oz. Orange Juice
½ oz. Falernum
¼ oz. Maraschino Liqueur

Shake with ice and strain into a cocktail glass.

FROSTY VINE

2 oz. Vanilla Ice Cream
1 oz. Brandy
1 oz. Port

Blend at a high speed until smooth. Serve straight up in a parfait glass.

FROTH BLOWER COCKTAIL

1 Egg White
1 tsp. Grenadine
2 oz. Gin

Shake with ice and strain into a cocktail glass.

FROTHY DAWN COCKTAIL

1½ oz. White Rum
1 oz. Orange Juice
2 tsp. Falernum
1 tsp. Maraschino Liqueur

Shake with ice and strain into a cocktail glass. Add ice.

FROTHY RIESLING

Rind of ⅓ Orange, grated
Rind of ⅓ Lemon, grated
Juice of ⅓ Orange
Juice of ⅓ Lemon
1 Egg White
1 tbsp. Sugar
8 oz. Riesling, chilled
1 scoop Lemon Sherbet
1 sprig Mint

Beat the egg white, adding sugar, grated rinds and fruit juices. When egg white becomes stiff, add chilled Wine. Beat until mixture becomes frothy. Pour into a pre-chilled Collins glass. Garnish with a scoop of lemon sherbet and a mint sprig.

FROU FROU

1½ oz. Gin
½ oz. Dry Vermouth
½ oz. Sweet Vermouth

Shake the ingredients together with a pineapple spear and an orange slice. Strain into a cocktail glass. Add a cherry.

FROUPE COCKTAIL

1½ oz. Sweet Vermouth
1½ oz. Brandy
1 tsp. Benedictine

Stir with ice and strain into a cocktail glass.

FROZEN ABSINTHE

1½ oz. Pernod
½ tsp. Sugar

Shake with ice and pour into a highball glass. Fill with soda and ice.

FROZEN APPLE

1½ oz. Applejack
1 tbsp. Lime Juice
1 tsp. Sugar
½ Egg White

Combine ingredients with a cup of crushed ice in a blender and blend at a low speed. Pour into an Old-fashioned glass.

FROZEN APPLE AND BANANA

1½ oz. Apple Brandy
½ oz. Banana Liqueur
2 tsp. Lime Juice

Shake with ice and strain into a cocktail glass. Garnish with a slice of banana.

FROZEN APPLE DAIQUIRI

1½ oz. Rum
½ oz. Applejack
½ oz. Lime Juice
1 tsp. Sugar

Blend with crushed ice and pour into a large cocktail glass packed with crushed ice. Add an apple wedge and a cherry.

FROZEN AQUAVIT

1½ oz. Aquavit
½ oz. Lime Juice
½ Egg White
1 tsp. Sugar
¼ oz. Kirschwasser

Blend with crushed ice and pour into a cocktail glass packed with crushed ice.

FROZEN BAPPLE

1½ oz. Applejack
½ oz. Creme de Bananes
½ oz. Lime Juice

Blend with crushed ice and pour into a cocktail glass packed with crushed ice. Add an apple wedge and a slice of banana.

FROZEN B.C.

1 oz. Creme de Cassis
1 oz. Pineapple Juice
1½ oz. Brandy

Blend with crushed ice and pour into a cocktail glass packed with crushed ice.

FROZEN BERKELEY

1½ oz. Rum
½ oz. Brandy
1 tbsp. Passion Fruit Syrup
1 tbsp. Lemon Juice

Combine ingredients with half a cup of crushed ice in a blender and blend at low speed. Pour into a champagne glass.

FROZEN BLACKBERRY TEQUILA

1½ oz. Tequila
1 oz. Blackberry Liqueur
2 tsp. Lemon Juice

Shake with ice and strain into a cocktail glass. Serve with a lemon slice.

FROZEN BLACKCURRANT

1 oz. Creme de Cassis
1 oz. Pineapple Juice
2 tsp. Brandy

Shake with ice and strain into a cocktail glass. Serve with an orange slice.

FROZEN BLACK TEQ

1½ oz. Tequila
1 oz. Blackberry Liqueur
½ oz. Lemon Juice

Blend with crushed ice and pour into a cocktail glass packed with crushed ice. Serve with a lemon wedge.

FROZEN BRANDY AND PORT

1 oz. Brandy
¾ oz. Port
1 Egg
1 tsp. Powdered Sugar

Shake with ice and strain into a cocktail glass. Sprinkle nutmeg on top.

FROZEN BRANDY AND RUM

1½ oz. Brandy
1 oz. Rum
1 tbsp. Lemon Juice
1 Egg Yolk
1 tsp. Powdered Sugar

Combine ingredients with a cup of crushed ice in a blender and blend at low speed. Pour into an Old-fashioned glass.

Here's to the girl with eyes
  of brown,
If you ask for a kiss she will
  call you down;
Here's to the girl with eyes
  of blue,
If you ask for one — she will
  say, yes, take two.

FROZEN DAIQUIRI

1½ oz. Rum
1 tbsp. Triple Sec
1½ oz. Lime Juice
1 tsp. Sugar
1 cup crushed Ice

Combine the ingredients in a blender and blend at a low speed for 5 seconds. Then blend at a high speed until firm. Pour into a champagne glass. Top with a cherry.

FROZEN GO

1½ oz. Rum
¾ oz. Guava Nectar
½ oz. Lime Juice
½ oz. Orange Juice

Blend with crushed ice and pour into a cocktail glass packed with crushed ice.

FROZEN GUAVA DAIQUIRI

1½ oz. Rum
1 oz. Guava Nectar
½ oz. Lime Juice
¼ oz. Creme de Bananes

Blend with crushed ice and pour into a cocktail glass packed with crushed ice.

FROZEN JULEP

2 oz. Bourbon
1 oz. Lemon Juice
1 oz. Sugar Syrup
6 oz. crushed Ice
Several Mint sprigs, crushed

Blend at high speed for 20 seconds. Serve straight up in a highball glass. Top with a cherry and a mint sprig.

FROZEN LIME DAIQUIRI

2 oz. White Rum
2 tsp. Lime Liqueur
2 tsp. Lime Juice

Shake with ice and strain into a cocktail glass. Serve with a lime wheel.

> O water, pure, free of pollution,
> I vainly wish that I dared trust it,
> But I've an iron constitution
> And much I fear that water'd rust it.

FROZEN MANDEE

1½ oz. Rum
1 oz. Mango Nectar
½ oz. Lime Liqueur
½ oz. Lime Juice

Blend with crushed ice and pour into a cocktail glass packed with crushed ice.

FROZEN MANGO-LIME DAIQUIRI

1½ oz. White Rum
1 oz. Mango Nectar
2 tsp. Lime Liqueur
2 tsp. Lime Juice

Pour into a champagne glass. Garnish with a slice of mango.

FROZEN MATADOR

1½ oz. Tequila
2 oz. Pineapple Juice
1 tbsp. Lime Juice

Combine all ingredients with a cup of crushed ice in a blender. Blend at a low speed and pour into an Old-fashioned glass. Add a pineapple stick.

FROZEN MINT DAIQUIRI

2 oz. Rum
1 tbsp. Lime Juice
6 Mint leaves
1 tsp. Sugar

Combine all ingredients with a cup of crushed ice in a blender, and blend at a low speed. Pour into an Old-fashioned glass.

FROZEN PASSION

1½ oz. Rum
½ oz. Passion Fruit Syrup
½ oz. Lime Juice
½ oz. Orange Juice
¼ oz. Lemon Juice
¼ tsp. Sugar

Blend with crushed ice and pour into a cocktail glass packed with crushed ice.

FROZEN PEACH DAIQUIRI

1½ oz. Rum
½ oz. Lime Juice
½ oz. Peach Liqueur or Peach Syrup
Several crushed Peach slices

Blend with crushed ice and pour into a large cocktail glass packed with crushed ice. Garnish with a peach slice.

FROZEN PINEAPPLE DAIQUIRI

1½ oz. Rum
4 Pineapple chunks (canned)
1 tbsp. Lime Juice
½ tsp. Sugar

Combine all the ingredients with a cup of crushed ice in a blender. Blend at a low speed and pour into a champagne glass.

FROZEN RUM HONEY

2 oz. 151-proof Rum
½ oz. Honey
2 tsp. Lemon Juice

Blend at a high speed for no more than 15 seconds. Strain into a cocktail glass and add ice.

FROZEN RUSSIAN APPLE

1½   oz. Vodka
½   oz. Applejack
½   oz. Lime Juice
Several pieces of Apple

Blend with crushed ice and pour into a cocktail glass packed with crushed ice.

FROZEN SCOTCH EL BORRACHO

Juice ½ Lemon
½   tsp. Sugar
1   dash Cointreau
1   dash Bitters
1   thin slice fresh Pineapple
1½   oz. Scotch

Blend with crushed ice and pour into an Old-fashioned glass. Garnish with a stick of pineapple.

FROZEN SESAME DAIQUIRI

1½   oz. Rum
½   oz. Sesame Syrup
2   tsp. Lime Juice
2   tsp. Dry Vermouth
2   tsp. Orange Juice

Shake with ice and strain into a cocktail glass.

FROZEN SOURSOP DAIQUIRI

1½   oz. White Rum
¼   oz. Jamaica Rum
1   oz. Soursop (Guanabana) Nectar
1   tsp. Lime Juice
2   oz. Bananas

Blend with ice and strain into a champagne glass.

FROZEN STEPPES

2   oz. Vanilla Ice Cream
2   tbsp. Vodka
1   tbsp. Dark Creme de Cacao

Blend at a high speed until smooth. Serve straight up in a cocktail glass.

FRUITED RHINE COOLER

2   oz. Pineapple Juice or Apricot Nectar
4   oz. Rhine Wine
1   tsp. Sugar
2   oz. Ginger Ale, chilled
Spears of Honeydew Melon and Pineapple
Mint sprigs

Combine pineapple juice, Wine and sugar in a Collins glass. Stir until the sugar is dissolved and add chilled ginger ale. Fill with crushed ice. Garnish with fruit and mint. Serve immediately.

> Let those love now who never loved before,
> Let those who always loved now love the more.

FULL HOUSE COCKTAIL NO. 1

1   dash Angostura Bitters
1   oz. Yellow Chartreuse
1   oz. Benedictine
1   oz. Applejack

Shake with ice and strain into a cocktail glass.

FULL HOUSE COCKTAIL NO. 2

1½   oz. Rum
½   oz. Swedish Punch
½   oz. Dry Vermouth

Stir with ice and strain into a cocktail glass.

FUN AND GAMES

1½   oz. Gin
½   oz. Creme de Cassis
½   oz. Lemon Juice
1   dash Angostura Bitters

Shake with ice and strain into a cocktail glass.

FUN IN BED COCKTAIL

1¼   oz. Whisky
1¼   oz. Grape Juice

Shake with ice and strain into a cocktail glass.

FURNACE CREEK COOLER

1½   oz. Rum
1½   oz. Apple Juice
¼   oz. Lemon Juice
¼   oz. Lime Juice
¼   oz. Maraschino Liqueur
¼   oz. Grenadine

Shake with ice and strain into a Collins glass. Fill with soda and ice.

FUTURITY

1½   oz. Sweet Vermouth
1½   oz. Sloe Gin
3   dashes Bitters
2   dashes Grenadine

Shake with ice and strain into a cocktail glass.

GABLES COLLINS

1½   oz. Vodka
1   oz. Creme d'Almond
1   tbsp. Lemon Juice
1   tbsp. Pineapple Juice

Shake with ice and strain into a Collins glass over ice cubes. Add soda. Decorate with a slice of lemon and a pineapple chunk.

G & C

Galliano
Cream

Fill a pony glass with Galliano and float cream on top.

GALAXY

1½ oz. Galliano
½ oz. Triple Sec or Orange Curacao
3 oz. Orange Juice
1 Egg White

Shake with ice and strain into a Collins glass. Add ice and serve with an orange slice.

GALLIANO GIMLET

1½ oz. Galliano
1 oz. Dry Vermouth
¾ oz. Lime Juice
1 dash Bitters

Shake with ice and strain into a highball glass. Fill with soda and ice.

GALLIANO ISLANDER

1 oz. Galliano
½ oz. Rum
2 oz. Hawaiian Punch
¼ oz. Lemon Juice

Shake with ice and strain into a double Old-fashioned glass containing crushed ice. Add a lemon wedge and flame 1 oz. of Galliano over the wedge.

GALLIANO L'AMORE

⅓ oz. White Creme de Menthe
⅓ oz. Dark Creme de Cacao
⅓ oz. Galliano

Pour carefully, in order given, into a pony glass so that each ingredient floats on the preceding one without mixing.

GALLIANO MARGARITA

1 oz. Galliano
1 oz. Tequila
½ oz. Lime Juice

Shake with ice and strain into a cocktail glass with a salted rim.

GALLIANO MILKSHAKE

2 oz. Galliano
1 scoop Vanilla Ice Cream
4 oz. Milk

Blend and serve in a Collins glass.

GALLIANO MIST

1½ oz. Galliano

Pour Galliano into an Old-fashioned glass filled with crushed ice. Add a squeeze of lime juice.

GALLIANO SCREWDRIVER

1 oz. Galliano
¼ oz. Lemon Juice

Mix in a Collins glass. Fill with orange juice and ice.

GALLIANO TODDY

1 oz. Galliano
1½ oz. Brandy
¼ oz. Grenadine

Mix the ingredients in an Old-fashioned glass and fill with hot water. Serve with a lemon wedge.

GALLIATINI

1¾ oz. Vodka
¾ oz. Galliano

Stir with ice and strain into a cocktail glass. Serve with a lemon twist.

GALLICE

¾ oz. Galliano
¾ oz. Grand Marnier

Mix in an Old-fashioned glass. Fill with crushed ice.

GAMAY COOLER

3 dashes Aromatic Bitters
½ oz. Orange-flavored Liqueur
1 oz. Lemon Juice
4 oz. Gamay
1 dash Grenadine
Chilled Soda

Shake all the ingredients (except soda) with ice and pour unstrained into a Collins glass. Fill with soda and stir. Garnish with fruit. Serve with straws.

GANGADINE

1¾ oz. Gin
½ oz. White Creme de Menthe
¼ oz. Pernod
¼ oz. Grenadine or Raspberry Syrup

Stir with ice and strain into a cocktail glass.

GARDEN OF EDEN

½ oz. Creme de Violette
½ oz. Apricot-flavored Brandy

Pour carefully, in order given, into a pony glass so that each ingredient floats on the preceding one without mixing.

GARDEN STARTER

1 oz. Galliano
1 oz. Apricot-flavored Brandy
½ oz. White Creme de Menthe

Shake with ice and strain into a cocktail glass.

GASLIGHT NO. 1

1¾ oz. Scotch Whisky
½ oz. Sweet Vermouth
¼ oz. Orange Curacao

Stir with ice and strain into a cocktail glass. Add a twist of orange peel and float a dash of Drambuie on top.

GASLIGHT NO. 2

1 oz. Metaxa Brandy
½ oz. Apricot-flavored Brandy
1 dash Galliano

Shake with ice and strain into a cocktail glass.

GASPER

1¾ oz. Gin
¾ oz. Apricot-flavored Brandy

(Pernod may be substituted for Brandy.) Stir with ice and strain into a cocktail glass.

GATSBY

2 oz. Cream
¾ oz. Amaretto
¾ oz. Light Creme de Cacao

Shake with ice and strain into a cocktail glass.

GAUGUIN

2 oz. Rum
1 tbsp. Passion Fruit Syrup
1 tbsp. Lemon Juice
1 tbsp. Lime Juice

Combine ingredients with a cup of crushed ice in a blender and blend at low speed. Serve in an Old-fashioned glass. Serve with a cherry.

GAY GALLIANO

½ oz. Lime Juice
1½ oz. Barbados Rum
¾ oz. Galliano

Shake with ice and strain into a cocktail glass. Add a squeeze of lime juice.

GAZETTE

1¼ oz. Brandy
1 oz. Sweet Vermouth
2 dashes Lemon Juice
1 tsp. Sugar Syrup

Shake with ice and strain into a cocktail glass.

GENE CORRIE

1¼ oz. Gin
1¼ oz. Pernod

Stir with ice and strain into a cocktail glass. Serve with a cherry.

GENERAL HARRISON'S EGGNOG NO. 1

1 whole Egg
1 tsp. superfine Sugar
½ cup crushed Ice
8 oz. Claret
Nutmeg

Put the egg, sugar and crushed ice in a cocktail shaker and shake vigorously. Strain into a Collins glass, fill with Claret and stir gently. Grate a little nutmeg on top. Serves 1.

GENERAL HARRISON'S EGGNOG NO. 2

1 Egg
1 tsp. Powdered Sugar

Shake with ice and strain into a Collins glass. Fill the glass with Claret or sweet cider and stir. Sprinkle nutmeg on top.

GENE TUNNEY

2 oz. Gin
1 oz. Dry Vermouth
1 dash Orange Juice
1 dash Lemon Juice

Stir with ice and strain into a cocktail glass. Serve with a cherry.

GENEVER COCKTAIL NO. 1

2 oz. Gin
2 dashes Angostura Bitters

Stir with ice and strain into a cocktail glass.

GENEVER COCKTAIL NO. 2

1½ oz. Gin
½ oz. Lime Juice
½ oz. Orange Juice
1 dash Angostura Bitters
½ tsp. Sugar

Shake with ice and strain into a cocktail glass.

GENOA

1 oz. Gin
½ oz. Sambuca
½ oz. Dry Vermouth
½ oz. Grappa

Stir with ice and strain into a cocktail glass. Serve with an olive.

GENTLE BEN

1 oz. Vodka
1 oz. Gin
1 oz. Tequila

Shake with ice and strain into a Collins glass over ice cubes. Fill with orange juice and stir. Decorate with an orange slice and a cherry.

GENTLE BULL

1½ oz. Tequila
¾ oz. Kahlua
1 tbsp. Heavy Cream

Shake with ice and strain into a cocktail glass. Add ice.

GENTLE JOHN

1¾ oz. Scotch Whisky
½ oz. Dry Vermouth
¼ oz. Cointreau
1 dash Bitters

Stir with ice and strain into a cocktail glass.

GENTLEMEN'S APERITIF

1 dash Pernod
2 dashes Simple Syrup
1 oz. Fernet Branca
2 oz. Sweet Vermouth

Stir with ice and strain into a cocktail glass.

GEORGE'S BEAUTY

1 oz. Lemon Juice
1 tsp. Sugar
1 Egg White
1½ oz. Brandy

Stir with ice and strain into a highball glass. Fill with soda and ice.

GEORGIA

1½ oz. Courvoisier
½ oz. Grand Marnier

Mix and serve in an Old-fashioned glass or a snifter.

GEORGIA MINT JULEP

2 sprigs Mint
1 tsp. Powdered Sugar
1½ oz. Brandy
1 oz. Peach-flavored Brandy

Place mint leaves in a Collins glass with ice. Add a tsp. sugar and a little water. Muddle and fill with Brandy and Peach-flavored Liqueur. Decorate with mint sprigs.

GEORGIAN

1 oz. Bourbon
½ oz. Orange Juice
½ oz. Creme de Cacao

Shake with ice and strain into a cocktail glass.

GEORGIA RUM COOLER

2½ oz. Rum
Several salted Peanuts
½ oz. Lemon Juice
¼ oz. Grenadine
¼ oz. Falernum

Shake with ice and strain into a Collins glass. Fill with soda and ice. Dust with cinnamon.

GIBSON (DRY)

2 oz. Gin
½ oz. Dry Vermouth

Stir with ice and strain into a cocktail glass. Serve with an onion.

GIBSON (SWEET)

¾ oz. Gin
¾ oz. Sweet Vermouth

Stir with ice and strain into a cocktail glass. Serve with an onion.

GIBSON GIRL

1¼ oz. Gin
1¼ oz. Dry Vermouth

Stir with ice and strain into a cocktail glass. Serve with a lemon twist.

GIGOLA

½ oz. Honey
1½ oz. Cream
1½ oz. Whisky

Mix in an Old-fashioned glass. Sprinkle nutmeg on top.

GIGOLO COCKTAIL

¾ oz. Parfait Amour
¾ oz. Sweet Cream
½ tsp. Honey

Stir the honey with the cream (use no ice). Add Liqueur and stir. Dust with nutmeg.

GILDED LADY

¾ oz. Gin
¾ oz. Rum
¾ oz. Peach-flavored Brandy
¾ oz. Orange Juice

Shake with ice and strain into a cocktail glass.

GILDED ORANGE

2 oz. Gin
3 tbsp. Orange Juice
2 tsp. Dark Rum
2 tsp. Sugar Syrup
A few drops Lemon Juice
1-2 dashes Almond Extract

Shake with ice and strain into a cocktail glass. Add ice.

> Here's champagne to our real friends
> And real pain to our sham friends.

GILROY COCKTAIL

Juice ¼ Lemon
1 tbsp. Dry Vermouth
¾ oz. Cherry-flavored Brandy
¾ oz. Gin
1 dash Orange Bitters

Shake with ice and strain into a cocktail glass.

GIM GALLI

1½ oz. Vodka
½ oz. Galliano
½ oz. Rose's Lime Juice

Shake with ice and strain into a cocktail glass.

GIMLET COCKTAIL

1 oz. Rose's Lime Juice
1 tsp. Powdered Sugar
1½ oz. Gin

Shake with ice and strain into a cocktail glass.

GIMLET HIGHBALL

2 oz. Gin
1 oz. Rose's Lime Juice

Shake with ice and pour into a highball glass. Fill with soda and ice. (Fresh lime juice and sugar may be substituted for Rose's Lime Juice.)

GIN

2¼ oz. Gin
2 dashes Orange Bitters

Stir with ice and strain into a cocktail glass. Serve with an orange or lemon twist.

GIN ALEXANDER

2 oz. Cream
1 oz. Gin
1 oz. Light Creme de Cacao

Shake with ice and strain into a cocktail glass. Sprinkle nutmeg on top.

GIN ALOHA

1½ oz. Gin
1½ tsp. Triple Sec or Orange Curacao
1 tbsp. unsweetened Pineapple Juice
1 dash Orange Bitters

Shake with ice and strain into a cocktail glass. Serve with a cherry.

GIN AND BITTERS

½ tsp. Bitters
Gin

Put Bitters into a cocktail glass and turn the glass until it is entirely coated with Bitters. Then fill with Gin. No ice is used in this drink.

GIN AND CAMPARI

1¼ oz. Gin
1¼ oz. Campari

Stir with ice and strain into a cocktail glass. Serve with a twist of orange peel.

GIN AND FRENCH

Dry Vermouth
2¼ oz. Gin

Coat the inside of a cocktail glass with Dry Vermouth and add Gin and ice.

GIN AND IT

2 oz. Gin
1 oz. Sweet Vermouth

Stir ingredients in a cocktail glass. No ice is used in this drink. ''IT'' refers to Italian (Sweet) Vermouth.

GIN AND LIME

1½ oz. Gin
½ oz. Lime Juice
½ oz. Orange Juice
¼ oz. Rose's Lime Juice

Shake with ice and strain into a cocktail glass. Serve with a lime wedge.

GIN AND SIN NO. 1

1 oz. Gin
1 oz. Lemon Juice
1 tbsp. Orange Juice
1 dash Grenadine

Shake with ice and strain into a cocktail glass.

GIN AND SIN NO. 2

2 oz. Gin
1 tbsp. Cinzano

Shake with ice and strain into a cocktail glass.

GIN AND TONIC

2½ oz. Gin
Tonic Water

Pour the Gin into a highball glass. Add ice, tonic and a twist of lemon.

GIN AQUAVIT

1½ oz. Gin
½ oz. Aquavit
½ oz. Lemon Juice
1 tsp. Sugar
½ Egg White
¼ oz. Cream

Shake with ice and strain into a cocktail glass.

GIN BENEDICTINE SANGAREE

1¼ oz. Gin
¼ oz. Benedictine
¼ oz. Grapefruit Juice

Mix in an Old-fashioned glass. Fill with ice and add a lemon wedge. Sprinkle nutmeg on top.

GIN BLIND

1¾ oz. Gin
½ oz. Orange Curacao
¼ oz. Cognac
1 dash Orange Bitters

Stir with ice and strain into a cocktail glass.

Three cups of this a prudent
   man may take;
The first of these for
   constitution's sake,
The second to the lass he
   loves the best,
The third and last to lull him
   to his rest.

GIN BRACE

2 oz. Gin
½ oz. Catsup
½ oz. Lemon Juice
1 dash Tabasco Sauce
1 dash Celery Salt
¼ oz. Worcestershire Sauce

Shake with ice and strain into a Collins glass. Fill with ice.

GIN BUCK

Juice ½ Lemon
1½ oz. Gin

Pour the ingredients into a highball glass and fill with ginger ale. Add ice cubes. Stir.

GIN CASSIS

1½ oz. Gin
½ oz. Lemon Juice
½ oz. Creme de Cassis

Shake with ice and strain into a cocktail glass.

GIN COBBLER

1 tsp. Powdered Sugar
2 oz. Soda
2 oz. Gin

In a goblet, dissolve sugar in soda. Then fill the goblet with ice and add Gin. Stir and decorate with fruits in season. Serve with straws.

GIN COCKTAIL

2¼ oz. Gin
2 dashes Angostura Bitters

Stir with ice and strain into a cocktail glass. Serve with a lemon twist.

GIN COCO

Fresh Coconut
2 oz. Gin

Cut the top off a fresh coconut and pour 4 oz. of coconut water into a wine glass. Add Gin and ice cubes and stir.

GIN COOLER

½ tbsp. Sugar
2 oz. Lemon Juice
2 oz. Gin
Ginger Beer

Put some ice in a Collins glass. Add sugar, lemon juice and Gin. Fill with ginger beer. Garnish with fruit.

GIN CRUSTA

1½ oz. Gin
½ oz. Lemon Juice
1 dash Bitters
¼ oz. Maraschino Liqueur
½ oz. Triple Sec

Shake with ice and strain into a cocktail glass in which the shell of a lemon has been fitted as a liner.

GIN CUP

1½ oz. Gin
½ oz. Lemon Juice
½ tsp. Sugar

Mix in a mug and fill with White Wine and ice.

GIN DAIQUIRI

1½ oz. Gin
½ oz. Rum
½ oz. Lime Juice
½ tsp. Sugar

Shake with ice and strain into a cocktail glass.

GIN DAISY NO. 1

Juice ½ Lemon
½ tsp. Powdered Sugar
1 tsp. Raspberry Syrup or Grenadine
2 oz. Gin

Shake with ice and strain into a stein. Add ice cubes and decorate with fruit.

GIN DAISY NO. 2

2 oz. Lemon Juice
1 tsp. Sugar
½ oz. Grenadine
2½ oz. Gin
½ oz. Orange Juice

Shake with ice and strain into a large cocktail glass.

GIN DAISY NO. 3

1½ oz. Gin
½ oz. Lemon Juice
½ oz. Grenadine

Shake with ice and strain into a highball glass. Fill with soda and ice.

GIN FIX

Juice ½ Lemon
1 tsp. Powdered Sugar
1 tsp. Water
2½ oz. Gin

Mix lemon juice, sugar and water in a highball glass. Stir and fill the glass with ice. Add Gin. Stir again, and add a slice of lemon. Serve with straws.

GIN FIZZ

1 oz. Lemon Juice
1 tsp. Sugar
1½ oz. Gin

Shake with ice and strain into a highball glass. Fill with soda and stir.

GINGERADE

3 cubes Ice
3 oz. Ginger Wine
8 oz. Tonic

Put ice cubes in a highball glass, pour in the Ginger Wine, fill with tonic and stir gently.

GINGER AND DUBONNET

3 oz. Dubonnet
Ginger Ale, chilled

Pour Dubonnet over ice cubes into a Collins glass. Fill with ginger ale. Stir lightly. Serve with a lemon twist.

GINGER FIZZ

1 oz. Lemon Juice
1 tsp. Sugar
1½ oz. Gin

Shake with ice and strain into a highball glass. Fill with ginger ale and ice.

GINGER HIGHBALL

1½ oz. Whisky
A large chunk fresh Ginger Root
Soda

Pour the Whisky into a highball glass; squeeze in the ginger root through a garlic press. Add ice and fill with soda, stir.

GINGER MIST

1½ oz. Irish Mist Liqueur

Pour into a highball glass. Fill with crushed ice and ginger ale.

GINGER ROGERS

1¼ oz. Port
1¼ oz. Cognac

Stir with ice and strain into a cocktail glass.

GINGER RUM TEA

1½ oz. Rum
1 . cup hot Tea

Pour into a Collins glass. Add a piece of preserved ginger and stir. This drink may be served iced.

GINGERSNAP

3 oz. Vodka
1 oz. Ginger Wine

Put 3-4 ice cubes in an Old-fashioned glass and pour in Vodka and Ginger Wine. Stir gently. Add soda to taste.

GIN GIMLET NO. 1

1¾ oz. Gin
¾ oz. Rose's Lime Juice

Shake with ice and strain into a cocktail glass. Add a squeeze of lime juice and a green cherry.

GIN GIMLET NO. 2

1½ oz. Gin
½ oz. Lime or Orange Juice
½ tsp. Sugar

Mix with ice and pour into a highball glass. Fill with soda and ice.

GINGUIVITIS

1½ oz. Gin
1¼ oz. Cream
¼ oz. Grenadine

Shake with ice and strain into a cocktail glass.

GIN HIGHBALL

2 oz. Gin

Pour into a highball glass over ice cubes and fill with ginger ale or soda. Add a twist of lemon peel, if desired, and stir.

GIN HO or GIN-ON-THE-ROCKS

Fill an Old-fashioned glass with cracked ice. Pour in the amount of Gin desired and serve. A twist of lemon peel may be added.

GIN JULEP

½ tsp. Sugar
2 oz. Gin
4 sprigs Mint

Muddle the mint with the sugar in a highball glass. Fill with crushed ice and add Gin. Stir and add additional mint sprigs.

GINKA

1¼ oz. Gin
1¼ oz. Vodka
½ oz. Dry Vermouth

Shake with ice and strain into a cocktail glass. Serve with a lemon twist and an olive.

GIN MILK PUNCH

1 tsp. Powdered Sugar
2 oz. Gin
1 cup Milk

Shake with ice and strain into a Collins glass. Sprinkle nutmeg on top.

GIN MINT FIX

1 tsp. Sugar dissolved in water
2 oz. Gin
½ oz. Lemon Juice
¼ oz. White Creme de Menthe

Mix in a highball glass. Fill with crushed ice and stir. Serve with a mint sprig.

GIN MINT PUNCH

4 sprigs Mint
1 tsp. Sugar
½ oz. Lemon Juice
2 oz. Gin

In a Collins glass muddle the 4 mint sprigs with the other ingredients. Fill with ice and ginger ale.

GIN OLD-FASHIONED

½ tsp. Sugar
2 dashes Bitters
1½ oz. Gin

Mix in an Old-fashioned glass. Fill with ice. Decorate with a cherry, an orange slice and a lemon twist.

GIN ORANGUTAN

½ oz. Lemon Juice
½ tsp. Sugar
2 dashes Orange Bitters
2 oz. Gin

Shake with ice and strain into a cocktail glass.

GIN PUFF

2 oz. Gin
2 oz. Milk or Cream

Mix in a highball glass. Fill with soda and ice.

GIN PUNCH

½ tsp. Sugar
1 Lemon twist
1 oz. Lemon Juice
½ oz. Maraschino Liqueur
2 oz. Gin

Mix in a Collins glass. Fill with soda and ice and stir.

GIN RICKEY NO. 1

Juice ½ Lime
1½ oz. Gin

Pour ingredients into a highball glass over ice cubes and fill with soda water. Stir. Add a wedge of lime.

GIN RICKEY NO. 2

1½ oz. Gin
1 oz. Dry Vermouth
¼ oz. Grenadine
¼ oz. Lemon Juice

Pour ingredients into a highball glass over ice cubes and fill with soda. Stir. Add a wedge of lemon.

GIN RISQUE

2 oz. Gin
3 tsp. Lime Juice

Shake with ice and strain into a highball glass. Add plenty of ice and fill with cold water. Serve with a twist of lime.

GIN SANGAREE

½ tsp. Sugar dissolved in water
2 oz. Gin

Mix in a highball glass. Fill with soda and ice. Stir. Float ½ oz. Port on top. Dust with nutmeg.

GIN SCAFFA

1 dash Angostura Bitters
1½ oz. Gin
¾ oz. Benedictine

Stir with ice and strain into a cocktail glass.

GINSICLE

½ oz. Sugar Syrup
1½ oz. Gin

Fill a cocktail glass with shaved ice and add sugar and Gin.

GIN SIDECAR

1½ oz. Gin
1 oz. Triple Sec or Orange Curacao
1 oz. Lemon Juice

Shake with ice and strain into an Old-fashioned glass. Add ice.

GIN SLING

Juice ½ Lemon
1 tsp. Powdered Sugar
1 tsp. Water
2 oz. Gin

Dissolve the sugar in the water and the lemon juice. Add Gin and pour over ice cubes in an Old-fashioned glass. Stir. Serve with a mint sprig.

GIN SMASH

1 lump Sugar
1 oz. Soda
4 sprigs Mint
2 oz. Gin

Muddle the sugar with water and mint, then add Gin and an ice cube. Stir in an Old-fashioned glass. Serve with an orange slice, a cherry and a lemon twist.

GIN SOUR

Juice ½ Lemon
½ tsp. Powdered Sugar
2 oz. Gin
½ oz. Orange Juice

Shake with ice and strain into a Sour glass. Decorate with a half-slice of lemon and a cherry.

GIN SOUTHERN NO. 1

1½ oz. Gin
½ oz. Southern Comfort
¼ oz. Lemon Juice
¼ oz. Grapefruit Juice

Shake with ice and strain into a cocktail glass.

GIN SOUTHERN NO. 2

2 oz. Gin
½ oz. Orange Curacao
1 dash Orange Bitters

Stir with ice and strain into a cocktail glass.

GIN SQUIRT

1½ oz. Gin
1 tbsp. Powdered Sugar
1 tsp. Raspberry Syrup or Grenadine

Stir with ice and strain into a highball glass. Fill with soda and ice. Decorate with strawberries and cubes of pineapple.

GIN STINGER

2 oz. Gin
1 oz. White Creme de Menthe

Shake with ice and strain into a cocktail glass.

GIN SWIZZLE NO. 1

Into a Collins glass put:

Juice 1 Lime
1 tsp. Powdered Sugar
2 oz. Soda

Fill the glass with ice and stir with a swizzle stick. Then add:
2 dashes Bitters
2 oz. Gin

Fill with soda and serve with a swizzle stick.

GIN SWIZZLE NO. 2

1½ oz. Lime or Lemon Juice
1 Egg White
½ oz. Brandy
½ oz. Dry Vermouth
¼ oz. Cointreau
2 oz. Gin

Shake with ice and strain into a cocktail glass.

GIN THING

1½ oz. Gin
Juice ½ Lime

Pour Gin and lime juice into a highball glass. Add ice cubes and fill with ginger ale.

GIN TODDY

½ tsp. Powdered Sugar
2 tsp. Water
2 oz. Gin

In an Old-fashioned glass, mix sugar and water. Add Gin and an ice cube. Stir and add a twist of lemon peel.

GIN TODDY (HOT)

½ tsp. Sugar
2 oz. Gin

Put the sugar in an Old-fashioned glass. Add some hot water and the Gin. Serve with a lemon wedge. Sprinkle nutmeg on top.

GIN TROPICAL

1 oz. Gin
1 oz. Passion Fruit Syrup
½ oz. Blue Curacao

Shake with ice and strain into a Collins glass. Fill with soda and ice. Serve with a cherry.

GIN ZOOM

Dissolve 1 tsp. of honey with boiling water in an Old-fashioned glass.

Add:
1 tsp. Cream
2 oz. Gin

Stir and add ice.

GLAD EYE COCKTAIL NO. 1

2 oz. Pernod
1 oz. Sugar Syrup
2 sprigs Mint

Crush the mint and shake with the other ingredients, plus ice. Strain into a chilled cocktail glass.

GLAD EYE COCKTAIL NO. 2

1 oz. Green Creme de Menthe
2 oz. Pernod

Shake with ice and strain into a cocktail glass.

GLAD EYE COCKTAIL NO. 3

1¾ oz. Pernod
¾ oz. Peppermint Schnapps

Shake with ice and strain into a cocktail glass.

GLASGOW NO. 1

1½ oz. Scotch Whisky
¾ oz. Lemon Juice
¼ oz. Dry Vermouth
¼ oz. Orgeat Syrup

Shake with ice and strain into a cocktail glass.

GLASGOW NO. 2

1¾ oz. Scotch Whisky
½ oz. Dry Vermouth
¼ oz. Pernod
1 dash Bitters

Stir with ice and strain into a cocktail glass.

GLOGG (INDIVIDUAL)

Heat in a small pot:

½ tsp. Sugar
1½ oz. Claret
1½ oz. Sherry
¾ oz. Brandy
1 dash Bitters
Raisins and/or Cloves, Orange Peels, Lemon Twists and Cinnamon Sticks.

Allow to simmer. Serve in an Old-fashioned glass. Garnish with almonds and raisins.

Were't the last drop in the well,
As I gasped upon the brink,
Ere my fainting spirit fell,
'Tis to thee that I would drink.
— To Thomas Moore, by Lord Byron

GLOGG (PUNCH)

1   bottle Tawny Port
1   bottle Madeira
1   bottle Medium-Dry Sherry
½   bottle Dry Red Wine
15 Cloves
15 Cardamom seeds
1   stick Cinnamon
½   lb. lump Sugar
½   cup Brandy
1   cup Raisins
1   cup blanched Almonds

Combine all ingredients except the sugar, Brandy, raisins and nuts in a heavy saucepan and heat slowly. When the wine mixture is hot, place a rack on top of the saucepan so that it covers half of it. Arrange the sugar cubes on the rack, warm the Brandy, pour it over the sugar and set it alight. Ladle the wine mixture over the flaming sugar until sugar is dissolved. Serve in mugs and garnish with the almonds and raisins. Makes about 10 servings.

GLOOM CHASER

1   oz. Lemon Juice
½   oz. Orange Curacao
¾   oz. Grand Marnier
¼   oz. Grenadine

Shake with ice and strain into a cocktail glass.

GLOOM LIFTER

Juice ½ Lemon
1   oz. Rye or Bourbon Whisky
½   oz. Brandy
1   tbsp. Raspberry Syrup
½   tsp. Sugar
½   Egg White

Shake with ice and strain into a highball glass over ice cubes.

GLOOM RAISER

1½ oz. Gin
½   oz. Dry Vermouth
¼   oz. Grenadine
¼   oz. Pernod

Stir with ice and strain into a cocktail glass.

GLORIA NO. 1

1½ oz. Gin
½   oz. Lemon Juice
1   Egg White
1   sprig Mint
½   oz. Grenadine

Shake with ice and strain into a cocktail glass.

GLORIA NO. 2

1   oz. Gin
1   oz. Dry Vermouth
¼   oz. Cointreau
¼   oz. Campari

Shake with ice and strain into a cocktail glass.

> I drink to the general joy of the whole table.
> — *Shakespeare*

GLUH WEIN NO. 1

1   Cinnamon stick
2   dashes ground Cinnamon
4   whole Cloves
1   slice Lemon Peel
1   slice Orange Peel
½   tsp. Sugar
4   oz. Burgundy

Put all the ingredients except the Wine into a preheated mug. Heat the Wine in a small saucepan to piping hot. Pour the hot Wine into the mug.

GLUH WEIN NO. 2

Heat in a small pot:

4   oz. Claret
3   sticks Cinnamon
½   tsp. Sugar
2   Orange Peels
2   Lemon Peels
1   Clove

Bring to a boil and serve in an Old-fashioned glass. (Cider can be substituted for Claret, add a dash of Rum or Apple Brandy.)

GOAT'S DELIGHT

¾   oz. Brandy
¾   oz. Kirschwasser
1   oz. Cream
¼   oz. Orgeat
¼   oz. Pernod

Shake with ice and strain into a cocktail glass.

GODDESS OF LOVE COCKTAIL

1½ oz. Pernod
½   oz. Anisette

Shake with ice and strain into a cocktail glass.

GODFATHER

1½ oz. Scotch or Bourbon Whisky
¾   oz. Amaretto

Float the Amaretto on top of the Whisky in an Old-fashioned glass with ice cubes.

GODMOTHER

1½ oz. Vodka
¾   oz. Amaretto

Serve in an Old-fashioned glass with ice cubes. (Float the Amaretto on top of the Whisky.)

GOLDEN APPLE

¾   oz. Apple Brandy
¾   oz. White Creme de Cacao
1   oz. Galliano

Coat the rim of a cocktail glass with cherry juice, and dip it into coconut snow. After shaking the ingredients with ice, strain into the prepared glass.

> May the most you wish for be the least you get.

I wish that my room had a floor;
I don't care so much for a door;
But this walking around
Without touching the ground
Is getting to be quite a bore.

GOLDEN BUNNY

1½   oz. Lime Juice
1   Egg White
½   oz. Galliano
½   oz. Dry Sherry
½   oz. Scotch

Shake with ice and strain into a cocktail glass.

GOLDEN CADILLAC

1   oz. Galliano
2   oz. White Creme de Cacao
1   oz. Sweet Cream

Combine the ingredients with half a cup of crushed ice in a blender at a low speed for 10 seconds. Strain into a champagne glass.

GOLDEN CHAIN

¾   oz. Lime Juice
1   oz. Galliano
1   oz. Brandy
1   dash Yellow Chartreuse

Shake with ice and strain into a cocktail glass. Add a lime slice and a cherry.

GOLDEN CHAMPAGNE COCKTAIL

1   Egg Yolk
1   tsp. Powdered Sugar
⅓   cup Brandy
Chilled Champagne

Shake first three ingredients with ice and strain into a champagne glass. Fill with chilled Champagne.

GOLDEN CLIPPER

¾   oz. Gin
¾   oz. Light Rum
¾   oz. Peach-flavored Brandy
¾   oz. Orange Juice

Shake with ice and strain into a cocktail glass.

GOLDEN DAWN NO. 1

1   oz. Apple Brandy
½   oz. Apricot-flavored Brandy
½   oz. Gin
1   oz. Orange Juice

Shake with ice and strain into an Old-fashioned glass over ice cubes. Add 1 tsp. Grenadine.

GOLDEN DAWN NO. 2

1½   oz. Gin
½   oz. Orange Juice
½   oz. Apricot-flavored Brandy

Shake with ice and strain into a cocktail glass.

GOLDEN DAWN NO. 3

¾   oz. Rum
¾   oz. Gin
¾   oz. Cointreau
¾   oz. Orange Juice

Shake with ice and strain into a cocktail glass.

GOLDEN DAZE

1½   oz. Gin
½   oz. Peach-flavored Brandy
1   oz. Orange Juice

Shake with ice and strain into a cocktail glass.

GOLDEN DRAGON NO. 1

1   oz. Galliano
¾   oz. Light Creme de Cacao
1   Egg Yolk
¼   oz. Cream

Shake with ice and strain into a cocktail glass.

GOLDEN DRAGON NO. 2

¾   oz. Yellow Chartreuse
¼   oz. Dry Vermouth

Stir with ice and serve in a pony glass or a snifter.

GOLDEN DREAM

1   tbsp. Orange Juice
½   oz. Triple Sec
1   oz. Galliano
1   tbsp. Sweet Cream

Shake with ice and strain into a cocktail glass.

GOLDEN EAGLE

1   oz. Galliano
1   oz. Peppermint Schnapps

Stir in an Old-fashioned glass. Fill with ice.

GOLDEN EARRING

¼-½   oz. Galliano
¼   oz. Anisette
¾   oz. Cream

Shake with ice and strain into a liqueur glass.

GOLDEN ERMINE

1½   oz. Gin
¾   oz. Dry Vermouth
¼   oz. Sweet Vermouth

Stir with ice and strain into a cocktail glass.

GOLDEN FIZZ NO. 1

Juice ½ Lemon
½ tbsp. Powdered Sugar
1½ oz. Gin
1 Egg Yolk

Shake with ice and strain into a highball glass. Fill with soda and ice.

GOLDEN FIZZ NO. 2

1 oz. Galliano
2 dashes Orange Flower Water
1 oz. Lemon or Lime Juice
2 oz. Cream

Shake with ice and strain into a highball glass. Fill with soda and ice.

GOLDEN FRAPPE

3 oz. Orange Juice
2 tsp. Lemon Juice
2 tsp. Sugar
3 oz. White Port

Mix and pour over crushed ice in a Collins glass. Serve with straws.

GOLDEN FREEZE COLLINS

1 oz. Lemon Juice
1 oz. Galliano
½ oz. Triple Sec or Orange Curacao

Blend with crushed ice and pour into a Collins glass. Top with soda. Garnish with fruit.

GOLDEN FROG

½ oz. Strega
¾ oz. Lemon Juice
½ oz. Galliano
½ oz. Vodka

Shake with ice and strain into a cocktail glass.

GOLDEN GATE COCKTAIL NO. 1

6 oz. Orange Juice
1½ oz. Gin

Shake well (use no ice). Serve in a Collins glass.

GOLDEN GATE COCKTAIL NO. 2

¾ oz. Gin
¾ oz. Rum
¼ oz. 151-proof Rum
½ oz. Lemon Juice
½ oz. Falernum
½ oz. Light Creme de Cacao

Shake with ice and strain into a cocktail glass. Serve with an orange slice.

GOLDEN GIN FIZZ

2½ oz. Gin
1½ tbsp. Lemon Juice
2½ tsp. Sugar Syrup
1 Egg Yolk

Shake with ice and strain into a Collins glass. Fill with soda and ice. Top with a lemon slice and nutmeg.

GOLDEN GIRL

1¾ oz. Gin
¾ oz. Sherry
1 dash Orange Bitters
1 dash Angostura Bitters

Stir with ice and strain into a cocktail glass.

GOLDEN GLOVES

1½ oz. Gold Rum
¾ oz. Lemon or Lime Juice
½ tsp. Sugar
¼ oz. Cointreau

Shake with ice and strain into a cocktail glass. Add an orange peel or lemon twist. (May also be served over crushed ice.)

GOLDEN GLOW NO. 1

1 oz. Galliano
1 oz. Drambuie
1 oz. Gin

Shake with ice and strain into a cocktail glass.

GOLDEN GLOW NO. 2

1¼ oz. Grenadine
½ tsp. Sugar
1½ oz. Bourbon
½ oz. Rum
1 oz. Orange Juice
½ oz. Lemon Juice

Pour the Grenadine into a cocktail glass, then shake the other ingredients with ice and strain into the glass.

GOLDEN GOPHER NO. 1

¾ oz. Creme de Cacao
1¾ oz. Brandy

Stir with ice and strain into a cocktail glass.

GOLDEN GOPHER NO. 2

¾ oz. Galliano
¾ oz. Brandy
¾ oz. Light Creme de Cacao
1½ oz. Cream

Shake with ice and strain into a cocktail glass.

GOLDEN HORNET

1½ oz. Gin
½ oz. Sherry
½ oz. Scotch Whisky

Stir with ice and strain into a cocktail glass. Serve with a lemon twist.

GOLDEN LEMONADE

2   oz. Lime Juice
1   Egg Yolk
1   oz. Amer Picon
2   tsp. Sugar
1½   oz. Goldwasser

Shake with ice and strain into a Collins glass. Fill with chilled soda.

GOLDEN LILLIE

1½   oz. Canadian Whisky
½   oz. Galliano
½   oz. Creme de Bananes

Shake with ice and strain into a cocktail glass.

GOLDEN MUSCATEL COCKTAIL

1   Egg
½   tsp. Sugar
½   oz. Heavy Cream
2   oz. Brandy
3   oz. Muscatel
½   cup cracked Ice

Blend with ice and strain into a highball glass. Sprinkle nutmeg on top.

GOLDEN NUT

¾   oz. Galliano
¾   oz. Creme de Noyaux
1   oz. Cream

Shake with ice and strain into a cocktail glass.

GOLDEN SCREW NO. 1

1½   oz. Vodka
3   oz. Orange Juice
1   dash Angostura Bitters

Shake with ice and strain into a cocktail glass.

GOLDEN SCREW NO. 2

4   oz. Orange Juice
1½   oz. Galliano

Stir in a Collins glass and fill with ice.

GOLDEN SLIPPER COCKTAIL NO. 1

¾   oz. Yellow Chartreuse
2   oz. Apricot-flavored Brandy

Stir with ice and strain into a cocktail glass. Float an unbroken egg yolk on top.

GOLDEN SLIPPER COCKTAIL NO. 2

¾   oz. Yellow or Green Chartreuse
¾   oz. Goldwasser

Stir with ice and strain into a cocktail glass. Float an unbroken egg yolk on top.

GOLDEN SPIKE

4   oz. Orange Juice
1½   oz. 100-proof Vodka
1   oz. Brandy

Stir with ice and strain into a Collins glass. Fill with ice.

GOLDEN STATE SHERRY COBBLER

1   tsp. Orange Juice
1   tsp. Sugar
6   oz. Medium Sherry

Fill a Collins glass two-thirds full with cracked ice. Add orange juice and sugar. Fill with Sherry. Stir gently. Garnish with an orange wheel and a maraschino cherry.

GOLDEN STING RAY

¾   oz. Galliano
1   oz. Bourbon

Stir with ice and strain into an Old-fashioned glass. Fill with ice.

GOLDEN WINE LEMONADE

Lemonade
Sherry or Muscatel

Fill a Collins glass three-quarters full with ice. Pour in lemonade and wine. Stir lightly. (Note: Use any proportions to suit yourself.)

GOLDEN WINE TONIC

4   oz. Sherry
4   oz. Tonic, chilled
Lime

Pour Wine and tonic over ice in a Collins glass. Stir. Add a squeeze of lime.

GOLDFINGER

1   oz. Pineapple Juice
1½   oz. Vodka
¾   oz. Galliano

Stir with ice and strain into a cocktail glass.

GOLDFISH

1   oz. Gin
1   oz. Danziger Goldwasser
½   oz. Cointreau
½   oz. Lemon Juice

Shake with ice and strain into a cocktail glass.

> Drink to the girls and drink to their mothers,
> Drink to their fathers and to their brothers;
> Toss their dear healths as long as you're able,
> And dream of their charms while under the table.

GOLD 'N BITTERS

1 dash Bitters
Gold Chablis, chilled
1 Orange slice
1 Maraschino Cherry

Dash Bitters on ice cubes in a Collins glass. Fill with Gold Chablis. Garnish with an orange slice and a maraschino cherry.

GOLF COCKTAIL

1½ oz. Gin
¾ oz. Dry Vermouth
2 dashes Bitters

Stir with ice and strain into a cocktail glass.

GOLF LINKS HIGHBALL

2 oz. Bourbon
½ oz. Loganberry Juice
¼ oz. Pineapple Juice
¼ oz. Lemon Juice
¼ tsp. Sugar

Shake with ice and strain into a highball glass. Fill with soda and ice.

GOOD FELLOW

1¼ oz. Benedictine
1¼ oz. Brandy
1 dash Bitters
1 pinch Sugar

Shake with ice and strain into a cocktail glass. Serve with a lemon twist.

GOOD LIFE

1½ oz. Brandy
½ oz. Orange Curacao

Stir with ice and strain into an Old-fashioned glass. Fill with ice.

GOOD MORNING FIZZ

1 oz. Lemon Juice
1 tsp. Sugar
2 oz. Gin
½ oz. Anisette
1 Egg White

Shake with ice and strain into a Collins glass. Fill with soda and ice.

GOOD NITE COCKTAIL

1½ oz. Fernet Branca
Sweet Vermouth, well chilled

Pour Fernet Branca into a cocktail glass. Fill with Vermouth. Place a twist of lemon peel in the drink and stir lightly.

GOOSEBERRY

¾ oz. Whisky
¾ oz. Sherry
1 oz. Lemon Juice
1 tsp. Sugar

Shake with ice and strain into a cocktail glass.

GORDON

2 oz. Gin
½ oz. Amontillado Sherry

Stir with ice and strain into a cocktail glass.

GORILLA SWEAT

½ tsp. Sugar
1½ oz. Tequila

Put the ingredients into an Old-fashioned glass, fill with boiling water and stir in 1 pat of butter. Sprinkle cinnamon and/or nutmeg on top or serve with a cinnamon stick.

GOSSAMER

2 oz. Gin
½ oz. White Creme de Menthe

Stir with ice and strain into a highball glass. Fill with Champagne and ice and add an orange slice.

GOSSIP'S CUP

12 oz. Ale
1½ oz. Cognac
1 tsp. Brown Sugar
Grated Lemon Rind
A pinch of Ginger and Nutmeg

Mix in a saucepan; heat but do not allow to boil. Serve in mugs. Add extra garnish to taste.

GOTHAM

1 dash Bitters
1½ oz. Brandy
1½ oz. Sweet Vermouth

Stir with ice and strain into a cocktail glass.

GOURMET COCKTAIL

1½ oz. Gin
1 tbsp. Dry Vermouth
1 dash of Campari Bitters

Stir with ice and serve in a chilled 4 oz. cocktail glass with a sliver of grapefruit peel.

GOURMET'S ULTIMATE REFRESHER

1 tsp. Benedictine
1 tsp. Orange-flavored Liqueur
1 tsp. Brandy
4 oz. Ruby Cabernet
Brut Champagne, chilled

Place 3-4 ice cubes in a Collins glass, and add all ingredients except Champagne. Then fill with Champagne. Stir lightly.

GRABA VODKA

¾ oz. Vodka
¾ oz. Brandy
¾ oz. Grand Marnier

Stir with ice and strain into a snifter.

GRACE'S DELIGHT

1 oz. Whisky
1½ oz. Dry Vermouth
½ oz. Framboise (Raspberry Brandy)
½ oz. Orange Juice
1 dash Orange Bitters
1 dash Orange Flower Water
1 pinch Cinnamon
1 pinch Nutmeg

Chill for ten minutes. Shake without ice and strain into a cocktail glass.

GRADEAL NO. 1

1½ oz. Rum
½ oz. Apricot-flavored Brandy
½ oz. Gin

Stir with ice and strain into a cocktail glass.

GRADEAL NO. 2

1 oz. Rum
½ oz. Lemon Juice
½ oz. Gin
½ oz. Apricot-flavored Brandy

Shake with ice and strain into a cocktail glass.

GRANADA

1 oz. Dry Sherry
1 oz. Brandy
½ oz. Curacao

Shake with ice and strain into a Collins glass. Fill with tonic water and ice.

GRAND

1½ oz. Bourbon
¾ oz. Sweet Vermouth
¼ oz. Anisette

Stir with ice and strain into a cocktail glass. Add an orange peel twist.

GRAND BRETAGNA

1½ oz. Gin
½ oz. Apricot-flavored Brandy
½ oz. Lime Juice
½ Egg White
1 dash Orange Bitters
½ tsp. Sugar

Shake with ice and strain into a cocktail glass. (Or substitute Kirschwasser for Brandy and peach for Orange Bitters. Add ¼ oz. Cordial Medoc.)

GRAND CENTRAL

1½ oz. Bourbon
1 tsp. Sugar Syrup
A few dashes of Angostura Bitters

Shake with ice and strain into a cocktail glass. Add ice.

GRAND MARNIER QUETSCH

1 oz. Grand Marnier
1 tsp. Quetsch Plum Brandy
1 tsp. Orange Juice

Combine without ice; stir well. Pour over crushed ice in a champagne cocktail glass. Serve with a lemon slice.

GRAND OL' MAN

2 dashes Orange Bitters
2 dashes Pernod
2 dashes Orange-flavored Liqueur
2 oz. Brandy
2 oz. Dry Vermouth

Stir with ice and strain into an Old-fashioned glass. Add a twist of lemon and a maraschino cherry.

GRAND ORANGE BLOSSOM

1½ oz. Gin
2 tbsp. Orange Juice
1 tbsp. Grand Marnier
1 tsp. Sugar Syrup

Shake with ice and strain into a cocktail glass. Add ice.

GRAND PASSION

2 oz. Gin
1 oz. Passion Fruit Nectar
1 dash Angostura Bitters

Stir with ice and strain into a cocktail glass.

GRAND PLUM

1½ oz. Grand Marnier
½ oz. Plum Brandy (Quetsch)

Stir with ice and strain into a cocktail glass.

GRAND ROYAL

1½ oz. Gin
¼ oz. Grenadine
1 oz. Lemon Juice
1 Egg
½ tsp. Sugar

Shake with ice and strain into a cocktail glass.

GRAND ROYAL CLOVER CLUB

Juice ½ Lemon
3 oz. Gin
1 tbsp. Grenadine
1 Egg

Shake with ice and strain into a Old-fashioned glass.

> May these ladies distrust
> man in general,
> But not us in particular!

GRAND ROYAL FIZZ

Juice ¼ Orange
Juice ½ Lemon
1   tsp. Powdered Sugar
2   oz. Gin
½   tsp. Maraschino Liqueur
2   tsp. Sweet Cream

Shake with ice and strain into a highball glass over two ice cubes. Fill with soda and stir.

GRAND SLAM NO. 1

1½   oz. Swedish Punch
½   oz. Sweet Vermouth
½   oz. Dry Vermouth

Stir with ice and strain into a cocktail glass.

GRAND SLAM NO. 2

½   oz. Gin
½   oz. Brandy
¾   oz. Apricot-flavored Brandy
½   oz. Lime Juice

Shake with ice and strain into a cocktail glass.

GRANVILLE

1½   oz. Gin
¼   oz. Grand Marnier
¼   oz. Calvados
¼   oz. Lemon Juice

Shake with ice and strain into a cocktail glass.

GRAPEFRUIT COCKTAIL

1   oz. Grapefruit Juice
1   oz. Gin
1   tsp. Maraschino Liqueur

Shake with ice and strain into a cocktail glass. Serve with a cherry.

> May the juice of the grape
> enliven each soul,
> And good humour preside at
> the head of each bowl.

GRAPEFRUIT COOLER

2   oz. Blended Whisky
4   oz. Grapefruit Juice
¼   oz. Lemon Juice
¼   oz. Grenadine

Shake with ice and strain into a Collins glass. Fill with soda and ice. Garnish with lemon and orange slices.

GRAPEFRUIT HIGHBALL

1½   oz. Puerto Rican Rum
Grapefruit Juice

Pour the Rum into a highball glass; add ice and fill with grapefruit juice. Stir well.

GRAPEFRUIT NOG

1½   oz. Brandy
½   cup unsweetened Grapefruit Juice
1   oz. Lemon Juice
1   tbsp. Honey
1   Egg

Blend all ingredients with a cup of crushed ice at low speed and pour into a Collins glass over ice cubes.

GRAPE VINE

1½   oz. Gin
½   oz. Lemon Juice
½   oz. Grape Juice
Grenadine to taste

Shake with ice and strain into a cocktail glass.

GRAPE VODKA FROTH

1½   oz. Vodka
1   oz. Grape Juice
1   Egg White
1   oz. Lemon Juice

Shake with ice and strain into an Old-fashioned glass over ice cubes.

GRAPE WINE COCKTAIL

Juice ¼ Lemon
½   oz. Grape Juice
1¼   oz. Gin
¼   tsp. Grenadine

Stir with ice and strain into a cocktail glass.

GRAPPA STREGA

1   oz. Grappa
1   oz. Strega
1   tsp. Lemon Juice
1   tsp. Orange Juice

Shake with ice and strain into a cocktail glass. Serve with a lemon twist.

GRASSHOPPER COCKTAIL

¾   oz. Green Creme de Menthe
¾   oz. White Creme de Cacao
¾   oz. Light Cream

(Kahlua may be substituted for Creme de Cacao.) Shake with ice and strain into a cocktail glass.

GRAVEL GERTIE

1   oz. Vodka
1   oz. Tomato Juice
1   oz. Clam Juice
1   dash Tabasco Sauce

Stir with ice and strain into a cocktail glass. Fill with ice.

GREAT SECRET

1¾   oz. Gin
¾   oz. Lillet
1   dash Angostura Bitters

Stir with ice and strain into a cocktail glass. Serve with a twist of orange peel.

GREEK BUCK

1½ oz. Metaxa
½   oz. Lemon Juice
¼   oz. Ouzo

Stir with ice and strain into a high-ball glass. Fill with ginger ale and ice.

GREENBACK

1½ oz. Gin
1   oz. Green Creme de Menthe
1   oz. Lemon Juice

Shake with ice and strain into an Old-fashioned glass over ice cubes.

GREENBRIAR NO. 1

1¾ oz. Sherry
¾   oz. Dry Vermouth
1   dash Peach Bitters

Stir with ice and strain into a cocktail glass. Add a sprig of mint.

GREENBRIAR NO. 2

1¼ oz. Gin
1¼ oz. Sweet Vermouth

Stir with ice and strain into a cocktail glass. Serve with a mint sprig.

GREEN BULLET

½   oz. 151-proof Rum
½   oz. Green Chartreuse

Pour into a pony glass and flame.

GREEN DEVIL

1½ oz. Gin
1½ tsp. Green Creme de Menthe
1   tbsp. Lime Juice

Shake with ice and strain into an Old-fashioned glass over ice cubes. Serve with a mint sprig.

GREEN DRAGON NO. 1

½   oz. Lemon Juice
½   oz. Kummel
1½ oz. Gin
½   oz. Green Creme de Menthe
4   dashes Orange or Peach Bitters

Shake with ice and strain into a cocktail glass.

GREEN DRAGON NO. 2

1   oz. Green Creme de Menthe
1   oz. Vodka
½   oz. Cointreau

Shake with ice and strain into a cocktail glass.

GREEN DRAGON NO. 3

1   oz. Green Creme de Menthe
1½ oz. Milk
1½ oz. Cream
½   oz. Pernod

Shake with ice and strain into a cocktail glass.

GREEN-EYED MONSTER

1¼ oz. Irish Whisky
1   oz. Sweet Vermouth
¼   oz. Green Creme de Menthe
1   dash Bitters

Stir with ice and strain into a cocktail glass.

GREEN EYES

1½ oz. Lillet
½   oz. Green Creme de Menthe
1   dash Orange Bitters

Stir with ice and strain into a cocktail glass. Add a green cherry.

GREEN FIRE

1½ oz. Gin
2   tsp. Green Creme de Menthe
2   tsp. Kummel

Shake with ice and strain into a cocktail glass. Add ice.

GREEN FIZZ

Juice ½ Lemon
1   tsp. Powdered Sugar
1   Egg White
2   oz. Gin
1   tsp. Green Creme de Menthe

Shake with ice and strain into a highball glass over two ice cubes. Fill with soda and stir.

GREEN HOPPER

⅓   oz. Green Creme de Menthe
⅓   oz. Light Creme de Cacao
⅓   oz. Cream

Pour carefully, in order given, into a pony glass so that each ingredient floats on the preceding one without mixing.

GREEN HORNET

1½ oz. Whisky
½   oz. Green Creme de Menthe

Pour Whisky into an Old-fashioned glass. Float Creme de Menthe on top. Serve with a beer chaser.

GREEN HORNET (DRY)

2   oz. Lime Vodka
Soda

Into a Collins glass pour Vodka over ice cubes. Fill with soda, stir, and add half a slice of lime.

O thrice accursed
Be a champagne thirst,
When the price of beer's all
we've got.

GREEN JADE

1   oz. Gin
½   oz. Green Creme de Menthe
½   Egg White
1   oz. Cream

Shake with ice and strain into a cocktail glass. Add a green cherry and a mint sprig.

GREEN LIZARD

¾   oz. Green Chartreuse
¼   oz. 151-proof Rum

Serve in an Old-fashioned glass. Add ice.

GREEN MIST

¾   oz. Galliano
¾   oz. Sweet Vermouth
¾   oz. Dry Vermouth
¾   oz. Green Chartreuse

Stir with ice and strain into a cocktail glass.

GREEN OPAL COCKTAIL

½   oz. Gin
½   oz. Anisette
1   oz. Pernod

Shake with ice and strain into a cocktail glass

GREEN ORCHID

1   Egg White
¾   oz. Green Creme de Menthe
½   oz. Pernod

Shake with ice and strain into a highball glass. Fill with soda and ice.

GREEN ROOM

1½   oz. Dry Vermouth
¾   oz. Brandy or Cognac
2   dashes Orange Curacao

Stir with ice and strain into a cocktail glass.

GREEN SNATCHER

1½   oz. Galliano
Tonic
Lime

Pour the Galliano into an Old-fashioned glass; add a squirt of tonic and a squeeze of lime juice. Add ice and stir.

GREEN SPIDER

1½   oz. Vodka
½   oz. Green Creme de Menthe

Stir with ice and strain into an Old-fashioned glass.

GREEN STAR

1½   oz. Kirschwasser
½   oz. Green Creme de Menthe
½   oz. Orange Curacao

Shake with ice and strain into a cocktail glass. Add sugar to taste.

GREEN SWIZZLE

1½   oz. Gin
1½   oz. Lime Juice
1   tsp. Sugar
½   oz. Green Creme de Menthe

In a Collins glass pour Gin, lime juice and sugar. Fill with crushed ice and stir until frosted. Fill with soda. Float ½ oz. Creme de Menthe on top.

GREEN TREE

Juice ½ Lemon
2   oz. Light Rum
½   oz. Green Creme de Menthe

Shake with ice and strain into a cocktail glass.

GRENADIER

1¾   oz. Brandy
¾   oz. Ginger-flavored Brandy
¼   tsp. Sugar
A sprinkle of Ginger

Stir with ice and strain into a cocktail glass.

GRENADINE COCKTAIL

½   oz. Grenadine
½   oz. Pernod
½   oz. White Creme de Menthe
1   oz. Gin

Shake with ice and strain into a cocktail glass.

GRENADINE FIZZ

1½   oz. Gin
1   oz. Lemon Juice
1   oz. Grenadine

Shake with ice and strain into a highball glass. Fill with soda and ice.

GRENADINE RICKEY

Juice ½ Lime
1½   oz. Grenadine

Pour into a highball glass over ice cubes and fill with soda. Stir and put a piece of lime in the glass.

GROG

2   oz. Dark Rum
1   cube Sugar
3   Cloves
1   Cinnamon stick
1   tbsp. Lemon Juice
1   Lemon slice
Boiling Water

Place all ingredients except the boiling water in an 8 oz. mug. Stir to dissolve the sugar, leaving the spoon in the mug. Pour in boiling water to fill, and stir.

GUANABANA

1½   oz. Rum
1   oz. Guanabana Nectar
½   oz. Lime Juice

Shake with ice and strain into a cocktail glass.

GUARDS

2 oz. Gin
1 oz. Sweet Vermouth
¼ oz. Orange Curacao

Stir with ice and strain into a cocktail glass. Serve with a twist of orange peel or a cherry.

GUAVA COOLER

1½ oz. Rum
1½ oz. Guava Nectar
½ tsp. Sugar
½ oz. Maraschino Liqueur
½ oz. Lemon Juice
½ oz. Pineapple Juice

Shake with ice and strain into a Collins glass. Fill with soda and ice.

GUAVA WATER

1½ oz. Rum
1½ oz. Guava Nectar
2 tsp. Lemon Juice
2 tsp. Pineapple Juice
2 tsp. Maraschino Liqueur
1 tsp. Sugar Syrup
1 Guava Shell
Soda

Combine (except the shell and the soda) with ice; shake. Strain into a Collins glass and add ice and soda. Top with the guava shell or a slice of lemon.

GUNGA DIN

1¾ oz. Gin
½ oz. Dry Vermouth
¾ oz. Orange Juice

Shake with ice and strain into a cocktail glass. Add a slice of pineapple.

GYPSY COCKTAIL NO. 1

1½ oz. Sweet Vermouth
1½ oz. Gin

Stir with ice and strain into a cocktail glass. Serve with a cherry.

GYPSY COCKTAIL NO. 2

1¾ oz. Vodka
¾ oz. Benedictine
1 dash Bitters

Stir with ice and strain into a cocktail glass. Serve with a cherry.

GYPSY COCKTAIL NO. 3

1½ oz. Vodka
½ oz. Benedictine
¼ oz. Lemon Juice
¼ oz. Orange Juice

Shake with ice and strain into a cocktail glass. Serve with an orange slice.

GYPSY PUNCH

1½ oz. Rum
¼ oz. Grenadine
½ oz. Lemon Juice
¼ tsp. Sugar

Stir with ice and strain into a highball glass. Fill with soda and ice. Sprinkle nutmeg on top.

HABITANT

1½ oz. Whisky
1 oz. Lemon Juice
1 tsp. Maple Sugar Syrup

Shake with ice and strain into a cocktail glass. Serve with an orange slice and a cherry. (Cognac may be substituted for Whisky.)

HABIT ROUGE

1½ oz. Gin
2 tbsp. Grapefruit Juice
2 oz. Cranberry Juice
1 tsp. Honey
2 oz. crushed Ice

Blend ingredients at a high speed to the consistency of snow. Serve unstrained in a fizz glass.

HAGUE

1½ oz. Bourbon
¾ oz. Green Chartreuse
¼ oz. Dry Vermouth

Stir with ice and strain into a cocktail glass. Serve with a cherry.

HAIR OF THE DOG

1½ oz. Scotch Whisky
½ oz. Cream
½ oz. Honey

Shake with ice and strain into a cocktail glass.

HAIR RAISER COCKTAIL

1½ oz. 100-proof Vodka
½ oz. Rock and Rye
1 tbsp. Lemon Juice

Shake with ice and strain into a cocktail glass.

HAITIAN COCKTAIL

1½ oz. Haitian Rum
1 oz. Lime Juice
1 tsp. Sugar

Shake with ice and strain into a cocktail glass.

HAKAM

1½ oz. Gin
1½ oz. Sweet Vermouth
¼ oz. Curacao
1 dash Orange Bitters

Stir with ice and strain into a cocktail glass. Serve with a cherry.

HALF & HALF AND DUBONNET

1 tbsp. Orange Juice
1 tbsp. Dubonnet
1 oz. Sweet Vermouth
1 oz. Dry Vermouth

Stir with ice and strain into an Old-fashioned glass.

HALF AND HALF COCKTAIL

Porter
Ale

Into a tall glass or beer mug, pour equal amounts of Porter and Ale.

HAMLET NO. 1

1½   oz. Aquavit
Bitter Lemon

Pour into a highball glass. Fill with ice and Bitter Lemon.

HAMLET NO. 2

1   oz. Cherry Heering
1½   oz. Aquavit

Stir with ice and strain into a cocktail glass.

HAMMOCK DELIGHT

2   tsp. Sugar
1   tbsp. Water
1   tbsp. Orange Juice
Burgundy

Dissolve the sugar in the water in a tall glass. Add orange juice and ice cubes. Fill with Wine. Garnish with a lemon slice.

H AND H

2   oz. Gin
1   oz. Lillet
¼   oz. Orange Curacao

Stir with ice and strain into a cocktail glass. Serve with a twist of orange peel.

HANKY-PANKY

2   oz. Gin
1   oz. Sweet Vermouth
¼   oz. Fernet Branca

Stir with ice and strain into a cocktail glass. Serve with a twist of orange peel.

HAOTE PIKIA

1   oz. Okolehao
1   oz. Rum
1   dash Angostura Bitters

Mix in a Collins glass. Fill with lemon soda and ice.

HAPA TIQI

1   oz. White Rum
1   oz. Orange Juice
1   tbsp. Lemon Juice
2   tsp. Brandy
1   tsp. Almond Extract

Shake with ice and strain into a cocktail glass.

HAPPY APPLE RUM TWIST

1½   oz. Rum
3   oz. Apple Juice or Cider
1½   tbsp. Lime Juice

Shake with ice and strain into a cocktail glass. Serve with a lime twist.

> Let schoolmasters puzzle
>   their brain
> With grammar and nonsense
>   and learning;
> Good liquor, I stoutly main-
>   tain,
> Gives genius a better
>   discerning.
> — *Goldsmith*

HAPPY THOUGHT

½   oz. Anisette
½   oz. Light Creme de Cacao
½   oz. Cognac
½   oz. Creme de Rose
½   oz. White Creme de Menthe
½   oz. Creme de Violette

Shake with ice and pour over crushed ice into a cocktail glass.

HARBOR LIGHT

¾   oz. Galliano
¼   oz. Metaxa

Mix in a pony glass and flame.

HARBORMASTER SWIZZLE

2½   oz. Jamaica Rum
1½   tsp. Lime Juice
1½   tsp. Sugar Syrup
Several dashes Demerara Bitters

Shake with ice and strain into a Collins glass. Add cold water to fill. Stir gently until the glass begins to frost.

HARD FOUR

¾   oz. Galliano
¾   oz. Parfait Amour
¾   oz. Cognac
¼   Egg White

Shake with ice and strain into a cocktail glass.

HARI KARI

1   oz. Lemon Juice
1½   oz. Whisky
½   tsp. Sugar

Shake with ice and strain into a Brandy glass. Fill with Apollinaris Water.

HARLEM COCKTAIL

¾   oz. Pineapple Juice
1½   oz. Gin
½   tsp. Maraschino Liqueur

Shake with ice and strain into a cocktail glass. Decorate with two pineapple chunks.

HARMONY

1½   oz. Brandy
¼   oz. Strawberry Syrup
¼   oz. Maraschino Liqueur
1   dash Orange Bitters

Mix in an Old-fashioned glass. Fill with ice.

HARPO'S SPECIAL

1 oz. Lemon Juice
½ tsp. Sugar
2 oz. Rum
1 dash Bitters
½ oz. Orange Curacao

Shake with ice and strain into a cocktail glass.

HARRITY

1½ oz. Whisky
1 oz. Gin
1 dash Bitters

Stir with ice and strain into a cocktail glass.

HARROVIAN

3 oz. Gin
1 tsp. Orange Juice
1 dash Lemon Juice
1 dash Angostura Bitters

Stir with ice and strain into a cocktail glass.

HARRY LAUDER

1½ oz. Scotch Whisky
1½ oz. Sweet Vermouth
¼ oz. Sugar Syrup

Stir with ice and strain into a cocktail glass.

HARRY'S

2 oz. Gin
1 oz. Sweet Vermouth
¼ oz. Pernod
2 sprigs fresh Mint

Shake with ice and strain into a cocktail glass. Serve with a mint sprig.

HARRY'S PICK-ME-UP

3 oz. Brandy or Cognac
¼ oz. Grenadine
1 oz. Lemon Juice

Shake with ice and strain into a Collins glass. Fill with chilled Champagne.

HART'S DELIGHT COCKTAIL

2 oz. Jamaica Rum
1 oz. Sweet Vermouth
1 dash Angostura Bitters

Shake with ice and strain into a cocktail glass. Serve with a maraschino cherry.

HARVARD COCKTAIL

1½ oz. Brandy
¾ oz. Sweet Vermouth
1 dash Bitters
1 tsp. Grenadine
2 tsp. Lemon Juice

Shake with ice and strain into a cocktail glass.

HARVARD COOLER

½ tsp. Powdered Sugar
2 oz. Soda
2 oz. Apple Brandy
Ginger Ale

Put the sugar and soda into a Collins glass. Stir. Then add some ice cubes and the Brandy. Fill with ginger ale and stir again. Add a twist of orange or lemon peel (or both) and dangle end over rim of glass. (Lemon juice may be added to taste.)

HARVARD FIZZ

½ oz. Sweet Vermouth
¼ tsp. Sugar
1 dash Orange Bitters
1½ oz. Brandy

Mix in a highball glass. Fill with soda and ice.

HARVARD SPECIAL

1 oz. Galliano
1 oz. Pimm's No. 1

Mix in a highball glass. Fill with ginger ale and ice. Serve with an orange slice.

HARVARD WINE

1 oz. Dry Vermouth
¾ oz. Brandy
1 dash Orange Bitters

Stir with ice and strain into a cocktail glass. Fill with soda.

HARVEY WALLBANGER

1 oz. Vodka
4 oz. Orange Juice
½ oz. Galliano

Pour Vodka and orange juice into a Collins glass over ice cubes. Stir. Float Galliano on top.

HASTY COCKTAIL

¾ oz. Dry Vermouth
1½ oz. Gin
¼ tsp. Pernod
1 tsp. Grenadine

Stir with ice and strain into a cocktail glass.

HAVANA BEACH

1½ oz. Rum
1 oz. Pineapple Juice

Shake with ice and strain into a cocktail glass. Add sugar to taste.

HAVANA CLUB

1¾ oz. Gold Rum
¾ oz. Dry Vermouth

Stir with ice and strain into a cocktail glass.

HAVANA CLUB RICKEY

Juice ½ Lime
1½ oz. Rum
Soda

Squeeze lime juice into a highball glass, leaving the shell in the glass. Add ice and soda. Add sugar to taste.

HAVANA COCKTAIL NO. 1

1½ oz. Pineapple Juice
½ tsp. Lemon Juice
¾ oz. Rum

Shake with ice and strain into a cocktail glass.

HAVANA COCKTAIL NO. 2

1¼ oz. Apricot-flavored Brandy
½ oz. Swedish Punch
½ oz. Gin
1 dash Lemon Juice

Stir with ice and strain into a cocktail glass.

HAVANA COCKTAIL NO. 3

1¼ oz. Pineapple Juice
1¼ oz. Rum
1 dash Lemon Juice

Shake with ice and strain into a cocktail glass.

HAVANA COCKTAIL NO. 4

1 oz. Rum
1 oz. Sherry
1 dash Lemon Juice

Shake with ice and strain into a cocktail glass. Serve with a pickled onion.

HAVANA DAIQUIRI

2 oz. White Rum
1 oz. Lemon Juice
1 tbsp. Banana Liqueur
1 tsp. Sugar Syrup

Shake with ice and strain into a cocktail glass.

HAVANA RAINBOW PLUS

1/7 oz. Grenadine
1/7 oz. Anisette
1/7 oz. Parfait Amour
1/7 oz. Green Creme de Menthe
1/7 oz. Orange Curacao
1/7 oz. Yellow Chartreuse
1/7 oz. Jamaica Rum

Pour carefully, in order given, into a pony glass so that each ingredient floats on the preceding one without mixing. Flame and serve.

HAVE A HEART

1½ oz. Gin
¾ oz. Swedish Punch
¼ oz. Grenadine
¾ oz. Lime Juice

Shake with ice and strain into a cocktail glass. Serve with a wedge of pineapple and a cherry.

HAVELOCK HIGHBALL

1½ oz. Brandy
3 oz. Ginger Wine

Mix in a highball glass. Fill with soda and ice. Serve with a lemon twist.

HAWAIIAN BRANDY

1½ oz. Apple Brandy
½ oz. Pineapple Juice
¼ oz. Maraschino Liqueur
¼ oz. Lemon Juice

Shake with ice and strain into a cocktail glass.

HAWAIIAN BULL

1½ oz. Scotch Whisky
½ oz. Orgeat
Crushed Ice
Fresh Pineapple

Put Whisky in a double Old-fashioned glass. Fill the glass with crushed ice and pineapple. Add Orgeat.

HAWAIIAN COCKTAIL NO. 1

2 oz. Gin
1 tbsp. Pineapple Juice
½ oz. Triple Sec

Shake with ice and strain into a cocktail glass.

HAWAIIAN COCKTAIL NO. 2

1 oz. Applejack
½ oz. Pineapple Juice
1 dash Maraschino Liqueur
1 dash Lemon Juice
½ tsp. Sugar Syrup

Shake with ice and strain into a cocktail glass.

HAWAIIAN COCKTAIL NO. 3

2 oz. Gin
1 oz. Curacao
1 oz. Orange Juice

Shake with ice and strain into a cocktail glass.

HAWAIIAN COCKTAIL NO. 4

1½ oz. Gin
½ oz. Pineapple Juice
1 dash Orange Bitters
1 Egg White

Shake with ice and strain into a cocktail glass.

HAWAIIAN COFFEE

1 cup Iced Coffee
8 oz. Coffee Ice Cream
4 oz. Pineapple Juice
2 oz. White Rum

Blend ingredients at a high speed until smooth. Split between two Collins glasses.

HAWAIIAN COLLINS

1½ oz. Pineapple Juice
1½ oz. White Rum

Shake with ice and strain into a Collins glass. Add ice and garnish with a slice of orange and a cherry.

HAWAIIAN COOLER NO. 1

1½ oz. Vodka
2   oz. Pineapple Juice
¼   oz. Green Creme de Menthe
1   slice fresh Pineapple

Blend with ice and strain into a Collins glass. Add a pineapple spear, cherry and a mint sprig.

HAWAIIAN COOLER NO. 2

2-3 oz. Rye Whisky
Soda Water, chilled

Place some ice cubes and the Whisky in a Collins glass and add a twist of orange peel. Fill the glass with chilled soda water.

> Then who'd be grave when
>   wine can save
> The heaviest soul from
>   sinking,
> And magic grapes give
>   angel-shapes
> To ev'ry girl we're drinking.

HAWAIIAN DAISY

1½ oz. Rum
½   oz. Pineapple Juice
¼   oz. Lime Juice
¼   oz. Grenadine

Shake with ice and strain into a large cocktail or fizz glass. Fill with soda and float ¼ oz. of 151-proof Rum on top.

HAWAIIAN EYE NO. 1

1½ oz. Bourbon
1   oz. each of Vodka, Kahlua
    and Cream
2   tsp. Pernod
1   Egg White
2   oz. Cherry Juice
3   oz. crushed Ice

Blend at a high speed for 15 seconds and strain into a Collins glass. Decorate with slices of pineapple and a cherry.

HAWAIIAN EYE NO. 2

3   oz. Grapefruit Juice
1½ oz. Guava Juice
¾   oz. Demerara 86-proof Rum
¾   oz. Jamaica Rum
¼   oz. Gold Rum
2   dashes Angostura Bitters
1   dash Rock Candy Syrup

Blend with ice and strain into a double Old-fashioned glass.

HAWAIIAN HIGHBALL

3   oz. Irish Whisky
2   tsp. Pineapple Juice
1   tsp. Lemon Juice

Mix in a highball glass. Fill with soda and ice.

HAWAIIAN HONEYMOON

1½ oz. Rum
2   oz. Orange Juice
1   oz. Pineapple Juice
1   dash Lemon Juice
1   dash Grenadine

Mix in a highball glass. Float some Pernod on top. Garnish with a cherry, a slice of pineapple and an orange slice.

HAWAIIAN NECTAR KISS

3   oz. unsweetened Pineapple
    Juice
3   oz. Apricot Nectar
3   oz. Light Muscat

Have all ingredients well chilled. Fill a Collins glass half full with cracked ice. Pour chilled ingredients over ice. Stir well. Garnish with a sprig of mint.

HAWAIIAN SCREWDRIVER

1   oz. Galliano
1   oz. Vodka
3   oz. Hawaiian Orange Punch
¼   oz. Lemon Juice

Mix in a Collins glass. Fill with ice and add a lemon twist.

HAWAIIAN SOUR

½   oz. Sugar Syrup
½   oz. Lemon Juice
1   oz. Pineapple Juice
2   oz. Bourbon

Shake with ice and strain into a Sour glass. Add a slice of pineapple.

HAWAII BREAKER

1   oz. unsweetened Pineapple
    Juice, chilled
3   oz. Extra Dry Champagne,
    chilled
1   dash Aromatic Bitters

Pour pineapple juice and Champagne into a pre-chilled champagne glass. Add Bitters. Put a pineapple chunk on a swizzle stick and place in the drink. Stir gently.

HAWAII COCKTAIL

1	oz. Gin
¾	oz. Pineapple Juice
½	Egg White
1	dash Orange Bitters

Shake with ice and strain into a cocktail glass.

H-BOMB

¾	oz. Yellow Chartreuse
¾	oz. Green Chartreuse
¾	oz. Brandy
¾	oz. Bourbon Whisky

Shake with ice and strain into a cocktail glass.

HEADLESS HORSEMAN

2	oz. Vodka
3	dashes Bitters

Pour into a Collins glass. Add several cubes of ice. Fill with dry ginger ale and stir. Decorate with a slice of orange.

HEADLONG HALL

1	oz. Gin
1	oz. Dry Vermouth
¼	oz. Pernod
¼	oz. Benedictine

Stir with ice and strain into a cocktail glass.

> When you go up the hill of Prosperity
> May you never meet any friend coming down.

HEAD SHRINKER

1	oz. Rum
1	oz. Galliano
1	oz. Blue Curacao
1	dash Vermouth

Shake with ice and strain into a cocktail glass.

HEARN'S

¾	oz. Whisky (Bourbon or Irish)
¾	oz. Sweet Vermouth
¾	oz. Pernod
1	dash Bitters

Stir with ice and strain into a cocktail glass.

HEARST

1¼	oz. Gin
1¼	oz. Sweet Vermouth
1	dash Orange Bitters
1	dash Angostura Bitters

Stir with ice and strain into a cocktail glass.

HEARTBEAT

1	oz. Lemon Juice
¾	oz. Galliano
1	oz. Vodka
¼	oz. Green Chartreuse

Shake with ice and strain into a cocktail glass.

HEART WARMER

3	oz. Cognac
1	Egg Yolk
1	pinch Paprika

Shake with ice and strain into a brandy snifter.

HEATHER

2	oz. Scotch Whisky
1	dash Angostura Bitters
½	oz. Dry Vermouth

Stir with ice and strain into a cocktail glass. (1 dash Orange Bitters and ¼ oz. Grenadine optional.)

HEAT WAVE

1	oz. Dark Jamaica Rum
1	oz. Triple Sec
1	oz. Rock and Rye
½	oz. Lemon Juice

Mix in an Old-fashioned glass. Fill with hot water. Add an orange slice and a cinnamon stick.

HEAVENLY COCKTAIL

1	dash Aromatic Bitters
1	oz. Apple Brandy
1	oz. White Dubonnet

Stir with ice and strain into a cocktail glass.

HELEN'S OWN

1	oz. Gin
1	oz. Dry Vermouth
¼	oz. Apricot-flavored Brandy
¼	oz. Orange Juice

Shake with ice and strain into a cocktail glass.

HELL COCKTAIL

1½	oz. Cognac or Brandy
1	oz. Green Creme de Menthe

Pour into an Old-fashioned glass. Dust with red pepper.

HELON'S RUSSIAN

1	oz. Vodka
¾	oz. Kahlua

Mix in an Old-fashioned glass. Fill with ice; add a dash of soda and a squeeze of lime juice.

HE LOVES ME

1	oz. Gin
½	oz. Sweet Vermouth
¼	oz. Grenadine
¼	oz. Pineapple Juice
1	Egg White

Shake with ice and strain into a cocktail glass. Serve with a pineapple spear.

HERE'S HOW

1½ oz. Port
1 oz. Jamaica Ginger
1½ oz. Brandy

Stir with ice and strain into a highball glass. Fill with soda and ice. Serve with a lemon twist and dust with nutmeg.

HESITATION

1½ oz. Swedish Punch
½ oz. Rye Whisky
1 dash Lemon Juice

Stir with ice and strain into a cocktail glass.

HET PINT

2 quarts Ale
1 whole Nutmeg, grated
Superfine Sugar to taste
2 whole Eggs and 1 yolk
1 cup Scotch Whisky

Pour the Ale into a heavy saucepan with the grated nutmeg, bring just to a boil and add sugar to taste. Remove from the heat. Beat the eggs with the extra yolk and slowly whisk into the hot ale. Add the Scotch. Pour the liquid from a height into a heated tankard and continue pouring it back and forth until it foams. Serve at once in warmed 8 oz. mugs. Makes about 8 servings.

> May Dame Fortune ever smile on you
> But never her daughter —
> Miss Fortune.

HEY HEY

¾ oz. Lemon Juice
¾ oz. Cointreau
¾ oz. Brandy
¾ oz. Lillet

Shake with ice and strain into a cocktail glass.

H. G. WELLS

1¾ oz. Bourbon
½ oz. Dry Vermouth
¼ oz. Pernod

Stir with ice and strain into a cocktail glass. Serve with a lemon twist.

HIBISCUS

1½ oz. Rum
½ oz. Lemon Juice
¼ oz. Dry Vermouth
¼ oz. Grenadine

Shake with ice and strain into a cocktail glass.

HI-DE-HO SPECIAL

Juice ½ Lemon
2 oz. Orange-flavored Gin
1 tsp. Powdered Sugar

Shake with ice and strain into a highball glass. Fill with soda and stir. Decorate with a slice of lemon.

HIGH C

2 oz. Orange Juice
2 oz. Champagne, chilled

Pour orange juice and chilled Champagne into a pre-chilled champagne glass. Stir lightly.

HIGH HAT NO. 1

½ oz. Kijafa or Cherry Heering
1 oz. Lemon Juice
1½ oz. Bourbon or Rye Whisky

Shake with ice and strain into a cocktail glass.

HIGH HAT NO. 2

1¼ oz. Brandy
1¼ oz. Grapefruit Juice
Sugar to taste

Shake with ice and strain into a cocktail glass.

HIGHLAND COCKTAIL

1 dash Orange Bitters
1½ oz. Scotch Whisky
1½ oz. Sweet Vermouth

Shake with ice and strain into a cocktail glass.

HIGHLAND COOLER

½ tsp. Sugar
2 oz. Soda
2 oz. Scotch Whisky

Dissolve sugar in soda and pour into a Collins glass. Fill with ice and add Scotch. Fill the glass up with soda or ginger ale. Garnish with lemon twists or orange peels. (Optional: 1 dash lemon juice and 1 dash Bitters.)

HIGHLAND FLING NO. 1

1½ oz. Scotch Whisky
1 tsp. Sugar
3 oz. Milk

Shake with ice and strain into a highball glass. Fill with ice and dust with nutmeg.

HIGHLAND FLING NO. 2

¾ oz. Sweet Vermouth
1½ oz. Scotch Whisky
2 dashes Orange Bitters

Stir with ice and strain into a cocktail glass. Serve with an olive.

HIGHLAND SCREW

1½ oz. Scotch Whisky
Orange Juice

Pour Scotch into a Collins glass and fill the glass up with ice and orange juice.

HIGHLAND WITCH

1½ oz. Scotch Whisky
¾ oz. Strega

Mix in an Old-fashioned glass. Fill with ice and add an orange slice.

HIGH LIFE NO. 1

½ oz. Cherry Heering
1 oz. Lemon Juice
2 oz. Rye or Scotch Whisky

Shake with ice and strain into a cocktail glass.

HIGH LIFE NO. 2

¾ oz. Brandy
¾ oz. Port
½ tsp. Sugar
½ Egg White

Shake with ice and strain into a cocktail glass.

HI HO

1¾ oz. Gin
¾ oz. White Port
1 dash Orange Bitters

Stir with ice and strain into a cocktail glass.

HILL BILLY HIGHBALL

2 oz. Corn Whisky

Pour into a highball glass over ice cubes and fill with Mountain Dew. Then add a twist of lemon peel, if desired, and stir.

HILLIARD COCKTAIL

1 dash Peychaud's Bitters
1 oz. Sweet Vermouth
2 oz. Gin

Shake with ice and strain into a cocktail glass.

HILLSBORO

1¾ oz. Gin
¾ oz. Dry Vermouth
1 dash Orange Bitters
1 dash Angostura Bitters

Stir with ice and strain into a cocktail glass.

HILLYCROFT COOLER

2 oz. Gin
Ginger Ale

Pour Gin into a Collins glass and fill the glass up with ice and ginger ale.

HIT AND RUN

2 oz. Gin
1 tbsp. Port
2-3 drops Anisette

Shake with ice and strain into a cocktail glass.

HOBBY

1¼ oz. Bourbon
1 oz. Gin
¼ oz. Orange Curacao
1 dash Orange Bitters

Stir with ice and strain into a cocktail glass.

HOBSON

1½ oz. Sloe Gin
½ oz. Orange Curacao
¼ oz. Pernod

Shake with ice and strain into a cocktail glass.

HOCUS POCUS

1 oz. Gin
1 oz. Cointreau
1 oz. Lemon Juice

Shake with ice and pour over crushed ice in a cocktail glass.

HOFFMAN HOUSE COCKTAIL

¾ oz. Dry Vermouth
1½ oz. Gin
2 dashes Orange Bitters

Stir with ice and strain into a cocktail glass. Serve with an olive. (Angostura may be substituted for Orange Bitters, and lemon twists or orange peels for the olive.)

HOFFMAN HOUSE FIZZ

2 oz. Gin
1 oz. Lemon Juice
1 tsp. Sugar
¼ oz. Maraschino Liqueur
¼ oz. Cream

Shake with ice and strain into a highball glass. (Optional: ¼ oz. Grenadine and ½ oz. orange juice.)

HO-HUM COCKTAIL

¾ oz. Rum
½ oz. Lime Juice
½ tsp. Honey

Shake with ice and strain into a cocktail glass.

HOKKAIDO COCKTAIL

1½ oz. Gin
1 oz. Sake
½ oz. Triple Sec

Shake with ice and strain into a cocktail glass.

HOLE-IN-ONE COCKTAIL

1¾ oz. Scotch Whisky
¾ oz. Dry Vermouth
¼ tsp. Lemon Juice
1 dash Orange Bitters

Shake with ice and strain into a cocktail glass.

HOLIDAY

1½ oz. Tequila
2 tsp. Lemon Juice
1-2 drops Grenadine

Shake with ice and strain into a cocktail glass. Add a green cherry.

HOLIDAY CHABLIS

1 Egg Yolk
2 tsp. Orange-flavored Liqueur
1 tbsp. Sugar
3 oz. Chablis

Place all ingredients in the top of a double boiler. Mix until smooth. Then, over piping hot water, beat mixture constantly with a beater. (Watch the mixture, as it will foam and rise due to the heat.) When the foam rises to within 1 inch of the top, it is ready. Serve in preheated mugs.

HOLLAND COCKTAIL

1 oz. Holland Gin
1 oz. Orange Bitters
1 oz. White Curacao

Shake with ice and strain into a cocktail glass.

HOLLAND GIN COCKTAIL

1 dash Angostura Bitters
1½ oz. Holland Gin

Stir with ice and strain into a cocktail glass.

HOLLAND HOUSE

1¾ oz. Holland Gin
¾ oz. Dry Vermouth
½ oz. Lemon Juice
¼ oz. Maraschino Liqueur

Shake with ice and strain into a cocktail glass. Add a fresh pineapple, coarsely chopped.

HOLLAND HOUSE FIZZ

1½ oz. Holland Gin
1 oz. Lemon Juice
1 tsp. Sugar

Mix in a highball glass. Fill with soda and ice.

HOLLYWOOD

1½ oz. Rum
½ Egg White
½ oz. Grenadine
½ oz. Grapefruit Juice

Shake with ice and strain into a cocktail glass. Sprinkle nutmeg on top. (Half an ounce of Gin may be substituted for ½ oz. of Rum.)

HOLLYWOOD COOLER

2 oz. frozen Orange Juice
5 oz. Sauterne

Stir in a Collins glass. Add ice. Sweeten to taste and garnish with mint and an orange slice.

HOME ON THE RANGE

1 oz. Bourbon
1 oz. Dubonnet
½ oz. Cointreau
1 dash Angostura Bitters

Stir with ice and strain into a cocktail glass. Add orange and lemon peel.

HOMESTEAD COCKTAIL NO. 1

1½ oz. Gin
¾ oz. Sweet Vermouth

Stir with ice and strain into a cocktail glass. Serve with an orange slice.

HOMESTEAD COCKTAIL NO. 2

1 oz. Galliano
¾ oz. Orange Juice
½ oz. Grenadine
½ oz. Cream

Pour over crushed ice into a cocktail glass.

HONEST JOHN

3 oz. Bourbon
1 dash Ginger Ale
2 lumps Ice

Serve in an Old-fashioned glass. Fill with soda water and top with a twist of lemon peel.

HONEYBEE

2 oz. Light Rum
½ oz. Lemon Juice
1 tbsp. Honey

Shake with ice and strain into a cocktail glass.

HONEYDEW COOLER

2-3 pieces Honeydew Melon
1½ oz. Gin
¼ oz. Pernod
¼ oz. Cream
¾ oz. Lemon Juice
½ tsp. Sugar

Blend with ice and strain into a Collins glass. Fill with soda and ice.

HONEYMOON COCKTAIL

¾ oz. Benedictine
¾ oz. Apple Brandy
1 oz. Lemon Juice
1 tsp. Triple Sec

Shake with ice and strain into a cocktail glass.

HONEYSUCKLE

1½   oz. Golden Rum
1   tsp. Honey
½   oz. Lime Juice

Shake with ice and strain into a cocktail glass.

HONG KONG NO. 1

1   oz. Gin
1   oz. Dry Vermouth
¼   oz. Lime Juice
1   dash Angostura Bitters
¼   tsp. Sugar

Shake with ice and strain into a cocktail glass.

HONG KONG NO. 2

1   oz. Gin
½   oz. Dry Vermouth
½   oz. Orange Juice
¼   oz. Lemon Juice
¼   oz. Kirschwasser

Shake with ice and strain into a cocktail glass.

HONI HONI

1½   oz. Rum
½   oz. Apricot-flavored Brandy
½   oz. Lemon Juice

Shake with ice and strain into a cocktail glass.

HONOLULU NO. 1

1   dash Bitters
¼   tsp. Orange Juice
¼   tsp. Pineapple Juice
¼   tsp. Lemon Juice
½   tsp. Powdered Sugar
1½   oz. Gin

Shake with ice and strain into a cocktail glass.

HONOLULU NO. 2

¾   oz. Gin
¾   oz. Maraschino Liqueur
¾   oz. Benedictine

Stir with ice and strain into a cocktail glass.

HONOLULU NO. 3

½   slice fresh Pineapple
½   oz. Lemon Juice
¼   oz. Rock Candy Syrup
1   dash Grenadine
1½   oz. Rum

Blend and strain into a fizz glass. Fill with crushed ice.

HONOLULU CAFE

¾   oz. Gin
¾   oz. Dry Vermouth
¾   oz. Cream
½   oz. Pineapple Juice

Shake with ice and strain into a cocktail glass.

> May the roof over your head
> never fall in,
> And those beneath it never
> fall out.

HONOLULU PUNCH

2   medium-sized ripe Pineapples
1   cup superfine Sugar
1   cup Lemon Juice
1   pint Brandy
1   pint Dark Rum
1   block Ice
4   bottles chilled Champagne

Peel the pineapples, grate them and sprinkle them with sugar. Let stand for an hour or so. Add lemon juice, Brandy and Rum, stir well, cover and refrigerate overnight. When ready to serve, pour mixture into a punch bowl with the ice and add the champagne. Stir gently and serve in 4 oz. punch glasses. Makes about 45 servings.

HONORABLE

1½   oz. Bourbon
½   oz. Dry Vermouth
½   oz. Sweet Vermouth

Stir with ice and strain into a cocktail glass.

HOOP LA COCKTAIL

¾   oz. Lemon Juice
¾   oz. Lillet
¾   oz. Cointreau
¾   oz. Brandy

Shake with ice and strain into a cocktail glass.

HOOSIER HONEY

½   oz. Galliano
½   oz. Scotch
½   oz. White Creme de Menthe

Mix in an Old-fashioned glass. Fill with ice.

HOOT MON COCKTAIL

¾   oz. Sweet Vermouth
1½   oz. Scotch Whisky
1   tsp. Benedictine

Stir with ice and strain into a cocktail glass. Serve with a twist of lemon peel. (Substitute: ½ oz. Lillet for Benedictine; use ½ oz. (instead of ¾ oz.) Sweet Vermouth.)

HOOVER

1¼   oz. Rum
1   oz. Sweet Vermouth
¼   oz. Orange Curacao

Stir with ice and strain into a cocktail glass.

HOP FROG

1   oz. Brandy
1½   oz. Lime Juice
Sugar to taste
Shake with ice and strain into a cocktail glass.

HOP TOAD COCKTAIL

Juice ½ Lime
¾ oz. Apricot-flavored Brandy
¾ oz. Light Rum

Stir with ice and strain into a cocktail glass.

HORNET

1 oz. Sloe Gin
½ oz. Peppermint Schnapps

Pour into a Collins glass. Fill with ice and Cola. Serve with a lemon wedge.

HORSECAR

1 oz. Rye Whisky
¾ oz. Sweet Vermouth
¾ oz. Dry Vermouth
1 dash Angostura Bitters

Stir with ice and strain into a cocktail glass. Serve with a cherry.

HORSE MARY

1½ oz. Vodka
5 oz. Tomato Juice
1½ tsp. Lemon Juice
2 tsp. grated Horse Radish
1 Egg White
1-2 drops Worcestershire Sauce
1-2 drops Tabasco Sauce
Salt and Pepper to taste

Shake with ice and strain into a Collins glass.

HORSE SHOE

½ oz. Gin
½ oz. Anisette

Mix in a pony glass or in an Old-fashioned glass.

Here's to the bottle which
   holds a store
Of imprisoned joy and
   laughter!
Here's to this bottle,
Many more bottles,
And others to follow after.

HORSE'S HIGHBALL

2 oz. Brandy
¼ oz. Pernod
¼ oz. Lemon Juice
1 Egg
½ tsp. Sugar

Shake with ice and strain into a highball glass. Fill with soda and ice. Sprinkle nutmeg on top.

HORSE'S NECK NO. 1

2 oz. Rye Whisky
Ginger Ale

Place a lemon twist (peeled from a whole lemon) in a Collins glass, dangling one end over the rim. Fill the glass with ice cubes. Add Whisky and fill with ginger ale. Stir well.

HORSE'S NECK NO. 2

1½ oz. Brandy
2 dashes Angostura Bitters

Prepare exactly as above, except use Brandy and Angostura Bitters in place of Whisky.

HOT APPLE TODDY

2 oz. Apple Brandy
2 oz. hot Baked Apple
2 tsp. Cider

Mix in a heated mug, fill with very hot water and stir. Sprinkle nutmeg on top.

HOT AUTUMN SPICED TEA

2 oz. hot Tea
2 oz. medium Sherry
1 dash Nutmeg
1 dash Cinnamon

Pour hot tea into a preheated mug. Add Sherry and dashes of nutmeg and cinnamon.

HOT BENEFACTOR

2 lumps Sugar dissolved in hot water
1½ oz. Jamaica Rum
2 oz. Burgundy

Mix in an Old-fashioned glass. Fill with hot water. Serve with a lemon wedge and dust with nutmeg.

HOT BRANDY

1 tsp. Sugar
2 oz. Brandy

Mix in an Old-fashioned glass. Fill with hot water and sprinkle nutmeg on top.

HOT BRANDY FLIP

1 Egg
1 tsp. Powdered Sugar
1½ oz. Brandy

Beat together the egg, sugar and Brandy, pour the mixture into a mug. Fill with hot milk. Stir and dust with nutmeg.

HOT BRICK TODDY

1 tsp. Butter
1 tsp. Powdered Sugar
3 pinches Cinnamon
1 oz. hot Water
1½ oz. Rye Whisky

Put the first four ingredients into a whisky glass and dissolve thoroughly. Then add the Rye, fill the glass with boiling water and stir.

HOT BURGUNDY

1 Egg Yolk
1 tbsp. Honey
1 tsp. Sugar
2 tsp. Orange-flavored Liqueur
3 oz. Burgundy or Claret

Mix egg yolk, honey and sugar in a small saucepan. Add the liqueur and Wine. Heat until mixture is piping hot. Do not boil. Serve in a preheated mug. Place a lemon slice and a pinch of cinnamon in each serving.

HOT BUTTERED APPLEJACK

1   quart Sweet Cider
4   tsp. superfine Sugar
Nutmeg
4   twists Lemon Peel
4   sticks Cinnamon
4   oz. Applejack
4   pats Butter

Heat the cider to just under the boiling point. In each of four 10-oz. mugs put a teaspoon of sugar, a grating of nutmeg, a twist of lemon peel, a cinnamon stick and an ounce of applejack. Fill the mugs up with cider and put a pat of butter on top. Stir with the cinnamon stick.

> Here's to the prettiest,
> Here's to the wittiest,
> Here's to the truest of all
>   who are true,
> Here's to the neatest one,
> Here's to the sweetest one,
> Here's to them all in one —
>   here's to you.

HOT BUTTERED COMFORT

1¼   oz. Southern Comfort
1   Cinnamon stick
1   Lemon slice

Mix with boiling water in a mug. Stir with the cinnamon stick. Float 1 pat of butter on top.

HOT BUTTERED RUM NO. 1

½   tsp. Sugar
1   pat of Butter
1½   oz. Rum

Put sugar and butter in a mug or an Old-fashioned glass. Fill with boiling water or cider and add Rum. Sprinkle nutmeg on top.

HOT BUTTERED RUM NO. 2

In an Old-fashioned glass or mug put:

1½   oz. Jamaica Rum
1   Lemon twist
1   Cinnamon stick
½   pat Butter

Fill with boiling cider or water and stir. (Other spices, Rums or Liqueurs of your choice may be used.)

HOT BUTTERED RUM COW

In a warmed-up Old-fashioned glass pour:

1   tsp. Pre-made Mix
1½   oz. Rum
½   oz. Jamaica Rum

Stir, fill with hot milk and dust with nutmeg.

HOT BUTTERED RUM DE CACAO

2   oz. Jamaica Rum
1   oz. Dark Creme de Cacao
2   tsp. Brown Sugar
Whole cloves, a Cinnamon stick
Nutmeg, Butter

Combine spices and sugar in a warm mug; add a little boiling water and allow to steep a minute or two. Add Rum and Creme de Cacao. Fill the mug with boiling water and stir well. Add a twist of lemon and top with a bit of butter.

HOT BUTTERED TODDY

In a warmed-up Old-fashioned glass pour:

1½   oz. Whisky
½   oz. Orange Juice
¼   tsp. Sugar

Fill with hot water and float ¼ pat butter on top.

HOT BUTTERED WINE

½   cup Muscatel
¼   cup Water
1   tsp. Butter
2   tsp. Maple Syrup

Heat the water just to simmering (do not boil) and mix with the wine. Then pour this mixture into a warmed mug or cup. Add butter and maple syrup. Stir and sprinkle nutmeg on top. Serve at once.

HOT CREOLE

1½   oz. White Rum
1   tsp. Lemon Juice
1-2 dashes Tabasco Sauce
Beef Bouillon

Stir the first three ingredients with ice and strain into a highball glass. Add ice and the bouillon. Stir well, and add salt and pepper to taste.

HOT DECK

1¾   oz. Rye Whisky
½   oz. Sweet Vermouth
1   dash Jamaica Ginger

Shake with ice and strain into a cocktail glass.

HOT DRAMBUIE TODDY

½   oz. Lemon Juice
1½   oz. Drambuie

Pour into a warmed-up Old-fashioned glass. Fill with hot water. Garnish with an orange slice, a lemon wedge and stir with a cinnamon stick.

HOT EGGNOG

1   Egg
1   tsp. Sugar
1   oz. Rum
1   oz. Brandy

Mix together in a warmed-up highball glass. Fill with hot milk. Sprinkle nutmeg on top.

HOTEL BRISTOL SPECIAL COCKTAIL

1 oz. Cointreau
1 oz. Peach-flavored Brandy

Shake with ice and strain into a Collins glass. Fill with Champagne.

HOTEL DRAKE VESUVIUS

1 oz. Lemon Juice
½ tsp. Sugar
1½ oz. Orange Juice
1 oz. Gold Rum
1 oz. Jamaica Rum
½ oz. Grenadine

Shake with ice and strain into a highball glass. Fill with crushed ice and garnish with fruit and a mint sprig.

> I drink to your health when
> I'm with you,
> I drink to your health when
> I'm alone,
> I drink to your health so
> often
> I'm beginning to worry
> about my own!

HOTEL PLAZA COCKTAIL

¾ oz. Sweet Vermouth
¾ oz. Dry Vermouth
¾ oz. Gin

Stir with ice and strain into a cocktail glass. Decorate with a crushed slice of pineapple.

HOT FLASHES

2 oz. Whisky
½ oz. Campari
¼ oz. White Vermouth

Mix the ingredients with ice and strain into a cocktail glass. Add a lemon twist.

HOT GIN TODDY

2 cubes Sugar
2 tbsp. Lemon Juice
2-3 oz. Gin

Put sugar and lemon juice in an Old-fashioned glass and stir to dissolve the sugar. Add Gin, fill with boiling water, stir and decorate with lemon peel or a slice of lemon. (Lemon juice may be omitted and the toddy served with nutmeg on top.)

HOT IRISH PUNCH

4 oz. Irish Whisky
2 cubes Sugar
Few drops Lemon Juice

Combine sugar with a few drops of hot water in a mug. Stir until the sugar is dissolved. Add Whisky and lemon juice to the hot water and stir. Top with a lemon slice and nutmeg.

HOT JAMAICAN GROG

1½ oz. Jamaica Rum
1 tsp. Sugar
1 slice Lemon
Whole Cloves

Place sugar, lemon slice and cloves in a mug; add Rum and fill with boiling water. Stir and allow to steep for a few minutes. Drink piping hot.

HOT LEMONADE

2 oz. Lemon Juice
1 tsp. Sugar

Put the ingredients in a highball glass. Fill with hot water and stir. (1½ oz. Rum, Whisky or Brandy may be added.)

HOT LIGHT

½ oz. Orange Curacao
½ oz. 151-proof Rum

Mix ingredients in a pony glass. Flame.

HOT LOCOMOTIVE

6 oz. Burgundy
2 tbsp. Honey
1 tbsp. Sugar Syrup
1 tbsp. Curacao
1 Egg Yolk

Combine the egg yolk, sugar and honey without ice in a mug. Stir well and pour the Curacao and Burgundy into a saucepan. Add the honey/egg mixture and heat until boiling, stirring constantly. Serve steaming hot. Top with a lemon slice and cinnamon.

HOT MILK PUNCH

1 tsp. Sugar
1 dash Angostura Bitters
1 oz. Jamaica Rum
1 oz. Brandy
1 cup hot Milk

Dissolve sugar in a little hot milk and mix thoroughly with Bitters, liquor and a cup of hot milk. Pour into a Collins glass and dust with nutmeg.

HOT MINT BURGUNDY DELIGHT

3 sprigs Mint
1 tsp. Sugar
½ oz. Maraschino Cherry Juice
3 oz. Burgundy
Lemon peel, Cinnamon stick

Muddle mint sprigs in an Old-fashioned glass, then mix with sugar, a lemon twist and maraschino juice. Add Burgundy and fill with hot water. Stir with a cinnamon stick.

HOT PANTS

1½ oz. Tequila
½ oz. Peppermint Schnapps
1 tbsp. unsweetened Grapefruit Juice
1 tsp. Powdered Sugar

Shake with ice and strain into an Old-fashioned glass rimmed with salt.

HOT PORT FLIP

3 oz. Port
1 oz. Cognac
½ oz. Coffee
1 Egg
1 oz. Heavy Cream

Combine and preheat the first three ingredients. Beat egg until foamy. Stir the cream into the egg. Pour the mixtures into a preheated mug and sprinkle nutmeg on top.

HOT RUBY SANGAREE

4 oz. Ruby Port
1 tsp. Sugar Syrup
3 oz. boiling Water

In a preheated mug pour Wine and sugar syrup. Stir in boiling water. Sprinkle nutmeg on top.

HOT RUM

1 tsp. Sugar
1 oz. Lemon Juice
1½ oz. Dark Rum

Mix in an Old-fashioned glass. Fill with hot water and sprinkle nutmeg or cinnamon on top.

HOT RUM COW

1 tsp. Sugar
1 dash Angostura Bitters
1½ oz. Rum

Mix in a highball glass. Fill with hot milk. Sprinkle nutmeg on top.

HOT RUM LEMONADE

1 tsp. Sugar
1 oz. Lemon Juice
1½ oz. Rum

Mix in a preheated mug. Fill with hot water and serve with a lemon wedge.

HOT RUM SLING

1 tsp. Sugar
2 dashes Bitters
1 oz. Lemon Juice
2 oz. Rum

Mix in a mug. Fill with hot water.

HOT RYE

1 tsp. Sugar dissolved in water
1 piece Cinnamon
2 oz. Rye Whisky

Mix in an Old-fashioned glass. Fill with hot water. (Lemon juice may be added to taste.)

HOT SANGAREE

1 tsp. Sugar dissolved in water
2 oz. Brandy

Mix in an Old-fashioned glass. Fill with hot water. Sprinkle nutmeg on top. (Any Port, Liquor, Gin, Whisky or Sherry may be substituted for Brandy.)

HOT SCOTCH NO. 1

1 tsp. Sugar
½ oz. Lemon Juice
1½ oz. Scotch Whisky

Mix in an Old-fashioned glass. Fill with hot water and dust with nutmeg.

HOT SCOTCH NO. 2

½ tsp. Sugar
1 oz. Lemon Juice
½ oz. Drambuie
1½ oz. Scotch Whisky

Mix in an Old-fashioned glass. Fill with hot water. Sprinkle nutmeg on top.

HOT SLING

1 tsp. Sugar dissolved in water
1 dash Angostura Bitters
1 oz. Lemon Juice
2 oz. Brandy

Mix in an Old-fashioned glass. Fill with hot water. (Rum, Whisky or Gin may be substituted for Brandy.)

HOT SPICED PORT

1½ oz. Port
1 cube Sugar
1 pinch Nutmeg
Whole Cloves, Allspice

Dissolve the sugar with a few drops of warm water in a mug; add spices and Port and fill the mug with boiling water. Stir well. Garnish with grated lemon rind. (Sherry, Madeira, Brandy, Rum or Claret can be used instead of Port.)

HOT SPICED RUM

1¼ oz. Jamaica Rum
2 tsp. Sugar
2 tsp. Butter
2-3 dashes ground Cloves and Cinnamon

Mix with boiling water in a mug. Stir well.

HOT SPOT

1 oz. Galliano
½ oz. Brandy
½ oz. Ginger Wine

Shake with ice and strain into an Old-fashioned glass. Fill with ice and garnish with lemon and orange slices.

HOT SPRINGS COCTAIL

1½ oz. Dry White Wine
1 tbsp. Pineapple Juice
½ tsp. Maraschino Liqueur
1 dash Orange Bitters

Shake with ice and strain into a cocktail glass.

HOT TAWNY PORT FLIP

1 Egg
1 tsp. Powdered Sugar
4 oz. Tawny Port

Place ingredients in a small saucepan. Heat well, stirring constantly. Serve in a preheated mug.

> Here's that we may all go up the hill of Prosperity and never meet a friend — coming down.

HOT TAWNY PORT WINE

4 tbsp. Water
1 tsp. Sugar
1 pinch Allspice
1 small piece Orange Peel
4 oz. Tawny Port

Put all ingredients in a small saucepan. Stir until sugar dissolves. Heat until mixture foams. Do not boil. Strain into a preheated mug.

HOT TODDY, SPECIAL

1 oz. Lime Juice
½ oz. Drambuie
¼ oz. Grenadine
1½ oz. Scotch Whisky

Mix in an Old-fashioned glass. Fill with hot water. (Any sweet liqueur and fruit juices may be substituted for lime juice and Drambuie.)

HOT WHISKY LEMONADE

1½ oz. Lemonade
1 tsp. Sugar
1½ oz. Whisky

Mix in a Collins glass. Fill with hot water and sprinkle nutmeg on top.

HOT WHITE PORT

2 oz. White port
2 tbsp. boiling Water
1 oz. Creme d'Almond
Butter

Pour Port into a preheated mug. Add boiling water, Creme d'Almond and a bit of butter. Stir. Dust with nutmeg.

HOT WINE LEMONADE

2 oz. Red Wine
1½ oz. Lemon Juice
1½ tsp. Sugar

Mix in a Collins glass. Fill with boiling water and serve with a lemon twist.

HOUR GLASS HIGHBALL

1 oz. Cognac
½ oz. Pernod
½ oz. Cointreau

Shake with ice and strain into a highball glass. Fill with soda and ice and add a lemon twist.

H.P.W. NO. 1

1½ oz. Gin
1½ oz. Dry Vermouth

Stir with ice and strain into a cocktail glass. Serve with a twist of orange peel.

H.P.W. NO. 2

2 oz. Gin
¼ oz. Dry Vermouth
¼ oz. Sweet Vermouth

Stir with ice and strain into a cocktail glass. Serve with a twist of orange peel.

H.R.W.

Muddle several cherries and shake with:

1¾ oz. Gin
¾ oz. Dry Vermouth

Shake with ice and strain into a cocktail glass.

HUAPALA

½ oz. Lime Juice
¾ oz. Gin
1 oz. Rum
¼ oz. Grenadine

Shake with ice and strain into a cocktail glass.

HUDSON BAY

1 oz. Gin
½ oz. Wild Cherry-flavored Brandy
1½ tsp. 151-proof Rum
1 tbsp. Orange Juice
1½ tsp. Lime Juice

Shake with ice and strain into a cocktail glass.

HUGO BRACER

1 oz. Lime Juice
1 oz. Apple Brandy
½ oz. Amer Picon
½ oz. Grenadine

Shake with ice and strain into a cocktail glass.

HUGO RICKEY

¾   oz. fresh Lime Juice
1½   oz. Gin
½   oz. Grenadine

Mix in a highball glass (leaving ½ of the lime shell in the glass). Fill with soda and ice. Serve with a pineapple spear.

HUGO SPECIAL

Muddle orange and pineapple slices in an Old-fashioned glass.

Add: 1½ oz. Gin
      ¾ oz. Sweet Vermouth

Fill with ice.

HUKILLAU

1   oz. Lemon Juice
2   oz. Orange Juice
1½   oz. Gold Rum
½   oz. Demerara Rum
½   oz. Orgeat Syrup

Blend and strain into a double Old-fashioned glass. Add a pineapple spear and a mint sprig. Fill with crushed ice.

HULA-HULA COCKTAIL

¾   oz. Orange Juice
1½   oz. Gin
¼   tsp. Powdered Sugar

Shake with ice and strain into a cocktail glass.

HUMPTY DUMPTY

2   oz. Dry Vermouth
1   oz. Maraschino Liqueur

Stir with ice and strain into a cocktail glass.

HUNDRED PERCENT

1½   oz. Swedish Punch
½   tbsp. Lemon Juice
½   tbsp. Orange Juice
2   dashes Grenadine

Stir with ice and strain into a cocktail glass.

HUNTER'S COCKTAIL

1½   oz. Rye Whisky
1   tbsp. Cherry-flavored Brandy

Stir with ice and strain into a cocktail glass. Serve with a cherry.

HUNTINGTON SPECIAL

1½   oz. Gin
2   tsp. Lemon Juice
1   tsp. Grenadine

Shake with ice and strain into a cocktail glass.

HUNTSMAN COCKTAIL

1½   oz. Vodka
½   oz. Jamaica Rum
Juice ½ Lime
Powdered Sugar to taste

Shake with ice and strain into a cocktail glass.

> Let us toast the fools; but for them the rest of us could not succeed.
> — *Mark Twain*

HURRICANE NO. 1

1   oz. Dark Rum
1   oz. Light Rum
1   tbsp. Passion Fruit Syrup
2   tsp. Lime Juice

Shake with ice and strain into a cocktail glass.

HURRICANE NO. 2

1   oz. Whisky
1   oz. Gin
1   oz. White Creme de Menthe
¾   oz. Lemon Juice

Shake with ice and strain into a cocktail glass.

HURRICANE COOLER

1   oz. White Rum
1   oz. Jamaica Rum
1   oz. Lime Juice
2   oz. Orange Juice
1   tbsp. Sugar Syrup
2   tsp. Orange Bitters
3   drops Pernod

Shake with ice and strain into a Collins glass. Decorate with a pineapple stick and a cherry.

HURRICANE PUNCH NO. 1

1   oz. Lemon Juice
1   oz. Lime Juice
2   oz. Passion Fruit Syrup
2   oz. Rum

Shake with ice and strain into a highball glass. Fill with crushed ice. Add a pineapple spear and mint sprigs.

HURRICANE PUNCH NO. 2

2   oz. Dark Rum
2   oz. Hawaiian Punch
1   oz. Lemon Juice

Mix in a highball glass. Fill with crushed ice. Serve with an orange slice and a cherry.

HUSTLER

2   oz. Bourbon
1   oz. Orange Curacao
1   oz. Sweet Vermouth
2   tsp. Lime Juice

Shake with ice and strain into a cocktail glass.

IAN'S FIZZ

1 oz. Lemon Juice
½ oz. Cointreau
½ oz. Orgeat Syrup
½ oz. Orange Juice
1½ oz. Gin

Shake with ice and strain into a highball glass. Fill with soda and ice.

I.B.F. PICK ME UP

1½ oz. Brandy
¼ oz. Orange Curacao
¼ oz. Fernet Branca

Mix in a highball glass. Fill with Champagne and ice. Serve with a lemon twist.

ICEBERG

2 oz. Orange Sherbet
1 oz. Galliano
2 tsp. Cointreau

Blend with ice and strain into a cocktail glass.

ICEBREAKER

2 oz. Tequila
2 oz. Grapefruit Juice
1 tbsp. Grenadine
2 tsp. Cointreau
Crushed Ice

Blend at a low speed for 15 seconds. Strain into a Sour glass.

ICE CREAM FLIP

1 Egg
1 oz. Maraschino Liqueur
1 oz. Triple Sec or Orange Curacao
1 small scoop Vanilla Ice Cream

Shake with ice and strain into a flip glass. Sprinkle nutmeg on top.

ICED COFFEE COCKTAIL

1½ oz. Jamaica Rum
1½ oz. Iced Coffee
2 tsp. Dark Creme de Cacao
1 tsp. Sugar

Shake with ice and strain into a highball glass. Add ice. Serve with a cherry.

ICED COFFEE FILLIP

8 oz. strong black Coffee
1 tsp. (or more to taste) Tia Maria or other Coffee Liqueur

Pour the coffee over ice cubes in a Collins glass. Stir in the Tia Maria.

ICED RUM COFFEE

1½ oz. Rum
½ oz. Jamaica Rum

Shake and pour into a Collins glass. Fill with coffee. Add sugar to taste and top off with whipped cream.

ICED RUM TEA

1½ oz. Rum
½ oz. 151-proof Rum
1 tsp. Sugar
½ oz. Falernum
½ oz. Lemon Juice

Mix in a Collins glass. Fill with tea and ice. Serve with a lemon wedge.

> Here's to the heart that fills as the bottle empties.

ICHBEIN

1½ oz. Brandy
½ oz. Curacao
1 Egg Yolk
4 oz. Milk

Shake with ice and strain into a highball glass. Sprinkle nutmeg on top.

I.C.U.

2 oz. Brandy
1 oz. Sweet Vermouth
1 oz. Dry Vermouth
3 dashes Orange-flavored Liqueur
1 dash Grenadine Syrup

Shake with ice and strain into an Old-fashioned glass.

IDEAL COCKTAIL NO. 1

1 oz. Dry Vermouth
1 oz. Gin
¼ tsp. Maraschino Liqueur
½ tsp. Grapefruit or Lemon Juice

Shake with ice and strain into a cocktail glass. Serve with a cherry.

IDEAL COCKTAIL NO. 2

1 oz. Dry Vermouth
1 oz. Gin
¼ oz. Grapefruit or Lemon Juice
1 dash Angostura Bitters
¼ tsp. Sugar

Shake with ice and strain into a cocktail glass. Serve with a lemon twist.

I DIED

1 oz. Rum
1 oz. Apricot-flavored Brandy

Mix in an Old-fashioned glass. Fill with ice and add a splash of water.

I DON'T CARE

1 oz. Bourbon
1 oz. White Creme de Menthe
½ oz. Grenadine

Shake with ice and strain into a cocktail glass.

I DON'T KNOW

1½   oz. Cream
¾   oz. Cheri-Suisse
¾   oz. Light Creme de Cacao

Shake with ice and strain into a cocktail glass.

IGUANA

¾   oz. Tequila
¾   oz. Vodka
1   oz. Kahlua

Mix in an Old-fashioned glass. Fill with ice. Add a squeeze of lime juice, if desired.

IL MAGNIFICO

¾   oz. Tuaca
¾   oz. Orange Curacao
1   oz. Cream

Shake with ice and strain into a cocktail glass.

IMPERIAL COCKTAIL NO. 1

1½   oz. Dry Vermouth
1½   oz. Gin
½   tsp. Maraschino Liqueur
1   dash Bitters

Stir with ice and strain into a cocktail glass. Serve with a cherry or an olive.

IMPERIAL COCKTAIL NO. 2

¾   oz. Orange Curacao
¾   oz. Port
1   oz. Cognac

Shake with ice and strain into a cocktail glass.

> Happy are we met, happy have we been,
> Happy may we part and happy meet again.

IMPERIAL DELIGHT

1   oz. Brandy
¼   oz. Fernet Branca
¼   oz. Orange Curacao

Mix in a highball glass. Fill with Champagne and ice. Serve with a lemon twist.

IMPERIAL FIZZ

Juice ½ Lemon
½   oz. Light Rum
1½   oz. Rye or Bourbon Whisky
1   tsp. Powdered Sugar

Shake with ice and strain into a highball glass. Add two ice cubes. Fill with soda and stir. (Champagne may be substituted for soda.)

IMPERIAL HOTEL FIZZ

1½   oz. Whisky
¾   oz. Light Rum
1   tsp. Lemon Juice
1½   tbsp. Lime Juice
1   tsp. Sugar

Shake with ice and strain into a highball glass. Fill with soda.

IMPERIAL PUNCH

1½   oz. Bourbon
½   oz. Orange Curacao
½   oz. Lemon Juice

Shake with ice and serve in a Collins glass. Fill with Champagne and ice and garnish with fruit.

INCA COCKTAIL

1   dash Orgeat Syrup
1   dash Orange Bitters
¾   oz. Gin
¾   oz. Dry Sherry
¾   oz. Sweet Vermouth
¾   oz. Dry Vermouth

Stir with ice and strain into a cocktail glass.

INCIDER COCKTAIL

1½   oz. Blended Whisky
Apple Cider

Mix Whisky with a generous helping of Apple Cider. Serve over ice in an Old-fashioned glass and garnish with a slice of apple.

INCOME TAX COCKTAIL

1½   tsp. Dry Vermouth
1½   tsp. Sweet Vermouth
1   oz. Gin
1   dash Bitters
Juice ¼ Orange

Shake with ice and strain into a cocktail glass.

INDEPENDENCE SWIZZLE

2   oz. Dark Rum
3   dashes Angostura Bitters
¼   oz. Honey
½   oz. Lime Juice
1   tsp. Sugar

Shake with ice and strain into a Collins glass. Fill with crushed ice. Swizzle thoroughly until glass frosts. Serve with a lime wheel.

INDIAN

1½   oz. Sloe Gin
½   oz. Dry Vermouth
1   dash Orange Bitters

Shake with ice and strain into a cocktail glass.

INDIAN RIVER

1½   oz. Whisky
½   oz. Grapefruit Juice
¼   oz. Grenadine or Raspberry Liqueur
¼   oz. Sweet Vermouth

Shake with ice and strain into a cocktail glass.

INDISPENSABLE

1½ oz. Gin
½ oz. Dry Vermouth
½ oz. Sweet Vermouth
¼ oz. Pernod

Stir with ice and strain into a cocktail glass.

INFERNO

1½ oz. Tuaca
Hot Coffee
Whipped Cream

Flame Tuaca in a cocktail glass. Fill with hot coffee and top off with whipped cream.

INK STREET

1½ oz. Rye Whisky
¾ oz. Orange Juice
¾ oz. Lemon Juice

Shake with ice and strain into a cocktail glass. Add sugar to taste.

INSTANT BRUNCH BEVERAGE

8 oz. Orange-flavored Instant Drink
3 oz. Marsala

Combine ingredients and chill well. Pour into a frosted Collins glass. Serve with a lemon twist.

INSTANT EGGNOG

1 oz. Bourbon
1 oz. Rum
Vanilla Ice Cream

Mix Bourbon and Rum in a highball glass. Fill the glass with ice cream and stir until creamy. Sprinkle nutmeg on top.

INSTANT EGGNOG PUNCH

2 quarts French Vanilla Ice Cream
1 bottle Bourbon
½ cup Dark Rum
Nutmeg

Put the ice cream in a punch bowl. Stir in the Bourbon and Rum until thoroughly blended. Sprinkle nutmeg on top. Serve in punch glasses. Makes about 24 servings.

INTERNATIONAL

1 oz. Cognac
2 tsp. Anisette
2 tsp. Triple Sec
1 tsp. Vodka

Shake with ice and strain into a cocktail glass.

INTERNATIONAL STINGER

1 oz. Galliano
¾ oz. Metaxa

Mix in an Old-fashioned glass. Fill with ice.

INVIGORATING

3 dashes Aromatic Bitters
3 oz. Port

Dash bitters into a cocktail glass. Pour in Port. Stir lightly.

IQUIQUE COCKTAIL

4 oz. Gin
1 oz. Lemon Juice
3 tsp. Powdered Sugar
2-3 drops Angostura Bitters

Shake with ice and strain into a highball glass. Add ice.

IRIS NO. 1

1½ oz. Brandy
½ oz. Sweet Vermouth
½ oz. Lemon Juice
Sugar to taste

Shake with ice and strain into a cocktail glass.

IRIS NO. 2

¾ oz. Gin
¾ oz. Sherry
½ oz. Dry Vermouth
1 dash Bitters
¼ oz. Orgeat Syrup

Shake with ice and strain into a cocktail glass.

IRISH CANADIAN SANGAREE

1¼ oz. Rye Whisky
½ oz. Irish Mist
¼ oz. Orange Juice

Mix in an Old-fashioned glass. Fill with ice. Sprinkle nutmeg on top.

IRISH COCKTAIL NO. 1

1½ oz. Irish Whisky
¼ oz. Pernod
¼ oz. Orange Curacao
1 dash Maraschino Liqueur
1 dash Angostura Bitters

Stir with ice and strain into a cocktail glass. Add an orange peel or lemon twist.

IRISH COCKTAIL NO. 2

1¾ oz. Irish Whisky
¾ oz. Sweet Vermouth

Stir with ice and strain into a cocktail glass. Serve with a cherry. (Dry Vermouth may be substituted for Sweet Vermouth, or a mixture of both may be used.)

IRISH COCKTAIL NO. 3

2 oz. Green Creme de Menthe
1 oz. Dry Vermouth
1 dash Orange Bitters

Shake with ice and strain into a cocktail glass.

IRISH COFFEE

1½ oz. Irish Whisky
Strong Coffee
Chilled Whipped Cream

Pour the whisky into a stemmed glass or cup rimmed with sugar. Fill glass to within ½ inch of top with hot, black coffee. Cover surface to brim with cream.

IRISH COFFEE A LA KAHLUA

1½ oz. Irish Whisky
¾ oz. Kahlua
Coffee

Mix Whisky and Kahlua in a cup or fizz glass. Fill the glass with hot black coffee. Top with whipped cream. Float some Kahlua on top of the whipped cream.

IRISH COFFEE DELUXE

1½ oz. Irish Whisky
¾ oz. Dark Creme de Cacao

Mix in a cup or fizz glass. Fill with hot black coffee. Top with whipped cream.

IRISH COFFEE SUPREME

1½ oz. Irish Whisky
½ oz. Irish Mist
Green Creme de Menthe

Mix in a cup or fizz glass. Fill the cup or glass with hot, black coffee. Top with whipped cream. Float Green Creme de Menthe on top of the whipped cream.

IRISH COOLER

1½ oz. Irish Whisky

Pour into a Collins glass. Fill with soda and ice. Decorate with twists of lemon and orange peel.

IRISH COW

1 cup hot Milk
1 tsp. Sugar
1½ oz. Irish Whisky

Pour the hot milk into a highball glass; add the sugar and stir until dissolved. Add Whisky (2 oz. of Rum may be used instead of Irish Whisky). Stir gently. Sprinkle nutmeg on top.

IRISH CRESTA

1 oz. Irish Whisky
½ oz. Irish Mist
½ oz. Orange Juice
1 Egg White

Shake with ice and strain into a cocktail glass.

IRISH DREAM

1 oz. Cream
½ oz. Galliano
½ oz. White Creme de Cacao
½ oz. Green Creme de Menthe

Shake with ice and strain into a cocktail glass.

IRISH ELEGANCE

1½ oz. Jamaica Rum
½ oz. Brandy
1 tsp. Creme de Violette
½ oz. Pineapple Juice
½ tsp. Sugar
Juice 1 Lime

Blend with ice and strain into a cocktail glass.

IRISH EYES

1½ oz. Irish Whisky
2 oz. Green Creme de Menthe
2 oz. Fresh Cream

Shake with ice and strain into a champagne glass. Serve with a cherry.

IRISH FIX

1 tsp. Sugar dissolved in water
1½ oz. Irish Whisky
½ oz. Lemon Juice

Mix in a highball glass. Fill with ice. Garnish with an orange slice and a lemon wedge.

IRISH FIZZ

1 oz. Lemon Juice
½ tsp. Sugar
½ oz. Orange Curacao
1½ oz. Irish Whisky

Shake with ice and strain into a highball glass. Fill with soda and ice.

IRISH RICKEY

Juice ½ Lime
1½ oz. Irish Whisky

Put the ingredients in a highball glass. Fill the glass with soda and ice cubes. Stir, and add a piece of lime.

IRISH ROSE

1½ oz. Irish Whisky
½ oz. Lemon Juice
½ oz. Grenadine

Shake with ice and strain into a cocktail glass.

My love, thy red mouth is a cup divine,
It is crowned with kisses sweeter than wine,
And from it I drink to your love — and mine.

IRISH SHILLELAGH

Juice ½ Lemon
1   tsp. Powdered Sugar
1½   oz. Irish Whisky
1   tbsp. Sloe Gin
1   tbsp. Light Rum

Shake with ice and strain into a punch glass. Decorate with fresh raspberries, strawberries, a cherry and two peach slices.

IRISH WHISKY COCKTAIL

½   tsp. Triple Sec
½   tsp. Pernod
¼   tsp. Maraschino Liqueur
1   dash Bitters
2   oz. Irish Whisky

Stir with ice and strain into a cocktail glass. Serve with an olive.

IRISH WHISKY HIGHBALL

2   oz. Irish Whisky

Pour into a highball glass over ice cubes and fill with ginger ale or soda. Serve with a lemon twist.

IRRESISTIBLE COCKTAIL

1   oz. Sweet Vermouth
½   tsp. Benedictine
½   tsp. Lemon Juice
2   oz. White Rum

Shake with ice and strain into a cocktail glass. (¼ oz. Apricot-flavored Brandy may be used instead of Benedictine.)

ISABELITA

1½   oz. Gin
½   oz. Orange Juice
½   oz. Sweet Vermouth
¼   oz. Grenadine

Shake with ice and strain into a cocktail glass.

ISLANDER

1   oz. Tuaca
1   oz. Rum
1   oz. Cream
1   scoop Vanilla Ice Cream

Blend and serve in a cocktail glass.

ISLAND IN THE SUN

1   oz. Galliano
2   oz. Pineapple Juice
½   oz. Dark Rum
½   oz. Apricot-flavored Brandy
½   oz. Lemon Juice
Sugar to taste

Shake with ice and strain into a Collins glass. Fill with crushed ice. Serve with an orange slice and a cherry.

ISLE OF PINES

½   oz. Sugar Syrup
1   oz. Grapefruit Juice
2   oz. Rum

Shake with ice and strain into a cocktail glass.

ISLE OF THE BLESSED COCONUT

1½   oz. White Rum
2   tsp. Coconut Cream
2   tsp. Lime Juice
1   tsp. Lemon Juice
1   tsp. Orange Juice
1   tsp. Sugar Syrup
3   oz. crushed Ice

Blend at a low speed for 15 seconds. Strain into a Collins glass. Serve with coconut slices on the side.

I.T. (ITALIAN TEA)

1   oz. Galliano
Hot Tea

Pour Galliano into a cup. Fill with tea and stir. Add a lemon wedge.

ITALIAN

2   oz. Sweet Vermouth
1   oz. Fernet Branca
2   dashes Sugar Syrup
1   dash Pernod

Stir with ice and strain into a cocktail glass.

ITALIAN APERITIF

3   oz. Punt e Mes
1   dash Dry Vermouth
1   dash Campari
Lemon

Pour Punt e Mes over ice cubes in an Old-fashioned glass. Add Vermouth, Campari and a squeeze of lemon juice. Add a lemon slice.

> Here's a bumper of wine;
> fill thine, fill mine: —
> Here's a health to old Noah,
> who planted the vine!

ITALIAN BANANA

¾   oz. Tuaca
¾   oz. Creme de Bananes
½   oz. Vodka

Mix in an Old-fashioned glass. Fill with ice.

ITALIAN COCKTAIL

1   dash Aromatic Bitters
3   oz. Brandy
2   dashes Orange-flavored Liqueur
1   oz. Sweet Vermouth

Shake with ice and strain into an Old-fashioned glass.

ITALIAN EGGNOG

1   Egg
1   oz. Galliano
1   oz. Brandy

Shake with ice and strain into a highball glass. Fill with milk. Sprinkle nutmeg or chocolate chips on top.

ITALIAN FASCINATION

1	oz. Galliano
½	oz. Kahlua
¼	oz. Triple Sec
1	oz. Cream

Shake with ice and strain into a cocktail glass.

ITALIAN HEATHER

| 2 | oz. Scotch Whisky |
| ¼ | oz. Galliano |

Stir with ice and strain into a cocktail glass. Serve with a lemon twist.

ITALIAN MARTINI

| 2¼ | oz. Gin |
| ¼ | oz. Galliano |

Stir with ice and strain into a cocktail glass. (Amaretto, Tuaca or Strega may be used instead of Galliano.)

ITALIAN MOUSSE

| 1 | oz. Vodka |
| ¾ | oz. Chocolate Mint Liqueur |

Cream

Fill an Old-fashioned glass with ice. Add Vodka and Chocolate Mint Liqueur. Float cream on top.

ITALIAN ORANGE BLOSSOM

1¼	oz. Orange Juice
1	oz. Galliano
¼	oz. Tequila

Shake with ice and strain into a cocktail glass.

ITALIAN SOMBRERO

| 1½ | oz. Amaretto |
| 3 | oz. ice-cold Milk |

Put in a blender or shake well. Serve over ice cubes or straight up in a stem champagne glass.

ITALIAN STALLION

| 1¾ | oz. Metaxa |
| ¾ | oz. Galliano |

Shake with ice and strain into a cocktail glass.

ITALIAN STINGER NO. 1

| 1¾ | oz. Galliano |
| ¾ | oz. White Creme de Menthe |

Shake with ice and strain into a cocktail glass. (Brandy may be used instead of Creme de Menthe.)

ITALIAN STINGER NO. 2

| ¾ | oz. Galliano |
| ¾ | oz. Tuaca |

Mix in an Old-fashioned glass. Fill with ice.

ITALIAN STREAKER

1½	oz. Cream
½	oz. Tuaca
½	oz. Anisette

Shake with ice and strain into a cocktail glass. (Galliano may be used instead of Tuaca.)

ITALIAN WINE

½	oz. Grenadine
¾	oz. Orgeat Syrup
½	oz. Lemon Juice

Mix in a Collins glass. Fill with crushed ice and wine. Add a splash of water. Garnish with fruit.

ITALIAN ZINGER

| 1 | oz. Vodka |
| ½ | oz. Galliano |

Mix in an Old-fashioned glass. Fill with ice.

ITCHIBAN

1½	oz. Brandy
¼	oz. Light Creme de Cacao
¼	oz. Benedictine
1	Egg

Shake with ice and strain into a highball glass. Fill with ice and sprinkle nutmeg on top.

ITCHY BITCHY

¾	oz. Vodka
¾	oz. Brandy
¼	oz. Grand Marnier

Mix in an Old-fashioned glass. Fill with ice.

JABBERWOCK

¾	oz. Gin
¾	oz. Dry Sherry
¾	oz. Dubonnet
2	dashes Orange Bitters

Stir with ice and strain into a cocktail glass. Serve with a lemon twist and a cherry.

JABON CANDIDO

1	oz. Lemon Juice
1	tsp. Sugar
½	Egg White
1½	oz. Rum

Shake with ice and strain into a cocktail glass.

JACK DEMPSEY

½	oz. Lemon Juice
1½	oz. Rum
½	oz. Gin
¾	tsp. Sugar

Shake with ice and strain into a cocktail glass.

Here's to old Adam's crystal ale,
Clear, sparkling and divine,
Fair H_2O, may long you flow!
We drink your health (in wine).

JACKIE O'S ROSE

1 oz. White Rum
2 tsp. Orange Cointreau
2 tsp. Lime Juice
1 tsp. Sugar Syrup

Shake with ice and strain over crushed ice into a cocktail glass.

JACK IN THE BOX COCKTAIL NO. 1

1 oz. Apple Brandy
1 oz. Pineapple Juice
1 dash Bitters

Shake with ice and strain into a cocktail glass.

JACK IN THE BOX COCKTAIL NO. 2

1½ oz. Apple Brandy
1 oz. Lemon Juice
½ oz. Pineapple Juice
2 dashes Bitters

Shake with ice and strain into a cocktail glass.

JACK KEARNS

1½ oz. Gin
¾ oz. Rum
¼ oz. Lemon Juice
½ tsp. Sugar

Shake with ice and strain into a cocktail glass.

JACK PINE

1¾ oz. Gin
½ oz. Dry Vermouth
½ oz. Orange Juice
1 slice Pineapple

Shake with ice and strain into a cocktail glass.

JACK RABBIT

1½ oz. Applejack
½ oz. Maple Syrup
¼ oz. Lemon Juice
¼ oz. Orange Juice

Shake with ice and strain into a cocktail glass.

JACK ROSE COCKTAIL

1½ oz. Apple Brandy
½ oz. Lime or Lemon Juice
½ oz. Grenadine

Shake with ice and strain into a cocktail glass.

JACK SLOAT

1½ oz. Gin
¼ oz. Dry Vermouth
½ oz. Sweet Vermouth
2 slices Pineapple
½ oz. Orange Juice (optional)

Shake with ice and strain into a cocktail glass.

JACKSON COCKTAIL

2 dashes Orange Bitters
1½ oz. Orange Gin
1½ oz. Dubonnet

Stir with ice and strain into a cocktail glass.

JACK WITHERS

¾ oz. Gin
¾ oz. Dry Vermouth
¾ oz. Sweet Vermouth
¾ oz. Orange Juice

Shake with ice and strain into a cocktail glass.

> Here's to the girl that I love,
> And here's to the girl that
> loves me,
> And here's to all those that
> love her that I love,
> And to those that love her
> that loves me.

JADE

1½ oz. Dark Rum
½ tsp. Green Creme de Menthe
½ tsp. Triple Sec
1 tbsp. Lime Juice
1 tsp. Powdered Sugar

Shake with ice and strain into a cocktail glass. Add a lime slice.

JAILAI

¾ oz. Kahlua
1½ oz. Bourbon
1 Cinnamon stick

Shake with ice and strain into a snifter or a small wine glass.

JAMAICA COFFEE

1 oz. Coffee-flavored Brandy
¾ oz. Jamaica Rum
Hot Coffee

Serve in a mug. Top with whipped cream and dust with nutmeg.

JAMAICA GLOW COCKTAIL

1 oz. Gin
1 tbsp. Claret
1 tbsp. Orange Juice
1 tsp. Jamaica Rum

Shake with ice and strain into a cocktail glass.

JAMAICA GRANITO

1 small scoop Lemon or Orange Sherbet
1½ oz. Brandy
1 oz. Triple Sec

Combine ingredients in a Collins glass. Fill the glass up with soda and stir. Sprinkle nutmeg on top.

JAMAICA HOP

1 oz. Coffee-flavored Brandy
1 oz. White Creme de Cacao
1 oz. Light Cream

Shake with ice and strain into a cocktail glass.

JAMAICA JULEP

1½ oz. Jamaica Rum
9 sprigs Mint
Powdered Sugar

Mash 6 mint sprigs with sugar and water. Strain into a bar glass half full of ice. Add Rum and shake. Strain the mixture into a tumbler filled with shaved ice. Add 3 sprigs of fresh mint dipped into powdered sugar. Garnish with berries and other fresh fruits.

JAMAICAN ELEGANCE

1½ oz. Gold Rum
½ oz. Brandy
½ oz. Pineapple Juice
½ oz. Lime Juice
1 tsp. Sugar

Shake with ice and strain into a cocktail glass.

JAMAICAN GINGER NO. 1

1¾ oz. Jamaica Rum
¼ oz. Maraschino Liqueur
¼ oz. Orange Curacao
¼ oz. Grenadine
1 dash Angostura Bitters

Shake with ice and strain into a cocktail glass.

Here's to champagne, the
   drink divine,
That makes us forget our
   troubles;
It's made of a dollar's worth
   of wine
And eight dollars' worth of
   bubbles.

JAMAICAN GINGER NO. 2

¾ oz. Gin
¾ oz. Orange Juice
¾ oz. Burgundy
¼ oz. Jamaican Ginger extract

Shake with ice and strain into a cocktail glass.

JAMAICAN GINGER NO. 3

1½ oz. Rum
½ oz. Dark Jamaica Rum
½ oz. 151-proof Rum
½ oz. Falernum
½ oz. Lime Juice

Shake with ice and strain into a Collins glass. Fill with ginger beer and ice. Add a pineapple spear soaked in White Creme de Menthe, and a piece of ginger.

JAMAICAN HONEY BEE

½ oz. Lemon Juice
2 oz. Jamaica Rum
½ oz. Honey

Shake with ice and strain into a cocktail glass.

JAMAICA R.D.

½ oz. Lime Juice
2 oz. Jamaica Rum
½ tsp. Sugar

Shake with ice and strain into a cocktail glass.

JAMAICA RUM COBBLER

3 oz. Jamaica Rum
1 tsp. Sugar

Fill a wine glass a quarter full with cracked ice. Add sugar and Rum. Fill with water and stir. Garnish with half a slice of orange, a maraschino cherry and a pineapple stick.

JAMAICA RUM COLLINS

Juice ½ Lemon
½ tsp. Powdered Sugar
2 oz. Jamaica Rum

Shake with ice and strain into a Collins glass. Fill with soda and ice.

JAMAICA RUM SOUR

Juice ½ Lemon
½ tsp. Powdered Sugar
1½ oz. Jamaica Rum

Shake with ice and strain into Delmonico glass. Add a dash of soda, half a slice of orange and a maraschino cherry.

JAMAICA RUM SWIZZLE

2 oz. Jamaica Rum
½ oz. Lime Juice
½ tsp. Sugar

Mix in a Collins glass. Fill with crushed ice and swizzle until the glass frosts.

JAMAICA SHANDY

1 bottle Beer
1 pint Ginger Beer, ice cold

Pour into a stein or beer glass. Stir gently and add ice.

JAMAICA WONDER

1 oz. Tia Maria
1 oz. Dark Rum
2 oz. Lime Juice
½ tsp. Sugar

Blend with ice and strain into a Collins glass. Fill with ice.

JAMOCHA

1½   oz. Jamaica Rum
½   tsp. Sugar
1   pinch Cinnamon
1   tbsp. of Whipped Cream
Coffee

Mix the Rum, sugar and cinnamon in a mug; fill with hot coffee and stir. Top with whipped cream.

JANET HOWARD

2½   oz. Brandy
¼   oz. Orgeat Syrup
1   dash Angostura Bitters

Stir with ice and strain into a cocktail glass. Add ice cubes and a lemon twist.

JAPALAC

1¼   oz. Rye Whisky
1¼   oz. Dry Vermouth
1   tbsp. Orange Juice
1-2 dashes Raspberry Syrup

Shake with ice and strain into a cocktail glass. Add ice.

JAPANESE

2   oz. Brandy
1½   tsp. Orgeat Syrup
1   tbsp. Lime Juice
1   dash Bitters

Shake with ice and strain into a cocktail glass. Add a twist of lime peel.

JAPANESE FIZZ

Juice ½ Lemon
1   tsp. Powdered Sugar
1½   oz. Rye Whisky
1   tbsp. Port
1   Egg White (optional)

Shake with ice and strain into a highball glass. Add two cubes of ice. Fill with soda and stir. Serve with a pineapple slice. (More Whisky may be used.)

JAUNTY

Extra Dry Champagne, chilled
1   oz. Muscatel, chilled
1   large grape

Pour Muscatel into a pre-chilled champagne glass. Fill with Champagne. Stir lightly. Drop a large grape into the drink.

JAVA COOLER

¾   oz. Lime Juice
1½   oz. Gin
3   dashes Angostura Bitters

Mix in a Collins glass. Fill with soda. Add ice and a lime wheel.

JEAN DE LA LUNE

¾   oz. Cognac
¾   oz. White Creme de Menthe
¼   oz. Anisette
1   dash Angostura Bitters

Shake with ice and strain into a cocktail glass. Serve with a lemon twist.

JEAN LAFITTE COCKTAIL

1   oz. Gin
½   oz. Triple Sec
½   oz. Pernod
1   tsp. Powdered Sugar
1   Egg Yolk

Shake with ice and strain into a cocktail glass.

JELLYBEAN

¾   oz. V.O.
¾   oz. Anisette

Fill an Old-fashioned glass with ice and add both ingredients.

JERSEY

½   oz. Green Chartreuse
½   oz. Cognac

Pour carefully, in order given, into a pony glass so that each ingredient floats on the preceding one without mixing.

JERSEY CITY

2   oz. Applejack
½   oz. Pineapple Juice
1   dash Angostura Bitters
½   tsp. Sugar

Shake with ice and strain into a cocktail glass.

JERSEY COCKTAIL

½   oz. Sloe Gin
¾   oz. Sweet Vermouth
1   dash Peychaud's Bitters
1   dash Cherry Liqueur

Stir with ice and strain into a cocktail glass.

JERSEY DEVIL

1½   oz. Apple Brandy
1   oz. Cranberry Juice
2   tbsp. Lime Juice
2   tsp. Cointreau
1   tsp. Sugar Syrup

Shake with ice and strain into a Sour glass. Decorate with an apple slice.

JERSEY HIGHBALL

2   oz. Applejack
1   dash Angostura Bitters
½   tsp. Sugar

Mix in a highball glass. Fill with cider, ice and add a lemon twist.

Happy are we met, happy
have we been,
Happy may we part, and
happy meet again.

JERSEY LIGHTHOUSE

2½ oz. Applejack
1 tsp. Sugar
1 dash Angostura Bitters
Several Cloves

Mix sugar, Bitters and cloves in a pre-heated cocktail glass. Add a lemon peel twist and 2½ oz. Applejack—flamed.

JERSEY LIGHTNING NO. 1

2-3 oz. Applejack
1 dash Angostura Bitters
Sugar Syrup to taste

Shake with ice and strain into a cocktail glass.

JERSEY LIGHTNING NO. 2

1½ oz. Apple Brandy
½ oz. Sweet Vermouth
Juice 1 Lime

Shake with ice and strain into a cocktail glass.

JERSEY LILY

⅔ oz. Green Chartreuse
⅓ oz. Cognac

Pour carefully, in order given, into a pony glass so that each ingredient floats on the preceding one without mixing.

JERSEY MUG

2 oz. Applejack
1 dash Bitters
Cloves

Mix in a mug, fill with hot water. Float more Applejack on top and flame.

JERSEY SOUR

½ oz. Lemon Juice
½ tsp. Sugar
2 oz. Applejack

Shake with ice and strain into a Sour glass. Serve with a cherry.

JEWEL COCKTAIL

¾ oz. Green Chartreuse
¾ oz. Sweet Vermouth
¾ oz. Gin
1 dash Orange Bitters

Stir with ice and strain into a cocktail glass. Fill with crushed ice.

JEYPLAK COCKTAIL

1½ oz. Gin
¾ oz. Sweet Vermouth
¼ tsp. Pernod

Stir with ice and strain into a cocktail glass. Serve with a cherry.

JIMMIE WALKER

1½ oz. Bourbon
½ oz. Sweet Vermouth
¼ oz. Lemon Juice
¼ oz. Grenadine

Shake with ice and strain into a cocktail glass.

JIMMY BLANC

1¾ oz. Gin
¾ oz. Lillet
¼ oz. Dubonnet

Stir with ice and strain into a cocktail glass. Serve with a twist of orange peel.

JINX

1¾ oz. Gin
½ oz. Pineapple Juice
¼ oz. Grenadine

Shake with ice and strain into a cocktail glass.

JO'BURG

1½ oz. Light Rum
1½ oz. Dubonnet
½ tsp. Orange Bitters

Shake with ice and strain into a cocktail glass. (2 dashes Angostura Bitters may be used instead of Orange Bitters.)

JOCKEY CLUB COCKTAIL NO. 1

1 dash Bitters
¼ tsp. Creme de Cacao
1½ oz. Gin
Juice ¼ Lemon

Shake with ice and strain into a cocktail glass.

JOCKEY CLUB COCKTAIL NO. 2

2 oz. Gin
2 dashes Creme de Noyaux
1 dash Orange Bitters
1 dash Angostura Bitters
¼ tsp. Lemon Juice

Stir with ice and strain into a large cocktail glass.

JOCOSE JULEP

2½ oz. Bourbon
½ oz. Green Creme de Menthe
1 oz. Lime Juice
1 tsp. Sugar
5 chopped Mint Leaves

Combine all ingredients in a blender. Pour into a Collins glass over ice cubes. Fill with soda and decorate with a sprig of mint.

JOHN

1 oz. Sloe Gin
1 oz. Sweet Vermouth
½ oz. Cherry Heering
1 dash Peychaud's Bitters

Shake with ice and strain into a cocktail glass.

JOHN ALDEN

1   oz. Gold Rum
1   oz. Coffee Liqueur
1   oz. Orange Curacao

Shake with ice and strain into a cocktail glass.

JOHN COLLINS

Juice ½ Lemon
1   tsp. Powdered Sugar
2   oz. Bourbon or Rye Whisky

Shake with ice and strain into a Collins glass. Add several cubes of ice, fill with soda and stir. Decorate with a slice of orange, lemon and a cherry. Serve with straws.

JOHN HOLT'S COCKTAIL

½   oz. Irish Whisky
1   oz. Sweet Vermouth
½   oz. Lemon Juice
¼   oz. Kummel
1   dash Angostura Bitters

Shake with ice and strain into a cocktail glass.

JOHN McCLAIN

2   oz. Scotch Whisky
½   tsp. Sugar
2   dashes Bitters

Stir with ice and strain into a cocktail glass.

JOHNNIE COCKTAIL

¾   oz. Triple Sec
1½   oz. Sloe Gin
1   tsp. Anisette

Shake with ice and strain into a cocktail glass.

JOHNNY

1½   oz. Sloe Gin
¾   oz. Orange Curacao
¼   oz. Anisette (or Pernod)

Stir with ice and strain into a cocktail glass.

JOHNSON DELIGHT

¾   oz. Lime Juice
1   oz. Pernod
¾   oz. Cointreau

Shake with ice and strain into a cocktail glass.

JOHN WOOD

1   oz. Sweet Vermouth
¾   oz. Irish Whisky
½   oz. Lemon Juice
¼   oz. Kummel
1   dash Angostura Bitters

Shake with ice and strain into a cocktail glass.

JOKER

¼   oz. Anisette
¼   oz. Creme de Violette
¼   oz. Benedictine
¼   oz. Cream

Pour carefully, in order given, into a pony glass so that each ingredient floats on the preceding one without mixing.

JOLLY ST. NICK'S

Cracked Ice
1   tsp. Sugar
4   oz. Orange-flavored Liqueur
4   oz. Brandy
4   oz. Tawny Port
Orange and Pineapple slices
Grapes, halved

Fill a tall glass half full with cracked ice. Add sugar, Liqueur, Brandy and Port. Stir well. Garnish with fruit.

JONKANOO SCREWDRIVER

¾   oz. Galliano
1   oz. Rum

Mix in a Collins glass. Fill with orange juice and ice.

JORIO

¾   oz. Gin
¾   oz. Dry Vermouth
¾   oz. Sweet Vermouth
¼   oz. Pineapple Juice
¼   oz. Orgeat Syrup

Shake with ice and strain into a cocktail glass.

J.O.S.

¾   oz. Gin
¾   oz. Dry Vermouth
¾   oz. Sweet Vermouth
¼   tsp. Brandy
¼   tsp. Orange Bitters
¼   tsp. Lemon or Lime Juice

Stir with ice and strain into a cocktail glass. Serve with a lemon twist.

JOSCOE JULEP

2   oz. Bourbon
½   oz. Green Creme de Menthe
3   sprigs Mint
1   oz. Lime Juice
1   tsp. Sugar

Shake with ice and strain into a Collins glass. Fill with crushed ice and soda. Add a mint sprig.

JOSEPH'S DANDY

2   cubes Ice
1½   oz. Brandy
Champagne, chilled
Juice of 1 Lemon

Place ice cubes in a Collins glass. Add lemon juice and Brandy. Fill with Champagne.

JOSETTE

¾   oz. Cognac
¾   oz. Anisette
¾   oz. Orange Curacao
½   Egg White

Shake with ice and strain into a cocktail glass. Sprinkle nutmeg on top.

JOULOUVILLE

1 oz. Gin
½ oz. Apple Brandy
1½ tsp. Sweet Vermouth
1 tbsp. Lemon Juice
2 dashes Grenadine

Shake with ice and strain into a cocktail glass.

JOURNALIST COCKTAIL

1½ tsp. Dry Vermouth
1½ tsp. Sweet Vermouth
1½ oz. Gin
½ tsp. Lemon Juice
½ tsp. Triple Sec
1 dash Bitters

Shake with ice and strain into a cocktail glass.

JUBILEE FIZZ

1 oz. Gin
1 oz. Pineapple Juice

Mix in a cocktail glass. Fill with chilled Champagne.

JUDGE JR. COCKTAIL

Juice ¼ Lemon
¾ oz. Gin
¾ oz. Rum
½ tsp. Powdered Sugar
¼ tsp. Grenadine

Shake with ice and strain into a cocktail glass.

JUDGETTE COCKTAIL

¾ oz. Peach-flavored Brandy
¾ oz. Gin
¾ oz. Dry Vermouth
Juice ¼ Lime

Shake with ice and strain into a cocktail glass. Serve with a cherry.

JULEP

3 oz. Bourbon Whisky
1 cube Sugar
Mint sprigs

Dissolve the sugar with a few drops of water in a highball glass. Add a few mint sprigs; fill the glass with ice and add Bourbon. Stir and add more mint.

JUMP UP AND KISS ME

1 oz. Galliano
1 oz. Pineapple Juice
1 oz. Rum
¼ oz. Apricot-flavored Brandy
¼ oz. Lemon Juice
1 Egg White

Shake with ice and strain into a Collins glass. Fill with ice.

JUNE BRIDE

1½ oz. Gin
½ Egg White
½ oz. Lemon Juice
1 tsp. Sugar or
Liqueur of your choice

Shake with ice and strain into a cocktail glass.

JUNGLE

1 oz. Gin
¾ oz. Sweet Vermouth
¾ oz. Sherry

Stir with ice and strain into a cocktail glass.

JUNGLE FIRE SLING

1 oz. Cherry-flavored Brandy
½ oz. Benedictine
½ oz. Parfait Amour
1 oz. Brandy

Mix in a Collins glass. Fill with crushed ice and ginger ale.

JUNIOR

1½ oz. Rye Whisky
½ oz. Lime Juice
½ oz. Benedictine
1 dash Bitters

Shake with ice and strain into a cocktail glass.

JUNIPER

2 oz. Gin
½ oz. Dry Vermouth
1 dash Grenadine

Stir with ice and strain into a cocktail glass.

JUPITER COCKTAIL

1 tsp. Orange Juice
1 tsp. Parfait Amour
½ oz. Dry Vermouth
1½ oz. Gin

Shake with ice and strain into a cocktail glass.

JUSCHU COCKTAIL

1½ oz. Tequila
2 tsp. Honey, strained
1 tsp. Lime Juice
1 dash Angostura Bitters

Shake with ice and strain into a cocktail glass.

JUST A SONG AT TWILIGHT COCKTAIL

½ oz. Sweet Vermouth
¼ tsp. Grenadine
¼ tsp. Lemon Juice
2 oz. Bourbon Whisky

Shake with ice and strain into a cocktail glass.

Here's to the Chaperone,
May she learn from Cupid
Just enough blindness
To be sweetly stupid.

KAFE ALEXANDER

2 oz. Heavy Cream
2 oz. Brandy
1 oz. Creme de Cafe

Shake with ice and strain into an Old-fashioned glass.

KAFE COCKTAIL

1 oz. strong cold Coffee
½ oz. Creme de Cafe
Cracked Ice

Blend well. Pour into a cocktail glass. Serve with short straws.

KAFE DE MENTHE

3 oz. White Creme de Menthe
1 oz. Creme de Cafe

Mix and pour over ice cubes in an Old-fashioned glass.

KAFE FROST

4 oz. Vanilla Ice Cream, softened
½ oz. Brandy
1 oz. Creme de Cafe

Blend until smooth. Pour into a frosted cocktail glass.

KAHLUA ALEXANDER

1 oz. Kahlua
1 oz. Cream
1 oz. Brandy

Shake with ice and strain into a cocktail glass.

KAHLUA BORDER SHAKE

2 oz. Kahlua
2 scoops Vanilla Ice Cream
2 oz. Cream

Blend and pour into a Collins glass.

KAHLUA EXPRESSO (VIENNESE)

1 oz. Kahlua
1 oz. Triple Sec
1 tsp. Expresso Coffee

Shake and pour over crushed ice into an Old-fashioned glass.

KAHLUA MARTINI

2 oz. Gin
½ oz. Kahlua

Stir with ice and strain into a cocktail glass. Serve with a lemon twist.

KAHLUA SOUR

1½ oz. Kahlua
1 oz. Lemon Juice
½ tsp. Sugar

Shake with ice and strain into a Sour glass. Serve with a lemon wedge and a cherry.

KAHLUA SUPREME

1 tsp. Instant Coffee
1 scoop Vanilla Ice Cream
2 oz. Kahlua
¼ oz. White Creme de Menthe

Dissolve instant coffee in boiling water. Add remaining ingredients. Blend with ice and strain into a cocktail glass.

KAHLUA TOREADOR

1 oz. Kahlua
2 oz. Brandy
1 Egg White

Shake with ice and strain into a cocktail glass.

KAH SET

½ oz. Anisette
1½ oz. Kahlua

Mix in an Old-fashioned glass. Fill with ice.

KAILUA COCKTAIL

1½ oz. Rum
1 oz. Pineapple Juice
½ oz. Lemon Juice
½ oz. Grenadine

Shake with ice and strain into a cocktail glass.

KAISER

1½ oz. Gin
¾ oz. Kummel
¼ oz. Dry Vermouth

Stir with ice and strain into a cocktail glass.

KALTE ENTE

Rind 1 Lemon
3 oz. Curacao
1 bottle chilled Moselle
1 bottle sparkling Moselle, chilled

Put the lemon rind in a large pitcher and add the remaining ingredients. Serve in wineglasses. Makes about 12 servings.

KAMEHAMEHA RUM PUNCH

½ cup crushed Ice
1 oz. Light Rum
2 oz. Pineapple Juice
1 tbsp. Lemon Juice
1 tsp. Grenadine
1 tsp. Blackberry-flavored Brandy
1 tsp. Sugar

Stir with ice and strain into a highball glass. Add ice and float 1 oz. Dark Rum on top. Decorate with a pineapple stick and a cherry.

KANGAROO COCKTAIL

1½ oz. Vodka
¾ oz. Dry Vermouth

Shake with ice and strain into a cocktail glass. Serve with a lemon twist.

KANSAS CITY CUTIE

2 oz. Early Times
½ oz. White Creme de Menthe
½ oz. Coffee Liqueur

Mix in an Old-fashioned glass. Fill with ice and stir.

KAPPA SPECIAL OLD- FASHIONED COCKTAIL

1 tsp. Sugar
3 dashes Bitters
¼ tsp. Lemon Juice
2 oz. Rye or Bourbon Whisky

Put first three ingredients in an Old-fashioned glass. Add enough water to cover sugar and muddle well. Add Rye or Bourbon Whisky, fill the glass with cracked ice and stir well. Add a twist of lemon and decorate with a slice of orange, lemon and a cherry. Serve with a swizzle stick.

KARETTO

1 oz. Vodka
1 oz. Amaretto

Fill an Old-fashioned glass with ice and add Vodka and Amaretto.

KATINKA

1½ oz. Gin
½ oz. Cordial Medoc
½ oz. Green Chartreuse
1 dash Angostura Bitters

Stir with ice and strain into a cocktail glass.

KATZ' MEOW

1½ oz. Vodka
¾ oz. Dry Vermouth

Stir with ice and strain into a cocktail glass. Serve with a lemon twist.

KAYSER SOUR

1 bottle chilled Rhine Wine
3 cups Lemon Juice
6 tbsp. superfine Sugar
Ice cubes

Dissolve the sugar in the lemon juice. Add Wine and stir to blend. Put a dozen ice cubes in a pitcher, pour the wine mixture over them, and serve in punch glasses. Or put 1 or 2 ice cubes in wineglasses and fill with 4 oz. of the mixture. Makes about 12 servings.

K.C.B. COCKTAIL

½ oz. Kummel
1½ oz. Gin
¼ tsp. Apricot-flavored Brandy
¼ tsp. Lemon Juice

Shake with ice and strain into a highball glass. Serve with a lemon twist. (Kirsch may be used instead of Kummel.)

KE KALI NEI AU

½ cup crushed Ice
1½ oz. Light Rum
1½ oz. Passion Fruit Juice
1½ oz. Kirsch
2 tbsp. Lemon Juice
1 oz. Sugar Syrup
Green Coconut with top cut off, drained
1 oz. Dark Rum
Fruit for garnish
Red Hibiscus

Put the ice in a mixing glass and add the Rum, Passion-Fruit juice, Kirsch, lemon juice and sugar syrup. Stir well. Pour into the green coconut. Float the dark Rum on top and decorate with fruit and hibiscus. Serve with straws. (If coconut is not available, use an Old-fashioned glass.)

KENNY

1½ oz. Applejack
¼ oz. Sweet Vermouth
¾ oz. Lemon Juice
½ oz. Grenadine
1 dash Angostura Bitters

Shake with ice and strain into a cocktail glass.

KENTUCKY NO. 1

1¼ oz. Pineapple Juice
1¼ oz. Kentucky Bourbon

Shake with ice and strain into a cocktail glass.

KENTUCKY NO. 2

1½ oz. Bourbon
½ oz. Lemon Juice
½ oz. Pineapple Juice
¼ oz. Maraschino Liqueur

Shake with ice and strain into a sugar-rimmed cocktail glass.

KENTUCKY COLONEL COCKTAIL

½ oz. Benedictine
1½ oz. Bourbon Whisky

Stir with ice and strain into a cocktail glass. Serve with a lemon twist.

KENTUCKY HORSE'S NECK

1½ oz. Bourbon
Ginger Ale

Half fill an Old-fashioned glass with crushed ice. Add Bourbon and fill with ginger ale and serve with a lemon twist.

A bumper of good liquor
Will end a contest quicker
Than Justice, Judge or
Vicar.

KENTUCKY TODDY

1 ½ oz. Bourbon
1 tsp. Sugar

Dissolve the sugar with a little water in a mug. Add Bourbon and ice; stir briskly. To make a hot Kentucky Toddy, add 3 oz. boiling water to the mug.

KENTUCKY WONDER

1 oz. Galliano
1 oz. Sloe Gin
¼ Egg White
1 oz. Maraschino Liqueur or Grenadine

Shake with ice and strain into a cocktail glass.

KEOKE COFFEE

1 oz. Irish Whisky
½ oz. Dark Creme de Cacao
½ oz. Brandy

Mix in a fizz glass. Fill with hot black coffee and top with whipped cream.

KERRY COOLER

1 ½ oz. Irish Whisky
1 oz. Sherry or Madeira Wine
¾ oz. Orgeat
1 oz. Lemon Juice

Shake with ice and strain into a Collins glass. Fill with soda and ice. Serve with a lemon wedge.

KEY COCKTAIL

1 ½ oz. Gin
½ oz. Lime Juice
¼ oz. Falernum
¼ oz. Dark Jamaica Rum

Shake with ice and strain into a cocktail glass. Serve with a pineapple slice.

KEY WEST

1 ½ oz. Rum
½ tsp. Sugar
½ tsp. Allspice
½ tsp. Butter

Stir in a highball glass with hot water. Grate nutmeg on top.

KICKER COCKTAIL

1 oz. Calvados or Apple Brandy
2 oz. Rum
¼ oz. Sweet Vermouth

Shake with ice and strain into a cocktail glass.

KIDDIE CAR

1 ¾ oz. Apple Brandy
½ oz. Lime Juice
¼ oz. Triple Sec

Shake with ice and strain into a cocktail glass.

KILTIE NO. 1

1 ¼ oz. Bourbon
1 ¼ oz. Dry Vermouth
1 dash Angostura Bitters

Stir with ice and strain into a cocktail glass. Serve with a lemon twist.

KILTIE NO. 2

1 ¼ oz. Bourbon
1 ¼ oz. Sweet Vermouth
1 dash Orange Bitters

Stir with ice and strain into a cocktail glass.

KIM

1 oz. Brandy
¾ oz. Galliano
¾ oz. Triple Sec or Orange Curacao
Sugar to taste

Shake with ice and strain into a cocktail glass.

KINA

1 ½ oz. Gin
½ oz. Sweet Vermouth
½ oz. Lillet

Stir with ice and strain into a cocktail glass. Serve with a cherry.

KING ALPHONSE

1 oz. Creme de Cacao
¼ oz. Heavy Cream

Pour the Creme de Cacao into a pony glass and carefully float the cream on top.

KING COLE COCKTAIL

1 slice Orange
1 slice Pineapple
½ tsp. Powdered Sugar
2 oz. Rye Whisky
2 cubes Ice

Muddle the first three ingredients in an Old-fashioned glass and add Rye Whisky and ice cubes. Stir well.

KING'S CROSS NUT

1 Coconut
2 cubes Ice
2 oz. Brandy
1 oz. Tia Maria
Nutmeg

Take the top off the coconut and remove milk. Place half the milk and ice cubes into a cocktail shaker. Add Brandy and Tia Maria. Shake and strain back into the coconut. Dust with nutmeg and serve with a spoon and drinking straws.

KING'S DAIQUIRI

½ oz. Lemon Juice
½ oz. Parfait Amour
1 ½ oz. Rum
¼ tsp. Sugar
1 dash Egg White

Blend with ice and strain into a champagne glass.

KING'S MEN

½   oz. Galliano
½   oz. White Creme de Menthe
½   oz. White Creme de Cacao
½   oz. Metaxa
½   oz. Cognac

Fill an Old-fashioned glass with crushed ice and add all ingredients.

KING'S PEG

1   cube Ice
2   oz. Brandy
6   oz. Chilled Champagne

Place the ice cube in a wine glass or goblet and add the Brandy and Champagne.

KINGSTON NO. 1

1   oz. Dark Rum
½   oz. Kummel
½   oz. Orange Juice
1   dash Pimento Dram

Shake with ice and strain into a cocktail glass.

KINGSTON NO. 2

1½   oz. Jamaica Rum
¾   oz. Lime or Lemon Juice
½   oz. Gin
½   oz. Grenadine

Shake with ice and strain into a cocktail glass.

KING'S TOUCH

Aromatic Bitters
Brut Champagne, chilled
1   Sugar cube
1   dash Brandy

Put the sugar cube in a champagne glass. Saturate cube with Bitters and pour in Champagne. Top the drink with a dash of Brandy.

KIPINSKI

1   oz. White Rum
1   oz. Triple Sec
1   oz. Grapefruit Juice

Shake with ice and strain into a cocktail glass.

KIR

6   oz. Dry White Wine
1   tbsp. Creme de Cassis

Pour into a goblet or large wine glass. Add ice and serve with a lemon twist.

KIRSCH AND CASSIS

1   oz. Kirschwasser
½   oz. Creme de Cassis

Mix in a highball glass. Fill with soda and ice.

KIRSCH CUBA LIBRE

1½   oz. Kirschwasser
2   tsp. Lime Juice
Cola

Mix in an Old-fashioned glass. Add ice and Cola and stir.

KIRSCH FRAISETTE HIGHBALL

1½   oz. Kirschwasser
1   oz. Strawberry Liqueur

Stir with ice and strain into a highball glass. Fill with soda and ice.

KIRSCH HIGHBALL

1½   oz. Grenadine
1½   oz. Kirschwasser

Stir with ice and strain into a highball glass. Fill with soda and ice.

KIRSCH RICKEY

1½   oz. Kirschwasser
¼   oz. Lime Juice (leave lime shell in glass)

Pour into a highball glass. Fill with soda and ice. Serve with sliced maraschino cherries.

KIRSCHWASSER PUNCH

1   tsp. Powdered Sugar
½   oz. Lemon Juice
½   oz. Chartreuse
1½   oz. Kirschwasser

Shake with ice and strain into a cocktail glass.

KISS

¾   oz. Dubonnet
¾   oz. Sweet Vermouth
¾   oz. Gin
¼   oz. Maraschino Liqueur

Stir with ice and strain into a cocktail glass.

KISS FROM HEAVEN COCKTAIL

1   oz. Drambuie
1   oz. Dry Vermouth
1   oz. Cognac

Stir with ice and strain into a cocktail glass.

KISS IN THE DARK COCKTAIL

¾   oz. Gin
¾   oz. Cherry-flavored Brandy
¾   oz. Dry Vermouth

Stir with ice and strain into a cocktail glass.

KISS LIKE WINE

1¼   oz. Dry Vermouth
¼   oz. Dubonnet

Stir with ice and strain into a cocktail glass.

KISS ME QUICK HIGHBALL

1½ oz. Pernod
2 dashes Angostura Bitters
1 tsp. Curacao

Shake with ice and strain into a highball glass. Fill with soda and ice.

KISS OF FIRE

Tuaca
2-3 Coffee Beans

Pour Tuaca into a pony glass, add coffee beans and flame.

KISS THE BOYS GOODBYE

¾ oz. Sloe Gin
¾ oz. Brandy
½ Egg White
Juice 1 Lemon

Shake with ice and strain into a cocktail glass.

KITCHEN SINK

¾ oz. Rye Whisky
¾ oz. Gin
1 Egg
½ oz. Orange Juice
½ oz. Lemon Juice
½ tsp. Sugar
¼ oz. Apricot-flavored Brandy

Shake with ice and strain into a cocktail glass.

KITTY HIGHBALL

3 oz. Claret

Stir with ice in a highball glass. Fill with ginger ale and ice.

KLONDIKE

1¼ oz. Applejack
1¼ oz. Dry Vermouth
1 dash Orange Bitters

Stir with ice and strain into a cocktail glass.

KLONDIKE COOLER

½ tsp. Powdered Sugar
2 oz. Soda
2 oz. Rye Whisky

Put sugar and soda into a Collins glass. Stir, and fill the glass with ice. Add Rye Whisky. Fill with soda or ginger ale and stir again. Decorate with a twist of orange or lemon peel (or both) and dangle end over rim of glass.

KLONDIKE HIGHBALL

1 oz. Dry Vermouth
1 oz. Sweet Vermouth
½ oz. Lemon Juice
½ tsp. Sugar

Mix in a highball glass. Fill with soda and ice.

KNICKERBEIN NO. 1

1 oz. Maraschino Liqueur
1½ oz. Brandy
1 Egg Yolk
½ oz. Grenadine

Shake with ice and strain into a cocktail glass.

KNICKERBEIN NO. 2

¾ oz. Benedictine
¾ oz. Yellow Chartreuse
¾ oz. Kummel
1 dash Bitters
1 Egg

Place Bitters in the bottom of a large cocktail glass. Add egg yolk and the liquors. Float beaten egg white.

KNICKERBEIN NO. 3

¾ oz. Benedictine
¾ oz. Kummel
½ oz. Creme de Rose
1 Egg Yolk
1 dash Orange Bitters

Shake with ice and strain into a cocktail glass.

KNICKERBOCKER COCKTAIL

¼ tsp. Sweet Vermouth
¾ oz. Dry Vermouth
1½ oz. Gin

Stir with ice and strain into a cocktail glass. Serve with a lemon twist.

KNICKERBOCKER SPECIAL COCKTAIL

1 tsp. Raspberry Syrup
1 tsp. Lemon Juice
1 tsp. Orange Juice
2 oz. Rum
½ tsp. Triple Sec

Shake with ice and strain into a cocktail glass. Decorate with a small slice of pineapple.

KNIGHT

1½ oz. Brandy
½ oz. Lemon Juice
¼ oz. Cointreau
¼ oz. Yellow Chartreuse

Shake with ice and strain into a cocktail glass.

KNIGHTLY COCKTAIL

1½ oz. Brandy
Brut Champagne, chilled

Pour Brandy over an ice cube in an Old-fashioned glass. Fill with Champagne. Add a twist of orange peel.

KNOCK-OUT COCKTAIL

½ oz. Pernod
¾ oz. Gin
¾ oz. Dry Vermouth
1 tsp. White Creme de Menthe

Stir with ice and strain into a cocktail glass. Serve with a cherry.

KNUCKLEBUSTER

1½ oz. Scotch Whisky
¾ oz. Drambuie

Fill an Old-fashioned glass with ice and add liquor.

K.O. COCKTAIL

1 dash Apricot Liqueur
1 dash Lemon Juice
½ oz. Kirschwasser
1½ oz. Gin

Shake with ice and strain into a cocktail glass.

KOFFEE KOCKTAIL

1 oz. Creme de Cafe
3 oz. Chablis
2 cubes Ice

Pour ingredients over ice cubes in an Old-fashioned glass.

KOFFEE KOOLER

2 oz. Kahlua
6 oz. Rhine Wine
Ice cubes

Pour ingredients over ice cubes in a Collins glass. Stir gently.

KOLA COCKTAIL

1½ oz. Gin
1 oz. Cola
1 dash Orange Bitters

Stir with ice and strain into a cocktail glass. Serve with a cherry.

KOOL BURGUNDY

1 dash Maraschino Liqueur
1 tsp. Lemon Juice
1 tsp. Sugar
Burgundy Wine
Fresh Fruit

Fill a Collins glass half full with cracked ice. Add liqueur, lemon juice and sugar. Fill with Burgundy and stir. Garnish with fresh fruit in season.

KOOL CHIANTI

Juice ½ Lemon
Juice ½ Orange
1 tsp. Sugar
Chianti
Rum extract to taste

Mix lemon juice, orange juice and sugar in a Collins glass. Stir until sugar is dissolved. Fill the glass half full with cracked ice. Fill with Wine. Stir gently and float Rum extract on top. Serve with an orange slice.

KOOL KOOLER

4 oz. Haut Sauterne, chilled
4 oz. Lemon-flavored Soda, chilled

Mix and pour over cracked ice in a Collins glass.

KOPMAN CAPRICE

1 oz. Blackberry-flavored Brandy
1½ oz. Gin
Juice ½ Lemon
Soda

Pour Brandy, Gin and lemon juice into a Collins glass. Fill with shaved ice and 2-3 oz. soda. Mix. Garnish with a few blackberries and a lemon slice.

KREMLIN COLONEL

2 oz. Vodka
2 tsp. Lime Juice
1½ tsp. Sugar Syrup

Shake with ice and strain into a cocktail glass. Add ice and top with mint leaves.

KREMLIN COOLER

2 oz. Vodka
½ oz. Lime Juice
½ tsp. Sugar

Shake with ice and strain into a cocktail glass. Fill with soda and ice.

KRETCHMA COCKTAIL

1 oz. Vodka
1 oz. White Creme de Cacao
1 tbsp. Lemon Juice
1 dash Grenadine

Shake with ice and strain into a cocktail glass.

KUALA LAMPUR COOLER

2 oz. Gin
1 oz. Pineapple Juice
2 tsp. Lime Juice

Stir with ice and strain into a highball glass. Add ice and club soda. Decorate with a chunk of pineapple.

KUMMEL BLACKBERRY FRAPPE

½ oz. Kummel
2 tsp. Blackberry-flavored Brandy
1 tsp. Lemon Juice

Stir without ice and strain over crushed ice in a cocktail glass.

KUMMEL COCKTAIL

1 oz. Kummel
1 oz. Gin
2 dashes Dry Vermouth

Shake with ice and strain into a cocktail glass.

KUNGSHOLM COCKTAIL

½ oz. Dry Vermouth
½ oz. Liqueur d' Or
1½ oz. Rye Whisky

Shake with ice and strain into a cocktail glass. Serve with a cherry.

KUP'S INDISPENSABLE COCKTAIL

½   oz. Sweet Vermouth
½   oz. Dry Vermouth
1½ oz. Gin
1   dash Bitters

Stir with ice and strain into a cocktail glass.

LA BELLE CREME

1   oz. Vodka
1   oz. Heavy Cream
2   tsp. White Creme de Cacao
2   tsp. Cointreau

Shake with ice and strain into a cocktail glass.

LA CREOLE

¼   oz. Raspberry Syrup or Grenadine
¼   oz. Maraschino Liqueur
¼   oz. Yellow Chartreuse
¼   oz. Green Chartreuse

Pour carefully, in order given, into a pony glass so that each ingredient floats on the preceding one without mixing.

LADIES' CHOICE

1¾ oz. Gin
½   oz. Dry Vermouth
¼   oz. Kummel

Stir with ice and strain into a cocktail glass.

LADIES' COCKTAIL

1¾ oz. Rye Whisky
½   tsp. Anisette
2   dashes Bitters

Stir with ice and strain into a cocktail glass. Serve with a pineapple stick on top.

LADIES' PUNCH

1   tsp. Sugar
1   Egg
¾   oz. Maraschino Liqueur
1½ oz. Light Creme de Cacao
4   oz. Milk

Shake with ice and strain into a Collins glass. Add ice. Decorate with an orange peel.

LADIES' SUB BOURBON

2   oz. Bourbon
½   oz. Orange Curacao
1   dash Angostura Bitters

Mix in an Old-fashioned glass. Fill with ice and add a squirt of soda.

LA DOLCE PRIMA

1½ oz. Amaretto
1½ oz. Cream

Shake with ice and strain into a cocktail glass.

LADY ALEXANDER

1   oz. Creme de Cacao
1   oz. Sloe Gin
1   Egg White
1   dash Bitters

Shake with ice and strain into a cocktail glass.

LADY BE GOOD

1½ oz. Brandy
½   oz. White Creme de Menthe
½   oz. Sweet Vermouth

Shake with ice and strain into a cocktail glass.

LADY FINGER

1   oz. Gin
½   oz. Kirschwasser
1   oz. Wild Cherry-flavored Brandy

Shake with ice and strain into a cocktail glass.

LADY GODIVA

1½ oz. Cream
1   oz. Light Creme de Cacao
¾   oz. Anisette

Shake with ice and strain into a cocktail glass.

LADY HOPKINS

1½ oz. Southern Comfort
½   oz. Passion Fruit Juice
¾   oz. Lime Juice

Shake with ice and strain into a cocktail glass. Serve with a cherry, an orange slice and a mint sprig.

LADY KAHLUA

1½ oz. Kahlua
½   oz. White Creme de Menthe

Mix in an Old-fashioned glass. Fill with ice.

LADY LOVE FIZZ

Juice ½ Lemon
1   tsp. Powdered Sugar
1   Egg White
2   oz. Gin
2   tsp. sweet Cream

Shake with ice and strain into a highball glass. Add two ice cubes. Fill with soda and stir.

LAFAYETTE

1½ oz. Rye Whisky
½   oz. Dry Vermouth
½   oz. Dubonnet
1   dash Angostura Bitters

Stir with ice and strain into a cocktail glass.

Here's to childhood, youth, old age,
Here's to prophet, bard and sage,
Here's a health to every one,
Peace on earth, and heaven won!

LAFAYETTE PUNCH

6   Oranges
1   cup superfine Sugar
1   bottle chilled Moselle Wine
1   block Ice
4   bottles chilled Champagne

Peel oranges, carefully removing all the white pith. Slice thinly and place in a shallow bowl. Sprinkle with sugar, pour the Moselle Wine over them, and refrigerate for an hour or more. When ready to serve, slide the orange and wine mixture into a punch bowl, add the block of ice and pour in the Champagne. Serve in 4 oz. punch glasses. Makes about 30 servings.

LAFITTE

1   oz. Gin
½   oz. Dry Vermouth
½   oz. White Creme de Menthe
½   oz. Pernod

Stir with ice and strain into a cocktail glass.

LA FLORIDA RUM DAISY

2   oz. Rum
1   dash Angostura Bitters
½   oz. Yellow Chartreuse
1   oz. Lemon Juice·
1   tsp. Sugar

Shake with ice and strain into a fizz glass. Fill with crushed ice. Garnish with berries and fruit.

LA JOLLA

1½   oz. Brandy
½   oz. Creme de Bananes
1   tsp. Orange Juice
2   tsp. Lemon Juice

Shake with ice and strain into a cocktail glass.

LAKE SIDE

1   oz. Brandy
½   oz. Light Creme de Cacao
½   oz. Cointreau
½   oz. White Creme de Menthe

Shake with ice and strain into a cocktail glass.

LALLAH ROOKH COCKTAIL

1½   oz. Cognac
½   oz. Dark Rum
¼   oz. Cream
½   oz. Creme de Vanille

Shake with ice and strain into a cocktail glass.

LA MA DONE

¾   oz. Ginger-flavored Brandy
¾   oz. Cordial Medoc
½   oz. Benedictine
½   oz. Kummel

Stir with ice and strain into a cocktail glass.

LAMB'S CLUB

¾   oz. Gin
¾   oz. Dry Vermouth
¾   oz. Sweet Vermouth
¼   oz. Benedictine

Stir with ice and strain into a cocktail glass.

L'AMOUR COCKTAIL

Muddle mint sprigs with:

¾   oz. Lemon Juice
1½   oz. Gin
½   oz. Cherry Cordial

Shake with ice and strain into a cocktail glass.

> The Happy Couple — May we all live to be present at their golden wedding.

LAMP COCKTAIL

¾   oz. Brandy
¾   oz. Creme de Menthe
¾   oz. Cointreau
1   oz. Creme de Cacao

Shake with ice and strain into a cocktail glass.

LAND LADY

1½   oz. Gin
1   Egg White
½   oz. Grenadine

Shake with ice and strain into a cocktail glass.

LAND'S END

1   oz. Lemon Juice
1½   oz. Jamaica Rum
¼   oz. Orange Juice
¼   oz. Framboise

Shake with ice and strain into a cocktail glass. Serve with a lemon twist.

LA NEGRESSA BLONDE

¾   oz. Light Creme de Cacao
¾   oz. Cream
½   oz. Gin
½   oz. Cognac

Shake with ice and strain into a cocktail glass.

LA PIROUETTE

1¼   oz. Sherry
1¼   oz. Dry Vermouth
1   dash Orange Bitters
1   dash Angostura Bitters

Stir with ice and strain into a cocktail glass. Serve with a lemon twist.

LA PLACE

1¼   oz. Bourbon
1¼   oz. Sweet Vermouth
1   dash Orange Bitters

Stir with ice and strain into a cocktail glass.

LARCHMONT

1½   oz. Rum
½   oz. Lime Juice
½   oz. Grand Marnier
¼   tsp. Sugar

Shake with ice and strain into a cocktail glass. Serve with a twist of orange peel.

LASKY COCKTAIL

¾   oz. Grape Juice
¾   oz. Swedish Punch
¾   oz. Gin

Shake with ice and strain into a cocktail glass.

LAST KISS

1½   oz. Rum
½   oz. Gin
¼   oz. Brandy
¼   oz. Dry Vermouth
¼   oz. Lemon Juice
¼   tsp. Sugar

Shake with ice and strain into a cocktail glass.

LAST RESORT

1   oz. Port
½   oz. Brandy
1   Egg Yolk
½   tsp. Sugar

Shake with ice and strain into a cocktail glass. Sprinkle nutmeg on top.

LAST ROSE COCKTAIL

¾   oz. Port
½   tsp. Sugar Syrup
½   oz. Brandy
½   Egg Yolk

Shake with ice and strain into a cocktail glass. Sprinkle nutmeg on top.

LAST ROUND

1   oz. Gin
1   oz. Dry Vermouth
¼   oz. Brandy
¼   oz. Pernod

Stir with ice and strain into a cocktail glass.

LAST THOUGHT COCKTAIL

¾   oz. Brandy
¾   oz. Champagne

Stir with ice and strain into a cocktail glass.

LAS VEGAS

2   oz. Vodka
½   oz. Galliano
1   drop Lemon Juice

Stir with ice and strain into a cocktail glass.

LAS VEGAS JULEP

1   oz. Bourbon
1   oz. Lemon Juice
2   tsp. Galliano
1   tsp. Sugar Syrup

Shake with ice and strain over crushed ice into a highball glass. Decorate with mint.

LATIN BITTERS

1½   oz. Campari
1   tbsp. Sweet Vermouth

Mix in a highball glass. Fill with soda and ice. Stir and serve with a lemon twist.

LATIN LOVER NO. 1

1½   oz. Valentino
1   oz. Tequila
2   tsp. Lemon Juice
1-2   dashes Grenadine

Shake with ice and strain into a cocktail glass.

LATIN LOVER NO. 2

1   oz. Kahlua
1   oz. Gold Rum

Mix in an Old-fashioned glass. Fill with ice.

LATIN WELCOME

1   dash Orange Bitters
1   dash Grenadine Syrup
2   oz. Sweet Vermouth
2   oz. Dry Vermouth

Stir with ice and strain into a cocktail glass. Serve with a lemon twist and a maraschino cherry.

Eat, drink and be merry, for tomorrow ye diet.

LAUGHING BOY

½   tsp. Sugar
1   dash Angostura Bitters
½   oz. Sweet Vermouth
2   oz. Rum

Dissolve sugar with the Bitters and Vermouth. Mix in an Old-fashioned glass. Add the Rum and serve with a lemon wedge and orange slice.

LAUGHING SOUP

1½   oz. Gin
½   oz. Lemon Juice
½   oz. Dry Vermouth
½   tsp. Sugar

Shake with ice and strain into a cocktail glass.

LAWHILL COCKTAIL

¾   oz. Dry Vermouth
1½   oz. Rye Whisky
¼   tsp. Pernod
¼   tsp. Maraschino Liqueur
1   dash Bitters

Stir with ice and strain into a cocktail glass.

LAW'S FLIP

1 Egg Yolk
1 oz. Port
½ oz. Brandy
1 tsp. Sugar

Shake with ice and strain into a flip glass. Sprinkle nutmeg on top.

LAYER CAKE

⅓ oz. Creme de Cacao
⅓ oz. Apricot-flavored Brandy
⅓ oz. Heavy Cream
1 Maraschino Cherry

Pour carefully, in order given, into a pony glass so that each ingredient floats on the preceding one without mixing. Carefully place the cherry on top. Chill before serving.

LAYERED-LOOK

½ cup Lemonade
Ruby Chablis, chilled

Pour the lemonade into a Collins glass. Add enough ice cubes to come above the lemonade. Slowly pour chilled Ruby Chablis over the cubes. (The wine will float on the lemonade, giving the drink a layered look.) Garnish with a lime wheel.

LA ZARAGOZANA

1/6 oz. Creme de Cacao
1/6 oz. Cognac
1/6 oz. Cointreau
1/6 oz. Chartreuse
1/6 oz. Benedictine
1/6 oz. Apricot-flavored Brandy

Pour carefully, in order given, into a pony glass so that each ingredient floats on the preceding one without mixing.

LEAD BALLOON

½ oz. Grand Marnier
1½ oz. Brandy

Mix in an Old-fashioned glass and fill with ice.

LEAP FROG

¾ oz. Lime Juice
1 oz. Rum
1 oz. Apricot-flavored Brandy
½ oz. Grenadine

Shake with ice and strain into a cocktail glass.

LEAP FROG HIGHBALL

Juice ½ Lemon
2 oz. Gin

Pour into a highball glass. Add ice cubes and fill with ginger ale. Stir.

LEAP YEAR COCKTAIL

1¼ oz. Gin
½ oz. Orange-flavored Gin or Grand Marnier
½ oz. Sweet Vermouth
¼ tsp. Lemon Juice

Shake with ice and strain into a cocktail glass.

LEATHERNECK

Juice ½ Lime
1½ oz. Rye Whisky
½ oz. Curacao

Shake with ice and strain into a cocktail glass.

LEAVE IT TO ME NO. 1

½ oz. Apricot-flavored Brandy
½ oz. Dry Vermouth
1 oz. Gin
¼ tsp. Lemon Juice
¼ tsp. Grenadine

Shake with ice and strain into a cocktail glass.

Here's to woman, — once our superior, now our equal.

LEAVE IT TO ME NO. 2

1 tsp. Raspberry Syrup
1 tsp. Lemon Juice
¼ tsp. Maraschino Liqueur
1½ oz. Gin

Stir with ice and strain into a cocktail glass.

LEAVE IT TO ME NO. 3

1½ oz. Rum
½ oz. Lime Juice
¼ oz. Grenadine
¼ oz. Maraschino Liqueur

Shake with ice and strain into a cocktail glass.

LEAVE IT TO ME NO. 4

1½ oz. Gin
¼ oz. Lemon Juice
¼ oz. Grenadine

Shake with ice and strain into a highball glass. Fill with soda and ice.

LE COQ HARDY

Fernet Branca
Grand Marnier
Champagne
Cognac
Angostura Bitters
1 Sugar cube

Place the sugar cube on the bottom of a saucer champagne glass; top it with a drop of Fernet Branca, Grand Marnier, Cognac and Bitters. Fill the glass with Champagne; stir gently until the sugar has dissolved. Decorate with a slice of orange and a cherry.

LEEWARD

1½   oz. Rum
½   oz. Calvados
½   oz. Sweet Vermouth

Stir with ice and strain into a cocktail glass. Serve with a lemon twist.

LE MASCHERE

1   oz. Scotch Whisky
½   oz. Galliano
½   oz. Lime Juice

Shake with ice and strain into a highball glass. Fill with crushed ice.

LEMONADE (CLARET)

2   tsp. Powdered Sugar
2   oz. Claret
Juice 1 Lemon

In a Collins glass, dissolve the sugar in the lemon juice. Then add ice and enough water to fill the glass, leaving room to float the Claret. Decorate with slices of orange and lemon and a cherry. Serve with straws.

LEMONADE (MODERN)

1   Lemon
2   tsp. Powdered Sugar
1½   oz. Sherry
1   oz. Sloe Gin

Cut the lemon in quarters and muddle well with the sugar. Add Sherry and Sloe Gin. Shake with ice and strain into a Collins glass. Fill the glass with soda.

LEMON RUM COOLER

½   oz. Lemon Juice
2   oz. Rum
¼   oz. 151-proof Rum
2   oz. Pineapple Juice
½   oz. Falernum

Shake with ice and strain into a Collins glass. Fill with Bitter Lemon soda and ice.

LENA COCKTAIL

1½   oz. Bourbon
½   oz. Sweet Vermouth
½   oz. Dry Vermouth
1   tsp. Campari
1   tsp. Galliano

Stir with ice and strain into a cocktail glass. Serve with a cherry.

LEO SPECIAL

1½   oz. Gin
½   oz. Lime Juice
½   oz. Cointreau
¼   oz. Pernod

Shake with ice and strain into a cocktail glass.

LEPRECHAUN

2   oz. Irish Whisky
3   oz. Tonic Water

Put the Whisky and tonic water in an Old-fashioned glass. Add ice cubes and stir gently. Serve with a lemon twist.

LEPRECHAUN DANCER

2   oz. Irish Whisky
2   oz. Lemon Juice

Mix in a Collins glass. Add soda and ginger ale in equal parts. Fill with ice. Serve with a lemon twist.

LES PETITS POIS COCKTAIL

1   oz. Cognac
¾   oz. Gin
¾   oz. Izarra

Stir with ice and strain into a cocktail glass.

> May you live all the days of your life.
>   — Swift

LET'S SLIDE

1½   oz. Brandy
½   oz. Port
½   oz. Blackberry-flavored Brandy

Stir with ice and strain into a cocktail glass.

LEVIATHAN COCKTAIL

1½   oz. Brandy
½   oz. Sweet Vermouth
½   oz. Orange Juice

Shake with ice and strain into a cocktail glass.

LEVIATHAN 477

¼   oz. Sugar Syrup
½   oz. Lemon Juice
½   oz. Orange Juice
1½   oz. Scotch Whisky

Shake with ice and strain into a cocktail glass.

LIANO

1½   oz. Cognac
½   oz. Galliano
½   oz. Grand Marnier

Shake with ice and strain into a cocktail glass.

LIAR'S COCKTAIL

1½   oz. Gin
½   oz. Dry Vermouth
¼   oz. Orange Curacao
¼   oz. Sweet Vermouth

Stir with ice and strain into a cocktail glass.

LIBERAL NO. 1

1½   oz. Whisky
½   oz. Sweet Vermouth
¼   oz. Amer Picon
1   dash Orange Bitters

Stir with ice and strain into a cocktail glass.

LIBERAL NO. 2

1¼ oz. Bourbon
1¼ oz. Amer Picon
¼ tsp. Sugar

Shake with ice and strain into a cocktail glass. Serve with a lemon twist.

LIBERTY COCKTAIL NO. 1

¾ oz. Rum
1½ oz. Apple Brandy
¼ tsp. Sugar Syrup

Stir with ice and strain into a cocktail glass.

LIBERTY COCKTAIL NO. 2

1½ oz. Applejack
½ oz. Rum
½ oz. Lemon Juice
½ tsp. Sugar

Shake with ice and strain into a cocktail glass.

LIEBFRAUMILCH

1 oz. Light Creme de Cacao
1 oz. Cream
1 oz. Lime Juice

Shake with ice and strain into a cocktail glass.

LICIA ALBANESE

1½ oz. Gin
½ oz. Campari

Mix in an Old-fashioned glass. Fill with ice. Serve with a lemon twist.

LIL' APPLE

1¼ oz. Lillet
1¼ oz. Calvados

Stir with ice and strain into a cocktail glass. Serve with an orange slice.

LILLANE

¾ oz. Cognac
¾ oz. Light Creme de Cacao
¾ oz. Kirschwasser
¼ oz. Grenadine

Shake with ice and strain into a cocktail glass.

LILLET COCKTAIL

1½ oz. Lillet
1 oz. Gin

Stir with ice and strain into a cocktail glass. Serve with a lemon twist.

LILLIAN RUSSELL

⅓ oz. Creme de Rose
⅓ oz. Creme de Violette
⅓ oz. Cream

Pour carefully, in order given, into a pony glass so that each ingredient floats on the preceding one without mixing.

LILLIAN WALDORF

¼ oz. Creme d'Yvette
¾ oz. Maraschino Liqueur

Pour carefully, in order given, into a pony glass so that each ingredient floats on the preceding one without mixing. Float cream on top (optional).

LILLY

¾ oz. Gin
¾ oz. Creme de Noyaux
¾ oz. Lillet
¼ oz. Lemon Juice

Stir with ice and strain into a cocktail glass.

May their joys be as deep
   as the ocean,
Their sorrows as light as its
   foam;
May the sunlight of love
   ever brighten
Their lives and shine into
   their home.

LIL NAUE

1 oz. Brandy
½ oz. Port
½ oz. Apricot-flavored Brandy
1 tsp. Powdered Sugar
1 Egg Yolk

Shake with ice and strain into a wine glass. Dust with cinnamon.

LIL' NUT

1¼ oz. Lillet
1 oz. Gin
¼ oz. Creme de Noyaux

Stir with ice and strain into a cocktail glass. Serve with a twist of orange peel.

LIMBO COW

1½ oz. Tia Maria

Pour into a highball glass. Fill with milk and ice.

LIME DAIQUIRI

1½ oz. Rum
½ oz. Lime Juice
½ oz. Lime Liqueur

Shake with ice and strain into a cocktail glass. Serve with a lime wedge.

LIME DEMI TASSE

Heat 1 oz. Lime Liqueur
½ oz. Rum
½ oz. Pineapple Juice
¼ oz. Lime Juice
½ oz. Water

Mix in a cup or a fizz glass.

LIME GIANT

Put ice cubes in a Collins glass.

Add: 2 oz. Lime Vodka

Fill with lemon and lime soda and decorate with a slice of lime.

LIME RICKEY

1½   oz. Gin
½   oz. Lime Juice

Mix in a highball glass. (Leave lime shell in glass.) Fill with soda and ice.

LIMEY

1   oz. Rum
1   oz. Lime Liqueur
½   oz. Triple Sec or Orange Curacao
2   tsp. Lime Juice

Combine ingredients and half a cup of crushed ice in a blender. Blend at low speed and pour into a champagne glass. Add a twist of lime peel.

LINSTEAD COCKTAIL

1   oz. Rye Whisky
1   oz. Pineapple Juice
½   tsp. Powdered Sugar
¼   tsp. Pernod
¼   tsp. Lemon Juice

Shake with ice and strain into a cocktail glass.

LION TAMER

1½   oz. Gin
1   oz. Raspberry Ice

Shake with ice and strain into a cocktail glass.

LIQUID SYMPHONY

¼   oz. Creme de Rose
¼   oz. Creme de Menthe
¼   oz. Yellow Chartreuse
¼   oz. Cognac

Pour carefully, in order given, into a pony glass so that each ingredient floats on the preceding one without mixing.

LITTLE BEN

2   oz. Brandy
2   oz. Sweet Vermouth
1   tsp. Benedictine

Shake with ice and strain into an Old-fashioned glass.

LITTLE COLONEL

½   oz. Lime Juice
¾   oz. Bourbon
1½   oz. Southern Comfort

Shake with ice and strain into a cocktail glass.

LITTLE DEVIL

Juice ¼ Lemon
1½   tsp. Triple Sec
¾   oz. Rum
¾   oz. Gin

Shake with ice and strain into a cocktail glass.

(A) LITTLE PORT

½   tbsp. Orgeat Syrup
½   tbsp. Sugar
1   dash Lemon Juice
¼   cup Water
Tawny Port

Put Orgeat Syrup, sugar, lemon juice and water in a Collins glass. Stir until sugar is dissolved. Fill the glass nearly full with cracked ice. Fill with Port. Garnish with fresh fruit.

LITTLE PRINCESS COCKTAIL

1½   oz. Sweet Vermouth
1½   oz. Rum

Stir with ice and strain into a cocktail glass.

> Here's to the love that lies
> in woman's eyes,
> And lies, and lies, and lies.

LIVELY ROSE CIDER

4   oz. Apple Cider, chilled
4   oz. Vin Rose, chilled

Mix cider and Vin Rose. Pour over ice cubes into a Collins glass. Serve with a lime wedge.

LIZARD SKIN

Hollow out half an orange, fill with Brandy and flame.

LOCHAN ORA BREEZE

1½   oz. Lochan Ora
½   oz. White Creme de Menthe

Fill a cocktail glass with crushed ice. Add Lochan Ora and Creme de Menthe.

LOCH LOMOND

1½   oz. Scotch Whisky
1   tsp. Sugar
3   dashes Angostura Bitters

Shake with ice and strain into a cocktail glass.

LOCOMOTIVE

5   oz. Claret
½   oz. Orange Curacao
1   oz. Honey
1½   tsp. Sugar
1   lightly beaten Egg

Stir first 4 ingredients. Add the egg and bring the mixture to a simmer. Top with cinnamon. Serve in a mug.

LOENSKY

1½   oz. Kummel
1   oz. Scotch Whisky

Stir with ice and strain into a cocktail glass.

LOFTUS

1   oz. Pernod
¾   oz. Sweet Vermouth
¾   oz. Dry Vermouth

Stir with ice and strain into a cocktail glass.

LOLITA

1½   oz. Tequila
3   tsp. Lime Juice
1   tsp. Honey
1-2   dashes Angostura Bitters

Shake with ice and strain into a cocktail glass. Add ice.

LOLLIPOP

¾   oz. Cointreau
¾   oz. Green Chartreuse
¾   oz. Kirschwasser
1   dash Maraschino

Shake with ice and strain into a cocktail glass.

LOMA BONITA

1½   oz. Tequila
3   oz. Pineapple Juice

Shake with ice and strain into an Old-fashioned glass. Add ice.

LONDON NO. 1

1½   oz. Rye Whisky
½   oz. Orgeat Syrup
2   dashes Orange Flower Water
1   Egg

Shake with ice and strain into a cocktail glass. Sprinkle nutmeg on top.

LONDON NO. 2

2   oz. Gin
2   dashes Orange Bitters
¼   oz. Maraschino Liqueur
¼   tsp. Sugar

Stir with ice and strain into a cocktail glass. Serve with a lemon twist. (Pernod may be used instead of Maraschino Liqueur.)

LONDON BUCK

2   oz. Gin
Juice ½ Lemon

Pour into a highball glass over ice cubes. Fill with ginger ale and stir.

LONDON DOCK

1½   oz. Burgundy
2   tbsp. Dark Rum
2   tsp. Sugar

Dissolve the sugar with a few drops of hot water in a mug. Add everything else, including a cinnamon stick and lemon peel. Fill with boiling water and stir. Garnish with nutmeg. (Bordeaux wine may be used instead of the Burgundy.)

LONDON FOG NO. 1

1   tbsp. White Creme de Menthe
1   tbsp. Anisette
1-2   dashes Angostura Bitters

Stir with ice and strain into a cocktail glass.

LONDON FOG NO. 2

1¾   oz. Gin
½   oz. Pernod

Fill a cocktail glass with crushed ice and pour in Gin and Pernod.

LONDON SPECIAL NO. 1

1   cube sugar
1   cube Ice
2   dashes Peychaud's Bitters
8   oz. chilled Champagne

Drop the sugar cube into a highball glass, add an orange peel, the ice cube and Bitters, and fill with Champagne.

LONDON SPECIAL NO. 2

½   Orange shell
1   tsp. Sugar
2   dashes Bitters
Champagne

Place the orange shell in a large cocktail glass, add the sugar and Bitters and fill the glass with Champagne.

LONE TREE COCKTAIL NO. 1

¾   oz. Sweet Vermouth
1½   oz. Gin

Stir with ice and strain into a cocktail glass.

LONE TREE COCKTAIL NO. 2

1   oz. Gin
¾   oz. Dry Vermouth
¾   oz. Sweet Vermouth
2   dashes Orange Bitters (optional)

Stir with ice and strain into a cocktail glass. Serve with a cherry.

LONE TREE COOLER NO. 1

½   tsp. Powdered Sugar
2   oz. Soda
2   oz. Gin
1   tbsp. Dry Vermouth

Put the first two ingredients into a Collins glass, stir, fill the glass with ice and add Gin and Vermouth. Fill the glass with soda or ginger ale and stir again. Decorate with an orange or lemon peel twist (or both) and dangle end over the rim of the glass.

> Here's to the triple alliance — Friendship, Freedom and Wine.

LONE TREE COOLER NO. 2

½ oz. Lemon Juice
½ oz. Orange Juice
½ oz. Dry Vermouth
1½ oz. Gin
¾ oz. Grenadine

Shake with ice and strain into a Collins glass. Fill with soda and ice.

LONG TOM COOLER

1 oz. Lemon Juice
1 tsp. Sugar
2 oz. Gin

Shake with ice and strain into a Collins glass. Fill with soda and ice. Serve with an orange slice.

LONG WHISTLE

2 oz. Brandy
3 oz. Milk
½ tsp. Sugar

Shake with ice and strain into a highball glass. Fill with ice, add milk and sprinkle nutmeg on top.

LOOK OUT BELOW

Juice ¼ Lemon
1½ oz. 151-proof Rum
1 tsp. Grenadine

Shake with ice and strain into an Old-fashioned glass. Add ice cubes.

LORD SUFFOLK

1¾ oz. Gin
¼ oz. Cointreau
¼ oz. Sweet Vermouth
¼ oz. Maraschino Liqueur

Stir with ice and strain into a cocktail glass. Serve with a lemon twist.

LORENZO

½ oz. Lime Juice
1 oz. Vodka
1 oz. Tuaca

Shake with ice and strain into a cocktail glass with a sugared rim.

LOS ANGELES COCKTAIL

Juice ½ Lemon
1 tsp. Powdered Sugar
1 Egg
¼ tsp. Sweet Vermouth
1½ oz. Rye Whisky

Shake with ice and strain into a flip glass.

LOS ANGELES LUV

1 oz. Early Times
1 oz. Creme de Bananes
½ oz. Triple Sec
½ oz. Lemon Juice
2 oz. Pineapple Juice

Shake with ice and strain into a highball glass. Fill with ice. Serve with a pineapple stick.

LOUD SPEAKER

¾ oz. Gin
¾ oz. Brandy
½ oz. Cointreau
½ oz. Lemon Juice

Shake with ice and strain into a cocktail glass.

LOUIS

1½ oz. Gin
½ oz. Dry Vermouth
¼ oz. Grand Marnier
¼ oz. Cointreau

Stir with ice and strain into a cocktail glass.

LOUISIANA LULLABY

1½ oz. Jamaica Rum
2 tsp. Dubonnet
1-2 drops Grand Marnier

Shake with ice and strain into a cocktail glass. Serve with a lemon twist.

LOUIS SPECIAL

1 oz. Gin
1 oz. Pineapple Juice
¼ oz. Sweet Vermouth
¼ oz. Dry Vermouth

Shake with ice and strain into a cocktail glass.

LOUISVILLE STINGER

1½ oz. Early Times
½ oz. White Creme de Menthe
1 dash Bitters

Mix in an Old-fashioned glass, the rim of which has been rubbed with lemon. Fill with ice, stir and serve with a lemon twist.

LOVE COCKTAIL

2 oz. Sloe Gin
1 Egg White
½ tsp. Lemon Juice
½ tsp. Raspberry Juice

Shake with ice and strain into a cocktail glass.

LOVER'S BALM

1 quart Cider
3 oz. Cognac
2 oz. Curacao
1½ oz. Sugar
3 tsp. Lemon Juice

Dissolve the sugar with the lemon juice in a large pot. Add grated lemon rinds, Brandy, Curacao and cider. Stir until foamy and well-blended. Store in the refrigerator until ready to use. Serve in mugs with ice and soda.

LOVER'S DELIGHT NO. 1

¾ oz. Cointreau
¾ oz. Forbidden Fruit
1 oz. Cognac

Shake with ice and strain into a cocktail glass.

LOVER'S DELIGHT NO. 2

1½ oz. Gin
Orange Sherbet

Shake with ice and strain into a cocktail glass.

LOVUM' AND LEAVEM'

¾ oz. Lime Juice
1 Egg White
1 oz. Gin
½ oz. Triple Sec
¼ oz. Grenadine

Shake with ice and strain into a cocktail glass.

LUCHOW'S GRAND PRIZE

1 oz. Bourbon
1 oz. Cherry Liqueur
1 oz. Lime Juice

Shake with ice and strain into a Sour glass. Add ice.

LUCIE

¾ oz. Lime Juice
¾ oz. Rum
¾ oz. Grand Marnier
¼ oz. Orange Curacao

Shake with ice and strain into a cocktail glass.

LUCIEN GAUDIN

1 oz. Gin
½ oz. Cointreau
½ oz. Campari
½ oz. Dry Vermouth

Stir with ice and strain into a cocktail glass.

LUCKY "4"

1 tsp. Lemon Juice
1 tsp. Sugar Syrup
1½ oz. Brandy
1½ oz. Sweet Vermouth

Stir with ice and strain into a cocktail glass.

LUGGER

1 oz. Brandy
1 oz. Apple Brandy
1 dash Apricot-flavored Brandy

Shake with ice and strain into a cocktail glass.

LUIGI

¾ oz. Tangerine Juice
1 oz. Gin
½ oz. Dry Vermouth
¼ oz. Grenadine
¼ oz. Cointreau

Shake with ice and strain into a cocktail glass. Serve with a lemon twist.

Here's to ourselves
And wishing all
The wish they wish
themselves!

LUNE DE MIEL COCKTAIL

¾ oz. White Cocoa
¾ oz. Parfait Amour
¾ oz. Kummel
1 Egg Yolk

Pour into a Kummel glass.

LUPE VELEZ

1¼ oz. Rum
½ oz. Kummel
½ oz. Orange Juice
¼ oz. Pimento Dram

Shake with ice and strain into a cocktail glass.

LUTKINS SPECIAL

1 oz. Gin
1 oz. Dry Vermouth
¼ oz. Apricot-flavored Brandy
¼ oz. Orange Juice

Stir with ice and strain into a cocktail glass.

LUXURY COCKTAIL

3 oz. Brandy
2 dashes Orange Bitters
3 oz. chilled Champagne

Stir and pour into a champagne glass.

MABEL BERRA

¾ oz. Lime Juice
¾ oz. Sloe Gin
1 oz. Swedish Punch

Shake with ice and strain into a cocktail glass.

MABEL TEA

1½ oz. Brandy
½ oz. Amer Picon
½ oz. Lime Juice

Shake with ice and strain into a cocktail glass.

MAC (WHISKY)

1 oz. Scotch Whisky
1 oz. Ginger Wine

Mix in an Old-fashioned glass.

MACARONI

1½ oz. Pernod
½ oz. Sweet Vermouth

Shake with ice and strain into a cocktail glass.

MA CHERIE COCKTAIL

2 oz. Dry Gin
1 oz. Cherry Liqueur

Shake with ice and strain into a cocktail glass.

MACHINE-GUN KELLY

1½ oz. Whisky
1 oz. Sweet Vermouth
1 oz. Dry Vermouth
1 dash Orange Bitters

Shake with ice and strain into a champagne glass. Serve with a lemon twist.

MACHO

¾ oz. Pernod
¾ oz. Tequila

Fill an Old-fashioned glass with crushed ice and add Pernod and Tequila. Serve with a squeeze of lemon juice.

MACKA

1 dash Creme de Cassis
1 oz. Gin
1 oz. Sweet Vermouth
1 oz. Dry Vermouth

Fill a highball glass half full with cracked ice. Add all the ingredients and stir. Serve with an orange slice.

MACKINNON

½ oz. Lemon Juice
½ oz. Lime Juice
1½ oz. Drambuie
½ oz. Rum

Shake with ice and strain into a Collins glass. Fill with soda and ice.

MACLEAY STREET

1 oz. Bourbon
½ oz. Galliano
1 dash Grenadine
Orange Juice

Shake with ice and strain into a highball glass.

MADAM LOU

1½ oz. Dry Vermouth
¾ oz. Gin
¼ oz. Pineapple Juice

Shake with ice and strain into a cocktail glass.

MAD BULL

1½ oz. Aquavit
¾ oz. Lime Juice
2 oz. Tomato Juice
1 oz. Beef Bouillon
Sprinkle of Celery Salt

Pour into a highball glass. Fill with crushed ice.

MADEIRA COCKTAIL

1 oz. Madeira Wine
¾ oz. Strega
¾ oz. Cognac

Stir with ice and strain into a cocktail glass.

MADEIRA MINT FLIP

1½ oz. Madeira Wine
1 oz. Chocolate Mint Liqueur
1 Egg
1 tsp. Sugar

Shake with ice and strain into a flip glass. Sprinkle nutmeg on top.

Here's to the health of the happy pair,
May good luck meet them everywhere,
And may each day of wedded bliss
Be always just as sweet as this!

MADEIRA PUNCH

12 Ice cubes
1 bottle Medium Dry Madeira
½ cup Brandy
Superfine Sugar, to taste
Lemon and Orange slices
Fresh Peach slices
Halved, fresh Strawberries
1 quart chilled Club Soda

Put ice cubes in a large pitcher, pour the Madeira and Brandy over them and sweeten to taste. Garnish with fruit and pour in the club soda. Serve in punch glasses. Makes approximately 14 servings.

MADEIRA WINE COCKTAIL

1 Egg Yolk
1 tsp. Grenadine
½ oz. Orange-flavored Liqueur
½ oz. Brandy
1 oz. Madeira Wine

Shake with ice and strain into a cocktail glass.

May you live as long as you like, and have all you like as long as you live.

MADELAINE NO. 1

½ oz. Lemon Juice
½ oz. Lime Juice
1 oz. Rum
1 oz. Drambuie

Shake with ice and strain into a cocktail glass.

MADELAINE NO. 2

1¾ oz. Gin
½ oz. Pernod
¼ oz. Grenadine

Shake with ice and strain into a cocktail glass. Serve with a lemon twist.

MAD HATTER

Juice ¼ Lemon
Juice ¼ Lime
1 tsp. Sugar
1½ oz. Whisky

Shake with ice and strain into a cocktail glass. Add a dash of Pernod.

MADISON AVENUE

2 oz. Vodka
2 oz. Clam Juice
2 oz. Tomato Juice
1-2 drops Lemon Juice
1-2 dashes Worcestershire Sauce
Pinch of salt

Shake with ice and strain into a highball glass.

MAE WEST

1½ oz. Brandy
1 Egg Yolk
1 tsp. Sugar

Shake with ice and strain into a Sour glass. Sprinkle cayenne pepper on top.

MAGNOLIA NO. 1

2 oz. Gin
1 oz. Heavy Cream
2 tbsp. Lemon Juice
½ tsp. Grenadine

Shake with ice and strain into a large cocktail glass.

MAGNOLIA NO. 2

1 oz. Brandy
½ oz. Orange Curacao
1 Egg Yolk

Shake with ice and strain into a fizz glass. Fill with Champagne.

MAGNOLIA BLOSSOM

1½ oz. Gin
½ oz. Cream
½ oz. Lemon Juice

Shake with ice and strain into a cocktail glass.

MAGNOLIA HIGHBALL

1½ oz. Brandy
½ tsp. Curacao
½ tsp. Sugar Syrup
1 Egg Yolk

Shake with ice and strain into a highball glass. Fill with Champagne and ice.

MAH JONGG

1½ oz. Gin
½ oz. Rum
½ oz. Cointreau

Stir with ice and strain into a cocktail glass. Serve with a lemon twist.

MAHUKONA NO. 1

1 oz. White Rum
2 tsp. Triple Sec
2 tsp. Lemon Juice
1-2 drops Rock Candy Syrup
1-2 dashes Angostura Bitters

Shake and strain over crushed ice in an Old-fashioned glass. Garnish with a pineapple slice and mint leaves.

MAHUKONA NO. 2

1 dash Angostura Bitters
½ oz. Triple Sec
1½ oz. Rum
½ oz. Lemon Juice
½ tsp. Sugar
Several pieces Pineapple and juice

Fill a Collins glass with shaved ice and add all ingredients. Serve with a cherry.

MAIBOWLE

1 quart ripe Strawberries
6-8 tbsp. superfine Sugar
3 bottles chilled Moselle Wine
1 bottle chilled Champagne
1 block Ice

Prepare the strawberries by washing and hulling them. Sprinkle with sugar and pour Moselle over them. Refrigerate for several hours. To serve, put a large block of ice in a punch bowl, add the strawberry mixture, the remaining 2 bottles of Moselle and the Champagne. Stir gently. Serve in punch glasses, with a strawberry in each. Makes about 24 servings.

MAIDEN'S BLUSH NO. 1

¼ tsp. Lemon Juice
1 tsp. Triple Sec
1 tsp. Grenadine
1½ oz. Gin

Shake with ice and strain into a cocktail glass.

MAIDEN'S BLUSH NO. 2

1½ oz. Gin
¾ oz. Pernod
1 tsp. Grenadine

Stir with ice and strain into a cocktail glass.

> Woman — she needs no
>   eulogy;
> She speaks for herself.

MAIDEN'S KISS

1/5 oz. Creme de Rose
1/5 oz. Orange Curacao
1/5 oz. Maraschino Liqueur
1/5 oz. Yellow Chartreuse
1/5 oz. Benedictine

Pour carefully, in order given, into a pony glass so that each ingredient floats on the preceding one without mixing.

MAIDEN'S PRAYER NO. 1

1½   oz. Gin
½   oz. Triple Sec
1   oz. Lemon Juice
1   oz. Orange Juice

Shake with ice and strain into a cocktail glass.

MAIDEN'S PRAYER NO. 2

¾   oz. Gin
¾   oz. Cointreau
1   tsp. Lemon Juice
1   tsp. Orange Juice

Shake with ice and strain into a cocktail glass. (Lillet can be used instead of Cointreau, with 2 tsps. each of Calvados and Apricot-flavored Brandy instead of the juices.)

MAI KAI NO

1   oz. White Rum
1   oz. 151-proof Rum
2   tsp. Jamaica Rum
2   tsp. Passion Fruit Juice
2   tsp. Honey
1   shot Lime Juice
1-2   dashes Angostura Bitters

Mix and pour over crushed ice into a Collins glass. Top off with a squirt of soda and garnish with a pineapple stick and a few mint sprigs.

MAINBRACE

¾   oz. Gin
¾   oz. Triple Sec
¾   oz. Grape Juice

Shake with ice and strain into a cocktail glass.

> Here's to the future, what-
> ever it brings,
> And hoping we'll never
> swerve
> From doing right and
> thinking right,
> And getting what we
> deserve.

MAI TAI NO. 1

½   tsp. Powdered Sugar
2   oz. Rum
1   oz. Triple Sec
1   tbsp. Orgeat or Almond-flavored Syrup
1   tbsp. Grenadine
1   tbsp. Lime Juice

Shake with ice and strain into a large Old-fashioned glass about ⅓ full of crushed ice. Decorate with a maraschino cherry speared to a wedge of fresh pineapple. For a hair raiser, top with a dash of 151-proof Rum and for a real Hawaiian effect float an orchid on each drink. Serve with straws.

MAI TAI NO. 2

2   oz. Dark Rum
½   oz. Curacao
½   oz. Apricot-flavored Brandy
1½   tbsp. Lime Juice

Shake with ice and strain into a cocktail glass. Serve with a pineapple stick.

MAI TAI NO. 3

1   oz. Light Rum
1   oz. Dark Rum
1½   oz. Lime Juice
½   oz. Orange Curacao
¼   oz. Grenadine
½   oz. Orgeat Syrup
¼   oz. Falernum

Shake with ice and strain into a double Old-fashioned glass. Fill with crushed ice and garnish with fruit.

MAJOR BAILEY

1½   tsp. Lime Juice
1½   tsp. Lemon Juice
½   tsp. Powdered Sugar
12   Mint leaves
2   oz. Gin

Muddle well and pour into a Collins glass. Fill the glass with ice and add Gin. Stir until glass is frosted. Decorate with a sprig of mint and serve with straws.

MAKALLE

1½   oz. Galliano
1   oz. Vodka
1   oz. Coffee
1   dash Angostura Bitters

Shake with ice and strain into a cocktail glass. Serve with a coconut slice.

MALAHUT PUNCH

1½   oz. Brandy
¼   oz. Pernod
½   oz. Lemon Juice
½   tsp. Sugar

Shake with ice and strain into a highball glass. Fill with crushed ice. Top with soda.

MALIBU

¾   oz. Cointreau
¾   oz. Anisette
¾   oz. Orange Curacao

Shake with ice and strain into a cocktail glass. Serve with a lemon twist.

MALMAISON

Juice ½ Lemon
1   oz. Rum
½   oz. Sweet Sherry

Shake with ice and strain into a cocktail glass rimmed with Anisette.

MAMA'S LEMONADE

1   tsp. Lemon Juice
1   oz. Orgeat Syrup
2   oz. Raspberry Syrup
4   oz. Chianti

Pour lemon juice, orgeat syrup and raspberry syrup into a Collins glass. Fill the glass ¾ full with cracked ice. Add Chianti. Fill with cold water. Stir well and garnish with fresh fruit.

MAMIE GILROY

Juice ½ Lime
2 oz. Scotch Whisky
1 dash Bitters

Pour into a Collins glass. Add ice cubes and fill with soda. Stir.

MAMIE'S SISTER

1 Lime
2 oz. Gin
Ginger Ale

Squeeze the juice of 1 lime into a Collins glass, drop in the lime rind, and add Gin. Fill the glass with ginger ale and ice. Stir.

MAMIE TAYLOR

Juice ½ Lime
2 oz. Scotch Whisky

Fill a Collins glass with ginger ale and ice. Add a slice of lemon and stir.

MANANA

1½ oz. Rum
½ oz. Lemon Juice
¼ oz. Grenadine
¼ oz. Apricot-flavored Brandy

Shake with ice and strain into a cocktail glass.

MANDARIN

1 oz. Gin
1 oz. Dry Vermouth
¼ oz. Orange Curacao
¼ oz. Mandarinette

Stir with ice and strain into a cocktail glass.

MANDARIN FIZZ

1½ oz. Gin
1½ oz. Mandarin Juice
2 tsp. Sugar Syrup

Shake with ice and strain into a fizz glass. Fill with soda and ice. Decorate with a mandarin slice.

MANDEVILLE

1½ oz. Light Rum
1 oz. Dark Rum
1 tsp. Pernod
1 tbsp. Lemon Juice
1 tbsp. Coca Cola
¼ tsp. Grenadine

Shake with ice and strain into an Old-fashioned glass. Add ice cubes.

MANGANN

½ oz. Lemon Juice
¾ oz. Gin
¾ oz. Dubonnet
½ oz. Orange Curacao

Shake with ice and strain into a cocktail glass.

MANGO COOLER

1½ oz. Vodka
1½ oz. Orange Juice
½ oz. Lemon Juice
½ oz. Cointreau
3 oz. Mango Nectar

Mix in a Collins glass. Fill with ice. Serve with a mango slice.

MANGO DAIQUIRI

2 oz. Light Rum
1 oz. Curacao
½ cup Mango Puree
2 tbsp. Lime Juice
1 tbsp. Sugar
1 cup crushed Ice

Blend with ice and strain into a champagne glass. Serve with straws.

MANGO MINT

1 oz. Rum
½ oz. Cream
½ oz. White Creme de Menthe
1½ oz. Mango Nectar

Shake with ice and strain into a cocktail glass.

MANHASSET

1½ oz. Rye Whisky
1½ tsp. Dry Vermouth
1½ tsp. Sweet Vermouth
1 tbsp. Lemon Juice

Shake with ice and strain into a cocktail glass.

MANHATTAN COCKTAIL

¾ oz. Sweet Vermouth
1½ oz. Bourbon or Rye Whisky
1 dash Angostura Bitters

Stir with ice and strain into a cocktail glass. Serve with a cherry.

MANHATTAN COCKTAIL (DRY)

¾ oz. Dry Vermouth
1½ oz. Rye Whisky

Stir with ice and strain into a cocktail glass. Serve with an olive.

MANHATTAN COCKTAIL (FRENCH)

½ oz. Sweet Vermouth
1 dash Angostura Bitters
1 dash Cointreau
1 oz. Bourbon Whisky

Stir with ice and strain into a cocktail glass. Serve with a cherry.

MANHATTAN COCKTAIL (PERFECT)

1¾ oz. Bourbon or Rye Whisky
¼ oz. Dry Vermouth
¼ oz. Sweet Vermouth

Stir with ice and strain into a cocktail glass. Serve with a lemon twist.

> The good die young; here's hoping you may live to a ripe old age.

MANHATTAN COOLER

4	oz. Claret
3	dashes Rum
2	tbsp. Lemon Juice
1-2	tsp. Sugar

Stir with ice and strain into a high-ball glass. Garnish with citrus fruit slices.

MANHATTAN DELUXE

1¾	oz. Southern Comfort
¾	oz. Dry Vermouth
1	dash Bitters

Stir with ice and strain into a cocktail glass. Serve with a lemon twist and a cherry.

MANHATTAN MANEATER

1½	oz. Whisky
2	tbsp. Southern Comfort
1-2	dashes Orange Bitters

Shake with ice and strain into a cocktail glass. Serve with a lemon twist.

MANHATTAN SPECIAL NO. 1

1½	oz. Whisky
½	oz. Sweet Vermouth
½	oz. Benedictine
1	dash Bitters

Stir with ice and strain into a cocktail glass. Serve with a cherry.

MANHATTAN SPECIAL NO. 2

1¾	oz. Rye Whisky
¾	oz. Sweet Vermouth
2	dashes Campari

Stir with ice and strain into a cocktail glass. Serve with a cherry.

MANHATTAN VIEUX CARRE

2	oz. Bourbon
1	oz. Sweet Vermouth
1-2	drops Sugar Syrup

Mix without ice and refrigerate in a small sealed jar for a day or two. Serve in a cocktail glass with a cherry.

MANILA FIZZ

2	oz. Gin
1	Egg
1	tsp. Powdered Sugar
3	oz. Sarsaparilla
Juice 1 Lime or ½ Lemon	

Shake with ice and strain into a highball glass. Add two cubes of ice.

MANILA HOTEL JULEP

2	oz. Bourbon
½	oz. Dark Rum
1	tsp. Sugar
Mint sprigs	

Muddle sugar and 2 mint sprigs with water in a highball glass. Fill the glass about half full with ice and muddle with more mint sprigs. Add more crushed ice and more mint sprigs. Add Bourbon and float Rum on top. Serve with mint leaves and a pineapple stick.

> Landlord, fill the flowing
>   bowl
> Until it doth run over;
> For tonight we'll merry be,
> Tomorrow we'll be sober.
> — *18th-century song*

MANYANN

1½	oz. Gin
1½	oz. Dubonnet
2	dashes Curacao
Juice 1 Lemon	

Shake with ice and strain into a cocktail glass.

MAPLE LEAF

1½	oz. Bourbon
½	oz. Maple Syrup
½	oz. Lemon Juice

Shake with ice and strain into a cocktail glass.

MARAGATO

1	oz. Rum
½	oz. Dry Vermouth
½	oz. Sweet Vermouth
¼	oz. Lemon Juice
¼	oz. Lime Juice
½	tsp. Sugar
¼	oz. Kirschwasser

Shake with ice and strain into a cocktail glass.

MARBLE HILL COCKTAIL

¾	oz. Dubonnet
¾	oz. Orange Juice
1½	oz. Gin

Shake with ice and strain into a cocktail glass.

MARCIA DELANO

1	tsp. Sugar
1	beaten Egg
1	oz. Rum
½	oz. Brandy

Mix in a highball glass. Fill with hot water. Sprinkle nutmeg on top.

MARCONI WIRELESS

1¾	oz. Applejack
¾	oz. Sweet Vermouth
2	dashes Orange Bitters

Stir with ice and strain into a cocktail glass.

MARGAES COCKTAIL

1½ oz. Gin
½ oz. Lemon Juice
½ oz. Pear Juice
Sugar to taste

Shake with ice and strain into a cocktail glass.

MARGARET DUFFY

1½ oz. Swedish Punch
½ oz. Brandy
2 dashes Angostura or other Bitters

Stir with ice and strain into a cocktail glass.

MARGARITA COCKTAIL

1½ oz. Tequila
½ oz. Triple Sec or Orange Curacao
2 3/4 oz. Lemon or Lime Juice *froza* *frozen OJ*

Rub the rim of a cocktail glass with the rind of a lemon or lime and dip rim in salt. Shake ingredients with ice and strain into the salt-rimmed glass.

MARGUERITE NO. 1

2 oz. Gin
1 oz. Dry Vermouth
1 dash Orange Bitters
1 twist Orange Peel

Stir with ice and strain into a cocktail glass. Serve with a cherry.

MARGUERITE NO. 2

1 oz. Gin
¼ oz. Pernod
½ Egg White
¼ oz. Grenadine
½ oz. Lime Juice
¼ tsp. Sugar

Shake with ice and strain into a cocktail glass.

MARGUERITE FIZZ

1½ oz. Gin
1 dash Bitters
¼ oz. Grenadine
¼ oz. Lemon Juice

Shake with ice and strain into a highball glass. Fill with soda and ice.

MARIA

2 oz. Sweet Sherry
1 oz. Gin

Stir with ice and strain into a cocktail glass. Serve with a cherry.

MARIA THERESA

2 oz. Tequila
2 tbsp. Cranberry Juice
1½ tsp. Lime Juice

Shake with ice and strain into an Old-fashioned glass. Add ice.

MARINER'S GROG

1½ oz. Jamaica Rum
1 lump Sugar
1 small stick Cinnamon
1 slice Lemon
Juice ½ Lemon
Several Cloves

Place all ingredients in a heavy mug. Fill with boiling water, stir and serve.

MARIPOSA COCKTAIL

1 oz. Rum
½ oz. Brandy
1 tbsp. Lemon Juice
1 tbsp. Orange Juice
1 dash Grenadine

Shake with ice and strain into a cocktail glass.

MARLBOROUGH

1¼ oz. Sherry
1¼ oz. Sweet Vermouth
1 dash Orange Bitters

Stir with ice and strain into a cocktail glass.

MARNEY COCKTAIL

1 oz. Grand Marnier
2 oz. Gin

Shake with ice and strain into a cocktail glass.

MARSALA MANHATTAN

3 oz. Marsala
1 oz. Sweet Vermouth
1 dash Aromatic Bitters

Stir with ice and strain into a cocktail glass. Serve with a cherry.

MARSALA MARTINI

1 oz. Gin
¾ oz. Dry Vermouth
¾ oz. Marsala

Stir with ice and strain into a cocktail glass. Serve with a lemon twist.

MARTHA

1½ oz. Bourbon
1 dash Orange Bitters
¼ oz. Maraschino Liqueur
¼ oz. Pernod

Fill an Old-fashioned glass with ice. Add Bourbon, Bitters and Maraschino Liqueur. Float Pernod. Serve with a lemon twist.

MARTINEZ COCKTAIL NO. 1

1 dash Orange Bitters
1 oz. Dry Vermouth
¼ tsp. Triple Sec
1 oz. Gin

Stir with ice and strain into a cocktail glass. Serve with a cherry.

MARTINEZ COCKTAIL NO. 2

1¼ oz. Gin
1¼ oz. Sweet Vermouth
1 dash Bitters
1 dash Sugar Syrup

Stir with ice and strain into a cocktail glass.

MARTINI (TRADITIONAL 2 to 1)

1½ oz. Gin
¾ oz. Dry Vermouth

Serve with an olive.

MARTINI (DRY 5 to 1)

1⅔ oz. Gin
⅓ oz. Dry Vermouth

Serve with an olive.

MARTINI (EXTRA DRY 7 to 1)

1¾ oz. Gin
¼ oz. Dry Vermouth

Serve with an olive.

MARTINI (MEDIUM)

1½ oz. Gin
½ oz. Dry Vermouth
½ oz. Sweet Vermouth

Serve with an olive.

MARTINI (SWEET)

1 oz. Gin
1 oz. Sweet Vermouth

Serve with an olive.

MARTINI HOLLAND STYLE

2 oz. Holland Gin
½ oz. Dry Vermouth

Stir with ice and strain into a cocktail glass. Serve with a lemon twist.

MARTINIQUE

¾ oz. Benedictine
¾ oz. Light Rum
4 oz. Pineapple Juice

Shake with ice and pour into a cocktail glass.

MARTINIQUE SWIZZLE

1½ oz. Martinique Rum
1 dash Angostura Bitters
½ oz. Lemon Juice
¼ tsp. Sugar
¼ oz. Pernod

Shake with ice and strain into a highball glass. Fill with shaved ice. Swizzle.

MARVEL

2 oz. Jamaica Rum
¼ oz. Grenadine
¼ oz. Sirop de Citron or Lemon Juice

Shake with ice and strain into a cocktail glass.

MARY ANN COCKTAIL NO. 1

1 oz. Dubonnet
1 oz. Dry Vermouth
1 oz. Orange Juice

Shake with ice and strain into a cocktail glass.

MARY ANN COCKTAIL NO. 2

1 oz. Rum
1 oz. Kahlua

Shake with ice and strain into an Old-fashioned glass. Fill with ice.

> Life is but a merry spree
> With its joy and trouble.
> Woman is the tempting glass,
> Flirtation is the bubble.

MARY GARDEN COCKTAIL

1½ oz. Dubonnet
¾ oz. Dry Vermouth

Stir with ice and strain into a cocktail glass.

MARY JANE

¾ oz. Gin
¾ oz. Dubonnet
½ oz. Dry Vermouth
½ oz. Orange Juice

Shake with ice and strain into a cocktail glass.

MARY PICKFORD COCKTAIL

1 oz. Light Rum
1 oz. Pineapple Juice
¼ tsp. Grenadine
¼ tsp. Maraschino Liqueur

Shake with ice and strain into a cocktail glass.

MARY ROSE COCKTAIL

¾ oz. Cherry Liqueur
¾ oz. Gin
1½ oz. Port Wine

Shake with ice and strain into a cocktail glass. Serve with a cherry.

MASTER OF THE HOUNDS

1½ oz. Rye Whisky
½ oz. Cherry-flavored Brandy
2 dashes Angostura Bitters

Stir with ice and strain into a cocktail glass.

MATADOR

1   oz. Tequila
2   oz. Pineapple Juice
1   tbsp. Lime Juice

Shake with ice and strain into an Old-fashioned glass. Add ice.

MATINEE

1   oz. Gin
½   oz. Sambuca
½   Egg White
½   oz. Lime Juice
¼   oz. Cream

Shake with ice and strain into a cocktail glass. Sprinkle nutmeg on top.

MAUDI COCKTAIL

1½   oz. Creme de Fine Champagne
1   dash Angostura Bitters

Shake with ice and strain into a champagne glass. Fill with Champagne.

> Here's to love and unity,
> Dark corners and opportunity.

MAUI COCKTAIL

1   oz. Vodka
½   oz. Banana Liqueur
2   tsp. Pineapple Juice concentrate
1   tsp. Lemon Juice

Shake with ice and strain into a cocktail glass.

MAURICE COCKTAIL NO. 1

Juice ¼ Orange
½   oz. Sweet Vermouth
½   oz. Dry Vermouth
1   oz. Gin
1   dash Bitters

Shake with ice and strain into a cocktail glass.

MAURICE COCKTAIL NO. 2

1   oz. Cognac
2   oz. Port Wine

Stir with ice and strain into a cocktail glass.

MAURICE COCKTAIL NO. 3

2   oz. Gin
¼   oz. Orange Curacao
¼   oz. Prunella
1   dash Lemon Juice

Stir with ice and strain into a cocktail glass.

MAX BAER

1   oz. Gin
1   oz. Apple Brandy
¼   oz. Grenadine
¼   oz. Pernod

Stir with ice and strain into a cocktail glass.

MAXIM

1½   oz. Gin
1   oz. Dry Vermouth
1   dash Creme de Cacao

Shake with ice and strain into a cocktail glass.

MAXIMILLIAN

1½   oz. Galliano
¾   oz. Gin

Fill an Old-fashioned glass with ice and pour in Galliano. Float Gin on top.

MAYAKA HOTEL SPECIAL

1   oz. Gin
¾   oz. Cointreau
½   oz. Pineapple Juice
¼   oz. Lime Juice

Shake with ice and strain into a cocktail glass.

MAY BLOSSOM FIZZ

Juice ½ Lemon
1   tsp. Grenadine
2   oz. Swedish Punch

Shake with ice and strain into a highball glass. Add two ice cubes. Fill with soda and stir.

MAY COCKTAIL

1½   oz. Whisky
¼   oz. Kirschwasser
¼   oz. Strawberry Liqueur

Shake with ice and strain into a highball glass. Fill with May Wine and ice. Serve with a lemon wedge.

MAYFAIR

1½   oz. Gin
½   oz. Apricot-flavored Brandy
½   oz. Orange Juice
1   dash Pimento Dram

Shake with ice and strain into a cocktail glass.

MAYFLOWER COCKTAIL NO. 1

2   oz. Dubonnet
¾   oz. Applejack

Shake with ice and strain into a cocktail glass.

MAYFLOWER COCKTAIL NO. 2

1   oz. Rum
1   oz. Grapefruit Juice
½   tsp. Sugar

Shake with ice and strain into a cocktail glass.

McBRANDY

1½   oz. Brandy
¾   oz. Apple Juice
¼   oz. Lemon Juice

Shake with ice and strain into a cocktail glass. Serve with a lemon slice.

McCLELLAND COCKTAIL

¾ oz. Triple Sec
1½ oz. Sloe Gin
1 dash Orange Bitters

Shake with ice and strain into a cocktail glass.

McCRORY

1½ oz. Whisky
2 dashes Bitters
½ tsp. Sugar

Mix in a highball glass. Fill with soda and ice.

McGREGOR'S EGG NOG

2 oz. Sherry
½ oz. Cognac
¼ oz. Rum
1 tsp. Sugar
1 beaten Egg

Shake with ice and strain into a highball glass. Fill with milk. Sprinkle nutmeg and cinnamon on top.

McKINLEY PUNCH

1½ oz. Bourbon
½ oz. Lemon Juice
1½ oz. Grenadine

Shake with ice and strain into a cocktail glass. Fill with soda and ice.

McKINLEY'S DELIGHT

1½ oz. Bourbon
½ oz. Sweet Vermouth
¼ oz. Pernod
¼ oz. Cherry-flavored Brandy (or Cherry Liqueur)

Shake with ice and strain into a cocktail glass.

McLAUGHLIN

1½ oz. Light Creme de Cacao
1 dash Angostura Bitters

Shake with ice and strain into a cocktail glass. Fill with Champagne and ice. Serve with a lemon twist.

McMENOMY COCKTAIL

Juice ½ Lime
2 dashes Grenadine
2 dashes Pernod
¾ oz. Rum
¾ oz. Swedish Punch

Shake with ice and strain into a cocktail glass.

MECCA

¾ oz. Gin
¾ oz. Dry Vermouth
½ oz. Sweet Vermouth
½ oz. Orange Juice

Shake with ice and strain into a cocktail glass.

MEDFORD COCKTAIL

¾ oz. Dry Vermouth
¾ oz. Orange Gin
¾ oz. Gin

Shake with ice and strain into a cocktail glass.

MEDFORD RUM PUNCH

1 tsp. Powdered Sugar
½ oz. Lemon Juice
2 oz. Rum
1 dash Jamaica Rum

Fill a cocktail glass with shaved ice and pour in sugar, lemon juice and Rums. Stir. Garnish with fruit.

MEDIEVAL CANDLE

½ oz. White Creme de Menthe
½ oz. Southern Comfort (100-proof, if available)

Flame in a pony glass.

MEEHOULAND

1½ oz. Sloe Gin
½ oz. Sweet Vermouth
½ oz. Dry Vermouth
1 dash Orange Bitters

Stir with ice and strain into a cocktail glass. Serve with a lemon twist.

MELBA

¾ oz. Light Rum
2 dashes Pernod
¾ oz. Swedish Punch
2 dashes Grenadine
Juice ½ Lime

Shake with ice and strain into a cocktail glass.

MELBA CHAMPAGNE

½ oz. Himbeergeist (Raspberry Brandy)
Champagne
Raspberry Sherbet

Put Himbeergeist into a cocktail glass. Fill with Champagne. Add a small scoop of raspberry sherbet and float a fresh raspberry on top.

> While there's life on the lips,
> While there's warmth in the wine,
> One deep health I'll pledge,
> And that health shall be thine.

MELON COCKTAIL

2 oz. Gin
¼ tsp. Lemon Juice
¼ tsp. Maraschino Liqueur

Shake with ice and strain into a cocktail glass. Serve with a cherry.

MEMPHIS BELLE

½   Peach
1   Maraschino Cherry
Southern Comfort

Place the peach and the cherry in a champagne glass. Add shaved ice and fill with Southern Comfort. Serve with short straws and a spoon.

MEMPHIS SLING SHOT

1   oz. Early Times
¾   oz. Sloe Gin
1½   oz. 7-Up
3   dashes Rose's Lime Juice

Mix in a Sour glass. Fill with ice. Serve with an orange slice.

MENLO CLUB

1   oz. Lemon Juice
½   oz. Gin
½   oz. Cointreau
½   oz. Rum
½   tsp. Sugar

Shake with ice and strain into a cocktail glass.

MERRY GO ROUND NO. 1

1½   oz. Bourbon Whisky
¼   oz. Curacao
¼   oz. Dubonnet

Stir with ice and strain into a cocktail glass. Serve with a twist of orange peel.

MERRY GO ROUND NO. 2

1½   oz. Gin
½   oz. Sweet Vermouth
½   oz. Dry Vermouth

Stir with ice and strain into a cocktail glass. Serve with an olive or a lemon twist.

MERRY WIDOW COCKTAIL NO. 1

1¼   oz. Gin
1¼   oz. Dry Vermouth
½   tsp. Benedictine
½   tsp. Pernod
1   dash Orange Bitters

Stir with ice and strain into a cocktail glass. Serve with a lemon twist.

MERRY WIDOW COCKTAIL NO. 2

1¼   oz. Maraschino Liqueur
1¼   oz. Wild Cherry-flavored Brandy

Stir with ice and strain into a cocktail glass. Serve with a cherry.

MERRY WIDOW COCKTAIL NO. 3

1¼   oz. Dubonnet
1¼   oz. Dry Vermouth

Stir with ice and strain into a cocktail glass. Serve with a lemon twist.

MERRY WIDOW COCKTAIL NO. 4

1¼   oz. Gin
1¼   oz. Byrrh

Stir with ice and strain into a cocktail glass.

MERRY WIDOWER

1   oz. Gin
1   oz. Dry Vermouth
1-2 drops Pernod
1-2 drops Benedictine
1-2 dashes Peychaud's Bitters

Shake with ice and strain into a cocktail glass. Add ice and serve with a lemon twist.

MERRY WIDOW FIZZ

Juice ½ Orange
Juice ½ Lemon
1   Egg White
1   tsp. Powdered Sugar
1½   oz. Sloe Gin

Shake with ice and strain into a highball glass. Add two ice cubes. Fill with soda and stir.

METROPOLE COCKTAIL

1   dash Peychaud's Bitters
1   dash Orange Bitters
1½   oz. Dry Vermouth
1½   oz. Brandy

Stir with ice and strain into a cocktail glass. Serve with a cherry.

METROPOLITAN COCKTAIL NO. 1

1   oz. Dubonnet
1   oz. Cognac
2   oz. White Creme de Menthe

Shake with ice and strain into a cocktail glass.

METROPOLITAN COCKTAIL NO. 2

1¼   oz. Brandy
1¼   oz. Sweet Vermouth
1   dash Bitters
¼   tsp. Sugar

Stir with ice and strain into a cocktail glass.

MEURICE COCKTAIL

1   oz. Vodka
1   oz. Creme de Bananes
1   oz. Heavy Cream

Shake with ice and strain into a cocktail glass.

MEXICANA

1½ oz. Tequila
1 oz. Lemon Juice
1 tbsp. Pineapple Juice
1 tsp. Grenadine

Shake with ice and strain into a cocktail glass.

MEXICAN BANANA NO. 1

1½ oz. Tequila
½ oz. Creme de Bananes

Fill an Old-fashioned glass with ice and pour in liquor.

MEXICAN BANANA NO. 2

½ oz. Kahlua
½ oz. Vodka
½ oz. Creme de Bananes

Fill an Old-fashioned glass with ice and pour in liquor.

MEXICAN BANGER NO. 1

1½ oz. Tequila
Orange Juice
½ oz. Galliano

Pour Tequila into a Collins glass. Fill with orange juice and ice. Float Galliano.

> May your joy be as deep as the ocean,
> Your trouble as light as its foam.

MEXICAN BANGER NO. 2

1½ oz. Vodka
Orange Juice
Kahlua

Pour Vodka into a Collins glass. Fill with orange juice and float Kahlua on top.

MEXICAN COFFEE

1 tsp. Brown (or regular) Sugar
1½ oz. Tequila
Whipped Cream
Hot Coffee
Kahlua (optional)

Pour Sugar and Tequila into a fizz glass. Fill with hot coffee. Top with whipped cream. (Float ¼ oz. Kahlua on cream.)

MEXICAN EL DIABLO

¾ oz. Lime Juice (leave shell in glass)
½ oz. Creme de Cassis
1½ oz. Tequila

Mix in a highball glass. Fill with ginger ale.

MEXICAN FLAG

⅓ oz. Grenadine
⅓ oz. Green Creme de Menthe
⅓ oz. 151-proof Rum

Pour carefully, in order given, into a pony glass so that each ingredient floats on the preceding one without mixing. Flame.

MEXICAN GRASSHOPPER

1½ oz. Cream
¾ oz. Kahlua
¾ oz. White Creme de Menthe

Shake with ice and strain into a cocktail glass.

MEXICAN MOTHER

1½ oz. Kahlua
½ oz. Orange Curacao

Fill an Old-fashioned glass with ice and pour in Kahlua and Orange Curacao.

MEXICANO

2 oz. Light Rum
½ oz. Kummel
½ oz. Orange Juice
1 dash Angostura Bitters

Shake with ice and strain into a cocktail glass.

MEXICAN SCREW

1½ oz. Tequila

Pour into a Collins glass. Fill with ice and orange juice.

MEXICAN STINGER

1½ oz. Tequila
½ oz. White Creme de Menthe

Mix in an Old-fashioned glass. Fill with ice.

MEXICAN ZIPPER

Fill an Old-fashioned glass with ice.

Add: 1½ oz. Tequila
½ oz. Green Creme de Menthe

MEXICOLA

2 oz. Tequila
Juice ½ Lime

Fill a Collins glass with ice cubes. Add Tequila and lime juice, and fill balance with Cola. Stir.

MEXICO MARTINI

1½ oz. Tequila
1 tbsp. Dry Vermouth
3 drops Vanilla Extract

Shake with ice and strain into a cocktail glass. Add ice.

MEXICO PACIFICO

1½ oz. Tequila
½ oz. Lime Juice
½ oz. Passion Fruit Syrup

Shake with ice and strain into a cocktail glass. Serve with a lime wheel.

MEXICO ROSE

1½ oz. Tequila
½ oz. Lime Juice
½ oz. Creme de Cassis

Shake with ice and strain into a cocktail glass.

MEXITINI

1½ oz. Dry Vermouth
1 tbsp. Tequila
1 Chili Bean

Pour Vermouth and Tequila into a cocktail glass, and stir. Top with the bean.

MIAMI

1½ oz. Rum
½ oz. White Creme de Menthe

Shake with ice and strain into a cocktail glass.

MIAMI BEACH COCKTAIL NO. 1

¾ oz. Scotch Whisky
¾ oz. Dry Vermouth
¾ oz. Grapefruit Juice

Shake with ice and strain into a cocktail glass.

MIAMI BEACH COCKTAIL NO. 2

1½ oz. Rum
¾ oz. Cointreau
¼ oz. Lemon or Lime Juice

Shake with ice and strain into a cocktail glass.

MIAMI SUNSET

Fill a highball glass with ice.

Add: 2 oz. Early Times
1 oz. Triple Sec or Orange Curacao

Fill with orange juice and stir. Float ½ oz. Grenadine on top.

MICKEY (OR MICKIE)

1 oz. Jamaica Rum
¾ oz. Orange Curacao
¾ oz. Bourbon
1 dash Grenadine

Stir with ice and strain into a cocktail glass.

MICKEY BOY

1½ oz. Gin
½ oz. Dry Vermouth
¼ oz. Pernod
¼ oz. White Creme de Menthe

Stir with ice and strain into a cocktail glass.

MICKEY FINN

1 oz. Gin
1 oz. Dry Vermouth
¼ oz. Pernod
¼ oz. White Creme de Menthe

Stir with ice and strain into a cocktail glass. Serve with a cherry.

MICKIE WALKER

2 oz. Scotch Whisky
¾ oz. Sweet Vermouth
1 dash Lemon Juice
1 dash Grenadine

Shake with ice and strain into a cocktail glass.

> May we never murmur without cause,
> and never have cause to murmur.

MIDDLETON COCKTAIL

1½ oz. Jamaica Rum
¾ oz. Grenadine
¾ oz. Holland Gin
1 Egg White
1 oz. Lemon Juice

Shake with ice and strain into a cocktail glass.

MIDNIGHT COCKTAIL NO. 1

1 oz. Apricot-flavored Brandy
½ oz. Triple Sec or Orange Curacao
1 tbsp. Lemon Juice

Shake with ice and strain into a cocktail glass.

MIDNIGHT COCKTAIL NO. 2

¾ oz. Gin
¾ oz. Sweet Vermouth
¾ oz. Dry Vermouth
¼ oz. Pernod
1 dash Orange Juice

Shake with ice and strain into a cocktail glass.

MIDNIGHT SUN

1½ oz. Aquavit
½ oz. Grapefruit Juice
½ oz. Lemon Juice
½ tsp. Sugar
¼ oz. Grenadine

Shake with ice and strain into a cocktail glass. Serve with an orange slice.

MIGUEL LIGERO

1 oz. Lemon Juice
1½ oz. Rum
½ oz. Orange Curacao
1 dash Angostura Bitters
½ tsp. Sugar

Shake with ice and strain into a cocktail glass.

MIKADO NO. 1

2 oz. Brandy
¼ oz. Orange Curacao
¼ oz. Light Creme de Cacao
2 dashes Bitters

Stir with ice and strain into a cocktail glass.

MIKADO NO. 2

1¾ oz. Brandy
¼ oz. Orange Curacao
¼ oz. Creme de Noyaux
¼ oz. Orgeat Syrup
2 dashes Bitters

Stir with ice and strain into a cocktail glass.

MIKE'S MUDDLER

1 oz. Bourbon
2 oz. Creme de Bananes
½ oz. Triple Sec
1 oz. Cream

Blend with ice and strain into a champagne glass.

MILAN

1 oz. Bourbon
1 oz. Rum
½ oz. Orange Juice

Shake with ice and strain into a cocktail glass. Serve with a lemon twist.

MILANO

1 oz. Galliano
¾ oz. Gin
¾ oz. Lime Juice

Shake with ice and strain into a cocktail glass. Serve with a cherry.

MILK AND HONEY

1½ oz. Irish Mist

Pour into a highball glass. Fill with ice and Milk. Dust with cinnamon.

MILK PUNCH NO. 1

1 tsp. Sugar
2 oz. Whisky

Shake with ice and strain into a Collins glass. Fill with milk and ice. Sprinkle nutmeg on top.

MILK PUNCH NO. 2

1½ oz. Cognac
½ oz. Rum
½ oz. Orange Curacao
½ tsp. Sugar

Shake with ice and strain into a Collins glass. Fill with milk. Sprinkle nutmeg on top.

MILK PUNCH NO. 3

1 dash Jamaica Rum
2 oz. Brandy
1 oz. Benedictine
4 oz. Milk

Shake with ice and strain into a Collins glass. Add a dash of soda. Sprinkle nutmeg on top.

MILK TODDY

2 oz. Rum (Brandy or Whisky)
2 oz. Milk

Stir liquor with hot milk in a highball glass. Sprinkle nutmeg on top.

MILLIE NO. 1

½ oz. Drambuie
½ oz. Grand Marnier

Pour into a snifter.

MILLIE NO. 2

½ oz. Drambuie
½ oz. Grand Marnier

Fill an Old-fashioned glass with ice and add liquor.

MILLIE SPECIAL COCKTAIL

1½ oz. Jamaica Rum
¾ oz. Bourbon
¾ oz. Curacao
1 dash Grenadine

Shake with ice and strain into a highball glass. Fill with crushed ice.

MILLION

1½ oz. Jamaica Rum
½ oz. Lime Juice
½ tsp. Sugar
1 dash Angostura Bitters

Shake with ice and strain into a cocktail glass. Serve with a cherry.

MILLIONAIRE NO. 1

1½ oz. Gin
¾ oz. Pernod
1 dash Anisette
1 Egg White

Shake with ice and strain into a cocktail glass.

MILLIONAIRE NO. 2

1½ oz. Bourbon
½ oz. Curacao
1 Egg White
1 dash Grenadine

Shake with ice and strain into a cocktail glass.

MILLIONAIRE NO. 3

1½ oz. Rye Whisky
½ oz. Pernod
½ oz. Grenadine
1 dash Curacao
½ Egg White

Shake with ice and strain into a cocktail glass.

MILLIONAIRE NO. 4

Juice 1 Lime
1 dash Grenadine
1 oz. Sloe Gin
1 oz. Apricot-flavored Brandy
1 oz. Jamaica Rum

Shake with ice and strain into a cocktail glass.

MILLION DOLLAR COCKTAIL

2   tsp. Pineapple Juice
1   tsp. Grenadine
1   Egg White
¾   oz. Sweet Vermouth
1½   oz. Gin

Shake with ice and strain into a cocktail glass.

MILLIONS COCKTAIL

1½   oz. Gin
1   tbsp. Sweet Vermouth
2   tsp. Pineapple Juice
1   Egg White
1-2 drops Grenadine

Shake with ice and strain into a cocktail glass. Add ice.

MILWAUKEE

2   oz. Rye Whisky
½   oz. Apricot-flavored Brandy

Stir with ice and strain into a cocktail glass. Serve with a green cherry.

MILWAUKEE MADNESS

1   oz. Early Times
¾   oz. Peppermint Schnapps
1   dash Bitters

Mix in an Old-fashioned glass. Fill with ice and stir.

MIMOSA

1   Ice cube
¼   cup Orange Juice
4   oz. Champagne

Place the ice cube in a wine glass, add the orange juice, pour in the Champagne and stir.

MINCE PIE COCKTAIL

⅔   oz. Creme de Menthe
⅓   oz. Cognac

Serve in a pony glass.

MINGO'S DELIGHT

1½   oz. Galliano
¾   oz. Lime Juice
½   Egg White

Shake with ice and strain into a cocktail glass.

MINNEAPOLIS COCKTAIL

1   oz. Sloe Gin
½   oz. Dry Vermouth
½   oz. Sweet Vermouth
1   dash Orange Bitters

Shake with ice and strain into a cocktail glass.

MINNEAPOLIS HUSTLER

2   oz. Early Times
1   oz. Sweet Vermouth
1   oz. Orange Curacao
½   oz. Lime Juice

Shake with ice and strain into a cocktail glass.

> May all single men be married,
> And all married men be happy.

MINNEHAHA

1   oz. Gin
½   oz. Dry Vermouth
½   oz. Sweet Vermouth
½   oz. Orange Juice

Shake with ice and strain into a cocktail glass. (Optional: float Pernod on top.)

MINT

1½   oz. White Wine
¾   oz. Gin
¼   oz. White Creme de Menthe

Stir with ice and strain into a cocktail glass. Serve with several mint sprigs.

MINT BREEZE

2   cubes Sugar
8   oz. Extra Dry Champagne, chilled
Mint (amount desired)

Fill a Collins glass three-quarters full with cracked ice. Add mint and the sugar cubes. Pour the Champagne over the ice.

MINT COLLINS NO. 1

Juice ½ Lemon
2   oz. Mint-flavored Gin

Shake with ice and strain into a Collins glass. Add several cubes of ice, fill with soda and stir. Decorate with slices of lemon and orange and a cherry. Serve with straws.

MINT COLLINS NO. 2

2   oz. Gin
1   oz. Lemon Juice
4   Mint sprigs
1   tsp. Sugar

Shake with ice and strain into a Collins glass. Fill with soda and ice. Serve with a lemon wedge and mint sprigs.

MINT COOLER

1½   oz. Scotch Whisky
½   oz. White Creme de Menthe

Pour into a highball glass. Fill with soda and ice.

MINT DELIGHT

4   oz. White Creme de Menthe
6   oz. Vanilla Ice Cream
4   oz. Light Cream

Blend at high speed until smooth. Serve in cocktail glasses.

MINTED GIN

1¾ oz. Gin
¾ oz. Lemon Juice
¾ tsp. Sugar

Shake with ice and strain into a cocktail glass. Serve with a lemon wedge and a mint leaf.

MINT GIN COCKTAIL

1 oz. Mint-flavored Gin
1 oz. White Port
1½ tsps. Dry Vermouth

Stir with ice and strain into a cocktail glass.

MINT HIGHBALL

2 oz. Green Creme de Menthe
Ginger Ale or Soda

Pour into a highball glass over ice cubes and fill with ginger ale or soda. Add a twist of lemon, if desired, and stir.

MINT JULEP NO. 1

4 Mint sprigs
1 tsp. Powdered Sugar
2½ oz. Bourbon Whisky

Muddle mint and sugar in a Collins glass. Fill the glass with ice and add Whisky. Stir until glass is frosted. Decorate with orange, lemon and pineapple slices, and a cherry. Top off with 5-6 mint sprigs. Serve with straws.

MINT JULEP NO. 2

1½ oz. Brandy
4 Mint sprigs
¾ oz. Peach-flavored Brandy
1 tsp. Sugar Syrup

Muddle first two ingredients in a Collins glass before adding remaining ingredients. Fill with soda and ice. Stir and decorate with mint sprigs and fruit.

MINT JULEP (SOUTHERN STYLE)

2½ oz. Bourbon Whisky
1 tsp. Powdered Sugar
Mint Leaves

In a Collins glass, dissolve sugar in 2 tsp. water. Then fill the glass with shaved ice and add Bourbon. Stir until glass is heavily frosted. Decorate with 5-6 sprigs of fresh mint.

MINT ON ROCKS

2 oz. Green Creme de Menthe

Pour Creme de Menthe on ice cubes in an Old-fashioned glass.

MINT TEQUILA

1½ oz. Tequila
½ oz. Lemon Juice
1 tsp. Sugar

Shake with ice and strain into a cocktail glass. Serve with several mint sprigs.

MIRACLE

¾ oz. Gin
¾ oz. Lillet
½ oz. Cointreau
½ oz. Lemon Juice
1 dash Pernod

Shake with ice and strain into a cocktail glass.

MISS AILEEN

¾ oz. Advokaat
¾ oz. Chocolate Mint Liqueur
¾ oz. Galliano

Shake with ice and strain into a cocktail glass.

Here's to the lasses we've loved, my lad,
Here's to the lips we've pressed;
For of kisses and lasses,
Like liquor in glasses,
The last is always the best.

MISSIONARY DOWNFALL

1½ oz. Lime Juice
3-7 Mint sprigs
¼ oz. Rock Candy Syrup
½ slice fresh Pineapple
½ oz. Peach-flavored Brandy
1 oz. Rum

Blend with ice and strain into a Collins glass. Fill with shaved ice.

MISSISSIPPI MULE

1½ oz. Gin
¼ oz. Creme de Cassis
¼ oz. Lemon Juice

Shake with ice and strain into a cocktail glass.

MISSISSIPPI PLANTER'S PUNCH

Juice 1 Lemon
1 tbsp. Powdered Sugar
¾ oz. Rum
¾ oz. Bourbon Whisky
1½ oz. Brandy

Shake with ice and strain into a Collins glass. Add ice cubes. Fill with soda and stir.

MISSOURI COOLER

1½ oz. Applejack
¾ oz. Light Creme de Cacao

Shake with ice and strain into a highball glass. Fill with milk and ice. Sprinkle nutmeg on top.

MISSOURI MULE NO. 1

2 oz. Southern Comfort
¼ oz. Lemon Juice

Pour into a Collins glass. Fill with ginger beer and ice.

MISSOURI MULE NO. 2

2 oz. Gin
¼ oz. Lemon Juice
¼ oz. Creme de Cassis

Shake with ice and strain into a cocktail glass.

MISS RUBY

1 dash Aromatic Bitters
1 dash Orange Bitters
2 dashes Orange-flavored Liqueur
3 oz. Port

Shake with ice and strain into a cocktail glass.

MISTY MANHATTAN

2 oz. Canadian Mist Whisky
1 tbsp. Sweet Vermouth
1-2 dashes Angostura Bitters

Shake with ice and strain into a cocktail glass. Serve with a cherry.

MIXED BLESSING

4 oz. Pineapple Juice
2 tbsp. Gold Rum
2 tbsp. crushed Pineapple
2 tsp. 151-proof Rum
1-2 drops Lime Juice
2 oz. crushed Ice

Blend with ice and strain into an Old-fashioned glass.

```
May we live to learn well,
And learn to live well.
```

MIXED MOCHA FRAPPE

¾ oz. Coffee Liqueur
¼ oz. White Creme de Menthe
¼ oz. Light Creme de Cacao
¼ oz. Triple Sec

Fill a cocktail glass with crushed ice and add all ingredients.

M.J.

1¾ oz. Gin
½ oz. Sweet Vermouth
¼ oz. Light Creme de Cacao

Stir with ice and strain into a cocktail glass.

MOBILE MULE

2 oz. Rum
½ oz. Lime Juice

Pour into a Collins glass. Fill with ginger beer and ice. Serve with a lime wheel.

MOCHA MINT

¾ oz. Coffee-flavored Brandy
¾ oz. White Creme de Cacao
¾ oz. White Creme de Menthe

Shake with ice and strain into a cocktail glass.

MOCKINGBIRD

1½ oz. Tequila
1 oz. Lime Juice
1 tbsp. White Creme de Menthe

Shake with ice and strain into a cocktail glass. Serve with a lime slice.

MODDER RIVER COCKTAIL

1½ oz. Gin
½ oz. Dry Vermouth
½ oz. Dubonnet

Stir with ice and strain into a cocktail glass. Serve with a lemon twist.

MODERN COCKTAIL NO. 1

1½ oz. Scotch Whisky
½ tsp. Lemon Juice
¼ tsp. Pernod
½ tsp. Jamaica Rum
1 dash Orange Bitters

Shake with ice and strain into a cocktail glass. Serve with a cherry.

MODERN COCKTAIL NO. 2

1½ oz. Sloe Gin
¾ oz. Scotch Whisky
1 dash Pernod
1 dash Orange Bitters
1 dash Grenadine

Shake with ice and strain into a cocktail glass.

MODERN LEMONADE

1½ oz. Sherry
1½ oz. Sloe Gin
2 tbsp. Sugar
4 tbsp. Lemon Juice

Shake with ice and strain into a Collins glass. Fill with soda and ice. Serve with a lemon twist.

MODERN MAID

1¾ oz. Scotch Whisky
¼ oz. Lemon Juice
¼ oz. Pernod
¼ oz. Jamaica Rum
1 dash Orange Bitters

Shake with ice and strain into a cocktail glass.

MOFUCO

2 oz. Rum
1 Egg
1 dash Angostura Bitters
1 tsp. Sugar

Stir with ice and strain into a cocktail glass. Serve with a lemon twist.

MOGEL'S MILLIONS

1 Egg White
¼ tsp. Grenadine
½ oz. Curacao
1½ oz. Whisky

Shake with ice and strain into a cocktail glass.

MOJITO

2 oz. Light Rum
½ Lime
1 tsp. Sugar
Club Soda

Pour Rum into a highball glass, squeeze in lime juice and drop in the peel. Add sugar and enough crushed ice to fill two-thirds of the glass. Fill with soda, stir gently and garnish with mint leaves.

MOLDAU

1½ oz. Gin
½ oz. Plum Brandy
¼ oz. Orange Juice
¼ oz. Lemon Juice

Shake with ice and strain into a cocktail glass. Serve with a brandied cherry.

MOLL

1 oz. Gin
¾ oz. Sloe Gin
¾ oz. Dry Vermouth
1 dash Orange Bitters
½ tsp. Sugar

Stir with ice and strain into a cocktail glass.

MOLLY PICON

1 oz. Gin
1 oz. Amer Picon
½ oz. Sweet Vermouth

Stir with ice and strain into a cocktail glass.

MOMINETTE

1¾ oz. Pernod
½ oz. Anisette
¼ oz. Grenadine

Shake with ice and strain into a cocktail glass. Serve with a lemon twist.

MOM'S APERITIF SPECIAL

1 dash Pernod
1 oz. Brandy
1 oz. Dubonnet

Stir with ice and strain into a cocktail glass.

MONAHAN

1½ oz. Whisky
½ oz. Sweet Vermouth
½ oz. Amer Picon

Stir with ice and strain into a cocktail glass.

MONARCH COOLER

1 dash Aromatic Bitters
1 tsp. Orange-flavored Liqueur
1 oz. Brandy
1 oz. Tawny Port
Extra Dry Champagne, well chilled

Shake the first four ingredients with ice and strain into a Collins glass. Fill the glass with Champagne. Garnish with an orange wheel.

MONKEY

1 oz. Rum
1 oz. Pineapple Juice
½ oz. Orange Curacao

Shake with ice and strain into a cocktail glass.

MONKEY GLAND

1½ oz. Gin
¾ oz. Orange Juice
3 dashes Benedictine
3 dashes Grenadine

Shake with ice and strain into a cocktail glass.

MONTANA

1½ oz. Brandy
1 oz. Port
½ oz. Dry Vermouth

Stir and serve on the rocks in an Old-fashioned glass.

MONTAUK RIDING CLUB

1½ oz. Calisay
1½ oz. Brandy
3 dashes Lime Juice
2 dashes Sugar Syrup

Shake with ice and strain into a cocktail glass.

MONTE CARLO

1¾ oz. Rye or Bourbon Whisky
¾ oz. Benedictine
2 dashes Angostura Bitters

Stir with ice and strain into a cocktail glass. Serve with a lemon twist.

MONTE CARLO IMPERIAL HIGHBALL

2 oz. Gin
½ oz. White Creme de Menthe
Juice ¼ Lemon

Shake with ice and strain into a highball glass. Add ice cubes. Fill glass with Champagne and stir.

MONTEGO SQUIRREL

1½ oz. Tia Maria
½ oz. Rum
1½ oz. Cream

Blend with ice and strain into a cocktail glass.

MONTEMARTE SPECIAL

1½ oz. Rum
¾ oz. Cream
¼ oz. Grenadine

Shake with ice and strain into a cocktail glass. Sprinkle nutmeg on top.

MONTEZUMA

1½ oz. Tequila
1 oz. Madeira
1 Egg Yolk
½ cup crushed Ice

Mix in a blender at low speed and serve in a champagne glass.

MONTIGNI

¾ oz. Cordial Medoc
¾ oz. Cream
½ oz. Cognac
½ oz. Orange Curacao

Shake with ice and strain into a cocktail glass. Sprinkle nutmeg on top.

MONTMARTRE COCKTAIL

1¼ oz. Gin
½ oz. Sweet Vermouth
½ oz. Triple Sec

Stir with ice and strain into a cocktail glass. Serve with a cherry.

MONTPELIER

1¾ oz. Gin
¾ oz. Dry Vermouth

Stir with ice and strain into a cocktail glass. Serve with an onion.

MONTREAL CLUB BOUNCER

1½ oz. Gin
½ oz. Pernod

Pour into an Old-fashioned glass. Add ice cubes and stir.

MONTREAL GIN SOUR

1 oz. Gin
1 oz. Lemon Juice
½ Egg White
1 tsp. Powdered Sugar

Shake with ice and strain into a Sour glass. Add a slice of lemon.

MONTY

2 oz. Cream
1 oz. Rum
¾ oz. Apricot-flavored Brandy
½ oz. Light Creme de Cacao
½ oz. Pineapple Juice (and fresh pineapple if available)
½ oz. Creme de Noyaux
½ oz. Orgeat Syrup

Shake with ice and strain into a large cocktail glass.

MONTY SPECIAL

1 large scoop Vanilla Ice Cream
1 oz. Rum
½ oz. Light Creme de Cacao
½ oz. Creme de Bananes
½ oz. Creme de Noyaux

Blend with ice and strain into a double Old-fashioned glass.

MOOD INDIGO

1 oz. Gin
½ oz. Parfait Amour
½ oz. Cognac
½ Egg White

Shake with ice and strain into a cocktail glass.

MOOMBA COCKTAIL

¾ oz. Rum
¾ oz. Grand Marnier
½ oz. Orange Juice
¼ oz. Lemon Juice
1 dash Grenadine

Shake with ice and strain into a cocktail glass. Serve with a twist of orange peel.

MOON CRATER

1 oz. Vodka
1 oz. Advokaat

Pour into a highball glass. Fill with Fanta and crushed ice. Top with cream. Sprinkle nutmeg on top. Serve with a cherry.

MOON DUST

1 oz. Rum
¾ oz. Galliano
½ oz. Lemon Juice
¼ oz. Orgeat
¼ oz. Grenadine

Shake with ice and strain into a cocktail glass. Serve with a green cherry.

MOONGLOW NO. 1

1½ oz. Brandy
1½ oz. White Creme de Menthe

Mix without ice and pour into a chilled cocktail glass.

MOONGLOW NO. 2

1 oz. Benedictine
1 oz. Creme de Cacao
1 oz. Light Cream

Shake with ice and pour into a cocktail glass.

MOONLIGHT COCKTAIL NO. 1

1 oz. White Wine
2 dashes Kirschwasser
1 tsp. Grapefruit Juice
1 oz. Gin

Shake with ice and strain into a cocktail glass.

MOONLIGHT COCKTAIL NO. 2

3 oz. Calvados
3 tsp. Lemon Juice
2 tsp. Sugar Syrup

Shake with ice and strain into an Old-fashioned glass. Fill with soda and ice. Top with fruit slices.

May our eyes be no keener when we look
Upon the faults of others
Than when we survey our own.

MOONLIGHT COOLER

Juice 1 Lemon
2 oz. Apple Brandy
1 tsp. Powdered Sugar

Shake with ice and strain into an Old-fashioned glass. Add ice cubes.

MOON QUAKE SHAKE

1½ oz. Dark Rum
1 oz. Coffee-flavored Brandy
1 tbsp. Lemon Juice

Shake with ice and strain into a cocktail glass.

MOON RAKER

¾ oz. Brandy
¾ oz. Dubonnet
¾ oz. Peach-flavored Brandy
¼ oz. Pernod

Shake with ice and strain into a cocktail glass.

MOON RAY COCKTAIL

¾ oz. Gin
¾ oz. Dry Vermouth
¾ oz. Strega
¼ oz. Anisette
1 dash Angostura Bitters

Stir with ice and strain into a cocktail glass.

MOON'S ECLIPSE

1 oz. Campari
1 oz. Drambuie
1 oz. Amsterdam
1 oz. Orange Juice
1 oz. fresh Cream

Shake with ice and strain into a champagne glass. Sprinkle nutmeg on top. Serve with a cherry.

MOONSHINE

1¾ oz. Gin
½ oz. Dry Vermouth
¼ oz. Maraschino Liqueur
2 dashes Pernod

Stir with ice and strain into a cocktail glass.

MOOR

1¾ oz. Gin
¾ oz. Sweet Vermouth

Stir with ice and strain into a cocktail glass. Serve with a lemon twist.

MOOSE

1¾ oz. Bourbon
¾ oz. Apricot-flavored Brandy
1 dash Angostura Bitters

Stir with ice and strain into a cocktail glass. Serve with a pineapple stick.

MOOSE MILK

2 oz. Kahlua

Pour into a Collins glass. Fill with ice and milk.

MORNING

1 oz. Brandy
1 oz. Dry Vermouth
¼ tsp. Triple Sec
¼ tsp. Maraschino Liqueur
¼ tsp. Pernod
2 dashes Orange Bitters

Stir with ice and strain into a cocktail glass. Serve with a cherry.

MORNING AFTER NO. 1

1 oz. Pernod
½ oz. Anisette
1 Egg White

Shake with ice and strain into a highball glass. Fill with Squirt and ice.

MORNING AFTER NO. 2

2 oz. Champagne, chilled
Brandy

Pour Champagne into a champagne glass. Place a teaspoon bottomside up across the top of the glass. Float some Brandy by pouring slowly over the rounded surface of the spoon.

MORNING CALL

1 oz. Pernod
¾ oz. Lemon Juice
¾ oz. Maraschino Liqueur

Shake with ice and strain into a cocktail glass.

MORNING FIZZ

½ oz. Lemon Juice
¼ oz. Pernod
1½ oz. Whisky
½ Egg White

Shake with ice and strain into a highball glass. Fill with Squirt and ice.

MORNING GLORY NO. 1

1 oz. Bourbon or Rye Whisky
¾ oz. Brandy
2 dashes Bitters
¼ oz. Pernod or Anisette
¼ oz. Orange Curacao
¼ tsp. Sugar

Shake with ice and strain into a highball glass. Fill with soda and ice.

MORNING GLORY NO. 2

½ oz. Cointreau
½ oz. Cherry-flavored Brandy
1 dash Angostura Bitters

Mix in a Collins glass. Fill with Champagne and ice. Garnish with an orange slice and pineapple spear.

MORNING GLORY NO. 3

1½ oz. Gin
¾ oz. Lime Juice
1 Egg
¼ oz. Green Creme de Menthe
½ tsp. Sugar

Shake with ice and strain into a cocktail glass.

MORNING GLORY NO. 4

1 oz. Gin
½ oz. Whisky
½ oz. Grenadine
1 Egg White
½ oz. Lemon Juice

Shake with ice and strain into a cocktail glass.

MORNING GLORY DAISY

½ Egg White
½ tsp. Sugar
2 oz. Bourbon, Scotch, Gin or Vodka
¼ oz. Pernod

Shake with ice and strain into a large cocktail glass. Top with Squirt.

MORNING GLORY FIZZ

Juice ½ Lemon or 1 Lime
1 tsp. Powdered Sugar
1 Egg White
½ tsp. Pernod
2 oz. Scotch Whisky

Shake with ice and strain into a highball glass. Add two ice cubes. Fill with soda and stir.

MORNING MIST

1 oz. Galliano
Orange Juice

Fill an Old-fashioned glass with crushed ice and add Galliano. Fill with orange juice.

MORNING ROSE

½ oz. Lemon Juice
1½ oz. Rum
¼ oz. Grenadine
¼ oz. Orange Curacao

Shake with ice and strain into a cocktail glass.

MORNING SUN

1½ oz. Gin
2 tbsp. Grapefruit Juice
2 tbsp. Orange Juice
1-2 dashes Angostura Bitters
1-2 drops Cherry Juice

Shake with ice and strain into an Old-fashioned glass. Add ice.

MOROCCAN COCKTAIL

1 oz. Gin
1 oz. Cointreau
1 oz. Mandarin Liqueur

Shake with ice and strain into a cocktail glass.

MORRO

1 oz. Gin
½ oz. Dark Rum
1 tbsp. Pineapple Juice
1 tbsp. Lime Juice
½ tsp. Powdered Sugar

Shake with ice and strain into a sugar-rimmed Old-fashioned glass over ice cubes.

MOSCOW MULE

3 cubes Ice
2 oz. Vodka
1 oz. Lemon Juice
Ginger Beer

Put the ice in a highball glass and add Vodka and lemon juice. Fill with ginger beer.

MOSCOW WITCH

1 oz. Vodka
¾ oz. Strega

Mix in an Old-fashioned glass. Fill with ice. Serve with a lemon twist and a lime squeeze.

MOSELLE CUP

12 Ice cubes
3 Peaches, peeled and sliced
12 Maraschino cherries
1½ oz. Benedictine
1 bottle chilled Moselle
1 bottle sparkling Moselle, chilled

Put the ice cubes in a large pitcher and add the peaches, cherries, Benedictine and Moselle. When ready to serve pour in the sparkling Moselle. Serve in wineglasses. Makes about 12 servings.

MOTHER

1½ oz. Gin
½ oz. Orange Juice
½ oz. Cherry Heering

Shake with ice and strain into a cocktail glass.

MOTHER SHERMAN

2 oz. Apricot-flavored Brandy
1 oz. Orange Juice
4 dashes Orange Bitters

Shake with ice and strain into a cocktail glass.

MOTHER'S MILK

1½ oz. Gin
1 oz. Cream
½ tsp. Sugar

Shake with ice and strain into a cocktail glass. Sprinkle nutmeg on top.

MOULIN ROUGE NO. 1

1¾ oz. Sloe Gin
¾ oz. Sweet Vermouth
1 dash Bitters

Stir with ice and strain into a cocktail glass.

MOULIN ROUGE NO. 2

1 oz. Orange Juice
½ oz. Lemon Juice
¾ oz. Apricot-flavored Brandy
¼ oz. Grenadine

Stir with ice and strain into a cocktail glass.

MOUNTAIN COCKTAIL

1 Egg White
¼ tsp. Lemon Juice
¼ tsp. Dry Vermouth
¼ tsp. Sweet Vermouth
1½ oz. Rye Whisky

Shake with ice and strain into a cocktail glass.

MOUNT BAKER BEAKER

2 oz. Dark Rum
1 oz. Lemon Juice
1 tsp. Sugar
¾ oz. Pineapple Juice
¾ oz. Water

Mix in a highball glass. Fill with crushed ice.

MOUNT FUJI

1½ oz. Gin
3 tsp. Lemon Juice
2 tsp. Heavy Cream
1 tsp. Pineapple Juice
1 Egg White
1-2 drops Maraschino Liqueur

Shake with ice and strain into a Sour glass. Garnish with a cherry.

MOVE OVER

1½ oz. Gin
½ oz. Dry Vermouth
¼ oz. Sweet Vermouth
¼ oz. Cherry Heering
1 dash Bitters

Stir with ice and strain into a cocktail glass. Serve with a lemon twist.

MOVIE LOT

1 oz. Gin
1 oz. Grape Juice
½ oz. Caloric

Shake with ice and strain into a cocktail glass.

MOVITO

1½ oz. Rum
¾ oz. Lime Juice
½ tsp. Sugar

Shake with ice and strain into a highball glass. Fill with soda and ice. Serve with a mint sprig.

MR. ERIC SUTTON'S GIN BLIND

1½ oz. Gin
¾ oz. Curacao
½ oz. Brandy
1 dash Orange Bitters

Stir with ice and strain into a cocktail glass.

MR. MANHATTAN COCKTAIL

Muddle a lump of sugar with:

4 sprigs Mint
¼ tsp. Lemon Juice
1 tsp. Orange Juice
1½ oz. Gin

Shake with ice and strain into a cocktail glass.

MRS. SOLOMON

2 oz. Brandy
½ oz. Orange Curacao
2 dashes Bitters

Shake with ice and strain into a cocktail glass with a sugared rim.

MS. MANHATTAN

2½ oz. Gin
1 tsp. Orange Juice
1 tsp. Sugar Syrup
1-2 drops Lemon Juice
1-2 Mint leaves, crushed

Shake with ice and strain into an Old-fashioned glass.

MUDDY RIVER

1½ oz. Dark Creme de Cacao
1 oz. Kahlua
3 oz. Cream
1 oz. Vodka (optional)

Fill a double Old-fashioned glass with ice and add ingredients. Stir.

MUD PIE

½ Sugar cube
2 dashes Peychaud's Bitters
4 dashes Curacao
1 large cube Ice
1½ oz. Whisky

In an Old-fashioned glass muddle sugar cube with Peychaud's Bitters, Curacao and ice cube. Decorate with fruit, and serve Whisky on the side.

MUFTI COCKTAIL

1 oz. Pernod
½ oz. Maraschino Liqueur
½ oz. Lemon Juice

Shake with ice and strain into a cocktail glass.

> May we never have friends
> who, like shadows,
> Keep close to us in the
> sunshine,
> Only to desert us on a
> cloudy day or in the night.

MULAHAT PUNCH

1½ oz. Brandy
½ oz. Pernod
1 tsp. Lemon Juice
1 tsp. Sugar Syrup

Shake with ice and strain into a highball glass. Fill with soda and ice.

> Come, a health! And it's not
> to be slighted with sips,
> A cold pulse, or a spirit
> supine —
> All the blood in my heart
> seems to rush to my lips
> To commingle its flow with
> the wine.

MULE

1½ oz. Gin
½ oz. Lemon Juice
½ oz. Creme de Cassis

Shake with ice and strain into a cocktail glass.

MULE'S HIND LEG

½ oz. Gin
½ oz. Applejack
½ oz. Benedictine
½ oz. Apricot-flavored Brandy
½ oz. Maple Syrup

Stir with ice and strain into a cocktail glass.

MULLED BOURBON

2½ oz. Madeira Wine
1 oz. Bourbon
1 oz. Lillet
2 dashes Orange Bitters
4 oz. Water
1 tsp. Brown Sugar

Mix in a small, heavy saucepan and heat—but do not boil. Place a lemon wedge, some cloves and a cinnamon stick in a mug and add the hot mixture.

MULLED BURGUNDY

3 oz. Water
½ tsp. Sugar
2 oz. Burgundy Wine
1 dash Aromatic Bitters
Pinch Allspice
Cloves
Small piece Cinnamon
Large twist Lemon peel

Combine all ingredients in a small saucepan. Heat to piping hot. Do not boil. Strain into a preheated mug.

MULLED CIDER

1 tsp. Sugar
1 oz. Lemon Juice
½ tsp. Cinnamon
½ tsp. Nutmeg
8 oz. Cider
½ oz. Rum

Mix ingredients in a small, heavy saucepan and heat—but do not boil. Strain into an 8 oz. mug.

MULLED WINE

8 oz. Claret or other dry Red Wine
1 dash Angostura Bitters
2-3 Cloves
1 tsp. Sugar
pinch Allspice
small piece Cinnamon stick
twist Lemon peel

Combine all ingredients in a small, heavy saucepan and heat (do not boil). Strain into an 8 oz. mug.

MURPHY'S DREAM

3 oz. Irish Mist
3 oz. Gin
3 oz. Lemon Juice
1 Egg White
Several dashes Orange Bitters

Shake with ice and strain into an Old-fashioned glass. Add ice.

MUSCAT BASIL COOLER

¼ cup Basil leaves, crushed
6 oz. Light Muscat
1 tsp. fresh Lemon Juice

Steep crushed basil leaves in wine for 1-2 hours. Strain. Pour Wine mixture over ice in a Collins glass. Stir and add lemon juice.

MUSCATEL FLIP

1 oz. Brandy
1½ oz. Muscatel
1 Egg
1 tsp. Sugar
1 tbsp. Heavy Cream

Blend with ice and strain into a large cocktail glass. Sprinkle nutmeg on top.

MUSCATEL TWIST

2 oz. Lemon Juice
6 oz. Muscatel
Powdered Sugar to taste
Cracked Ice

Shake with ice and strain into a Collins glass.

MUSKMELON

1½ oz. Rum
½ tsp. Sugar
½ oz. Lime Juice
½ oz. Orange Juice

Shake with ice and strain into a cocktail glass. Garnish with a piece of ripe cantaloupe.

MUSTAPHA

1½ oz. Gin
½ oz. Creme de Cassis
½ Egg White
¼ oz. Lime Syrup
1 dash Tabasco Sauce

Shake with ice and strain into a cocktail glass.

MY COCKTAIL

2 oz. Gin
½ oz. Grand Marnier

Stir with ice and strain into a cocktail glass.

MY OWN

1½ oz. Gin
½ oz. Orange Juice
½ oz. Cointreau

Shake with ice and strain into a cocktail glass.

MY PLEASURE

1 tsp. Orange Bitters
2 oz. Orange Juice
4 oz. Apricot-flavored Brandy
Extra Dry Champagne, chilled

Combine all ingredients except Champagne and stir well. Strain into a Collins glass. Fill with Champagne.

MYRTLE BANK PUNCH

1½ oz. 151-proof Demerara Rum
1½ tbsp. Lime Juice
1 tsp. Grenadine
1 tsp. Sugar

Shake with ice and strain into a Collins glass. Fill with ice and soda. Float ½ oz. Maraschino Liqueur on top.

> Pleasure has its time;
> so, too, has Wisdom.
> Make love in thy youth,
> And in old age attend to thy
> salvation.

MY SIN

1 oz. Pernod
1 oz. Anisette
1 dash Bitters
1 Egg White

Shake with ice and strain into a cocktail glass.

NACIONAL

1 oz. Rum
¾ oz. Apricot-flavored Brandy
¾ oz. Lime Juice
Sugar to taste

Shake with ice and strain into a cocktail glass.

NAKED LADY

1 oz. Light Rum
1 oz. Sweet Vermouth
1 tsp. Apricot-flavored Brandy
½ tsp. Grenadine
1 tsp. Lemon Juice

Shake with ice and strain into a cocktail glass.

NAPA HIGHBALL

1½ oz. Gin
½ oz. Lemon Juice
½ tsp. Sugar

Shake with ice and strain into a highball glass. Fill with soda and ice.

NAPLES DELIGHT

1 oz. Cream
¾ oz. Galliano
¾ oz. Dark Creme de Cacao

Shake with ice and strain into a cocktail glass.

NAPOLEON

3 oz. Gin
1 dash Dubonnet
1 dash Curacao
1 dash Fernet Branca

Shake with ice and strain into a cocktail glass. Serve with a lemon twist.

NAPOLI

1 oz. Galliano
1½ oz. Vodka

Stir with ice and strain into a highball glass. Fill with ice and ginger ale.

NARRAGANSETT

1½ oz. Bourbon Whisky
1 oz. Sweet Vermouth
1 dash Anisette

Stir ingredients in an Old-fashioned glass over ice cubes. Add a twist of lemon peel.

NARRAGANSETT COBBLER

2 oz. Whisky
½ tsp. Sugar

Fill a double Old-fashioned glass with crushed ice and add ingredients. Fill with ginger ale. Serve with a twist of orange peel and straws.

NATIONAL NO. 1

1½ oz. Rum
½ oz. Pineapple Juice
½ oz. Apricot-flavored Brandy

Shake with ice and strain into a cocktail glass. Serve with a pineapple stick and a cherry.

NATIONAL NO. 2

1½ oz. Rum
½ oz. Lime Juice
¼ oz. Apricot-flavored Brandy
½ oz. Pineapple Juice

Shake with ice and strain into a cocktail glass.

NATURAL

1 oz. Rum
½ oz. Brandy
¼ oz. Grenadine
¼ oz. Orgeat Syrup
¼ oz. Lemon Juice

Shake with ice and strain into a cocktail glass.

NAVAL COCKTAIL

1¼ oz. Gin
1¼ oz. Sweet Vermouth

Stir with ice and strain into a cocktail glass. Serve with an olive and a lemon twist.

NAVY GROG NO. 1

1   oz. Dark Rum
½   oz. Rum
½   oz. Lime Juice
½   oz. Orange Juice
½   oz. Pineapple Juice
½   oz. Guava Nectar
¼   oz. Falernum

Shake with ice and strain into a double Old-fashioned glass. Serve with a mint sprig.

NAVY GROG NO. 2

1   oz. Demerara Rum
1   oz. Jamaica Rum
¾   oz. Lemon Juice
¾   oz. Grapefruit Juice
1   oz. Rum

Shake with ice and strain into a double Old-fashioned glass. Fill with soda.

NAVY GROG NO. 3

1½ oz. Lime Juice
¾   oz. Grapefruit Juice
1   dash Rock Candy Syrup
1   oz. Rum
1   oz. Dark Rum
1   oz. Demerara Rum
¼   oz. Pineapple Juice
¼   oz. Orange Juice
¼   oz. Guava Nectar

Shake with ice and strain into a double Old-fashioned glass.

NEAPOLITAN

1½ oz. Rum
½   oz. Cointreau
½   oz. Grand Marnier

Stir with ice and strain into a cocktail glass.

NECTARINE COOLER

2   oz. Vodka
3   oz. Orange Juice
1   tsp. Sugar
Several pieces ripe Nectarine

Shake with ice and strain into a Collins glass. Fill with Squirt and ice. Serve with a slice of nectarine.

NEGRITA GROG

½   oz. Brandy
½   oz. Rum
½   tsp. Sugar
½   oz. Orange Curacao
1   oz. strong Tea

Mix in an Old-fashioned glass. Fill with hot water. Serve with a lemon wedge.

NEGRONI

¾   oz. Campari
¾   oz. Sweet Vermouth
1   tbsp. Gin

Shake with ice and strain into a cocktail glass. Top with a twist of lemon.

> There is not in life a pleasure
>   so sweet
> As to sit near a window and
>   tilt up your feet
> To puff a Havana, whose
>   flavor just suits,
> And gaze at the world,
>   through the toes of your
>   boots.

NEGRONI COOLER

¾   oz. Gin
¾   oz. Campari
¾   oz. Sweet or Dry Vermouth

Stir with ice and strain into a cocktail glass. A splash of soda may be added. Serve with a lemon twist.

NELSON'S BLOOD

1½ oz. Rum
1   pat Butter

Pour into an Old-fashioned glass. Fill with hot water and add butter. Stir.

NETHERLAND

1   oz. Brandy
1   oz. Triple Sec or Orange Curacao
1   dash Orange Bitters

Stir with ice and strain into an Old-fashioned glass. Add ice cubes.

NEVADA COCKTAIL

Juice 1 Lime
1½ oz. Rum
1   oz. Grapefruit Juice
1   dash Bitters
3   tsp. Powdered Sugar

Shake with ice and strain into a cocktail glass.

NEVINS

1½ oz. Bourbon Whisky
1½ tsp. Apricot-flavored Brandy
1   tbsp. Grapefruit Juice
1½ tsp. Lemon Juice
1   dash Bitters

Shake with ice and strain into a cocktail glass.

NEWBURY

1   oz. Gin
1   oz. Sweet Vermouth
½   oz. Orange Curacao

Stir with ice and strain into a cocktail glass. Serve with a lemon twist.

NEW DEAL

1½ oz. Whisky
½   oz. Amer Picon
¼   tsp. Sugar

Mix in an Old-fashioned glass. Fill with ice. Serve with a twist of orange peel.

NEW LIFE

½   oz. Lemon Juice
1   oz. Cointreau
½   oz. Pernod
½   oz. Rum
Sugar to taste

Shake with ice and strain into a cocktail glass.

NEW ORLEANS NO. 1

1½   oz. Bourbon
1   dash Anisette
2   dashes Pernod
2   dashes Angostura Bitters
1   dash Orange Bitters
½   tsp. Sugar

Stir with ice and strain into a cocktail glass. Serve with a lemon twist.

NEW ORLEANS NO. 2

1½   oz. White Rum
2   tsp. Lime Juice
2   tsp. Orange Juice
1-2   dashes Peychaud's Bitters

Shake with ice and strain into a highball glass. Fill with ice. Add ginger ale and stir.

NEW ORLEANS BUCK

1½   oz. Rum
1   oz. Orange Juice
½   oz. Lemon Juice
2   dashes Peychaud's Bitters

Shake with ice and strain into a Collins glass. Add ice cubes, fill with ginger ale and stir.

Here's to the girl that's good
   and sweet,
Here's to the girl that's true,
Here's to the girl that rules
   my heart —
In other words, here's to
   you.

NEW ORLEANS GIN FIZZ

Juice ½ Lemon
Juice ½ Lime
1   tsp. Powdered Sugar
1   Egg White
2   oz. Gin
1   tbsp. sweet Cream
½   tsp. Orange Flower Water

Shake with ice and strain into a highball glass. Add two ice cubes, fill with soda and stir.

NEW ORLEANS MINT JULEP

2   oz. Bourbon Whisky
1   lump Sugar
4   Mint leaves

Fill a Collins glass with crushed ice and set aside. In an Old-fashioned glass muddle sugar and mint leaves. Add Whisky and mix. Pour over crushed ice in Collins glass. Stir until outside of glass is frosted. Decorate with a mint sprig and sprinkle with powdered sugar.

NEW ORLEANS PUNCH

1½   oz. Bourbon
1   dash Cherry Liqueur
Juice ½ Lime

Shake with ice and strain into a Collins glass. Fill with cold black tea.

NEW ORLEANS TRUMPETER

1½   oz. Early Times
1   oz. Green Creme de Menthe
½   tsp. Sugar

Shake with ice and strain into a cocktail glass. Add a squirt of 7-Up. Serve with a cherry.

NEWPORT

1   oz. Galliano
½   oz. White Creme de Menthe
¾   oz. Orange Juice
½   oz. Cream

Shake with ice and strain into a cocktail glass.

NEWTON'S APPLE COCKTAIL

1¾   oz. Apple Brandy
¾   oz. Orange Curacao
1   dash Angostura Bitters

Stir with ice and strain into a cocktail glass.

To Friendship:
Here's to the tears of friendship!
May they crystallize as they
   fall and be worn
As gems in the memory of
   those we love.

NEWTON'S SPECIAL

1¾   oz. Brandy
¾   oz. Cointreau
1   dash Angostura Bitters

Stir with ice and strain into a cocktail glass.

NEW WORLD

1½   oz. Blended Whisky
½   oz. Lime Juice
½   oz. Grenadine

Shake with ice and strain into a cocktail glass. Serve with a lime wedge.

NEW YORK

1½   oz. Whisky
½   oz. Lime or Lemon Juice
¼   oz. Grenadine
¼   tsp. Sugar

Shake with an orange peel and strain into a cocktail glass. Serve with a lemon twist.

NEW YORKER NO. 1

1½ oz. Bourbon
½ oz. Claret
½ oz. Lemon Juice
½ tsp. Sugar

Shake with ice and strain into a highball glass. Fill with soda and ice.

NEW YORKER NO. 2

½ oz. Gin
1½ oz. Dry Vermouth
½ oz. Dry Sherry
1 dash Cointreau

Stir with ice and strain into a cocktail glass.

NEW YORKER NO. 3

2 oz. Southern Comfort
½ oz. Lime Juice

Stir with ice and strain into a cocktail glass.

> To our noble selves:
> Why not toast ourselves,
> And praise ourselves,
> Since we have the best means
> Of knowing all the good in ourselves?

NEW YORKER NO. 4

¾ oz. Galliano
1 oz. Inca Pisco
1 oz. Grapefruit Juice
½ oz. Lime Juice
1 tsp. Sugar

Shake with ice and strain into a cocktail glass.

NEW YORKER NO. 5

1½ oz. Blended Whisky
½ oz. Lime Juice
½ tsp. Sugar
¼ oz. Grenadine

Shake with ice and strain into a cocktail glass. Serve with a lemon twist and an orange peel.

NEW YORKER NO. 6

1½ oz. Bourbon
½ oz. Lemon Juice
½ tsp. Sugar
½ oz. Claret

Mix the first three ingredients in a highball glass, fill with soda and ice and float Claret on top.

NEW YORK EXPERIENCE

1 oz. Early Times
1 oz. Dry Vermouth
1 oz. Triple Sec or Orange Curacao

Stir with ice and strain into a cocktail glass. Serve with a lemon twist.

NEW YORK SOUR

Juice ½ Lemon
1 tsp. Powdered Sugar
2 oz. Rye Whisky
Claret

Shake the first three ingredients with ice and strain into a Sour glass, leaving about ½ inch on which to float Claret. Decorate with half a slice of lemon and a cherry.

NICKEL FEVER

⅓ oz. Southern Comfort
⅓ oz. Galliano
⅔ oz. fresh Orange Juice
⅔ oz. fresh Cream
¼ oz. Blue Curacao

Shake with ice and strain into a champagne glass. Add ice chips and 8 drops of Blue Curacao.

NICK'S OWN

1½ oz. Brandy
1½ oz. Sweet Vermouth
1 dash Angostura Bitters
1 dash Pernod

Stir with ice and strain into a cocktail glass. Add a squeeze of lemon juice and serve with a cherry.

NICKY'S FIZZ

1½ oz. Gin
1 oz. Pineapple Juice

Shake with ice and strain into a highball glass. Fill with soda and ice.

NICOLASKI

2-3 oz. Brandy

Chill Brandy with ice. Pour into a cocktail glass and add 1 slice of lemon dipped in powdered sugar.

NICOLOSCAR

1 square slice Lemon Peel
Coarsely-ground Coffee
Sugar
1½ oz. Brandy

Place the coffee and the sugar on the lemon peel wafer-like and chew it. Wash it down with the Brandy.

NIGHT CAP NO. 1

2 oz. Rum
1 tsp. Powdered Sugar

Add enough warm milk to fill a highball glass and stir. Sprinkle a little nutmeg on top.

NIGHT CAP NO. 2

¾ oz. Brandy
¾ oz. Anisette
¾ oz. Orange Curacao
1 Egg Yolk

Shake with ice and strain into a cocktail glass. Sprinkle nutmeg on top.

NIGHT FLIGHT

1½ oz. Rum
½ oz. Lime Juice
½ oz. Maple Syrup

Shake with ice and strain into a cocktail glass.

NIGHTMARE

1½ oz. Gin
½ oz. Dubonnet
½ oz. Cherry-flavored Brandy
1 tsp. Orange Juice

Shake with ice and strain into a cocktail glass.

NIGHT SHADE

1½ oz. Bourbon
½ oz. Sweet Vermouth
½ oz. Orange Juice
1 dash Yellow Chartreuse

Shake with ice and strain into a cocktail glass. Serve with an orange slice and lemon wedge.

NINE-PICK

1 oz. Pernod
1 oz. Curacao
1 oz. Brandy
1 Egg Yolk

Shake with ice and strain into a cocktail glass.

NINETEEN NO. 1

3 oz. Dry Vermouth
½ oz. Gin
½ oz. Kirschwasser
1 dash Pernod
3 dashes Sugar Syrup

Shake with ice and strain into a cocktail glass.

NINETEEN NO. 2

¾ oz. Gin
¾ oz. Kirschwasser
¾ oz. Dry Vermouth
1 dash Angostura Bitters
¼ tsp. Sugar Syrup

Shake with ice and strain into a cocktail glass. Serve with a cherry.

NINETEEN FOURTEEN COCKTAIL

1 oz. Curacao
1 oz. sweet Cream
1 oz. Gin

Shake with ice and strain into a cocktail glass.

NINETEEN-PICK-ME-UP

1½ oz. Pernod
¾ oz. Gin
1 dash Angostura Bitters
1 dash Orange Bitters
1 dash Sugar Syrup

Shake with ice and strain into a cocktail glass. Add a dash of soda.

NINETEEN-TWENTY NO. 1

1 oz. Gin
½ oz. Dry Vermouth
½ oz. Kirschwasser
1 dash Orange Bitters
1 tsp. Groseille Syrup

Shake with ice and strain into a cocktail glass.

NINETEEN-TWENTY NO. 2

1½ oz. Rye Whisky
½ oz. Sweet Vermouth
½ oz. Dry Vermouth
1 dash Orange Bitters

Shake with ice and strain into a cocktail glass. Serve with a lemon twist.

NINETEEN-TWENTY NO. 3

1½ oz. Dry Vermouth
½ oz. Gin
½ oz. Kirschwasser
1 dash Pernod

Shake with ice and strain into a cocktail glass.

There are many good
reasons for drinking
And one has just entered
my head.
If a man doesn't drink when
he's living
How the hell can he drink
when he's dead.

NINETEEN-TWENTY HIGHBALL

1½ oz. Pernod
1 oz. Gin
1 dash Angostura Bitters
1 dash Orange Bitters
½ tsp. Sugar

Mix in a highball glass. Fill with soda and ice.

NINETY MILES

1½ oz. Sloe Gin
1½ oz. Applejack

Shake with ice and strain into a cocktail glass.

NINOTCHKA COCKTAIL

1½ oz. Vodka
½ oz. Creme de Cacao
1 tbsp. Lemon Juice

Shake with ice and strain into a cocktail glass.

NONE BUT THE BRAVE

1½ oz. Brandy
¾ oz. Pimento Dram
1 tsp. Sugar
1 dash Jamaica Ginger
1 dash Lemon Juice

Shake with ice and strain into a cocktail glass.

NOON

1 oz. Gin
½ oz. Sweet Vermouth
½ oz. Dry Vermouth
½ oz. Orange Juice
1 Egg White
1 dash Bitters

Shake with ice and strain into a cocktail glass.

NORMANDY

1 oz. Sweet Cider
¾ oz. Brandy
½ oz. Apple Brandy
¼ oz. Gin

Stir with ice and strain into a cocktail glass.

NORTH EXPRESS

1 oz. Canadian Whisky
1 oz. Dry Vermouth
1 oz. Cordial Medoc

Mix without ice until well blended. Pour over ice in a cocktail glass. Decorate with a cherry.

NORTH POLE COCKTAIL

1 Egg White
½ oz. Lemon Juice
½ oz. Maraschino Liqueur
1 oz. Gin

Shake with ice and strain into a cocktail glass. Top with whipped cream.

NORTHSIDE SPECIAL

2½ oz. Orange Juice
½ oz. Lemon Juice
1 tsp. Sugar
1½ oz. Rum

Shake with ice and strain into a Collins glass. Fill with soda and ice.

NORTHWEST PASSAGE

1 pat Butter
1 oz. 151-proof Demerara Rum

Put into an Old-fashioned glass, fill with hot water and stir. Serve with a lemon twist.

NOURMAHAL PUNCH

¾ oz. Lime Juice
2 oz. Jamaica Rum
2 dashes Angostura Bitters

Put lime juice and the lime shell into a Collins glass and fill the glass with ice. Add Rum and Bitters and top off with soda.

NUDE EEL COCKTAIL

¾ oz. Dubonnet
¾ oz. Chartreuse
¾ oz. Cognac
¾ oz. Gin
1 dash Dry Vermouth

Shake with ice and strain into a cocktail glass.

NUGENT

1 oz. Lemon Juice
½ Egg White
1 tsp. Sugar
1½ oz. Rum

Shake with ice and strain into a cocktail glass.

NUMBER 3

1¾ oz. Gin
½ oz. Dry Vermouth
1 dash Orange Bitters
¼ oz. Anisette

Stir with ice and strain into a cocktail glass.

NUMBER 6

1½ oz. Gin
¾ oz. Sweet Vermouth
1 twist Orange Peel
3 dashes Curacao

Shake with ice and strain into a cocktail glass. Serve with a cherry.

NUPCIAL

1 oz. Tequila
1 tbsp. White Creme de Cacao
1 tbsp. White Syrup
1¼ oz. Evaporated Milk
4 oz. crushed Ice

Blend at a low speed for a minute and a half. Strain into an Old-fashioned glass. Top with a cherry.

NUPTIAL

1½ oz. Gin
¾ oz. Kirschwasser
¼ oz. Orange Curacao
¼ oz. Lemon Juice
¼ oz. Orange Juice

Shake with ice and strain into a cocktail glass.

> Here's a sigh to those who love me,
> And a smile to those who hate;
> And whatever skies above me,
> Here's a heart for every fate.

NUT

1½ oz. Vodka
½ oz. Amaretto

Fill an Old-fashioned glass with ice and add Vodka and Amaretto.

OASIS COOLER

1½ oz. Gin
1½ oz. Dry Vermouth
½ oz. Lemon Juice

Shake with ice and strain into a Collins glass. Fill with soda and ice.

OASIS DAIQUIRI

1	oz.	Rum
¼	oz.	Peach-flavored Brandy
½	oz.	Lemon Juice
1	oz.	Orange Juice

Peach pieces (ripe)

Blend with ice and strain into a cocktail glass. Serve with a cherry.

OBEAH PRINCESS

¾	oz.	Galliano
¼	oz.	Green Creme de Menthe
1	oz.	Barbados Rum
1		Egg White

Shake with ice and strain into a cocktail glass. Serve with an orange slice.

OCEAN SHORE

½	oz.	Lemon Juice
1	oz.	Sloe Gin
½	oz.	Gin
½		Egg White
¼	oz.	Orgeat Syrup

Shake with ice and strain into a cocktail glass.

OCHO RIOS

1½	oz.	Jamaica Rum
1	oz.	Guava Nectar
½	oz.	Cream
½	oz.	Lime Juice
½	tsp.	Sugar

Shake with ice and strain into a cocktail glass.

ODDBALL

1½	oz.	Pernod
1	oz.	Orange Juice

Shake with ice and strain into a cocktail glass.

ODD McINTYRE

¾	oz.	Brandy
¾	oz.	Cointreau
¾	oz.	Lillet
¾	oz.	Lemon Juice

Shake with ice and strain into a cocktail glass.

OF COURSE

1½	oz.	Cream
¾	oz.	Amaretto
¾	oz.	Brandy

Shake with ice and strain into a cocktail glass.

OFF SHORE

1	oz.	Apple Brandy
¾	oz.	Caloric
¾	oz.	Rum

Shake with ice and strain into a cocktail glass.

OGGE

4		Egg Yolks
2	oz.	Sugar Syrup
1	quart	Beer

Nutmeg

Beat the egg yolks until light and lemon-colored, then stir in the sugar syrup. Heat the Beer to just under the boiling point and slowly add to the sweetened egg yolks, beating constantly. Serve in warmed mugs and dust a little nutmeg on top of each. Serves 4.

O'HEARN SPECIAL

2	oz.	Brandy
1	twist	Orange peel
2		Mint sprigs

Place in a Collins glass with ice cubes. Fill with ginger ale. Stir and serve.

OH HENRY! COCKTAIL

1	oz.	Benedictine
1	oz.	Bourbon
1	oz.	Ginger Ale

Stir with ice and strain into a cocktail glass.

OJEN

2½	oz.	Ojen
2	dashes	Peychaud's Bitters

Stir with ice and strain into a cocktail glass.

> Inspiring bold John Barley-corn,
> What dangers thou canst make us scorn!
> — *Robert Burns*

OLAFFSON'S PUNCH

1½	oz.	Lime Juice
1¼	oz.	Orange Juice
2	oz.	Haitian Rum
1½	tsp.	Sugar

Shake with ice and strain into a Collins glass. Fill with soda and ice.

OLD BOURBON COOLER

3	oz.	Bourbon
2	tsp.	Grenadine
1	tsp.	Powdered Sugar
1-2	drops	White Creme de Menthe
1-2	dashes	Orange Bitters

Shake with ice and strain into a Collins glass. Fill with soda and ice. Top with a slice of orange, a cherry and a pineapple stick.

OLD CASTLE PUNCH

1½	oz.	Rum

Pour into a Collins glass. Fill with Rhine Wine and ice. Add sugar to taste.

OLD CHARLES

2 oz. Galliano
1 oz. Barbados Rum
2 oz. Grapefruit Juice
1 dash Grenadine
½ oz. Lime Juice

Shake with ice and strain into a cocktail glass. Serve with a lime wheel.

OLD CHARLIE

1 dash Sugar Syrup
2 dashes Aromatic Bitters
2 oz. Brandy
2 oz. Sweet Vermouth

Shake with ice and strain into an Old-fashioned glass. Serve with a cherry.

OLD CHARTER

1½ oz. Bourbon
½ oz. Lemon Juice
1 dash Grenadine

Stir with ice and strain into a cocktail glass.

OLD ETONIAN

1¼ oz. Gin
1¼ oz. Lillet
2 dashes Orange Bitters
2 dashes Creme de Noyaux

Stir with ice and strain into a cocktail glass. Serve with a twist of orange peel.

OLD FALL RIVER LINE

¾ oz. Gin
¾ oz. Brandy
½ oz. White Creme de Menthe
½ oz. Maraschino Liqueur

Shake with ice and strain into a cocktail glass.

OLD-FASHIONED APPETIZER

1 dash Peychaud's Bitters
¼ oz. Pernod
¼ oz. Orange Curacao
¾ oz. Rye or Bourbon Whisky
¾ oz. Dubonnet

Mix in an Old-fashioned glass. Fill with ice. Serve with an orange slice and a lemon twist.

OLD-FASHIONED COCKTAIL

1 dash Angostura Bitters
2 oz. Rye or Bourbon Whisky

In an Old-fashioned glass put a small cube of sugar, Angostura Bitters and a tsp. of water and muddle well. Add Whisky. Stir and add a lemon twist and ice cubes. Decorate with a slice of orange, lemon and a cherry. Serve with a swizzle stick.

OLD MAN'S MILK

2 oz. Scotch Whisky
2 tsp. Drambuie
2 tsp. Sugar Syrup
1 Egg, beaten
8 oz. Milk

Combine in a saucepan; heat but do not allow to boil. Stir constantly to prevent the milk from scalding and serve in a double Old-fashioned glass.

OLD PAL NO. 1

¾ oz. Rye Whisky
¾ oz. Dry Vermouth
¾ oz. Campari

Shake with ice and strain into a cocktail glass.

OLD PAL NO. 2

1½ oz. Whisky
½ oz. Sweet Vermouth
½ oz. Grenadine

Stir with ice and strain into a cocktail glass.

OLD PEPPER

Juice ½ Lemon
2 oz. Whisky
1 tsp. Worcestershire Sauce
1 tsp. Chili Sauce
2 dashes Angostura Bitters
1 dash Tabasco Sauce

Shake with ice and strain into a Sour glass.

OLD PUSS

1 oz. Gin
1 oz. Calvados
¼ oz. Pernod
¼ oz. Grenadine

Shake with ice and strain into a cocktail glass.

OLD SAN FRANCISCO

⅓ oz. Kirschwasser
⅓ oz. Keuck
2 dashes Lime Cordial
2 dashes Grenadine

Stir with ice and strain into a cocktail glass. Float whipped cream on top. Sprinkle with Nescafe.

OLD SMOOTHIE

½ oz. Galliano
1 oz. Vodka
½ oz. Lime Juice

Shake with ice and strain over crushed ice in a cocktail glass.

OLD TIME APPETIZER

¾ oz. Rye or Bourbon Whisky
¾ oz. Dubonnet
¼ oz. Orange Curacao
¼ oz. Pernod
1 dash Peychaud's Bitters

Mix in an Old-fashioned glass. Fill with ice. Serve with an orange slice, a lemon twist and a pineapple spear.

OLD TOM

2 oz. Gin
¼ oz. Pernod
1 dash Orange Bitters
¼ tsp. Sugar

Shake with ice and strain into a cocktail glass.

OLD VERMONT

1½ oz. Gin
½ oz. Maple Syrup
¼ oz. Lemon Juice
¼ oz. Orange Juice
1 dash Angostura Bitters

Shake with ice and strain into a cocktail glass.

OLE

1½ oz. Tequila
1 oz. Kahlua
1 tbsp. Sugar Syrup

Mix without ice and pour over crushed ice in a cocktail glass. Float 1 tbsp. heavy cream on top.

OLIVETTE

2 oz. Gin
½ tsp. Sugar Syrup
2 dashes Orange Bitters

Stir with ice and strain into a cocktail glass. Serve with a twist of lemon peel, and an olive if desired. (¼ oz. Anisette may be used—omit lemon twist.)

OLSEN COCKTAIL

1½ oz. Sweet Vermouth
1½ oz. Russian Kummel
2 dashes Scotch Whisky

Shake with ice and strain into a cocktail glass.

OLSON

1½ oz. Bourbon
½ oz. Cream
½ oz. Honey

Shake with ice and strain into a cocktail glass. Sprinkle nutmeg on top.

OLYMPIA

1½ oz. Dark Rum
1 oz. Cherry-flavored Brandy
Juice ½ Lime

Shake with ice and strain into a cocktail glass.

OLYMPIC COCKTAIL NO. 1

¾ oz. Orange Juice
¾ oz. Triple Sec or Orange Curacao
¾ oz. Brandy

Shake with ice and strain into a cocktail glass.

God made man as frail as a bubble,
God made love, and love made trouble,
God made wine, so is it a sin,
For man to drink wine to drown trouble in?

OLYMPIC COCKTAIL NO. 2

1¾ oz. Gin
½ oz. Sweet Vermouth
¼ oz. Pernod

Stir with ice and strain into a cocktail glass.

OLYMPIC COCKTAIL NO. 3

¾ oz. Plymouth Gin
¾ oz. Dry Vermouth
¾ oz. Sweet Vermouth
¼ oz. Orange Juice

Shake with ice and strain into a cocktail glass. Serve with a lemon twist.

OLYMPIC COCKTAIL NO. 4

½ oz. Cognac or Brandy
1 oz. Kahlua
1 Egg
4 oz. Half & Half

Shake with ice and strain into a Collins glass. Fill with ice.

OMAR'S DELIGHT

1½ oz. 100-proof Southern Comfort
½ tsp. Curacao
⅓ oz. Lemon Juice
½ tsp. Sugar
Juice ½ small Lime

Shake with ice and strain into a champagne glass.

ONCE MORE

1½ oz. Dry Vermouth
½ oz. Kirschwasser
½ oz. Mandarinette
1 dash Angostura Bitters

Stir with ice and strain into a cocktail glass.

ONE EXCITING NIGHT

¾ oz. Gin
¾ oz. Dry Vermouth
¾ oz. Sweet Vermouth
¼ oz. Orange Juice

Stir with ice and strain into a cocktail glass. Serve with a lemon twist.

ONE HUNDRED PERCENT COCKTAIL

½ oz. Orange Juice
½ oz. Lemon Juice
1½ oz. Swedish Punch
2 dashes Grenadine

Shake with ice and strain into a cocktail glass.

ONE IRELAND

1 oz. Irish Whisky
1 tbsp. Green Creme de Menthe
2 oz. Vanilla Ice Cream

Blend at a high speed until smooth and pour into a Martini glass.

ONE OF MINE

1½ oz. Gin
¾ oz. Dry Vermouth
¾ oz. Sweet Vermouth
1 dash Bitters
Juice ¼ Orange

Stir with ice and strain into a cocktail glass.

ONE SPOT

1½ oz. Gin
1½ oz. Pernod
½ oz. Lemon Juice
1 dash Angostura Bitters

Shake with ice and strain into a cocktail glass.

OOM PAUL

1 oz. Calvados or Applejack
1 oz. Dubonnet
1 dash Angostura Bitters

Stir with ice and strain into a cocktail glass.

OPAL COCKTAIL

1 oz. Gin
½ oz. Triple Sec
1 tbsp. Orange Juice
¼ tsp. Powdered Sugar
½ tsp. Orange Flower Water

Shake with ice and strain into a cocktail glass.

OPENHEIM

1½ oz. Bourbon
½ oz. Grenadine
½ oz. Sweet Vermouth

Stir with ice and strain into a cocktail glass. Serve with a cherry.

OPENING COCKTAIL

½ oz. Grenadine
½ oz. Sweet Vermouth
1½ oz. Rye Whisky

Stir with ice and strain into a cocktail glass.

OPERA COCKTAIL NO. 1

1 tbsp. Maraschino Liqueur
½ oz. Dubonnet
1½ oz. Gin

Stir with ice and strain into a cocktail glass.

OPERA COCKTAIL NO. 2

1 oz. Gin
¾ oz. Dubonnet
¾ oz. Mandarinette

Stir with ice and strain into a cocktail glass.

ORACABESSA

1 oz. Banana Liqueur
½ oz. Lemon Juice
½ oz. 151-proof Rum

Shake with ice and strain into a cocktail glass. Garnish with a lemon wedge and a banana slice dipped in lemon juice.

Here's to love, a thing so divine,
Description makes it but the less;
'Tis what we feel, but cannot define;
'Tis what we know, but cannot express.

ORAL FIZZ

Juice ½ Lemon
1 tsp. Sugar
¾ oz. Jamaica Rum
¾ oz. Port Wine
1 Egg White

Shake with ice and strain into a fizz glass. Fill with soda and ice.

ORANGE BLOOM

1 oz. Gin
½ oz. Sweet Vermouth
½ oz. Cointreau

Stir with ice and strain into a cocktail glass. Serve with a cherry.

ORANGE BLOSSOM BLENDER

2 oz. Orange Juice
2 tbsp. Gin
2 tsp. Lemon Juice
2 tsp. Curacao
1-2 drops Orange Flower Water
2 oz. crushed Ice

Blend at a low speed for 10 seconds. Strain into an Old-fashioned glass and top with an orange slice.

ORANGE BLOSSOM COCKTAIL NO. 1

1 oz. Gin
1 oz. Orange Juice
¼ tsp. Powdered Sugar

Shake with ice and strain into a cocktail glass.

ORANGE BLOSSOM COCKTAIL NO. 2

1 oz. Orange Juice
¾ oz. Gin
¾ oz. Sweet Vermouth

Shake with ice and strain into a cocktail glass.

ORANGE BLOSSOM COOLER

Juice ½ Orange
2-3 oz. Gin
1 tsp. Sugar

Shake with ice and strain into a highball glass. Fill with soda and ice. Garnish with fruit or mint.

ORANGE BUCK

1½   oz. Gin
1   oz. Orange Juice
1   tbsp. Lime Juice

Shake with ice and strain into a highball glass. Add ice cubes, fill with ginger ale and stir.

ORANGE CADILLAC

1   oz. Galliano
¾   oz. Light Creme de Cacao
¼   oz. Orange Juice
1   oz. Cream

Shake with ice and strain into a cocktail glass.

ORANGE CHAMPAGNE

½   oz. Orange Curacao

Pour into a champagne glass. Fill with Champagne. Serve with a twist of orange peel.

ORANGE COCKTAIL

1½   oz. Gin
½   oz. Orange Juice
¼   oz. Dry Vermouth
¼   tsp. Sugar
1   dash Orange Bitters

Shake with ice and strain into a cocktail glass. Serve with a twist of orange peel.

ORANGE COMFORT

½   oz. Southern Comfort
½   oz. Anisette
¾   oz. Orange Juice
½   oz. Lemon Juice

Shake with ice and strain into a cocktail glass. Serve with an orange slice.

> Once more fill a bumper —
> ne'er talk of the hour;
> On hearts thus united, old
> Time has no power.

ORANGE COOLER

1   oz. 151-proof Rum
½   oz. Orange Curacao
½   oz. Lime Juice
1   tsp. Sugar

Shake with ice and strain into a highball glass. Fill with soda and ice.

ORANGE COUNTY SPECIAL

3   oz. Brandy
1   oz. Sweet Vermouth
1   dash Pernod
1   dash Orange Juice

Stir with ice and strain into a cocktail glass.

ORANGE FIZZ NO. 1

1½   oz. Gin
1¼   oz. Orange Juice
1   dash Grenadine

Shake with ice and strain into a highball glass. Fill with soda and ice.

ORANGE FIZZ NO. 2

1½   oz. Gin
1   oz. Orange Juice
½   oz. Lemon Juice
½   oz. Lime Juice
Sugar to taste

Shake with ice and strain into a highball glass. Fill with soda and ice.

ORANGE FIZZ NO. 3

1½   oz. Gin
½   oz. Lemon Juice
1½   oz. Orange Juice
¼   oz. Triple Sec
½   tsp. Sugar
2   dashes Orange Bitters

Shake with ice and strain into a Collins glass. Serve with an orange slice.

ORANGE FLOWER

1   oz. Orange Curacao
½   oz. Cherry Liqueur
½   oz. Orange Juice
¼   oz. Lemon Juice
1   dash Orange Flower Water

Shake with ice and strain into a cocktail glass.

ORANGE GIN COLLINS

Juice ½ Lemon
2   oz. Orange-flavored Gin

Shake with ice and strain into a Collins glass. Add several cubes of ice, fill with soda and stir. Decorate with slices of lemon and orange and a cherry. Serve with straws.

ORANGE GIN FIZZ

Juice ½ Lemon
1   tsp. Powdered Sugar
2   oz. Orange-flavored Gin
1   dash Grenadine

Shake with ice and strain into a highball glass. Add two ice cubes, fill with soda and stir.

ORANGE GIN HIGHBALL

2   oz. Orange-flavored Gin

Pour into a highball glass. Add ice cubes and fill with ginger ale or soda. Add a twist of lemon peel, if desired, and stir.

ORANGE GIN RICKEY

Juice ½ Lime
2   oz. Orange-flavored Gin

Pour into a highball glass. Add ice cubes and fill with soda. Add a wedge of lime and stir.

ORANGE MARTINI

1¾ oz. Gin
½ oz. Dry Vermouth
¼ oz. Sweet Vermouth

Stir with ice and strain into a cocktail glass. Grate some orange rind and mix with the drink. Serve with a twist of orange peel.

ORANGE MILK FIZZ

Juice ½ Lemon
1 tsp. Sugar
2 oz. Orange-flavored Gin
2 oz. Milk

Shake with ice and strain into a highball glass. Fill with soda and ice.

ORANGE MIST

1½ oz. Irish Mist Liqueur

Pour into a highball glass. Fill with crushed ice and orange juice.

I drink it as the Fates
   ordain it.
Come, fill it and have done
   with the rhymes;
Fill up the lonely glass and
   drain it,
In memory of dear old times.

ORANGE OASIS

1½ oz. Gin
½ oz. Cherry Liqueur
4 oz. Orange Juice

Mix in a Collins glass. Fill with ginger ale and ice. Serve with an orange slice.

ORANGE SANGAREE

4 oz. Claret or Bordeaux
2 oz. Orange Juice
1½ oz. Sugar
2 tbsp. Lemon Juice
1 whole Clove
Allspice

Shake with ice and strain into a 12 oz. glass. Chill for one hour. Fill with soda.

ORANGE SMILE

Juice 1 large Orange
1 Egg
½ oz. Raspberry Syrup or Grenadine

Shake with ice and strain into a highball glass. (Liquor of your choice may be added if desired.)

ORANGE SPARKLER

Ice cubes
Juice 1 Orange
Pink Champagne, well chilled

Pour orange juice over ice cubes in a Collins glass. Fill with Champagne. Stir lightly.

ORANGE WARMER PUNCH

6 cups boiling Water
6 tsp. Tea
6 cups Orange Juice
½ cup superfine Sugar
1 cup Grand Marnier or Cointreau
Orange slices, halved
Whole Cloves

Combine the tea and the boiling water. Steep the tea for 3 minutes. Strain into a punch bowl. Meanwhile, heat the orange juice with the sugar, stirring until the sugar is dissolved. Add to the punch bowl, together with the Grand Marnier or Cointreau. Garnish with orange slices studded with whole cloves. Serve in mugs. Makes about 12 servings.

ORCHARD PUNCH

2 tsp. Maple Syrup
3 dashes Lime Juice
½ oz. Pineapple Syrup
1½ oz. Brandy

Mix the first three ingredients in a Collins glass. Fill the glass with shaved ice and add Brandy. Shake well and garnish with fruits. Float a dash of Port Wine on top.

ORCHID

1½ oz. Gin
1 Egg White
¼ oz. Creme d'Yvette

Shake with ice and strain into a cocktail glass.

ORGEAT COCKTAIL

1 oz. Gin
¾ oz. Orgeat Syrup
¾ oz. Orange Juice

Shake with ice and strain into a cocktail glass.

ORGEAT FIZZ

2 oz. Orgeat Syrup
¾ oz. Lime Juice

Shake with ice and strain into a highball glass. Fill with soda and ice.

ORGEAT HIGHBALL

1¾ oz. Orgeat Syrup

Pour into a highball glass. Fill with soda and ice.

ORGEAT PUNCH

¾ oz. Orgeat Syrup
2 oz. Brandy
1 oz. Lemon Juice

Shake with ice and strain into a Collins glass. Fill with crushed ice. Garnish with fruit and float a dash of Port Wine on top.

ORIENTAL COCKTAIL NO. 1

1 oz. Whisky
½ oz. Sweet Vermouth
½ oz. Curacao
Juice ½ Lime

Shake with ice and strain into a cocktail glass.

ORIENTAL COCKTAIL NO. 2

1 oz. Gin
½ oz. Dry Vermouth
½ oz. Sweet Vermouth
½ oz. Orange Juice
1 Egg White

Shake with ice and strain into a cocktail glass. Serve with a pineapple stick.

ORIENTE

1½ oz. Rum
1½ oz. Pineapple Juice
¼ oz. Amer Picon
½ oz. Lime Juice
½ tsp. Sugar

Shake with ice and strain into a cocktail glass.

ORIGINAL KOENIG'S PUNCH

½ tsp. Parfait Amour
1½ oz. Rye Whisky

Shake with ice and strain into a highball glass. Add several mint sprigs. Fill with soda and ice.

ORLENA

½ tsp. Sugar
¼ oz. Pernod
¼ oz. Brandy
Champagne

Pour the first three ingredients into a cocktail glass. Fill the glass with Champagne and serve with a lemon twist.

ORONOFF

1 oz. Gin
¾ oz. Prunella
¾ oz. Kirschwasser

Stir with ice and strain into a cocktail glass. Serve with a twist of orange peel.

OSTEND FIZZ NO. 1

1½ oz. Creme de Cassis
1½ oz. Kirschwasser

Mix in a highball glass. Fill with soda and ice.

OSTEND FIZZ NO. 2

1½ oz. Kirschwasser
½ oz. Creme de Cassis
½ oz. Lemon Juice
½ tsp. Sugar

Shake with ice and strain into a highball glass. Fill with soda and ice. Serve with a lemon wedge.

OTTO'S JOY

1 dash Aromatic Bitters
1 dash Pernod
2 oz. Brandy
2 oz. Sweet Vermouth

Stir with ice and strain into an Old-fashioned glass. Add a twist of lemon and a maraschino cherry.

OUZOG RICKEY

1 oz. Ouzo
1 oz. Cognac
½ oz. Lime Juice

Mix in a highball glass. Leave lime shell in glass. Fill with soda and ice.

OVER HILL 'N' DALE

1½ oz. Apple Brandy
2 tbsp. White Creme de Menthe
1-2 drops Pernod

Shake with ice and strain into a brandy snifter.

PABLO

1 oz. Rum
½ oz. Cointreau
½ oz. Advokaat
1 slice Pineapple

Shake with ice and strain into a champagne glass. Serve with a cherry.

PACEMAKER

1½ oz. Gin
½ oz. Triple Sec
½ oz. Lemon Juice
1 dash Blue Food Coloring

Shake with ice and strain into a cocktail glass.

PACIFIC

1½ oz. Gin
½ oz. Cherry-flavored Brandy
½ oz. Cointreau

Stir with ice and strain into a cocktail glass.

PACIFIC PACIFIER

1 oz. Cointreau
1 tbsp. Banana Liqueur
1 tbsp. Light Cream

Shake with ice and strain into a cocktail glass. Strain over crushed ice.

> Then wreath the bowl with flowers of soul
> The brightest wit can find us;
> We'll take a flight toward heaven tonight
> And leave dull earth behind us!

PADDY COCKTAIL NO. 1

1½ oz. Irish Whisky
1½ oz. Sweet Vermouth
1 dash Bitters

Stir with ice and strain into a cocktail glass.

PADDY COCKTAIL NO. 2

2 oz. Rye Whisky
½ oz. Lemon Juice
1 dash Angostura Bitters

Stir with ice and strain into a cocktail glass.

PAGO PAGO

1½   oz. Gold Rum
½   oz. Lime Juice
¼   oz. Green Chartreuse
¼   oz. Light Creme de Cacao
½   oz. Pineapple Juice

Shake with ice and strain into a cocktail glass.

PAISLEY MARTINI

2   oz. Gin
½   oz. Dry Vermouth
1   tsp. Scotch Whisky

Stir with ice and strain into an Old-fashioned glass. Add ice cubes. Serve with a lemon twist.

PALACE MARTINI

3   oz. Gin
1   tbsp. Dry Vermouth
1   tbsp. Cordial Medoc

Shake with ice and strain into a Martini glass.

PALE DEACON

1¼   oz. Gin
1¼   oz. Grapefruit Juice
½   tsp. Sugar

Shake with ice and strain into a cocktail glass.

PALISADES COCKTAIL

1   oz. Gin
1   oz. Cider
1   dash Angostura Bitters

Shake with ice and strain into a cocktail glass.

PALL MALL

1½   oz. Gin
½   oz. Sweet Vermouth
½   oz. Dry Vermouth
½   oz. White Creme de Menthe

Stir with ice and strain into an Old-fashioned glass. Add ice cubes.

PALM BEACH NO. 1

1½   oz. Gin
1½   tsp. Sweet Vermouth
1½   tsp. Grapefruit Juice

Shake with ice and strain into a cocktail glass.

PALM BEACH NO. 2

1   oz. Galliano
1   oz. Vodka
1   Egg White

Shake with ice and strain into a highball glass. Fill with soda and ice. Serve with a lime wedge.

PALMER COCKTAIL

2   oz. Bourbon or Rye Whisky
1   dash Bitters
½   tsp. Lemon Juice

Stir with ice and strain into a cocktail glass.

PALMETTO NO. 1

1½   oz. Light Rum
1½   oz. Sweet Vermouth
2   dashes Orange Bitters

Stir with ice and strain into a cocktail glass. Serve with a lemon twist.

PALMETTO NO. 2

1¼   oz. Rum
1¼   oz. Dry Vermouth
2   dashes Bitters

Stir with ice and strain into a cocktail glass.

PALMETTO NO. 3

¾   oz. Rum
¾   oz. Apricot-flavored Brandy
½   oz. Cointreau
½   oz. Lime Juice

Shake with ice and strain into a cocktail glass.

PALMS

1½   oz. Gin
½   oz. Dry Vermouth
½   oz. Sweet Vermouth
¼   oz. Orange Curacao
½   Egg White

Shake with ice and strain into a cocktail glass.

PANACHE

Fill a Collins glass with:

½   Beer
½   Lemonade

PANAMA

1½   oz. Dark Rum
¾   oz. Creme de Cacao
¾   oz. Heavy Cream

Shake with ice and strain into a cocktail glass.

PANAMA COCKTAIL

1   oz. Creme de Cacao
1   oz. Sweet Cream
1   oz. Brandy

Shake with ice and strain into a cocktail glass.

PANAMA COOLER

1   oz. Orange Juice
¼   oz. Lime Juice
2   oz. Rhine Wine
2   oz. Dry Sherry
½   oz. Maraschino Liqueur
1   dash Angostura Bitters

Shake with ice and strain into a Collins glass. Fill with soda and ice. Serve with a lemon wedge.

PAN AMERICAN

¼   Lemon, peeled
1   tsp. Sugar
1½   oz. Rye Whisky

Muddle the lemon and sugar in an Old-fashioned glass, fill the glass with ice and add Whisky.

PANCHO VILLA

1	oz. Light Rum
1	oz. Gin
1	oz. Apricot-flavored Brandy
1	tsp. Cherry-flavored Brandy
1	tsp. Pineapple Juice

Shake with ice and strain into a cocktail glass.

PANSY

1½	oz. Pernod
½	oz. Grenadine
2	dashes Angostura Bitters

Shake with ice and strain into a cocktail glass.

PANTHER

1½	oz. Tequila

Pour into an Old-fashioned glass. Top with lemon mix. Fill with ice if desired.

PANTHER'S BREATH

½	oz. Orange Curacao
½	oz. Cream

Pour carefully, in order given, into a pony glass so that each ingredient floats on the preceding one without mixing. Add 1 drop of Angostura Bitters.

PANTOMIME

1½	oz. Dry Vermouth
1	dash Grenadine
1	dash Orgeat Syrup
1	Egg White

Shake with ice and strain into a cocktail glass.

PANZERWAGEN

1	oz. Vodka
1	oz. Gin
1	oz. Cointreau

Shake with ice and strain into a cocktail glass. Add ice.

PAPAYA COCKTAIL

1½	oz. Papaya Juice
1	oz. Sherry

Shake with ice and strain into a cocktail glass.

PAPAYA SLING

Juice 1 Lime	
1½	oz. Gin
1	dash Bitters
1	tbsp. Papaya Syrup

Shake with ice and strain into a highball glass. Add ice cubes, fill with soda and stir. Serve with a pineapple stick.

PARACHUTE PUNCH

1½	oz. Brandy
1½	oz. Kirschwasser
1½	oz. Coffee
1	Egg White

Shake with ice and strain into a Collins glass. Fill with soda and ice.

PARADISE COCKTAIL NO. 1

1	oz. Apricot-flavored Brandy
¾	oz. Gin
Juice ¼ Orange	

Shake with ice and strain into a cocktail glass.

PARADISE COCKTAIL NO. 2

1¼	oz. Rum
1¼	oz. Apricot-flavored Brandy

Stir with ice and strain into a cocktail glass.

Here's to the sparkling wine;
Here's to your sweetheart
  and mine;
May he be faithful and she
  be true.
Say, I'd leave my happy
  home for you.

PARADISE COOLER

1	oz. White Rum
1	oz. Orange Juice
2	tsp. Falernum
1	tsp. Cherry-flavored Brandy
1½	tsp. Lime Juice

Shake with ice and strain into a Collins glass. Garnish with mint sprigs dipped in powdered sugar and a cherry. Serve with straws.

PARDO BAR COCKTAIL

1½	oz. Rum
1	dash Amer Picon
1	dash Pernod

Shake with ice and strain into a cocktail glass.

PARFAIT AMOUR COCKTAIL

1½	oz. Parfait Amour
1½	oz. Gin
1	dash Maraschino Liqueur

Shake with ice and strain into a cocktail glass.

PARIS

¾	oz. Gin
¾	oz. Grand Marnier
½	oz. Cherry Liqueur
½	oz. Lemon Juice

Shake with ice and strain into a cocktail glass.

PARIS BY NIGHT

1	oz. Pernod
1	oz. Strega
½	oz. Amsterdam

Pour into a highball glass. Top with lemonade. Serve with an orange slice and a cherry.

PARISETTE

½ oz. Grenadine
Cold Milk

Pour Grenadine into a highball glass and fill with cold milk and ice.

PARISIAN

1 oz. Gin
1 oz. Dry Vermouth
½ oz. Creme de Cassis

Shake with ice and strain into a cocktail glass.

PARISIAN BLONDE COCKTAIL

¾ oz. sweet Cream
¾ oz. Triple Sec or Orange Curacao
¾ oz. Dark Rum

Shake with ice and strain into a cocktail glass.

PARISIEN

1/5 oz. Framboise
1/5 oz. Maraschino Liqueur
1/5 oz. Orange Curacao
1/5 oz. Green Chartreuse
1/5 oz. Champagne

Pour carefully, in order given, into a pony glass so that each ingredient floats on the preceding one without mixing.

PARIS MIDI

1 oz. Cognac
¾ oz. Cordial Medoc
¾ oz. Orange Juice

Shake with ice and strain into a cocktail glass. Float ½ oz. Champagne on top.

PARK AVENUE

1½ oz. Gin
¾ oz. Sweet Vermouth
1 tbsp. Pineapple Juice

Stir with ice and strain into a cocktail glass.

PARLOR PUNCH

12 Lemons
2 lb. Sugar
2 tbsp. English Breakfast or Darjeeling Tea
1 cup Dark Rum
1 cup Raspberry Syrup
Club Soda (optional)

Grate the rinds of 3 lemons into the sugar. Add 1 quart of water and bring to boil over high heat. Boil for 15 minutes and strain. When cool add the juice of the 12 lemons. Pour 1 pint of boiling water over the tea and steep for ½ hour. Strain into the sweetened lemon mixture. Refrigerate overnight. When ready to serve, add Rum and Raspberry Syrup and blend well. Put 2 or 3 ice cubes in 10-oz. tumblers and fill with punch, or punch and a dash of soda. Makes about 20 servings.

PASSENGER LIST

¾ oz. Brandy
¾ oz. Gin
½ oz. Parfait Amour
½ oz. Yellow Chartreuse
1 dash Pernod

Shake with ice and strain into a cocktail glass.

PASSION

½ oz. Dark Rum
1 oz. Light Rum
1 oz. Lime Juice
1 oz. Honey

Shake with ice and strain into a cocktail glass.

PASSION DAIQUIRI COCKTAIL

Juice 1 Lime
1½ oz. Light Rum
1 tsp. Powdered Sugar
1 tbsp. Passion Fruit Juice

Shake with ice and strain into a cocktail glass.

PASSION FRUIT COOLER

1 oz. Orange Juice
½ oz. Lemon Juice
½ oz. Gin
1½ oz. Rum
2 oz. Passion Fruit Nectar

Shake with ice and strain into a Collins glass. Fill with ice.

PASSIPE COCKTAIL

1 oz. Dry Vermouth
1½ oz. Gin
Juice 1 Orange

Shake with ice and strain into a cocktail glass.

PAT BRA

1½ oz. Gin
½ oz. Sweet Vermouth
¼ oz. Maraschino Liqueur
¼ oz. Lime Juice

Shake with ice and strain into a cocktail glass.

PATIO COCKTAIL

1½ oz. Gin
1 tbsp. Dry Vermouth
1 tbsp. Sweet Vermouth
1-2 drops Cointreau

Shake with ice and strain into a cocktail glass.

PATIO RETREAT

3 Ice cubes
1 tsp. Benedictine
1 tsp. Orange-flavored Liqueur
1 tsp. Brandy
4 oz. Burgundy
Extra Dry Champagne, chilled
Fresh Fruit

Put ice cubes in a Collins glass. Add Benedictine, Orange-flavored liqueur, Brandy and Burgundy. Fill with Champagne. Stir. Garnish with fresh fruit.

PATRICK GAVIN DUFFY'S PUNCH

3	oz. Brandy
1½	oz. Benedictine
½	tsp. Sugar
2½	oz. Orange Juice

Shake with ice and strain into a Collins glass. Fill with ice. Serve with mint sprigs.

PAT'S SPECIAL

¾	oz. Gin
¾	oz. Sherry
¾	oz. Quinquina
¼	oz. Creme de Cassis
¼	oz. Apricot-flavored Brandy

Shake with ice and strain into a cocktail glass. Serve with an orange peel and a cherry.

PAULA STAFFORD

½	oz. Gin
1	oz. Pimm's No. 1
1	oz. Cleopatra

Shake with ice and strain into a cocktail glass.

PAULINE

1¼	oz. Rum
1	oz. Lemon Juice
½	tsp. Sugar
¼	oz. Pernod

Shake with ice and strain into a cocktail glass. Sprinkle nutmeg on top.

PAVILLON SPECIAL

1	oz. Gin
½	oz. Sweet Vermouth
½	oz. Dry Vermouth
½	oz. Cherry Brandy
½	oz. Kirschwasser
2	dashes Orange Bitters

Stir with ice and strain into a cocktail glass. Serve with a twist of orange peel and a cherry.

PEACH AND HONEY COCKTAIL

1	tsp. Honey
1½	oz. Peach-flavored Brandy

Shake with ice and strain into a cocktail glass.

PEACH BLOSSOM

1	tsp. Lemon Juice
½	tsp. Powdered Sugar
2	oz. Gin
½	Peach

Shake with ice and strain into a highball glass. Add ice cubes, fill with soda and stir.

PEACH BLOW

1½	oz. Peach-flavored Brandy
¼	oz. Grenadine
½	oz. Lemon Juice
½	oz. Cream

Shake with ice and strain into a highball glass. Fill with soda and ice.

PEACH BLOW FIZZ NO. 1

	Juice ½ Lemon
1	Egg White
2	tsp. Grenadine
½	tsp. Powdered Sugar
1	oz. sweet Cream
2	oz. Gin

Shake with ice and strain into a highball glass. Add ice cubes, fill with soda and stir.

Sparkling and bright in the
  liquid light
Does the wine of our goblets
  gleam in,
With hue as red as the rosy
  bed
Which a bee would choose
  to dream in.

PEACH BLOW FIZZ NO. 2

1½	oz. Gin
½	oz. Strawberry Liqueur
½	oz. Lemon Juice
½	tsp. Sugar
½	oz. Cream

Shake with ice and strain into a highball glass. Fill with soda and ice. Serve with a lemon wedge and a fresh strawberry.

PEACH BLOW FIZZ NO. 3

1½	oz. Gin
¾	oz. Cream
1	tsp. Sugar
4	fresh Strawberries (or fresh Peach slices)
1	oz. Lemon Juice
½	oz. Lime Juice

Shake with ice and strain into a highball glass. Fill with soda and ice.

PEACH BOWL

1	fresh Peach
6	oz. chilled Champagne

Place the peach in a highball glass, prick several times to release the flavor, and cover with chilled Champagne. The peach may be eaten after the drink is finished. (A brandied peach may be used—pour ½ oz. peach syrup over it.)

PEACH BRANDY JULEP

6	sprigs Mint
1	tsp. Water
2	oz. Cognac
¾	oz. Peach-flavored Brandy

In a highball glass muddle 3 mint sprigs with the water. Fill the glass one-third full with crushed ice and add the remaining mint sprigs. Add Cognac and the Brandy. Decorate with a mint sprig and a peach slice.

PEACH BUCK

1½ oz. Vodka
½ oz. Peach-flavored Brandy
½ oz. Lemon Juice

Mix in a highball glass. Fill with ginger ale and ice. Serve with a lemon wedge and peach slice.

PEACH BUNNY

¾ oz. Peach-flavored Brandy
¾ oz. White Creme de Cacao
¾ oz. Light Cream

Shake with ice and strain into a cocktail glass.

PEACH COCKTAIL NO. 1

1½ oz. Peach-flavored Brandy
¾ oz. Dry Vermouth
¼ oz. Grenadine

Shake with ice and strain into a cocktail glass.

PEACH COCKTAIL NO. 2

1 fresh Peach, peeled
Pink Champagne, chilled

Place peach in a pre-chilled large goblet. Pierce the peach with a fork until it is well perforated. Fill the goblet with Pink Champagne.

PEACH DAIQUIRI

2 oz. Light Rum
½ Peach, fresh, peeled or canned
1 tbsp. Lime Juice
1 tsp. Sugar

Blend with ice and serve, with short straws, in a large saucer champagne glass.

PEACH EXTRAVAGANZA

1 fresh Peach, peeled
2 oz. Brandy
8 oz. Extra Dry Champagne, chilled
1 Mint sprig

Place peach in a pre-chilled, large snifter. Pierce the peach with a fork until it is well-perforated, then pour Brandy over it. Add Champagne. Garnish with a mint sprig.

PEACH FLIP

2 oz. Vodka
1 oz. Almond Extract
3 tsp. Lemon Juice
2 ripe Peaches
3 oz. crushed Ice

Peel and dice the peaches and blend with the remaining ingredients at a high speed until smooth. Strain into a Collins glass.

PEACH SANGAREE

2 oz. Peach-flavored Brandy
1 tsp. Port

Put Brandy in a highball glass with ice cubes. Fill the glass with soda and stir, leaving enough room to float Port on top. Sprinkle nutmeg on top.

PEACH VELVET

½ oz. Peach-flavored Brandy

Pour into a highball glass. Place a peeled peach on the bottom of the glass. Fill with Champagne.

PEACHY PINK

1 small Peach, peeled and sliced
3 pieces of cracked Ice
1 dash Peach-flavored Brandy
3 oz. Pink Champagne, chilled

Place peach slices in a champagne glass. Add cracked ice, Peach-flavored Brandy and Champagne.

PEACHY RHINE CLASSIC

⅓ cup frozen Peaches, partially thawed
1 drop Almond Extract
1 dash Lemon Juice
6 oz. Rhine Wine, chilled

Blend until smooth and pour into a pre-chilled tall glass. Sprinkle nutmeg on top.

PEACOCK

1½ oz. Brandy
½ oz. Amer Picon
½ oz. Pernod

Shake with ice and strain into a cocktail glass.

PEACOCK ALLEY

2 oz. Rum
1 oz. Maple Syrup
Juice ½ Lime

Shake with ice and strain into a cocktail glass.

PEAR RICKEY

1½ oz. Pear Brandy
½ oz. Lime Juice

Mix in a highball glass. Leave lime shell in the glass. Fill with soda and ice and serve with pear slices.

PEBBLE BEACH COMBER

1½ oz. Grand Marnier
Juice ½ Orange

Shake with ice and strain into a champagne glass.

PECK

1½ oz. Gin
½ oz. Dry Vermouth
½ oz. Apricot-flavored Brandy

Stir with ice and strain into a cocktail glass.

PEDIATRICIAN

1 oz. Gin
½ oz. Grape Juice
¾ oz. Lemon Juice
½ oz. Grenadine

Shake with ice and strain into a cocktail glass.

PEGGY COCKTAIL

¾ oz. Dry Vermouth
1½ oz. Gin
¼ tsp. Pernod
¼ tsp. Dubonnet

Stir with ice and strain into a cocktail glass.

PEG O MY HEART COCKTAIL

¾ oz. Lime Juice
¾ oz. Rum
1 dash Grenadine

Shake with ice and strain into a cocktail glass.

PEGU CLUB COCKTAIL

1 dash Angostura Bitters
1 dash Orange Bitters
1 tsp. Lime Juice
¾ oz. Curacao
2 oz. Gin

Shake with ice and strain into a cocktail glass.

PEKING

1½ oz. Rum
½ oz. Lemon Juice
¼ oz. Grenadine
¼ oz. Pernod

Shake with ice and strain into a cocktail glass.

PEKING EXPRESS

½ oz. Cointreau
1 oz. Gin
1 Egg White
1 drop Creme de Menthe

Shake with ice and strain into a cocktail glass.

PENANG

¾ oz. Gin
1½ oz. Pineapple Juice
½ oz. Green Creme de Menthe

Pack a cocktail glass with ice and add all ingredients.

PENDENNIS NO. 1

1½ oz. Gin
¾ oz. Peach-flavored Brandy
1 dash Peach Bitters
1 oz. Lemon or Lime Juice

Shake with ice and strain into a cocktail glass.

PENDENNIS NO. 2

1 oz. Gin
¾ oz. Apricot-flavored Brandy
¾ oz. Dry Vermouth

Shake with ice and strain into a cocktail glass.

PENDENNIS EGGNOG

1 bottle Bourbon
1 lb. superfine Sugar
12 Eggs, separated
2 quarts Heavy Cream
Nutmeg

Pour the Bourbon into a bowl and stir in the sugar. Set aside for 2 hours. Beat the egg yolks until light and then slowly beat in the Bourbon. Set aside for another 2 hours. When ready to serve, beat the cream until stiff; beat the egg whites until they stand in peaks. Pour the Bourbon mixture into a punch bowl and fold in the cream, then the egg whites. Grate a little nutmeg on top. Serve in punch glasses. Makes about 30 servings.

PENDENNIS TODDY

1 lump Sugar
2 oz. Bourbon

Muddle sugar with 1 tsp. water in a Sour glass. Fill with ice and add Bourbon. Decorate with two slices of lemon.

PENNSYLVANIA

2 oz. Rum
½ oz. Pineapple Juice
1 dash Grenadine

Shake with ice and strain into a cocktail glass.

PENSACOLA

1½ oz. Rum
½ oz. Guava Nectar
½ oz. Orange Juice
½ oz. Lemon Juice
3 oz. crushed Ice

Blend at low speed for 15 seconds and strain into an Old-fashioned glass.

PEOPLE EATER

1 oz. 151-proof Rum
¼ oz. Lime Juice

Mix in a highball glass. Fill with 7-Up and ice and add a squeeze of lime.

PEPPERMINT FIZZ

2 oz. Peppermint Chocolate
1 oz. fresh Cream
Ginger Beer
Creme de Menthe

Pour chocolate and cream into a highball glass. Top with ginger beer. Float Creme de Menthe. Decorate with a cherry and sprinkle chocolate on top.

PEPPERMINT ICEBERG

2 oz. Peppermint Vodka

Pour Vodka over ice cubes into an Old-fashioned glass. Stir and serve with a peppermint-candy swizzle stick.

PEPPERMINT PATTIE

1 oz. White Creme de Cacao
1 oz. White Creme de Menthe

Shake with ice and strain into an Old-fashioned glass. Add ice cubes.

PEPPERMINT STICK NO. 1

1 oz. Peppermint Vodka
1½ oz. White Creme de Cacao
1 oz. sweet Cream

Shake with ice and strain into a champagne glass.

PEPPERMINT STICK NO. 2

1½ oz. Brandy
½ oz. Orange Curacao
½ oz. Peppermint Schnapps
1 dash Orange Bitters

Shake with ice and strain into a cocktail glass.

PEPPER TREE PUNCH

1½ oz. White Rum
1 tbsp. Dark Rum
1 tbsp. Lime Juice
2 tsp. Sugar
1-2 dashes Angostura Bitters
1 pinch Cinnamon
1 pinch Cayenne Pepper

Shake with ice and strain into a Collins glass. Add ice.

PERFECT COCKTAIL

1½ tsp. Dry Vermouth
1½ tsp. Sweet Vermouth
1½ oz. Gin
1 dash Bitters

Stir with ice and strain into a cocktail glass.

PERFECTION

1¾ oz. Gin
½ oz. Sweet Vermouth
¼ oz. Orange Juice

Shake with ice and strain into a cocktail glass.

PERFECT LADY

1 oz. Gin
½ oz. Peach-flavored Brandy
½ oz. Lemon Juice
1 tsp. Egg White

Shake with ice and strain into a cocktail glass.

PERFECT MARTINI

1½ oz. Gin
2 tsp. Dry Vermouth
2 tsp. Sweet Vermouth

Shake with ice and strain into a Martini glass. Serve with an olive.

PERFECTO

1¾ oz. Bourbon Whisky
½ oz. Dry Vermouth
¼ oz. Sweet Vermouth
1 dash Orange Bitters
1 dash Angostura Bitters

Stir with ice and strain into a cocktail glass.

PERFECT ROYAL

¾ oz. Gin
¾ oz. Dry Vermouth
¾ oz. Sweet Vermouth
¼ oz. Pernod

Stir with ice and strain into a cocktail glass. Serve with a green cherry.

PERIDOT

¾ oz. Gin
¾ oz. White Creme de Menthe
1 oz. Cream

Shake with ice and strain into a cocktail glass. Serve with a mint sprig.

PERNOD

2 oz. Pernod
½ oz. Water
1 dash Sugar Syrup
1 dash Angostura Bitters

Shake with ice and strain into a cocktail glass.

PERNOD CURACAO FRAPPE

2 tsp. Pernod
2 tsp. Curacao
2 tsp. Orange Juice
1 tsp. Lemon Juice

Stir well and pour over crushed ice in a cocktail glass. Serve with an orange slice.

PERNOD DRIP

1½ oz. Pernod
1 cube Sugar

Pour the Pernod into a cocktail glass. Place the sugar cube in a tea strainer above the glass, pack the strainer with crushed ice and wait until the ice melts, dissolves the sugar and drips into the Pernod. Stir gently and add ice to taste.

PERNOD FLIP NO. 1

1 oz. Pernod
½ oz. Cointreau
½ oz. Lemon Juice
1 Egg
1 tsp. Sugar

Shake with ice and strain into a flip glass. Sprinkle nutmeg on top.

PERNOD FLIP NO. 2

1½ oz. Pernod
1 oz. Heavy Cream
1 Egg White
2 tsp. Almond Extract
4 oz. crushed Ice

Blend at high speed for 5 seconds. Strain into an Old-fashioned glass.

PERNOD FRAPPE

1½ oz. Pernod
½ oz. Anisette
2 dashes Angostura Bitters

Shake with ice and strain into a cocktail glass.

PERNOD MARTINI

2 oz. Gin
½ oz. Dry Vermouth
1 dash Pernod

Stir with ice and strain into a cocktail glass.

PERNOD PARACHUTE

1½ oz. Pernod
3 oz. Cranberry Juice
3 oz. Pineapple Juice

Fill a Collins glass with crushed ice and pour in all ingredients.

PERPETUAL

1½ oz. Sweet Vermouth
1½ oz. Dry Vermouth
4 dashes Creme d'Yvette
2 dashes Creme de Cacao

Stir with ice and strain into a cocktail glass.

PERPIGNAN

¾ oz. Galliano
¾ oz. Dubonnet
¾ oz. Scotch Whisky
¾ oz. Vodka

Shake with ice and strain into a cocktail glass.

PERSONALITY

1½ oz. Gin
½ oz. Calvados
½ oz. Pernod
1 dash Angostura Bitters

Stir with ice and strain into a cocktail glass.

PET

1½ oz. Rum
¼ oz. Jamaica Rum
¼ oz. Cointreau
¼ oz. Grenadine
¼ oz. Lemon Juice

Shake with ice and strain into a cocktail glass.

PETER ARNO

1¼ oz. Gin
¾ oz. Apricot-flavored Brandy
½ oz. Lemon Juice
4 Mint sprigs

Shake with ice and strain into a cocktail glass.

PETER PAN COCKTAIL NO. 1

2 dashes Bitters
¾ oz. Orange Juice
¾ oz. Dry Vermouth
¾ oz. Gin

Shake with ice and strain into a cocktail glass.

PETER PAN COCKTAIL NO. 2

¾ oz. Gin
¾ oz. Dry Vermouth
¾ oz. Orange Juice
¾ oz. Peach-flavored Brandy

Shake with ice and strain into a cocktail glass.

> May we kiss whom we please,
> And please whom we kiss.

PETER TOWER

1½ oz. Brandy
½ oz. Light Rum
1 tsp. Grenadine
1 tsp. Curacao
1 tsp. Lemon Juice

Shake with ice and strain into a cocktail glass.

PETION

¾ oz. Rum
¾ oz. Benedictine
¾ oz. Clarion
¼ oz. Lime Juice
Sugar to taste

Shake with ice and strain into a cocktail glass.

PETO

1½ oz. Gin
¾ oz. Sweet Vermouth
¾ oz. Dry Vermouth
2 dashes Maraschino Liqueur
Juice ¼ Orange

Shake with ice and strain into a cocktail glass.

PHILADELPHIA COOLER

Mint sprigs
1 tsp. Sugar
Champagne

Fill a Collins glass with ice. Add several mint sprigs, sugar and fill with Champagne.

PHILADELPHIA FILLY

1 oz. Early Times
1 oz. Dark Creme de Cacao
1 oz. Cream

Blend with ice and strain into a cocktail glass.

PHILADELPHIAN

1   oz. Port
1   oz. Applejack
½   oz. Orange Juice

Shake with ice and strain into a cocktail glass. Fill with soda and ice.

PHILADELPHIA PUNCH

2   tsp. Powdered Sugar
1   dash Lemon Juice
1½   oz. Rum
¾   oz. Brandy

Stir with ice and strain into a cocktail glass. Garnish with fruit.

PHILADELPHIA SCOTCHMAN COCKTAIL

1½   oz. Applejack
1½   oz. Port
Juice 1 Orange

Mix in a highball glass. Fill with ginger ale and ice.

PHILIP BROWN'S PUNCH

4   bottles Dry White Wine
1   bottle Brandy
1   bottle Golden Rum
3   oz. frozen Lemonade
1   block Ice
2   quarts Club Soda

Mix the Wine, Brandy, Rum and lemonade concentrate in a punch bowl and allow to stand for about an hour. When ready to serve, add ice and the club soda. Stir lightly and serve in punch glasses. Makes about 50 servings.

PHILLY SPECIAL

1   oz. Bourbon Whisky
1   oz. Heavy Cream
1   oz. Dark Creme de Cacao

Shake with ice and strain into a cocktail glass.

PHILOMEL

2   oz. Sherry
¾   oz. Rum
1½   oz. Quinquina
1½   oz. Orange Juice
1   pinch Pepper

Shake with ice and strain into an Old-fashioned glass.

PHOEBE SNOW COCKTAIL

1½   oz. Dubonnet
1½   oz. Brandy
½   tsp. Pernod

Stir with ice and strain into a cocktail glass.

PHOENIX BIRD

1   oz. Early Times
½   oz. Creme de Bananes
½   oz. Triple Sec
1   oz. Cream

Blend with ice and strain into a cocktail glass.

PHOTO FINISH

1½   oz. Rum
¾   oz. Curacao
Juice ½ Lime

Shake with ice and strain into an Old-fashioned glass. Serve with a lime wheel.

PHYLLIS

1   oz. Brandy
½   oz. Orange Curacao
½   oz. Maraschino Liqueur
½   oz. Lemon Juice

Shake with ice and strain into a cocktail glass.

PICADOR

2   oz. Tequila
1   oz. Kahlua
½   cup crushed Ice

Stir with ice and strain into a cocktail glass. Serve with a lemon twist.

PICASSO

1½   oz. Cognac
½   oz. Dubonnet
½   oz. Lime Juice
1   tsp. Sugar

Shake with ice and strain into a cocktail glass. Serve with a twist of orange peel.

PICCA

1½   oz. V.O.
½   oz. Galliano
½   oz. Punt e Mes

Stir with ice and strain into a cocktail glass. Serve with an orange peel and a cherry.

PICCADILLY COCKTAIL

¾   oz. Dry Vermouth
1½   oz. Gin
¼   tsp. Pernod
¼   tsp. Grenadine

Stir with ice and strain into a cocktail glass.

PICKEN'S PUNCH

¾   oz. Peach-flavored Brandy
¾   oz. Cherry Liqueur
¾   oz. White Creme de Menthe

Shake with ice and strain into a cocktail glass.

PICKFAIR

1½   oz. Brandy
½   oz. Cola
½   oz. Lemon Syrup

Shake with ice and strain into a cocktail glass.

PICK ME UP NO. 1

¾ oz. Cognac
¾ oz. Dry Vermouth
¾ oz. Pernod

Stir with ice and strain into a cocktail glass.

PICK ME UP NO. 2

1 dash Angostura Bitters
1 tsp. Sugar
2 oz. Brandy
6 oz. Milk

Shake with ice and strain into a highball glass. Add a squirt of soda.

PICK ME UP NO. 3

½ oz. Dubonnet
½ oz. Cognac
¾ oz. Anisette
1 Egg White

Shake with ice and strain into a cocktail glass. Serve with a lemon twist.

PICK ME UP NO. 4

2 oz. Brandy
¼ oz. Orange Curacao
¼ oz. Orange Juice

Shake with ice and strain into a highball glass. Fill with Champagne and ice. Float ¼ oz. Pernod on top.

PICKUP

1½ oz. Rye Whisky
¾ oz. Fernet Branca
3 dashes Pernod

Stir with ice and strain into a cocktail glass. Serve with a lemon wedge.

PICON NO. 1

1½ oz. Amer Picon
1½ oz. Dry Vermouth

Stir with ice and strain into a cocktail glass. (Sweet Vermouth may be used instead of Dry Vermouth.)

PICON NO. 2

1½ oz. Amer Picon
½ oz. Lime Juice
½ oz. Grenadine

Stir with ice and strain into a cocktail glass.

PICON CURACAO HIGHBALL

1½ oz. Amer Picon
½ oz. Orange Curacao

Mix in a highball glass. Fill with soda and ice.

PICON GRENADINE

1½ oz. Amer Picon
¾ oz. Grenadine

Shake with ice and strain into an Old-fashioned glass. Fill with soda and ice.

PICON ME

1½ oz. Amer Picon
½ oz. Lemon Juice
Squirt of soda

Pour into an Old-fashioned glass. Fill with ice. Serve with a lemon wedge.

PICON PICON

1½ oz. Amer Picon
1½ oz. chilled, fresh Orange Juice

Shake with ice and strain into a cocktail glass. Add chilled soda.

PICON POMPIER COCKTAIL

1½ oz. Amer Picon
½ oz. Grenadine

Pour into a highball glass. Fill with soda and ice.

PICON PUNCH NO. 1

1½ oz. Amer Picon
¼ oz. Grenadine

Pour into a highball glass. Fill with soda and ice. Float ½ oz. Cognac on top. Serve with a lemon twist.

PICON PUNCH NO. 2

1½ oz. Amer picon
½ oz. Grenadine
½ oz. Lemon Juice

Pour into a highball glass. Fill with soda and ice. Serve with a lemon twist.

PICON PUNCH NO. 3

1½ oz. Amer Picon
½ oz. Lime Juice

Pour into a highball glass. Fill with ginger ale and ice. Serve with a squeeze of lime.

PICON WHISKY

1¼ oz. Whisky
1¼ oz. Amer Picon
¼ tsp. Sugar

Stir with ice and strain into a cocktail glass. Serve with a lemon twist.

PIKAKI

2 oz. Jamaica Rum
¼ oz. Orange Juice
¼ oz. Lemon Juice
1 dash Grenadine

Shake with a pineapple spear and ice. Strain into a cocktail glass.

PIKE'S PEAK COCKTAIL

Juice ½ Lemon
1 tsp. Powdered Sugar
1 Egg

Shake with ice and strain into a Collins glass over cracked ice. Fill with cider and stir. Add a twist of orange or lemon peel (or both) and dangle end over rim of glass.

> What harm in drinking can
>   there be,
> Since punch and life so well
>   agree?

PILGRIM COCKTAIL

1½ oz. Rum
½ oz. Lemon Juice
½ oz. Cointreau
½ tsp. Sugar

Shake with ice and strain into a cocktail glass.

PILGRIM HOT BUTTERED RUM

2 oz. Jamaica Rum
Cloves, Cinnamon stick
Lemon twist

Put into a mug or Old-fashioned glass. Fill with hot cider. Float a pat of butter on top.

PIMM'S CUP

1 thin slice Lemon
1 small piece Cucumber Peel
2 oz. Pimm's No. 1, 2 or 3
Lemon soda, Tom Collins mix or soda

Place ice, lemon slice and cucumber peel in a highball glass. Add Pimm's mixture, fill with one of the three mixers and stir gently. If you use club soda, add 2 tbsp. lemon juice and a tsp. of sugar syrup.

PINA COLADA

2 oz. Golden Rum
2 oz. Coconut Cream
4 oz. Pineapple Juice
Coconut Snow

Blend the first three ingredients with crushed ice and strain into a Collins glass. Add 1 tsp. Coconut Snow and serve with a pineapple spear and a cherry.

PINA FIZZ

1 cup crushed Ice
1½ oz. Light Rum
½ oz. Dark Rum
2 oz. Pineapple Juice
3 tbsp. Lime Juice
½ oz. Orgeat Syrup
½ oz. Falernum

Blend with ice and strain into a Collins glass. Serve with a pineapple spear.

PINA FRIA

1 oz. White Rum
2 oz. Pineapple Juice
1 oz. Lemon Juice
2 Pineapple rings, torn in pieces
3 oz. crushed Ice

Blend at high speed for 15 seconds. Strain into a Collins glass. Serve with mint and straws.

PINATA

1 oz. Tequila
1 tbsp. Banana Liqueur
1 oz. Lime Juice

Shake with ice and strain into a cocktail glass.

> Then fill tonight, with hearts
>   as light,
> To love as gay and fleeting,
> As bubbles that swim on the
>   beaker's rim,
> And break on the lips while
>   meeting.

PINCHGUT PERIL

½ oz. Gin
1 oz. Whisky
½ oz. Lime Juice
2 dashes Grenadine
½ slice Pineapple

Blend with ice and strain into a highball glass. Fill with crushed ice. Garnish with pineapple chunks and a slice of orange.

PINEAPPLE COCKTAIL NO. 1

¾ oz. Pineapple Juice
1½ oz. Light Rum
½ tsp. Lemon Juice

Shake with ice and strain into a cocktail glass.

PINEAPPLE COCKTAIL NO. 2

1½ oz. Gin
½ oz. Pineapple Juice
½ oz. Grenadine

Shake with ice and strain into a cocktail glass.

PINEAPPLE COOLER NO. 1

2 oz. Pineapple Juice
½ tsp. Powdered Sugar
2 oz. Soda
2 oz. Dry White Wine

Put pineapple juice, sugar and soda into a Collins glass. Stir, and add ice cubes and the Wine. Fill with soda and stir again. Place a twist of orange or lemon peel (or both) on the rim of glass.

PINEAPPLE COOLER NO. 2

1 oz. Galliano
1 oz. Lemon Juice
1¼ oz. Orange Juice
3 oz. Pineapple Juice
½ tsp. Sugar

Stir with ice and strain into a Collins glass. Fill with crushed ice.

PINEAPPLE DAIQUIRI

2 oz. Light Rum
½ oz. Cointreau
½ cup Pineapple Juice
1 tsp. Lime Juice

Blend with ice and strain into a champagne glass.

PINEAPPLE DELIGHT

1½ oz. Chablis
1½ oz. Sherry
2 oz. crushed Pineapple
1 tbsp. White Rum
2 tsp. Lime Juice
2 tsp. Cointreau

Mix without ice and refrigerate for several hours. Serve unstrained in a Collins glass and add ice. Decorate with pineapple chunks.

PINEAPPLE DREAM COCKTAIL

Juice ½ Lime
½ oz. Pineapple Juice
1 oz. Rum

Shake with ice and strain into a cocktail glass.

PINEAPPLE FIZZ NO. 1

1 oz. Pineapple Juice
½ tsp. Powdered Sugar
2 oz. Light Rum or Gin
1 dash Lime Juice

Shake with ice and strain into a highball glass. Add two ice cubes, fill with soda and stir.

PINEAPPLE FIZZ NO. 2

1 oz. Pineapple Juice
1½ oz. Rum
¼ tsp. Sugar

Shake with ice and strain into a highball glass. Fill with soda and ice.

PINEAPPLE LEMONADE

2 slices Pineapple, coarsely chopped
1 tsp. Sugar
1½ oz. Brandy
1 dash Raspberry Syrup

Muddle the pineapple and sugar thoroughly in a cocktail shaker. Add Brandy, raspberry syrup and some crushed ice. Shake and strain into a highball glass. Fill with soda and decorate with a lemon peel and a pineapple stick.

PINEAPPLE MINT COOLER

1½ oz. Gin
½ oz. White Creme de Menthe
3 oz. Pineapple Juice
1 oz. Lemon Juice

Shake with ice and strain into a Collins glass. Fill with Squirt and ice. Serve with a pineapple stick and a cherry.

PINEAPPLE MIST

2 oz. crushed Pineapple
1 oz. crushed Ice
1½ oz. Light Rum

Put the pineapple and ice in an Old-fashioned glass and mix lightly. Pour in the Rum and decorate with a cherry.

PINEAPPLE-OKOLEHAO PUNCH

1 block Ice
2 bottles chilled Okolehao
1½ quarts chilled Pineapple Juice
1 cup chilled Lemon Juice
1 pint chilled Club Soda
Strawberries

Put the ice in a punch bowl and add all ingredients except strawberries. Stir lightly, then garnish with the berries. Serve in punch glasses. Makes about 30 servings.

PINEAPPLE SANGAREE

4 oz. Claret or Bordeaux
1½ oz. Sugar
1 tbsp. Orange Juice
1 tsp. Lemon Juice
4 oz. crushed Pineapple

Shake with ice and chill for 1 hour. Strain into a highball glass. Fill with soda and ice. Sprinkle with allspice.

PINEAPPLE SUNRISE

1½ oz. Tequila
1½ oz. Pineapple Juice
1 tbsp. Grenadine
1½ tbsp. Lime Juice

Shake with ice and strain into an Old-fashioned glass. Decorate with a cherry and a slice of pineapple.

PINEAPPLE SWIZZLE COCKTAIL

Juice ½ Orange
1 dash Orange Bitters
3 oz. Sweet Vermouth

Shake with ice and strain into an Old-fashioned glass. Serve with a pineapple chunk on a swizzle stick.

> Let us drink and be merry,
> dance, joke, and rejoice,
> With claret and sherry,
> theorbo and voice!

PINE ROOM PIPPEN

1½   oz. Scotch Whisky
½   oz. Dubonnet
1   dash Angostura Bitters
¼   tsp. Sugar
Juice ½ Lemon

Shake with ice and strain into a cocktail glass.

PING PONG NO. 1

1½   oz. Sloe Gin
½   oz. Dry Vermouth
½   oz. Sweet Vermouth

Stir with ice and strain into a cocktail glass.

PING PONG NO. 2

½   oz. Lemon Juice
1   Egg White (optional)
1   oz. Sloe Gin
1   oz. Creme d'Yvette

Shake with ice and strain into a cocktail glass.

PING PONG NO. 3

1   oz. Sloe Gin
1   oz. Sweet Vermouth
½   oz. Orange Curacao
1   dash Angostura Bitters

Stir with ice and strain into a cocktail glass. Serve with a lemon twist and a cherry.

PINK ALMOND

½   oz. Creme de Noyaux
½   oz. Orgeat Syrup
1   oz. Blended Whisky
½   oz. Kirschwasser
½   oz. Lemon Juice

Shake with ice and strain into a cocktail glass. Serve with a lemon wedge.

PINK AND GOLD

1½   oz. frozen Pink Lemonade Concentrate
3½   oz. Chablis, chilled

Stir with ice and strain into a Collins glass. Add ice and a lemon slice.

PINK ANGEL

1   oz. Rum
½   oz. Advokaat
½   oz. Cherry-flavored Brandy
1   Egg White
1   oz. fresh Cream

Shake with ice and strain into a champagne glass.

PINK BABY

1½   oz. Gin
¾   oz. Grenadine
¾   oz. Sirop de Citron
1   Egg White

Shake with ice and strain into a cocktail glass.

PINK CALIFORNIA SUNSHINE

4   oz. chilled Pink Champagne
4   oz. chilled Orange Juice
1   dash Creme de Cassis

Pour the Champagne into a champagne glass. Add orange juice and Cassis.

PINK CHAMPAGNE COCKTAIL

1   Sugar cube
1   dash Aromatic Bitters
1   small Ice cube
Pink Champagne, chilled

Rub sugar cube along the side of a ripe lemon, scraping off as much lemon oil onto the cube as possible. Place the sugar in a champagne glass and dash Bitters on it. Add the ice cube. Fill the glass with Pink Champagne. Stir gently until sugar is dissolved. Add a twist of lemon.

PINK CREOLE

1½   oz. Rum
1   tbsp. Lime Juice
1   tsp. Grenadine
1   tsp. sweet Cream

Shake with ice and strain into a cocktail glass. Add a black cherry soaked in Rum.

PINK DEATH

1   oz. Light Cuban Rum
1   oz. 151-proof Rum
1   tsp. Cointreau
1   dash Lime Juice
¼   Peach (fresh or canned)

Shake with ice and strain into a large cocktail glass. Serve with a cherry.

PINK ELEPHANT

¾   oz. Vodka
¾   oz. Galliano
¾   oz. Creme de Noyaux or Almond Liqueur
¾   oz. fresh Orange Juice
¾   oz. fresh Cream
1   dash Grenadine

Shake with ice and strain into a champagne glass. Dust with cinnamon.

PINK GARTER NO. 1

1½   oz. Gin
¼   oz. Lemon Juice
¼   oz. Orange Juice
½   oz. Grenadine

Shake with ice and strain into a cocktail glass.

PINK GARTER NO. 2

1½   oz. Gin
½   oz. Lemon Juice
½   oz. Grenadine
1   dash Angostura Bitters

Shake with ice and strain into a highball glass. Fill with soda and ice. Serve with a lemon twist.

PINK GIN

2 dashes Angostura Bitters
2 oz. Gin
2 oz. Water or
2-3 cubes Ice

Pour Bitters into an 8 oz. wine glass and stir. Add Gin and dilute with water or add ice cubes.

PINK GOODY

¾ oz. Gin
¾ oz. Rum
¾ oz. Lemon Juice
¼ oz. Maraschino Liqueur

Shake with ice and strain into a cocktail glass. (Pineapple spear optional.)

PINK LADY NO. 1

1½ oz. Gin
1½ oz. Calvados or Applejack
1 tbsp. Grenadine
3 tbsp. Lemon Juice
1 Egg White

Shake with ice and strain into a cocktail glass.

PINK LADY NO. 2

1 Egg White
1 tsp. Grenadine
1 tsp. Sweet Cream
1½ oz. Gin

Shake with ice and strain into a cocktail glass.

PINK LADY NO. 3

1 oz. Cream
1 oz. Gin
½ oz. Grenadine

Shake with ice and strain into a cocktail glass.

PINK LADY NO. 4

1½ oz. Gin
½ oz. Lemon Juice
½ oz. Grenadine
1 Egg White

Shake with ice and strain into a cocktail glass.

PINK LADY FIZZ

1½ oz. Gin
½ oz. Lemon Juice
½ oz. Grenadine
1 Egg White

Shake with ice and strain into a Collins glass. Fill with soda and ice.

PINK LEMONADE

3 oz. Rose Wine
2 oz. Orange Juice
2 oz. Lemon Juice
½ oz. Kirschwasser
2 tsp. Sugar

Mix in a Collins glass. Fill with ice, water or soda. Serve with a lemon wedge and a cherry.

PINK MINTIE

1 oz. Fresh Cream
1 dash Grenadine
1 oz. Creme de Menthe

Shake with ice and strain into a cocktail glass.

PINK PEARL

1½ oz. Grapefruit Juice
¼ oz. Lemon Juice
½ oz. Grenadine
½ Egg White
1½ oz. Rum

Shake with ice and strain into a cocktail glass.

PINK PICON

1½ oz. Amer Picon
½ oz. Grenadine

Mix in a highball glass. Fill with soda and ice.

PINK PUSSY CAT

1½ oz. Vodka or Gin
Pineapple or Grapefruit Juice
1 dash Grenadine

Into a highball glass almost filled with ice, put Vodka or Gin. Fill balance of glass with juice. Add Grenadine for color and stir.

PINK ROSE

1 oz. Gin
1 tsp. Grenadine
1 tsp. Lemon Juice
1 tsp. Cream
1 Egg White

Shake with ice and strain into a cocktail glass.

PINK ROSE FIZZ

Juice ½ Lemon
1 tsp. Powdered Sugar
1 Egg White
2 tsp. Sweet Cream
2 oz. Gin

Shake with ice and strain into a highball glass. Add two ice cubes, fill with soda and stir.

PINK RUM AND TONIC

1½ oz. Rum
½ oz. Lime Juice
¼ oz. Grenadine

Shake with ice and strain into a Collins glass. Fill with tonic and ice. Serve with a lime wheel.

PINK SPARKLE

4 oz. Pink Chablis, chilled
4 oz. Citrus Mixer, chilled
Mint Leaf

Fill a Collins glass two-thirds full with ice. Pour in Chablis and mixer. Decorate with a mint leaf.

PINK SQUIRREL

1   oz. Creme de Noyaux
1   tbsp. White Creme de Cacao
1   tbsp. Sweet Cream

Shake with ice and strain into a cocktail glass.

PINK TOP

1½   oz. Gin
¾   oz. Grand Marnier
¼   oz. Lemon Juice
1   dash Grenadine

Shake with ice and strain into a cocktail glass.

PINK TREAT

2   oz. Pink Grapefruit Juice
2   oz. Brandy
2   oz. Sweet Vermouth

Have all ingredients well chilled. Pour into a pre-chilled highball glass. Stir.

PINK VERANDA

1   oz. Gold Rum
½   oz. Dark Jamaica Rum
1½   oz. Cranberry Juice
½   oz. Lime Juice
1   tsp. Sugar
½   Egg White

Shake with ice and strain into a cocktail glass.

PINK WHISKERS

¾   oz. Apricot-flavored Brandy
¾   oz. Dry Vermouth
2   dashes White Creme de Menthe
1   tsp. Grenadine
2   tbsp. Orange Juice

Shake with ice and strain into a cocktail glass. Float 1 oz. Port Wine on top.

PINKY

1½   oz. Gin
1½   oz. Grenadine
1   Egg White

Shake with ice and strain into a cocktail glass.

PINO FRIO

1½   oz. Gold Rum
1   tsp. Sugar
½   oz. Pineapple Juice
Several Pineapple pieces

Shake with ice and strain into a Collins glass. Fill with soda and ice.

PINO ROYAL

1   oz. Passion Fruit Juice
1   oz. Orange Juice
¼   slice fresh Pineapple
1   dash Grenadine
1   oz. Lemon Juice
1½   oz. Gold Rum
½   oz. 86-proof Demerara Rum

Blend with ice and strain into a Collins glass.

PINOT COBBLER

1½   tbsp. Sugar
2   oz. chilled Soda
3   oz. White Pinot, chilled

Place sugar and soda in a Collins glass. Stir until sugar is dissolved. Fill the glass with crushed ice. Pour in Wine. Stir gently. Garnish with fresh fruit and mint. Serve with straws.

PIONEER

2   oz. Jamaica Rum
2   tsp. Lime Juice
2   drops Orange Curacao
2   drops Grenadine

Shake with ice and strain into a cocktail glass. Add ice.

PIRATE'S NO. 1

1½   oz. Dark Rum
¾   oz. Sweet Vermouth
1   dash Angostura Bitters

Shake with ice and strain into a cocktail glass.

PIRATE'S NO. 2

¾   oz. Rum
¾   oz. Cognac
½   oz. Grenadine
½   oz. Lemon Juice

Shake with ice and strain into a cocktail glass.

PIROUETTER

1   oz. Gin
½   oz. Grand Marnier
1   oz. Orange Juice
¼   oz. Lemon Juice

Shake with ice and strain into a cocktail glass. Serve with a lemon twist.

PISCO PUNCH

1   Ice cube
1   tsp. Lime Juice
1   tsp. Pineapple Juice
1   cube Pineapple
3   oz. Pisco (Peruvian) Brandy

Place in a highball glass. Fill with iced water and stir.

PISCO SOUR

2   oz. Pisco
1   tsp. Sugar
1   tsp. Lime or Lemon Juice
1   tbsp. Egg White

Shake with ice and strain into a cocktail glass. Shake 2-3 dashes Angostura Bitters on top.

PLAIN SHERRY COCKTAIL

2 oz. Sherry
2 dashes Maraschino Liqueur
2 dashes Pernod

Shake with ice and strain into a cocktail glass.

PLAIN VERMOUTH

2 oz. Dry Vermouth
¼ oz. Maraschino Liqueur
¼ oz. Pernod

Stir with ice and strain into a cocktail glass. Serve with a cherry.

PLANTATION COFFEE

1 cup Iced Coffee
4 oz. Brandy
1 small Banana, sliced

Combine in blender at high speed until smooth. Serve straight up in a mug.

PLANTATION PUNCH NO. 1

2 oz. Planter's Punch Rum
1 oz. Puerto Rican Dark Rum
½ oz. Barbados Rum
2 oz. Ginger Beer
2 oz. frozen Pineapple Juice
2 dashes Bitters
2 dashes Pernod
Juice 1 Lime

Shake with ice and strain into a Collins glass. Decorate with a slice of lemon, orange and pineapple, and a cherry. Serve with straws.

Here's to you my dear,
And to the dear that's not
    here, my dear;
But if the dear that's not
    here, my dear,
Were here, my dear,
I'd not be drinking to you,
    my dear.

PLANTATION PUNCH NO. 2

1½ oz. Southern Comfort
½ oz. Lemon Juice
½ oz. Rum
½ tsp. Sugar

Mix in a double Old-fashioned glass. Fill with soda and ice. Serve with an orange peel (or a cherry) and an orange slice.

PLANTER'S NO. 1

1½ oz. Light or Golden Rum
1½ oz. Orange Juice
1 dash Lemon Juice

Shake with ice and strain into a cocktail glass.

PLANTER'S NO. 2

½ oz. Lemon Juice
2 oz. Jamaica Rum
½ tsp. Sugar

Shake with ice and strain into a cocktail glass.

PLATINUM BLOND COCKTAIL

¾ oz. sweet Cream
¾ oz. Orange Curacao
1 oz. Rum

Shake with ice and strain into a cocktail glass. (Cointreau may be used instead of Orange Curacao.)

PLATOON

1¾ oz. Sweet Vermouth
½ oz. Gin
¼ oz. Orange Curacao

Stir with ice and strain into a cocktail glass.

PLAYBOY COOLER

1½ oz. Gold Rum
1¼ oz. Jamaican Coffee Liqueur
3 oz. Pineapple Juice
½ oz. Lemon Juice

Shake with ice and strain into a Collins glass. Fill with Cola and ice. Serve with a pineapple stick.

PLAZA COCKTAIL

¾ oz. Sweet Vermouth
¾ oz. Dry Vermouth
¾ oz. Gin

Shake with ice and strain into a cocktail glass. Add a strip of pineapple.

PLAZA MARTINI

1 tbsp. Gin
1 tbsp. Dry Vermouth
1 tbsp. Sweet Vermouth
1-2 drops Pineapple Juice

Shake with ice and strain into a Martini glass.

PLUIE d'OR

¾ oz. Gin
¾ oz. Vieille Cure
½ oz. Orange Curacao
½ oz. Kummel

Stir with ice and strain into a cocktail glass.

PLUM APERITIF

1½ oz. Dry Vermouth
½ oz. Cognac
½ oz. Prunelle

Stir with ice and strain into a cocktail glass. Serve with a lemon wedge.

PLUM BLOSSOMS

¾   oz. Dry Gin
¾   oz. Plum Brandy
⅛   oz. Grenadine
Juice ½ Lemon

Shake with ice and strain into a cocktail glass. Decorate with 2 small rose petals.

PLUM RICKEY

1½   oz. Plum Brandy
½   oz. Lime Juice

Mix in a highball glass. Leave lime shell in glass. Fill with soda and ice. Serve with a plum slice.

PLUSH HORSE COCKTAIL

1   dash Angostura Bitters
1   oz. Grand Marnier
2   oz. Gin

Shake with ice and strain into a cocktail glass.

PLYMOUTH COCKTAIL

2½   oz. Gin
2   dashes Orange Bitters

Stir with ice and strain into a cocktail glass.

POET'S DREAM

1   oz. Gin
¾   oz. Dry Vermouth
¾   oz. Benedictine

Stir with ice and strain into a cocktail glass. Serve with a lemon twist.

POKER COCKTAIL

1½   oz. Sweet Vermouth
1½   oz. Rum

Stir with ice and strain into a cocktail glass.

POLICHINELLE HIGHBALL

1½   oz. Creme de Cassis
¾   oz. Kirschwasser

Mix in a highball glass. Fill with soda and ice.

POLISH SIDECAR

¾   oz. Gin
¾   oz. Lemon Juice
1   oz. Polish Blackberry Liqueur

Shake with ice and strain into a cocktail glass. Float a fresh blackberry on top.

POLLYANNA COCKTAIL

3   slices Pineapple
3   slices Orange
2   oz. Gin
½   oz. Sweet Vermouth
½   tsp. Grenadine

Muddle all ingredients together. Shake with ice and strain into a cocktail glass.

POLLY OR POPPY

2   oz. Gin
1   oz. Creme de Cacao

Stir with ice and strain into a cocktail glass.

POLLY'S SPECIAL

1½   oz. Scotch Whisky
¾   oz. unsweetened Grapefruit Juice
¾   oz. Curacao

Shake with ice and strain into a cocktail glass.

> Oh, 'tis jesting, dancing, drinking
> Spins the heavy world around.
> — A. E. Housman

POLO COCKTAIL NO. 1

1   tbsp. Lemon Juice
1   tbsp. Orange Juice
1   oz. Gin

Shake with ice and strain into a cocktail glass.

POLO COCKTAIL NO. 2

1½   oz. Dark Rum
½   oz. Lemon Juice
½   oz. Orange Juice

Shake with ice and strain into a cocktail glass.

POLO COCKTAIL NO. 3

1   oz. Gin
½   oz. Dry Vermouth
½   oz. Sweet Vermouth
½   oz. Lime Juice

Shake with ice and strain into a cocktail glass.

POLO LOUNGE

½   oz. Rum
½   oz. Apricot-flavored Brandy
½   oz. Amer Picon

Shake with ice and strain into a Collins glass. Decorate with a slice of apple.

POLONAISE

1½   oz. Brandy
½   oz. Blackberry Liqueur
½   oz. Dry Sherry
¼   oz. Lemon Juice
2   dashes Orange Bitters

Shake with ice and strain into a cocktail glass.

POLYNESIA

1½   oz. Rum
1   oz. Passion Fruit Syrup
¼   oz. Lime Juice
½   Egg White

Shake with ice and strain into a cocktail glass.

POLYNESIAN APPLE

1¼   oz. Applejack
½   oz. Brandy
¾   oz. Pineapple Juice

Shake with ice and strain into a cocktail glass. Serve with a pineapple stick.

POLYNESIAN COCKTAIL

1½   oz. Vodka
¾   oz. Cherry-flavored Brandy
Juice 1 Lime

Rub the rim of a cocktail glass with lime and dip into powdered sugar. Shake above ingredients with ice and strain into the glass.

POLYNESIAN HURRICANE

¾   oz. Gin
1   oz. Brandy
¾   oz. Apricot-flavored Brandy
1   oz. Rum
1½   oz. Pineapple Juice
1½   oz. Orange Juice
1½   oz. Lemon Juice
1   tsp. Sugar

Shake with ice and strain into a double Old-fashioned glass.

POLYNESIAN PARADISE

1½   oz. Gold Rum
1   tsp. Brown Sugar
¾   oz. Lime Juice
½   oz. Sweet Vermouth
¼   oz. Triple Sec

Shake with ice and strain into a cocktail glass.

POLYNESIAN PICK ME UP

1½   oz. Vodka
¼   oz. Lemon Juice
½   oz. Cream
½   tsp. Curry Powder
2   dashes Tabasco Sauce
Several fresh Pineapple pieces

Shake with ice and strain into a cocktail glass. Sprinkle cayenne on top.

POLYNESIAN SLING

1   oz. Lemon Juice
½   tsp. Sugar
1½   oz. Gin
½   oz. Blackberry-flavored Brandy

Shake with ice and strain into a Collins glass. Fill with soda or 7-Up. Serve with a lemon wedge and a cherry.

POLYNESIAN SOUR

2   oz. White Rum
1   oz. Orange Juice
1½   tsp. Lemon Juice
1-2 drops Almond Extract
1-2 drops Rock Candy Syrup

Shake with ice and strain into a Sour glass. Add ice. Serve with a mint sprig.

POMPANO

1   oz. Gin
½   oz. Dry Vermouth
1   oz. Grapefruit Juice

Shake with ice and strain into a cocktail glass.

POMPIER

2   oz. Dry Vermouth
1   oz. Creme de Cassis

Mix in a highball glass. Fill with soda and ice.

POM POM

1½   oz. Dry Vermouth
¾   oz. Gin
2   dashes Orange Bitters

Stir with ice and strain into a cocktail glass.

POMPONETTE

¼   oz. Dry Vermouth
¼   oz. Creme de Cassis
¼   oz. Kirschwasser
¼   oz. Cognac

Pour carefully, in order given, into a pony glass so that each ingredient floats on the preceding one without mixing.

PONCE DE LEON NO. 1

½   oz. Grapefruit Juice
½   oz. Cointreau
½   oz. Rum
½   oz. Cognac

Shake with ice and strain into a champagne glass. Fill with Champagne.

PONCE DE LEON NO. 2

1½   oz. Rum
½   oz. Grapefruit Juice
½   oz. Mango Nectar
¼   oz. Lemon Juice

Shake with ice and strain into a cocktail glass.

PONDO PUNCH

2   oz. Rum
½   oz. Orange Curacao
¼   oz. Grenadine
1   oz. Orange Juice

Shake with ice and strain into a Collins glass. Fill with soda and ice.

PONTALBA PUNCH

1½ oz. Rum
¾ oz. Orange Juice
½ oz. Apricot-flavored Brandy

Shake with ice and strain into a highball glass. Fill with soda and ice.

POOH BAH COCKTAIL

1 oz. Rum
1 dash Apricot-flavored Brandy
1 oz. Swedish Punch
1 oz. Gin

Shake with ice and strain into a cocktail glass.

POOLSIDE MIST

1 tsp. Lemon Juice
1 tsp. Sugar
Riesling, chilled

Fill a Collins glass half full with cracked ice. Add lemon juice and sugar. Stir gently. Fill with chilled Riesling. Add a twist of lemon. Garnish with mint.

POOP DECK PAPPY COCKTAIL

1½ oz. Blackberry-flavored Brandy
¾ oz. Port Wine
¾ oz. Cognac

Shake with ice and strain into a cocktail glass.

POOR DEAR OLD THING

1½ oz. Rum
½ oz. Sherry
½ oz. Lemon Juice

Shake with ice and strain into a cocktail glass. Serve with a lemon twist.

P.O.P.

3 oz. Pineapple-Orange Juice concentrate, frozen
3 oz. Water
3 oz. White Port, chilled
Cinnamon

Blend until foamy and serve in a Collins glass. Dust with cinnamon.

POPO E IXTA

1 tbsp. Kahlua
1 tsp. Tequila

Pour into a pony glass. Stir well. Serve straight up.

POPPY NO. 1

1¾ oz. Gin
¾ oz. Light Creme de Cacao

Stir with ice and strain into a cocktail glass.

POPPY NO. 2

1¾ oz. Gin
¾ oz. Sherry
1 dash Orange Bitters
1 dash Angostura Bitters

Stir with ice and strain into a cocktail glass.

POP'S DUBONNET COCKTAIL

1 dash Aromatic Bitters
1 dash Orange-flavored Liqueur
¾ oz. Brandy
1 oz. Dubonnet

Stir with ice and strain into a cocktail glass.

PORT NO. 1

3 oz. Port
1 dash Brandy
3-4 Ice cubes

Shake with ice and strain into a cocktail glass. Twist an orange peel over the top of the glass, then drop peel in.

PORT NO. 2

3 oz. Port
2 dashes Curacao
1 dash Orange Bitters
1 dash Angostura Bitters

Stir with ice and strain into a cocktail glass.

PORT AND SHERRY COBBLER

2½ oz. Sherry
½ oz. Orange Curacao

Mix in a highball glass. Fill with shaved ice and float ½ oz. Port on top. Serve with a fruit garnish and straws.

PORT AND SODA

½ tsp. Sugar Syrup
4 oz. Port
Chilled Soda
½ oz. Brandy

Pour Sugar syrup and Port over ice cubes in a highball glass. Add soda and float Brandy on top.

PORT AND STARBOARD

1 tbsp. Grenadine
½ oz. Green Creme de Menthe

Pour carefully into a pony glass so that the Creme de Menthe floats on the Grenadine.

PORT ANTONIO

1 oz. Gold Rum
½ oz. Dark Rum
½ oz. Lime Juice
½ oz. Coffee Liqueur
¼ oz. Falernum

Shake with ice and strain into a cocktail glass. Serve with a lime wheel.

PORT COBBLER NO. 1

1   tsp. Orange Juice
1   tsp. Curacao
4   oz. Port

Fill a highball glass two-thirds full with crushed ice, add orange juice and Curacao, and stir. Pour in the Port and decorate with orange slices and a pineapple stick.

PORT COBBLER NO. 2

4   oz. Tawny Port
¾   oz. Brandy
½   tsp. Sugar

Mix in a highball glass. Fill with crushed ice. Garnish with a lemon twist, orange peel and mint sprig.

PORT COCKTAIL NO. 1

2¼   oz. Port
¼   oz. Brandy

Stir with ice and strain into a cocktail glass. Serve with a lemon twist and an orange peel.

PORT COCKTAIL NO. 2

2¼   oz. Port
¼   oz. Orange Curacao
1   dash Orange Bitters
1   dash Angostura Bitters

Stir with ice and strain into a cocktail glass.

PORTER SANGAREE

½   tsp. Sugar
Porter

Place sugar in a double Old-fashioned glass. Fill with Porter. Sprinkle nutmeg on top.

PORT FLIP

2   dashes Aromatic Bitters
1   tsp. Sugar Syrup
1   Egg
2   oz. Port

Shake with ice and strain into a cocktail glass. Sprinkle nutmeg on top.

PORT LIGHT HIGHBALL NO. 1

2   oz. Red Creme de Menthe

Stir with ice in a highball glass. Serve with straws.

PORT LIGHT HIGHBALL NO. 2

2   oz. White Creme de Menthe
½   oz. Grenadine

Mix in a highball glass. Fill with soda and ice.

PORT MARIA

1½   oz. Rum
¾   oz. Pineapple Juice
½   oz. Lemon Juice
¼   oz. Falernum

Shake with ice and strain into a cocktail glass. Sprinkle nutmeg on top.

PORT MILK PUNCH

1   tsp. Powdered Sugar
2   oz. Port
1   cup Milk

Shake with ice and strain into a Collins glass. Sprinkle nutmeg on top.

> If all be true that I do think,
> There are five reasons we
>   should drink;
> Good wine — a friend —
>   or being dry —
> Or lest we should be by and
>   by —
> Or any other reason why.

PORTOFINO COCKTAIL

¼   oz. Galliano
1½   oz. Gin
½   oz. Lemon Juice
½   oz. Orange Juice
¼   oz. Green Creme de Menthe

Shake with ice and strain into a cocktail glass.

PORTO FLIP

1½   oz. Port
1   tsp. Sugar
1   Egg
¼   oz. Benedictine

Shake with ice and strain into a flip glass. Sprinkle nutmeg on top. Float ¼ oz. Yellow Chartreuse on top.

PORT OF SAN JUAN

1½   oz. Rum
½   oz. Pineapple Juice
½   oz. Orange Curacao

Shake with ice and strain into a Collins glass. Fill with crushed ice and soda. Float ½ oz. Port on top. Serve with mint sprigs.

PORTO RICO

1½   oz. Rum
½   oz. Molasses
½   oz. Pimento Dram

Stir with ice and strain into a cocktail glass.

PORTO RICO RICKEY

1½   oz. Rum
½   oz. Lime Juice

Pour into a highball glass. Fill with soda and ice. Squeeze in the lime juice, leaving the shell in the glass. (¼ oz. Grenadine optional.)

PORT SANGAREE

½ tsp. Sugar
2 oz. Port
2 cubes Ice
1 tbsp. Brandy
Club Soda

Put sugar in a highball glass and add enough water to dissolve. Add Port, ice cubes and fill with soda. Float Brandy on top. Dust with nutmeg.

PORT WINE COBBLER

1 tsp. Powdered Sugar
2 oz. Soda
3 oz. Port

Dissolve sugar in water, then fill a goblet with shaved ice and add Port. Stir and decorate with fruits. Serve with straws.

PORT WINE COCKTAIL

2½ oz. Port
½ tsp. Brandy

Stir with ice and strain into a cocktail glass.

PORT WINE EGGNOG

1 Egg
1 tsp. Powdered Sugar
3 oz. Port
6 oz. Milk

Shake with ice and strain into a Collins glass. Sprinkle nutmeg on top.

PORT WINE FLIP

1 Egg
1 tsp. Powdered Sugar
1½ oz. Port
2 tsp. Sweet Cream (if desired)

Shake with ice and strain into a flip glass. Sprinkle nutmeg on top.

PORT WINE NEGUS

1 tbsp. Sugar
3 oz. Port
Boiling Water

Put sugar in a small, heavy saucepan and add just enough water to dissolve it. Add Port and lemon peel and heat. Pour into a warmed mug or punch glass, fill with boiling water and stir. Dust with nutmeg.

PORT WINE PUNCH

½ tsp. Sugar dissolved in
½ oz. Lemon Juice
1 oz. Orange Juice
2½ oz. Port

Mix sugar and the juices in a Collins glass. Fill with crushed ice and add Port. Serve with a fruit garnish.

PORT WINE SANGAREE

½ tsp. Powdered Sugar
1 tsp. Water
2 oz. Port
1 tbsp. Brandy

Dissolve sugar in water in a highball glass. Add Port and ice cubes. Fill the glass with soda, leaving enough room for the Brandy. Stir. Float Brandy on top. Sprinkle nutmeg on top.

POTTED PARROT

2 oz. White Rum
2 oz. Orange Juice
1 oz. Lemon Juice
2 tsp. Orange Curacao
1 tsp. Almond Extract
1 tsp. Rock Candy Syrup

Shake with ice and strain into an Old-fashioned glass. Add ice. Serve with a mint sprig.

POTTS POINT SPECIAL

¾ oz. unsweetened Pineapple Juice
¾ oz. Vodka
¾ oz. White Curacao

Shake with ice and strain into a champagne glass. Serve with ¼ slice pineapple.

POUSSE CAFE NO. 1

⅓ oz. Peach Liqueur
⅓ oz. Kirschwasser
⅓ oz. Pernod

Pour carefully, in order given, into a pony glass so that each ingredient floats on the preceding one without mixing.

POUSSE CAFE NO. 2

¼ oz. Orgeat Syrup
¼ oz. Creme de Noyaux
¼ oz. Orange Curacao
¼ oz. Cream

Pour carefully, in order given, into a pony glass so that each ingredient floats on the preceding one without mixing.

POUSSE CAFE NO. 3

¼ oz. Passion Fruit Syrup
¼ oz. Green Creme de Menthe
¼ oz. Strawberry Liqueur
¼ oz. Ouzo

Pour carefully, in order given, into a pony glass so that each ingredient floats on the preceding one without mixing.

POUSSE CAFE NO. 4

¼ oz. Grenadine
¼ oz. Light Creme de Cacao
¼ oz. Drambuie
¼ oz. Cream

Pour carefully, in order given, into a pony glass so that each ingredient floats on the preceding one without mixing.

POUSSE CAFE NO. 5

¼   oz. Creme de Noyaux
¼   oz. Anisette
¼   oz. Tuaca
¼   oz. Whipped Cream

Pour carefully, in order given, into a pony glass so that each ingredient floats on the preceding one without mixing.

POUSSE CAFE NO. 6

¼   oz. Grenadine
¼   oz. Light Creme de Cacao
¼   oz. Triple Sec
¼   oz. Forbidden Fruit

Pour carefully, in order given, into a pony glass so that each ingredient floats on the preceding one without mixing.

POUSSE CAFE NO. 7

1/5 oz. Dark Creme de Cacao
1/5 oz. Maraschino Liqueur
1/5 oz. Creme de Rose
1/5 oz. Yellow Chartreuse
1/5 oz. Cognac

Pour carefully, in order given, into a pony glass so that each ingredient floats on the preceding one without mixing.

POUSSE CAFE NO. 8

¼   oz. Parfait Amour
¼   oz. Cherry Liqueur
¼   oz. Anisette
¼   oz. Cream

Pour carefully, in order given, into a pony glass so that each ingredient floats on the preceding one without mixing.

Here's to man from morning
    till night;
Here's to the man with
    courage to fight —
The courage to fight and the
    courage to live —
The courage to learn, and to
    love, and forgive.

POUSSE CAFE NO. 9

¼   oz. Light Creme de Cacao
¼   oz. Cherry Liqueur
¼   oz. Kummel
¼   oz. Whipped Cream

Pour carefully, in order given, into a pony glass so that each ingredient floats on the preceding one without mixing.

POUSSE CAFE NO. 10

¼   oz. Green Creme de Menthe
¼   oz. Galliano
¼   oz. Blackberry-flavored Liqueur
¼   oz. Kirschwasser

Pour carefully, in order given, into a pony glass so that each ingredient floats on the preceding one without mixing.

POUSSE CAFE NO. 11

1/5 oz. Maraschino Liqueur
1/5 oz. Orange Curacao
1/5 oz. Green Chartreuse
1/5 oz. Anisette
1/5 oz. Cognac

Pour carefully, in order given, into a pony glass so that each ingredient floats on the preceding one without mixing.

POUSSE CAFE NO. 12

1/6 oz. Grenadine
1/6 oz. Yellow Chartreuse
1/6 oz. Creme d'Yvette
1/6 oz. White Creme de Menthe
1/6 oz. Green Chartreuse
1/6 oz. Cognac

Pour carefully, in order given, into a pony glass so that each ingredient floats on the preceding one without mixing.

POUSSE CAFE NO. 13

1/5 oz. Grenadine
1/5 oz. Maraschino Liqueur
1/5 oz. Creme de Violette
1/5 oz. Green Chartreuse
1/5 oz. Brandy

Pour carefully, in order given, into a pony glass so that each ingredient floats on the preceding one without mixing.

POUSSE CAFE NO. 14

1/6 oz. Grenadine
1/6 oz. Maraschino Liqueur
1/6 oz. Green Creme de Menthe
1/6 oz. Yellow Chartreuse
1/6 oz. Orange Curacao
1/6 oz. Brandy

Pour carefully, in order given, into a pony glass so that each ingredient floats on the preceding one without mixing.

POUSSE CAFE NO. 15

⅓   oz. Banana Liqueur
⅓   oz. Cherry Heering
⅓   oz. Cognac

Pour carefully, in order given, into a pony glass so that each ingredient floats on the preceding one without mixing.

POUSSE CAFE NO. 16

1/7 oz. Grenadine
1/7 oz. Anisette
1/7 oz. Parfait Amour
1/7 oz. Yellow Chartreuse
1/7 oz. Green Chartreuse
1/7 oz. Orange Curacao
1/7 oz. Cognac

Pour carefully, in order given, into a pony glass so that each ingredient floats on the preceding one without mixing.

POUSSE CAFE (PAREE)

⅓ oz. Benedictine
⅓ oz. Curacao
⅓ oz. Kirschwasser

Pour carefully, in order given, into a pony glass so that each ingredient floats on the preceding one without mixing.

POUSSE CAFE (ST. MORITZ)

1/7 oz. Raspberry Syrup
1/7 oz. Anisette
1/7 oz. Parfait Amour
1/7 oz. Creme de Violette
1/7 oz. Yellow Chartreuse
1/7 oz. Green Chartreuse
1/7 oz. Cognac

Pour carefully, in order given, into a pony glass so that each ingredient floats on the preceding one without mixing.

POUSSE L'AMOUR NO. 1

1 tbsp. Maraschino Liqueur
1 Egg Yolk
½ oz. Benedictine
½ oz. Brandy

Pour carefully, in order given, into a pony glass so that each ingredient floats on the preceding one without mixing.

POUSSE L'AMOUR NO. 2

⅓ oz. Grenadine
1 Egg Yolk
⅓ oz. Maraschino Liqueur
⅓ oz. Champagne

Pour carefully, in order given, into a pony glass so that each ingredient floats on the preceding one without mixing.

POUSSE L'AMOUR NO. 3

¼ oz. Maraschino Liqueur
1 Egg Yolk
½ oz. Creme de Vanille
½ oz. Brandy

Pour carefully, in order given, into a pony glass so that each ingredient floats on the preceding one without mixing.

POWERHOUSE

1 oz. Galliano
½ oz. Vodka
½ oz. 151-proof Rum
1 oz. Sweet & Sour Lemon Mix
1 oz. Orange Juice
1 dash Grenadine

Shake with ice and strain into a Collins glass. Fill with crushed ice.

PRADO

1½ oz. Tequila
¾ oz. Lemon Juice
1 tbsp. Maraschino Liqueur
½ Egg White
1 tsp. Grenadine

Shake with ice and strain into a Sour glass. Add a slice of lime and a cherry.

PRAIRIE CHICKEN

1 oz. Gin
1 Egg
Salt and Pepper

Open egg without breaking the yolk and put in a wine glass. Pour Gin on top. Add salt and pepper.

Come in the evening, or come in the morning —
Come when you're looked for, or come without warning;
A thousand welcomes you'll find here before you,
The oftener you come here the more I'll adore you!

PRAIRIE OYSTER COCKTAIL NO. 1

1 oz. Brandy
1 tbsp. Worcestershire Sauce
1 tsp. Tomato Catsup
1 tbsp. Vinegar
1 pinch Pepper

Shake with ice and strain into an Old-fashioned glass. Add two ice cubes. Place an egg yolk on top without breaking it. Add a dash of cayenne pepper.

PRAIRIE OYSTER COCKTAIL NO. 2

1½ oz. Cognac
½ oz. Cider Vinegar
½ oz. Worcestershire Sauce
1 tsp. Catsup
2 dashes Angostura Bitters
1 Egg Yolk placed on top without breaking

Pour ingredients into a cocktail glass, sprinkle cayenne on top and swallow in one gulp.

PREAKNESS COCKTAIL

¾ oz. Sweet Vermouth
1½ oz. Rye Whisky
1 dash Bitters
½ tsp. Benedictine

Stir with ice and strain into a cocktail glass. Serve with a lemon twist.

PRESBYTERIAN

2-3 oz. Bourbon Whisky
2 oz. chilled Ginger Ale
2 oz. chilled Club Soda

Mix in a highball glass. Add ice and a twist of lemon.

PRESCRIPTION

1   oz. Gin
¾   oz. Grenadine
1   dash Orange Bitters
¾   oz. Lemon Juice

Shake with ice and strain into a cocktail glass.

PRESIDENT

1½   oz. Rum
1   oz. Orange Juice
1   dash Grenadine

Shake with ice and strain into a cocktail glass.

PRESIDENTE

1½   oz. White Rum
1   tbsp. Dry Vermouth
1-2 dashes Grenadine
1-2 dashes Orange Curacao

Shake with ice and strain into a cocktail glass. Add ice.

PRESIDENTE VINCENT

1½   oz. Rum
½   oz. Dry Vermouth
½   oz. Lime Juice
½   tsp. Sugar

Shake with ice and strain into a cocktail glass.

PRESTO COCKTAIL

1   tbsp. Orange Juice
½   oz. Sweet Vermouth
1½   oz. Brandy
¼   tsp. Pernod

Shake with ice and strain into a cocktail glass.

PREVIEW

1½   oz. Gin
½   oz. Cointreau
1   dash Pernod

Shake with ice and strain into a cocktail glass.

PRIMA VERA NO. 1

¾   oz. Rum
¾   oz. Gin
¾   oz. Anisette
1   dash Angostura Bitters

Shake with ice and strain into a cocktail glass.

PRIMA VERA NO. 2

1   oz. Orange Juice
1   oz. Gin
½   oz. Galliano

Shake with ice and strain into a cocktail glass.

PRIMOS

1   oz. Bourbon Whisky
1   oz. Brandy
½   oz. Grand Marnier

Shake with ice and strain into a cocktail glass.

PRINCE

1   dash Orange Bitters
1½   oz. Rye Whisky
½   oz. White Creme de Menthe

Mix the first two ingredients in an Old-fashioned glass, fill with ice and add Creme de Menthe.

PRINCE EDWARD

1¾   oz. Scotch Whisky
½   oz. Lillet
¼   oz. Drambuie

Stir with ice and strain into a cocktail glass. Serve with an orange slice.

PRINCE GEORGE

1½   oz. Rum
½   oz. Grand Marnier
½   oz. Lime Juice

Shake with ice and strain into a cocktail glass. Serve with a lemon twist.

PRINCE OF WALES COCKTAIL NO. 1

2   oz. Gin
1   Egg White
1   oz. Pineapple Juice

Shake with ice and strain into a cocktail glass.

PRINCE OF WALES COCKTAIL NO. 2

1   dash Angostura Bitters
1   tsp. Curacao
1   oz. Madeira
1   oz. Brandy
6   oz. chilled Champagne

Shake with ice and strain into a champagne glass. Serve with an orange slice.

PRINCE'S SMILE COCKTAIL

½   oz. Apricot-flavored Brandy
½   oz. Apple Brandy
1   oz. Gin
¼   tsp. Lemon Juice

Shake with ice and strain into a cocktail glass.

PRINCESS

¾   oz. Apricot-flavored Brandy
¼   oz. Cream

Pour carefully, in order given, into a pony glass so that each ingredient floats on the preceding one without mixing.

PRINCESS DREAM

¾   oz. Galliano
¾   oz. Pineapple Juice
½   oz. Light Creme de Cacao
¼   oz. Cream

Shake with ice and strain into a cocktail glass.

PRINCESS HIGHBALL

1½ oz. Apricot-flavored Brandy
½ oz. Cream

Mix in a highball glass. Fill with soda and ice.

PRINCESS MARY

1½ oz. Gin
1½ oz. Creme de Cacao
1½ oz. Heavy Cream

Shake with ice and strain into a cocktail glass.

PRINCESS MARY'S PRIDE

1½ oz. Calvados or Apple Brandy
¾ oz. Dubonnet
¾ oz. Dry Vermouth

Stir with ice and strain into a cocktail glass. (Sweet Vermouth may be used instead of Dry Vermouth.)

PRINCESS POUSSE CAFE

¾ oz. Apricot-flavored Brandy
1½ tsp. Sweet Cream

Pour the cream carefully on top of the Brandy, so that the two don't mix. Use a pousse cafe or pony glass.

PRINCETON NO. 1

1½ oz. Gin
½ oz. Port
2 dashes Orange Bitters

Stir with ice and strain into a cocktail glass. Serve with a lemon twist.

PRINCETON NO. 2

1 oz. Gin
1 oz. Dry Vermouth
Juice ½ Lime

Stir with ice and strain into a cocktail glass.

PRINCETON NO. 3

1½ oz. Gin
2 dashes Orange Bitters

Mix in a highball glass. Fill with soda and ice.

PROHIBITION COCKTAIL

1½ oz. Gin
1½ oz. Lillet
2 dashes Orange Juice
1 dash Apricot Liqueur

Shake with ice and strain into a cocktail glass. Serve with a lemon twist.

PRUNEAUX

1 oz. Gin
1 oz. Sherry
¼ oz. Orange Juice
¼ oz. Prune Syrup

Shake with ice and strain into a cocktail glass.

PRUNELLA NO. 1

1½ oz. Dry Vermouth
¾ oz. Gin
¼ oz. Prunelle

Stir with ice and strain into a cocktail glass.

PRUNELLA NO. 2

1½ oz. Cognac
½ oz. Prunelle
½ oz. Lime Juice

Shake with ice and strain into a cocktail glass.

PRUNELLE ALEXANDER

¾ oz. Gin (or Brandy)
¾ oz. Prunelle
1 oz. Cream
Cinnamon

Shake with ice and strain into a cocktail glass.

PUERTO APPLE

1½ oz. Applejack
¾ oz. Rum
1 tbsp. Lime Juice
1 oz. Orgeat Syrup

Shake with ice and strain into an Old-fashioned glass. Add ice cubes and decorate with a lime slice.

PUERTO RICAN COCKTAIL NO. 1

Juice ½ Lime
½ oz. Pineapple Juice
2 oz. Puerto Rican Rum

Shake with ice and strain into a champagne glass.

PUERTO RICAN COCKTAIL NO. 2

1½ oz. Puerto Rican Rum
½ oz. Dry Vermouth
½ oz. Lime Juice
¼ oz. Grenadine

Shake with ice and strain into a cocktail glass.

PUERTO RICAN COCKTAIL NO. 3

1½ oz. Puerto Rican Rum
½ oz. Lime Juice
¼ tsp. Sugar
¼ oz. Maraschino Liqueur

Shake with ice and strain into a cocktail glass.

PUERTO RICAN PINK LADY

1½ oz. Gold Rum
¾ oz. Lemon Juice
½ Egg White
½ oz. Grenadine

Shake with ice and strain into a cocktail glass.

PUERTO RICAN RUM SWIZZLE NO. 1

½ oz. Lime Juice
1 oz. Dry Vermouth
1 oz. Rum
½ tsp. Sugar

Mix in a highball glass. Fill with crushed ice. Swizzle until glass frosts. Top with soda.

PUERTO RICAN RUM SWIZZLE NO. 2

1 oz. Lime Juice
2 oz. Rum
1 tsp. Sugar
2 dashes Angostura Bitters

Mix in a Collins glass. Fill with crushed ice. Swizzle until glass frosts. Top with soda.

PUMPKIN COACH COCKTAIL

1 oz. Cesoriac
2 tsp. Sweet Vermouth
2 tsp. Cherry Juice

Mix and pour over crushed ice in a pony glass. Serve with a twist of lime.

PUMP ROOM BATH CURE

3 oz. 151-proof Rum
1½ oz. Vodka
1½ oz. Lemon Juice
3 oz. Milk
1 dash Grenadine
1 tsp. Sugar

Shake with ice and strain into a Collins glass.

> And fill them high with
>   generous juice,
> As generous as your mind,
> And pledge me in the
>   generous toast —
> The whole of human kind!
>   — *Robert Burns.*

PUMP ROOM SPECIAL

1½ oz. Vodka
½ oz. White Creme de Menthe
½ oz. Cognac

Pour carefully, in order given, into a pony glass so that each ingredient floats on the preceding one without mixing.

PUNCH ROMAINE

1 oz. Rye Whisky
1 oz. Jamaica Rum
3 tsp. Lemon Juice
2 tsp. Sugar Syrup

Shake with ice and strain into an Old-fashioned glass. Add ice.

PUNT E MES NEGRONI

¾ oz. Gin
¾ oz. Sweet Vermouth
¾ oz. Punt e Mes

Stir with ice and strain into a cocktail glass. Serve with a lemon twist and add a squirt of soda, if desired.

PURITAN

1¾ oz. Gin
½ oz. Dry Vermouth
¼ oz. Yellow Chartreuse
1 dash Orange Bitters

Stir with ice and strain into a cocktail glass.

PURPLE BUNNY

¾ oz. Cherry-flavored Brandy
¾ oz. Light Creme de Cacao
1 oz. Cream

Shake with ice and strain into a cocktail glass.

PURPLE COW

1 oz. Blackberry-flavored Brandy
1 oz. Light Cream
1 tsp. Almond Extract

Shake with ice and strain into an Old-fashioned glass. Fill with crushed ice.

PURPLE MASK

1 oz. Vodka
1 oz. Grape Juice
½ oz. White Creme de Cacao

Shake with ice and strain into a cocktail glass.

PURPLE PASSION

1½ oz. Vodka

Pour into a highball glass. Fill with grape juice and ice.

PURPLE PEOPLE EATER

1½ oz. Parfait Amour
1½ oz. Gin
1-2 drops Lemon Juice

Shake with ice and strain into a cocktail glass.

PURPLE SHELL

¾ oz. Sloe Gin
½ oz. Gin
½ oz. Parfait Amour
1½ oz. Fresh Cream

Shake with ice and strain into a champagne glass.

PURPLE TWISTER

2 oz. Grape Vodka
Cola

Pour Vodka into a Collins glass over ice cubes. Fill with Cola, add a slice of lemon and stir.

PUSSYCAT

1½   oz. Early Times
3   oz. cold Water
1   package Instant Pussycat

Blend with ice and strain into a cocktail glass. Fill with crushed ice. Serve with a cherry and a lime slice.

QUAKER'S COCKTAIL NO. 1

¾   oz. Light Rum
¾   oz. Brandy
2   tsp. Raspberry Syrup
Juice ¼ Lemon

Shake with ice and strain into a cocktail glass.

QUAKER'S COCKTAIL NO. 2

1   oz. Rye Whisky
1   oz. Brandy
1   tsp. Raspberry Syrup or Grenadine
1   tbsp. Lime Juice

Shake with ice and strain into a cocktail glass.

QUARTER DECK COCKTAIL NO. 1

⅓   oz. Sweet Sherry
1½   oz. Dark Rum
Juice ½ Lime

Stir with ice and strain into a cocktail glass.

QUARTER DECK COCKTAIL NO. 2

1½   oz. Jamaica Rum
¾   oz. Dry Sherry
¾   oz. Scotch Whisky
1   tsp. Sugar Syrup
1   dash Orange Bitters

Shake with ice and strain into a cocktail glass.

QUEBEC

1½   oz. Canadian Whisky
½   oz. Dry Vermouth
1½   tsp. Amer Picon
1½   tsp. Maraschino Liqueur

Shake with ice and strain into a cocktail glass rimmed with sugar.

QUEEN BEE NO. 1

2   oz. Sloe Gin
1   oz. Curacao
1   dash Anisette

Shake with ice and strain into a cocktail glass.

QUEEN BEE NO. 2

1½   oz. Lime Vodka
1   oz. Coffee-flavored Brandy
½   oz. Sweet Sherry

Shake with ice and strain into a cocktail glass.

QUEEN CHARLOTTE

2   oz. Claret
1   oz. Raspberry Syrup or Grenadine

Pour into a Collins glass. Add ice cubes, fill with lemon soda and stir.

QUEEN CHARLOTTE COOLER

3   oz. Framboise
½   oz. Orgeat Syrup

Mix in a Collins glass. Fill with soda and ice.

QUEEN ELIZABETH COCKTAIL NO. 1

1½   oz. Gin
½   oz. Dry Vermouth
1½   tsp. Benedictine

Stir with ice and strain into a cocktail glass.

QUEEN ELIZABETH COCKTAIL NO. 2

1½   oz. Brandy
1½   oz. Sweet Vermouth
1   dash Curacao

Stir with ice and strain into a cocktail glass. Serve with a cherry.

QUEEN ELIZABETH COCKTAIL NO. 3

1¾   oz. Gin
¼   oz. Cointreau
¼   oz. Lemon Juice
¼   oz. Pernod

Stir with ice and strain into a cocktail glass.

QUEEN ELIZABETH WINE

1   oz. Dry Vermouth
1½   oz. Benedictine
1   tbsp. Lime or Lemon Juice

Stir with ice and strain into a cocktail glass.

QUEEN'S COCKTAIL NO. 1

Muddle slices of pineapple in a shaker and stir with:

1½   oz. Gin
½   oz. Sweet Vermouth
½   oz. Dry Vermouth

Pour into a cocktail glass.

QUEEN'S COCKTAIL NO. 2

½   oz. Gin
½   oz. Dry Vermouth
½   oz. Sweet Vermouth
½   oz. Pineapple Juice

Shake with ice and strain into a cocktail glass. Serve with a cherry and a piece of pineapple.

QUEEN'S DELIGHT

1½ oz. Tuaca
1½ oz. Orange Juice
1½ oz. Cream
½ oz. Lime Juice
½ tsp. Sugar

Shake with ice and strain into a cocktail glass. Fill with crushed ice.

QUEEN'S PARK SWIZZLE

Juice ½ Lime (plus shell)
¾ oz. Lime Juice
1½ oz. Dark Rum
1 dash Angostura Bitters
3 Mint sprigs
½ tsp. Sugar

Put all ingredients into a highball glass. Fill with crushed ice. Swizzle until glass frosts. Serve with a mint sprig.

QUEEN'S PEG

¾ oz. Gin
Champagne

Place an ice cube in a large wine glass. Add Gin and fill with chilled Champagne.

QUEEN'S PICK

¾ oz. Brandy
Champagne

Place an ice cube in a large wine glass. Add Brandy and fill with chilled Champagne.

QUELLE VIE

1½ oz. Brandy
¾ oz. Kummel

Stir with ice and strain into a cocktail glass.

QUENCHER COOLER

1½ oz. Cognac
½ tsp. Sugar
½ oz. Lemon Juice
1 Egg

Shake with ice and strain into a Collins glass. Fill with ginger ale and ice.

QUICK COCKTAIL

1 oz. Port
1 oz. Grand Marnier
1 dash Angostura Bitters

Shake with ice and strain into a cocktail glass.

QUICKLY

1 oz. Brandy
1 oz. Anisette
½ oz. Orange Curacao
2 dashes Angostura Bitters

Shake with ice and strain into a cocktail glass.

QUININE SURPRISE

2 oz. Ruby Port
4 oz. Tonic Water, chilled

Pour wine and tonic water over crushed ice in a Collins glass. Stir gently. Garnish with a lemon slice.

QUIN QUINA

¾ oz. Cognac
¾ oz. Peach-flavored Brandy
¾ oz. Quinquina
¼ oz. Pernod

Shake with ice and strain into a cocktail glass.

Here's to the host and the hostess,
We're honored to be here tonight;
May they both live long and prosper,
May their star of hope ever be bright.

RABBIT'S FOOT

¾ oz. Apple Brandy
¾ oz. Rum
½ oz. Orange Juice
½ oz. Lemon Juice
¼ oz. Grenadine

Shake with ice and strain into a cocktail glass. Serve with an orange slice.

RACQUET CLUB COCKTAIL

1½ oz. Gin
¾ oz. Dry Vermouth
1 dash Orange Bitters

Stir with ice and strain into a cocktail glass. (Orange peel optional.)

RACQUET CLUB FIZZ

1½ oz. Rum
1 oz. Lemon Juice
1 tsp. Sugar
1 Egg

Shake with ice and strain into a Collins glass. Add a piece of pineapple. Fill with soda and ice.

R.A.C. SPECIAL

1½ oz. Gin
¾ oz. Sweet Vermouth
¾ oz. Dry Vermouth
2 dashes Orange Bitters

Shake with ice and strain into a cocktail glass. Serve with a twist of orange peel.

RAFFAELLO

½ oz. Galliano
½ oz. Inca Pisco
½ oz. Sweet Vermouth, White
1 dash Angostura Bitters
¼ oz. Grand Marnier or Triple Sec

Shake with ice and strain into an Old-fashioned glass. Fill with ice.

RAFFLES HOTEL SLING

1 oz. Gin
1 oz. Cherry-flavored Brandy
1 oz. Benedictine

Shake with ice and strain into a Collins glass. Fill with soda and ice. Serve with a lime wheel.

RAH RAH RUT

2¼ oz. Rye Whisky
¼ oz. Pernod
2 dashes Peychaud's Bitters

Stir with ice and strain into a cocktail glass.

RAIDME

1¾ oz. Gin
½ oz. Pernod
¼ oz. Campari

Shake with ice and strain into a cocktail glass.

RAIL SPLITTER

1 oz. Lemon Juice
1 tsp. Sugar
1½ oz. Liquor of your choice

Mix in a Collins glass. Fill with ginger ale and ice.

RAINBOW NO. 1

1/7 oz. Creme de Violette
1/7 oz. Light Creme de Cacao
1/7 oz. Maraschino Liqueur
1/7 oz. Yellow Chartreuse
1/7 oz. Green Chartreuse
1/7 oz. Benedictine
1/7 oz. Brandy

Pour carefully, in order given, into a pony glass so that each ingredient floats on the preceding one without mixing.

RAINBOW NO. 2

1/7 oz. Creme de Cassis
1/7 oz. Creme de Violette
1/7 oz. Maraschino Liqueur
1/7 oz. Green Creme de Menthe
1/7 oz. Orange Curacao
1/7 oz. Yellow Chartreuse
1/7 oz. Cherry-flavored Brandy

Pour carefully, in order given, into a pony glass so that each ingredient floats on the preceding one without mixing.

RAINBOW OLD-FASHIONED

2 oz. Rye Whisky
1¼ oz. Sugar Syrup
1 tsp. Cherry Juice
1-2 dashes Angostura Bitters

Mix in an Old-fashioned glass. Add ice. Decorate with a strawberry, a slice of orange, a cherry and a twist of lemon.

RAJAH

1¼ oz. Brandy
1¼ oz. Champagne

Stir with ice and strain into a cocktail glass.

RAMON

1½ oz. Gin
½ oz. Dry Vermouth
½ oz. Hercules

Stir with ice and strain into a cocktail glass.

RAMONCITA LOPEZ SPECIAL

1 tsp. Sugar
2 oz. Rum
½ oz. Lime Juice
1 Egg White

Shake with ice and strain into a cocktail glass.

RAMOS FIZZ

Juice ½ Lemon
1 Egg White
1 tsp. Powdered Sugar
2 oz. Gin
1 tbsp. sweet Cream
½ tsp. Orange Flower Water
1½ tbsp. Lime Juice

Shake with ice and strain into a highball glass. Add ice cubes, fill with soda and stir.

RAMOS FIZZ A LA KAHLUA

1 oz. Gin
¾ oz. Lemon Juice
2 oz. Milk
½ Egg White
3 dashes Orange Flower Water
¾ oz. Kahlua

Shake with ice and strain into a Collins glass. Fill with soda and ice.

RANGER

¾ oz. Gin
¾ oz. Rum
¾ oz. Lemon Juice
½ tsp. Sugar

Shake with ice and strain into a cocktail glass.

RANGE RIDER

1 tbsp. Orange Juice
1 tsp. Powdered Sugar
2 oz. Sweet Vermouth
2 oz. Dry Vermouth

Stir with ice and strain into a large cocktail glass.

RANGIRORA MADNESS

1½ oz. Jamaica Rum
2 tbsp. Pineapple Juice
2 tbsp. Orange Juice

Shake with ice and strain into a Collins glass. Add ice and fill with lemon soda. Float 1 tsp. 151-proof Rum; decorate with a cherry.

RANGOON RUBY

2   oz. Vodka
2   tbsp. Cranberry Juice

Mix in an Old-fashioned glass. Squeeze in the juice of a lime and drop in the peel. Add ice and fill with soda. Stir.

RAPUNSIL

½   oz. Galliano
½   oz. Light Creme de Cacao
¾   oz. Cream
¾   oz. Pineapple Juice

Shake with ice and strain into a cocktail glass.

RASPBERRY NO. 1

1½   oz. Gin
¼   oz. Kirschwasser
¾   oz. White Wine
Several Raspberries

Shake with ice and strain into a cocktail glass.

RASPBERRY NO. 2

3   Raspberries, muddled
¾   oz. Gin
¾   oz. Sweet Vermouth
¾   oz. Dry Vermouth

Shake with ice and strain into a cocktail glass.

RASPBERRY CLARET CUP

4   oz. Red Wine
1   oz. Brandy
1   oz. Himbeergeist (Raspberry Brandy)
¾   oz. Grenadine
1   oz. Lemon Juice

Mix in a Collins glass. Fill with soda and ice. Serve with a fresh raspberry.

RASPBERRY FOAM

6   oz. Pink Chablis, chilled
Raspberry Sherbet
Lemon-lime soda, chilled

Pour Chablis into a Collins glass. Scoop in raspberry sherbet. Fill with soda and stir gently.

RASPBERRY HIGHBALL

1½   oz. Gin
1   oz. Raspberry Syrup or Grenadine
½   oz. Lemon Juice

Shake with ice and strain into a highball glass. Fill with soda and ice.

RASPBERRY RICKEY

1½   oz. Himbeergeist (Raspberry Brandy)
½   oz. Lime Juice (Leave shell in glass)

Mix in a highball glass. Fill with soda and ice. Serve with a fresh raspberry.

RASPBERRY TWINKLE

Juice ½ Lemon
1½   oz. Raspberry Syrup
1½   oz. Brandy
Brut Champagne, Chilled

Place ice cubes in a Collins glass. Add lemon juice, raspberry syrup and Brandy. Stir and fill with Champagne.

RASPUTIN

2   oz. Vodka
½   oz. Clam Juice

Stir with ice and strain into a cocktail glass. Serve with an anchovy-stuffed olive.

RATTLER

¾   oz. Gin
¾   oz. Sweet Vermouth
¾   oz. Dry Vermouth
½   oz. Orange Juice

Shake with ice and strain into a cocktail glass.

RATTLESNAKE COCKTAIL

1½   oz. Rye Whisky
1   Egg White
1   tsp. Lemon Juice
½   tsp. Powdered Sugar
¼   tsp. Pernod

Shake with ice and strain into a cocktail glass.

RAY LONG

2   oz. Brandy
1   oz. Sweet Vermouth
4   dashes Pernod
1   dash Angostura Bitters

Stir with ice and strain into a cocktail glass.

RAYMOND

1¾   oz. Sweet Vermouth
¾   oz. Orange Juice
1   dash Orange Bitters

Shake with ice and strain into a cocktail glass.

RAYMOND HITCHCOCKTAIL

3   oz. Sweet Vermouth
¼   cup Orange Juice
1   dash Orange Bitters

Stir with ice and strain into a highball glass. Serve with a pineapple slice.

RAZZBERRY COCKTAIL

1 oz. Applejack
1 oz. Raspberry Syrup
1 oz. Yellow Chartreuse

Stir with ice and strain into a cocktail glass.

READY GO

¾ oz. Rum
¾ oz. Cointreau
¾ oz. Anisette
¼ oz. Pineapple Juice

Shake with ice and strain into a cocktail glass.

REBEL CHARGE

1 oz. Bourbon Whisky
½ oz. Triple Sec
1 tbsp. Orange Juice
1 tbsp. Lemon Juice
½ Egg White

Shake with ice and strain into an Old-fashioned glass over ice cubes. Add an orange slice.

RECRUIT

1 oz. Galliano
1 oz. Kirschwasser

Mix in a highball glass. Fill with soda and ice and Champagne. Serve with several black cherries.

RED APPLE

1 oz. 100-proof Vodka
1 oz. Apple Juice
1 tbsp. Lemon Juice
1 tsp. Grenadine

Shake with ice and strain into a cocktail glass.

RED CLOUD

1½ oz. Gin
½ oz. Apricot-flavored Brandy
1 tbsp. Lemon Juice
1 tsp. Grenadine

Shake with ice and strain into a cocktail glass.

RED DEVIL COCKTAIL NO. 1

¾ oz. Brandy
¾ oz. Creme de Menthe
1 dash Red Pepper

Shake with ice and strain into a cocktail glass.

RED DEVIL COCKTAIL NO. 2

2 oz. Irish Whisky
1½ oz. Clam Juice
1½ oz. Tomato Juice
1 dash Worcestershire Sauce
¼ oz. Lime Juice
Pinch of Pepper

Shake with ice and strain into a highball glass. Fill with ice.

RED EYE

½ Cold Beer
½ Tomato Juice

Mix in a Collins glass.

RED GAVILAN

1 oz. Tequila
4 oz. Tomato Juice
2 dashes Angostura Bitters

Shake with ice and strain into an Old-fashioned glass. Add ice. Decorate with a lime wheel.

RED HEAD

1½ oz. Whisky
⅛ oz. Kirschwasser
⅛ oz. Raspberry Cordial or Syrup
Juice ½ Lemon

Shake with ice and strain into a cocktail glass. Serve with a twist of orange peel.

RED LION NO. 1

2 oz. Grand Marnier
1 oz. Gin
1 tbsp. Orange Juice
1 tbsp. Lemon Juice

Shake with ice and strain into a cocktail glass. Serve with a lemon twist.

RED LION NO. 2

¾ oz. Gin
¾ oz. Grand Marnier
½ oz. Lime Juice
½ oz. Grenadine

Shake with ice and strain into a cocktail glass.

RED RAIDER

1 oz. Bourbon Whisky
½ oz. Triple Sec
1 oz. Lemon Juice
1 dash Grenadine

Shake with ice and strain into a cocktail glass.

RED ROBBIN

1 oz. Vodka
1 oz. Dubonnet

Mix in an Old-fashioned glass. Fill with ice. Serve with a lemon twist.

RED RUSSIAN

1 oz. Vodka
1 oz. Cherry Heering

Mix in an Old-fashioned glass. Fill with ice.

RED SEA NO. 1

1	oz. Dry Vermouth
¾	oz. Rye Whisky
¾	oz. Strega

Stir with ice and strain into a cocktail glass.

RED SEA NO. 2

2	oz. Tomato Juice
2	oz. Clam Juice
2	tsp. fresh Lemon Juice
1	oz. Dry Sherry
2	drops Tabasco Sauce
Salt and Pepper to taste

Combine all ingredients in a small saucepan. Heat to piping hot. Do not boil. Serve in preheated mugs.

REDSKIN

1¾	oz. Bourbon
¾	oz. Dry Vermouth
1	dash Angostura Bitters

Stir with ice and strain into a cocktail glass.

RED SWIZZLE

1½	oz. Lime Juice
1½	oz. Gin
1	tsp. Sugar
2	oz. Soda

Mix in a Collins glass. Fill with crushed ice. Add 2 dashes of Bitters. Swizzle until glass frosts. (Liquor of your choice may be used instead of Gin.)

RED (OR WHITE) WINE COOLER

2	tsp. Sugar
1	tsp. Cold Water
1	tbsp. Orange Juice
Chilled Red or White Wine

Put sugar and water in a highball glass and stir until sugar is dissolved. Add orange juice and ice cubes and fill with chilled red or white Wine. Garnish a Red Wine Cooler with a slice of lemon, a White Wine Cooler with a slice of orange.

REFORM COCKTAIL

¾	oz. Dry Vermouth
1½	oz. Dry Sherry
1	dash Orange Bitters

Stir with ice and strain into a cocktail glass. Serve with a cherry.

REGAL FIZZ

1½	oz. Brandy
¾	oz. Benedictine
1	tsp. Lemon Juice
1	tsp. Sugar Syrup

Shake with ice and strain into a highball glass. Fill with soda.

REGENT PUNCH NO. 1

3	oz. White Wine
1½	oz. Madeira Wine
1	oz. Rum

Mix in a Collins glass. Fill with hot tea.

The Frenchman loves his
   native wine;
The German loves his beer;
The Englishman loves his
   'alf and 'alf,
Because it brings good cheer.
The Irishman loves his
   "whiskey straight,"
Because it gives him dizziness.
The American has no choice
   at all,
So he drinks the whole
   damned business.

REGENT PUNCH NO. 2

½	oz. Brandy
½	oz. Swedish Punch
¼	oz. Orange Curacao
1½	oz. Jamaica Rum
1	oz. Lemon Juice
2	oz. strong Tea
1	dash Angostura Bitters

Mix in a highball glass. Fill with Champagne and ice.

Here's wishing good health
and long life to you,
And the choice of the girls
for a wife to you,
And your land without penny
of rent to you:
If these three blessings are
sent to you,
Then there'll be peace and
content to you.
       — *An Irish Toast*

RELAXER

2	oz. Brandy
1	oz. Apple Brandy
1	oz. Sweet Vermouth

Stir with ice and strain into a cocktail glass.

REMSEN COOLER

½	tsp. Sugar
2	oz. Soda
2½	oz. Scotch Whisky
Soda or Ginger Ale

Put sugar and soda in a Collins glass. Stir to dissolve sugar and add ice, Scotch and stir. Fill with soda or ginger ale and garnish with lemon peel.

RENAISSANCE COCKTAIL

1½	oz. Gin
½	oz. Dry Sherry
1	tbsp. Sweet Cream

Shake with ice and strain into a cocktail glass. Sprinkle nutmeg on top.

RENDEZVOUS COCKTAIL NO. 1

1½	oz. Gin
½	oz. Kirschwasser
¼	oz. Campari

Shake with ice and strain into a cocktail glass. Serve with a lemon twist.

RENDEZVOUS COCKTAIL NO. 2

1 oz. Cognac
¾ oz. Strega
¾ oz. Cherry-flavored Brandy

Stir with ice and strain into a cocktail glass. Serve with a pineapple slice.

RENO SPLIT

1½ oz. Early Times
1 oz. Apricot-flavored Brandy
2 oz. Pineapple Juice

Shake with ice and strain into a highball glass. Fill with soda and ice. Serve with a pineapple stick.

RENOVATOR COCKTAIL

1 Egg
¾ oz. Benedictine

Shake with ice and strain into a cocktail glass. Fill with sweet cream.

RESOLUTE COCKTAIL

Juice ¼ Lemon
½ oz. Apricot-flavored Brandy
1 oz. Gin

Shake with ice and strain into a cocktail glass.

RETREAT FROM MOSCOW

1½ oz. Gin
¾ oz. Kummel
¾ oz. Lemon Juice

Shake with ice and strain into a cocktail glass.

REVE D'ALSACE

1 oz. Prunelle
¾ oz. Cherry Liqueur
½ oz. Brandy
¼ oz. Benedictine

Stir with ice and strain into a cocktail glass.

REVELATION

1¾ oz. Benedictine
½ oz. Kummel
¼ oz. White Creme de Menthe

Shake with ice and strain into a cocktail glass. Serve with a lemon twist.

REVIGORATOR

1½ oz. Gin
½ oz. Cola
½ oz. Sirop de Citron

Shake with ice and strain into a cocktail glass.

REVIVER COOLER

1½ oz. Brandy
½ oz. Framboise
3 oz. Milk

Shake with ice and strain into a highball glass. Fill with soda.

REVIVIA

¾ oz. Gin
¾ oz. Dubonnet
½ oz. Pernod
½ oz. Lemon Juice

Shake with ice and strain into a cocktail glass.

REX

1¾ oz. Gin
¾ oz. Sweet Vermouth
1 dash Orange Bitters

Stir with ice and strain into a cocktail glass.

RHAPSODY

1½ oz. Gin
½ oz. Yellow Chartreuse
1 dash Orange Bitters

Shake with ice and strain into a cocktail glass. Serve with a cherry.

RHETT BUTLER

1½ oz. Southern Comfort
2 tsp. Lime Juice
1 tbsp. Lemon Juice
1 tsp. Curacao
½ tsp. Sugar

Shake with ice and strain into a cocktail glass.

RHINE FRAPPE

6 Ice cubes
4 oz. Rhine Wine
1 tsp. Lime Juice
1 tbsp. Sugar

Blend until smooth. Pour into a Collins glass. Garnish with an orange twist. Serve with straws.

RHINE SPRITZER

4 oz. Rhine Wine, chilled
4 oz. chilled Soda

Pour Wine and soda over ice in a Collins glass. Stir.

RHINE WINE COBBLER

1 tsp. Sugar
1 tsp. Lemon Juice
Rhine Wine

Fill a tumbler half full with cracked ice and add sugar and lemon juice. Stir lightly and fill with Rhine Wine. Serve with a lemon twist and mint.

Here's to the heart,
Though another's it be;
Here's to the cheeks,
Though they bloom not for me.

RHINE WINE CUP

Ice cubes
1 bottle Rhine Wine
Fruits in season
½ oz. Triple Sec
½ oz. Curacao
6 oz. Club Soda
Cucumber peel
Mint sprigs

Put 12-16 ice cubes in a large pitcher and add the Rhine Wine, fruits, Triple Sec, Curacao and club soda. Decorate with the cucumber peel and mint sprigs. Serve in wine glasses. Serves 8.

RHINE WINE PUNCH

½ oz. Brandy
½ oz. Maraschino Liqueur
2 oz. strong Tea
½ tsp. Sugar

Mix in a Collins glass. Fill with ice and Rhine Wine.

RHINE WINE PUNCH BOWL

1 block Ice
1 cup Sugar Syrup
2 cups Lemon Juice
1 pint Dry Sherry
½ pint Brandy
½ pint cold black Tea
3 quarts chilled dry Rhine Wine
8-10 thin strips Cucumber peel
1 quart chilled Club Soda

Put the ice in a punch bowl and pour in all the liquid ingredients except the club soda. Stir, add cucumber peel and let punch steep for 15 minutes. Remove peel. Add club soda, stir and serve in punch glasses. Makes about 40 servings.

RICHELIEU

2 oz. Bourbon
1 oz. White Dubonnet
1 tsp. Vieille Cure

Shake with ice and strain into a fizz glass. Add ice and a twist of orange.

RICHMOND

2 oz. Gin
1 oz. Lillet

Stir with ice and strain into a cocktail glass. Serve with a lemon twist.

RICKEY FIZZ

1½ oz. Gin
¼ oz. Pernod
½ oz. Lemon Juice
½ tsp. Sugar

Shake with ice and strain into a highball glass. Fill with lime rickey.

RICO LLIANO

½ oz. Galliano
½ oz. Lime Juice
1 tsp. Sugar
1½ oz. Rum

Shake with ice and strain into a Collins glass. Fill with crushed ice and soda. Serve with a pear spear, a cherry and an orange slice.

RIDING LESSON

1¾ oz. Whisky
½ oz. Sweet Vermouth
¼ oz. Benedictine
1 dash Angostura Bitters

Stir with ice and strain into a cocktail glass. Serve with a cherry.

RIESLING SPRITZER

2 oz. Dry Sherry
4 oz. Riesling, chilled
4 oz. chilled Soda

Mix and pour over ice cubes in a Collins glass.

You are welcome, my fair guests; that noble lady, Or gentleman that is not freely merry, Is not my friend: This to confirm my welcome: And to you all good health.
— Henry VIII.

RING OF FROST

1 dash Aromatic Bitters
1 dash Orange-flavored Liqueur
1½ oz. Apple Brandy
Extra Dry Champagne, chilled

Combine all ingredients except Champagne and stir well. Strain into a sugar-rimmed champagne glass. Fill with Champagne.

RITZ OF LONDON

1½ oz. Gin
¾ oz. Lemon Juice
¾ oz. Dry Vermouth
1 dash Orange Bitters
1-2 grains Sugar

Shake with ice and strain into a cocktail glass.

RITZ OF MADRID

Juice ¾ Lemon
Juice ½ Orange
1 tsp. Sugar
1½ oz. Triple Sec

Shake with ice and strain into a cocktail glass.

RITZ OF PARIS

¾ oz. Brandy
⅛ oz. Cointreau
Juice ¼ Orange
Champagne

Shake and strain ingredients into a champagne glass until the glass is half full. Fill the glass with chilled Champagne.

RIVIERA

½ oz. Galliano
1 oz. Vodka
½ oz. Creme de Cassis
¾ oz. Lime Juice
½ oz. Cranberry Juice

Shake with ice and strain into a cocktail glass.

ROBBER

1¾ oz. Scotch Whisky
¾ oz. Sweet Vermouth
1 dash Bitters

Stir with ice and strain into a cocktail glass. Serve with a cherry.

ROBERT BURNS

1¾ oz. Scotch Whisky
½ oz. Sweet Vermouth
¼ oz. Pernod
1 dash Orange Bitters

Stir with ice and strain into a cocktail glass.

ROBERT E. LEE COOLER

Juice ½ Lime
½ tsp. Powdered Sugar
2 oz. Soda
¼ tsp. Pernod
2 oz. Gin

Put the first three ingredients into a Collins glass. Stir and add ice cubes and Pernod and Gin. Fill with ginger ale and stir again. Add a twist of orange or lemon peel (or both) and dangle the end over the rim of the glass.

ROBIN'S NEST

1 oz. Vodka
1 oz. Cranberry Juice
½ oz. White Creme de Cacao

Shake with ice and strain into a cocktail glass.

ROBINSON CRUSOE

1¼ oz. Rum
1¼ oz. Pineapple Juice

Shake with ice and strain into a cocktail glass.

ROB ROY

2 oz. Scotch Whisky
1 oz. Sweet Vermouth
2 dashes Angostura Bitters

Stir with ice and strain into a cocktail glass. Serve with a lemon twist.

ROB ROY HOLIDAY STYLE

2 oz. Scotch Whisky
¼ oz. Dry Vermouth
¼ oz. Sweet Vermouth

Stir with ice and strain into a cocktail glass coated inside with ¼ oz. Drambuie. Serve with a cherry.

ROBSON COCKTAIL

2 tsp. Lemon Juice
1 tbsp. Orange Juice
1½ tsp. Grenadine
1 oz. Dark Rum

Shake with ice and strain into a cocktail glass.

ROC-A-COE

1½ oz. Gin
1½ oz. Sherry

Stir with ice and strain into a cocktail glass. Serve with a cherry.

ROCK AND RYE NO. 1

1 piece Rock Candy
3 oz. Rye Whisky
½ tsp. Lemon Juice

Dissolve the rock candy in the Whisky, add lemon juice and serve in a cocktail glass.

ROCK AND RYE NO. 2

1 oz. Rock and Rye
1 oz. White Port
½ oz. Dry Vermouth

Stir with ice and strain into a cocktail glass.

ROCK AND RYE COOLER

1 oz. Rock and Rye
1½ oz. Vodka
1 tbsp. Lime Juice

Shake with ice and strain into a highball glass. Add ice cubes, fill with bitter-lemon soda and stir.

ROCK AND RYE TODDY (HOT)

2 oz. Rock and Rye
2 dashes Angostura Bitters
1 Lemon wedge

Mix in an Old-fashioned glass. Fill with hot water. Add a cinnamon stick. Sprinkle nutmeg on top.

ROCKETTE

Juice ½ Lemon
1 tsp. Sugar
3 sprigs fresh Mint
1½ oz. Vodka

Shake with ice and strain into a cocktail glass.

ROCKY DANE

1 oz. Gin
½ oz. Dry Vermouth
½ oz. Cherry Heering
¼ oz. Kirschwasser

Stir with ice and strain into a cocktail glass. Serve with a lemon twist.

ROCKY GREEN DRAGON

1 oz. Gin
¾ oz. Cognac
¾ oz. Green Chartreuse

Stir with ice and strain into a cocktail glass.

ROCKY MOUNTAIN COCKTAIL

2 oz. Brandy
1 oz. Sweet Vermouth
1 oz. White Creme de Menthe

Stir with ice and strain into a cocktail glass.

ROCKY MOUNTAIN COOLER

2 oz. Applejack
1 Egg
1 tsp. Sugar
½ oz. Lemon Juice

Shake with ice and strain into a Collins glass. Fill with ice and apple cider. Sprinkle nutmeg on top.

ROCOCO

1 oz. Cherry Vodka
1 oz. Orange Juice
½ oz. Triple Sec

Shake with ice and strain into a cocktail glass.

ROFFIGNAC

3 oz. Whisky
1 tbsp. Raspberry Syrup
Soda

Mix in a Sour glass. Fill with soda and ice.

ROLLER DERBY

1¾ oz. Gin
¼ oz. Dry Vermouth
¼ oz. Sweet Vermouth
¼ oz. Benedictine

Stir with ice and strain into a cocktail glass.

The bubble winked at me
   and said:
"You'll miss me, brother,
   when you're dead."

ROLLS ROYA

1¼ oz. Gin
½ oz. Sweet Vermouth
½ oz. Dry Vermouth
¼ oz. Benedictine

Stir with ice and strain into a cocktail glass.

ROLLS ROYCE A PARIS

1 oz. Cointreau
1 oz. Orange Juice
1 tbsp. Cognac

Shake with ice and strain into a cocktail glass. Add ice.

ROLLS ROYCE COCKTAIL NO. 1

½ oz. Dry Vermouth
½ oz. Sweet Vermouth
1½ oz. Gin
¼ tsp. Benedictine

Stir with ice and strain into a cocktail glass.

ROLLS ROYCE COCKTAIL NO. 2

1 oz. Cointreau
1 oz. Cognac
1 oz. Orange Juice

Shake with ice and strain into a cocktail glass.

ROMA

1½ oz. Gin
½ oz. Sweet Vermouth
½ oz. Dry Vermouth
3 fresh Strawberries

Shake with ice and strain into a cocktail glass.

ROMAN CANDLE

1 oz. Campari
1 oz. Cranberry Juice
½ oz. Lemon Juice

Shake with ice and strain into an Old-fashioned glass. Fill with ice. Serve with a lemon twist.

ROMAN COFFEE

1 tsp. Sugar
1 oz. Galliano

Mix in a cup. Add hot black coffee. (Cream optional.)

ROMAN COOLER

1½ oz. Gin
½ oz. Punt e Mes
½ oz. Lemon Juice
1 tsp. Sugar

Shake with ice and strain into a Collins glass. Fill with soda and ice. Serve with a lemon twist.

ROMAN FRULLATI

3 oz. Gin
2 oz. diced Apples
2 oz. diced Pears
2 oz. sliced Peaches
1 oz. Maraschino Liqueur
1 oz. Almond Extract

Blend with ice and strain into a double Old-fashioned glass. Add crushed ice.

ROMAN PUNCH NO. 1

1 oz. Lemon Juice
1 oz. Grenadine
1 oz. Rum
1 oz. Brandy

Mix in a Collins glass. Fill with crushed ice. Float ½ oz. Port on top.

ROMAN PUNCH NO. 2

1½ oz. Cognac
½ oz. Orange Curacao
½ oz. Lemon Juice
½ oz. Rum
¼ oz. Grenadine
¼ tsp. Sugar

Shake with ice and strain into a highball glass. Fill with ice and decorate with a fruit garnish.

ROMAN SNOWBALL

2 oz. Sambuca
3 Coffee Beans

Pack an 8 oz. wine glass half full with crushed ice. Pour Sambuca over ice and top with coffee beans. (Beans are chewed after they have absorbed the flavor of the liqueur.)

ROME BEAUTY

1 oz. Galliano
½ oz. Rose's Lime Juice
½ oz. Cherry Heering

Mix in an Old-fashioned glass. Fill with ice.

Love is the inspiring wine
Mingling tears and laughter;
Marriage is the never failing
Headache the day after.

RON CACAO

1½ oz. Rum
½ oz. Light Creme de Cacao
½ oz. Dry Vermouth

Shake with ice and strain into a cocktail glass.

ROOM AND BOARD

3 oz. Jamaica Rum
¾ oz. Falernum

Pour into an Old-fashioned glass. Decorate with an orange slice and a lemon peel.

ROOSEVELT

1¾ oz. Haitian Rum
½ oz. Dry Vermouth
¼ oz. Orange Juice
¼ tsp. Sugar

Shake with ice and strain into a cocktail glass.

ROOT BEER FLOAT

2 oz. Cream
1½ oz. Galliano

Fill a Collins glass with crushed ice and cola. Add cream and Galliano. Stir well and serve.

RORY O'MORE

¾ oz. Sweet Vermouth
1½ oz. Irish Whisky
1 dash Orange Bitters

Stir with ice and strain into a cocktail glass.

ROSA NO. 1

1½ oz. Gin
½ oz. Kirschwasser
½ oz. Apricot-flavored Brandy

Stir with ice and strain into a cocktail glass.

ROSA NO. 2

½ oz. Grand Marnier
1½ oz. Gin

Stir with ice and strain into a cocktail glass.

ROSE COCKTAIL NO. 1

¾ oz. Cherry-flavored Brandy
¾ oz. Kirschwasser
1½ oz. Gin

Stir with ice and strain into a cocktail glass.

ROSE COCKTAIL NO. 2

1½ oz. Kirsch
1½ oz. Dry Vermouth
1 tsp. Grenadine

Stir with ice and strain into a cocktail glass.

ROSE COCKTAIL (ENGLISH)

½ oz. Apricot-flavored Brandy
½ oz. Dry Vermouth
1 oz. Gin
½ tsp. Lemon Juice
1 tsp. Grenadine

Moisten rim of cocktail glass with lemon juice and dip into powdered sugar. Shake above ingredients with ice and strain into prepared glass.

ROSE COCKTAIL (FRENCH)

½ oz. Cherry-flavored Brandy
½ oz. Dry Vermouth
1½ oz. Gin

Stir with ice and strain into a cocktail glass.

ROSE DU BOY

1½ oz. Gin
½ oz. Dry Vermouth
¼ oz. Cherry-flavored Brandy
¼ oz. Kirschwasser

Stir with ice and strain into a cocktail glass.

ROSE HALL

1 oz. Dark Rum
1 oz. Orange Juice
½ oz. Banana Liqueur
¼ oz. Lemon Juice

Shake with ice and strain into a cocktail glass.

ROSE IN JUNE FIZZ

1½	oz. Gin
1½	oz. Framboise
½	cup Orange Juice
4	tbsp. Lime Juice

Shake with ice and strain into a highball glass. Fill with soda and ice.

ROSE LEMONADE PUNCH

2	bottles California Rose Wine
2	6-oz. cans frozen Lemonade concentrate
1	quart Club Soda
Ice cubes	

Thoroughly chill Wine and club soda. Pour Wine into a large pitcher, add lemonade concentrate and stir to blend. Add club soda and a dozen ice cubes, and stir gently. Serve in 4 oz. punch or wine glasses. Makes about 20 servings.

ROSELYN COCKTAIL NO. 1

¾	oz. Dry Vermouth
1½	oz. Gin
½	tsp. Grenadine

Stir with ice and strain into a cocktail glass. Serve with a lemon twist.

ROSELYN COCKTAIL NO. 2

1½	oz. Gin
¼	oz. Pernod
¼	oz. Grenadine
¼	oz. Lime Juice
½	Egg White

Shake with ice and strain into a cocktail glass.

ROSE MARIE

1¼	oz. Gin
½	oz. Dry Vermouth
¼	oz. Armagnac
¼	oz. Cherry-flavored Brandy
¼	oz. Campari

Stir with ice and strain into a cocktail glass.

ROSEMARY COCKTAIL NO. 1

1	oz. Whisky
1	oz. Grand Marnier
1	oz. Lemon Juice

Shake with ice and strain into a cocktail glass.

ROSEMARY COCKTAIL NO. 2

| 1¼ | oz. Whisky |
| 1¼ | oz. Dry Vermouth |

Stir with ice and strain into a cocktail glass.

ROSE OF PICARDY

1½	oz. Gin
2	tsp. Cherry Kijafa
2	tsp. Dubonnet
1	tsp. Dry Vermouth

Shake with ice and strain into an Old-fashioned glass. Add ice.

ROSE OF WARSAW

| 1¾ | oz. Polish Vodka |
| ¾ | oz. Cherry Cordial |

Stir with ice and strain into a cocktail glass.

ROSETTE COCKTAIL

¾	oz. Gin
½	oz. Claret
½	oz. Orange Juice

Shake with ice and strain into a cocktail glass.

ROSINGTON

| 2 | oz. Gin |
| 1 | oz. Sweet Vermouth |

Stir with ice and strain into a cocktail glass. Serve with a twist of orange peel.

ROSITA

1	oz. Tequila
½	oz. Dry Vermouth
½	oz. Sweet Vermouth
1	oz. Campari

Stir in an Old-fashioned glass with cracked ice. Serve with a lemon twist and short straws.

ROSY

1½	oz. Gin
½	oz. Claret
½	oz. Orange Juice

Shake with ice and strain into a cocktail glass.

ROSY DAWN

1	oz. Gin
¾	oz. Orange Curacao
¾	oz. Cherry-flavored Brandy
¼	oz. Rose's Lime Juice

Shake with ice and strain into a cocktail glass.

ROSY DEACON

¾	oz. Gin
¾	oz. Sloe Gin
1	oz. Grapefruit Juice
Sugar to taste	

Shake with ice and strain into a cocktail glass.

ROSY SQUASH

| 1 | oz. Lemon Juice |
| ½ | oz. Grenadine |

Mix in a highball glass. Fill with soda and ice.

ROTOTO

¾ oz. Brandy
½ oz. Benedictine
½ oz. Maraschino Liqueur
½ oz. Orange Curacao
¼ oz. Vouvray

Shake with ice and strain into a cocktail glass.

ROULETTE NO. 1

¾ oz. Swedish Punch
¾ oz. Rum
1½ oz. Calvados

Shake with ice and strain into a cocktail glass.

ROULETTE NO. 2

¾ oz. Galliano
½ oz. Gin
¼ oz. Creme de Violette
½ Egg White
1 dash Orange Flower Water

Shake with ice and strain into a cocktail glass.

ROYAL NO. 1

1 oz. Gin
1 oz. Dry Vermouth
1 oz. Cherry-flavored Brandy

Stir with ice and strain into a cocktail glass.

ROYAL NO. 2

1 Egg
1 oz. Lemon or Lime Juice
1 tsp. Sugar
1½ oz. Gin

Shake with ice and strain into a cocktail glass.

ROYAL NO. 3

1¾ oz. Gin
¾ oz. Dubonnet
1 dash Orange Bitters
1 dash Angostura Bitters

Shake with ice and strain into a cocktail glass.

ROYAL ANNE COCKTAIL

1 dash Aromatic Bitters
1 dash Maraschino Liqueur
2 oz. Sweet Vermouth
2 oz. Dry Vermouth

Stir with ice and strain into a cocktail glass. Serve with a cherry.

ROYAL BERMUDA

Juice 1 Lime
2 oz. Barbados Rum
¼ oz. Sugar Syrup
1 dash Cointreau

Shake with ice and strain into a cocktail glass.

ROYAL CANADIAN

1½ oz. Whisky
2 tsp. Maple Syrup
Juice ½ Lemon

Shake with ice and strain into a cocktail glass.

ROYAL CLOVER CLUB COCKTAIL

Juice 1 Lime
1 tbsp. Grenadine
1 Egg Yolk
1½ oz. Gin

Shake with ice and strain into a flip glass.

ROYAL FIZZ

1¼ oz. Gin
1½ tsp. Sugar Syrup
1½ tsp. Lemon Juice
1 Egg

Shake with ice and strain into a fizz glass. Fill with soda and ice.

ROYAL GIN FIZZ

Juice ½ Lemon
1 tsp. Powdered Sugar
2 oz. Gin
1 Egg

Shake with ice and strain into a highball glass. Add two cubes of ice, fill with soda and stir.

ROYAL HAWAIIAN

1½ oz. Gin
1½ oz. Pineapple Juice
½ oz. Lime Juice
1 tsp. Cointreau

Cut the top off a pineapple, hollow it out and pour in the drink (or serve in a goblet). Serve with straws.

ROYAL LADY

1 oz. Pernod
1 oz. Sweet Vermouth
1 oz. Dry Vermouth

Stir with ice and strain into a cocktail glass.

ROYAL MILK PUNCH

1½ oz. Rum
1 tsp. Sugar
1 Egg Yolk
3 oz. Milk

Shake with ice and strain into a Collins glass. Fill with soda and ice. Sprinkle nutmeg on top.

ROYAL MONCEAU

1 oz. Gin
½ oz. Liqueur Suze
½ oz. Lemon Juice

Shake with ice and strain into a cocktail glass.

ROYAL RESERVE

1½ oz. Rum

Pour into a Collins glass. Fill with ginger ale and ice.

ROYAL RICKEY

1½ oz. Gin
½ oz. Lime Juice (leave shell in glass)
¾ oz. Sweet Vermouth
½ oz. Grenadine

Shake with ice and strain into a highball glass. Fill with soda or ginger ale and ice. (Dry Vermouth may be substituted for Sweet Vermouth and lemon juice may be used instead of lime juice.)

ROYAL ROMANCE COCKTAIL

1 oz. Gin
1 oz. Grand Marnier
1 oz. Orange Juice

Shake with ice and strain into a cocktail glass.

ROYAL RUBY REFRESHER

Juice ½ Orange
2 dashes Lemon Juice
½ tbsp. Sugar
Ruby Port

Put orange juice, lemon juice, sugar and a little water in a Collins glass. Stir until sugar is dissolved. Fill glass with crushed ice. While adding Port to fill, stir to mix well. Garnish with fresh fruit.

ROYAL SMILE NO. 1

Juice ¼ Lemon
1 tsp. Grenadine
½ oz. Gin
1 oz. Apple Brandy

Stir with ice and strain into a Collins glass.

ROYAL SMILE NO. 2

1 oz. Gin
1 oz. Grenadine
2 dashes Lemon Juice

Stir with ice and strain into a cocktail glass.

ROYAL SNOWCAP

¾ oz. Rum
¾ oz. Dry Vermouth
½ oz. Parfait Amour
1 dash Lemon Juice
1 Egg White

Shake with ice and strain into a cocktail glass. Sprinkle chocolate flakes on top.

ROYAL WELCOME

½ oz. Lemon Juice
1 tsp. Powdered Sugar
1½ oz. Brandy
Extra Dry Champagne, chilled

Fill a Collins glass half full with cracked ice. Add lemon juice, sugar and Brandy. Fill with Champagne.

ROY HOWARD LILLET

2 oz. Lillet
1 oz. Brandy
1 oz. Orange Juice
2 dashes Grenadine

Shake with ice and strain into a cocktail glass.

RUBAN BLEU

1½ oz. Rum
2 dashes Creme d'Yvette
Juice ½ Lemon

Shake with ice and strain into a cocktail glass.

RUBY NO. 1

½ oz. Galliano
1 oz. Brandy
½ oz. Cherry Kijafa
½ oz. Orange Juice

Shake with ice and strain into a cocktail glass.

RUBY NO. 2

1¾ oz. Sloe Gin
½ oz. Sweet Vermouth
¼ oz. Cherry Liqueur
1 dash Orange Bitters

Shake with ice and strain into a cocktail glass.

RUBY NO. 3

¾ oz. Sloe Gin
¾ oz. Gin
½ oz. Dry Vermouth
½ oz. Sweet Vermouth
¼ oz. Benedictine

Shake with ice and strain into a cocktail glass.

RUBY NO. 4

1½ oz. Rum
1 oz. Orange Juice
¼ oz. Blackberry-flavored Brandy
Sugar to taste

Shake with ice and strain into a cocktail glass.

RUBY NO. 5

1½ oz. Gin
¾ oz. Applejack
¼ oz. Grenadine

Shake with ice and strain into a cocktail glass.

RUBY NO. 6

1½ oz. Cherry-flavored Brandy
½ oz. Dry Vermouth
¼ oz. Maraschino Liqueur
1 dash Orange Bitters

Shake with ice and strain into a cocktail glass.

RUBY AND SHERRY

½   tbsp. Sugar
1   oz. Pineapple Juice
6   oz. Medium Sherry
1   oz. Ruby Port

Put the sugar, a little water and pineapple juice in a Collins glass. Stir to dissolve the sugar and fill the glass three-quarters full with cracked ice. Pour in Sherry. Stir and float Port. Garnish with fresh fruit.

RUBY FIZZ

Juice ½ Lemon
1   tsp. Powdered Sugar
1   Egg White
1   tsp. Grenadine
2   oz. Sloe Gin
1   tsp. Raspberry Syrup

Shake with ice and strain into a highball glass. Add ice cubes, fill with soda and stir.

RUBY PORT COBBLER

1   tsp. Orange-flavored Liqueur
1   tsp. Orange Juice
Ruby Port

Fill a Collins glass two-thirds full with cracked ice. Add liqueur and orange juice. Fill with Port. Stir lightly. Garnish with a lime wheel and a cherry.

RUBY PORT COCKTAIL

1   dash Orange-flavored Liqueur
2   dashes Aromatic Bitters
1½   oz. Brandy
1½   oz. Port

Stir with ice and strain into a cocktail glass.

RUBY PUNCH

½   oz. Lemon Juice
1   oz. Orange Juice
½   oz. Brandy
½   oz. Orange Curacao
½   oz. Grenadine
3   oz. Sparkling Burgundy

Mix in a Collins glass. Fill with ice. Add a squirt of soda.

RUBY RANGOON

1½   oz. Gin
1½   oz. Cranberry Juice

Mix in a highball glass. Fill with ginger ale and ice. Serve with a squeeze of lime juice.

RUBY RED

2   oz. Cranberry Juice Cocktail
3   oz. Ruby Port

Mix and pour over ice cubes in a Collins glass.

RUBY SILVER

¾   oz. Sloe Gin
¾   oz. Sweet Vermouth
¼   oz. Cherry Liqueur
1   dash Orange Bitters
½   Egg White

Shake with ice and strain into a cocktail glass. Sprinkle nutmeg on top.

RUDDY MARY

1½   oz. Aquavit
3   oz. Tomato Juice
½   oz. Cream
1   dash Tabasco Sauce
½   Egg Yolk
¼   oz. Lemon Juice
¼   oz. Catsup

Shake with ice and strain into a double Old-fashioned glass.

RUM ALEXANDER

1½   oz. Jamaica Rum
¾   oz. Cream
¾   oz. Light Creme de Cacao

Shake with ice and strain into a cocktail glass.

RUMAN

1½   oz. Rum
½   oz. Cointreau
½   oz. Lemon Juice

Shake with ice and strain into a cocktail glass.

RUM AND COCONUT COOLER

2   oz. Rum
1   oz. Coconut Cream
½   oz. Lemon Juice

Shake with ice and strain into a Collins glass. Fill with ice and Squirt. Serve with a lemon wedge and a cherry.

RUM AND FRUIT

¾   oz. Jamaica Rum
¾   oz. Orange Juice
½   oz. Benedictine
¼   oz. Lemon Juice
½   oz. Kummel

Shake with ice and strain into a cocktail glass.

RUM AND GIN

1½   oz. Rum
½   oz. Gin
½   oz. Lemon Juice

Shake with ice and strain into a cocktail glass.

Here's a toast to great ambition,
About which people rant.
It makes you want to do the thing
That everyone knows you can't.

RUM AND PINEAPPLE COOLER

2   oz. Rum
2   oz. Pineapple Juice
½   oz. Lemon Juice
¼   oz. 151-proof Rum
1   tsp. Sugar
1   dash Angostura Bitters

Shake with ice and strain into a Collins glass. Fill with ice and Squirt. Serve with a pineapple stick and a cherry.

RUM AND SHERRY

1¾   oz. Rum
¾   oz. Sherry

Stir with ice and strain into a cocktail glass. Serve with a cherry.

RUM APERITIF

1   oz. Rum
1   oz. Dry Vermouth
¼   oz. Dark Rum
¼   oz. Grenadine
½   oz. Lemon Juice

Shake with ice and strain into a cocktail glass.

RUMBA

1½   oz. Rum
¼   oz. Lemon Juice
¾   oz. Pernod

Shake with ice and strain into a cocktail glass.

RUMBLE

1   oz. Kahlua
1   oz. Rum

Mix in a Collins glass. Fill with soda and ice.

RUM BLOODY MARY

1½   oz. Puerto Rican Rum
4   oz. Tomato Juice
1   tbsp. Lime Juice
3   drops Worcestershire Sauce
3   drops Tabasco Sauce
1   pinch Salt

Shake with ice and strain into a Sour glass.

RUM BUCK

1½   oz. Rum
½   oz. Lemon Juice

Fill with ginger ale and ice. Serve with a lemon twist. (Soda may be used instead of ginger ale.)

RUM CITRUS COOLER

2   oz. Rum
1   oz. Orange Juice
½   oz. Lime Juice
½   oz. Cointreau
1   tsp. Sugar

Shake with ice and strain into a Collins glass. Fill with 7-Up and ice. Serve with a lemon wedge and a lime wheel.

RUM COBBLER

1   tsp. Powdered Sugar
2   oz. Soda
2   oz. Jamaica Rum

In a goblet, dissolve sugar in soda. Fill the goblet with shaved ice and add Rum. Stir and decorate with fruits. Serve with straws.

RUM COCONUT COOLER

2½   oz. White Rum
1   oz. Coconut Cream
2   tsp. Lemon Juice
Soda

Shake with ice and strain into a highball glass. Fill with soda and ice.

RUM COCONUT FIZZ

2   oz. Rum
½   oz. Coconut Cream
½   oz. Lime Juice

Shake with ice and strain into a Collins glass. Fill with soda and ice. Serve with a lime wheel.

RUM COFFEE COCKTAIL

1½   oz. Jamaica Rum
⅔   cup Coffee

Mix in a cup.

RUM COLLINS

Juice 1 Lime
1   tsp. Powdered Sugar
2   oz. Rum

Shake with ice and strain into a Collins glass. Add ice and fill with soda. Stir and decorate with a lemon slice and a cherry. Serve with straws.

RUM COOLER

½   tsp. Powdered Sugar
2   oz. Soda
2   oz. Rum

In a Collins glass, dissolve sugar in soda. Stir and fill the glass with ice and add Rum. Fill with ginger ale and stir again. Insert a twist of orange or lemon peel (or both) and dangle the end over the rim of the glass.

RUM COW

1½   oz. Light Rum
2   drops Vanilla
1   dash Angostura Bitters
2   tsps. Sugar
1   cup Milk

Shake with ice and strain into a highball glass. Sprinkle nutmeg on top and add ice.

RUM CRUSTA

1½ oz. Rum
¼ oz. Maraschino Liqueur
1 dash Bitters
½ oz. Lemon Juice
¼ oz. Orange Curacao

Stir with ice and strain into a sugar-rimmed cocktail glass. Serve with a lemon twist.

RUM CUIT

1½ oz. Rum
3 tsp. Lime Juice
1-2 drops Dark Molasses

Shake with ice and strain into a cocktail glass.

May the right person say the right thing
To the right person in the right way.
At the right time, in the right place.

RUM CURACAO COOLER

1 oz. Dark Rum
1 oz. Orange Curacao
½ oz. Lime Juice

Shake with ice and strain into a Collins glass. Fill with ice and Squirt. Serve with a lime wheel and an orange slice.

RUM CURE

1 oz. each Jamaica, White and 151-proof Rum
1 oz. each Pineapple, Lemon and Orange Juice
2 tsp. Brandy
2 tbsp. Grenadine

Shake with ice and strain into an Old-fashioned glass. Fill with crushed ice. Decorate with slices of fruit and float a few drops of Curacao on top.

RUM DAISY

Juice ½ Lemon
½ tsp. Powdered Sugar
1 tsp. Raspberry Syrup or Grenadine
2 oz. Rum

Shake with ice and strain into a stein or metal cup. Add an ice cube and decorate with fruit.

RUM DOUBLOON

1 oz. each Jamaica, White and 151-proof Rum
1 oz. Grapefruit Juice
1 oz. Orange Juice
1-2 drops Orange Curacao
1-2 drops Pernod

Shake with ice and strain into an Old-fashioned glass. Fill with crushed ice.

RUM DUBONNET

1½ oz. Light Rum
1½ tsps. Dubonnet
1 tsp. Lemon Juice

Shake with ice and strain into a cocktail glass.

RUM EGGNOG

1 Egg
1 tsp. Powdered Sugar
2 oz. Rum
6 oz. Milk

Shake with ice and strain into a Collins glass. Sprinkle nutmeg on top.

RUM FIX

Juice ½ Lemon or 1 Lime
1 tsp. Powdered Sugar
1 tsp. Water
2½ oz. Rum

Stir the first three ingredients together in a highball glass and fill with ice. Add Rum and stir. Add a slice of lemon. Serve with straws.

RUM FIZZ

1½ oz. Rum
¾ oz. Cherry-flavored Brandy
½ tsp. Sugar
2 tbsp. Lemon Juice

Shake with ice and strain into a Collins glass. Fill with soda and ice.

RUM FLIP

1½ oz. Rum
1 tsp. Sugar
1 Egg

Shake with ice and strain into a flip glass. Sprinkle nutmeg on top. (½ oz. cream may be added.)

RUM FLOAT

¾ oz. Lime Juice
3 oz. Soda
1 oz. Dark Rum

Mix the first 2 ingredients in a highball glass. Fill with ice and float Rum on top.

RUM FRAPPE

1 scoop Orange or Lemon Sherbet
2 oz. Light Rum

Put the sherbet in a saucer champagne or cocktail glass, pour the Rum over it and stir.

RUM FUSTIAN

6 Egg yolks
1 quart Beer or Ale
1 pint Gin
1 pint Medium-Dry Sherry
1 stick Cinnamon
1 dash Nutmeg
1 twist Lemon peel

Beat the egg yolks until lemony and frothy. Add the beer; then the Gin. Put the Sherry in a saucepan with the cinnamon, nutmeg and lemon peel and heat (but do not boil). Remove the cinnamon. Beat the hot Wine into the egg mixture, and serve at once, while it is still warm, in heated mugs.

RUM HIGHBALL

2 oz. Rum
Ginger ale or soda

Pour Rum in a highball glass over ice and fill with ginger ale or soda. Add a twist of lemon, if desired, and stir.

RUM JULEP NO. 1

Several Mint sprigs
1 tsp. Sugar
1 oz. Water
1½ oz. Rum

Muddle the mint sprigs in a Collins glass with sugar and water. Fill the glass with crushed ice and add Rum. Stir until the glass frosts. Serve with a few mint sprigs.

RUM JULEP NO. 2

Several Mint sprigs
1 tsp. Sugar and Water
4 ripe Peach slices
1½ oz. Rum
¾ oz. Lime Juice
½ tsp. Sugar

Muddle the mint sprigs with the sugar water in a double Old-fashioned glass. Fill the glass half full with crushed ice. Place peach slices in the glass and mix. Stir together Rum, lime juice and sugar and strain over the prepared glass. Serve with several mint sprigs.

RUM KUM

1½ oz. Rum
¾ oz. Lime Juice
½ oz. Orange Curacao
¼ oz. Jamaica Rum

Shake with ice and strain into a cocktail glass. Serve with a kumquat.

RUM MANHATTAN

1½ oz. Rum
1 oz. Sweet Vermouth
1 dash Orange Bitters

Stir with ice and strain into a cocktail glass. Serve with a lemon twist.

RUM MARTINI

1½ oz. Rum
1 oz. Dry Vermouth
1 dash Orange Bitters

Stir with ice and strain into a cocktail glass. Serve with an olive, an onion or a lemon twist.

RUM MILK PUNCH

1 tsp. Powdered Sugar
2 oz. Rum
1 cup Milk

Shake with ice, strain into a Collins glass and sprinkle nutmeg on top.

RUM MINT SQUASH

2 oz. Gold Rum
½ doz. Mint sprigs
1-2 dashes Peychaud's Bitters
1-2 dashes Rock Candy Syrup

Muddle the mint with the Bitters and candy syrup in 1 oz. of cold water in an Old-fashioned glass. Add ice and Rum. Stir briskly. Serve with a twist of lemon peel.

> Then here's to thee, old
> friend; and long
> May thou and I thus meet,
> To brighten still with wine
> and song
> The short life ere it fleet.

RUM MOCHA

1 scoop Vanilla Ice Cream
2 oz. Martinique Rum
Black Coffee

Fill a Collins glass one-third full with crushed ice. Add ice cream and Rum. Fill with hot coffee.

RUMMY

1 oz. Jamaica Rum
¾ oz. Dry Vermouth
½ oz. Lime Juice
½ oz. Grenadine

Shake with ice and strain into a cocktail glass.

RUMOLA

1½ oz. Gin
½ oz. Lemon Juice
½ oz. Rumola

Shake with ice and strain into a cocktail glass.

RUM OLD-FASHIONED

½ tsp. Powdered Sugar
1 dash Bitters
1 tsp. Water
1½ oz. Light Rum
1 tsp. 151-proof Rum

Stir sugar, Bitters and water in an Old-fashioned glass. When the sugar is dissolved, add ice cubes and golden Rum. Add a twist of lime peel and float 151-proof Rum on top.

RUM ON THE ROCKS

2 oz. Light Rum
2-3 Ice cubes
Twist of Lemon Peel

Put the ice in an Old-fashioned glass, pour in Rum and drop in the lemon peel.

RUM ORANGE COCKTAIL

1½ oz. Rum
½ oz. Orange Juice
½ oz. Sweet Vermouth

Shake with ice and strain into a cocktail glass. Dust with cinnamon.

RUM PICK-UP

2 oz. Gold or Dark Rum
2 oz. Milk

Mix in a highball glass. Fill with soda and ice.

RUM PINEAPPLE FIZZ

2 oz. Gold Rum
½ oz. 151-proof Rum
½ Egg White
1 tsp. Sugar
½ oz. Lime Juice
½ oz. Lemon Juice
Several fresh Pineapple pieces

Blend with ice and strain into a Collins glass. Fill with soda and ice. Serve with a lime wheel.

RUM PUFF

1½ oz. Rum
3 oz. Milk

Mix in a highball glass. Fill with soda and ice.

RUM PUNCH NO. 1

1½ oz. Rum
¼ oz. Orange Curacao
½ oz. Lemon Juice
¼ tsp. Sugar

Shake with ice and strain into a highball glass. Fill with crushed ice and soda. Decorate with a fruit garnish.

RUM PUNCH NO. 2

2 oz. Orange Juice
2 oz. Pineapple Juice
2 oz. Papaya Nectar
1 oz. Lime Juice
2 oz. Medium-dark Rum

Mix fruit juices together and chill thoroughly. When ready to serve, put ice cubes in a double Collins glass, add Rum and chilled juices, stir to mix and garnish with mint or fruit.

RUM PUNCH BOWL

1 bottle Medium-dark Rum
2 Vanilla Beans
Large block of Tea Ice
1 cup fresh Lime Juice
4 cups cold black Tea

Put vanilla beans in the bottle of Rum and allow to steep for 2 to 3 hours. Strain. Set the tea ice in a punch bowl and add Rum, lime juice and tea. Stir. Serve in 4 oz. punch glasses. Makes about 16 servings.

RUM RAMSEY

1¾ oz. Rum
¼ oz. Bourbon Whisky
¼ oz. Lime Juice
¼ tsp. Sugar
1 dash Peychaud's Bitters

Stir with ice and strain into a cocktail glass.

RUM RICKEY NO. 1

Juice ½ Lime
1½ oz. Rum

Pour into a highball glass over ice cubes and fill with soda. Stir and add a wedge of lime.

RUM RICKEY NO. 2

1½ oz. Rum
¾ oz. Benedictine
½ oz. Lemon Juice
¼ oz. Grenadine

Pour into a highball glass. Fill with soda and ice.

RUM ROYALE

1 oz. Rum
2 oz. Sauterne
1½ oz. Lemon Juice
2 oz. Pineapple Juice
1 tsp. Sugar
1 dash Peychaud's Bitters

Shake with ice and strain into a Collins glass. Serve with a pineapple spear and a cherry.

RUM RUMMY

½ oz. Galliano
½ oz. Tio Pepe
1 oz. Pineapple Juice
1 oz. Grapefruit Juice
1 oz. Rum
1 dash Angostura Bitters
¼ oz. Grenadine

Shake with ice and strain into a highball glass. Fill with bitter lemon soda and add ice. Serve with a cherry and slices of lemon and orange.

RUMRUNNER NO. 1

1½ oz. White Rum
1 tbsp. Orange Juice
2 tsp. Lime Juice
1½ tsp. Sugar Syrup
1-2 dashes Orange Bitters

Shake with ice and strain into an Old-fashioned glass. Add ice and an orange twist.

RUMRUNNER NO. 2

Juice 1 Lime
1½ oz. Gin
1 oz. Pineapple Juice
1 tsp. Sugar
1 dash Peychaud's Bitters

Shake with ice and strain over ice cubes in an Old-fashioned glass rimmed with salt.

RUM SCAFFA

1 dash Angostura Bitters
1¼ oz. Rum
1¼ oz. Benedictine

Pour into a cocktail glass. Stir and serve without ice.

RUM SCREWDRIVER

1½ oz. Rum
5 oz. Orange Juice

Combine ingredients in a highball glass with ice cubes.

RUM SHAKE

3	oz. Jamaica Rum
1½	oz. Pernod
4	oz. Pineapple Juice

Shake with ice and strain into a highball glass. Add ice.

RUM SIDECAR

1	oz. Rum
¾	oz. Lemon or Lime Juice
¾	oz. Cointreau

Shake with ice and strain into a cocktail glass.

RUM SMASH

½	tsp. Sugar dissolved in Water
1½	oz. Rum
Soda	
Mint sprigs	

Muddle mint and sugar water in a highball glass. Fill with crushed ice, add Rum and a squirt of soda. Serve with a mint sprig.

RUM SOUR NO. 1

3	oz. Dark Rum
3	tbsp. Lime Juice
Sugar Syrup to taste	

Shake with ice and strain into an Old-fashioned glass. Serve with an orange slice and a cherry.

RUM SOUR NO. 2

¾	oz. Lemon Juice
¼	oz. Orange Juice
1½	oz. Rum
1	tsp. Sugar

Shake with ice and strain into a cocktail glass. Float 151-proof Rum on top. Serve with a lemon wedge.

RUM STINGER

1¾	oz. Rum
¾	oz. White Creme de Menthe

Shake with ice and strain into a cocktail glass.

RUM SWIRL

1	oz. White Rum
2	oz. Banana Liqueur
1	tsp. Lime Juice

Shake with ice and strain into an Old-fashioned glass. Add ice.

RUM SWIZZLE NO. 1

¾	oz. Lime Juice
1½	oz. Rum
1	dash Angostura Bitters
½	oz. Falernum

Stir with ice and strain into a highball glass.

RUM SWIZZLE NO. 2

½	oz. Lime Juice
1	tsp. Sugar dissolved in
2	oz. Soda
2	dashes Bitters
1½	oz. Rum

Pour the lime juice and sweetened soda into a Collins glass. Fill with crushed ice and stir. Add Bitters and Rum. Top off with more soda and stir.

RUM TEA

3-4	oz. Jamaica Rum
1	pot hot Tea
Whole Cinnamon sticks and Cloves	
Nutmeg	
Mint sprigs	

In a mug, steep the spices in the tea for several minutes; add Rum when ready to serve.

RUM TODDY

½	tsp. Powdered Sugar
2	tsps. Water
2	oz. Rum

In an Old-fashioned glass dissolve the sugar in the water. Stir and add Rum and a cube of ice. Stir again and add a twist of lemon peel.

RUM TODDY (HOT)

2	oz. Rum
Boiling Water	
1	lump Sugar

Put sugar in a hot whisky glass and fill two-thirds full with boiling water. Add Rum and stir. Decorate with a slice of lemon. Sprinkle nutmeg on top.

RUM ZOOM

1	tsp. Honey
1	tsp. Cream
3	oz. Rum

Dissolve honey in a cup with a little boiling water. Pour into a shaker with cream and Rum. Add ice and shake well. Strain into a cocktail glass.

RUNT'S AMBITION

¾	oz. Rum
¾	oz. Gin
½	oz. Whisky
½	oz. Port

Shake with ice and strain into a cocktail glass.

RURAL PUNCH

2	Lemon twists
½	tsp. Sugar
1	dash Angostura Bitters
1½	oz. Applejack
Cider	

Muddle lemon twists, sugar and Bitters in a highball glass. Add Applejack and fill with cider and ice.

RUSSELL HOUSE (DOWN THE HATCH)

2	oz. Rye Whisky
3	dashes Blackberry-flavored Brandy
2	dashes Sugar Syrup
2	dashes Orange Bitters

Stir with ice and strain into a cocktail glass.

RUSSIAN NO. 1

1   oz. Gin
1   oz. Vodka
1   oz. Creme de Cacao

Stir with ice and strain into a cocktail glass.

RUSSIAN NO. 2

1¾   oz. Brandy
½   oz. Orange Juice
¼   oz. Pernod
1   dash Orange Bitters

Stir with ice and strain into a cocktail glass.

RUSSIAN NO. 3

1½   oz. Cognac
1   dash Angostura Bitters

Mix in a cocktail glass. Fill with Champagne and stir.

RUSSIAN BEAR COCKTAIL

1   oz. Vodka
½   oz. White Creme de Cacao
1   tbsp. sweet Cream

Stir with ice and strain into a cocktail glass.

RUSSIAN COFFEE COCKTAIL

¾   oz. Coffee Liqueur
¾   oz. Vodka
¾   oz. Cream

Shake with ice and strain into a cocktail glass.

RUSSIAN COFFEE (HOT)

1   tsp. Brown or White Sugar
1½   oz. Vodka

Mix in a cup. Fill with hot black coffee. Top with whipped cream.

RUSSIAN ESPRESSO

1½   oz. Vodka
½   oz. Coffee Liqueur
¼   oz. Lemon Juice

Shake with ice and strain into a cocktail glass. Serve with a lemon twist.

RUSSIAN PUNCH

1   oz. Cognac
1   oz. Kummel

Mix in a highball glass. Fill with Champagne and ice.

RUSSIAN ROULETTE

½   oz. Galliano
½   oz. Vodka
½   oz. Banana-flavored Brandy
½   oz. Orange Juice
¼   oz. Lemon Juice

Shake with ice and strain into a cocktail glass. Serve with several fresh banana pieces.

RUSTY NAIL

¾   oz. Scotch Whisky
¾   oz. Drambuie

Serve in an Old-fashioned glass with ice cubes.

RYE AND DRY

1½   oz. Rye Whisky
1   oz. Dry Vermouth
1   dash Orange Bitters

Stir with ice and strain into a cocktail glass.

RYE COCKTAIL

2   oz. Rye Whisky
1   tsp. Sugar Syrup
2   dashes Angostura Bitters

Shake with ice and strain into a cocktail glass. Add ice.

RYE EGGNOG

1½   oz. Rye Whisky
1   Egg
1   tsp. Sugar
½   pint Milk

Shake with ice and strain into a Collins glass.

RYE FLIP

1   Egg
1½   oz. Rye Whisky
1   tsp. Sugar
(½ oz. Cream optional)

Shake with ice and strain into a flip glass. Sprinkle nutmeg on top.

RYE HIGHBALL

2   oz. Rye Whisky
Ginger Ale or soda

Put Whisky in a highball glass over ice cubes and fill with ginger ale (or soda) and ice cubes. Add a twist of lemon peel, if desired, and stir.

RYE LEMONADE

1½   oz. Rye Whisky
Lemonade

Pour Rye into a cocktail glass with a sugared rim. Fill with fresh lemonade.

RYE OLD-FASHIONED

1½   oz. Rye Whisky
1   dash Bitters
1   cube Sugar

Muddle sugar and bitters in an Old-fashioned glass with a dash of soda. Add ice, Rye and a lemon twist. Stir.

RYE RICKEY

1½   oz. Rye Whisky
Juice and rind ½ Lime

Place in a Collins glass. Fill with soda and ice.

RYE SAZERAC

¼ oz. Pernod
½ tsp. Sugar
2 dashes Angostura or
   Peychaud's Bitters
¼ oz. Water
2 oz. Rye Whisky
Several Ice cubes

Coat the inside of an Old-fashioned glass with the Pernod, then add the remaining ingredients. Stir and serve with a lemon twist.

RYE WHISKY COCKTAIL

1 dash Bitters
1 tsp. Powdered Sugar
2 oz. Rye Whisky

Shake with ice and strain into a cocktail glass. Serve with a cherry.

RYE WHISKY PUNCH

2 oz. Rye Whisky
½ oz. Lemon Juice
½ tsp. Sugar

Shake with ice and pour unstrained into a highball glass. Fill with ice. Serve with an orange slice.

SABBATH CALM COCKTAIL

¾ oz. Brandy
¾ oz. Black Coffee
¾ oz. Port
1 Egg
2 oz. Cream

Shake with ice and strain into a goblet. Sprinkle nutmeg on top.

SAGUENAY

1 oz. Rum
1 oz. Dry Vermouth
¼ oz. Creme de Cassis
¼ oz. Lemon Juice

Shake with ice and strain into a cocktail glass.

SAINT AUGUSTINE

1½ oz. Rum
1   oz. Grapefruit Juice
¼   oz. Cointreau

Shake with ice and strain into a cocktail glass with a sugared rim. Serve with a lemon twist.

ST. CHARLES PUNCH

1 oz. Brandy
½ oz. Triple Sec
3 oz. Port
1 tsp. Sugar
   Juice 1 Lemon

Shake all ingredients with ice except Port. Strain into a Collins glass with ice. Top with Port. Add a slice of lemon and a cherry.

ST. CROIX COOLER

2   oz. Rum
½   oz. Dark Rum
1   oz. Brandy
1   tsp. Brown Sugar
2½   oz. Orange Juice
1½   oz. Lemon Juice
1   dash Orange Flower Water

Shake with ice and strain into a Collins glass. Fill with Squirt and ice.

ST. CROIX MILK PUNCH

1   oz. Jamaica Rum
1   oz. Cognac
1   oz. Gin
1-2 dashes Angostura Bitters
3   oz. Milk
     Sugar

Mix Rum, Cognac and Gin in a mug. Warm the milk and add to the liquors. Sweeten to taste. Add Bitters and stir well. Serve warm, garnished with nutmeg.

ST. FRANCIS SPECIAL MARTINI

3 oz. Gin
1 oz. Vermouth

Stir with ice and strain into a cocktail glass. Serve with an olive.

ST. GERMAIN

1½ oz. Green Chartreuse
1   Egg White
1   oz. Lemon or Grapefruit Juice

Shake with ice and strain into a cocktail glass.

ST. LO

1½ oz. Gin
½   oz. Calvados
½   oz. Lemon Juice
1   tsp. Sugar

Shake with ice and strain into a cocktail glass.

ST. LOUIS BLIZZARD

2   oz. Early Times
¾   oz. Cranberry Juice
1   oz. Lemon Juice
1   tbsp. Sugar

Blend with lots of ice and strain into an Old-fashioned glass.

ST. MARK

1   oz. Gin
1   oz. Dry Vermouth
½   oz. Cherry-flavored Brandy
½   oz. Groseille Syrup

Stir with ice and strain into a cocktail glass.

ST. MORITZ COCKTAIL NO. 1

1 oz. Dry Vermouth
1 oz. Rye Whisky
1 oz. Goldwasser
1 dash Orange Bitters

Shake with ice and strain into a cocktail glass.

ST. MORITZ COCKTAIL NO. 2

1   oz. Kummel
1   oz. Scotch Whisky

Pack a cocktail glass with crushed ice. Add Kummel and Scotch and top with a lemon wedge.

ST. PATRICK'S DAY COCKTAIL

¾   oz. Green Creme de Menthe
¾   oz. Green Chartreuse
¾   oz. Irish Whisky
1   dash Bitters

Stir with ice and strain into a cocktail glass.

ST. RAPHAEL AND VODKA

3   oz. St. Raphaël
1½   oz. Vodka

Put 2 or 3 ice cubes into a goblet, add St. Raphaël and Vodka and a little soda. Stir lightly and serve with a lemon twist.

ST. REGIS

2   oz. Applejack
¼   oz. Lemon Juice
¼   oz. Grenadine

Shake with ice and strain into a cocktail glass.

ST. VINCENT

¾   oz. Galliano
1   oz. Rum
¾   oz. Gin
1   dash Grenadine

Shake with ice and strain into a cocktail glass.

SAKE HIGHBALL

3   oz. Sake
1   tsp. Castor Sugar
Juice ¼ Lemon

Stir with ice and strain into a highball glass. Fill with ice and soda. Serve with a lemon slice.

SAKETINI

2   oz. Gin
½   oz. Sake

Stir with ice and strain into a cocktail glass. Serve with a lemon twist or an olive.

SALOME NO. 1

1   oz. Gin
1   oz. Dry Vermouth
1   oz. Dubonnet

Stir with ice and strain into a cocktail glass.

SALOME NO. 2

¾   oz. Dubonnet
¾   oz. Sweet Vermouth
2   dashes Pernod

Shake with ice and strain into a cocktail glass.

SALT LAKE SPECIAL

¾   oz. Galliano
2   oz. Grapefruit Juice
¾   oz. Gin
1   dash Orange Bitters

Shake with ice and strain into a highball glass. Fill with ice and 7-Up.

SALTY DOG NO. 1

1½   oz. Gin
5   oz. Grapefruit Juice
¼   tsp. Salt

Pour into a highball glass over ice cubes. Stir well.

SALTY DOG NO. 2

2   oz. Vodka
4   oz. Grapefruit Juice

Rub the rim of an Old-fashioned glass with lemon, and dip it in salt. Add ice cubes, Vodka and grapefruit juice and stir gently.

SALUBRIOUS SALUTATIONS

½   oz. Galliano
½   oz. Drambuie
½   oz. Gin
½   oz. Benedictine
1   oz. Fresh Cream

Shake with ice and strain into a cocktail glass.

SALUTE

1   tbsp. Campari
6   oz. chilled Champagne

Place an ice cube in a goblet and pour Campari over it. Fill the glass slowly with Champagne.

SAMBUCA COFFEE FRAPPE

1   oz. Sambuca
½   oz. Coffee Liqueur

Pack a cocktail glass with crushed ice and stir Sambuca with liqueur. Strain over ice in a cocktail glass. Add several roasted coffee beans.

SAMMY

2¼   oz. chilled Vodka
¼   oz. Galliano

Pour Vodka into a cocktail glass. Float Galliano on top. Serve with a cucumber slice.

SAM WARD COCKTAIL

Green Chartreuse

Cut a small lemon and fill with fine ice. Add Green Chartreuse and serve with straws.

SANCTUARY

2	oz. Dubonnet
1	oz. Amer Picon
1	oz. Cointreau

Stir with ice and strain into a cocktail glass.

SAND GROGG

½	tsp. Sugar
1	oz. Whisky
1	oz. Orange Curacao
1	oz. Jamaica Rum

Mix in a highball glass. Fill with hot water. Sprinkle nutmeg on top.

SAN DIEGO

1	oz. Bourbon Whisky
1	oz. Dubonnet
½	oz. Orange Curacao
1	dash Bitters

Stir with ice and strain into a cocktail glass.

> Here's to the bride and the bridegroom,
> We'll ask their success in our prayers,
> And through life's dark shadows and sunshine
> That good luck may ever be theirs.

SAND-MARTIN COCKTAIL

1	tsp. Green Chartreuse
1½	oz. Sweet Vermouth
1½	oz. Gin

Stir with ice and strain into a cocktail glass.

SAN FRANCISCO COCKTAIL

¾	oz. Sloe Gin
¾	oz. Sweet Vermouth
¾	oz. Dry Vermouth
1	dash Bitters
1	dash Orange Bitters

Shake with ice and strain into a cocktail glass. Serve with a cherry.

SAN FRANCISCO TROLLEY

2	oz. Early Times
4	oz. Pineapple Juice
2	oz. Cranberry Juice

Shake with ice and strain into a highball glass. Fill with ice and stir. Serve with an orange slice.

SANGAREE

¼	tsp. Sugar
2	oz. Liquor (your choice)
½	oz. Port

Dissolve sugar in water in a double Old-fashioned glass. Fill with crushed ice and add liquor of your choice. Float Port on top. Sprinkle nutmeg on top.

SANGAREE (GIN) COCKTAIL

2	oz. Gin
1	tsp. Sugar
1	tsp. Sherry

Pour Gin into a cocktail glass and add sugar. Fill with crushed ice and add Sherry.

SANGAREE COMFORT

1	oz. Bourbon
1	oz. Southern Comfort
¼	oz. Peach-flavored Brandy
¼	oz. Lemon Juice
½	tsp. Sugar

Mix in a double Old-fashioned glass. Fill with ice. Top with Squirt. Sprinkle nutmeg on top.

> Drink, for faith and hope are high —
> None so true as you and I —
> Drink the lover's litany —
> "Love like ours can never die!"

SANGRIA NO. 1

1	Orange, sliced
1	Lemon, sliced
1	Apple, cored and cut into 8 wedges
1	bottle Dry Red Wine
2	oz. Brandy
1	pint chilled Club Soda
¼	cup superfine Sugar
Ice	

Combine fruits and sugar in a large glass pitcher, pour in the Wine and Brandy and stir. Refrigerate. At serving time add club soda and ice cubes, stir and serve in 8 oz. goblets. Makes about 6 servings.

SANGRIA NO. 2

| 1 | quart Dry Red Wine |
| 1 | quart chilled Club Soda |

Orange, Lemon and Lime slices
Peel of 1 Orange
Sugar Syrup to taste
Ice cubes

Blend all the ingredients except the ice cubes. Put about 12 ice cubes in a large glass pitcher and pour the wine mixture and garnishes over them. Serve in 4 oz. punch glasses or small wineglasses. Makes 16 servings.

SANGRIA NO. 3

½ cup Sugar Syrup
1 Orange, thinly sliced
1 Lime, thinly sliced
1 bottle chilled Red Wine
Ice cubes

Pour the sugar syrup over the orange and lemon slices in a bowl. Let them marinate for at least 4 hours. Put a dozen or so ice cubes in a large pitcher, add the fruit mixture and the Wine. Stir well and serve in wine or punch glasses with a slice of both fruits in each serving. Makes about 8 servings.

SANGRIA CALIFORNIA STYLE

2 gallons California Zinfandel
1 cup Brandy
½ cup Cointreau or Strega
2 quarts Orange Juice
2 cups Lemon Juice
Ice cubes
2 quarts chilled Club Soda
3 Oranges, thinly sliced
3 Lemons, thinly sliced
1 cup superfine Sugar

Chill all ingredients. Pour the Wine, Brandy and Cointreau (or Strega) into a large punch bowl. Stir orange and lemon juice with the sugar until sugar has dissolved. Then add to the bowl and stir to blend. Add a dozen ice cubes. Mix in the soda. Garnish with fruit slices. Serve in 4 oz. punch or wineglasses. Makes about 100 drinks.

SANGRIA DE OPORTO

1 oz. Lemon Juice
1½ oz. light Corn Syrup
4 oz. Soda
4 oz. Tawny Port, chilled

Stir gently and pour over ice cubes in a Collins glass. Serve with a straw.

SANGROLE CHAMPAGNE COCKTAIL

2 oz. Sangrolé, chilled
3 oz. Champagne, chilled

Pour ingredients into a pre-chilled champagne glass.

Here's to friends both near and far;
Here's to woman, man's guiding star;
Here's to friends we've yet to meet,
Here's to those here; all here I greet;

SAN JUAN

1½ oz. Rum
1 oz. Grapefruit Juice
¼ oz. Coconut Cream
½ oz. Lime Juice
½ oz. 151-proof Rum

Shake all ingredients (except the 151-proof Rum) with ice and strain into a cocktail glass. Float the remaining ingredient on top.

SAN JUAN SLING

¾ oz. Rum
¾ oz. Cherry Liqueur
¾ oz. Benedictine
½ oz. Lime Juice

Shake with ice and strain into a Collins glass. Fill with soda and ice. Serve with a lime wedge.

SAN MARTIN

¾ oz. Gin
¾ oz. Dry Vermouth
¾ oz. Sweet Vermouth
¼ oz. Anisette
1 dash Bitters

Stir with ice and strain into a cocktail glass with a sugared rim.

SANO GROG

1 tbsp. Whisky
1 tbsp. Curacao
1 tbsp. Jamaica Rum
1 tsp. Powdered Sugar

Mix in a mug. Fill with boiling water.

SAN SEBASTIAN

1 oz. Gin
1½ tsp. Rum
1 tbsp. Grapefruit Juice
1½ tsp. Triple Sec
1 tbsp. Lemon Juice

Shake with ice and strain into a cocktail glass.

SANS FACON

2 oz. Brandy
¼ oz. Cointreau
¼ oz. Creme de Noyaux
1 dash Angostura Bitters
Sugar to taste

Stir with ice and strain into a cocktail glass.

SANS SOUCI

1 oz. Galliano
1 oz. White Port
1 dash Falernum
1 dash Orange Bitters

Stir with ice and strain into a cocktail glass. Serve with a twist of orange peel.

SANTA BARBARA NO. 1

1¾ oz. Bourbon
½ oz. Grapefruit Juice
¼ oz. Apricot-flavored Brandy
Sugar to taste

Shake with ice and strain into a cocktail glass.

SANTA BARBARA NO. 2

1 oz. Cream
¾ oz. Light Creme de Cacao
¾ oz. Vodka

Shake with ice and strain into a cocktail glass.

SANTA CRUZ FIX

1 oz. Lemon Juice
1 tsp. Sugar Syrup
2 oz. Rum

Mix lemon juice and syrup in a high-ball glass. Fill with crushed ice. Add Rum. Serve with a lemon wedge.

SANTA CRUZ RUM DAISY

½ tsp. Sugar
¼ oz. Maraschino Liqueur
1 oz. Lemon Juice
¼ oz. Orange Curacao
2 oz. Rum

Fill a fizz glass half full with crushed ice. Add all ingredients and stir gently.

SANTA FE

1½ oz. Brandy
½ oz. Grapefruit Juice
½ oz. Dry Vermouth
¼ oz. Lemon Juice

Shake with ice and strain into a cocktail glass with a sugared rim.

SANTIAGO COCKTAIL NO. 1

½ tsp. Powdered Sugar
¼ tsp. Grenadine
1½ oz. Light Rum
Juice 1 Lime

Shake with ice and strain into a cocktail glass.

SANTIAGO COCKTAIL NO. 2

1½ oz. Rum
¼ oz. Orange Curacao
½ oz. Lime Juice
¼ oz. Jamaica Rum

Shake with ice and strain into a cocktail glass.

SANTIAGO COCKTAIL NO. 3

1½ oz. Rum
¾ oz. Lime Juice
¼ oz. Grenadine

Shake with ice and strain into a cocktail glass. Serve with a lemon wedge.

SANTIAGO JULEP

4 Mint sprigs
½ oz. Grenadine
1½ oz. Lime Juice
½ oz. Pineapple Juice
2 oz. Rum

Muddle mint sprigs with Grenadine in a Collins glass. Add crushed ice. Pour in remaining ingredients, and add several sugar-frosted mint sprigs. Stir.

> When two people get married, they become one; The argument is usually — which one?

SANTINI'S POUSSE CAFE

¼ oz. Brandy
1 tbsp. Maraschino Liqueur
¼ oz. Triple Sec or Orange Curacao
¼ oz. Rum

Pour carefully, in order given, into a pony glass so that each ingredient floats on the preceding one without mixing.

SAP BUCKET SPECIAL

2 oz. Dark Rum
1 oz. Lemon Juice
2 tsp. Maple Syrup

Warm the maple syrup over a low flame. Mix with the Rum and juice in a warmed wine glass. Stir gently.

SAPPHIRE COCKTAIL

¾ oz. Dry Gin
¾ oz. Blue Curacao
2 tsp. Heavy Cream

Shake with ice and strain into a cocktail glass.

SARA'S SPECIAL

1½ oz. Amontillado
2 tbsp. Sweet Vermouth

Pour into an Old-fashioned glass and stir gently. Touch up with ice and a twist of lemon.

SARATOGA COCKTAIL NO. 1

2 oz. Brandy
2 dashes Bitters
1 tsp. Lemon Juice
1 tsp. Pineapple Juice
½ tsp. Maraschino Liqueur

Shake with ice and strain into a cocktail glass.

SARATOGA COCKTAIL NO. 2

¾ oz. Applejack
¾ oz. Sweet Vermouth
¾ oz. Dubonnet
¼ oz. Orange Juice

Shake with ice and strain into a cocktail glass.

SARATOGA COCKTAIL NO. 3

2 oz. Brandy
¼ oz. Pineapple Syrup
¼ oz. Maraschino Liqueur
2 dashes Bitters

Mix in a Collins glass. Fill with soda and ice.

SARATOGA COCKTAIL NO. 4

2 oz. Brandy
1 oz. Lemon Juice
½ tsp. Sugar
2 dashes Angostura Bitters

Fill with ginger ale and ice.

SARATOGA COOLER

Fill a Collins glass with cracked ice. Fill with Sarsaparilla. Add a twist of lemon and dangle end over rim of glass.

SARATOGA FIZZ

1½ oz. Rye or Bourbon Whisky
½ oz. Lemon Juice
1 tsp. Lime Juice
1 tsp. Sugar
1 Egg White

Shake with ice and strain into a cocktail glass. Serve with a cherry.

SARDI'S DELIGHT

1½ oz. Gin
¼ oz. Passion Fruit Juice
¼ oz. Lemon Juice
¼ oz. Grenadine
¼ oz. Pernod
1 dash Angostura Bitters

Shake with ice and strain into a cocktail glass.

SARONNO NO. 1

1½ oz. Amaretto
1 tbsp. Galliano
3 oz. Milk

Mix in a blender or shake well with ice. Strain into a cocktail glass.

SARONNO NO. 2

¾ oz. Amaretto
¾ oz. Brandy
1 oz. Cream

Shake with ice and strain into a cocktail glass.

SATAN COCKTAIL

3 dashes Peychaud's Bitters
1 dash Pernod
½ oz. Sweet Vermouth
2 oz. Bourbon

Stir with ice and strain into a cocktail glass.

SATIN'S WHISKERS

½ oz. Gin
½ oz. Dry Vermouth
½ oz. Sweet Vermouth
½ oz. Orange Juice
¼ oz. Grand Marnier
¼ oz. Orange Bitters

Stir with ice and strain into a cocktail glass.

SATYRE

1½ oz. Dry Vermouth
½ oz. Cognac
½ oz. Prunelle

Stir with ice and strain into a cocktail glass.

SAUCY SUE COCKTAIL

½ tsp. Apricot-flavored Brandy
½ tsp. Pernod
2 oz. Apple Brandy

Stir with ice and strain into a cocktail glass.

SAUTERNE COBBLER

Fill a double Old-fashioned glass with crushed ice. Sprinkle fine sugar over ice. Fill with Sauterne. Garnish with fruits and berries.

SAUTERNE COOLER

½ tsp. Sugar Syrup
3 oz. Sauterne

Pour sugar syrup into a Collins glass. Fill with ice and add Sauterne. Fill with soda. Decorate with lemon and orange twists.

SAUTERNE CUP

½ tsp. Sugar
1 oz. Lemon Juice
½ oz. Orange Curacao
Sauterne

Fill a Collins glass half full with ice. Add the first three ingredients and fill with Sauterne.

SAUTERNE PUNCH

1½ oz. Brandy
1½ oz. Curacao
1½ oz. Maraschino
2 bottles chilled Sauterne
8 oz. chilled Club Soda
Lemon and Orange slices

Combine all ingredients except the fruit in a large pitcher or punch bowl, stir gently and set in a bed of crushed ice. Garnish with the lemon and orange slices. Serve in wineglasses. Makes about 15 servings.

SAUTERNE SANGAREE

½ tsp. Sugar Syrup
2½ oz. Sauterne

Pour sugar syrup into a double Old-fashioned glass. Fill with ice and add Sauterne. Stir. Sprinkle nutmeg on top.

SAUZALIKY

2 oz. Tequila
4 oz. Orange Juice
1 tsp. Lemon Juice
1 very ripe Banana
3 oz. crushed Ice

Blend with ice and strain into a cocktail glass. Serves two.

SAVANNAH

1 oz. Gin
1 dash White Creme de Cacao
1 Egg White
Juice ½ Orange

Shake with ice and strain into a cocktail glass.

SAVOY HOTEL

⅓ oz. Dark Creme de Cacao
⅓ oz. Benedictine
⅓ oz. Brandy

Pour carefully, in order given, into a pony glass so that each ingredient floats on the preceding one without mixing.

SAVOY HOTEL RICKEY

Limes
1½ oz. Gin
½ oz. Grenadine

Squeeze ¾ oz. of lime juice into a highball glass. Leave some lime shell in the glass. Add Gin. Fill with soda and ice. Float Grenadine on top.

SAVOY HOTEL SPECIAL NO. 1

2 oz. Gin
1 oz. Dry Vermouth
2 dashes Grenadine
1 dash Pernod

Stir with ice and strain into a cocktail glass. Serve with a lemon twist.

SAVOY HOTEL SPECIAL NO. 2

2 oz. Gin
1 oz. Dry Vermouth
2 dashes Dubonnet

Stir with ice and strain into a cocktail glass. Serve with a twist of orange peel.

SAVOY-PLAZA

¾ oz. Jamaica Rum
½ oz. Apricot-flavored Brandy
½ oz. Lemon Juice

Shake with ice and strain into a cocktail glass.

SAVOY TANGO

1½ oz. Sloe Gin
1½ oz. Applejack or Calvados

Shake with ice and strain into a cocktail glass.

SAXON COCKTAIL

Juice ½ Lime
½ tsp. Grenadine
1¾ oz. Rum

Shake with ice and strain into a cocktail glass. Serve with a twist of orange peel.

SAZ

2 oz. Bourbon Whisky
3 dashes Peychaud's Bitters
3 drops Pernod

Shake Bourbon and Bitters with ice and strain into a cocktail glass, the inside of which has been coated with Pernod. Add a twist of lemon peel.

SAZERAC

2 oz. Rye Whisky
1 dash Pernod
1 dash Peychaud's Bitters

Stir with ice and strain into a cocktail glass. Serve with a lemon twist.

SCANDIA

2 oz. Aquavit
1 oz. Lime Juice
2 tsp. Grenadine

Shake with ice and strain into a cocktail glass.

SCARLETT O'HARA

2 oz. Southern Comfort
2 oz. Cranberry Juice
2 tsp. Lime Juice

Shake with ice and strain into a cocktail glass.

SCHNORKEL

1½ oz. Gold Rum
½ oz. Pernod
1 oz. Lime Juice
½ tsp. Sugar

Shake with ice and strain into a cocktail glass.

SCHNOZZLE

¾ oz. Gin
¾ oz. Dry Vermouth
½ oz. Sherry
¼ oz. Pernod
¼ oz. Orange Curacao

Stir with ice and strain into a cocktail glass.

SCHUSSBOOMER'S DELIGHT

¾ oz. Lime Juice
1½ oz. Cognac

Pour into a Collins glass. Fill with ice and Champagne.

SCOFF-LAW

1 oz. Rye Whisky
1 oz. Dry Vermouth
½ oz. Lemon Juice
½ oz. Grenadine
1 dash Orange Bitters

Stir with ice and strain into a cocktail glass.

SCOOP

¾   oz. Applejack
¾   oz. Brandy
¾   oz. Rum
1   dash Apricot-flavored Brandy
2   tsp. Grenadine

Shake with ice and strain into a large cocktail glass. Serve with a mint sprig.

SCOOTER

1   oz. Amaretto
1   oz. Brandy
1   oz. Sweet Cream

Combine in a blender or shake well with cracked ice. Strain into a cocktail glass.

SCORPION NO. 1

1   oz. Brandy
1   oz. Rum
2   oz. Orange Juice
1   oz. Lemon Juice
½   oz. Orgeat Syrup

Shake with ice and strain into a double Old-fashioned glass. Float ½ oz. 151-proof Rum on top.

SCORPION NO. 2

½   oz. Gin
½   oz. Brandy
2½ oz. Rum
1   oz. Orgeat
2   oz. Orange Juice
3   oz. Lemon Juice

Shake with ice and strain into a double Old-fashioned glass. Fill with ice. Serve with several mint sprigs.

SCOTCH AND VODKA

2½ oz. Vodka
2   tsp. Dry Vermouth
3   drops Scotch Whisky

Pour into a highball glass. Stir until well blended. Pour straight up and serve with a twist of lemon.

SCOTCH BIRD FLYER

1½ oz. Scotch Whisky
1   Egg Yolk
½   oz. Triple Sec
½   tsp. Powdered Sugar
1   oz. sweet Cream

Shake with ice and strain into a champagne glass.

SCOTCH BISHOP COCKTAIL

1   oz. Scotch Whisky
1   tbsp. Orange Juice
½   oz. Dry Vermouth
½   tsp. Triple Sec
¼   tsp. Powdered Sugar

Shake with ice and strain into a cocktail glass. Serve with a lemon twist.

SCOTCH COBBLER

2   oz. Scotch Whisky
½   tsp. Curacao
½   tsp. Brandy

Mix in a highball glass. Add ice. Decorate with a slice of lemon and some mint.

SCOTCH COOLER

2   oz. Scotch Whisky
3   dashes White Creme de Menthe

Pour into a highball glass over ice cubes. Fill with chilled soda and stir.

SCOTCH FIZZ

1   oz. Lemon Juice
1   tsp. Sugar
1½ oz. Scotch Whisky

Shake with ice and strain into a fizz glass. Fill with soda.

SCOTCH FLING

2   oz. Scotch Whisky
1   tsp. Lime Juice

Shake with ice and strain into a highball glass. Add ice and fill with ginger ale.

SCOTCH FLIP

2   oz. Scotch Whisky
1   Egg White
2   tsp. Sugar Syrup

Shake with ice and strain into a flip glass. Fill with soda and ice.

Here's to today — the tomorrow you worried about yesterday.

SCOTCH FROG

½   oz. Galliano
1   oz. Vodka
½   oz. Cointreau
1   oz. Lime Juice
1   dash Angostura Bitters
¼   oz. Maraschino Cherry Juice

Shake with ice and strain into a cocktail glass.

SCOTCH HIGHBALL

1½ oz. Scotch Whisky

Pour into a highball glass. Fill with soda or ginger ale and ice. Serve with a lemon twist.

SCOTCH HOLIDAY SOUR

1½ oz. Scotch Whisky
1   oz. Cherry-flavored Brandy
½   oz. Sweet Vermouth
1   oz. Lemon Juice

Shake with ice and strain into an Old-fashioned glass. Add a slice of lemon.

SCOTCH HORSE'S NECK

¼ oz. Sweet Vermouth
¼ oz. Dry Vermouth
1½ oz. Scotch Whisky

Mix in a Collins glass. Fill with ginger ale and ice. Serve with a lemon twist.

SCOTCH MILK PUNCH

2 oz. Scotch Whisky
6 oz. Milk
1 tsp. Powdered Sugar

Shake with ice and strain into a Collins glass. Sprinkle nutmeg on top.

SCOTCH MIST

2 oz. Scotch Whisky

Pack an Old-fashioned glass with crushed ice. Add Whisky and a twist of lemon peel. Serve with straws.

SCOTCH OLD-FASHIONED

2 dashes Bitters
½ tsp. Sugar
1½ oz. Scotch Whisky

Mix in an Old-fashioned glass. Fill with ice. Serve with an orange slice and a cherry.

SCOTCH ON THE ROCKS

2 oz. Scotch or other Whisky
Cold Water (optional)

Put ice cubes in an Old-fashioned glass and pour in Whisky. Drop in a lemon peel. Add cold water to taste.

SCOTCH ORANGE FIX

1 tsp. Sugar
½ oz. Lemon Juice
1 Orange twist
1½ oz. Scotch Whisky
¼ oz. Orange Curacao

In a highball glass, dissolve sugar in water. Add all ingredients (except the Curacao). Float Curacao on top.

SCOTCH RICKEY

1½ oz. Scotch Whisky
Juice ½ Lime

Pour into a highball glass over ice and fill with soda. Add a lime rind. Stir.

SCOTCH SANGAREE

½ tsp. Honey dissolved in soda
2 oz. Scotch Whisky

Into a double Old-fashioned glass pour honey dissolved in soda. Fill with ice and add Scotch. Serve with a lemon twist. Sprinkle nutmeg on top.

SCOTCH SAZ

¼ oz. Sweet Vermouth
1½ oz. Scotch Whisky
Pernod

Coat the inside of an Old-fashioned glass with Pernod. Add Sweet Vermouth and Scotch. Add ice and stir.

SCOTCH SIDECAR

1½ oz. Scotch or other Whisky
¾ oz. Cointreau
¾ oz. Lemon Juice

Shake with ice and strain into a cocktail glass.

SCOTCH SMASH

1 tsp. Sugar
3 Mint sprigs
1½ oz. Scotch Whisky

Muddle sugar with mint sprigs in an Old-fashioned glass. Add ice and Scotch. Stir.

SCOTCH SOLACE

1½ oz. Scotch Whisky
½ oz. Honey
½ oz. Triple Sec
4 oz. Milk
½ oz. Cream

Mix in a Collins glass. Add ice and stir. Sprinkle grated orange peel on top.

SCOTCH SOUR

1½ oz. Scotch Whisky
½ tsp. Powdered Sugar
Juice ½ Lime

Shake with ice and strain into a Sour glass. Decorate with a half-slice of lemon and a cherry.

SCOTCH STINGER

1½ oz. Scotch Whisky
¾ oz. White Creme de Menthe

Mix in an Old-fashioned glass. Fill with ice.

> May all mankind make free to enjoy the blessings of liberty, but never take the liberty to subvert the principles of freedom.

SCOTCH STONE FENCE

1½ oz. Scotch Whisky
2 dashes Peychaud's Bitters

Mix in a highball glass. Fill with soda and ice. Serve with a lemon twist.

SCOTCH WHISKY HIGHBALL

2　oz. Scotch Whisky

Put Whisky in a highball glass with ice cubes and fill with ginger ale or soda. Add a twist of lemon, if desired, and stir.

SCOTTISH GUARDS

1　oz. Scotch Whisky
½　oz. Lemon Juice
¾　oz. Orange Juice
¾　oz. Grenadine

Shake with ice and strain into a cocktail glass.

SCREWDRIVER

1½　oz. Gin
3　oz. Orange Juice

Put ice cubes in an Old-fashioned glass, add Gin and orange juice. Stir gently.

SEABOARD

1　oz. Blended Whisky
1　oz. Gin
1　tbsp. Lemon Juice
1　tsp. Powdered Sugar

Shake with ice and strain into an Old-fashioned glass over ice. Decorate with mint leaves.

SEA BREEZE COOLER

1½　oz. Gin
¾　oz. Apricot-flavored Brandy
¼　oz. Grenadine
1　oz. Lemon Juice

Mix in a highball glass. Fill with soda and ice. Serve with a mint sprig.

SEA CAPTAIN'S SPECIAL

½　tsp. Sugar
2　dashes Bitters
1½　oz. Rye Whisky

Mix in an Old-fashioned glass. Fill with ice and Champagne. Float ¼ oz. Pernod on top.

SEA ISLAND

½　oz. Dry Vermouth
½　oz. Grenadine
½　oz. Apricot-flavored Brandy
1½　oz. Van der Hum

Stir with ice and strain into a cocktail glass.

SEAPEA FIZZ

1　oz. Lemon Juice
2　oz. Pernod

Shake with ice and strain into a highball glass. Fill with soda and ice.

SECOND REGIMENT PUNCH

2　tsp. Powdered Sugar
1　tsp. Lemon Juice
1½　oz. Brandy
1½　oz. Muscatel
½　oz. Raspberry Syrup

Shake with ice and strain into a large cocktail glass. Fill with crushed ice. Garnish with fruit and add a dash of Jamaica Rum.

SECRET

1½　oz. Scotch Whisky
3　dashes White Creme de Menthe

Stir with ice and strain into a cocktail glass. Fill with soda.

SEESAW

1½　oz. Cognac
1　tsp. Benedictine
1　tsp. Dry Vermouth
1　dash Bitters

Shake with ice and strain into a cocktail glass.

SEE-THROUGH

1　oz. White Rum
½　oz. Cointreau
½　oz. Orange Gin
1　dash Curacao

Stir gently with ice and strain into a cocktail glass. Serve with an onion.

SEIGNIORY CLUB SPECIAL

1½　oz. Rye Whisky
1　oz. Grapefruit Juice
1　tsp. Maple Syrup
1　dash Rum
½　Egg White

Shake with ice and strain into a cocktail glass.

SELF-STARTER

1　oz. Gin
½　oz. Lillet
¼　oz. Apricot-flavored Brandy
2　dashes Pernod

Stir with ice and strain into a cocktail glass.

SENSATION COCKTAIL NO. 1

1½　oz. Gin
1　tsp. Maraschino Liqueur
Juice ¼ Lemon

Shake with ice and strain into a cocktail glass. Serve with a mint sprig.

SENSATION COCKTAIL NO. 2

1¾ oz. Port
¾ oz. Brandy

Stir with ice and strain into a cocktail glass. Serve with a lemon twist.

SEPARATOR

1 oz. Brandy
1 oz. Kahlua

Pour into a Collins glass. Fill with ice and milk or cream.

SEPTEMBER MORN COCKTAIL

1 Egg White
1½ oz. Light Rum
1 tsp. Grenadine
Juice ½ Lime

Shake with ice and strain into a cocktail glass.

SERPENT'S STING

¾ oz. Rum
¾ oz. Galliano
¾ oz. Creme de Noyaux or Almond Liqueur
¾ oz. fresh Orange Juice
¾ oz. fresh Cream

Stir with ice and strain into a cocktail glass. Serve with a cherry.

SERPENT'S TOOTH

1 oz. Irish Whisky
2 oz. Sweet Vermouth
2 oz. Lemon Juice
½ oz. Kummel
1 dash Angostura Bitters

Stir with ice and strain into a cocktail glass.

SESAME

1½ oz. Rum
½ oz. Lime Juice
½ oz. Sesame Seed Syrup

Shake with ice and strain into a cocktail glass.

> This night is ours, then strew with flowers
> The moments as they roll:
> For if any pain or care remain,
> Why, drown it in the bowl.
> This lesson oft in life I sing,
> And from any grave I still shall cry,
> Drink, mortal, drink, while time is young,
> Ere death has made thee old as I.
> — Moore.

SESQUI

1 oz. Brandy
1 oz. Aquavit
1 oz. Whisky
2 dashes Creme de Violette

Shake with ice and strain into a cocktail glass.

SETTLER HIGHBALL

1½ oz. Cognac
1½ oz. Creme de Cassis

Shake with ice and strain into a highball glass. Fill with soda and ice.

SEVEN FRUITS

1¾ oz. Bourbon Whisky
¾ oz. Seven Fruits Liqueur
1 dash Orange Bitters
1 dash Angostura Bitters

Shake with ice and strain into a cocktail glass.

SEVENTH HEAVEN COCKTAIL NO. 1

2 tsp. Grapefruit Juice
1 tbsp. Maraschino Liqueur
1½ oz. Gin

Shake with ice and strain into a cocktail glass. Decorate with a sprig of fresh mint.

SEVENTH HEAVEN COCKTAIL NO. 2

1¼ oz. Gin
1 oz. Dubonnet
¼ oz. Maraschino Liqueur
1 dash Angostura Bitters

Stir with ice and strain into a cocktail glass. Serve with an orange peel and a cherry.

SEVENTH REGIMENT

1¾ oz. Gin
¾ oz. Sweet Vermouth

Pour into a cocktail glass. Stir.

SEVILLA COCKTAIL NO. 1

½ tsp. Powdered Sugar
1 Egg
1 oz. Port
1 oz. Light Rum

Shake with ice and strain into a flip glass.

SEVILLA COCKTAIL NO. 2

1 oz. Dark Rum
1 oz. Sweet Vermouth

Stir with ice and strain into a cocktail glass. Serve with a twist of orange peel.

SEVILLA FLIP

1 oz. White Rum
1 oz. Port
1 tsp. Sugar Syrup
1 Egg

Shake with ice and strain into an Old-fashioned glass. Add ice.

SEVILLE

1 oz. Gin
½ oz. Fino Sherry
½ oz. Orange Juice
½ oz. Lemon Juice
½ tsp. Sugar

Shake with ice and strain into a cocktail glass with a sugared rim.

S.G.

¾ oz. Rye Whisky
¾ oz. Lemon Juice
¾ oz. Orange Juice
¼ oz. Grenadine

Shake with ice and strain into a cocktail glass.

SHADY GROVE

1½ oz. Gin
1 tsp. Powdered Sugar
Juice ½ Lemon

Shake with ice and strain into a highball glass with ice cubes. Fill with ginger beer.

SHALOM

1½ oz. 100-proof Vodka
1 oz. Madeira
1 tbsp. Orange Juice

Shake with ice and strain into an Old-fashioned glass over ice cubes. Add an orange slice.

May friendship, like wine, improve as time advances, and may we always have old wine, old friends, and young cares.

SHALUTA COCKTAIL

¾ oz. Gin
¾ oz. Lemon Juice
¾ oz. Claret
2 tsp. Sugar Syrup

Shake with ice and strain into a cocktail glass.

SHAMROCK COCKTAIL NO. 1

1½ oz. Irish Whisky
½ oz. Dry Vermouth
1 tsp. Green Creme de Menthe
1 tsp. Green Chartreuse

Stir with ice and strain into a cocktail glass. Serve with an olive.

SHAMROCK COCKTAIL NO. 2

¾ oz. Gin
½ oz. Green Creme de Menthe
½ oz. Orange Juice
½ oz. Lemon Juice
½ Egg White

Shake with ice and strain into a cocktail glass.

SHANDYGAFF

½ Ale
½ Ginger Ale

Fill a Collins glass with half of each ingredient.

SHANGHAI COCKTAIL

1 tsp. Anisette
1 oz. Jamaica Rum
½ tsp. Grenadine
Juice ¼ Lemon

Shake with ice and strain into a cocktail glass.

SHARK'S TOOTH NO. 1

1½ oz. Gold Rum
¼ oz. Lemon Juice
¼ oz. Passion Fruit Syrup
¼ oz. Sweet Vermouth
¼ oz. Sloe Gin
1 dash Angostura Bitters

Shake with ice and strain into a cocktail glass with a sugared rim. Serve with an orange peel and a cherry.

SHARK'S TOOTH NO. 2

2 oz. Rum
1 oz. Lemon Juice
½ oz. Grenadine

Shake with ice and strain into a cocktail glass. Fill with crushed ice and soda.

SHARK'S TOOTH NO. 3

1½ oz. Rum
¼ oz. Lemon Juice
¼ oz. Sloe Gin
¼ oz. Dry Vermouth
¼ oz. Passion Fruit Syrup

Shake with ice and strain into a Collins glass. Fill with crushed ice and soda.

SHARKY HIGHBALL

1½ oz. Applejack
½ oz. Bourbon Whisky
½ oz. Lemon Juice
½ tsp. Sugar

Mix in a highball glass. Fill with soda and ice.

SHARKY PUNCH COCKTAIL

2 oz. Calvados or Apple Brandy
½ oz. Rye Whisky
¼ tsp. Sugar

Shake with ice and strain into a cocktail glass. Add a squirt of soda.

SHAUN BANIGAN

1 oz. Light Rum
1 oz. Dark Rum
½ oz. Lemon Juice
½ tsp. Sugar
1 dash Bitters

Shake with ice and strain into a cocktail glass.

SHAVETAIL

1½ oz. Peppermint Vodka
1   oz. Pineapple Juice
1   oz. Sweet Cream

Shake with ice and strain into an Old-fashioned glass.

SHEIK'S BREATH

1   oz. Gin
¾   oz. Caloric
¾   oz. Lemon Juice

Shake with ice and strain into a cocktail glass.

SHERATON SHEHERAZADE

1   oz. Galliano
2   oz. Orange Juice
¼   oz. Lemon Juice
½   oz. Apricot-flavored Brandy
¼   oz. Triple Sec

Shake with ice and strain into a Collins glass. Fill with ice. Serve with a pineapple stick and a cherry.

SHERMAN

1½ oz. Whisky
½   oz. Port
½   oz. Jamaica Rum
1   dash Orange Bitters
1   dash Angostura Bitters

Stir with ice and strain into a cocktail glass.

SHERMAN BILLINGSLEY SPECIAL

¾   oz. Cherry-flavored Brandy
½   oz. Triple Sec
½   oz. Peach-flavored Brandy
Juice 1 Lime

Shake with ice and strain into a Collins glass.

SHERRIED COFFEE COCKTAIL

1¼ oz. Oloroso Sherry
1¼ oz. Coffee Liqueur

Shake with ice and strain into a cocktail glass. Float ½ oz. cream on top.

SHERRIED CORDIAL MEDOC FRAPPE

½   oz. Amontillado Sherry
1   oz. Cordial Medoc

Pack a cocktail glass with crushed ice and add both ingredients.

SHERRIED SCOTCH

1½ oz. Scotch Whisky
1½ oz. Cream Sherry
1   tsp. Honey
1   oz. Orange Juice

Heat and pour into an Old-fashioned glass. Add a dash of Angostura Bitters. Serve with a cinnamon stick and an orange slice. Stir.

SHERRY AND BITTERS COCKTAIL

1   dash Angostura Bitters
1½ oz. Sherry

Pour into a cocktail glass.

SHERRY AND DUBONNET

2   oz. chilled Sherry
2   oz. chilled Dubonnet

Pour into a pre-chilled cocktail glass. Stir gently.

SHERRY AND EGG COCKTAIL

1   Egg
Sherry

Place an egg in a cocktail glass, being careful not to break the yolk. Fill the glass with Sherry.

SHERRY COBBLER NO. 1

3   oz. Sherry
½   tsp. Port Wine
½   tsp. Curacao

Stir with ice and strain into a highball glass. Fill with crushed ice. Add a dash of Port on top.

SHERRY COBBLER NO. 2

½   tsp. Sugar
1   oz. Brandy
½   oz. Orange Juice
2½ oz. Sherry

Mix in a Collins glass. Fill with crushed ice. Serve with an orange slice.

SHERRY COBBLER NO. 3

3   oz. Sherry
1   tsp. Powdered Sugar
1   tsp. Orange Juice

Mix and pour over crushed ice in an Old-fashioned glass. Decorate with a pineapple stick or mint and a slice of orange.

SHERRY COCKTAIL NO. 1

2   oz. Sherry
½   oz. Dry Vermouth
2   dashes Orange Bitters

Stir with ice and strain into a cocktail glass.

SHERRY COCKTAIL NO. 2

1   oz. Sherry
¾   oz. Gin
¾   oz. Lemon Juice

Stir with ice and strain into a cocktail glass.

SHERRY COCKTAIL NO. 3

1 oz. Sherry
½ oz. Applejack
1 dash Angostura Bitters
1 tsp. Orange Juice
½ tsp. Sugar Syrup

Shake with ice and strain into a cocktail glass.

SHERRY EGG FRAPPE

¼ cup crushed Ice
2 oz. Pineapple Juice
4 oz. Orange Juice
4 oz. Cream Sherry
1 Egg White
Mint sprigs

Combine the first four ingredients in a shaker. Beat egg white slightly in a bowl, add to the shaker and shake until frothy. Strain into a Collins glass. Garnish with mint sprigs.

SHERRY EGGNOG

1 Egg
1 tsp. Powdered Sugar
2 oz. Sherry

Shake above ingredients with ice and strain into a Collins glass. Fill the glass with milk and stir. Sprinkle nutmeg on top.

> Who loves not women, wine, and song
> Will be a fool his whole life long.

SHERRY FLIP

1 Egg
1 tsp. Powdered Sugar
1½ oz. Sherry
2 tsp. Sweet Cream (if desired)

Shake with ice and strain into a flip glass. Sprinkle nutmeg on top.

SHERRY-GRAPEFRUIT FIZZ

3 oz. Grapefruit Juice
1 oz. Sherry
1 Egg White

Stir with ice and strain into a Collins glass. Add sugar to taste and plenty of cracked ice. Stir vigorously.

SHERRY KAFE FLIP

1 Egg
1 tsp. Sugar
⅓ cup crushed Ice
½ tsp. Creme de Cafe
1½ oz. Medium Sherry

Blend until well mixed. Pour into a pre-chilled large cocktail glass. Sprinkle nutmeg on top.

SHERRY MILK FRAPPE

1 tsp. Sugar
2 oz. Medium Sherry
4 oz. Milk

Place sugar, Wine and ice in a mixing glass. Pour in milk and shake well. Strain into a Collins glass. Sprinkle nutmeg on top.

SHERRY MILK PUNCH

1 tsp. Powdered Sugar
2 oz. Sherry
½ pt. Milk

Shake with ice and strain into a Collins glass. Sprinkle nutmeg on top.

SHERRY OLD-FASHIONED

½ tsp. Sugar dissolved in water
2 dashes Orange Bitters
1½ oz. Sherry

Mix in an Old-fashioned glass. Fill with ice. Serve with an orange slice and a cherry.

SHERRY ORANGE FRAPPE

1 cup crushed Ice
4 oz. Orange Juice, chilled
4 oz. Medium Sherry, chilled
1 tbsp. Honey
1 tbsp. Lemon Juice
1 drop Mint Extract

Blend all ingredients until well mixed. Pour into a pre-chilled Collins glass. Garnish with mint leaves. Serve with straws.

SHERRY PUNCH

4 oz. Sherry
½ oz. Lemon Juice
½ tsp. Sugar

Shake with ice and strain into a Collins glass. Fill with soda and ice.

SHERRY SANGAREE

½ tsp. Powdered Sugar
1 tsp. Water
2 oz. Sherry
Soda
Port

In an Old-fashioned glass dissolve sugar in water. Add Sherry and stir. Add ice cubes and a splash of soda, leaving enough room to float a tablespoon of Port on top. Dust with nutmeg.

SHERRY TWIST COCKTAIL NO. 1

1 oz. Sherry
½ oz. Brandy
½ oz. Dry Vermouth
½ oz. Triple Sec or Cointreau
½ tsp. Lemon Juice

Shake with ice and strain into a cocktail glass. Top with a pinch of cinnamon and a twist of orange peel.

SHERRY TWIST COCKTAIL NO. 2

1½	oz. Sherry
¾	oz. Whisky
½	oz. Cointreau
1	oz. Orange Juice
½	oz. Lemon Juice

Shake with ice and strain into a cocktail glass. Top with a pinch of cayenne pepper and cloves.

SHERRY WINE PUNCH

½	oz. Lemon Juice
1	oz. Orgeat Syrup
1½	oz. Sherry

Shake with ice and strain into a highball glass. Fill with crushed ice.

SHERRY'S HAT

2	oz. Orgeat Syrup
2	dashes Lemon Juice
6	oz. Medium Sherry
1	oz. Chianti

Put Orgeat Syrup and lemon juice in a Collins glass. Fill the glass three-quarters full with cracked ice. Stir, pouring in Sherry. Float Chianti. Garnish with fresh fruit.

SHILLELAGH

1	oz. Irish Whisky
1	oz. Dry Vermouth
½	oz. Pernod
1	dash Angostura Bitters

Stir with ice and strain into a cocktail glass.

SHIP

4	oz. Sherry
½	oz. Whisky
2	dashes Rum
2	dashes Prune Syrup
2	dashes Orange Bitters

Shake with ice and strain into a large cocktail glass.

SHOOT

1	oz. Scotch Whisky
1	oz. Dry Sherry
¼	oz. Lemon Juice
¼	oz. Orange Juice
½	tsp. Sugar

Shake with ice and strain into a cocktail glass.

SHOT IN THE ARM

1½	oz. Brandy
1½	oz. Cream
¾	oz. White Creme de Menthe
¼	oz. Grenadine

Shake with ice and strain into a highball glass. Fill with soda and ice.

SHRAPNEL

1¼	oz. Bourbon Whisky
½	oz. Dry Vermouth
½	oz. Sweet Vermouth
¼	oz. Apricot-flavored Brandy

Stir with ice and strain into a cocktail glass. Serve with an orange slice.

SHRINER COCKTAIL

1½	oz. Brandy
1½	oz. Sloe Gin
2	dashes Bitters
½	tsp. Sugar Syrup

Stir with ice and strain into a cocktail glass. Serve with a lemon twist.

SICILIAN KISS

1	oz. Southern Comfort
1	oz. Amaretto

Mix in an Old-fashioned glass. Fill with soda and ice.

SIDECAR COCKTAIL

Juice ¼ Lemon	
½	oz. Triple Sec
1	oz. Brandy

Shake with ice and strain into a cocktail glass with a sugared rim.

SIDNEY FIELDS

2	oz. Dry Sherry
1	oz. Gin

Shake with ice and strain into a cocktail glass.

> A health to our sweethearts, our friends and our wives, And may fortune smile on them the rest of their lives.
>
> Here's to the girl who loves me And here's to the many who don't; Here's to the girl who accepts me, And here's to the many who won't.

SIERRA DAWN

1	slice Orange
1	tbsp. fresh Lemon Juice
1	oz. Framboise
Extra Dry Champagne, well chilled	

Fill a Collins glass half full with ice cubes. Add the lemon juice, Framboise and orange slice. Fill with Champagne. Stir gently. Serve with straws.

SILK PURSE

1½	oz. Kahlua
1½	oz. Cream
1½	oz. Lemon Mix

Shake with ice and strain into a Collins glass. Fill with ice.

SILVER

1	oz. Dry Vermouth
1	oz. Gin
2	dashes Orange Bitters
¼	tsp. Sugar Syrup
½	tsp. Maraschino Liqueur

Stir with ice and strain into a cocktail glass. Serve with a lemon twist.

SILVER BALL FIZZ

2   oz. Rhine Wine
1   Egg White
½   oz. Grapefruit Juice
½   tsp. Sugar
1   dash Orange Flower Water

Shake with ice and strain into a highball glass. Fill with soda and ice.

SILVER BULLET NO. 1

1   oz. Gin
1   oz. Kummel
1   tbsp. Lemon Juice

Shake with ice and strain into a cocktail glass.

SILVER BULLET NO. 2

1½   oz. Gin
½   oz. Lillet
½   oz. Lemon Juice

Shake with ice and strain into a cocktail glass.

SILVER BULLET NO. 3

2   oz. Gin
¼   oz. Dry Vermouth

Stir with ice and strain into a cocktail glass. Float ¼ oz. Scotch on top.

May the sunshine of plenty dispel the clouds of care.

SILVER DAWN

1   oz. Galliano
1   oz. Gin
1   oz. Lemon Juice
¾   oz. Maple Syrup

Shake with ice and strain into a cocktail glass.

SILVER FIZZ

Juice ½ Lemon
1   tsp. Powdered Sugar
2   oz. Dry Gin
1   Egg White

Shake with ice and strain into a highball glass over two cubes of ice. Fill with soda and stir.

SILVER FLASH

1¾   oz. Sloe Gin
¾   oz. Benedictine
1   dash Orange Bitters

Stir with ice and strain into a cocktail glass.

SILVER KING COCKTAIL

1   Egg White
1½   oz. Gin
½   tsp. Powdered Sugar
2   dashes Orange Bitters
Juice ¼ Lemon

Shake with ice and strain into a cocktail glass.

SILVER KIRSCH

1   oz. Kirschwasser
1½   oz. Positano
½   oz. Lemon Juice
½   Egg White
1   tsp. Sugar

Shake with ice and strain into a cocktail glass.

SILVER STALLION FIZZ NO. 1

1   scoop Vanilla Ice Cream
2   oz. Gin

Shake with ice and strain into a highball glass. Fill with soda and stir.

SILVER STALLION FIZZ NO. 2

1½   oz. Gin
2   scoops Vanilla Ice Cream
½   oz. Lime Juice
½   oz. Lemon Juice
½   Egg White (optional)

Shake with ice and strain into a Collins glass. Fill with soda.

SILVER STREAK

1½   oz. Gin
1   oz. Kummel

Shake with ice and strain into a cocktail glass.

SIMPLE WINE COBBLER

1½   tbsp. Sugar
2   oz. cold Water
6   oz. Riesling, chilled

Stir with ice and pour over ice cubes in a Collins glass.

SINGAPORE

1½   oz. Rye Whisky
¼   oz. Sloe Gin
¼   oz. Rose's Lime Juice
½   oz. Lemon Juice

Shake with ice and strain into a cocktail glass.

SINGAPORE SLING

Juice ½ Lemon   ½ ounce Cherry Liquer
1   tsp. Powdered Sugar ½ oz Grenadine
2   oz. Gin

Shake with ice and strain into a Collins glass. Add ice cubes and fill with soda. Float ½ oz. Cherry-flavored Brandy on top. Decorate with fruits in season and serve with straws.

SINK OR SWIM

2 oz. Brandy
¾ oz. Sweet Vermouth
1 dash Angostura Bitters

Stir with ice and strain into a cocktail glass.

SIR CHARLES PUNCH

1 tsp. Sugar
1 oz. Port
¾ oz. Brandy
½ oz. Orange Curacao

Pour into a Collins glass. Stir. Decorate with an orange slice, a pineapple spear and a grape.

SIR KNIGHT COCKTAIL

1 oz. Cointreau
1 oz. Cognac
1 oz. Chartreuse
2 drops Angostura Bitters

Shake with ice and strain into a cocktail glass. Serve with a lemon twist.

SIR RIDGEWAY KNIGHT

1 oz. Brandy
1 oz. Triple Sec
1 oz. Yellow Chartreuse
2 dashes Angostura Bitters

Shake with ice and strain into a cocktail glass.

SIR WALTER COCKTAIL

¾ oz. Rum
¾ oz. Brandy
1 tsp. Grenadine
1 tsp. Triple Sec or Orange Curacao
1 tsp. Lemon Juice

Shake with ice and strain into a cocktail glass.

SIT DOWN STRIKER COCKTAIL

1 oz. Benedictine
1 oz. Pernod
1 oz. Lemon Juice

Shake with ice and strain into a cocktail glass. Float ½ oz. Cognac on top.

SIX CYLINDER

½ oz. Gin
½ oz. Cherry-flavored Brandy
½ oz. Campari
½ oz. Dubonnet
¼ oz. Dry Vermouth
¼ oz. Sweet Vermouth

Shake with ice and strain into a cocktail glass.

SIX DEGREE

1¼ oz. Gin
½ oz. Kirschwasser
½ oz. Cherry-flavored Brandy
¼ oz. Kummel

Shake with ice and strain into a cocktail glass.

SIX FEET UNDER

1 oz. Rum
¾ oz. Swedish Punch
¾ oz. Calvados

Shake with ice and strain into a cocktail glass. Serve with a lemon twist.

SIX O SIX

1¼ oz. Gin
½ oz. Cointreau
¼ oz. Lemon Juice
¼ oz. Pernod
¼ oz. Cochineal

Shake with ice and strain into a cocktail glass.

SKEET SHOOTER'S SPECIAL

1½ oz. Dark Rum
2 tbsp. each Pineapple, Grapefruit and Orange Juice
1 oz. Lemon Soda
1 tbsp. White Rum
1 pinch Cinnamon

Shake with ice and strain into a Collins glass. Add ice and decorate with cherries.

SKIDMORE '54 COCKTAIL

¼ oz. Orange Juice
¼ oz. Dubonnet
¾ oz. Dry Vermouth
¾ oz. Whisky

Shake with ice and strain into a cocktail glass.

SKIDMORE TIPPLE

2 oz. Cognac
2 oz. Kummel

Mix in a double Old-fashioned glass. Stir until blended. Serve straight up.

SKIER'S SMOOTHIE

1½ oz. Galliano

Pour into a cup and fill with hot strong tea.

SKIP AND GO NAKED

1½ oz. Gin
1 oz. Lemon Juice
½ tsp. Sugar

Mix in a Collins glass. Fill with beer and ice.

SKIPPER

1   oz. Gin
¾   oz. Maraschino Liqueur
½   oz. Lemon Juice
¼   oz. Grenadine

Shake with ice and strain into a cocktail glass.

SKIPPY

½   oz. Galliano
¾   oz. Rum
¾   oz. Triple Sec
½   oz. Apricot-flavored Brandy
¼   oz. Dry Vermouth
¼   oz. Prunelle
1   oz. Lemon Juice
1¼   oz. Orange Juice

Shake with ice and strain into a Collins glass. Fill with ice and Sprite. Decorate with a cherry, a mint sprig and a pineapple spear.

SKY CLUB

1½   oz. Whisky
3   oz. Orange Juice
2-3   drops 151-proof Rum

Mix in an Old-fashioned glass. Add ice and stir well.

SKY PILOT

1¼   oz. Applejack
¾   oz. Jamaica Rum
¼   oz. Lime Juice
¼   oz. Grenadine

Shake with ice and strain into a cocktail glass.

SKYSCRAPER

1/5   oz. Creme de Vanille
1/5   oz. Maraschino Liqueur
1/5   oz. Green Creme de Menthe
1/5   oz. Yellow Chartreuse
1/5   oz. Cognac

Pour carefully, in order given, into a pony glass so that each ingredient floats on the preceding one without mixing.

SLAM NO. 1

¾   oz. Cognac
¾   oz. Cointreau
½   oz. Apricot-flavored Brandy
½   oz. Lime Juice

Shake with ice and strain into a cocktail glass.

SLAM NO. 2

¾   oz. Gin
¾   oz. Brandy
½   oz. Apricot-flavored Brandy
½   oz. Lemon Juice

Shake with ice and strain into a cocktail glass.

SLEDGE HAMMER

1   oz. Brandy
1   oz. Rum
1   oz. Apple Brandy
1   dash Pernod

Shake with ice and strain into a cocktail glass.

SLEEPYHEAD

2½   oz. Brandy
3   Mint leaves, bruised
Ginger Ale

Pour Brandy into an Old-fashioned glass; add orange peel, mint leaves and ice. Fill with ginger ale.

SLEEPY HOLLOW

Mint sprigs
½   oz. Lemon Juice
¼   oz. Apricot-flavored Brandy
¼   tsp. Sugar
2   oz. Gin

Muddle lemon juice with mint sprigs, Brandy and sugar. Shake with Gin and strain into a cocktail glass.

SLEIGH RIDE'S END

Lemon peel
6   Mint leaves
1   tbsp. Sugar
2   whole Cloves
1   Cinnamon stick
2   drops Maraschino Syrup
2   oz. Claret
2   oz. Water, piping hot

Place lemon peel, mint leaves and sugar in a preheated mug. Muddle well. Add the rest of the ingredients and stir.

SLOEBERRY COCKTAIL

2½   oz. Sloe Gin
1   dash Angostura Bitters and/or
1   dash Orange Bitters

Stir with ice and strain into a cocktail glass.

SLOE BRANDY

1¾   oz. Brandy
½   oz. Sloe Gin
¼   oz. Lemon Juice

Shake with ice and strain into a cocktail glass. Serve with a lemon twist.

SLOE COMFORTABLE SCREW

1½   oz. Southern Comfort
½   oz. Sloe Gin
Orange Juice

Pour Southern Comfort into a Collins glass. Fill with orange juice and ice. Float Sloe Gin on top.

> Come, fill the bowl, each jolly soul;
> Let Bacchus guide our revels;
> Join cup to lip, with "hip, hip, hip,"
> And bury the blue devils.

SLOE COMFORTABLE SCREW UP AGAINST THE WALL

1 oz. Vodka
1 oz. Southern Comfort
½ oz. Sloe Gin
½ oz. Galliano
Orange Juice

Pour Vodka and Southern Comfort into a Collins glass. Fill with ice and orange juice. Add Sloe Gin and Galliano. Stir.

SLOE CRANBERRY COOLER

2 oz. Sloe Gin
4 oz. Cranberry Juice
1 oz. Lemon Juice

Pour into a Collins glass. Fill with ice. Serve with a lime wheel.

SLOE DRIVER

2 oz. Sloe Gin
Orange Juice

Put 2-3 ice cubes in a highball glass and add Sloe Gin. Fill with orange juice and stir.

SLOE GIN COCKTAIL

2 oz. Sloe Gin
1 dash Orange Bitters
¼ tsp. Dry Vermouth

Stir with ice and strain into a cocktail glass.

SLOE GIN COLLINS

Juice ½ Lemon
2 oz. Sloe Gin

Shake with ice and strain into a Collins glass. Add several ice cubes and fill with soda. Stir and decorate with slices of lemon and orange and a cherry. Serve with straws.

SLOE GIN FIZZ

Juice ½ Lemon
1 tsp. Powdered Sugar
2 oz. Sloe Gin

Shake with ice and strain into a highball glass. Add ice cubes, fill with soda and stir. Decorate with a slice of lemon.

SLOE GIN FLIP

1 Egg
1 tsp. Powdered Sugar
1 tbsp. Sloe Gin
2 tsp. Sweet Cream (if desired)

Shake with ice and strain into a flip glass. Sprinkle nutmeg on top.

SLOE GIN RICKEY NO. 1

Juice ½ Lime
2 oz. Sloe Gin

Pour into a highball glass over ice cubes and fill with soda. Stir. Drop lime rind into glass.

SLOE GIN RICKEY NO. 2

1½ oz. Sloe Gin
½ oz. Lemon Juice
¼ oz. Grenadine

Mix in a highball glass. Fill with 7-Up and ice.

SLOE LIME FRAPPE

¾ oz. Sloe Gin
¾ oz. Lime Liqueur
¾ oz. Rum

Mix without ice and pour into a cocktail glass packed with crushed ice. Serve with a lime wheel.

SLOE SCREW

1½ oz. Sloe Gin
Orange Juice

Pour Sloe Gin over ice in an Old-fashioned glass. Fill with orange juice and stir.

SLOE TEQUILA

1 oz. Tequila
½ oz. Sloe Gin
1 tbsp. Lime Juice

Combine ingredients with half a cup of crushed ice in a blender. Blend at low speed and pour into an Old-fashioned glass. Add ice cubes and cucumber peel.

SLOE VERMOUTH

1 oz. Sloe Gin
1 oz. Dry Vermouth
1 tbsp. Lemon Juice

Shake with ice and strain into a cocktail glass.

SLOPPY JOE'S COCKTAIL NO. 1

Juice 1 Lime
¼ tsp. Triple Sec
¼ tsp. Grenadine
¾ oz. Light Rum
¾ oz. Dry Vermouth

Shake with ice and strain into a cocktail glass.

SLOPPY JOE'S COCKTAIL NO. 2

¾ oz. Pineapple Juice
¾ oz. Brandy
¾ oz. Port
¼ tsp. Triple Sec
¼ tsp. Grenadine

Shake with ice and strain into a cocktail glass.

SLUSCIOUS LEMONADE

3 oz. Chablis
¾ oz. frozen Lemonade concentrate

Freeze Chablis until slushy. Blend with lemonade until smooth. Pour into a cocktail glass.

SMALL DINGER

¾ oz. Gin
½ oz. Rum
½ oz. Lemon Juice
½ oz. Grenadine

Shake with ice and pour over crushed ice in a cocktail glass.

SMART ALEC

1 oz. Cognac
¾ oz. Cointreau
¾ oz. Yellow Chartreuse
1 dash Orange Bitters

Stir with ice and strain into a cocktail glass.

Here's to a temperance supper
With water in glasses tall,
And coffee and tea to end with —
And me not there at all.

SMEDLEY

1 oz. Lemon Juice
1 oz. Galliano
1 oz. White Creme de Menthe

Shake with ice and strain into a cocktail glass.

SMILE COCKTAIL NO. 1

1 oz. Grenadine
1 oz. Dry Gin
½ tsp. Lemon Juice

Shake with ice and strain into a cocktail glass.

SMILE COCKTAIL NO. 2

1¾ oz. Gin
¾ oz. Strega
2 dashes Orange Bitters

Stir with ice and strain into a cocktail glass. Serve with a lemon twist.

SMILER COCKTAIL

½ oz. Sweet Vermouth
½ oz. Dry Vermouth
1 oz. Gin
1 dash Bitters
¼ tsp. Orange Juice

Shake with ice and strain into a cocktail glass.

SMILIN' JOE'S SPECIAL

½ oz. Brandy
1 oz. Medium Sherry
4 oz. chilled Soda
8 oz. chilled Riesling
1 slice each Orange and Lemon
Cucumber peel
Piece of Lemon rind

Mix with ice and pour into a Collins glass. Garnish with berries.

SMITH AND WESSON

1½ oz. Kahlua

Pour into a Collins glass. Fill with ice. Add 2 oz. milk or Half & Half cream. Fill with soda.

SMOOTHIE

1½ oz. Kahlua
½ oz. Gin
½ oz. Lemon Juice
1 tsp. Sugar

Shake ingredients together and pour over crushed ice in a large cocktail glass.

SNAPPER

1½ oz. Gin
½ oz. Green Creme de Menthe

Pour into an Old-fashioned glass. Fill with ice.

S 'N' D COCKTAIL

2 oz. Sweet Vermouth
2 oz. Dry Vermouth
Soda

Stir Vermouth with ice cubes and strain into a large cocktail glass. Fill with chilled soda and add a twist of lemon.

SNICKER

1½ oz. Gin
¾ oz. Dry Vermouth
½ tsp. Maraschino Liqueur
1 dash Orange Bitters
1 tsp. Sugar Syrup
1 Egg White

Shake with ice and strain into a cocktail glass.

SNIFTER

¾ oz. Galliano
¾ oz. Brandy
¼ oz. White Creme de Menthe

Pour into a snifter. Add ice and stir.

SNOOPY

1 oz. Galliano
1½ oz. Bourbon Whisky
1 oz. Campari
½ oz. Grand Marnier
2 drops Lemon Juice

Shake with ice and strain into a cocktail glass. Serve with a lemon twist.

SNOOPY'S GLEAM

1	oz. Bourbon Whisky
¼	oz. Orange Curacao
¼	oz. Grenadine
½	oz. Orangeade

Shake with ice and strain into a cocktail glass. Garnish with an orange slice and a cherry.

SNOWBALL COCKTAIL NO. 1

1½	oz. Gin
½	oz. Anisette
1	tbsp. Sweet Cream

Shake with ice and strain into a cocktail glass.

SNOWBALL COCKTAIL NO. 2

2	oz. Bourbon Whisky
1	Egg White

Shake with ice and strain into a highball glass. Fill with ice and decorate with mint sprigs and fruit.

SNOWBALL COCKTAIL NO. 3

1	oz. Gin
¼	oz. Creme de Violette
¼	oz. White Creme de Menthe
¼	oz. Anisette
¼	oz. Heavy Cream

Shake with ice and strain into a cocktail glass.

SNOW DROP

½	oz. Galliano
½	oz. Vodka
½	oz. White Creme de Cacao
½	oz. Triple Sec
1	oz. Cream
½	Egg White

Shake with ice and strain into a cocktail glass.

SNOWFLAKE

¾	oz. Galliano
¼	oz. Cointreau
¼	oz. Yellow Chartreuse
1¼	oz. Cream

Shake with ice and strain into a cocktail glass. Serve with a cherry.

SNOW JOB

1½	oz. Tuaca
1	oz. Cream
1	tsp. Coconut Snow

Shake with ice and strain into a cocktail glass.

SNOWSHOE NO. 1

1	oz. Vodka
1	oz. Anisette

Mix in an Old-fashioned glass. Fill with ice.

SNOWSHOE NO. 2

1	oz. Peppermint Schnapps
1	oz. Wild Turkey 101

Mix in an Old-fashioned glass. Fill with ice.

SNOW WHITE

1¾	oz. Rum
¼	oz. Lime Juice
¼	oz. Pineapple Juice
½	Egg White
¼	tsp. Sugar

Shake with ice and strain into a cocktail glass.

SNYDER

1½	oz. Gin
½	oz. Dry Vermouth
½	oz. Triple Sec or Orange Curacao

Shake with ice and strain into a cocktail glass. Serve with a lemon twist.

SOCIETY COCKTAIL

1½	oz. Gin
¾	oz. Dry Vermouth
¼	oz. Grenadine

Stir with ice and strain into a cocktail glass.

SODA APERITIF

3	oz. Dry Vermouth
¾	oz. Campari
¾	oz. Creme de Cassis
Soda	

Pour Vermouth into a goblet, add ice and fill three-quarters full with soda. Add Campari and Creme de Cassis. Stir gently.

SOFT TOUCH

1	oz. Galliano
2	oz. Milk
1	tsp. Honey

Shake with ice and strain into a cocktail glass.

SOHO

1	oz. Chianti
½	oz. Sweet Vermouth
½	oz. Grapefruit Juice

Shake with ice and strain into a cocktail glass.

SOL Y SOMBRA (SUN AND SHADE)

1¼	oz. Gin
1¼	oz. Spanish Brandy

Shake with ice and strain into a cocktail glass.

SOMBRERO

1½	oz. Coffee-flavored Brandy
1	oz. Sweet Cream

Pour Brandy into an Old-fashioned glass over ice cubes. Float cream on top.

SOME MOTHER

1¾ oz. Gin
½ oz. Dry Vermouth
¼ oz. Pernod

Stir with ice and strain into a cocktail glass. Serve with an onion.

SOMERSET

1½ oz. Rum
1 oz. Papaya Juice
½ oz. Creme de Bananes
¼ oz. Lemon Juice

Shake with ice and strain into a cocktail glass.

SONJA

1 oz. Yellow Chartreuse
½ oz. Blue Curacao
½ oz. Galliano
1 Maraschino Cherry
Fresh Cream

Stir the first three ingredients with ice and strain into a cocktail glass. Float cream on top. Sprinkle nutmeg on top. Serve with a cherry.

SONORA

1½ oz. Rum
1½ oz. Calvados or Applejack
2 dashes Apricot-flavored Brandy
1 dash Lemon Juice

Stir with ice and strain into a cocktail glass.

SONZA'S (WILSON)

1¼ oz. Gin
1 oz. Cherry-flavored Brandy
¼ oz. Lemon or Lime Juice
¼ oz. Grenadine

Stir with ice and strain into a cocktail glass.

SOOTHER COCKTAIL NO. 1

½ oz. Brandy
½ oz. Apple Brandy
½ oz. Triple Sec
1 tsp. Powdered Sugar
Juice ½ Lemon

Shake with ice and strain into a cocktail glass.

SOOTHER COCKTAIL NO. 2

1 oz. Rum
1 oz. Brandy
¼ oz. Apple Brandy
½ oz. Orange Curacao
¾ oz. Lime Juice
¾ tsp. Sugar

Shake with ice and strain into a cocktail glass.

SO-SO

1 oz. Gin
1 oz. Sweet Vermouth
½ oz. Calvados or Apple Brandy
½ oz. Grenadine

Stir with ice and strain into a cocktail glass.

SOUL KISS COCKTAIL NO. 1

1½ tsp. Orange Juice
1½ tsp. Dubonnet
¾ oz. Dry Vermouth
¾ oz. Bourbon Whisky

Shake with ice and strain into a cocktail glass. Serve with an orange slice.

SOUL KISS COCKTAIL NO. 2

1½ oz. Sweet Vermouth
1½ oz. Dry Vermouth
1 oz. Dubonnet
1 oz. Orange Juice

Mix in an Old-fashioned glass. Fill with crushed ice.

SOUPED-UP GIBSON

2 oz. Gin
2 tsp. Dry Vermouth

Mix in a Martini glass. Drop in several pearl onions.

SOUR KISSES

1¾ oz. Gin
¾ oz. Dry Vermouth
1 Egg White

Shake with ice and strain into a cocktail glass.

SOURTEQ

1½ oz. Tequila
1 oz. Lemon Juice
½ tsp. Sugar

Shake with ice and strain into a Sour glass. Serve with an orange slice and a cherry.

SOUTH AFRICAN "SUNDOWNER"

1½ oz. Brandy
½ oz. Van Der Hum Liqueur
¼ oz. Lemon Juice
¼ oz. Orange Juice

Shake with ice and strain into a cocktail glass.

SOUTH CAMP SPECIAL

½ oz. Jamaica Rum
½ oz. Gin
½ oz. Scotch Whisky
¼ oz. Lime Juice
¼ oz. Dry Vermouth
½ oz. Cherry-flavored Brandy

Shake with ice and strain into a cocktail glass.

SOUTHERLY BUSTER

2	Ice cubes
1	oz. Brandy
½	oz. Dry Vermouth
½	oz. Lime Cordial
	Dry Ginger Ale

Mix in a highball glass. Add ice and serve with drinking straws and a slice of lemon.

SOUTHERLY KISS

1	Sugar cube
¼	oz. Gin
1	oz. Parfait Amour
	Champagne

In a champagne glass, combine Gin and the sugar cube. Top up with Champagne. Pour Parfait Amour down the side of the champagne glass and serve.

SOUTHERN

¼	oz. Benedictine
¼	oz. Grenadine
½	oz. Lemon Juice
1½	oz. Bourbon Whisky

Mix in an Old-fashioned glass. Fill with ice. Serve with a lemon twist and a cherry.

SOUTHERN BANANA COMFORT

1	oz. Gold Rum
1	oz. Southern Comfort
½	oz. Lime Juice
1	tsp. Sugar
	Several pieces ripe Banana

Shake with ice and strain into a cocktail glass.

SOUTHERN BANGER

1½	oz. Vodka
½	oz. Southern Comfort
	Orange Juice

Pour Vodka into a Collins glass. Fill with ice and orange juice. Float Southern Comfort on top.

SOUTHERN BELLE

1	oz. Bourbon Whisky
1	oz. Heavy Cream
1	tbsp. Green Creme de Menthe
1	tbsp. White Creme de Cacao

Shake with ice and strain into a highball glass.

SOUTHERN BRIDE

1¾	oz. Gin
½	oz. Grapefruit Juice
¼	oz. Maraschino Liqueur

Shake with ice and strain into a cocktail glass.

SOUTHERN COFFEE

1½	oz. Southern Comfort
1	tsp. Brown Sugar

Mix in a cup. Fill with hot black coffee.

SOUTHERN COMFORT HIGHBALL

1½	oz. Southern Comfort

Pour into a highball glass. Fill with ice and soda. Serve with a lemon twist.

SOUTHERN COMFORT SPARKLE

2	oz. Southern Comfort
4	oz. Pineapple Juice
½	oz. Lemon or Lime Juice

Shake with ice and strain into a Collins glass. Fill with crushed ice. Add ginger ale. Garnish with a pineapple spear and an orange slice.

> Drink no longer water, but use a little wine for thy stomach's sake.
> — I Timothy 5:23

SOUTHERN COMFORT STRAWBERRY FRAPPE

1	tbsp. Southern Comfort
1	tbsp. Strawberry Liqueur

Mix without ice and stir well. Pour over crushed ice in an Old-fashioned glass. Decorate with a slice of lemon and an orange twist.

SOUTHERN CROSS

1	oz. Rum
1	oz. Brandy
¾	oz. Lime Juice
¾	tsp. Sugar
¼	oz. Orange Curacao

Shake with ice and strain into a highball glass. Fill with Squirt and ice.

SOUTHERN CROSS PUNCH

1	bottle Tawny Port
2	tbsp. superfine Sugar
½	tsp. mixed Spice
½	cup Grapefruit Juice
	Juice and rind of 1 Lemon
¼	cup Raisins
1	cup Water

Pour Wine into a heavy saucepan and add all ingredients except the raisins and water. Heat gently. Meanwhile, put the raisins into a small saucepan with the water and slowly bring to a boil. Add to the hot Wine mixture and pour into a metal punch bowl. Serve in punch glasses. Serves 8.

SOUTHERN DREAM

1	oz. Galliano
½	oz. Southern Comfort
½	oz. Orange Juice
1	oz. Cream (or 1 scoop Vanilla Ice Cream)

Shake with ice and strain into a cocktail glass.

SOUTHERN GAL

¾ oz. Galliano
¾ oz. Southern Comfort
¾ oz. Cointreau

Stir with ice and strain into a cocktail glass.

SOUTHERN GIN COCKTAIL

2 oz. Gin
2 dashes Orange Bitters
½ tsp. Triple Sec or Orange Curacao

Stir with ice and strain into a cocktail glass. Serve with a lemon twist.

SOUTHERN GINGER

1½ oz. 100-proof Bourbon
1 oz. Ginger Ale
¼ oz. Lemon Juice
¼ oz. Ginger-flavored Brandy

Shake with ice and strain into a cocktail glass. Serve with a lemon twist.

SOUTHERN HOSPITALITY

1 oz. Southern Comfort

Pour into a cocktail glass. Fill with Champagne.

SOUTHERN MINT JULEP

1 tsp. Sugar
3 sprigs Mint
2½ oz. Bourbon Whisky

Fill a highball glass half full with crushed ice. Add sugar, mint and 2 oz. Bourbon. Muddle these ingredients and fill the glass with crushed ice. Stir until the glass frosts. Add sugar-coated mint sprigs. Float ½ oz. Bourbon on top.

SOUTHERN PACIFIC

1½ oz. Brandy
½ oz. Lemon Juice
½ oz. Creme de Bananes
¼ oz. White Creme de Menthe

Shake with ice and strain into a cocktail glass. Serve with a pineapple stick.

SOUTHERN PEACH

1 oz. Southern Comfort
¾ oz. Peach Liqueur
¾ oz. Cream

Shake with ice and strain into a cocktail glass. Decorate with a peach slice.

SOUTHERN PINES

1 oz. Galliano
1 oz. Gin
½ tsp. Sugar
1 Egg White
¼ oz. Pernod
½ oz. Cream

Shake with ice and strain into a highball glass. Fill with soda and ice.

SOUTHERN PUNCH

1½ oz. Bourbon Whisky
½ oz. Brandy
1 oz. Lemon Juice
½ oz. Sugar Syrup

Shake with ice and strain into a Collins glass. Fill with soda and ice. Float ½ oz. Rum on top.

SOUTHERN STRAWBERRY FRAPPE

¾ oz. Southern Comfort
¾ oz. Strawberry Liqueur

Pack a cocktail glass with crushed ice and pour Southern Comfort and the liqueur over ice. Serve with an orange peel and a lemon wedge.

SOUTHERN-STYLE CHAMPAGNE

1 Mint sprig
1 Sugar cube
1 tbsp. Water
Brut Champagne, chilled

In a Collins glass crush the mint sprig and sugar cube with water. Drop in an ice cube. Pour Champagne in slowly, stirring lightly. Garnish with fresh fruit in season.

SOUTHGATE

1¼ oz. Whisky
½ tsp. Sugar Syrup
1-2 dashes Angostura Bitters

Shake with ice and strain into an Old-fashioned glass. Add ice. Serve with a twist of lemon.

SOUTH OF THE BORDER

1 oz. Tequila
¾ oz. Coffee-flavored Brandy
Juice ½ Lime

Shake with ice and strain into a Sour glass. Add a lime slice.

SOUTH PACIFIC

1½ oz. Brandy
2 tsp. Lemon Juice
1½ oz. Gin
1 tbsp. Grapefruit Juice
3 drops Maraschino Liqueur

Shake with ice and strain into a Collins glass. Add ice.

SOUTH SEA

1¼ oz. Rum
¾ oz. Lime Juice
½ oz. Orange Curacao

Shake with ice and strain into a cocktail glass.

SOUTH SEA DIPPER

½ tsp. Sugar
½ oz. Lemon Juice
¼ oz. Passion Fruit Liqueur
½ oz. Pineapple Juice
1½ oz. Rum

Shake with ice and strain into a highball glass. Fill with crushed ice. Float ½ oz. Port on top. Serve with a mint sprig.

SOUTH-SIDE COCKTAIL

Juice ½ Lemon
1 tsp. Powdered Sugar
1½ oz. Gin

Shake with ice and strain into a cocktail glass. Serve with a mint sprig.

SOUTH-SIDE FIZZ

Juice ½ Lemon
1 tsp. Powdered Sugar
2 oz. Gin

Shake with ice and strain into a highball glass. Add ice cubes, fill with soda and stir. Add fresh mint leaves.

SOUTHWEST ONE

1 oz. Vodka
¾ oz. Orange Juice
¾ oz. Campari

Shake with ice and strain into a cocktail glass.

SOVIET

1½ oz. Vodka
½ oz. Amontillado Sherry
½ oz. Dry Vermouth

Shake with ice and strain into an Old-fashioned glass. Add ice cubes. Serve with a lemon twist.

SOVIET SALUTE

1 oz. Vodka
¾ oz. Sherry
¾ oz. Dry Vermouth

Stir with ice and strain into a cocktail glass.

SOYER AU CHAMPAGNE

1 heaping tbsp. Vanilla Ice Cream
2 dashes Maraschino Liqueur
2 dashes Curacao
2 dashes Brandy
4 oz. chilled Champagne

Put the ice cream in the bottom of a large saucer champagne glass, add Maraschino, Curacao and Brandy and stir gently. Pour in the Champagne and decorate with an orange slice and a cherry.

SPANISH

2½ oz. Sweet Vermouth
2 dashes Angostura Bitters

Stir with ice and strain into a cocktail glass. Serve with a twist of orange peel.

SPANISH MOSS

1½ oz. Tequila
2 tbsp. Kahlua
3 drops Green Creme de Menthe

Shake with ice and strain into an Old-fashioned glass. Add an ice cube.

SPANISH ROCKET

1 oz. Galliano
1 oz. Tequila
1 oz. Orange Juice

Shake with ice and strain into a cocktail glass rimmed with sugar and cinnamon. Serve with a lemon wedge.

SPANISH TOWN COCKTAIL

2 oz. Light Rum
1 tsp. Triple Sec or Orange Curacao

Stir with ice and strain into a cocktail glass. Dust with nutmeg.

SPANISH VODKA MARTINI

2 oz. Vodka
½ oz. Dry Sherry

Mix in a cocktail glass. Add ice cubes and serve with a lemon twist.

SPARKLING BYRRH

2 tsp. Lemon Syrup
3 oz. Byrrh
3 oz. Soda

Pour all ingredients over ice cubes in a Collins glass. Stir gently.

SPARKLING CASSIS

Champagne
1 oz. Creme de Cassis
2 Ice cubes

Fill a pre-chilled Collins glass about two-thirds full with chilled Champagne. Add Creme de Cassis. Stir gently. Add ice cubes.

SPARKLING GALLIANO

½ oz. Galliano
¼ oz. Lemon Juice

Pour into a champagne glass. Fill with Champagne. Garnish with cucumber rind.

SPARKLING SHERRY

3 oz. Dry Sherry
5 oz. chilled Soda

Fill a Collins glass half full with cracked ice. Combine Sherry and soda and pour over ice. Serve with a lemon twist and an orange slice.

SPARKLING VANILLA COCKTAIL

1 tsp. Vanilla Ice Cream
2 dashes Orange-flavored Liqueur
2 dashes Maraschino Liqueur
2 dashes Brandy
Extra Dry Champagne, chilled

Combine first four ingredients in a champagne glass. Stir lightly. Fill with Champagne. Garnish with an orange slice and a cherry.

SPARKLING VERMOUTH

1½ oz. Orange-flavored Liqueur
3 oz. Dry Vermouth
Soda

Put Liqueur and Dry Vermouth in a Collins glass. Add ice cubes. Fill with chilled soda.

SPARTAN

1½ oz. Gin
½ oz. Orange Juice
½ oz. Orgeat Syrup

Shake with ice and strain into a cocktail glass.

SPECIAL MANHATTAN

1¾ oz. Bourbon or Rye Whisky
½ oz. Sweet Vermouth
¼ oz. Campari

Stir with ice and strain into a cocktail glass. Serve with a cherry.

SPECIAL ROUGH COCKTAIL

1½ oz. Apple Brandy
1½ oz. Brandy
½ tsp. Pernod

Stir with ice and strain into a cocktail glass.

SPENCER COCKTAIL

¾ oz. Apricot-flavored Brandy
1½ oz. Gin
1 dash Bitters
¼ tsp. Orange Juice

Shake with ice and strain into a cocktail glass. Serve with an orange slice and a cherry.

SPHINX COCKTAIL

1½ oz. Gin
1½ tsp. Sweet Vermouth
1½ tsp. Dry Vermouth

Stir with ice and strain into a cocktail glass. Serve with a cherry.

SPICED COFFEE

1 oz. Brandy, Rum or Bourbon
1 cup hot Coffee
Cinnamon, ground Cloves
Nutmeg

Wrap the spices in cheesecloth. Soak them in the coffee for several minutes. Add Brandy, Rum or Bourbon when ready. Serve in a mug.

SPICED ORANGE BLOSSOM

4 oz. Orange Juice
2 oz. Gin
2-3 drops Lemon Juice
1-2 Maraschino Cherries
1-2 dashes Angostura Bitters
1-2 pinches Cinnamon
2-3 drops Cherry Juice

Combine in a blender at a high speed until foamy. Serve unstrained in a Collins glass.

SPIKED ALE

1 quart Ale
4 oz. Brandy
1 tbsp. Sugar
Cloves, Nutmeg and Ginger

Combine in a large saucepan and heat, stirring constantly (do not bring to a boil). Strain and serve piping hot in mugs.

SPINNAKER

¾ oz. Benedictine
¾ oz. Gin
4 oz. Orange Juice

Shake with ice and pour into a cocktail glass with ice.

SPION KOP

1½ oz. Dry Vermouth
1½ oz. Dubonnet

Stir with ice and strain into a cocktail glass.

SPIRITED CHAMPAGNE

4 oz. Extra Dry Champagne, chilled
2 tsp. Brandy
2 tsp. Benedictine

Place an ice cube in a Collins glass. Pour in ingredients. Stir and garnish with an orange wheel, a maraschino cherry and fresh mint.

SPIRITED COOLER

1 oz. Orange-flavored Liqueur
1 oz. Brandy
Champagne, chilled

Fill a Collins glass half full with ice cubes. Add orange-flavored liqueur and Brandy. Fill with Champagne. Stir and garnish with mint.

SPIRITED DUBONNET

1 oz. Brandy
3 oz. Dubonnet

Stir with ice and strain into a cocktail glass.

SPIRITS OF '76

1 oz. Rum
½ oz. Applejack
½ oz. Papaya Juice
1 dash Lemon Juice

Shake with ice and strain into a cocktail glass.

SPRING COCKTAIL

1½ oz. Gin
½ oz. Benedictine
½ oz. Quinquina
1 dash Bitters

Shake with ice and strain into a cocktail glass. Serve with an olive.

SPRING FEELING COCKTAIL

1 tbsp. Lemon Juice
½ oz. Green Chartreuse
1 oz. Gin

Shake with ice and strain into a cocktail glass.

SPRINGTIME VERMOUTH

1 oz. Dry Vermouth
2 oz. Cranberry Juice
6 Strawberries

Shake the first two ingredients with ice and strain into a Collins glass. Fill with strawberries.

SPRITZER HIGHBALL

3 oz. Rhine Wine or Sauterne
Soda

Pour Rhine Wine or Sauterne into a highball glass with ice cubes. Fill balance with soda and stir gently.

SPUTNIK

1½ oz. Vodka
¾ oz. Fernet Branca
1 tsp. Lemon Juice
½ tsp. Sugar

Shake with ice and strain into a cocktail glass.

S.S. MANHATTAN

1¼ oz. Bourbon Whisky
1 oz. Orange Juice
¼ oz. Benedictine

Shake with ice and strain into a cocktail glass.

STAG LINES

1½ oz. Brandy
1 dash Angostura Bitters
2 dashes Orgeat Syrup

Shake with ice and strain into a cocktail glass. Serve with a lemon twist.

STANLEY COCKTAIL

Juice ¼ Lemon
1 tsp. Grenadine
¾ oz. Gin
¼ oz. Rum

Shake with ice and strain into a cocktail glass.

STARBOARD LIGHT NO. 1

1½ oz. Green Creme de Menthe
½ oz. Gin

Pour into an Old-fashioned glass. Fill with ice.

STARBOARD LIGHT NO. 2

1½ oz. Green Creme de Menthe
½ oz. Lemon Juice

Shake with ice and strain into a highball glass. Fill with soda and ice.

> A cheerful glass, a pretty lass,
> A friend sincere and true;
> Blooming health, good store of wealth
> Attend on me and you.

STAR COCKTAIL NO. 1

1 oz. Apple Brandy
1 oz. Sweet Vermouth
1 dash Bitters

Stir with ice and strain into a cocktail glass. Serve with a cherry.

STAR COCKTAIL NO. 2

1 oz. Gin
1 oz. Apple Brandy
¼ oz. Dry Vermouth
¼ oz. Sweet Vermouth
1 dash Grapefruit Juice

Stir with ice and strain into a cocktail glass.

STAR COCKTAIL NO. 3

1¼ oz. Applejack
1 oz. Dry Vermouth
¼ oz. Orange Curacao
1 dash Orange Bitters

Stir with ice and strain into a cocktail glass. Serve with a cherry.

STAR DAISY

Juice ½ Lemon
½ tsp. Powdered Sugar
1 tsp. Raspberry Syrup or Grenadine
1 oz. Gin
1 oz. Apple Brandy

Shake with ice and strain into a stein or metal cup. Add an ice cube and decorate with fruit.

STARLIGHT

1¾ oz. Gin
¾ oz. Orange Curacao
1 dash Angostura Bitters

Shake with ice and strain into a cocktail glass.

STARS AND STRIPES NO. 1

⅓ oz. Creme de Cassis
⅓ oz. Green Chartreuse
⅓ oz. Maraschino Liqueur

Pour carefully, in order given, into a pony glass so that each ingredient floats on the preceding one without mixing.

STARS AND STRIPES NO. 2

⅓ oz. Grenadine
⅓ oz. Heavy Cream
⅓ oz. Creme d'Yvette

Pour carefully, in order given, into a pony glass so that each ingredient floats on the preceding one without mixing.

STARS FELL ON ALABAMA

1¼ oz. Corn Whisky
1 tsp. Sugar Syrup
1-2 drops Pernod
1-2 drops Orange Flower Water
1-2 dashes Peychaud's and Angostura Bitters

Shake with ice and strain into a highball glass. Add ice.

STARS IN YOUR HAIR

1 oz. Gin
¾ oz. Forbidden Fruit Liqueur
¾ oz. White Creme de Menthe

Shake with ice and strain into a cocktail glass.

STEEPLEJACK

1½ oz. Apple Brandy
2½ oz. Apple Juice
¼ oz. Lime Juice

Mix in a Collins glass. Fill with soda and ice. Serve with a lime wheel.

STELLA ROMA

½ oz. Galliano
1 oz. Gin
¼ oz. Campari
½ Egg White
2 oz. 7-Up

Shake with ice and strain into a cocktail glass.

STEPHEN'S COCKTAIL

1 oz. Sherry
¾ oz. Dry Vermouth
¾ oz. Benedictine

Stir with ice and strain into a cocktail glass.

STERLING

1¼ oz. Rum
¾ oz. Orange Juice
½ oz. Benedictine

Shake with ice and strain into a cocktail glass.

STILETTO

Juice ½ Lemon
1½ tsp. Amaretto
1½ oz. Blended or Bourbon Whisky

Pour into an Old-fashioned glass over ice cubes and stir.

STINGER COCKTAIL

½ oz. White Creme de Menthe
1½ oz. Brandy

Shake with ice and strain into a cocktail glass.

STINGERING

1 oz. Bourbon Whisky
1 oz. Green Chartreuse

Stir with ice and strain into a cocktail glass.

STINGER RESERVE

1 oz. Orange Juice
1 oz. Rye Whisky
¼ oz. Dry Vermouth
¼ oz. Pernod

Shake with ice and strain into a cocktail glass.

STINGER ROYAL

1¾ oz. Brandy
½ oz. White Creme de Menthe
¼ oz. Pernod

Stir with ice and strain into a cocktail glass.

STIRRUP CUP NO. 1

1 oz. Cherry-flavored Brandy
1 oz. Brandy
1 tsp. Sugar
Juice ½ Lemon

Shake with ice and strain into an Old-fashioned glass over ice cubes.

STIRRUP CUP NO. 2

1½ oz. Cranberry Juice
¼ oz. Lemon Juice
1½ oz. Southern Comfort
½ oz. Grapefruit Juice

Mix in a double Old-fashioned glass. Fill with soda and ice. Serve with a mint sprig.

STOLEN KISSES

¾ oz. Gin
¾ oz. Pernod
½ Egg White
½ tsp. Sugar

Stir with ice and strain into a cocktail glass.

STOMACH REVIVER

¾ oz. Brandy
¾ oz. Kummel
½ oz. Fernet Branca
4 dashes Angostura Bitters

Stir with ice and strain into a cocktail glass.

STONE COCKTAIL

½ oz. Rum
½ oz. Sweet Vermouth
1 oz. Dry Sherry

Stir with ice and strain into a cocktail glass.

STONE FENCE NO. 1

2 dashes Bitters
2 oz. Scotch Whisky

Fill a highball glass with ice cubes. Add Scotch and Bitters and fill with soda or cider. Stir.

STONE FENCE NO. 2

3 oz. Applejack
2 dashes Angostura Bitters
Sweet Cider

Fill a highball glass with ice cubes. Add Applejack and Bitters and fill with soda or cider. Stir.

STONEHENGE COLLINS

3 oz. Gin
3 tsp. Lemon Juice
2 tsp. Sugar Syrup
1 tsp. White Creme de Menthe

Shake with ice and strain into a highball glass. Garnish with fruit slices or mint.

STONE SOUR

1½ oz. Bourbon Whisky
1 tbsp. Lemon Juice
1 tsp. White Creme de Menthe
Club Soda

Pour Bourbon, juice and Creme de Menthe over crushed ice in a Sour glass. Stir and fill the glass with soda. Sweeten to taste. Decorate with mint sprigs and a cherry.

STONYBROOK

1½ oz. Blended Whisky
½ oz. Triple Sec
½ Egg White
¼ oz. Orgeat Syrup

Shake with ice and strain into a cocktail glass. Serve with a lemon twist and an orange peel.

STORK CLUB FROST

½ oz. Triple Sec
3 oz. Orange Juice
1 oz. Curacao

Shake with ice and strain into a Collins glass.

STORMCLOUD

1 oz. Vodka
¾ oz. Light Creme de Cacao
1 oz. Lemon Juice
¼ oz. Grenadine

Shake with ice and strain into a cocktail glass.

STOUT SANGAREE

½ tsp. Sugar
2 oz. Soda
Stout

Dissolve sugar in soda in a double Old-fashioned glass. Fill with Stout and ice. Sprinkle nutmeg on top.

STRAIGHT LAW COCKTAIL

¾ oz. Gin
1½ oz. Dry Sherry

Stir with ice and strain into a cocktail glass. Serve with a lemon twist.

STRAITS SLING

1 oz. Lemon Juice
2 dashes Angostura Bitters
2 dashes Orange Bitters
1 oz. Gin
¼ oz. Benedictine
¼ oz. Cherry-flavored Brandy

Shake with ice and strain into a Collins glass. Fill with soda and ice.

STRATOSPHERE

1 oz. Rum
½ oz. Brandy
¼ oz. Cherry Liqueur
½ oz. Lemon Juice
1 tsp. Sugar

Shake with ice and strain into a cocktail glass.

STRAWBERRY BLONDE

1 oz. Strawberry Liqueur
3 fresh Strawberries, muddled
½ oz. Kirschwasser
3 oz. Rhine Wine

Mix in a Collins glass. Fill with ice and soda or Squirt. Top off with a strawberry.

STRAWBERRY COCKTAIL

1½ oz. Brandy
2 dashes Orange Bitters
1 oz. Strawberry Juice (from fresh berries)

Shake with ice and strain into a cocktail glass. Top off with a strawberry.

> I drink it as the fates ordain it,
> Come fill it, and have done with rhymes;
> Fill up the lonely glass and drain it
> In memory of dear old times.

STRAWBERRY CREAM COOLER

1½ oz. Gin
1-2 fresh Strawberries, muddled, or frozen Berries with juice
1 oz. Lemon Juice
½ oz. Cream
1 tsp. Sugar

Shake with ice and strain into a Collins glass. Fill with Squirt and ice.

STRAWBERRY FIZZ

1½ oz. Cream
1-2 crushed Strawberries
½ tsp. Sugar
1 oz. Lemon Juice
Liquor (your choice)

Shake with ice and strain into a fizz glass. Fill with soda and ice.

STRAWBERRY KISS

1 oz. Strawberry Liqueur
½ oz. Kirschwasser
½ oz. Rum
½ oz. Orange Juice
¼ oz. Lemon Juice

Shake with ice and strain into a cocktail glass. Top off with a fresh strawberry.

STRAWBERRY PUNCH

½ tsp. Sugar dissolved in water
1 oz. Lemon Juice
¼ oz. Strawberry Syrup or Liqueur
1½ oz. Brandy

Mix in a Collins glass. Fill with crushed ice and stir. Top off with a fresh strawberry.

> Here's to the fellow who smiles
> When life rolls along like a song,
> And here's to the chap who can smile
> When everything goes dead wrong.

STRAWBERRY RITA

1 oz. Tequila
2 oz. whole Strawberries
3 tsp. Sugar Syrup
3 oz. crushed Ice

Blend with ice and strain into a cocktail glass. Garnish with sliced strawberries and whipped cream, and a slice of lime.

STRAWBERRY RUM FLIP

1 oz. Strawberry Liqueur
1½ oz. Rum
¼ oz. Lemon Juice
1 Egg
1 tsp. Sugar

Shake with ice and strain into a flip glass. Sprinkle nutmeg on top.

STRAWBERRY SANGAREE

4 oz. Claret or Bordeaux
1½ oz. Sugar
1 tsp. Lemon Juice
4 oz. crushed Strawberries

Shake with ice and strain into a Collins glass. Leave the mixture in the glass and chill for at least one hour. Strain and add ice. Fill the glass with soda and decorate with slices of fruit.

STRAWBERRY SWIG

1½ oz. Gin
½ oz. Strawberry Liqueur
¼ oz. Lime Juice
1 dash Orange Bitters

Shake with ice and strain into a cocktail glass. Serve with a squeeze of lime juice.

STRAWBERRY VERMOUTH

Several crushed Strawberry pieces
2½ oz. Dry Vermouth
1 oz. Gin
2 tsp. Red Currant Syrup

Shake with ice and strain into a Collins glass. Fill with Squirt and ice and stir. Top off with a lemon wedge.

STREAKER

1 oz. Cream
¾ oz. Light Creme de Cacao
¾ oz. Anisette

Shake with ice and strain into a cocktail glass.

STREGA FIZZ

1 oz. Gin
1 oz. Strega
1 oz. Lemon Juice

Shake with ice and strain into a highball glass. Fill with soda and ice.

STREGA FLIP

1 Egg
1 oz. Strega
1 oz. Brandy
½ oz. Orange Juice
¼ oz. Lemon Juice
1 tsp. Sugar

Shake with ice and strain into a flip glass. Sprinkle nutmeg on top.

STREGA SOUR

1 oz. Gin
½ oz. Strega
½ oz. Lemon Juice

Shake with ice and strain into a cocktail glass with a sugared rim. Serve with a lemon wedge and a cherry.

STRIKE'S OFF

1½ oz. Gin
¾ oz. Swedish Punch
¾ oz. Lemon Juice

Stir with ice and strain into a cocktail glass.

STYRRUP

1¾ oz. Bourbon Whisky
¾ oz. Orange Juice
1 dash Angostura Bitters

Shake with ice and strain into a cocktail glass. Serve with a lemon twist.

SUBMARINE

1 ½   oz. Gin
½   oz. Dubonnet
½   oz. Dry Vermouth
1   dash Boker's Bitters

Stir with ice and strain into a cocktail glass.

SUBURBAN

1 ¾   oz. Bourbon Whisky
½   oz. Jamaica Rum
¼   oz. Port
1   dash Angostura Bitters
1   dash Orange Bitters

Stir with ice and strain into a cocktail glass.

SUDAN COOLER

1 ½   oz. Gin
1 ½   oz. Sweet Vermouth
1 ½   oz. Dry Vermouth
½   oz. Lime Juice

Shake with ice and strain into a Collins glass. Fill with soda and ice. (Cider may be used instead of soda.)

SUFFERING HAOLE

1   oz. Rose's Lime Juice
1   oz. Gin
½   oz. Brandy

Mix in a Collins glass. Fill with crushed ice and ginger beer and stir. Decorate with a mint sprig and fruit.

SUICIDE COCKTAIL

1 ½   oz. Haitian Rum
1   oz. Soda
½   oz. Light Creme de Cacao

Shake with ice and strain into a cocktail glass. Drop in a mint Lifesaver.

SUISSE

1 ½   oz. Pernod
½   oz. Anisette
1   Egg White

Shake with ice and strain into a cocktail glass.

SUISSESSE COCKTAIL NO. 1

2   oz. Anisette
1   Egg White

Shake with ice and strain into a cocktail glass.

SUISSESSE COCKTAIL NO. 2

1 ½   oz. Pernod
¼   oz. Anisette

Shake with ice and strain into a highball glass. Fill with soda and ice.

SUISSESSE COCKTAIL NO. 3

1 ¼   oz. Pernod
¾   oz. Anisette
1   Egg White
½   oz. Cream (optional)

Shake with ice and strain into a cocktail glass.

SUISSESSE MILANESE

1 ½   oz. Galliano
½   oz. Anisette
½   Egg White

Shake with ice and strain into a cocktail glass.

> Unto our doctors let us drink,
> Who cure our chills and ills,
> No matter what we really
>   think
> About their pills and bills.

SUISSETTE

½   oz. Sweet Vermouth
1   tsp. Sugar
1   oz. Brandy
1   Egg
½   oz. Pernod
1 ½   oz. Lemon Juice

Shake with ice and strain into a Collins glass. Fill with soda and ice.

SUMMER BOURBON

1 ½   oz. Bourbon Whisky
3   oz. Orange Juice
1   pinch Salt

Mix together Whisky, orange juice and salt and pour into an 8 oz. goblet half filled with crushed ice.

SUMMER CLARET NOG

½   cup Strawberries, sliced
1   Egg
2   tbsp. Sugar
3-4   grains Salt
4   oz. Milk
1   tsp. Lemon Juice
3   oz. Claret

Chill all ingredients, then blend everything together except lemon juice and Wine. Stir in lemon juice and Wine. Serve in a Collins glass.

SUMMER FIZZ

Several Mint sprigs, muddled
½   tsp. Sugar
1 ½   oz. Orange Juice
½   oz. Grenadine
Liquor—your choice (optional)

Shake with ice and strain into a Collins glass. Fill with ginger ale and ice.

SUMMER PUNCH (Individual)

3   tbsp. Creme de Cassis
1   dash Kirschwasser
10   oz. chilled Champagne

Put ice cubes in a 12 oz. goblet. Add Cassis and Kirschwasser and fill up with Champagne. Stir gently.

SUMMER PUNCH BOWL

1   block Ice
3   bottles Dry White Wine
1½   cups Creme de Cassis
12   Orange slices, halved
1   pint Strawberries

Put the ice in a punch bowl. Pour in Wine and Cassis, and stir. Float orange slices and strawberries on top. Serve in punch glasses. Makes about 18 servings.

SUMMER TIME

1½   oz. Gin
½   oz. Sirop de Citron

Mix in a highball glass. Fill with soda and ice.

SUMMERTIME REJUVENATOR

1   tbsp. Sugar Syrup
4   oz. chilled Soda
Chablis, chilled

Pour sugar syrup and soda over ice cubes in a Collins glass. Fill with Chablis. Garnish with an orange wheel and mint leaves.

SUN COCKTAIL

1½   oz. Brandy
¼   oz. Lemon Juice
¼   oz. Pineapple Syrup
¼   oz. Maraschino Liqueur
¼   oz. Orange Curacao
1   dash Angostura Bitters

Shake with ice and strain into a cocktail glass.

SUNDOWNER NO. 1

1½   oz. Brandy
½   oz. Van Der Hum
¼   oz. Orange Juice
¼   oz. Lemon Juice

Shake with ice and strain into a cocktail glass.

SUNDOWNER NO. 2

1½   oz. Rum
2   oz. Limeade

Blend with lots of crushed ice and pour into a large cocktail glass. Add ice and float Grenadine on top.

SUNDOWNER NO. 3

¾   oz. Benedictine
¾   oz. Light or Gold Rum
4   oz. Orange Juice

Shake with ice and pour into a cocktail glass with ice.

Here's to the whole world,
For fear some fool will be sore
Because he's left out.

SUNRISE NO. 1

1   oz. Tequila
½   oz. Galliano
½   oz. Creme de Bananes
½   oz. Cream
¼   oz. Grenadine
¼   oz. Lemon Juice

Shake with ice and strain into a cocktail glass.

SUNRISE NO. 2

¼   oz. Grenadine
¼   oz. Creme de Violette
¼   oz. Yellow Chartreuse
¼   oz. Cointreau

Pour carefully, in order given, into a pony glass so that each ingredient floats on the preceding one without mixing.

SUNRISE NO. 3

½   oz. Lime Juice
½   tsp. Sugar
1½   oz. warmed Cognac

Mix lime juice and sugar in a Sherry glass. Add Cognac and flame.

SUNSET NO. 1

1   oz. Cherry-flavored Brandy
1   oz. Advokaat
1   oz. fresh Cream
Lemonade

Shake with ice and strain into a highball glass. Fill with lemonade and serve.

SUNSET NO. 2

1   oz. Galliano
½   oz. Cointreau
½   oz. Papaya Juice
½   oz. Cream

Shake with ice and strain into a cocktail glass.

SUNSET NO. 3

1½   oz. Tequila
½   oz. Lime Juice
½   oz. Grenadine

Shake with ice and strain into a cocktail glass. Serve with a lime wedge.

SUNSET CLARET COCKTAIL

4   oz. Vanilla Ice Cream
1   oz. Light Cream
½   oz. Brandy
¾   oz. Claret

Blend until smooth. Pour into a large cocktail glass. Sprinkle nutmeg on top.

SUNSET LIMITED

2	oz. Muscatel
1	oz. Lemon Juice
1	dash Angostura Bitters

Mix in a Collins glass. Fill with soda, Chablis and ice. Serve with a mint sprig.

SUNSHADE

¾	oz. Pineapple Juice
¾	oz. Dry Vermouth
¾	oz. Rum
¼	oz. Grenadine

Stir with ice and strain into a cocktail glass.

SUNSHINE COCKTAIL NO. 1

¾	oz. Sweet Vermouth
1½	oz. Gin
1	dash Bitters

Stir with ice and strain into a cocktail glass. Serve with a twist of orange peel.

SUNSHINE COCKTAIL NO. 2

¾	oz. Rum
¾	oz. Dry Vermouth
¼	oz. Creme de Cassis
¾	oz. Lime or Lemon Juice

Shake with ice and strain into a cocktail glass.

SUNSHINE COCKTAIL NO. 3

1½	oz. Rum
¾	oz. Sweet Vermouth
1	dash Bitters

Stir with ice and strain into a cocktail glass. Serve with a twist of orange peel.

SUNSHINE COCKTAIL NO. 4

¾	oz. Rum
¾	oz. Orange Juice
½	oz. Maraschino Liqueur
¼	oz. Lemon Juice
1	dash Orange Bitters

Shake with ice and strain into a cocktail glass.

SUN TRAP

¾	oz. Tia Maria
¾	oz. Gin
½	oz. Lime Juice
½	oz. Dry Vermouth

Shake with ice and strain into a cocktail glass.

SUN VALLEY

4	oz. Jamaica Rum
1	quart Heavy Cream
4	Egg Yolks
2	tbsp. Powdered Sugar
Milk	

Pour the cream into a saucepan and bring almost to a boil; remove from heat. Beat the yolks with a little milk; add them plus the sugar to the cream. Pour in the Rum and stir well. Serve piping hot in small mugs.

SUN VALLEY SPECIAL

| 2½ | oz. Sweet Vermouth |

Pour into a cocktail glass. Serve with a lemon twist, a cherry and an orange slice.

SUPERIOR

1	oz. Rum
½	oz. Apricot-flavored Brandy
½	oz. Sweet Vermouth
½	oz. Lemon Juice

Shake with ice and strain into a cocktail glass.

SUPERIOR COCKTAIL

2	oz. Gin
1	oz. Lemon Juice
1-2	drops Dry Vermouth
1-2	dashes Kirschwasser
1	tsp. Sugar Syrup
Button Mushrooms	

Shake the liquids with ice and strain into a cocktail glass. Drop in the mushrooms.

SUPREME COCKTAIL

1	oz. Rum
½	oz. Benedictine
½	oz. Sweet Vermouth
½	oz. Lemon Juice

Shake with ice and strain into a cocktail glass.

SUPRISED

1½	oz. Jamaica Rum
½	oz. Kummel
½	oz. Orange Juice
1	dash Pimento Dram

Shake with ice and strain into a cocktail glass.

SUSIE TAYLOR

| Juice ½ Lime | |
| 2 | oz. Rum |

Pour into a Collins glass over ice cubes and fill with ginger ale. Stir.

We have toasted our sweet-
  hearts,
Our friends and our wives,
We have toasted each other
Wishing all merry lives;
Don't frown when I tell you
This toast beats all others
But drink one more toast —
A toast to — "Our
  Mothers."

SUTTON PLACE SLING

1½ oz. Jamaica Rum
2 tbsp. Orange Juice
1 tsp. 151-proof Rum
1-2 dashes Angostura Bitters
1-2 drops Lime Juice
1-2 drops Cherry Juice
Lemon Soda

Combine everything except the soda and 151-proof Rum with ice and shake well. Strain into a Collins glass, add ice and fill with lemon soda. Float 151-proof Rum on top.

SUTTON'S GIN BLIND

1½ oz. Gin
½ oz. Brandy
½ oz. Orange Curacao

Stir with ice and strain into a cocktail glass.

SVETLANA

1½ oz. 100-proof Vodka
½ oz. Sweet Vermouth
¼ oz. Kirschwasser
¼ oz. Orange Juice

Shake with ice and strain into a cocktail glass. Serve with a twist of orange peel.

SW 1

1 tbsp. Vodka
1 tbsp. Orange Juice
1 tbsp. Campari

Shake with ice and strain into a Collins glass. Fill with crushed ice.

SWAMP WATER

1½ oz. Green Chartreuse
4 oz. Pineapple Juice

Mix in a Collins glass. Fill with ice. Top off with a squeeze of lime juice.

SWAN

1 oz. Lime Juice
½ oz. Gin
¾ oz. Dry Vermouth
¼ oz. Pernod
2 dashes Abbot's Bitters

Shake with ice and strain into a cocktail glass.

SWAN SONG

¾ oz. Brandy
¾ oz. Applejack
¾ oz. Orange Juice
¼ oz. Grenadine

Shake with ice and strain into a cocktail glass.

SWEDISH HIGHBALL

2 oz. Swedish Punch
1 dash Bitters

Mix in a highball glass. Fill with soda and ice.

SWEDISH SNOWBALL

1½ oz. Advokaat
Lemon Soda

Pour Advokaat over ice in an Old-fashioned glass. Fill the glass with lemon soda and stir. Decorate with a lemon slice.

SWEENEY'S

1½ oz. Brandy
½ oz. Pineapple Juice
1 dash Maraschino Liqueur
3 dashes Angostura Bitters

Shake with ice and strain into a cocktail glass.

SWEET DREAM

¾ oz. Gin
¾ oz. Rum
¾ oz. Apricot-flavored Brandy
¼ oz. Pineapple Juice

Shake with ice and strain into a cocktail glass.

SWEETIE PIE

1 oz. Gin
¾ oz. Cherry-flavored Brandy
¾ oz. Yellow Chartreuse

Stir with ice and strain into a cocktail glass.

SWEET LILT

2 oz. Cognac
2 tbsp. Anisette
2 tbsp. Curacao

Shake with ice and strain into an Old-fashioned glass. Garnish with a chunk of fresh pineapple.

SWEET MARIA

1 tbsp. Sweet Cream
½ oz. Amaretto
1 oz. Vodka

Shake with ice and strain into a cocktail glass.

SWEET PATOOTIE COCKTAIL

1 oz. Gin
½ oz. Triple Sec
1 tbsp. Orange Juice

Shake with ice and strain into a cocktail glass.

SWEET SUMMER BREEZE

1½ oz. Brandy
¾ oz. Cointreau
2 Ice cubes

Mix in a highball glass. Add ice and fill with champagne.

SWEET VERMOUTH AND BITTERS

2 dashes Aromatic Bitters
2 dashes Orange Bitters
3 oz. Sweet Vermouth

Stir with ice and strain into a cocktail glass. Serve with a twist of orange peel.

SWEET VERMOUTH CASSIS

1   oz. Creme de Cassis
2   oz. Sweet Vermouth
Soda

Pour Creme de Cassis and Vermouth over ice cubes in an Old-fashioned glass. Fill with chilled soda.

SWEET VERMOUTH COCKTAIL

1   dash Orange Bitters
1   tbsp. Brandy
1   oz. Sweet Vermouth
Soda

Put all ingredients except soda in a highball glass. Stir and fill with chilled soda.

SWEET VERMOUTH HIGHBALL

1   dash Aromatic Bitters
1   oz. Sweet Vermouth
2   oz. chilled Soda

Combine Bitters, Vermouth and soda. Pour over ice cubes in a highball glass. Serve with a lemon twist.

SWEET VERMOUTH OLD-FASHIONED

1   tsp. Sugar Syrup
2   dashes Aromatic Bitters
1½   oz. Sweet Vermouth

Pour syrup, Bitters and Vermouth over ice cubes in an Old-fashioned glass. Stir and decorate with a twist of lemon and a cherry.

SWING HIGH, SWING LOW

¾   oz. Rum
¾   oz. Cointreau
¾   oz. Gin
¼   oz. Pernod

Stir with ice and strain into a cocktail glass.

SWISS

1¼   oz. Dubonnet
1¼   oz. Kirschwasser

Stir with ice and strain into a cocktail glass. Serve with a lemon twist.

SWISS ALEXANDER

1   oz. Cream
¾   oz. Cheri-Suisse
¾   oz. Brandy

Shake with ice and strain into a cocktail glass.

SWISS ALPS

¾   oz. Vodka
¾   oz. Light Creme de Cacao
¾   oz. Cheri-Suisse

Pack a cocktail glass with crushed ice and add all the ingredients.

SWISS CHOCOLATE

¾   oz. Anisette
¾   oz. Green Tea
¾   oz. Cherry-flavored Brandy

Shake with ice and strain into a cocktail glass. Float ½ oz. fresh cream on top. Serve with a cherry.

SWISS FAMILY COCKTAIL

½   tsp. Pernod
2   dashes Bitters
¾   oz. Dry Vermouth
1½   oz. Rye or Bourbon Whisky

Stir with ice and strain into a cocktail glass.

SWISS MISS

1   oz. Brandy
1   oz. Cheri-Suisse

Mix in an Old-fashioned glass. Fill with ice.

SWISSTZ

1   oz. Vodka
1   oz. Cheri-Suisse

Mix in an Old-fashioned glass. Fill with ice.

SWIZZLES

Juice 1 Lime
2   oz. Gin
1   dash Angostura Bitters
1   tsp. Sugar

Stir with swizzle stick until the mixture foams. Add ice.

SWORE

1½   oz. 100-proof Vodka
2   tsp. Sweet Vermouth
1   tsp. Kirschwasser
1   tsp. Orange Juice

Shake with ice and strain into a highball glass. Add ice. Serve with a twist of orange peel.

SYMPHONY OF MOIST JOY COCKTAIL

¼   oz. Creme de Rose or Grenadine
¼   oz. Yellow Chartreuse
¼   oz. Green Creme de Menthe
¼   oz. Cognac

Pour carefully, in order given, into a pony glass so that each ingredient floats on the preceding one without mixing.

TABOO

1   oz. Vodka
1   oz. White Rum
2   tbsp. Pineapple Juice
2   tsp. Lemon Juice
3   drops Rock Candy Syrup
2   oz. crushed Ice

Blend with ice and strain into a Sour glass. Garnish with slices of fruit and mint sprigs.

TABU

1½ oz. Rum
½ tsp. Sugar
½ oz. Lemon Juice
½ oz. Grenadine or Cranberry Syrup

Shake with ice and strain into a cocktail glass. Serve with a pineapple stick.

TAGO

1 oz. Gin
½ oz. Orange Juice
½ oz. Dry Vermouth
½ oz. Sweet Vermouth
¼ oz. Orange Curacao

Blend with ice and strain into a cocktail glass.

TAHITIAN HONEY BEE

½ oz. Honey
½ oz. Lemon Juice
1½ oz. Rum

Shake honey and lemon juice together. Add Rum and shake with ice. Strain into a cocktail glass.

> The grace that every man desires —
> The good graces of a woman.

TAHITIAN RUM PUNCH

¾ oz. Lime Juice (leave shell in glass)
½ tsp. Sugar
1½ oz. Martinique Rum

Mix lime juice and sugar in a Collins glass. Fill with crushed ice and add Rum. Stir. Garnish with a banana slice, a pineapple spear and an orange slice. Sprinkle nutmeg on top.

TAHITI CLUB

2 oz. Rum
1 tbsp. Lemon Juice
1 tbsp. Lime Juice
1 tbsp. Pineapple Juice
½ tsp. Maraschino Liqueur

Shake with ice and strain into an Old-fashioned glass over ice cubes. Add a slice of lemon.

TAHITI TANTALIZER

1½ oz. Vodka
1 tbsp. Pineapple Juice concentrate
2 tsp. Guava Nectar
2 tsp. Lemon Juice

Shake with ice and strain into an Old-fashioned glass. Add ice.

TAHITI TYPHOON

¾ oz. Lime Juice
1 oz. Cointreau
1 oz. Gin

Mix in a Collins glass. Fill with Champagne and ice.

TAHOE

1½ oz. Rum
½ oz. Lime Juice
½ oz. Creme de Kirsch

Shake with ice and strain into a cocktail glass.

TAILSPIN COCKTAIL

¾ oz. Gin
¾ oz. Sweet Vermouth
¾ oz. Green Chartreuse
1 dash Orange Bitters

Stir with ice and strain into a cocktail glass. Add a twist of lemon peel and a cherry or olive.

TAKE IT OR LEAVE IT

1 oz. Gin
½ oz. Apricot-flavored Brandy
½ oz. Dry Vermouth
¼ oz. Lemon Juice
¼ oz. Grenadine

Shake with ice and strain into a cocktail glass.

TALENT SCOUT

3 oz. Bourbon Whisky
1 dash Grand Marnier
1 dash Angostura Bitters

Shake and serve in an Old-fashioned glass with a twist of lemon peel.

TALL CHAMPAGNE

Juice ½ Lemon
Juice ½ Orange
1 tsp. Grenadine
2 oz. Brandy
4 oz. Dry Champagne, chilled

Combine all ingredients except Champagne and shake well. Strain into a Collins glass. Fill with Champagne.

TALL DUTCH EGGNOG

1½ oz. Advokaat
1½ oz. Rum
½ oz. 151-proof Rum
1 oz. Orange Juice
4 oz. Milk
1 tsp. Sugar

Shake with ice and strain into a Collins glass. Dust with cinnamon.

> Here's a toast to the future,
> A toast to the past,
> And a toast to our friends,
>   far and near.
> May the future be pleasant;
> The past a bright dream;
> May our friends remain
>   faithful and dear.

TALL ISLANDER

2	oz. Rum
3	oz. Pineapple Juice
1	oz. Lime Juice
¼	oz. Dark Rum
1	tsp. Sugar

Shake with ice and strain into a Collins glass. Fill with ice and add a squirt of soda. Serve with a lime wheel.

TAMAGOZAKE COCKTAIL

6	oz. Sake
1	tsp. Sugar
1	Egg

Bring Sake to a boil and light with a match. Allow to burn for 1 second. Remove from heat. Add egg and sugar and stir. Pour into a drinking cup and serve.

TAMARIND PUNCH

2	oz. Gin
½	tsp. Sugar
½	oz. Lemon Juice
2	oz. Tamarind

Mix in a Collins glass. Fill with soda and ice. Serve with a lemon twist.

TAMMANY

¾	oz. Gin
¾	oz. Sweet Vermouth
¾	oz. Dry Vermouth
¼	oz. Pernod

Stir with ice and strain into a cocktail glass.

TAM O'SHANTER

2	oz. Scotch Whisky
¼	oz. Lemon Juice
½	tsp. Sugar

Pour into a highball glass. Fill with hot water. Add spices (your choice), a cinnamon stick and sprinkle nutmeg on top.

TAMPA

1½	oz. Rum
¾	oz. Gin
¼	oz. Lemon Juice

Shake with ice and strain into a cocktail glass.

TAMPA TARPON

1½	oz. Early Times
½	oz. Triple Sec
3	oz. Orange Juice
½	tsp. Sugar

Blend with ice and strain into a highball glass. Fill with soda and ice. Serve with a pineapple stick.

TANGLEFOOT

1	oz. Light Rum
1	oz. Swedish Punch
½	oz. Orange Juice
½	oz. Lemon Juice

Shake with ice and strain into a cocktail glass.

TANGO COCKTAIL NO. 1

1	tbsp. Orange Juice
½	oz. Dry Vermouth
½	oz. Sweet Vermouth
1	oz. Gin
½	tsp. Triple Sec

Shake with ice and strain into a cocktail glass.

TANGO COCKTAIL NO. 2

½	oz. Orange Juice
½	oz. Sweet Vermouth
½	oz. Dry Vermouth
1	oz. Rum
½	oz. Benedictine

Shake with ice and strain into a cocktail glass.

TANTALUS COCKTAIL

1	oz. Lemon Juice
1	oz. Brandy
1	oz. Forbidden Fruit Liqueur

Shake with ice and strain into a cocktail glass.

TAPA PUNCH

¾	oz. Lime Juice
1¼	oz. Lemon Juice
½	tsp. Sugar
½	oz. Peach-flavored Brandy
½	oz. Demerara 86-proof Rum
1	oz. Gold Rum

Blend with ice and strain into a Collins glass. Fill with crushed ice and soda.

TARPON

3	oz. Orange Juice
2	tbsp. Bourbon Whisky
2	tsp. Triple Sec
1	tsp. Sugar

Shake with ice and strain into a highball glass. Fill with soda and ice. Decorate with pineapple.

TAXCO FIZZ

2	oz. Tequila
1½	tbsp. Lime Juice
½	tsp. Sugar
2	dashes Orange Bitters

Shake with ice and strain into a highball glass. Fill with soda and ice.

TCHOUPITOLAS STREET GUZZLE

| 1 | oz. Rum |
| 6 | oz. Ginger Beer |

Pour Rum into a highball glass over ice cubes. Add ginger beer.

TEA PUNCH

2 oz. Brandy
½ oz. Rum
½ oz. Lemon Juice
1 tsp. Sugar

Mix in a highball glass. Serve with a lemon twist.

TEA PUNCH BOWL

1½ quarts hot Tea
2 6-oz. cans frozen concentrated Lemonade
1 cup frozen concentrated Orange Juice
1 bottle Vodka
1 large block Ice
Lemon and Orange slices
Strawberries in season

Combine tea with frozen juices and allow to cool. Add Vodka and stir to mix well. Put ice in a punch bowl and pour in the vodka mixture. Decorate with orange and lemon slices, and strawberries in season. Serve in punch glasses. Makes about 20 servings.

TEGGIM

1¼ oz. Rose's Lime Juice
1¼ oz. Tequila

Stir with ice and strain into a cocktail glass.

TEMPTATION COCKTAIL NO. 1

1½ oz. Rye Whisky
½ tsp. Triple Sec
½ tsp. Pernod
½ tsp. Dubonnet

Shake with ice and strain into a cocktail glass. Add twists of lemon and orange peel.

TEMPTATION COCKTAIL NO. 2

1¼ oz. Pernod
¾ oz. Rum
½ oz. Lemon Juice

Shake with ice and strain into a cocktail glass.

TEMPTER COCKTAIL

1 oz. Port
1 oz. Apricot-flavored Brandy

Stir with ice and strain into a cocktail glass.

TENDER

¾ oz. Apricot-flavored Brandy
¾ oz. Apple Brandy
1½ oz. Gin
1 dash Lemon Juice

Shake with ice and strain into a cocktail glass.

TEN FURLONGS

1 oz. Vodka
1 oz. Apricot-flavored Brandy
½ oz. White Curacao
3 dashes Lime Juice

Stir well and pour without straining into a 10 oz. glass. Top up with Bitter Lemon Soda. Garnish with ½ a slice of pineapple and a cherry.

TENNESSEE COCKTAIL

1½ oz. Whisky
½ oz. Maraschino Liqueur
½ oz. Lemon Juice

Shake with ice and strain into a cocktail glass. Serve with a cherry.

May we never know any difference between our country and others save the oceans which separate them.

TENNESSEE MANHATTAN (DRY)

1½ oz. Tennessee Whisky
¾ oz. Dry Vermouth
1-2 dashes Angostura Bitters

Stir ingredients with ice and strain into a cocktail glass. Add a twist of lemon peel or an olive.

TENNESSEE SOUR

Juice ½ Lemon
½ tsp. Sugar
2 oz. Tennessee Whisky
Soda Water

Shake lemon juice, sugar and whisky and strain into a Sour glass. Top with soda water. Decorate with half a slice of orange and a cherry.

TENNIS GIRL COCKTAIL

2 oz. Dry Vermouth
½ oz. Scotch Whisky
1 dash Lime Juice

Shake with ice and strain into a cocktail glass.

TEN STRIKE

1¾ oz. Pernod
¾ oz. Gin
1 dash Angostura Bitters
1 dash Orange Bitters

Shake with ice and strain into a cocktail glass.

TEN TON COCKTAIL NO. 1

1½ oz. Rye Whisky
½ oz. Dry Vermouth
½ oz. Grapefruit Juice

Shake with ice and strain into a cocktail glass. Serve with a cherry.

TEN TON COCKTAIL NO. 2

1 oz. Gin
1 oz. Kummel
½ oz. Dry Vermouth

Stir with ice and strain into a cocktail glass.

TEQUILA A LA CANELA

1 oz. Tequila
2 tbsp. Condensed Milk

Mix in an Old-fashioned glass. Add ice and dust with cinnamon.

TEQUILA COCKTAIL NO. 1

2 oz. Tequila
1 oz. Dry Vermouth
3 drops Vanilla Extract

Stir with ice and strain into a cocktail glass.

TEQUILA COCKTAIL NO. 2

½ cup Grapefruit Juice
1 tbsp. Grenadine
2 tsp. Lime Juice
2 dashes Orange Bitters
2-3 oz. Tequila

Mix in an Old-fashioned glass. Add ice.

TEQUILA COLLINS

1 oz. Lemon Juice
1 tsp. Sugar
1½ oz. Tequila

Shake with ice and strain into a Collins glass. Fill with soda and ice. Garnish with an orange slice, a cherry and a lemon wedge.

TEQUILA DAIQUIRI

1½ oz. Tequila
1½ tsp. Lime Juice
1½ tsp. Sugar Syrup

Shake with ice and strain into a cocktail glass.

TEQUILA DUBONNET

1½ oz. Tequila
1½ oz. Dubonnet

Stir with ice and strain into an Old-fashioned glass. Add ice. Decorate with a slice of lemon.

TEQUILA FIZZ

2 oz. Tequila
¾ oz. Grenadine
1 tbsp. Lemon Juice
1 Egg White

Shake with ice and strain into a Collins glass. Add ice cubes, fill with ginger ale and stir.

TEQUILA FRESA

1½ oz. Tequila
¾ oz. Strawberry Liqueur
½ oz. Lime Juice
2 dashes Orange Bitters

Shake with ice and strain into a cocktail glass. Serve with a slice of lime and a strawberry.

TEQUILA FROZEN SCREWDRIVER

1½ oz. Tequila
3 oz. Orange Juice
3 oz. crushed Ice

Blend with ice and strain into a double Old-fashioned glass. Add ice and decorate with a slice of orange.

TEQUILA GHOST

2 oz. Tequila
1 oz. Pernod
2 tsp. Lemon Juice

Shake with ice and strain into an Old-fashioned glass. Add ice.

TEQUILA GUAYABA

1½ oz. Tequila
½ oz. Guava Syrup
½ oz. Orange Juice
½ oz. Lime Juice

Shake with ice and strain into a cocktail glass. Serve with a twist of orange peel.

TEQUILA MANHATTAN

2 oz. Tequila
1 oz. Sweet Vermouth
1 dash Lime Juice

Shake with ice and strain into an Old-fashioned glass. Add ice cubes, a cherry and an orange slice.

TEQUILA MATADOR

1½ oz. Tequila
3 oz. Pineapple Juice
Juice ½ Lime

Shake with crushed ice and strain into a champagne glass.

TEQUILA MOCKINGBIRD

1½ oz. Tequila
¾ oz. Green Creme de Menthe
Juice 1 Lime

Shake with ice and strain into a cocktail glass. Decorate with a lime slice.

TEQUILA OLD-FASHIONED

1½ oz. Tequila
½ tsp. Sugar
1 dash Bitters

Mix sugar, Bitters and a tsp. of water in an Old-fashioned glass. Add Tequila, ice and a splash of soda. Decorate with a pineapple stick.

TEQUILA PINK

1½ oz. Tequila
1 oz. Dry Vermouth
1 dash Grenadine

Shake with ice and strain into a cocktail glass.

TEQUILA PUP

1½ oz. Tequila
3 tsp. Lime Juice
1 tsp. Honey
2 dashes Angostura Bitters

Shake with ice and strain into an Old-fashioned glass. Add ice.

TEQUILA RICKEY

¾ oz. Lime Juice (leave shell in glass)
1½ oz. Tequila

Mix in a highball glass. Fill with soda and ice.

TEQUILA SCREWDRIVER

1½ oz. Tequila

Pour into a Collins glass. Fill with ice and orange juice.

TEQUILA SOUR

Juice ½ Lemon
1 tsp. Powdered Sugar
2 oz. Tequila

Shake with ice and strain into a Sour glass. Decorate with half a slice of lemon and a cherry.

TEQUILA STRAIGHT

¼ Lemon
1 pinch Salt
1½ oz. Tequila

Put salt between thumb and index finger on the back of your left hand. Hold a jigger of Tequila in same hand and the lemon wedge in the right hand. Taste the salt, drink the Tequila and then suck the lemon.

TEQUILA SUNRISE

2 oz. Tequila
3 dashes Grenadine ¾ oz
1 tbsp. Lime Juice 4oz OJ
½ tsp. Creme de Cassis
Lime peel

Pour into a highball glass. Fill with ice and soda and stir gently.

TEQUINI COCKTAIL

1½ oz. Tequila
½ oz. Dry Vermouth
1 dash Bitters (if desired)

Stir with ice and strain into a cocktail glass. Serve with a twist of lemon peel and an olive.

TEQUONIC

2 oz. Tequila
Juice ½ Lemon or Lime
Tonic Water

Pour Tequila over ice cubes in an Old-fashioned glass. Add juice, fill with tonic water and stir.

TERRACE GRILL

⅓ oz. Whisky
⅓ oz. Apricot-flavored Brandy
⅓ oz. Gin

Shake with ice and strain into a cocktail glass.

TERRAZZA

1½ oz. Galliano
1½ oz. Vodka
2 oz. Pineapple Juice
½ oz. Cream

Shake with ice and strain into a cocktail glass. Serve with a cherry and a pineapple spear.

TERRY SLOAN COOLER

1½ oz. Gin
½ oz. Creme de Cassis
½ oz. Lemon Juice
½ tsp. Sugar

Shake with ice and strain into a highball glass. Fill with soda and ice.

TEXAN

1½ oz. Bourbon Whisky
2 tsp. each Apricot-flavored Brandy, Lime Juice and Grenadine

Shake with ice and strain into an Old-fashioned glass. Add ice. Decorate with a slice of lime and a green cherry.

TEXAS FIZZ

2 oz. Gin
1 tsp. Orange Juice
½ tsp. Grenadine
½ tsp. Lemon Juice

Shake with ice and strain into a highball glass. Fill with Champagne or soda and ice.

TEXAS RANGER

½ oz. Gin
½ oz. Sweet Vermouth
½ oz. Dry Vermouth
¾ oz. Grapefruit Juice
¼ oz. Maraschino Liqueur

Shake with ice and strain into a cocktail glass.

TEXAS SPECIAL

¾ oz. Gin
¾ oz. Grapefruit Juice
¼ oz. Cognac
¼ oz. Dry Vermouth
½ oz. Cointreau

Shake with ice and strain into a cocktail glass.

TEX COLLINS

1½ oz. Gin
1½ oz. Grapefruit Juice
¾ oz. Honey

Shake with ice and strain into a Collins glass. Fill with soda and ice.

THANKSGIVING SPECIAL COCKTAIL

¾ oz. Apricot-flavored Brandy
¾ oz. Gin
¾ oz. Dry Vermouth
¼ tsp. Lemon Juice

Shake with ice and strain into a cocktail glass. Serve with a cherry.

THE DEVIL

1 oz. Brandy
1 oz. Green Creme de Menthe
1 pinch Red Pepper

Shake Brandy and Creme de Menthe together and strain into a cocktail glass. Sprinkle red pepper on top.

THE SHOOT

1 oz. Scotch Whisky
1 oz. Dry Sherry
1 tsp. Orange Juice
1 tsp. Lemon Juice
½ tsp. Powdered Sugar

Shake with ice and strain into a cocktail glass.

THE SMOOTHIE

1½ oz. Kahlua
½ oz. Gin
½ oz. Lemon Juice
½ tsp. Sugar

Shake and pour into a cocktail glass. Add crushed ice.

THE THIRD DEGREE COCKTAIL NO. 1

1½ oz. Gin
¾ oz. Dry Vermouth
1 tsp. Pernod

Stir with ice and strain into a cocktail glass.

THE THIRD DEGREE COCKTAIL NO. 2

1¾ oz. Gin
¼ oz. Dry Vermouth
¼ oz. Pernod
¼ oz. Orange Juice
1 dash Angostura Bitters

Stir with ice and strain into a cocktail glass.

THIN MAN

1 oz. Dry Gin
1 oz. Curacao
1 oz. Heavy Cream

Shake with ice and strain into a cocktail glass.

THIRD RAIL NO. 1

2-3 oz. Dry Vermouth
1-2 dashes Curacao
1-2 dashes Creme de Menthe

Stir with ice and strain into a cocktail glass. Serve with a lemon twist.

THIRD RAIL NO. 2

¾ oz. Rum
¾ oz. Apple Brandy
¾ oz. Brandy
¼ tsp. Pernod

Shake with ice and strain into a cocktail glass.

THIRD RAIL NO. 3

¾ oz. Dry Vermouth
1 dash Orange Juice
¾ oz. Sweet Vermouth
¾ oz. Gin

Shake with ice and strain into a cocktail glass with a sugared rim.

THISTLE COCKTAIL

1½ oz. Sweet Vermouth
1½ oz. Scotch Whisky
2 dashes Bitters

Stir with ice and strain into a cocktail glass.

THOMAS & JEREMIAH

1½ oz. Rum
½ tsp. Brown Sugar
½ oz. Lemon or Lime Juice

Mix in an Old-fashioned glass. Fill with hot cider.

THOMPSON

1¾ oz. Whisky
¾ oz. Sweet Vermouth

Stir with ice and strain into a cocktail glass. Serve with a lemon twist, orange peel and a pineapple spear.

> A toast of wine, to woman divine,
> I would toss off in haste, me think;
> To her eyes, to her hair, to her beauty so rare —
> But I haven't the wine to drink.

THREE FACES

1 oz. Galliano
1 oz. Rum
½ oz. Campari

Mix in an Old-fashioned glass. Fill with ice and a squirt of soda. Serve with a twist of orange peel.

THREE FOURTHS COCKTAIL

⅓ oz. Yellow Chartreuse
⅓ oz. Curacao
⅓ oz. Brandy

Pour carefully, in order given, into a pony glass so that each ingredient floats on the preceding one without mixing.

THREE MILLER COCKTAIL

1½ oz. Light Rum
¾ oz. Brandy
1 tsp. Grenadine
¼ tsp. Lemon Juice

Shake with ice and strain into a cocktail glass.

THREE ORBIT

1 oz. Drambuie
1 oz. Cointreau
1 oz. Vodka

Shake with ice and strain into a cocktail glass.

THREESOME

Juice ½ Orange
1 tsp. Creme de Menthe
½ tsp. Sugar
1 oz. Brandy
1 oz. Dry Vermouth
1 tsp. Burgundy

Pour Creme de Menthe into a Collins glass filled with crushed ice. Place orange juice, sugar, Brandy, Dry Vermouth and ice in a shaker. Shake well. Strain into the glass. Top off with Burgundy.

THREE STRIPES COCKTAIL

1 oz. Gin
½ oz. Dry Vermouth
1 tbsp. Orange Juice

Shake with ice and strain into a cocktail glass.

THREE TO ONE COCKTAIL

½ oz. Lime Juice
1 oz. Apricot-flavored Brandy
2 oz. Gin

Shake with ice and strain into a cocktail glass.

THUMPER NO. 1

1½ oz. Vodka
¾ oz. Tuaca

Mix in an Old-fashioned glass. Fill with ice. Serve with a lemon twist or a squeeze of lime juice.

THUMPER NO. 2

1¾ oz. Brandy
¾ oz. Tuaca

Stir with ice and strain into a cocktail glass. Serve with a lemon twist.

THUNDER COCKTAIL

1 tsp. Powdered Sugar
1 Egg Yolk
1½ oz. Brandy
1 pinch Cayenne Pepper

Shake with ice and strain into a cocktail glass.

THUNDER AND LIGHTNING COCKTAIL

1 Egg Yolk
1 tsp. Powdered Sugar
1½ oz. Brandy

Shake with ice and strain into a cocktail glass.

Here's to that most pro-voking man,
The man of wisdom deep,
Who never talks when he takes his rest,
But only smiles in his sleep.

THUNDERBIRD SPECIAL

1 oz. Bourbon
1 oz. Heavy Cream
2 tsp. Creme de Bananes
2 tsp. Cointreau

Shake with ice and strain into an Old-fashioned glass. Add an ice cube.

THUNDERCLAP COCKTAIL

¾ oz. Gin
¾ oz. Rye Whisky
¾ oz. Brandy

Shake with ice and strain into a cocktail glass.

TIA MINT

1½ oz. Tia Maria
½ oz. White Creme de Menthe

Mix in an Old-fashioned glass. Fill with ice.

TIDBIT

1 oz. Gin
1 scoop Vanilla Ice Cream
1 dash Dry Sherry

Blend at low speed and pour into a highball glass.

TIGER'S MILK NO. 1

1¼ oz. Sloe Gin
1¼ oz. Brandy

Shake with ice and strain into a cocktail glass. Serve with a lemon twist.

TIGER'S MILK NO. 2

1½ oz. Dark Rum
1½ oz. Brandy
4 oz. Heavy Cream
2 tsp. Sugar

Shake with ice and strain into a highball glass.

TIGER SPECIAL

2 oz. Light Rum
½ oz. Cointreau
Juice ½ Lime

Shake with ice and strain into a cocktail glass.

TIGER TAIL

1½ oz. Pernod

Pour into a Collins glass. Fill with ice and orange juice. Serve with a lime wheel.

TIJUANA SUNRISE

2 oz. Tequila
4 oz. Orange Juice
1 dash Angostura Bitters

Shake with ice and strain into a Sour glass.

TINTON

1½ oz. Applejack
¾ oz. Port

Shake with ice and strain into a cocktail glass.

TIN WEDDING

1 oz. Brandy
1 oz. Gin
1 oz. Sweet Vermouth
2 dashes Orange Bitters

Shake with ice and strain into a cocktail glass.

TIPPERARY COCKTAIL NO. 1

¾ oz. Irish Whisky
¾ oz. Green Chartreuse
¾ oz. Sweet Vermouth

Shake with ice and strain into a cocktail glass.

TIPPERARY COCKTAIL NO. 2

1 oz. Gin
½ oz. Sweet Vermouth
½ oz. Dry Vermouth
¼ oz. Orange Juice
¼ oz. White Creme de Menthe

Stir with ice and strain into a cocktail glass.

TIPPERARY COCKTAIL NO. 3

1 oz. Gin
1 oz. Dry Vermouth
½ oz. Orange Juice
½ oz. Grenadine

Shake with ice and strain into a cocktail glass. Garnish with mint sprigs.

TIPPERARY COCKTAIL NO. 4

1½ oz. Sloe Gin
½ oz. Dry Vermouth
1 dash Lemon Juice

Shake with ice and strain into a cocktail glass.

TIP TOE

1½ oz. Sloe Gin
½ oz. Dry Vermouth
½ oz. Lemon Juice

Stir with ice and strain into a cocktail glass.

TIPTOES

¾ oz. Gin
¾ oz. Whisky
½ oz. Sweet Vermouth
½ oz. Kirschwasser

Stir with ice and strain into a cocktail glass.

TIP TOP PUNCH

1½ oz. Brandy
½ oz. Lemon Juice
¼ tsp. Sugar
½ oz. Benedictine

Shake with ice and strain into a Collins glass. Fill with Champagne and ice.

TIVOLI SPECIAL

1½ oz. Cherry Heering
1 oz. Lemon Juice

Mix in a Collins glass. Fill with ginger ale and crushed ice.

T 'N' T

1½ oz. Tuaca
¾ oz. Tequila

Shake with ice and strain into a cocktail glass. Serve with a squeeze of lime. Add crushed ice.

T.N.T.

1½ oz. Rye Whisky
1½ oz. Pernod

Shake with ice and strain into a cocktail glass.

TOASTED ALMOND

1½ oz. Coffee Amaretto
1½ oz. Milk

Shake with ice and strain into a cocktail glass.

TOBAGO

1 oz. Gold Rum
1 oz. Gin
¼ oz. 151-proof Rum
½ oz. Lime Juice
¼ oz. Guava Syrup

Shake with ice and strain into a cocktail glass. Serve with a lime wedge.

TOKAY FLIP

2 oz. Tokay Wine
1 Egg
1 tsp. Sugar

Shake with ice and strain into a flip glass. Sprinkle nutmeg on top.

TOM AND JERRY

1 Egg, separated
1 tsp. Salt
1½ oz. Brandy
1½ oz. Dark Rum
⅓ cup hot Milk

Beat the egg white until it is stiff and beat the yolk until thick and lemon-colored. Combine them and beat in the sugar. Have ready a warmed 8 oz. mug. Add the egg mixture, Brandy and Rum, then fill with hot milk. Stir and top with a little grated nutmeg.

TOMATE

½ oz. Pernod
¼ oz. Grenadine

Mix in a highball glass. Fill with soda and ice.

TOMBOY

½ cup chilled Tomato Juice
½ cup cold Beer

Pour tomato juice into a highball glass. Add Beer.

TOM COLLINS

2 tbsp. Lemon Juice
1 tsp. Sugar
2 oz. Gin

Put lemon juice and sugar in a Collins glass. Stir to dissolve sugar. Add Gin and ice cubes and fill with soda. Stir quickly. Garnish with fruit slices and a cherry.

TOM JOHNSTON

1 oz. Scotch Whisky
½ oz. Lime Juice
½ oz. Sweet Vermouth
½ oz. Cointreau

Shake with ice and strain into a cocktail glass.

TOM MOORE

2 oz. Irish Whisky
1 oz. Sweet Vermouth
1 dash Angostura Bitters

Stir with ice and strain into a cocktail glass.

TONGA

1½ oz. Orange Juice
¾ oz. Lemon Juice
2 oz. Rum
¾ oz. Lime Juice
½ oz. Cognac
½ oz. Grenadine
¼ oz. Jamaica Rum
½ tsp. Sugar

Shake with ice and strain into a Collins glass.

TOP BANANA

1 oz. Vodka
1 oz. Creme de Bananes
Juice ½ Orange

Shake with ice and strain into an Old-fashioned glass. Add ice cubes.

TOP HAT

Juice 1 Orange
¾ tbsp. Sugar
6 oz. Burgundy, chilled
1 oz. Tawny Port

Place the first three ingredients in a Collins glass with ice. Stir. Float Port on top.

TOP HOT

½ oz. Grenadine
2 oz. Rum

Muddle Grenadine with a lemon wedge, orange slice and a pineapple spear. Add Rum. Shake with ice and strain into a cocktail glass.

TOP OF THE AFTERNOON

2 dashes Aromatic Bitters
3 oz. Muscatel
2 splashes Soda
Juice ½ Lemon
Rhine Wine

Pour all ingredients except Rhine Wine into a Collins glass. Fill with the chilled Wine.

TOP OF THE CROSS

1 oz. Pernod
1 oz. Blue Curacao

Mix in a highball glass. Fill with ginger beer and ice.

TOPPER COCKTAIL NO. 1

1 oz. Cognac
1 oz. Apricot Liqueur
1 oz. Creme de Menthe
1 dash Pernod

Shake with ice and strain into a cocktail glass.

TOPPER COCKTAIL NO. 2

1 scoop Vanilla Ice Cream
½ oz. Green Creme de Menthe
1 oz. Brandy or Cognac

Shake with ice and strain into a cocktail glass.

TOPPING

¾ oz. Sloe Gin
¾ oz. Dry Vermouth
½ oz. Creme de Violette

Shake with ice and strain into a cocktail glass. Serve with a cherry.

TOREADOR

1½ oz. Tequila
½ oz. Creme de Cacao
1 tbsp. sweet Cream

Shake with ice and strain into a cocktail glass. Top with a little whipped cream and a light sprinkling of cocoa.

TORERO

1½ oz. Kahlua
1 Egg White
1½ oz. Cognac

Shake with ice and strain into a cocktail glass.

TORONTO

2 oz. Rye Whisky
¼ oz. Fernet Branca
¼ tsp. Sugar
1 dash Angostura Bitters

Stir with ice and strain into a cocktail glass. Serve with an orange slice.

TORPEDO

2 oz. Calvados or Apple Brandy
1 oz. Brandy
1 dash Gin

Stir with ice and strain into a cocktail glass.

TORRIDORA COCKTAIL

1½ oz. Rum
½ oz. Coffee-flavored Brandy
1½ tsp. Sweet Cream

Shake with ice and strain into a cocktail glass. Float 1 tsp. of 151-proof Rum on top.

TORTUGA

½ oz. Orange Juice
½ oz. Lime Juice
½ oz. Lemon Juice
¾ oz. Sweet Vermouth
1 oz. 151-proof Rum
1 oz. Rum
½ oz. Grenadine
½ oz. Orange Curacao
¼ oz. Light Creme de Cacao

Shake with ice and strain into a Collins glass. Fill with ice.

TOUCH OF MAGIC

1 tsp. Sugar Syrup
1 oz. Brandy
1 oz. Dry Vermouth
Extra Dry Champagne, chilled

Combine ingredients except Champagne with ice and shake well. Strain into a champagne glass. Fill with Champagne.

TOVARICH COCKTAIL

1½ oz. Vodka
¾ oz. Kummel
Juice ½ Lime

Shake with ice and strain into a cocktail glass.

TOWER ISLE COCKTAIL

1½ oz. Rum
½ oz. Light Creme de Cacao
½ oz. Coconut Cream

Shake with ice and strain into a cocktail glass. Serve with a cherry.

TRADER VIC'S CHAMPAGNE APRICOT

1 Apricot
1 oz. Southern Comfort

Place apricot in a champagne glass. Pour in Southern Comfort and fill with Champagne and ice.

TRADER VIC'S PUNCH

1 oz. Orange Juice
1 oz. Lemon Juice
1¼ oz. Jamaica Rum
1¼ oz. Rum
1 tsp. Sugar
¼ oz. Orgeat Syrup
1 Pineapple spear

Shake with ice and strain into a Collins glass.

TRADER VIC'S RUM FIZZ

1½ oz. Rum
1 oz. Lemon Juice
1 Egg
1 tsp. Sugar
½ oz. Cream Soda

Shake with ice and strain into a fizz glass. Sprinkle grated orange peel on top.

TRADE WINDS

2 oz. Gold Rum
½ oz. Lime Juice
½ oz. Plum Brandy
1 tsp. Sugar

Shake with ice and strain into a cocktail glass.

TRAILER COCKTAIL

1 oz. Brandy
1 oz. Cointreau
1 oz. Lemon Juice

Shake with ice and strain into a cocktail glass.

TRAMINER REFRESHER

3 Ice cubes
3 dashes Aromatic Bitters
3 oz. Traminer, chilled
Chilled Soda

Dash Bitters on ice cubes in a Collins glass. Pour in chilled Wine. Fill with soda and stir. Serve with a lemon twist.

TRANQUILIZER

1½ oz. Bourbon Whisky
1 dash sweetened Lime Juice

Pour into a highball glass. Add ice cubes.

TRANSPLANT

1 oz. Rum
1 dash Galliano
1 dash Green Creme de Menthe

Mix in a highball glass. Fill with orange juice. Serve with a twist of orange peel.

TRANSVAAL

1½ oz. Gin
1½ oz. Dubonnet
3 dashes Orange Bitters

Stir with ice and strain into a cocktail glass.

TRAVELEX

½ oz. Galliano
¼ oz. Vodka
¼ oz. Creme de Bananes
½ oz. Lemon Juice
2 tsp. Kummel

Shake with ice and strain into a cocktail glass. Decorate with pineapple and serve.

TREASURE ISLAND SPECIAL

1 oz. Rum
1 oz. Jamaica Rum
¼ oz. Orange Curacao
¼ oz. Peach-flavored Brandy
½ oz. Lime Juice
2 oz. Pineapple Juice
½ oz. Sugar
2 drops Angostura Bitters

Shake with ice and strain into a double Old-fashioned glass.

TRILBY NO. 1

1½ oz. Gin
1½ oz. Sweet Vermouth
2 dashes Orange Bitters
1 tsp. Creme d'Yvette

Shake all ingredients except Creme d'Yvette and strain into a cocktail glass. Carefully float Creme d'Yvette on top.

TRILBY NO. 2

¾ oz. Scotch Whisky
¾ oz. Sweet Vermouth
¾ oz. Parfait Amour
2 dashes Pernod
2 dashes Angostura Bitters

Stir with ice and strain into a cocktail glass.

TRILBY NO. 3

1½ oz. Bourbon Whisky
¾ oz. Sweet Vermouth
2 dashes Orange Bitters

Stir with ice and strain into a cocktail glass.

TRINIDAD NO. 1

Juice ½ Lime
2 oz. Trinidad Rum
1 tsp. Powdered Sugar
3 dashes Angostura Bitters

Shake with ice and strain into a cocktail glass.

TRINIDAD NO. 2

1¼ oz. Trinidad Rum
1¼ oz. Dry Vermouth
1 dash Angostura Bitters

Stir with ice and strain into a cocktail glass.

> Here's to merry old world,
> And the days be they bright
>   or blue,
> Here's to the fates, let them
>   bring what they may —
> But the best of them all —
>   That's you.

TRINITY COCKTAIL NO. 1

¾ oz. Sweet Vermouth
¾ oz. Dry Vermouth
¾ oz. Gin

Stir with ice and strain into a cocktail glass.

TRINITY COCKTAIL NO. 2

1½ oz. Scotch Whisky
½ oz. Dry Vermouth
¼ oz. White Creme de Menthe
¼ oz. Apricot-flavored Brandy
1 dash Orange Bitters

Stir with ice and strain into a cocktail glass.

TRIO

¾ oz. Gin
¾ oz. Sweet Vermouth
¾ oz. Dry Vermouth

Stir with ice and strain into a cocktail glass.

TRIPLE C

1 oz. Cognac
2 whole Cardamom Seeds
Hot Coffee

Drop the seeds into a coffee mug and break them open with a muddler. Add Cognac and coffee; sugar to taste. Stir well.

TRIPLE COMFORT

1 tbsp. Lemon Juice
3 oz. Brandy
1 oz. Sweet Vermouth

Shake with ice and strain into an Old-fashioned glass.

TRIPLE DEATH

1   tsp. Orange-flavored Liqueur
2   dashes Pernod
1½   oz. Brandy
1   oz. Dry Vermouth
1   oz. Sweet Vermouth

Stir with ice and strain into a cocktail glass. Add ice.

TRIPLE DECIDER

1   tsp. Creme d'Yvette
1   tsp. Orange-flavored Liqueur
1½   oz. Apricot-flavored Brandy

Put Creme d'Yvette into a cocktail glass. Shake other ingredients with ice and strain into the cocktail glass with Creme d'Yvette. Do not mix. Fill the glass with Burgundy.

TRIPLE KONA CREAM

6   oz. chilled Coffee
1   oz. Creme de Cafe
Ice cubes
3   oz. Coffee Ice Cream

Mix coffee, Creme de Cafe and ice in a Collins glass. Stir well and top off with ice cream.

TRIPLICE

1   oz. Gin
¾   oz. Dry Vermouth
¾   oz. Benedictine

Stir with ice and strain into a cocktail glass.

TROCADERO

1½   oz. Sweet Vermouth
1½   oz. Dry Vermouth
1   dash Grenadine
1   dash Orange Bitters

Stir with ice and strain into a cocktail glass.

TROIS RIVIERES

1½   oz. Canadian Whisky
1   tbsp. Dubonnet
1½   tsp. Triple Sec

Shake with ice and strain into an Old-fashioned glass. Add ice cubes. Serve with a twist of orange peel.

TROLLEY

2   oz. Bourbon Whisky
Pineapple Juice
Cranberry Juice

Pour Bourbon over ice in a highball glass. Fill the glass with equal parts of pineapple and cranberry juices and stir gently. Serve with an orange slice.

TROPICAL COCKTAIL NO. 1

1½   oz. Brandy
½   oz. Creme de Vanille
1   dash Peychaud's Bitters

Shake with ice and strain into a cocktail glass.

TROPICAL COCKTAIL NO. 2

¾   oz. Dry Vermouth
¾   oz. Maraschino Liqueur
¾   oz. Light Creme de Cacao
1   dash Bitters

Stir with ice and strain into a cocktail glass.

TROPICAL COCKTAIL NO. 3

1½   oz. Rum
½   oz. Orange Curacao
½   oz. Lime Juice

Shake with ice and strain into a cocktail glass.

TROPICAL COCKTAIL NO. 4

3   oz. Gin
1   oz. Guava Nectar
1   oz. Frozen Pineapple Juice

Mix in an Old-fashioned glass.

TROPICALA

1½   oz. Dry Vermouth
2   tbsp. White Creme de Cacao
2   tbsp. Maraschino Liqueur
2   dashes Angostura and Orange Bitters

Shake with ice and strain into an Old-fashioned glass. Fill with crushed ice.

TROPICALE

1   oz. Galliano
1   oz. Rum
½   oz. Cointreau
½   oz. Grapefruit Juice
1   dash Angostura Bitters

Shake with ice and strain into a cocktail glass.

TROPICAL FIZZ

2   oz. Gin
½   oz. Pineapple Juice
1   oz. Lime Juice
1   Egg White

Shake with ice and strain into a fizz glass. Fill with soda and ice. Serve with a mint sprig.

TROPICAL ITCH

1   dash Angostura Bitters
¼   oz. Bourbon Whisky
½   oz. Orange Curacao
½   oz. Jamaica Rum
1   oz. 151-proof Rum
Passion Fruit Juice

Fill a double Old-fashioned glass with shaved ice and add Bitters, Bourbon, Curacao and Rum. Fill with Passion fruit juice. Decorate with a pineapple spear, mint sprigs and a cherry.

TROPICAL RUBY COOLER

2 oz. Tropical Fruit Punch
4 oz. Ruby Chablis
½ tsp. Lemon Juice

Mix and pour over ice cubes in a Collins glass.

TROPICAL SPECIAL

1½ oz. Gin
1 oz. each Orange and Lime Juice
2 tbsp. Grapefruit Juice
2 tsp. Sugar Syrup

Shake with ice and strain into a Sour glass. Decorate with fruit slices and a cherry.

TROPICAL TREASURE

1 oz. Galliano
1 oz. Orange Curacao
1 oz. Pineapple Juice
1 Egg White
1 dash Angostura Bitters

Shake with ice and strain into a cocktail glass.

TROPICANA

2 oz. Galliano
1 oz. Coconut Milk

Shake with ice and strain into a cocktail glass. Decorate with a fresh coconut slice and a banana slice.

TROPICANA BELLE

½ oz. Galliano
½ oz. Calvados
½ oz. Gin
¼ oz. Maraschino Cherry Juice

Blend with plenty of crushed ice and strain into a large snifter.

TROPIC JINKS

1½ oz. Gin
¾ oz. Lime Juice

Mix in a highball glass. Fill with tonic and ice.

TRUE BLUE

½ oz. Creme de Cacao
½ oz. Maraschino Liqueur
½ oz. Rum
½ oz. fresh Cream

Shake with ice and strain into a champagne glass half full of crushed ice. Float cream on top and serve with a cherry.

TRYST COCKTAIL

¾ oz. Scotch Whisky
¾ oz. Parfait Amour
¾ oz. Sweet Vermouth
¼ oz. Pernod
1 dash Orange Bitters

Stir with ice and strain into a cocktail glass.

T.S.I.T.E. COCKTAIL
(THEY SHALL INHERIT THE EARTH)

¾ oz. Brandy
¾ oz. Lemon Juice
½ oz. Cointreau
½ oz. Benedictine

Shake with ice and strain into a cocktail glass.

TUACA SOUR

1½ oz. Tuaca
1 oz. Lemon Juice
½ tsp. Sugar

Shake with ice and strain into a Sour glass. Serve with a lemon wedge and a cherry.

TUACA STINGER

1¾ oz. Tuaca
¾ oz. White Creme de Menthe

Shake with ice and strain into a cocktail glass.

TUACIAN

1½ oz. Tuaca
½ oz. Orange Curacao
¼ oz. Galliano
¾ oz. Lime Juice

Shake with ice and strain into a cocktail glass.

TUDOR TAYLOR

2¼ oz. Vodka
¼ oz. Grenadine

Stir with ice and strain into a cocktail glass.

TUESDAY WELD

¾ oz. Brandy
¾ oz. Dark Creme de Cacao
1 oz. Cream

Shake with ice and strain into a cocktail glass. Top off with an oreo cookie.

TULIP

¾ oz. Calvados or Applejack
¾ oz. Sweet Vermouth
½ oz. Apricot-flavored Brandy
1 tbsp. Lemon Juice

Stir with ice and strain into a cocktail glass.

TURF COCKTAIL

¼ oz. Pernod
2 dashes Bitters
1 oz. Dry Vermouth
1 oz. Gin

Stir with ice and strain into a cocktail glass. Serve with a twist of orange peel.

TURF REFRESHER

1 tsp. Grenadine
3 oz. Dry Vermouth
Chilled Soda

Pour Grenadine and Dry Vermouth over ice cubes in a Collins glass. Fill with chilled soda.

TURKISH COFFEE

1 cup Coffee, hot and black
2 tsp. Cognac
Sugar to taste

Stir in a mug and sip while still piping hot.

TURKISH HAREM COOLER

3 oz. Rose Wine

Pour into a highball glass. Fill with crushed ice and tonic.

TURRET COCKTAIL

½ oz. Grenadine
½ oz. Swedish Punch
½ oz. Calvados
½ oz. Lemon Juice
1 oz. Gin

Shake with ice and strain into a cocktail glass.

TUSCAN

1 oz. Tuaca
1 oz. Lemon Juice
½ oz. Maraschino Liqueur

Shake with ice and strain into a cocktail glass. Serve with a lemon wedge and a cherry.

TUXEDO NO. 1

3 oz. Sherry
¾ oz. Anisette
2 dashes Maraschino Liqueur
1 dash Peychaud's Bitters

Stir with ice and strain into a cocktail glass.

TUXEDO NO. 2

1½ oz. Gin
1½ oz. Dry Vermouth
¼ tsp. Maraschino Liqueur
¼ tsp. Pernod
2 dashes Orange Bitters

Stir with ice and strain into a cocktail glass. Serve with a cherry.

T.V. SET

1 oz. Tuaca
¾ oz. Anisette

Mix in an Old-fashioned glass. Add ice to taste.

TWELVE GAUGE GROG

1½ oz. Jamaica Rum
1 tbsp. 151-proof Rum
2 oz. Orange Juice
1 oz. Lemon Juice
3 dashes Angostura Bitters
Sugar to taste

Shake with ice and strain into a Collins glass. Fill with ice and grapefruit soda. Serve with an orange slice and a cherry.

TWELVE MILES OUT

¾ oz. Calvados or Applejack
¾ oz. Light Rum
¾ oz. Swedish Punch

Stir with ice and strain into a cocktail glass.

TWENTIETH CENTURY

¾ oz. Brandy
¾ oz. Light Creme de Cacao
1 oz. Cream

Shake with ice and strain into a cocktail glass.

TWILIGHT ZONE

2 oz. Rum
1 oz. Creme de Menthe
½ oz. Parfait Amour
½ oz. Lime Cordial
½ oz. fresh Cream

Shake with ice and strain into a champagne glass. Serve with a cherry.

TWIN HILLS

1½ oz. Blended Whisky
2 tsp. Benedictine
1½ tsp. Lemon Juice
1½ tsp. Lime Juice
1 tsp. Sugar

Shake with ice and strain into a Sour glass. Add a slice of lime and lemon.

TWINKLE TOES COCKTAIL

½ oz. Orange Juice
½ oz. Lemon Juice
1 oz. Rum
1 oz. Swedish Punch

Shake with ice and strain into a cocktail glass.

TWIN SIN COCKTAIL

1 oz. Gin
½ oz. Sweet Vermouth
¼ tsp. Grenadine
1 tbsp. Orange Juice
1 Egg White

Shake with ice and strain into a cocktail glass.

TWISTER

2 oz. Vodka
Juice ⅓ Lime

Pour into a Collins glass. Add several ice cubes, drop a lime rind into the glass. Fill with lemon soda and stir.

TWO FIFTY TWO

1 oz. 151-proof Rum
1 oz. Wild Turkey 101

Mix in an Old-fashioned glass. Fill with ice.

TWO RUTHS

Juice ½ Lemon
1½ oz. Light Rum
¾ oz. Pineapple Juice
¾ oz. Apricot-flavored Brandy

Blend with ice and strain into a cocktail glass packed with crushed ice.

TYPHOON

1 oz. Gin
½ oz. Anisette
1 oz. Lime Juice

Shake all ingredients with ice. Strain into a Collins glass. Add ice cubes Fill glass with chilled Champagne.

TYROL

1 oz. Galliano
½ oz. Brandy
½ oz. Green Chartreuse
½ oz. Cream

Shake with ice and strain into a cocktail glass.

> Let's drink to our friend and host.
> May his generous heart, like his good wine, only grow mellower with the years.

ULANDA COCKTAIL

¾ oz. Triple Sec or Orange Curacao
1½ oz. Gin
¼ tsp. Pernod

Stir with ice and strain into a cocktail glass.

ULYSSES

¾ oz. Cherry-flavored Brandy
¾ oz. Dry Vermouth
¾ oz. Brandy

Stir with ice and strain into a cocktail glass. Serve with a twist of orange peel.

UNCLE HARRY'S PUNCH

1 large block Ice
2 bottles chilled Rhine Wine
½ cup Orange Juice
½ cup Lemon Juice
¾ cup Curacao
¾ cup Golden Rum
2 quarts chilled Club Soda
2 bottles chilled Champagne
Mint leaves
Orange and Lemon slices

Put the block of ice in a punch bowl and pour in all ingredients (in the order listed) except the garnish. Stir gently to mix, float mint leaves, lemon and orange slices on top. Serve in 4 oz. punch glasses. Makes about 45 servings.

UNDERTAKER'S COCKTAIL NO. 1

¾ oz. Gin
¾ oz. Vodka
1 oz. Cream

Shake with ice and strain into a cocktail glass.

UNDERTAKER'S COCKTAIL NO. 2

¾ oz. Vodka
¾ oz. Gin
¾ oz. Light Creme de Cacao

Shake with ice and strain into a cocktail glass.

UNE IDEE

¾ oz. Gin
¾ oz. Sweet Vermouth
¾ oz. Cognac
½ oz. Apricot-flavored Brandy

Stir with ice and strain into a cocktail glass.

UNIE K

1½ oz. Galliano
1 oz. Vodka
1 oz. Lime Juice
¼ oz. Grenadine

Shake with ice and strain into a cocktail glass. Serve with a lemon wheel.

UNION JACK COCKTAIL NO. 1

¾ oz. Creme d'Yvette
1½ oz. Gin
½ tsp. Grenadine

Shake with ice and strain into a cocktail glass.

UNION JACK COCKTAIL NO. 2

⅓ oz. Green Chartreuse
⅓ oz. Maraschino Liqueur
⅓ oz. Grenadine

Pour carefully, in order given, into a pony glass so that each ingredient floats on the preceding one without mixing.

UNION LEAGUE

1¾ oz. Gin
¾ oz. Port
1 dash Orange Bitters

Stir with ice and strain into a cocktail glass.

UNISPHERE

1½ oz. Rum
¼ oz. Grenadine
½ oz. Lime Juice
¼ oz. Benedictine
¼ oz. Pernod

Shake with ice and strain into a cocktail glass.

UPISSIPPI

1½ oz. Gin
½   oz. Sweet Vermouth
½   oz. Dry Vermouth
¼   oz. Grenadine

Stir with ice and strain into a cocktail glass.

UPSTAIRS

3   oz. Dubonnet
1   tbsp. Lemon Juice

Pour into a fizz glass. Fill with soda and ice.

UPSTARTER

1½ oz. Galliano
1   oz. Vodka
¼   oz. Peach-flavored Brandy

Shake with ice and strain into a cocktail glass.

UP TO DATE

1½ oz. Rye Whisky
1½ oz. Sherry
2   dashes Angostura Bitters
2   dashes Grand Marnier

Stir with ice and strain into a cocktail glass.

VAIL COCKTAIL

½   oz. Dry Vermouth
½   oz. Benedictine
1¼ oz. Rye Whisky

Stir with ice and strain into a cocktail glass.

VALENCIA COCKTAIL NO. 1

1   tbsp. Orange Juice
1½ oz. Apricot-flavored Brandy
2   dashes Orange Bitters

Stir with ice and strain into a cocktail glass.

VALENCIA COCKTAIL NO. 2

1½ oz. Apricot-flavored Brandy
2   oz. Orange Juice

Shake with ice and strain into a Collins glass. Fill with Champagne and ice.

VAMPIRE

1   oz. Gin
1   oz. Dry Vermouth
½   oz. Lime Juice

Shake with ice and strain into a cocktail glass.

VAN

2   oz. Gin
1   oz. Dry Vermouth
2   dashes Grand Marnier

Stir with ice and strain into a cocktail glass.

VANCOUVER

1½ oz. Gin
¾   oz. Sweet Vermouth
¼   oz. Benedictine
1   dash Orange Bitters

Shake with ice and strain into a cocktail glass.

> Here's to the man who is
> wisest and best,
> Here's to the man who with
> judgment is blest,
> Here's to the man who's as
> smart as can be —
> I mean the man who agrees
> with me.

VANDERBILT COCKTAIL

¾   oz. Cherry-flavored Brandy
1½ oz. Brandy
1   tsp. Sugar Syrup
2   dashes Bitters

Stir with ice and strain into a cocktail glass.

VANDERMINT JULEP

1½ oz. Vandermint
1½ oz. Bourbon Whisky

Mix Bourbon and 1 oz. Vandermint in a highball glass. Fill with ice and stir. Float remaining Vandermint on top. Serve with a mint sprig.

VANDERMIST

2   oz. Vandermint

Pour into an Old-fashioned glass. Fill with crushed ice.

VANDERSPRITZ

1½ oz. Vandermint

Pour into a highball glass. Fill with soda and ice.

V AND V

1   oz. Vandermint
1   oz. Vodka

Mix in an Old-fashioned glass. Fill with ice.

VANILLA COOLER

2   oz. Brandy
1   scoop Vanilla Ice Cream
3   oz. Cream

Shake with ice and strain into a Collins glass. Fill with soda.

VANILLA PUNCH

2   tsp. Powdered Sugar dissolved in water
3   dashes Lemon Juice
3   dashes Curacao
1½ oz. Brandy
¾   oz. Vanilla Cordial

Shake with ice and strain into a Collins glass. Fill with soda and ice. Decorate with fruit.

VAN VLEET

3   oz. Rum
1   oz. Maple Syrup
1   oz. Lemon Juice

Shake with ice and strain into an Old-fashioned glass. Add ice cubes.

VAULTER PUNCH

2   oz. Rye Whisky
Cider

Stir Whisky with crushed ice. Add 2 pieces of lemon peel. Strain into a Collins glass filled with ice. Fill with Cider. Decorate with fruit.

VEL D'HIV COCKTAIL

1½   oz. Cognac
½   oz. Lemon Juice
½   oz. Benedictine
1   dash Angostura Bitters

Shake with ice and strain into a cocktail glass.

VELOCITY

1½   oz. Sweet Vermouth
¾   oz. Gin

Shake with ice and strain into a cocktail glass. Serve with an orange slice.

VELVET

1   oz. Gin
1   oz. Dubonnet
½   oz. Mandarinette

Shake with ice and strain into a cocktail glass.

VELVET CUP

½   cold Stout
½   chilled Champagne

Serve in a mug or Collins glass.

VELVET GAFF COOLER

4   oz. chilled Porter

Pour into a Collins glass. Fill with chilled Champagne.

VELVET HAMMER NO. 1

1½   oz. Vodka
1   tbsp. Creme de Cacao
1   tbsp. Sweet Cream

Shake with ice and strain into a cocktail glass.

VELVET HAMMER NO. 2

1½   oz. Strega
1   oz. Creme de Cacao
1   tbsp. Sweet Cream

Shake with ice and strain into a cocktail glass.

VELVET HAMMER NO. 3

¾   oz. Gin
¾   oz. Apricot-flavored Brandy
¾   oz. Dry Vermouth
¼   oz. Maraschino Liqueur
1   dash Orange Bitters

Stir with ice and strain into a cocktail glass. Serve with a cherry.

VELVET ORCHID

1   oz. Dry Vermouth
1   oz. White Creme de Cacao
3   drops Black Raspberry Syrup

Shake with ice and strain into a cocktail glass.

VENDOME

1   oz. Gin
1   oz. Dubonnet
½   oz. Dry Vermouth

Stir with ice and strain into a cocktail glass. Serve with a lemon twist.

VENETIAN COFFEE

1   oz. Brandy
½   oz. Dark Creme de Cacao

Pour into a cup. Fill with hot black coffee. (Brown sugar or Kahlua may be used instead of Creme de Cacao.)

VENICE

2   oz. Brandy
1   tsp. Sugar Syrup
1   Egg
1   tsp. Lemon Juice

Shake with ice and strain into a Collins glass. Fill with ice and ginger ale. Decorate with mint sprigs and a cherry.

VERACRUZ COCKTAIL

1½   oz. Jamaica Rum
2   oz. Lime Juice
1½   oz. Dry Vermouth
1-2 dashes Pineapple Juice

Shake with ice and strain into a large cocktail glass. Add ice.

VERA HIGHBALL

1½   oz. Pernod
1   tsp. Sugar Syrup

Stir in a highball glass with ice. Fill with ice water and stir again.

VERBOTEN

1½   oz. Gin
1   tbsp. Forbidden Fruit
1   tbsp. Orange Juice
1   tbsp. Lemon Juice

Shake with ice and strain into a cocktail glass. Add a brandied cherry.

VERITAS

¾ oz. Gin
¾ oz. Cointreau
¾ oz. Lime Juice

Shake with ice and strain into a cocktail glass. Float ¼ oz. Creme de Cassis on top.

VERMONT COCKTAIL

½ oz. Applejack
½ oz. Apricot-flavored Brandy
½ oz. Gin
½ oz. Benedictine
½ oz. Maple Syrup

Shake with ice and strain into a cocktail glass.

VERMOUTH AND CURACAO

1½ oz. Dry Vermouth
¾ oz. Curacao

Mix in a highball glass. Fill with soda.

VERMOUTH AND DUBONNET

2 oz. Sweet Vermouth
2 oz. Dubonnet

Stir with ice and strain into an Old-fashioned glass.

VERMOUTH AND FRIENDS

½ tsp. Orange-flavored Liqueur
1 tsp. Amer Picon
½ tsp. Powdered Sugar
1 dash Bitters
2 oz. Sweet Vermouth

Stir with ice and strain into a cocktail glass. Add a twist of lemon and a maraschino cherry.

VERMOUTH AND SPARKLING WATER

3 oz. Sweet Vermouth
Soda

Pour Vermouth over cracked ice in a Collins glass. Fill with chilled soda. Stir gently. Garnish with an orange wheel. Serve with straws.

VERMOUTH AND TONIC

4 oz. Sweet Vermouth
4 oz. Tonic Water

Place ice cubes in a Collins glass. Pour in Vermouth and chilled tonic water. Stir.

VERMOUTH APERITIF

Sweet Vermouth

Place cracked ice in a cocktail glass. Fill with Vermouth and serve with a twist of lemon peel.

VERMOUTH CASSIS

¾ oz. Creme de Cassis
1½ oz. Dry Vermouth

Stir in a highball glass with ice cubes and fill with soda. Stir again and serve. (Lemon wedge optional.)

VERMOUTH CASSIS COOLER

3 oz. Dry Vermouth
1½ oz. Creme de Cassis
Soda

Place ice cubes in a Collins glass. Add Dry Vermouth and Creme de Cassis. Fill with chilled soda. Stir gently. Add a twist of lemon peel.

VERMOUTH COCKTAIL NO. 1

1 oz. Dry Vermouth
1 oz. Sweet Vermouth
1 dash Orange Bitters

Stir with ice and strain into a cocktail glass. Serve with a cherry.

VERMOUTH COCKTAIL NO. 2

1½ oz. Dry Vermouth
½ oz. Pernod

Shake with ice and strain into a cocktail glass.

VERMOUTH COCKTAIL NO. 3

1½ oz. Sweet Vermouth
1 dash Angostura Bitters

Stir with ice and strain into a cocktail glass. Serve with an olive.

VERMOUTH COCKTAIL NO. 4

2 oz. Sweet Vermouth
1 tsp. Curacao
1 tsp. Amer Picon
½ tsp. Sugar
1 dash Angostura Bitters

Stir with ice and strain into a cocktail glass. Serve with a lemon twist and a cherry.

VERMOUTH COLLINS

Juice ½ Lemon
1 tsp. Sugar
2 oz. Dry Vermouth
Soda

Pour lemon juice, sugar and Vermouth over cracked ice in a Collins glass. Stir. Fill with chilled soda. Stir lightly.

VERMOUTH COOLER NO. 1

2 oz. Dry Vermouth
2 tbsp. Raspberry Syrup
Club Soda

Put ice cubes in a highball glass, add Vermouth and Raspberry Syrup. Fill with club soda. Serve with an orange slice.

VERMOUTH COOLER NO. 2

2 oz. Sweet Vermouth
1 oz. Vodka
½ oz. Lemon Juice
1 tsp. Sugar

Shake with ice and strain into a Collins glass. Fill with soda and ice. Serve with a lemon wedge.

VERMOUTH COOLER NO. 3

5 oz. Dry Vermouth
5 oz. chilled Soda
1 dash Bitters

Place ice cubes in a Collins glass. Add ingredients. Stir lightly. Garnish with a lemon slice.

VERMOUTH DAIQUIRI

2 oz. Liquid Daiquiri Mix
2 oz. Dry Vermouth

Stir with ice and strain into an Old-fashioned glass.

VERMOUTH DAIQUIRI FROST

⅓ cup crushed Ice
1 oz. Frozen Daiquiri Mix
2 oz. Dry Vermouth

Blend for about 10 seconds and pour into a large, frosted cocktail glass.

VERMOUTH FLIP

3 oz. Dry Vermouth
1 Egg White
1 oz. Cognac
1½ tsp. Lemon Juice
1 tsp. Powdered Sugar

Shake with ice and strain into a Collins glass. Fill with soda and stir gently.

VERMOUTH FRAPPE

2 oz. Sweet Vermouth
1 dash Angostura Bitters

Fill a cocktail glass with crushed ice and add Vermouth and Bitters.

VERMOUTH MARASCHINO

2 oz. Dry Vermouth
½ oz. Maraschino Liqueur
½ oz. Lemon Juice
2 dashes Orange Bitters

Shake with ice and strain into a cocktail glass. Serve with a cherry.

VERMOUTH ON THE ROCKS

4 oz. Dry or Sweet Vermouth, Vermouth Fraise or Vermouth Framboise

Put ice cubes in an Old-fashioned glass and pour in the preferred Vermouth.

VERMOUTH PICON COCKTAIL

2 oz. Amer Picon
2 oz. Dry Vermouth

Stir with ice and strain into a cocktail glass.

VERMOUTH TRIPLE SEC

1 oz. Dry Vermouth
1 oz. Gin
½ oz. Triple Sec
2 dashes Orange Bitters

Shake with ice and strain into a cocktail glass. Serve with a lemon twist.

VERMOUTH TWIST COCKTAIL

2 oz. Dry Vermouth
Chilled Soda

Pour Vermouth over ice cubes in a tall glass. Fill with soda. Add a twist of lemon.

VESPER

1¾ oz. Gin
¾ oz. Creme de Noyaux
1 dash Orange Bitters
1 dash Angostura Bitters

Shake with ice and strain into a cocktail glass.

VESUVIO

Juice ½ Lemon
1 oz. Rum
1 tsp. Powdered Sugar
½ Egg White
½ oz. Sweet Vermouth

Shake with ice and strain into an Old-fashioned glass. Add ice cubes.

VIA VENETO

1¾ oz. Brandy
½ oz. Sambuca
½ Egg White
½ oz. Lemon Juice
1 tsp. Sugar

Shake with ice and strain into a cocktail glass.

VICOMTE

1 oz. Gin
¾ oz. Dry Vermouth
¾ oz. Creme de Rose

Stir with ice and strain into a cocktail glass.

VICTOR

1½ oz. Gin
½ oz. Brandy
½ oz. Sweet Vermouth

Shake with ice and strain into a cocktail glass.

VICTORY

¾ oz. Dry Vermouth
¾ oz. Sweet Vermouth
¼ oz. Orange Juice
¼ oz. Lemon Juice
¼ oz. Grenadine

Shake with ice and strain into a cocktail glass.

VICTORY COLLINS

1½ oz. Vodka
3 oz. unsweetened Grape Juice
3 oz. Lemon Juice
1 tsp. Powdered Sugar

Shake with ice and strain into a Collins glass. Add ice cubes. Serve with an orange slice.

VICTORY HIGHBALL

1½ oz. Pernod
1½ oz. Grenadine

Shake with ice and strain into a cocktail glass. Fill with soda and ice.

VIENNESE ICED TEA

Sugar to taste
1½ oz. Rum or Brandy
Tea

Fill a Collins glass three-quarters full with crushed ice. Add a lemon slice, sugar and Rum or Brandy. Fill with freshly brewed tea and stir gently. Garnish with mint.

VIE ROSE

1 oz. Gin
1 oz. Kirschwasser
½ oz. Lemon Juice
½ oz. Grenadine

Shake with ice and strain into a cocktail glass.

VIKING

1½ oz. Galliano
½ oz. Aquavit

Pour Galliano into an Old-fashioned glass. Float Aquavit on top.

VILLA IGIEA

1 oz. Gin
1 oz. Sweet Vermouth
1 oz. Amaro

Shake with ice and strain into a Collins glass. Fill with crushed ice.

VILLA ROMA

1 oz. Galliano
4 oz. Orange Juice
¼ oz. Lime Juice

Shake with ice and strain into a large cocktail glass.

VIOLET FIZZ NO. 1

Juice ½ Lemon
½ tsp. Powdered Sugar
1½ oz. Gin
1 tbsp. Creme d'Yvette

Shake with ice and strain into a highball glass. Add two ice cubes, fill with soda and stir.

VIOLET FIZZ NO. 2

1½ oz. Gin
½ oz. Grenadine
½ oz. Cream
1 oz. Lemon Juice

Shake with ice and strain into a fizz glass. Fill with soda and ice.

VIRGIN

1 oz. Gin
½ oz. White Creme de Menthe
1 oz. Forbidden Fruit

Shake with ice and strain into a cocktail glass.

VIRGINIA JULEP

2 oz. Bourbon Whisky
1½ tsp. Sugar Syrup
Mint sprigs

Soak a few mint sprigs in the Bourbon for one hour. When ready, combine minted Bourbon with sugar syrup and ice and shake well. Strain over crushed ice in an Old-fashioned glass. Stir and decorate with fresh mint.

VIVA LA CAFE

3 oz. French Vanilla Ice Cream
1 oz. Creme de Cafe

Blend until smooth and serve in a cocktail glass.

VIVA VILLA

Juice 1 Lime
1 tsp. Sugar
1½ oz. Tequila

Shake with ice and strain into an Old-fashioned glass rimmed with salt.

VLADIVOSTOK VIRGIN

1 oz. Gin
1 oz. Vodka
½ oz. Grapefruit Juice
1 dash Angostura Bitters

Shake with ice and strain into a cocktail glass.

VODKA AND APPLE JUICE

2 oz. Vodka
Apple Juice

Put two or three ice cubes in a highball glass. Add Vodka. Fill with apple juice and stir.

VODKA AND BITTER LEMON

2 oz. Vodka
Bitter Lemon

Put ice cubes in a highball glass, add Vodka and fill with bitter lemon. Stir lightly.

VODKA AND TONIC

2 oz. Vodka
Tonic Water

Pour Vodka into a highball glass over ice cubes, add tonic water and stir.

VODKA-CHAMPAGNE PUNCH

¾ oz. Vodka
1 tbsp. White Rum
2 tsp. Lime Juice
2 tsp. Strawberry Liqueur
3 drops Grenadine

Shake with ice and strain into a champagne glass with a sugared rim. Decorate with a strawberry.

VODKA-CHAMPAGNE PUNCH BOWL

1 bottle iced Vodka
2 bottles chilled Champagne
Lemon slices
Strips Cucumber peel

Thoroughly chill a punch bowl. Pour in the Vodka and Champagne; garnish with lemon slices and strips of cucumber peel. Serve in 4 oz. punch glasses. Makes about 16 servings.

VODKA COCKTAIL NO. 1

1½ oz. Vodka
¾ oz. Cherry-flavored Brandy
Juice ½ Lemon or Lime

Shake with ice and strain into a cocktail glass.

VODKA COCKTAIL NO. 2

¾ oz. Vodka
¾ oz. Dry Vermouth
½ oz. Strega
½ oz. Cream

Shake with ice and strain into a cocktail glass.

VODKA COLLINS

1 oz. Lemon Juice
1 tsp. Sugar
1½ oz. Vodka

Shake with ice and strain into a Collins glass. Fill with soda and ice. Serve with a lemon wedge, a cherry and an orange slice.

VODKA COOLER

½ tsp. Sugar dissolved in
2 oz. Soda
1½ oz. Vodka

Pour sweetened soda into a Collins glass. Add ice and Vodka. Fill with soda or ginger ale. Decorate with twists of lemon and orange.

VODKA DAISY

Juice ½ Lemon
½ tsp. Powdered Sugar
1 tsp. Grenadine
2 oz. Vodka

Shake with ice and strain into a large cocktail glass. Add ice cubes and decorate with fruit.

VODKA FRAISE

¾ oz. Vodka
¾ oz. Rum
½ oz. Strawberry Liqueur
½ oz. Lime Juice
½ oz. Grenadine

Shake with ice and strain into a sugar-rimmed cocktail glass. Serve with a strawberry.

VODKA GIBSON

2 oz. Vodka
½ oz. Dry Vermouth

Stir with ice and strain into a cocktail glass. Serve with a pickled pearl onion.

VODKA GIMLET

1½ oz. Vodka
1 tsp. Sugar
1½ tbsp. Lime Juice

Stir with ice and strain into a cocktail glass. Top off with a squeeze of lime and a green cherry.

VODKA GRAND MARNIER

1½ oz. Vodka
½ oz. Lime Juice
½ oz. Grand Marnier

Shake with ice and strain into a cocktail glass. Serve with an orange slice.

VODKA GRASSHOPPER COCKTAIL

¾ oz. Vodka
¾ oz. Green Creme de Menthe
¾ oz. White Creme de Cacao

Shake with ice and strain into a cocktail glass.

VODKA GYPSY COCKTAIL

1½ oz. Vodka
¾ oz. Benedictine
1 dash Angostura Bitters

Stir with ice and strain into a cocktail glass.

VODKA ICEBERG

1½ oz. Vodka

Pour into an Old-fashioned glass. Fill with ice. Float ½ oz. Pernod on top.

VODKA MARTINI

2½ oz. Vodka
½ oz. Dry Vermouth

Stir with ice and strain into a cocktail glass. Serve with a lemon twist.

VODKA MILK PUNCH

1½ oz. Vodka
3 oz. Milk
½ oz. Peppermint Schnapps
½ tsp. Sugar

Shake with ice and strain into a highball glass. Fill with ice. Sprinkle nutmeg on top.

VODKA MIST

1½ oz. Vodka

Pour Vodka into a cocktail shaker. Add a lemon twist and serve unstrained in an Old-fashioned glass.

VODKA OLD-FASHIONED

½ tsp. Sugar
2 dashes Bitters
2 oz. Vodka

Mix in an Old-fashioned glass. Fill with ice. Serve with a lemon twist and a cherry.

VODKA ON THE ROCKS

2 oz. Vodka

Put two or three ice cubes in an Old-fashioned glass and add Vodka. Serve with a twist of lemon peel.

VODKA-ORANGE PUNCH

3 bottles iced Vodka
3 6-oz. cans frozen concentrated Orange Juice
1 cup Cointreau
1 dash Lemon Juice
Orange slices (optional)

Put the ingredients in a large jug, stir well and set in a bowl of ice. Serve in punch glasses, garnished with a slice of orange. Makes about 25 servings.

VODKA SALTY DOG

1½ oz. Vodka
5 oz. Grapefruit Juice
¼ tsp. Salt

Pour into a highball glass. Add ice cubes and stir well.

> So I'm for drinking honestly, and dying in my boots.
> — John Masefield

VODKA '7'

2 oz. Vodka
Juice ½ Lime

Pour into a Collins glass over ice cubes. Drop lime rind into the glass, fill the glass up with lemon soda and stir.

VODKA SLING

1 tsp. Sugar
2 oz. Vodka

Mix in an Old-fashioned glass. Fill with soda and ice. Serve with a twist of orange peel.

VODKA SOUR

Juice ½ Lemon
½ tsp. Powdered Sugar
2 oz. Vodka

Shake with ice and strain into a Sour glass. Decorate with half a slice of lemon and a cherry.

VODKA STINGER

1 oz. Vodka
1 oz. White Creme de Menthe

Shake with ice and strain into a cocktail glass.

VOLARE

1 oz. Galliano
1 oz. Apple Juice
1 oz. Lemon Juice
Sugar to taste

Shake with ice and strain into a cocktail glass.

VOLCANO

¾ oz. Lemon Juice
¾ oz. Vodka
¾ oz. Southern Comfort
1 dash Grenadine

Stir with ice and strain into a cocktail glass.

VOLGA BOATMAN

1½ oz. Vodka
1½ oz. Cherry-flavored Brandy
1½ oz. Orange Juice

Stir with ice and strain into a cocktail glass.

VOLGA COCKTAIL

1½ oz. Gin
¼ oz. Lemon Juice
2 tsp. Prune Juice

Shake with ice and strain into a cocktail glass.

VOLSTEAD

¾ oz. Swedish Punch
¾ oz. Rye Whisky
½ oz. Orange Juice
½ oz. Grenadine
½ oz. Anisette

Shake with ice and strain into a cocktail glass.

VONNIE'S DELIGHT

Milk
1 oz. Coffee Liqueur
½ oz. Galliano

Fill a highball glass with ice. Add Coffee Liqueur. Fill with milk. Float Galliano on top.

WAGNER

¾ oz. Sloe Gin
¾ oz. Sweet Vermouth
¾ oz. Cherry-flavored Brandy
1 dash Orange Bitters

Shake with ice and strain into a cocktail glass.

WAGON WHEEL

1½ oz. Southern Comfort
¾ oz. Cognac
½ oz. Lemon Juice
1 dash Grenadine

Shake with ice and strain into a cocktail glass.

WAHINE

2 oz. Rum
2 oz. Pineapple Juice

Shake with ice and strain into an Old-fashioned glass. Fill with crushed ice.

WAHINE'S DELIGHT

½ oz. Orgeat Syrup
1 oz. Lemon Juice
1 oz. Gold Rum

Shake with ice and strain into an Old-fashioned glass. Fill with crushed ice. Garnish with fruit.

WAIKIKI

1½ oz. Gin
1 oz. Orange Juice
1 oz. Pineapple Juice
1 dash Lemon Juice
1 dash Bitters
Powdered Sugar

Shake with ice and strain into a cocktail glass. Serve with a fresh pineapple stick.

WAIKIKI BEACHCOMBER

¾ oz. Gin
¾ oz. Triple Sec or Orange Curacao
1 tbsp. fresh Pineapple Juice

Shake with ice and strain into a cocktail glass.

WAILUC

1¾ oz. Sweet Vermouth
½ oz. Gin
¼ oz. Maraschino Liqueur

Stir with ice and strain into a cocktail glass. Serve with a lemon twist.

WALDORF NO. 1

2 oz. Swedish Punch
½ oz. Gin
½ oz. Lemon or Lime Juice

Stir with ice and strain into a cocktail glass.

WALDORF NO. 2

1 oz. Bourbon Whisky
1 oz. Pernod
1 oz. Sweet Vermouth
3 dashes Angostura Bitters

Stir with ice and strain into a cocktail glass.

WALLICK COCKTAIL

1½ oz. Dry Vermouth
1½ oz. Gin
1 tsp. Triple Sec or Orange Curacao

Stir with ice and strain into a cocktail glass.

WALLICKS

1¼ oz. Cherry-flavored Brandy
1¼ oz. Triple Sec or Orange Curacao

Shake with ice and strain into a cocktail glass.

WALLICK'S SPECIAL

1½ oz. Brandy
1½ oz. Cream
1 Egg White
½ tsp. Powdered Sugar
2 dashes Grenadine

Shake with ice and strain into a cocktail glass.

WALLIS BLUE COCKTAIL

1 oz. Triple Sec or Orange Curacao
1 oz. Gin
Juice 1 Lime

Moisten the rim of an Old-fashioned glass with lime juice and dip into powdered sugar. Shake ingredients with ice and strain into the prepared glass over ice cubes.

WALLY COCKTAIL NO. 1

¾ oz. Cointreau
¾ oz. Peppermint Schnapps
2 oz. Gin
Juice ½ Lemon

Shake with ice and strain into a highball glass. Fill with soda and ice.

WALLY COCKTAIL NO. 2

1 oz. Brandy
½ oz. Benedictine
Lemon Juice to taste

Shake with ice and pour into a champagne glass. Fill with Champagne.

WALSH CHAMPAGNE COCKTAIL

1 tsp. Sugar
1 Mint Sprig
1 Lemon Twist
Champagne

Mix the first 3 ingredients in a Collins glass. Fill with Champagne and ice. Serve with a cherry.

WALTERS

1½ oz. Scotch Whisky
1 tbsp. Orange Juice
1 tbsp. Lemon Juice

Shake with ice and strain into a cocktail glass.

WANDA COCKTAIL

1 oz. Kummel
2 oz. Cognac

Stir with ice and strain into a cocktail glass.

Come friends, come let us drink again,
This liquid from the nectar vine,
For water makes you dumb and stupid,
Learn this from the fishes —
They cannot sing, nor laugh, nor drink
This beaker full of sparkling wine.

WAR DAYS

¾ oz. Gin
¾ oz. Sweet Vermouth
¾ oz. Apple Brandy
¼ oz. Green or Yellow Chartreuse

Shake with ice and strain into a cocktail glass.

WARD EIGHT

Juice ½ Lemon
1 tsp. Powdered Sugar
1 tsp. Grenadine
2 oz. Rye or Bourbon Whisky

Shake with ice and strain into a goblet filled with cracked ice. Add slices of orange and lemon and a cherry. Serve with straws.

WARDEN

1½ oz. Gin
½ oz. Dry Vermouth
½ oz. Pernod

Stir with ice and strain into a cocktail glass.

WARD'S

¾ oz. Brandy
¾ oz. Chartreuse
1 twist Orange Peel

Arrange the orange peel in the bottom of a cocktail glass to form a circle. Fill the glass with cracked ice and add the Chartreuse and Brandy and decorate with fresh mint leaves. Different liqueurs may be used if desired.

WARSAW COCKTAIL

1½ oz. Vodka
½ oz. Blackberry-flavored Brandy
½ oz. Dry Vermouth
1 tsp. Lemon Juice

Shake with ice and strain into a cocktail glass.

WASHINGTON COCKTAIL

1½ oz. Dry Vermouth
¾ oz. Brandy
2 dashes Bitters
½ tsp. Sugar Syrup

Stir with ice and strain into a cocktail glass.

Here's a health to the future,
A sigh for the past;
We can love and remember,
And hope to the last;
And for all the base lies
That the almanacs hold,
While there's love in the heart,
We can never grow old.

WASSAIL

10 small Apples
10 tsp. Brown Sugar
2 bottles Dry Sherry or Dry Madeira
½ tsp. grated Nutmeg
1 tsp. ground Ginger
3 Cloves
3 Allspice Berries
1'' stick Cinnamon
2 cups superfine Sugar
½ cup Water
6 Eggs, separated
1 cup Brandy

Prepare the apples by coring them, then filling each with a teaspoon of brown sugar. Place them in a baking pan, add ⅛'' of water and bake at 350° until the apples are soft (about 30 minutes). In a large saucepan heat, but do not boil, the remaining ingredients except the eggs and the Brandy. Leave the saucepan on very low heat. Beat the egg yolks until lemon-colored and the whites until stiff. Fold the whites into the yolks. Now strain the wine mixture and add gradually to the eggs, stirring constantly. Add the Brandy. Finally, pour into a metal punch bowl, float the baked apples and serve in mugs. Makes about 10 servings.

WASSAIL BOWL— HOT SPICED BEER

12	small Apples
12	tsp. Brown Sugar
1	cup superfine Sugar
1	tsp. Cinnamon
½	tsp. Ginger
½	tsp. Nutmeg
1½	cups Orange Juice
1½	cups Cranberry Juice
2	quarts Beer or Ale

Prepare the apples as in the previous recipe. Combine the sugar and spices in a 4-quart saucepan. Add the juices and Beer and heat the mixture for 15 minutes without boiling. Pour the mixture into a metal punch bowl and float the baked apples on top. Serve in mugs. Makes 12 servings.

WATERBURY COCKTAIL

Juice ¼ Lemon or ½ Lime	
½	tsp. Powdered Sugar
1	Egg White
1½	oz. Brandy
½	tsp. Grenadine

Shake with ice and strain into a cocktail glass.

WATERMELON CASSIS

2	oz. Gin
1-2	pieces fresh Watermelon
¾	oz. Creme de Cassis
½	oz. Lemon Juice

Shake with ice and strain into a Collins glass. Fill with soda and ice. Serve with a lemon wedge.

> "Woman — the morning star of infancy, the day star of manhood, the evening star of old age; bless our stars and may they always be kept at a telescopic distance."
> — Bachelor's toast

WATERMELON COOLER

2¼	oz. White Rum
2	tsp. Lime Juice
1½	tsp. Sugar Syrup
4	oz. diced, seeded Watermelon

Blend with ice and strain into a double Old-fashioned glass. Fill with crushed ice. Decorate with a slice of lime.

WAVERLY

1¾	oz. Gin
½	oz. Orange Juice
½	oz. Creme de Cassis

Shake with ice and strain into a cocktail glass.

WAX

2½	oz. Gin
3	dashes Orange Bitters

Stir with ice and strain into a cocktail glass.

W.B.M. COCKTAIL

1	oz. Sloe Gin
1	oz. Brandy
1	oz. Dry Vermouth

Shake with ice and strain into a cocktail glass.

W.C.T.U.

1½	oz. Brandy
1¼	oz. Dry Vermouth
1	dash Angostura Bitters
1	dash Orange Bitters

Stir with ice and strain into a cocktail glass.

WEBSTER COCKTAIL

Juice ½ Lime	
1½	tsp. Apricot-flavored Brandy
½	oz. Dry Vermouth
1	oz. Gin

Shake with ice and strain into a cocktail glass.

WEDDING BELLE COCKTAIL

1½	tsp. Orange Juice
1½	tsp. Cherry-flavored Brandy
¾	oz. Gin
¾	oz. Dubonnet

Shake with ice and strain into a cocktail glass.

WEDDING MARCH

Juice ½ Lime	
2	oz. Light Rum
2	Egg Whites
2	dashes Angostura Bitters
1	tsp. Sugar

Shake with ice and strain into a cocktail glass.

WEDDING NIGHT

1¾	oz. Rum
½	oz. Maple Syrup
½	oz. Lime Juice

Shake with ice and strain into a cocktail glass.

WEEP-NO-MORE COCKTAIL

Juice ½ Lime	
¾	oz. Dubonnet
¾	oz. Brandy
¼	tsp. Maraschino Liqueur

Shake with ice and strain into a cocktail glass.

WEESUER SPECIAL

¾	oz. Gin
¾	oz. Curacao
¾	oz. Dry Vermouth
¾	oz. Sweet Vermouth
½	oz. Pernod

Stir with ice and strain into a cocktail glass.

WEIGHT WATCHERS' SPECIAL

5	oz.	Strawberry Liquid Diet Food
½	tsp.	Lemon Peel, grated
4	oz.	Tawny Port

Pour strawberry liquid diet food into an ice tray. Place in the freezer until center is almost firm, then put into a blender. Add grated lemon peel and Port. Blend until well mixed. Pour into a goblet. Add a maraschino cherry and serve with a spoon.

WEISSMULLER

1	oz.	Rum
1	oz.	Gin
½	oz.	Lemon Juice
¼	tsp.	Sugar
¼	oz.	Grenadine

Shake with ice and strain into a cocktail glass.

WELCOME STRANGER

½	oz.	Gin
½	oz.	Swedish Punch
½	oz.	Brandy
½	oz.	Grenadine
½	oz.	Lemon Juice
½	oz.	Orange Juice

Shake with ice and strain into a cocktail glass.

WELLINGTON

Juice ½ Lime		
1½	oz.	Gin
2	dashes	Swedish Punch
2	dashes	Cherry-flavored Brandy

Stir with ice and strain into a cocktail glass.

A little health, a little wealth,
A little house and freedom,
With some few friends for
  certain ends,
But little cause to need 'em.

WEMBLY COCKTAIL NO. 1

¾	oz.	Dry Vermouth
1½	oz.	Gin
¼	tsp.	Apricot-flavored Brandy
½	tsp.	Apple Brandy

Stir with ice and strain into a cocktail glass.

WEMBLY COCKTAIL NO. 2

1	oz.	Scotch Whisky
1	oz.	Dry Vermouth
1	oz.	Pineapple Juice

Shake with ice and strain into a cocktail glass.

WESTBROOK

1½	oz.	Gin
½	oz.	Sweet Vermouth
½	oz.	Bourbon Whisky
½	tsp.	Sugar

Shake with ice and strain into a cocktail glass.

WESTERNER

1	dash	Aromatic Bitters
2½	oz.	Brandy
1	oz.	Sweet Vermouth

Stir with ice and strain into a cocktail glass.

WESTERN ROSE COCKTAIL

½	oz.	Apricot-flavored Brandy
1	oz.	Gin
½	oz.	Dry Vermouth
¼	tsp.	Lemon Juice

Shake with ice and strain into a cocktail glass.

WEST INDIAN

2½	oz.	Gin
½	oz.	Angostura Bitters
1	tsp.	Sugar
1	tsp.	Lemon Juice
2		Ice cubes

Mix in a cocktail glass.

WEST INDIES YELLOW BIRD

1	oz.	Galliano
1½	oz.	Rum
¼	oz.	Creme de Bananes
2	oz.	Pineapple Juice
2	oz.	Orange Juice

Shake with ice and strain into a Collins glass. Decorate with an orange slice, a cherry and a pineapple spear.

WESTMINSTER

1	oz.	Bourbon Whisky
¾	oz.	Dry Vermouth
¾	oz.	Sweet Vermouth

Stir with ice and strain into a cocktail glass.

WETBACK

1½	oz.	Gin
½	oz.	Lime Juice
¼	oz.	White Creme de Menthe
¼	oz.	Pernod

Stir with ice and strain into a cocktail glass.

WHALER'S TODDY

2	oz.	Jamaica Rum
4	oz.	boiling Water
1	tsp.	Sugar

Pour boiling water into a mug; add sugar and stir until dissolved. Add Rum, 1 or 2 whole cloves and some cinnamon pieces. Stir gently and serve piping hot, garnished with nutmeg and decorated with a slice of lemon.

WHAT IS IT?

¾ oz. Port
1 oz. Rum
1 Egg White

Shake with ice and strain into a highball glass. Fill with soda and ice.

WHAT THE HELL

1 oz. Gin
1 oz. Dry Vermouth
1 oz. Apricot-flavored Brandy
1 dash Lemon Juice

Stir in an Old-fashioned glass over ice cubes.

WHEELER

1½ oz. Whisky
½ oz. Orange Juice
½ oz. Dry Vermouth
¼ oz. Grenadine

Shake with ice and strain into a cocktail glass.

WHICH WAY COCKTAIL

1 oz. Pernod
1 oz. Anisette
1 oz. Cognac

Shake with ice and strain into a cocktail glass.

WHILE ROME BURNS

1¾ oz. Rum
½ oz. Lemon Juice
¼ oz. Maple Syrup

Shake with ice and strain into a cocktail glass.

WHIP COCKTAIL

½ oz. Dry Vermouth
½ oz. Sweet Vermouth
1½ oz. Brandy
¼ tsp. Pernod
1 tsp. Triple Sec

Stir with ice and strain into a cocktail glass.

WHISKY AND HONEY

1 tsp. Honey
3 oz. Whisky

Put honey in an Old-fashioned glass with 2-3 ice cubes and a twist of lemon peel. Add Whisky and stir.

WHISKY BLOSSOM COCKTAIL

1½ oz. Whisky
½ oz. Sweet Vermouth
1 dash Pineapple Juice
1 dash Lemon Juice

Stir with ice and strain into a cocktail glass.

WHISKY COBBLER NO. 1

1 tsp. Powdered Sugar
2 oz. Soda
2 oz. Rye Whisky

In a goblet, dissolve sugar in the soda. Fill with shaved ice and add Whisky. Stir and decorate with fruits in season. Serve with straws.

WHISKY COBBLER NO. 2

2 oz. Scotch Whisky
4 dashes Curacao
4 dashes Brandy
1 slice Lemon

Fill a goblet with cracked ice. Add all the ingredients, stir and decorate with fruit and a mint sprig.

WHISKY COBBLER NO. 3

2½ oz. Blended Whisky
¾ oz. Lemon Juice
½ oz. Orange Juice
¾ oz. Orgeat Syrup

Shake with ice and strain into a Collins glass. Fill with crushed ice. Garnish with a peach slice and an orange slice.

WHISKY COCKTAIL

1 dash Angostura Bitters
1 tsp. Sugar Syrup
2 oz. Rye or Bourbon Whisky

Stir with ice and strain into a cocktail glass. Serve with a cherry.

WHISKY COLLINS

Juice ½ Lemon
1 tsp. Powdered Sugar
2 oz. Rye or Bourbon Whisky

Shake with ice and strain into a Collins glass. Add several ice cubes. Fill with soda and stir. Decorate with lemon slices, orange slices and a cherry. Serve with straws.

WHISKY COOLER

1½ oz. Rye or Bourbon Whisky
1 oz. Lemon Juice
1 tsp. Sugar

Mix in a highball glass. Fill with ginger ale and ice.

WHISKY CURACAO FIZZ

2 oz. Blended Whisky
½ oz. Orange Curacao
1 tsp. Sugar
1 oz. Lemon Juice

Shake with ice and strain into a Collins glass. Fill with soda and ice. Serve with an orange slice.

WHISKY DAISY NO. 1

Juice ½ Lemon
½ tsp. Powdered Sugar
1 tsp. Raspberry Syrup or Grenadine
2 oz. Rye or Bourbon Whisky

Shake with ice and strain into a highball glass. Add an ice cube and decorate with fruit.

WHISKY DAISY NO. 2

1½ oz. Blended Whisky
½ oz. Lemon Juice
½ oz. Grenadine
¼ oz. Yellow Chartreuse

Shake the first 3 ingredients with ice and strain into a highball glass. Fill with soda and ice. Float Chartreuse on top. Serve with a lemon wedge.

WHISKY DAISY NO. 3

1½ oz. Whisky
1 oz. Lemon Juice
½ tsp. Sugar
½ oz. Triple Sec

Shake with ice and strain into a highball glass. Fill with soda and ice. Garnish with fruit.

WHISKY EGGNOG

1 Egg
1 tsp. Powdered Sugar
2 oz. Rye or Bourbon Whisky

Shake ingredients with ice and strain into a Collins glass. Fill the glass with milk. Sprinkle nutmeg on top.

WHISKY FIX

Juice ½ Lemon
1 tsp. Powdered Sugar
2½ oz. Rye or Bourbon Whisky

Shake the lemon juice and sugar with ice and strain into a highball glass. Fill the glass with ice. Add Whisky and stir. Add a slice of lemon and serve with straws.

WHISKY FLIP

1 Egg
1 tsp. Powdered Sugar
1½ oz. Rye or Bourbon Whisky
2 tsp. sweet Cream (if desired)

Shake with ice and strain into a flip glass. Dust with nutmeg.

WHISKY HIGHBALL

2 oz. Whisky
Ginger Ale or Soda

Pour Whisky into a highball glass over ice cubes and fill with ginger ale or soda. Add a twist of lemon peel and stir.

WHISKY HOUND

1½ oz. 100-proof Bourbon Whisky
2 tsp. 151-proof Rum
2 tsp. Grapefruit Juice
2 tsp. Orange Juice
1 oz. Lemon Juice
1 tbsp. Sugar Syrup
1-2 drops Maraschino Cherry Juice

Shake with ice and strain into an Old-fashioned glass. Add ice.

WHISKY KUMQUAT

3 oz. Bourbon Whisky
4 drops Kumquat Juice
1 whole Kumquat

Mix the first two ingredients in a double Old-fashioned glass. Add the kumquat and some crushed ice.

WHISKY MAC

2 oz. Scotch Whisky
2 oz. Ginger Wine

Combine Whisky and Ginger Wine in a mixing glass with ice and stir well. Strain into a cocktail glass.

WHISKY MILK PUNCH

1 tsp. Powdered Sugar
2 oz. Rye or Bourbon Whisky
½ pint Milk

Shake with ice and strain into a Collins glass. Sprinkle nutmeg on top.

WHISKY ORANGE

Juice ½ Orange
1 tsp. Powdered Sugar
½ tsp. Pernod
1½ oz. Rye or Bourbon Whisky

Shake with ice and strain into a highball glass. Decorate with slices of orange and lemon.

WHISKY OUZO FIX

½ tsp. Sugar dissolved in water
2 oz. Blended Whisky
½ oz. Lemon Juice
¼ oz. Ouzo

Mix the first 3 ingredients in a highball glass. Fill with crushed ice. Stir and float Ouzo on top. Serve with a lemon twist.

WHISKY PEPPERMINT FLIP

1 Egg
½ tsp. Sugar
1½ oz. Whisky
½ oz. Peppermint Schnapps

Shake with ice and strain into a flip glass. Sprinkle nutmeg on top.

WHISKY PUFF

1½ oz. Whisky
2 oz. Milk

Pour into a highball glass. Fill with ice. Add milk and fill with soda.

WHISKY PUNCH NO. 1

2 oz. Whisky
1 tsp. Sugar
½ oz. Lemon Juice

Mix in a highball glass. Fill with soda and ice.

WHISKY PUNCH NO. 2

1½ oz. Bourbon or Rye Whisky
1 oz. Lemon Juice
1 tsp. Sugar
½ oz. Orange Curacao

Shake with ice and strain into a Collins glass. Fill with soda and ice. Float ¼ oz. Rum or Brandy on top.

WHISKY PUNCH BOWL

1½ cups Lemon Juice
4 cups Orange Juice
2 tbsp. superfine Sugar
1 block Ice
3 oz. Curacao
1½ bottles Bourbon, Rye or Blended Whisky
2 quarts chilled Club Soda, or
1 quart Iced Tea and
1 quart Club Soda
Fruits to garnish

Combine orange and lemon juice with sugar and stir until sugar is dissolved. Pour over the ice in a punch bowl and add all the remaining ingredients. Stir gently. Serve in punch glasses. Makes about 32 servings.

WHISKY RICKEY NO. 1

Juice ½ Lime
1½ oz. Rye Whisky

Pour into a highball glass over ice cubes and fill with soda. Stir and drop lime rind into glass.

WHISKY RICKEY NO. 2

1½ oz. Bourbon Whisky
½ tsp. Maraschino Liqueur
½ tsp. Brandy
½ tsp. Lemon Juice

Mix in a highball glass. Fill with soda. Decorate with fruit.

WHISKY RICKEY NO. 3

1½ oz. Bourbon Whisky
½ oz. Lime Juice
¼ oz. Benedictine

Shake with ice and strain into a highball glass. Fill with soda and ice.

WHISKY SANGAREE

½ tsp. Powdered Sugar
1 tsp. Water
2 oz. Rye or Bourbon Whisky

Combine sugar, water and Whisky in an Old-fashioned glass. Add ice and a splash of soda. Stir and float a tbsp. of Port on top. Sprinkle nutmeg on top.

WHISKY SCAFFA

1 dash Angostura Bitters
1½ oz. Rye or Bourbon Whisky
¾ oz. Benedictine

Mix in a cocktail glass and serve.

WHISKY SHAKE

2 oz. Whisky
2 tbsp. Lime Juice
1 tsp. Sugar Syrup

Shake with ice and strain into an Old-fashioned glass. Add ice.

WHISKY SKIN

Hot Water
1 lump Sugar
2 oz. Whisky

Put sugar into an Old-fashioned glass and fill two-thirds full with boiling water. Add Whisky and stir. Serve with a lemon twist.

WHISKY SLING

1 tsp. Powdered Sugar
1 tsp. Water
2 oz. Rye or Bourbon Whisky
Juice ½ Lemon

In an Old-fashioned glass, dissolve sugar in the water and lemon juice. Add ice cubes and Whisky and stir. Serve with a lemon twist.

WHISKY SMASH

1 lump Sugar
1 oz. Soda
4 Mint sprigs
2 oz. Rye or Bourbon Whisky

Muddle sugar in an Old-fashioned glass with soda and mint sprigs. Add Whisky and ice cubes. Stir and decorate with a slice of orange and a cherry. Add a twist of lemon peel.

WHISKY SOUR

2 oz. Rye or Bourbon Whisky
1 oz. Lemon Juice
½ tsp. Sugar
3 drops Egg White

Shake with ice and strain into a cocktail glass. Fill with soda. Garnish with an orange slice and a cherry.

WHISKY SOUR IN THE ROUGH

2 oz. Whisky
1 tsp. Sugar
Orange and Lemon slices

Muddle sugar with fruit slices. Add Whisky and ice and shake well. Pour (do not strain) into an Old-fashioned glass and allow to settle before drinking.

WHISKY SPECIAL

1½ oz. Whisky
½ oz. Dry Vermouth
½ oz. Orange Juice

Shake with ice and strain into a cocktail glass. Sprinkle nutmeg on top. Serve with a twist of orange peel.

WHISKY SQUIRT

1½ oz. Rye or Bourbon Whisky
1 tbsp. Powdered Sugar
1 tbsp. Raspberry Syrup or Grenadine

Shake with ice and strain into a highball glass. Fill with soda and ice cubes. Decorate with pineapple chunks and strawberries.

WHISKY SWIZZLE

1½ oz. Lime or Lemon Juice
1 tsp. Sugar
2 oz. Soda
2 dashes Bitters
2 oz. Whisky

Pour the first three ingredients into a Collins glass. Fill with crushed ice and stir thoroughly. Add Bitters and Whisky and stir until the glass frosts. Top with soda and decorate with mint sprigs.

WHISKY TODDY (COLD)

½ tsp. Powdered Sugar
2 tsp. Water
2 oz. Rye or Bourbon Whisky

Stir sugar and water in an Old-fashioned glass. Add ice cubes and Whisky and stir. Serve with a lemon twist.

WHISKY TODDY (HOT)

1 lump Sugar
2 oz. Whisky

Put the sugar into an Old-fashioned glass and fill two-thirds full with boiling water. Add Whisky and stir. Decorate with a lemon slice. Dust with nutmeg.

WHISKY ZOOM

½ oz. Honey
½ oz. Cream
1½ oz. Whisky

In a mixing glass, dissolve honey in hot water. Add the cream and the Whisky. Shake with ice and strain into a cocktail glass.

WHISPER

1 oz. Whisky
1 oz. Dry Vermouth
1 oz. Sweet Vermouth

Shake with ice and strain into a cocktail glass.

WHISPERS OF THE FROST COCKTAIL

¾ oz. Bourbon or Rye Whisky
¾ oz. Sherry
¾ oz. Port
1 tsp. Powdered Sugar

Stir with ice and strain into a cocktail glass. Serve with slices of lemon and orange.

WHIST NO. 1

1 oz. Calvados or Applejack
½ oz. Light Rum
½ oz. Sweet Vermouth

Stir with ice and strain into a cocktail glass.

WHIST NO. 2

1½ oz. Calvados or Apple Brandy
½ oz. Rum
½ oz. Swedish Punch

Stir with ice and strain into a cocktail glass.

WHITE BABY

1½ oz. Gin
¾ oz. Cointreau
¾ oz. Sirop de Citron

Stir with ice and strain into a cocktail glass.

WHITE CADILLAC NO. 1

1 oz. Cream
¾ oz. Cointreau
¾ oz. Light Creme de Cacao

Shake with ice and strain into a cocktail glass.

WHITE CADILLAC NO. 2

1 oz. Cream
¾ oz. Vodka
¾ oz. Light Creme de Cacao

Shake with ice and strain into a cocktail glass.

WHITE CADILLAC NO. 3

1 oz. Cream
¾ oz. Vodka
¾ oz. Triple Sec

Shake with ice and strain into a cocktail glass.

WHITE CAP

1¾ oz. Gin
½ oz. Sweet Vermouth
¼ oz. White Creme de Menthe
1 dash Angostura Bitters

Shake with ice and strain into a cocktail glass. Serve with a cherry.

WHITE CARGO COCKTAIL

1 small scoop Vanilla Ice Cream
1 oz. Gin

Shake until thoroughly mixed and add water or Sauterne if the mixture is too thick. Serve in an Old-fashioned glass.

WHITE CLOUD

1 oz. Cream
¾ oz. Creme de Bananes
¾ oz. White Creme de Menthe

Shake with ice and strain into a cocktail glass.

WHITE COBBLER

½ tsp. Sugar
2 oz. Soda
White Wine

Mix sugar and soda in a double Old-fashioned glass, and fill the glass with ice and wine.

WHITE COCKTAIL

1½ oz. Gin
½ oz. Anisette
2 dashes Orange Bitters

Shake with ice and strain into a cocktail glass.

WHITE DOVE

2 oz. White Rum
2 oz. Anisette

Shake with ice and strain into an Old-fashioned glass. Add soda.

WHITE DUBONNET

Juice ¼ Lemon
3 oz. White Dubonnet

Stir with ice and pour over ice cubes in a large cocktail glass. Fill with chilled soda.

WHITE ELEPHANT NO. 1

1½ oz. Gin
1 oz. Sweet Vermouth
1 Egg White

Shake with ice and strain into a cocktail glass.

WHITE ELEPHANT NO. 2

1 oz. Cream
¾ oz. Vodka
¾ oz. Light Creme de Cacao

Shake with ice and strain into a cocktail glass.

WHITE FLAME

2 oz. Gin
1 oz. Cointreau
Champagne

Shake with ice and strain into a champagne glass. Fill with chilled Champagne. Garnish with fruit.

WHITE HORSE

1 oz. Gin
1 oz. Heavy Cream
1 oz. Cointreau

Shake with ice and strain into a cocktail glass.

WHITE LADY COCKTAIL NO. 1

1 Egg White
1 tsp. Powdered Sugar
1 tsp. Sweet Cream
1½ oz. Gin

Shake with ice and strain into a cocktail glass.

WHITE LADY COCKTAIL NO. 2

2 oz. Gin
1 oz. Triple Sec
1 oz. Lemon Juice

Shake with ice and strain into a cocktail glass.

WHITE LADY COCKTAIL NO. 3

1½ oz. Cointreau
½ oz. Brandy
½ oz. White Creme de Menthe

Shake with ice and strain into a cocktail glass.

WHITE LILY COCKTAIL

¾ oz. Triple Sec
¾ oz. Rum
¾ oz. Gin
¼ tsp. Anisette

Shake with ice and strain into a cocktail glass.

WHITE LION COCKTAIL

Juice ½ Lemon
1 tsp. Powdered Sugar
2 dashes Bitters
½ tsp. Grenadine
1½ oz. Light Rum

Shake with ice and strain into a cocktail glass.

WHITE MAN'S BURDEN

1½ oz. Sloe Gin
½ oz. Apricot-flavored Brandy
Juice ½ Lime

Shake with ice and strain into a cocktail glass.

WHITE MINK

1 oz. Galliano
¾ oz. Light Creme de Cacao
½ oz. Brandy
1½ oz. Cream
1 scoop Vanilla Ice Cream

Blend with ice and strain into a large cocktail glass.

WHITE MULE

1 oz. Galliano
¾ oz. Vodka
¾ oz. Anisette

Shake with ice and strain into an Old-fashioned glass. Fill with ice.

WHITE PELICAN

1¾ oz. Gin
½ oz. Dry Vermouth
¼ oz. Sweet Vermouth

Stir with ice and strain into a cocktail glass.

> Laugh at all things,
> Great and small things,
> Sick or well, at sea or shore;
> While we are quaffing
> Let's have laughing,
> Who the devil cares for
> more.
> — *Byron.*

WHITE PLUSH NO. 1

2 oz. Rye or Bourbon Whisky
1 cup Milk
1 tsp. Powdered Sugar

Shake with ice and strain into a Collins glass.

WHITE PLUSH NO. 2

1½ oz. Gin
½ oz. Maraschino Liqueur
4 oz. cold Milk

Shake with ice and strain into a highball glass. Sprinkle nutmeg on top.

WHITE ROSE COCKTAIL NO. 1

Juice 1 Lime
¾ oz. Gin
1 tbsp. Orange Juice
½ oz. Maraschino Liqueur
1 Egg White
Sugar to taste

Shake with ice and strain into a cocktail glass.

WHITE ROSE COCKTAIL NO. 2

¾ oz. Gin
½ oz. Cream
¾ oz. Anisette
½ Egg White

Shake with ice and strain into a cocktail glass.

WHITE RUSSIAN

1 oz. Creme de Cacao
2 oz. Vodka
1 tbsp. Heavy Cream

Shake with ice and strain into a cocktail glass.

WHITE SHADOW

1 oz. Rye Whisky
1 oz. Pernod
1 oz. Cream

Shake with ice and strain into a cocktail glass. Sprinkle nutmeg on top.

WHITE SHAKE

2 oz. Triple Sec or Orange Curacao
½ oz. Lemon Juice
1 dash Angostura Bitters

Shake with ice and strain into a cocktail glass.

WHITE SHOULDER

1 oz. Cream
¾ oz. Vodka
¾ oz. Curacao

Shake with ice and strain into a cocktail glass.

WHITE SPIDER

¾ oz. Vodka
¾ oz. White Creme de Menthe
¾ oz. Light Creme de Cacao

Mix in an Old-fashioned glass. Add ice.

WHITE STRAP

½ oz. Lemon Juice
½ oz. Molasses
White Wine

Mix lemon juice and molasses in a highball glass. Fill with chilled White Wine.

WHITE SWAN

1½ oz. Amaretto
3 oz. Milk

Shake with ice and strain into a cocktail glass.

WHITE TIGER

1¼ oz. Cream
1¼ oz. Tuaca

Shake with ice and strain into a cocktail glass.

WHITE WAY COCKTAIL NO. 1

¾ oz. Brandy
¾ oz. Anisette
¾ oz. Pernod

Shake with ice and strain into a cocktail glass.

WHITE WAY COCKTAIL NO. 2

¾ oz. White Creme de Menthe
1½ oz. Gin

Shake with ice and strain into a cocktail glass.

WHITE WINE COOLER NO. 1

1 tbsp. Sugar Syrup
3-4 oz. Soda, chilled
White Wine

Place syrup and soda in a highball glass with ice cubes. Fill with chilled Wine. Garnish with mint and an orange slice.

WHITE WINE COOLER NO. 2

½ oz. Brandy
¼ oz. Kummel
½ oz. Lemon Juice
1 tsp. Sugar
1 dash Orange Bitters
White Wine

Mix all the ingredients except Wine in a highball glass. Then add Wine and ice.

WHITE WINE PUNCH

2 oz. White Wine
1 oz. Arrack
½ oz. Lemon Juice
½ tsp. Sugar

Shake with ice and strain into a highball glass. Add ice. Decorate with a pineapple spear and an orange slice.

WHITE WING

1¾ oz. Gin or Vodka
¾ oz. White Creme de Menthe

Shake with ice and strain into a cocktail glass.

WHITE WITCH

1 oz. White Rum
2 tsp. White Creme de Cacao
2 tsp. Cointreau
½ Lime

Shake with ice and strain into a Collins glass. Fill with soda and ice. Garnish with several mint sprigs coated with powdered sugar.

WHIZ BANG COCKTAIL

½ oz. Dry Vermouth
½ tsp. Grenadine
½ tsp. Pernod
2 dashes Orange Bitters
1 oz. Scotch Whisky

Stir with ice and strain into a cocktail glass.

WHIZZ DOODLE

¾ oz. Cream
¾ oz. Scotch Whisky
¾ oz. Gin
¾ oz. Light Creme de Cacao

Shake with ice and strain into a cocktail glass.

WHY MARRY

1½ oz. Brandy
½ oz. Gin
½ oz. Cointreau
½ oz. Lemon Juice

Shake with ice and strain into a cocktail glass.

WHY NOT?

1 oz. Gin
1 oz. Apricot-flavored Brandy
½ oz. Dry Vermouth
1 dash Lemon Juice

Shake with ice and strain into a cocktail glass.

WIDOW'S DREAM

3 oz. Benedictine
1 whole Egg
1½ oz. Heavy Cream

Shake with ice and strain into a large cocktail glass.

WIDOW'S KISS COCKTAIL NO. 1

¾ oz. Parfait Amour
¾ oz. Yellow Chartreuse
¾ oz. Benedictine
1 beaten Egg White

Mix the first three ingredients and pour into a cocktail glass. Top with beaten egg white and a strawberry slice.

WIDOW'S KISS COCKTAIL NO. 2

1 oz. Calvados or Applejack
½ oz. Yellow Chartreuse
½ oz. Benedictine
1 dash Angostura Bitters

Shake with ice and strain into a cocktail glass. Serve with a strawberry.

WILD COW

1½ oz. Bourbon
1 tsp. Sugar
Milk

Dissolve the sugar in the Bourbon on the bottom of a Collins glass. Add milk plus ice to fill glass. Stir gently. Dust with nutmeg.

WILD-EYED ROSE

3 oz. Irish Whisky
¾ oz. Grenadine
Juice ½ Lime

Mix in a large cocktail glass with 1 ice cube and fill with soda.

WILD JAFFA

1 oz. Galliano
1 oz. Vodka
1 oz. Cointreau
1 dash Lemon Juice
1 dash Sugar Syrup
3 drops Grenadine

Shake together all ingredients (except Grenadine) and strain into a cocktail glass, with 3 drops of Grenadine in the bottom.

WILD OATS

1½ oz. Gin
½ oz. Kirschwasser
1 dash Lemon Juice
1 dash Apricot-flavored Brandy

Shake with ice and strain into a cocktail glass.

WILD RED HEAD

1½ oz. Cherry Heering
2½ oz. Lemon Juice

Blend with ice and strain into a Sour glass.

WILD ROSE

1½ oz. Gin
½ oz. Dry Vermouth
½ oz. Sweet Vermouth
1 dash Orange Bitters
1 dash Angostura Bitters

Stir with ice and strain into a cocktail glass.

WILLAWA

1 oz. Brandy
½ oz. Galliano
½ oz. Cherry-flavored Brandy
½ oz. Cream

Shake with ice and strain into a cocktail glass. Sprinkle nutmeg on top.

WILLIAM OF ORANGE

1½ oz. Brandy
¾ oz. Curacao
¾ oz. Orange Bitters

Stir with ice and strain into a cocktail glass.

WILLIAMSON

1¾ oz. Rum
¾ oz. Orange Juice
¼ oz. Lemon Juice
¼ tsp. Sugar

Shake with ice and strain into a cocktail glass.

WILLIE SMITH

1¾ oz. Brandy
¾ oz. Maraschino Liqueur
½ oz. Lemon Juice

Stir with ice and strain into a cocktail glass.

WILL ROGERS

1½ oz. Gin
1 tbsp. Orange Juice
½ oz. Dry Vermouth
1 dash Triple Sec

Shake with ice and strain into a cocktail glass.

WILSON SPECIAL

2 oz. Gin
2 dashes Dry Vermouth
2 slices Orange

Shake with ice and strain into a cocktail glass.

WINCHELL

1 oz. Cognac
1 oz. Gin
¼ oz. Lemon Juice
¼ oz. Cointreau

Shake with ice and strain into a cocktail glass.

WINDJAMMER

2 oz. White Rum
2 tbsp. Rock and Rye
2 tbsp. Orange Curacao
An Orange peel, cut in a long strip
Brown Sugar

Coat the orange peel in brown sugar; place it on bottom of a mug. Heat the mug over a low flame until sugar melts on the peel. Add the remaining ingredients. Fill the mug with boiling water and stir well. Touch up with a twist of lemon peel.

WINDMILL

1½ oz. Vodka
½ oz. Galliano
½ oz. Light Creme de Cacao

Shake with ice and strain into a cocktail glass.

WINDSOR

1¾ oz. Gin
¾ oz. Green Creme de Menthe

Shake with ice and strain into a cocktail glass.

WINDY CORNER COCKTAIL

2 oz. Blackberry-flavored Brandy

Stir Brandy with ice and strain into a cocktail glass. Sprinkle nutmeg on top.

WINE COLLINS

1 oz. Lemon Juice
½ tsp. Sugar
Red or White Wine
Soda

Mix lemon juice and sugar in a Collins glass. Fill with Wine, ice and soda.

WINE COOLER

½ tsp. Sugar dissolved in Soda
½ oz. Orange Juice
Red Wine

Mix soda and juice in a Collins glass. Fill with Wine and ice. Serve with an orange slice.

WINE LEMONADE

2 oz. Lemonade
4 oz. Burgundy

Fill a Collins glass three-quarters full with cracked ice. Pour in lemonade and Wine. Stir lightly.

WINE MARGARITA

1 oz. Rose's Lime Juice
3 oz. Chablis

Rub the rim of a chilled cocktail glass with lime peel. Dip the rim in salt. Combine lime juice, Chablis and cracked ice in a blender until well mixed. Strain into the salt-rimmed cocktail glass.

WINE REFRESHER

1 bottle Rose Wine
3 cups unsweetened Grapefruit Juice
Ice cubes (optional)

Chill wine and grapefruit juice thoroughly, then pour into a pitcher and stir to blend. Put 1 or 2 ice cubes into 8 oz. wine glasses and pour 4 oz. of the wine punch over them. Or serve punch without ice, in 4 oz. wine glasses. Makes 12 servings.

WINE RICKEY

4 oz. Riesling
4 oz. chilled Soda
¼ tsp. Sugar

Fill a Collins glass two-thirds full with crushed ice. Add Riesling, soda and sugar. Squeeze a lime slice over the drink and then drop the slice in. Stir well.

WINE SOUR

1½ oz. Chablis, chilled
3 oz. Collins mix, chilled
1 dash Lemon Juice

Shake with ice and strain into a large cocktail glass. Serve with a cherry.

WISCONSIN COCKTAIL

1½ oz. Rye Whisky
¼ oz. Apricot-flavored Brandy

Shake with ice and strain into a cocktail glass. Serve with a green cherry.

WITCH A GO-GO

1 oz. Lemon Juice
1 tsp. Sugar
1 oz. Strega
½ oz. Rum

Shake with ice and strain into a cocktail glass.

WITCH DOCTOR

1½ oz. Brandy
2 oz. Cream
½ tsp. Sugar
¼ oz. Vanilla
¼ oz. Dark Creme de Cacao

Shake the first four ingredients with ice and strain into a cocktail glass. Top with the Creme de Cacao.

WITCHING EVE

¾ oz. Light Creme de Cacao
1 drop Angostura Bitters
¼ oz. Cream

Pour carefully, in order given, into a pony glass so that each ingredient floats on the preceding one without mixing.

WITCH'S BREW

1 oz. Cream
1 oz. Orange Juice
1 oz. Triple Sec
1½ oz. Strega

Shake with ice and strain into a large cocktail glass.

W. JOHNSON QUINN

1¾ oz. Brandy
¼ oz. Sweet Vermouth
¼ oz. Dry Vermouth
¼ oz. Orange Curacao
1 dash Pernod

Stir with ice and strain into a cocktail glass.

WONDER

1 oz. Gin
1 oz. Claret
¼ oz. Lemon Juice
¼ tsp. Sugar

Shake with ice and strain into a cocktail glass.

> May friendship propose the toast,
> And sincerity drink it.

WOODSTOCK

1½ oz. Gin
1 oz. Lemon Juice
1½ tsp. Maple Syrup
1 dash Orange Bitters

Shake with ice and strain into a cocktail glass.

WOODWARD COCKTAIL

1½ oz. Scotch Whisky
½ oz. Dry Vermouth
1 tbsp. Grapefruit Juice

Shake with ice and strain into a cocktail glass.

WOW COCKTAIL

1	oz. Cognac
¾	oz. Apple Brandy
¾	oz. Rum
¼	oz. Pernod

Stir with ice and strain into a cocktail glass.

WOXUM COCKTAIL

¾	oz. Yellow Chartreuse
1	oz. Applejack
¾	oz. Sweet Vermouth

Shake with ice and strain into a cocktail glass.

WRIGHT BROTHERS

1	oz. Rye Whisky
1	oz. Port
½	oz. Lemon Juice
½	tsp. Sugar

Shake with ice and strain into a cocktail glass. Top with 1 beaten egg white. Serve with a pineapple spear.

WYOMING SWING

2	oz. Sweet Vermouth
2	oz. Dry Vermouth
2	oz. fresh Orange Juice
1	tsp. Sugar

Stir with ice and strain into an Old-fashioned glass.

XANTHIA COCKTAIL

¾	oz. Cherry-flavored Brandy
¾	oz. Yellow Chartreuse
¾	oz. Gin

Stir with ice and strain into a cocktail glass.

XERES COCKTAIL

1	dash Orange Bitters
2	oz. Dry Sherry

Stir with ice and strain into a cocktail glass.

XOCHIMILCO

1½	oz. Kahlua
½	oz. Cream

Fill an Old-fashioned glass with ice and add Kahlua and cream.

X.Y.Z. COCKTAIL NO. 1

1	tbsp. Lemon Juice
½	oz. Cointreau
1	oz. Dark Rum

Shake with ice and strain into a cocktail glass.

X.Y.Z. COCKTAIL NO. 2

¾	oz. Gin
½	oz. Dry Vermouth
½	oz. Sweet Vermouth
½	oz. Lemon Juice
¼	tsp. Sugar

Shake with ice and strain into a cocktail glass.

YACHT CLUB PUNCH

2	oz. Rum
½	oz. Grenadine
½	oz. Lemon Juice
¼	oz. Pernod

Mix in a highball glass. Add crushed ice and stir. Top with soda. Garnish with fruit.

YACHTING CLUB

2	oz. Holland Gin
1	oz. Dry Vermouth
2	dashes Sugar Syrup
2	dashes Peychaud's Bitters
1	dash Pernod

Stir with ice and strain into a cocktail glass.

YALE COCKTAIL NO. 1

1½	oz. Gin
½	oz. Dry Vermouth
1	dash Bitters
1	tsp. Creme d'Yvette

Stir with ice and strain into a cocktail glass.

YALE COCKTAIL NO. 2

1¾	oz. Gin
½	oz. Dry Vermouth
2	dashes Orange Bitters
¼	oz. Maraschino Liqueur
Sugar to taste	

Shake with ice and strain into a cocktail glass.

YALE COCKTAIL NO. 3

1¾	oz. Gin
¾	oz. Sweet Vermouth
1	dash Orange Bitters

Shake with ice and strain into a cocktail glass.

YANKEE DOODLE

1¾	oz. Gin
¼	oz. Cream
¼	oz. Lemon Juice
¼	oz. Creme d'Yvette
Sugar to taste	

Shake with ice and strain into a cocktail glass.

YANKEE PRINCE COCKTAIL

1	oz. Apricot Liqueur
1	oz. Pernod
1	oz. Yellow Chartreuse

Shake with ice and strain into a cocktail glass.

YANUCK FEVER

½ oz. Dry Vermouth
½ oz. Sweet Vermouth
1¼ oz. Brandy
¼ tsp. Pernod
1 tsp. Curacao

Stir with ice and strain into a cocktail glass.

YASHMUK

¾ oz. Rye Whisky
¾ oz. Pernod
¾ oz. Dry Vermouth
1 dash Angostura Bitters
⅛ tsp. Sugar

Stir with ice and strain into a cocktail glass.

YELLOW BIRD NO. 1

½ oz. Galliano
1½ oz. Rum
½ oz. Triple Sec
1 oz. Lime Juice

Shake with ice and strain into a cocktail glass.

YELLOW BIRD NO. 2

1 oz. Rum
½ oz. Galliano
½ oz. Banana Liqueur
1 oz. Pineapple Juice

Shake with ice and strain into a cocktail glass.

YELLOW DAISY

1½ oz. Gin
½ oz. Dry Vermouth
¼ oz. Grand Marnier
¼ oz. Pernod

Stir with ice and strain into a cocktail glass. Serve with a cherry.

YELLOW DIAMOND

1 oz. Galliano
½ oz. Cointreau
1 oz. Cream
1 dash Gin

Shake with ice and strain into a cocktail glass.

YELLOW FEVER

½ tsp. Sugar
1 oz. Soda
¾ oz. Lemon Juice
1½ oz. Vodka

In a highball glass dissolve sugar in soda. Stir in lemon juice and Vodka. Fill with soda and ice. Stir.

YELLOW FINGERS

1 oz. Gin
1 oz. Blackberry-flavored Brandy
½ oz. Banana Liqueur
½ oz. Cream

Shake with ice and strain into a cocktail glass.

To the old, long life and
   treasure;
To the young, all health and
   pleasure.
             — Ben Jonson.

YELLOW GLOW COCKTAIL

1 oz. Gin
1 oz. Yellow Chartreuse
1 oz. Sweet Vermouth

Shake with ice and strain into a cocktail glass.

YELLOW JACKET

¾ oz. Benedictine
¾ oz. Vodka
4 oz. Orange Juice

Shake with ice and pour into a cocktail glass with ice.

YELLOW MONKEY

½ oz. Galliano
½ oz. Light Creme de Cacao
½ oz. Rum
1 oz. Cream
Several ripe Bananas

Blend with ice and strain into a cocktail glass.

YELLOW PARROT COCKTAIL

¾ oz. Anisette
¾ oz. Yellow Chartreuse
¾ oz. Apricot-flavored Brandy

Shake with ice and strain into a cocktail glass.

YELLOW PLUM

1½ oz. Plum Brandy
½ oz. Lemon Juice
½ oz. Orange Juice
¼ oz. Maraschino Liqueur
Sugar to taste

Shake with ice and strain into a cocktail glass.

YELLOW RATTLER

1 oz. Gin
1 tbsp. Orange Juice
½ oz. Dry Vermouth
½ oz. Sweet Vermouth

Shake with ice and strain into a cocktail glass. Serve with an onion.

YERREP COCKTAIL

1 oz. Advokaat
¼ oz. Grand Marnier
1 tbsp. Ice Cream
1 oz. Fresh Cream
2 dashes Ricard

Shake with ice and strain into a champagne glass. Serve with a cherry.

YES AND NO

2 oz. Brandy
½ oz. Orange Curacao
1 Egg White

Shake with ice and strain into a cocktail glass. Sprinkle nutmeg on top.

YODEL

1 Ice cube
2 oz. Fernet Branca
2 oz. Orange Juice
Soda

Place the ice cube in a highball glass and pour in Fernet Branca and orange juice. Fill with soda and ice.

YO HO

1 oz. Rum
1 oz. Swedish Punch
1 oz. Calvados or Apple Brandy

Shake with ice and strain into a cocktail glass. Serve with a twist of lemon peel.

YOKOHAMA COCKTAIL

½ oz. Orange Juice
¼ oz. Grenadine
¼ oz. Vodka
1 dash Pernod
1 oz. Gin

Shake with ice and strain into a cocktail glass.

YOLANDA

½ oz. Brandy
½ oz. Gin
½ oz. Anisette
1 oz. Sweet Vermouth
1 dash Grenadine

Shake with ice and strain into a cocktail glass. Serve with a twist of orange peel.

YORK SPECIAL

3 oz. Dry Vermouth
1 oz. Maraschino Liqueur
4 dashes Orange Bitters

Stir with ice and strain into a cocktail glass.

YOU NEVER KNOW

2 oz. Blackberry-flavored Brandy
½ oz. White Creme de Menthe

Shake with ice and strain into a cocktail glass. Sprinkle nutmeg on top.

YOUNG MAN

1¾ oz. Brandy
½ oz. Sweet Vermouth
¼ oz. Orange Curacao
1 dash Angostura Bitters

Stir with ice and strain into a cocktail glass.

YOUNG MAN'S COCKTAIL

1 dash Boonekamp Bitters
2 dashes Curacao
½ oz. Dry Vermouth
1½ oz. Cognac

Shake with ice and strain into a cocktail glass. Serve with an olive.

YOUR PLEASURE

Pernod
1 Sugar cube
1 Ice cube
Extra Dry Champagne, chilled
1 dash Brandy

Place the sugar cube in a highball glass. Soak it with Pernod. Add the ice cube. Fill the glass nearly full with Champagne. Add Brandy and a strip of lemon peel.

YUKON BLIZZARD

Juice ½ Orange
5 oz. Rose Wine
Citrus mixer or Soda

Pour the orange juice and Rose into a Collins glass. Add ice cubes. Fill with chilled soda or citrus mixer.

YUP

2½ oz. Gin
2 drops Scotch Whisky

Stir with ice and strain into a cocktail glass. Serve with an anchovy-stuffed olive.

YVETTE COCKTAIL

1½ oz. Gin
½ oz. Creme d'Yvette
½ oz. Lemon Juice
Sugar to taste

Shake with ice and strain into a cocktail glass.

YVETTE VICTORIA

¾ oz. Creme d'Yvette
¾ oz. Pernod

Pour Creme d'Yvette into a cocktail glass, then shake Pernod with ice and strain over the top.

ZAIVE'S NEW ORLEANS COCKTAIL

1½ oz. Bourbon Whisky
1 dash Orange Bitters
½ oz. Anisette
1 dash Angostura Bitters
½ lump Sugar
½ oz. Pernod

Shake with ice and strain into a Collins glass. Fill with crushed ice. Serve with a lemon twist.

ZANZIBAR

1½   oz. Dry Vermouth
½   oz. Gin
¼   oz. Lemon Juice
¼   tsp. Sugar

Shake with ice and strain into a cocktail glass. Serve with a lemon twist.

ZAZA COCKTAIL NO. 1

1½   oz. Gin
¾   oz. Dubonnet

Stir with ice and strain into a cocktail glass. Serve with a twist of orange peel.

ZAZA COCKTAIL NO. 2

1½   oz. Sherry
1½   oz. Dubonnet

Stir with ice and strain into a cocktail glass.

ZAZERAC

1   cube Sugar
1   dash Angostura Bitters
1   dash Soda
3   Ice cubes
1   oz. Bourbon or Rye Whisky
½   tsp. Pernod

Put the sugar in an Old-fashioned glass and add Angostura Bitters and soda to dissolve. Add the ice cubes and Bourbon (or Rye). Float Pernod on top and garnish with a slice of orange and a cherry. Add some lemon peel and serve with a swizzle stick.

ZED

1¼   oz. Pernod
1¼   oz. Apple Brandy

Stir with ice and strain into a cocktail glass.

ZENITH

½   oz. Pineapple Juice
1½   oz. Gin

Mix in a highball glass. Fill with soda and ice. Serve with a pineapple stick.

ZEPHYR

1¾   oz. Brandy
¼   oz. Orange Curacao
¼   oz. Pineapple Juice
¼   oz. Maraschino Liqueur
1   dash Angostura Bitters

Coat the inside of a cocktail glass with lemon juice and then shake all ingredients with ice. Strain into the prepared glass.

ZERO

1½   oz. Pernod
½   oz. Grenadine
½   oz. Orange Juice

Shake with ice and strain into a cocktail glass.

ZERO MINT

2   oz. Green Creme de Menthe
1   oz. Water

Chill Creme de Menthe mixed with water in the refrigerator for 2 hours or longer. (Does not have to be frozen solid.) Serve in a cocktail glass.

ZEUS

Ice cubes
2   oz. Campari
1   oz. Vodka

Put 2-3 ice cubes in an Old-fashioned glass and pour in Campari and Vodka. Stir lightly. Serve with a lemon twist.

ZINFANDEL LEMONADE

Juice 1 Lemon
1½   tsp. Sugar
Zinfandel, chilled
2   slices Lemon

Put lemon juice and sugar in a Collins glass. Stir until the sugar has dissolved. Half fill the glass with cracked ice. Fill with chilled Wine. Stir lightly. Garnish with lemon slices. Serve with straws.

ZOMBIE NO. 1

¾   oz. 90-proof Rum
1½   oz. 86-proof Golden Rum
¾   oz. 86-proof Light Rum
¾   oz. Pineapple Juice
¾   oz. Papaya Juice
3   tbsp. Lime Juice
3-4 Ice cubes
1   tsp. Sugar
1   tbsp. 151-proof Demerara Rum

Combine all the ingredients except the Demerara Rum and sugar in a cocktail shaker. Shake very thoroughly and strain into a highball glass. Garnish with a pineapple stick and a cherry. Carefully float Demerara Rum on top and lightly sprinkle with sugar.

ZOMBIE NO. 2

1   oz. Lemon or Lime Juice
4   dashes Passionola or Papaya Juice
4   dashes Apricot-flavored Brandy
4   dashes Cherry-flavored Brandy
1   oz. White Rum
1   oz. Dark Rum
1   oz. Jamaica Rum
151-proof Rum

Fill a highball glass with cracked ice. Add all the ingredients (except 151-proof Rum) and stir. Top with 151-proof Rum. Decorate with cherries and a slice of orange.

What you can make with a bottle of . . .

Irish Whisky

Rum